3495

SO-ATT-359

R424
1995

The Church as *Polis*

The Church as *Polis*

From Political Theology to Theological Politics
as Exemplified by Jürgen Moltmann and Stanley Hauerwas

ARNE RASMUSSON

University of Notre Dame Press
Notre Dame, Indiana

First published in 1994, copyright © Arne Rasmusson, by
Lund University Press in Sweden (Box 141, S-221 00 Lund) and in
Great Britain by Chartwell-Bratt Ltd. (Old Orchard, Bickley Road, Bromley, Kent BR1 2NE

Library of Congress Cataloging-in-Publication Data

Rasmusson, Arne,
 The Church as polis : from political theology to theological
politics as exemplified by Jürgen Moltmann and Stanley Hauerwas /
Arne Rasmusson.
  p.   cm.
 Includes bibliographical references and index.
 ISBN 0-268-00809-4 (cl) (alk. paper) 0-268-00810-8 (p) (alk. paper)
1. Christianity and Politics—History of doctrines—20th century.
2. Moltmann, Jürgen.   3. Hauerwas, Stanley, 194– . I. Title.
BR115.P7R424   1995
261.7'092'2—dc20   94-45054

Contents

Part Three

Towards a Theological Politics: Contemporary Radical Reformation Theology as an Alternative

Part Four

Conclusion

Preface

One theme Stanley Hauerwas and Jürgen Moltmann have in common is the importance of friendship. The writing of this book is a witness to this. Many people have given me much help during the years I have been working on this book. Per Erik Persson has followed my work all these years, even after his retirement from Lund University, and has always been generous with his time, given me much encouragement, and supported me in many practical ways. He is also known for being an extraordinarily close and careful reader, something I have greatly benefited from. His successor Per Frostin tragically died after only two years as professor. During that brief period he gave me some valuable help. Gösta Hallonsten has been of great assistance during the final work on the book and with gentle prods helped me at long last to finish the project.

Drafts of my manuscript have also been discussed several times by the seminar in systematic theology in Lund, as well as once in Göran Bexell's ethics seminar, and also once in Hans Ulrich's ethics seminar in Erlangen. I am grateful for the comments and criticisms the participants have given me.

Many other people have read parts of the manuscript and given helpful comments. Among them are Margareta Bertilsson, Colin Gunton, John Howard Yoder, James Wm. McClendon, Jr., Ted Koontz, Peter Kristiansson, Bengt Rasmusson, and Carl-Gustav Carlsson.

Two people should be especially mentioned, Reinhard Hütter and Roland Spjuth. Reinhard, who knows the issues I deal with in this book better than most, has read and discussed drafts of my manuscript and spent countless hours in Germany, USA, and Sweden discussing the issues it raises. He and his family were also especially helpful during my two stays in America.

No one, however, has spent more time reading and rereading drafts of my book than Roland Spjuth. After having written two books together, we have finally separated our writing projects, but our cooperation has continued. Our many discussions and his incisive criticisms have forced me to much rewriting, but also made this book much better than it otherwise would have been.

My parents Ruth and Stig Rasmusson, as well as my parents-in-law Tage and Gerd Bofeldt have also supported me and my family in various ways during this project, which has made my work much easier.

Several people have worked hard to make my "Swenglish" into something closer to English. The main work was done by Karin Eriksson, but Anders Jönsson, Pekka Mellergård, Christopher Meakin, and Lois Pettersson have also spent many hours with me discussing how to remake my sentences into a readable English. Sigurd Bergmann has proof-read the German references in the bibliography.

In respect to language, it should be said that I have followed the common Anglo-American convention using English translations of books written in other languages whenever they have been available to me. I have, moreover, translated citations. However, in the case of Moltmann I have also given the references to the German versions of his texts in parentheses.

Writing on living persons has its complications, especially when they are as productive as Moltmann and Hauerwas. But the positive side is the chance to learn to know them as persons and not only as authors. During a year in Tübingen I could follow Moltmann's lectures and his higher seminar, and he gave me also generously of his time for conversation, as he has done also later both in Tübingen and in Sweden. During six weeks in Durham, Hauerwas showed similar generosity with his time, discussing his theology and helping me with material. He has also been extremely helpful in continuously sending his newly written material to me.

Moltmann and Hauerwas stress the importance of the practical ecclesial context for the work of theology. For me, this has been the small church in Arlöv I am part of. Living with this church has taught me much that one can never learn from books and helped to keep my feet on the ground. It has also been a helpful place for testing my ideas. In one sense, this book can thus be described as a theoretical reflection on our common life as a church in Arlöv.

When I started writing this book I was single. Since then I have married and now have two boys. Although this changed my time plan, Moniqua, Clemens, and Theodore have greatly enriched my life, filling it with joy and love. However, a writing project like this is not the best way of starting a marriage. Moniqua has had to carry a heavy burden, and I cannot express how grateful I am for all her support and encouragement.

Part One

Introduction

Chapter 1

The Quest: An Introductory General Presentation

1. Political Theology

a) The Emergence and Basic Characteristics of Political Theology

Political theology has been one of the most influential theological movements both in church life and academy during the last three decades. It emerged out of the turbulence of the 1960s and was first formulated by the Catholic theologian Johann Baptist Metz and the Protestant Jürgen Moltmann.[1] It was an attempt to positively meet the challenges of modernity, characterized by industrialization, urbanization, science, technology, market economy and a growing state and its various ideological backbones in liberalism and socialism, with their common beliefs in progress and in politics as a mean for consciously forming the future. One result of modernity was the long term movement towards secularization of society, which accelerated during the 1960s. The church had during the previous two hundred years increasingly lost the privileged and established role it had in the West since the fourth century. Christian faith and practice were forced out of the public world into the sphere of private life.

The 1960s was a decade in which the beliefs and hopes of modernity were intensified. The human possibilities through science and technology seemed unlimited. The welfare state apparatus grew and with it the belief in social and political planning. Moral, religious and political traditions were severely criticized in

---

[1]The literature on political theology is overwhelming. One especially helpful overview of the context, development and discussion of political theology up to the mid-seventies is Wiedenhofer, *Politische Theologie*. This book includes a very extensive survey of literature. See also his discussion of the continuing development in his later article "Politische Theologie". A more recent work is Chopp, *The Praxis of Suffering*. Fiorenza's articles "Political Theology and Liberation Theology" and "Political Theology as Foundational Theology" are also particularly useful. I have (together with Roland Spjuth) in an earlier book, *Kristologiska perspektiv*, dealt with another prominent European Catholic political theologian, namely Edward Schillebeeckx.

the name of human autonomy. This criticism, however, was also increasingly directed against modern society itself. The discrepancy between the technological rationality and possibilities and the very slowly changing organization of society was increasingly felt. The economic and social systems were seen as unjust and irrational, as was also (and especially) the gulf between the First and the newly independent Third World. This made socialist and Marxist thought attractive in wide circles. In Germany the revisionist Marxism of Ernst Bloch was very influential. Later the critical theory of Theodor Adorno, Max Horkheimer, Jürgen Habermas, and others, became leading. The opposition to the liberal capitalist society and world system and the hopes for revolutionary changes became focused in the radical student movement and the so-called New Left. This also led to parallel changes and conflicts in the churches, especially symbolized in the Roman Catholic Church by Vatican II, and in the Protestant churches both by the World Council of Churches Conference on Church and Society in Geneva 1966 and its Fourth Assembly in Uppsala 1968.

Political theology emerged out of this socio-political and intellectual milieu. It was an attempt to positively meet the challenge to church and theology that modernity is. In this sense it has an apologetic intention. It wants to critically mediate the Christian tradition to the modern world. The modern project, understood as a demystification of nature and a concomitant humanization of the world, was interpreted in terms of Christian eschatology. Not cosmos but history became the basic framework for understanding reality. Society can be changed by common human effort and God is a God of the future who opens up reality. This made politics the basic horizon for also church and theology. Political theology did not wish to politicize theology or develop a theology of politics, but to analyse the political implications of actual Christian theology, practice and institutions, as well as of the Christian Gospel. There is, it was often said, no way to be apolitical, the issue is *how* one is political. So if one aim was apologetic, the other was hermeneutic. The aim was to articulate the political meaning and practice of Christianity as a public practice.

This political hermeneutics was developed in criticism of the then dominant individualistic, ahistorical and apolitical existential and transcendental understandings of Christianity (like Rudolf Bultmann and Karl Rahner) that accepted the modern privatization of Christian faith. The common-place American historiography of modern theology and especially of what they call neo-orthodoxy is however too undifferentiated.[2] Protestant political theology could more directly connect with earlier Protestant theology, especially with the tradition of the Confessing Church and the theologies of Dietrich Bonhoeffer and Karl Barth, than

---

[2]Chopp, *The Praxis of Suffering*, 29-33, is an example of this.

Catholic theology could, although Rahner's influence on the shape of Catholic political theology is unmistakable and clearly acknowledged.[3]

One part of this political hermeneutics was to analyse the modern bourgeois society in which the church lives and the concomitant bourgeois form of Christian religion. This made social and political theory a necessary instrument for theology. For political theology this has usually meant some form of (often revisionist) Marxist theory. The Marxist criticism of religion was also generally in the background of the development of political theology. Both Metz and Moltmann were at this time active in the Christian-Marxist dialogue. One important consequence of this was the reception from Marxist thought of a specific understanding of the relation between theory and praxis. How, exactly, that relation should be understood was and is not well clarified, but in general terms it means that the theological reflection takes place in the actual socio-political and ecclesial situation. In political terms, political theology has usually also defended some form of democratic socialism.

The tradition or program of political theology has developed in different forms. The positions of Metz and Moltmann are, for example, not identical. Their theologies have also developed extensively since the early formulations of the 1960s. One major change came after 1970 when the strong stress on eschatology and God as future was modified. One problem with this was that theology tended to become mainly critical, criticizing present reality in the light of a hoped for future, to which little content was given. The criticism became abstract with little to say about concrete positive alternatives. Both Metz and Moltmann therefore attempted to find ways to a more substantial and politically concrete theology.

With this conception the question of ecclesiology becomes highly significant. The church together with other progressive movements becomes the subject of God's transforming work in history. This makes the institutional form of the church crucial. Metz talks about base communities and Moltmann relates himself to the Free Church tradition. We saw that political theology in the 1960s related itself to the student movement. It has continued to be deeply related to what has been called the new social movements of the Western world, such as ecological, peace, and feminist movements, and to the liberation movements of the Third World. It is no exaggeration to say that the social and ecclesial base for this type of theology has been the Christians who are active in and related to these movements.

Political theology as a general program has had a much wider reception than the actual label "political theology".[4] It has also developed in different directions, some of which are rather critical of the original conception. Moltmann's own de-

---

[3]This is also Moltmann's own view. See "Political Theology and Liberation Theology", 213f. See further Wiedenhofer, *Politische Theologie*, 26-28, Wacker, "Politische Theologie", 387. For an extensive discussion of the relation between Barmen and political theology, see Weth, *"Barmen" als Herausforderung der Kirche*, esp. 37-82.

[4]Wiedenhofer, *Politische Theologie*, 13-19.

scription of this is as follows: "Political theology became the starting point for a whole series of mediating theologies . . . . : the theology of revolution, the theology of liberation, black theology, feminist theology and other regionally conditioned, 'contextual' theologies in Africa and Asia."[5] Especially Latin American liberation theology has become extremely influential also in Europe and North America, so that today many prefer to identify themselves as liberation theologians.[6] I use the designation "political theology" because I will specifically discuss the theology of Moltmann and this is the identification he himself uses. Furthermore, my interest is North Atlantic theology which reflects on church and Christian life in that type of society. To talk about liberation theology or liberationism would only confuse matters as it leads the thoughts to Latin American theology.[7]

b) Inherent Tensions

However, there are, as I will try to show, severe difficulties with the project of political theology, which have to do with deep tensions in its very conception. These tensions cannot be easily described in a short thesis form, but will be made clear throughout the exposition. The major tension, which works itself out in several ways, has to do with the inherent difficulties of combining the way one reads the Christian story about Israel, Jesus and the church with a hermeneutics that makes the politics of the world, interpreted in a certain emancipatory tradition, the primary horizon. Practically, it shows itself in the tension between making the church and ecclesial discipleship *or* political activism in social movements the primary context. The inner logic of the former tends in a different direction than the latter. This tension became clearer when political theology, in its second phase, developed a more substantial use of the Christian tradition, in contrast to its earlier (concerning politics and ethics) basically formal and critical use.

On another level, the project of political hermeneutics has tended to undermine itself. Political theology emerged as an attempt to mediate Christianity to modernity. It has, however, and this is more true for Moltmann than for Metz, become increasingly critical of modernity and its assumptions of reality, knowledge and praxis, assumptions that were intrinsic to the very conception of political theology. In this development the Christian tradition has been used to criticize basic assumptions of modernity and to this extent the two mentioned major tensions work together. The result of this is, first, that political theologies are drawn in different directions, and, second, that problems in the actual use of political theology for interpreting and guiding the life of the church in the modern world

---

[5]*ThT* 88 (95). See also *CJF* 27f (42f).
[6]Cf. Wogaman, *Christian Perspectives on Politics*, 53-71, who labels these theologies, Moltmann and Metz included, as "Christian liberationist perspectives".
[7]See Fiorenza, "Political Theology and Liberation Theology" for an early discussion of the differences. For a recent account of Moltmann's view of the relation, see Moltmann, "Political Theology".

arise. These allegations are, however, only possible to substantiate through an actual critical description of political theology.

c) Why Moltmann?

One question this sort of investigation raises is whether to treat political theology in general or to choose one or a few representatives of it. To discuss the entire movement has the advantage that one can cover the whole area and therefore be able to make claims about political theology in general. The problems with this approach are the sheer mass of the material and its high degree of diversity. One objection would probably be that nobody actually defends the model I would have constructed out of this diversity. On the other hand, to concentrate on one author has the advantage of describing and discussing an actual position and of doing this in certain analytical detail. The predictable response to this strategy is that there are other political theologians who have developed this position more powerfully and who are not vulnerable to the sort of criticism the analysis provides. One has to choose, and I have chosen the latter approach as the more fruitful, because of the more detailed discussion and analysis it allows. Much theological writing and analysis concentrates on method and general approach. I am, however, interested in the actual substantial performance, as only this finally helps in the critical evaluation of the fruitfulness of an approach. While method might be reduced to basic principles, performance cannot, but requires extensive description, and it is therefore better to base an investigation on one theologian rather than on several or a whole movement.[8]

For these reasons I have chosen to concentrate on one theologian, namely Jürgen Moltmann. I have chosen him for several reasons, the first being that his work is more comprehensive and wide ranging than the work of any other contemporary political theologian.[9] While Metz, as maybe most political theologians, has primarily worked as a fundamental theologian, Moltmann has developed a broad substantial theology. There are others who methodologically are more stringent, but nobody has made a comparable performance of political theology.[10] A second related reason is that the tensions I mentioned above are clearer in his case than in most others, primarily because he has performed political theology more extensively than others. Because of a concentration on the issues of funda-

---

[8]One can see the problem in Chopp's *The Praxis of Suffering*, which in a rather short space deals with Gutierrez, Metz, Míguez Bonino and Moltmann. Although a helpful and sophisticated work, it suffers both from lack of sustained exposition and therefore too easily falls into typical "liberationist jargon", and from lack of critical examination of the *actual* performances of these theologies, and instead concentrates too much on method and on what they *claim* that their theologies do.

[9]Dorrien, after having criticized aspects of his program, says that "I believe that Moltmann has nonetheless offered the most generative, socially valuable, and suggestive theological work of the past generation. More than any other contemporary theologian, he has revealed the enduring power of the biblical witness." (*Reconstructing the Common Good*, 99.)

[10]Another major exception from the common methodological concentration is parts of Latin American liberation theology and this seems to be one reason for its influence and importance.

mental theology and a high level of abstraction the tensions are not as visible in some other parallel projects of political theology. A third reason is his importance for contemporary theology in general. He might be, or so it is said, the most influential of the now active Protestant theologians.[11] A fourth reason is that he is a Protestant theologian, and I therefore avoid the added complexities of discussing a Roman Catholic theologian like Metz.[12]

2. Contemporary Radical Reformation Theology as an Alternative

I will suggest that one way out of the described impasse of political theology could be to more consistently follow what one might call Contemporary Radical Reformation theology. I will not try to argue that this is the only possibility, but neither is it an arbitrary suggestion. Moltmann has explicitly said that the future of the Reformation should be seen in the Radical Reformation and the Free Church tradition.[13] Furthermore, he has, as I will argue, following the inner logic of his theology, continuously moved in this direction and explicitly taken up central parts of Contemporary Radical Reformation theology. Though this is most explicit in the case of Moltmann, one can find similar developments in other parts of political theology.

In this book I use the designation Radical Reformation in a broad sense. It refers, first, to the Anabaptist movements of the sixteenth century and its direct descendants; second, to the broader tradition often called the Believers' Church or the Free Church movement; and, third, to a recurring phenomenon throughout all of church history, which means that this phenomenon is also found inside the established churches. All three uses have relevance for Radical Reformation theology as I understand it.[14]

This wide scope is important, but with the qualification "contemporary" I want to specify a particular contemporary form of Radical Reformation theology, which is as clearly identifiable as political theology. This is a theology with deep roots in both the general Christian tradition and in the Radical Reformation tradition, but which has a specific form. Just as Metz and Moltmann are the two most important formative figures of political theology, the Mennonite theologian John

---

[11]So Bauckham, who writes "that Jürgen Moltmann has probably had more influence worldwide than any other Protestant dogmatic theologian alive today" (*Moltmann*, 1).

[12]To this might now be added that the best critical discussion of political and liberation theology I am aware of, and which parallels my conclusions, John Milbank's *Theology and Social Theory*, 206-255, deals with the Catholic tradition of Metz and the Latin Americans. This was not a reason that determined my original choice, for the simple reason that Milbank's book was not published at that time. It has, however, been helpful in the final rewriting of this work and it also gives reason for believing that my analysis of Moltmann has relevance for political theology in general. See also his article "On Baseless Suspicion".

[13]*OC* 117 (142), *OHD* 140f (83f).

[14]I am not wholly satisfied with this label, but I have not found any better. It is the one Yoder prefers, though he points to its shortcomings. See Yoder, *The Priestly Kingdom*, 105-107, 197 n. 1, 203 n. 4.

Howard Yoder and the Methodist Stanley Hauerwas (who is the representative in this book) could be seen as having a corresponding position in Contemporary Radical Reformation theology (for convenience I will usually refer to this theology as Radical Reformation theology).

I will introduce this "position" at greater length than political theology for the reason that while political theology is well known and part of the curriculum of most theology programs, the same cannot be said for Contemporary Radical Reformation theology. My description of this theology and its roots is more ecclesial in nature than the more generally politically-oriented description of the contexts and roots of political theology. The reason for this is a basic difference between these two theologies. While both strongly stress the political nature of Christianity, they do this in different ways. Radical Reformation theology gives primacy not to politics understood as the struggle for control over the processes of social change (the politics of the world), but to the politics of the church as an alternative *polis*. This is the background not only of the title of this book, *The Church as Polis*, but also of the concept "theological politics" found in its subtitle (a designation I will also use for describing this theology).

a) Anabaptism

Yoder, who placed this position on the modern theological map, is a Mennonite, and thus a direct descendant of the Anabaptists. His theology has grown out of this tradition and experience. However, he does not defend any idea of a normative Anabaptism, in terms of founders or some original normative Anabaptist theology or Confession. This would be, first of all, for Radical Reformation theology a theological mistake, because it does not want to make (though it has sometimes done so) a specific history normative except the New Testament.[15] As we will see, in the case of Yoder and Hauerwas this entails no simple biblicism. In addition, there has never existed some "pure" Radical Reformation theology. Yoder writes:

> Anabaptism . . . was a very wide set of phenomena, too wide to be called a movement. They didn't come from the same place, they weren't going to the same place. They had in common only one or two practices which happened to put them in the same place in the eyes of establishment critics. There is no point in saying that one of these groups was le-

---

[15]"Perhaps a Calvinist or a Lutheran needs, for reasons which he can define theologically, to be faithful to his founder. The descendants of churches once led by Menno do not. By the nature of the case the tradition of the sixteenth century is not normative in the free church style. The free church tradition is also a *tradition*, so that guidance is also received from the past. But the *way* that guidance is received is much less firmly structured, and much less concerned for fidelity to any particular father." ("Reformed Versus Anabaptist Social Strategies", 5. See further ibid., 4-6 and "The Believers' Church Conferences in Historical Perspective", 10-13.)

gitimately Anabaptist and another wasn't, since there is no other criterion for the legitimacy of an Anabaptist.[16]

The position that stressed, among other things, separation from the world and non-resistance, became dominant only after 1540 because other positions disappeared.[17] If the outer ecclesial and political situation had been more favourable, the continuing theology of Anabaptism might have been significantly different.[18]

---

[16]*Christian Attitudes to War, Peace, and Revolution,* 191, see further ibid., 165-200.

[17]"The radicals who became Anabaptists did not set out with separatism as a forming principle, but it became a part of their identity. They had originally intended to challenge and reform the prevailing structure. It was by a kind of 'trial and error' that the radicals arrived at the fact and the idea of a separated church which stood as an alternative to existing structures." (Weaver, *Becoming Anabaptist,* 119)

[18]Anabaptist historiography is an interesting subject from many perspectives. Anabaptism was long a despised tradition whose history was written by its enemies and persecutors and mainly associated with Thomas Müntzer and Münster. During the nineteenth century a more adequate appraisal started to be made, but it was especially the work of Max Weber and Ernst Troeltsch that led to reinterpretations in wider circles. Inside the Mennonite community this twentieth century rewriting of history became important for the quest of their own identity during a time of radical change. Harold Bender's synthesis in terms of "the Anabaptist vision" as the consistent development of the Protestant tradition, making discipleship, non-resistance, and the church as voluntary community central, became very influential. (Bender, "The Anabaptist Vision". For historical accounts representing the end of this period, see Littell, *The Anabaptist View of the Church,* which includes a historiography up until mid-twentieth century on pp. 138-161, Estep, *The Anabaptist Story,* and the massive Williams, *The Radical Reformation,* which made the label in this book's title common usage.) In the 1960s and 1970s more socio-historical accounts emerged, that interpreted Anabaptism (and the Reformation in general) as part of more general social movements. It was further shown that there was not one genesis, but several, and that there were a great variety of theological and political views. There never existed some original "normative Anabaptism" of Bender's type. Earlier studies, especially in-group Mennonite history, were criticized for being too formed by theological assumptions. (See e.g. Stayer, *Anabaptists and the Sword,* Goertz, *Die Täufer,* Clasen, *Anabaptism,* Stayer, Packull, and Deppermann, "From Monogenesis to Polygenesis", Packull, "Between Paradigms". On the wider context, see also Goertz, *Pfaffenhaß und groß Geschrei,* and Blickle, *Gemeindereformation.* For both the history from the new perspective and a theological reflection, see Weaver, *Becoming Anabaptist.* For an interesting account of Williams' further research and for his appraisal of the new approach, see his "The Radical Reformation Revisited". For Yoder's recent thought on these matters, see e.g. *Christian Attitudes,* 165-200 and "The Believers' Church Conferences", 10f.) Reading some of this material I get the impression that there is place for some further revision. First, in some of these scholars one finds a questionably sharp dualism between, as it is said, "religious-idealist" and "socio-political" interpretations. In a sense the earlier so-called "purely religious" accounts are only turned up side down. The separation of the religious from the social is still assumed, only now the latter are seen as finally determinative. For criticism of this type of social history, see Milbank, *Theology and Social Theory,* e.g. 111-121. Second, it is hardly an accident that a socio-historical approach arose and that is was so positively received during the 1970s also inside the Mennonite tradition. As Stayer, himself a non-Mennonite, argues, the new perspective could be used for legitimating both always existing but also growing Mennonite pluralism and a growing identification with radical politics and political theology. In other words, we would then have a parallel to the use of the first revision. ("The Early Demise of a Normative Vision of Anabaptism". Goertz is one of many examples of this, see his "The Confessional Heritage in Its New Mold".) Stayer is also generally critical of the self-understanding of some of the later revisionists as "objective critical" historians in contrast to the more "confessional" historians. (Cf. also his critical comments in the new section in the second edition of *Anabaptist and the Sword,* esp. xi-xiii.)

So while Yoder does not want to write Mennonite theology, but theology for the universal church, his constructive theological reflection flows out of the resources of his Mennonite tradition, with its stress on community, separation from the world, discipleship and peace, and the specific historical experiences of this tradition.[19]

b) The Believers' Church or the Free Church Tradition

Because Yoder understands Anabaptism as one instance of a recurring phenomenon,[20] he sees Anabaptism and modern Mennonites as a part of what is also called the Believers' Church or the Free Church tradition.[21] This is a family of churches that could be interpreted as standing alongside the Roman Catholic, Orthodox, Lutheran, Reformed and Anglican traditions as a distinct type of tradition in its own right (but also as existing inside these other traditions in various ways).[22] It is, just like Anabaptism, more diverse than these other church traditions: it does not have, as some of these others, one recognizable founder; and it has never with the help of state coercion been formed into established churches with a single uniform organization. In the widest sense church groups like Baptists, Brethren, Mennonites, Methodists, Quakers, Pentecostals, Pietists, and others could be mentioned as being part of the Believers' Church tradition.

These churches have been formed at different times and circumstances, but still have some common themes, though in different combinations and with a varied development. To reflect on this, the work of James Wm. McClendon is useful. McClendon, a Baptist, is a third major proponent of Contemporary Radical Reformation theology and is working on a three-volume systematic theology from this position.[23] In his first chapter, he discusses what the vision of Radical

---

[19]It is also a deeply critical reflection on the faith and practice of historical and contemporary Mennonitism.

[20]Besides texts mentioned, see *The Priestly Kingdom*, 123-134.

[21]He also thinks that twentieth century Mennonites owe more to various other later Believers' Church traditions and to Lutheran and Reformed theology (depending on locations) than to sixteenth century Anabaptism (in addition to the specific historical experience of the Mennonites). See *Christian Attitudes*, 198f.

[22]Westin, *Den kristna friförsamlingen genom tiderna*, Littell, *The Free Church*, Durnbaugh, *The Believers' Church*, idem, "Characteristics of the Radical Reformation in Historical Perspective". Cf. also the way Piepkorn in *Protestant Denominations* talks about "Churches with origins in the Radical Reformation" as one of the main types of modern American Protestantism, although his characterizations are open to certain objections. In numerical terms this church group is much larger than either the Lutheran, Reformed or Anglican church groups, as a quick look in Barrett, *World Christian Encyclopedia*, 792f shows. If one measure in terms of active participation (only a tiny minority of e.g. European Lutherans are active) the difference becomes even larger.

[23]So far one volume has been published, *Systematic Theology: Ethics*. Another attempt to write a systematic theology from what he calls the Believer's Church perspective is Thomas Finger's two-volume work *Christian Theology*. Cf. McClendon's review article "In the Light of Last Things".

Reformation (or as he prefers baptist) theology could be.[24] By "vision" he does not mean "some end result of theoretical reflection", nor "a detachable baptist Ideal", but

> the guiding stimulus by which a people (or as here, a combination of peoples) shape their life and thought as that people or that combination; . . . the continually emerging theme and tonic structure of their common life. The vision is thus already present, waiting to be recognized and employed: it must not seem a stranger to those who share in baptist life or to their sympathetic observers. Yet once acknowledged for what it is, it should serve as the touchstone by which authentic baptist life is discovered and described, and also as the organizing principle around which a genuine baptist theology can take shape.[25]

After a long discussion of different proposals about how to understand this vision he summarizes his own suggestion in the following way: "first of all the awareness of the *biblical* story as our story, but also of *mission* as responsibility for costly witness, of *liberty* as the freedom to obey God without state help or hindrance, of *discipleship* as life transformed into obedience to Jesus' lordship, and of *community* as daily sharing in the vision."[26] This needs to be extensively interpreted, but it gives a first approximation, to which my description of Hauerwas' theology will give further elaboration.

These characteristics, however, can be understood and combined in many different ways. Radical Reformation or Believers' Church theology is a very diverse phenomenon. Far from all members and theologians in this stream of Christianity would accept the specific ways in which Yoder, Hauerwas and McClendon formulate Christian theology. Especially controversial is their strong emphasis on the political nature of salvation, and therefore on the church as a disciplined community and alternative society, as well as their making peace crucial for understanding the Christian faith-practice.[27] One explanation for these differences is the partly different origins of the Anabaptists (today Mennonites) on the one side, and, for example, of the Baptists, who have their origin partly in English separatist Puritanism, and Methodism that grew up inside the Anglican Church and was

---

[24]*Ethics*, 17-46, esp. 27-35. McClendon prefers the label "baptist" (not "Baptist"), which is Anabaptist without the prejudicial Ana-. It has for McClendon, however, the same broad sense as I have given Radical Reformation. In contemporary German, Täufer is used instead of Wiedertäufer. See ibid., 19. The problem with the baptist label is that it too easily becomes confused with the more narrow Baptist, and also because it might give the issue of believer's baptism a too central role for the whole phenomenon I describe.

[25]Ibid., 27f.

[26]Ibid., 35 and further pp. 27-35. See also Durnbaugh, *The Believers' Church*, 209-299, and idem, "Characteristics".

[27]It might be noted that in the classical Swedish, so-called, Free Church tradition with its origins in Lutheran Pietism, Baptism and (later) Pentecostalism, pacifism for a long time has been the normative (though not exclusive) practice. Sweden has compulsory military service, which make this question an issue for every male. There has not been much historical study on this, but one that has been done is Gustafsson, *Fred och försvar i frikyrkligt perspektiv 1900-1921*.

strongly influenced by Pietism, on the other side.[28] Although McClendon and Hauerwas represent the two latter traditions, it is Yoder's constructive work that has been decisive—a further reason to use the designation Radical Reformation.

c) The Ecumenical Claims of Radical Reformation Theology

Yoder describes this type of theology and practice as a form of Christianity that not only was, he thinks, dominant in the early church, but which has also existed in various forms throughout church history inside the established churches (monasticism in the Roman Catholic church is an obvious example).[29] So Contemporary Radical Reformation theology should not be understood in narrow confessional terms. It makes ecumenical claims. Yoder says that it "is a vision of unlimited catholicity"[30] and Hauerwas describes himself as "a servant to the church catholic".[31] I have related this position to specific church traditions because I want to stress that it has grown, and continues to grow, out of actual church life; that is, it is not a construction of independent "thinkers". It is written out of specific communities, but it is written for the "church catholic".

In contemporary theology, one also finds many examples of a similar direction in theologies from other church traditions, both independently developed and under the influence of Radical Reformation theology. Yoder and Hauerwas have been highly influential outside their own tradition, both generally in setting part of the agenda for modern theological debate and for positively influencing contemporary theology. Two quite remarkable examples of the latter might be especially mentioned. The first is the "Postmodern critical Augustinianism" of the English Anglo-Catholic theologian John Milbank, whose work shows a strong Hauerwas

---

[28]Yoder's discussion in "A Non-Baptist View of Southern Baptists" of temptations into which Southern Baptism easily falls indicates his view of the questions in which this difference of perspective becomes apparent. First, there is a tendency to a quasi-Constantinianism, in which God and church are intimately related to the established order. This is also expressed in the lowering of the baptismal age. Second, a strongly individualistic and inward understanding of conversion and sanctification (and salvation in general) which also leads to an uncritical attitude to the general individualism in American society. Third, a congregationalism that misses the churchly character of what is beyond the local congregation. Fourth, a social ethics that puts the stress on transformed individuals' influence on society. Fifth, an uncritical acceptance of modern nationalism over the church's cosmopolitanism. Sixth, a quasi-creedalism inherited from the fundamentalist controversy.

[29]This is also the view of Troeltsch in *The Social Teaching of the Christian Churches*. Cf. the discussion reported in Durnbaugh, *The Believers' Church*, 8-22.

[30]*The Priestly Kingdom*, 4. See further ibid., 1-6 and "Reformed Versus Anabaptist".

[31]"Will the Real Sectarian Stand Up", 92. "No theologian should desire anything less than that his or her theology reflect the catholic character of the church. Thus I hope my theology is catholic inasmuch as it is true to those Protestants and Roman Catholics who constitute the church catholic." (*PK* xxvi.) "Methodist identity makes sense only as it entails a commitment to discovering the unity of God's church through our different histories." ("The Testament of Friends", 214f.) So also *AN* 19 and "Protestants and the Pope", 84f.

influence,[32] who himself is one of the most perceptive commentators on Hauerwas' theology, and who has also, in turn, influenced Hauerwas.[33] The second example is the American Armenian Orthodox theologian Vigen Guroian, who is also strongly influenced by Hauerwas and Yoder in his attempt "to do ethics out of the Orthodox tradition within a North American context".[34]

In Roman Catholic theology, the most striking example of a position close to Radical Reformation theology is the work of the German exegete Gerhard Lohfink, who independently of Yoder and Hauerwas has formulated a very similar understanding of the church and the Christian life.[35] Among Reformed theologians Jacques Ellul and Lesslie Newbigin might be mentioned,[36] and also, as we will see, Moltmann. Actually, in an article co-written by Yoder and the Reformed philosopher and theologian Richard Mouw, the polarity traditionally seen between Anabaptist and Reformed ethics is questioned. This conflict is, they argue, better seen as a family quarrel that not only goes on between the two traditions, but also inside them. They especially point to commonalities in their use of Scripture and in their communal ethics.[37] If this analysis is accepted, it gives an additional explanation to Moltmann's positive attitude to the Radical Reformation and the general Free Church tradition (parts of which of course came from, and often still consider itself to be part of, the Reformed tradition).[38]

Although Hauerwas is usually critical of Lutheran theology,[39] the best work about Hauerwas is written by a German Lutheran, Reinhard Hütter, who himself is sympathetic to Hauerwas' position.[40] An interesting comparison could also be

---

[32]Generally on his theology, see his "Postmodern Critical Augustinianism". The label "postmodern" should be qualified, because in the end Milbank deconstructs postmodernity from a Christian perspective. See *Theology and Social Theory* and "Problematizing the Secular".

[33]On Hauerwas, see "Critical Study" and "Between Purgation and Illumination", 188-192, 196. For comments by Hauerwas, see "Epilogue", 151, 176f, "On being 'placed' by John Milbank", and "Creation, Contingency, and Truthful Non-Violence". Milbank is given an important place in Hauerwas' recent *AC* and "Virtue Christianly Considered".

[34]*Incarnate Love*, 1. In addition to this book, see also his "Tradition and Ethics".

[35]See esp. *Jesus and Community* and *Wem gilt die Bergpredigt?*

[36]I think especially of Newbigin's *The Gospel in a Pluralist Society*. Parts of his related book *Foolishness to the Greeks* seem to go in another direction. Of Ellul's many books *Éthique de la Liberté*, *The Subversion of Christianity*, and *Anarchy and Christianity* may be mentioned in this context.

[37]"Evangelical Ethics and the Anabaptist-Reformed Dialogue". See also Yoder, "Reformed Versus Anabaptist", Mouw, "Abandoning the Typology", idem, "Creational Politics", and idem, *The God Who Commands*, esp. 110-149.

[38]In her recent major analysis of Moltmann's ecclesiology, Mary Brink consistently describes and analyses Moltmann as a faithful Lutheran ("The Ecclesiological Dimensions of Jurgen Moltmann's Theology", v, 42-49, 183, 257, 260-269)! Although Moltmann uses Luther more than Calvin, his Reformed roots are very important for the understanding of his theology and especially his ecclesiology. I am, however, not sure if Brink is aware that not all Protestants are Lutherans, as she also describes Barth as a Lutheran theologian, and therefore the strong Barthian influence on Moltmann's theology as a Lutheran influence (pp. 42, 185f). Also Anabaptists and Mennonites are called Lutherans (p. 247).

[39]He actually started his teaching career (1968-1970) at the (Swedish) Lutheran Augustana College.

[40]See *Evangelische Ethik als kirchliches Zeugnis*, "Ethik in Traditionen", and "The Ecclesial Ethics of Stanley Hauerwas". Another Lutheran sympathetic to Hauerwas is Robert Jenson, which is shown in

made between Hauerwas and the influential Lutheran George Lindbeck. The similarities have often been noted, even by Lindbeck and Hauerwas themselves, although the differences between them are substantial.[41] Although not a contemporary theologian, one Lutheran theologian that should be mentioned is Dietrich Bonhoeffer whose ideas of discipleship, pacifism and the church as an alternative *polis* come close to the Radical position and who also deeply influenced Moltmann.[42] The Confessing Church is another often mentioned twentieth century expression of the general Believers' Church type.[43] Theologically this is the tradition out of which Moltmann came.[44] Finally, among American Evangelical theologians Robert Webber and Rodney Clapp (both Episcopalians) can be mentioned as examples of the influence of Yoder and Hauerwas.[45]

d) Hauerwas as a Radical Reformation Theologian

The theologian I have chosen to represent Contemporary Radical Reformation theology is Hauerwas. He is a Methodist theologian teaching theological ethics at Duke University. Previously for fourteen years he was at the Catholic University of Notre Dame. A natural alternative would have been Yoder. Although Yoder may be the more original, Hauerwas has developed Yoder's theology in a very

---

one of the most perceptive articles written on Hauerwas, "The Hauerwas Project". See also his "Hauerwas Examined". It is often noted that it is not too difficult to find texts by (especially the early) Luther that point in this direction. Durnbaugh even builds his developed definition of the Believers' Church on a quotation from Luther. See *The Believers' Church*, 3 and 32f.

[41]Lindbeck and Hauerwas are, together with people like Hans Frei and Ronald Thiemann, often described as leading so-called postliberal theologians. See Placher, "Postliberal Theology" and idem, *Unapologetic Theology*, 17-21, 154-174. For Hauerwas' discussion of his relation to Lindbeck's approach, see esp. *AN* 1-9. By Lindbeck, see esp. *The Nature of Doctrine*, "The Sectarian Future of the Church", "The Church's Mission to a Postmodern Culture", and "Confession and Community" (cf. p. 492 on Hauerwas). In his later writings Lindbeck sometimes leans in a more Neoconservative direction. Moreover, "postliberal" denotes more a way of doing theology than specific substantial positions and the similarity between Hauerwas and Lindbeck should therefore not be overemphasized. The differences are important. For a criticism of Lindbeck from a perspective similar to Hauerwas', see Milbank, *Theology and Social Theory*, 382-388.

[42]See esp. *The Cost of Discipleship* and *Life Together*, as well as McClendon, *Ethics*, 187-208 and Fowl and Jones, *Reading in Communion*, 135-164. For Moltmann on Bonhoeffer, see e.g. "The Lordship of Christ and Human Society", and on the relation between Bonhoeffer and Moltmann, Chapman, "Hope and the Ethics of Formation".

[43]Durnbaugh, *The Believers' Church*, 176-191.

[44]Moltmann's teachers in Göttingen Otto Weber, Hans Joachim Iwand and Ernst Wolf were not only strongly influenced by Barth, they were also leaders in the Confessing Church and critics of the restoration of the German church after the War. As Meeks shows in *Origins of the Theology of Hope*, 18-53, the importance of these theologians for the shape of Moltmann's theology can hardly be overemphasized. Furthermore, of especial importance for the purpose of this book is that Weber's *Versammelte Gemeinde* from 1949 (republished with an introduction by Moltmann in 1975) has a strong Radical Reformation character. Another of his mentors were the Russian-born Mennonite Johannes Harder. I owe these last points to Yoder.

[45]*People of the Truth.*

interesting direction and writes on a wider range of subjects than Yoder.[46] Especially interesting is his analysis of liberal society and the church's life in that sort of society. Yet, it could not be strongly enough stressed that Hauerwas' theology, as it is today, is unthinkable without the extensive influence of Yoder, who has developed the basic tenets of Radical Reformation theology more extensively than Hauerwas. The latter tends in this respect to build directly on these tenets. A further reason is Hauerwas' central and controversial role in especially contemporary American, but also increasingly European, theology and ethics. The Princeton philosopher Jeffrey Stout wrote 1987 following about Hauerwas' influence in North America:

> Over the last decade, he has done more than anyone but the liberation theologians to set the agenda for Christian ethics. It is hard to imagine what recent work on character, the virtues, narrative, and the relation between the church and liberal society might look like in the absence of Hauerwas' influence. Indeed, it is hard to know whether these topics would seem as central as they do had Hauerwas not helped make them unavoidable.[47]

What I mean with characterizing Hauerwas as a Contemporary Radical Reformation theologian will become clear from my actual exposition of his theology. Nonetheless, some initial reflections in relation to the foregoing might be appropriate here. Often quoted is his statement that "my ecclesial preference is to be a high-church Mennonite."[48] He also says that he "believes that the most nearly faithful form of Christian witness is best exemplified by the often unjustly ignored people called anabaptists or Mennonites."[49] The high-church part refers to his strong Catholic sympathies. But he has also interpreted the above statement in the following way: "by describing myself as a high-church Mennonite I am saying I am Methodist."[50] By this he means that "Methodists are a people with Catholic practices of Eucharist" that "have a free church ecclesiology."[51] This seemingly

---

[46]It seems that the largest part of Yoder's work is only available in semi-published and unpublished form. His work is in other words much more extensive and wider than most people suspect. Nigel Wright at the University of London is at the moment working on a dissertation about Yoder and Moltmann. He has already written a shorter study which has only been published in Swedish under the title *Makt och lärjungaskap*.

[47]Review of Hauerwas, *Suffering Presence*, 124. In Hans Ulrich's recent anthology *Evangelische Ethik* it is James Gustafson and Hauerwas that represent American Protestant ethics and in Ulrich's overview of North American theological ethics, Hauerwas has the most prominent place. See "Theologische Ethik im englischsprachigen Kontext", esp. 79-83. Reinhard Hütter's *Evangelische Ethik* is the first book about Hauerwas and one book by Hauerwas is presently being translated into German. When I started this work he was almost unknown in Sweden. That is no longer the case, which for example a recent theme issue on theological ethics in Sweden gives witness to. See Bexell and others, "Ämnespresentation: Etik."

[48]*CC* 6. In another context he describes himself as "a Mennonite camp follower". ("The Testament of Friends", 214.) On his ecclesiological background, see also *PK* xiv, xxvi and *CET* 39, 115-131.

[49]*CC* 6.

[50]"The Testament of Friends", 214.

[51]"Why *Resident Aliens* struck a chord", 427. See also "The Testament of Friends", 214 and "The Importance of Being Catholic", 28, 44 n. 3.

confusing picture gives a rather adequate portrait of the theology of Hauerwas and says something about Radical Reformation theology in general. In his early work *Character and the Christian Life*[52] he developed, partly using the work of Aristotle and Thomas Aquinas, a concept of character as a conceptually and ethically useful interpretation of the doctrine of sanctification in the works of John Calvin, John Wesley and Jonathan Edwards.[53] So, already here we find a combination of Methodist (as well as Reformed[54]) and Catholic traditions, together with a critique of the Lutheran use of the doctrine of justification. His fourteen years at Notre Dame only reinforced the Catholic character of his theology, as Catholicism became a major context for his theological work.[55]

However, it was also during this time that he discovered the work of Yoder, which helped him to develop an ecclesiology that was the necessary concomitant to his ethics of character and virtue and made his whole approach less abstract. This ecclesiology entailed both a specific christology and a pacifism that became crucial for his further theological development. He did not thus see this reception of Radical Reformation theology as a break with, but rather as a development entailed by his Catholic Methodist theology, although he was at first unwilling to take this path.[56]

He has also, although not at length, pointed to the similarities between Radical Reformation theology and both Methodism (or more exactly Wesley himself)[57] and Catholicism.[58] On the former he is supported (though maybe for him in a too Protestant way) by Howard Snyder's comparison between Wesley and Radical Reformation theology. Snyder mentions as central characteristics of the Radical tradition things like the church as a covenanted community in contrast to the world, mutual edification and discipline, lay movement, a practical use of

---

[52]This book, published 1975, is built on his dissertation from 1968. I do not know to what extent the latter was revised. For his own later evaluation and critique of this book, see the long introduction to the edition of 1985.

[53]His only other substantial discussion of Wesley is "Characterizing Perfection".

[54]Like for Moltmann and Yoder, Barth has also been important for Hauerwas, as other Reformed theologians like the Niebuhrs and his teacher at Yale James Gustafson have been. This might reinforce Yoder's and Mouw's contention above. In *PK* xix-xxv he discusses theologians and philosophers that in different ways have influenced him.

[55]On this, see esp. "Importance", 27-30. He even says "that most of the time I was at Notre Dame, I did not think of myself as a Protestant ethicist—I thought I was a Catholic" (p. 28). Cf. his reflections on this in the introductions to two books coming from the later part of this time, *CC* 6 and *PK* xxvi. Robert Jenson describes him as a "barely-crypto-Catholic" in "The Hauerwas Project", 292.

[56]The necessity of an ecclesial account was already stressed, but not developed, in *CCL* (e.g. 231f, cf. xxxif.) His encounter with Yoder came before all of his published writings. I do not know what his pre-Yoder ecclesiology was like, but already in an article that originally was delivered 1971, "The Future of Christian Social Ethics", 129-131, he seems to affirm what could be called a Radical Reformation ecclesiology. For his early work on Yoder, see *VV* 197-221, "Messianic Pacifism", and "The Ethicist as Theologian", 411f. On his encounter with Yoder, see "When the Politics of Jesus Makes a Difference".

[57]"Characterizing Perfection", 262 n. 27. Cf. also "A Pacifist Response to *In Defense of Creation*", esp. 5f.

[58]"Importance", 44 n. 2, *DFF* 212.

Scripture, primitivism and restitutionism, a pragmatic approach to church order, and the visibility of the church in the community of believers. His conclusion is that "[a]t practically every point Wesley incorporated the emphases and concerns of the Radical Protestant tradition. But he did so as an established churchman."[59] The latter comment refers to the modification of these features caused by the fact that Methodism at the time of Wesley was still a community inside the Church of England. It had not been forced to become a separate church.[60] Snyder, however, also mentions themes that were important for only some parts of the Radical tradition, and to which there is lesser commonality found in Wesley, "such as suffering, the eschatological vision, pacifism, consensus in decision making, ecumenism and separation from the state."[61] These are themes that became important in the Anabaptist tradition and that are crucial for Hauerwas, who says that "the most determinative difference" between Methodism and Anabaptism concerns the understandings of non-violence and forgiveness.[62]

On the relation between sixteenth century Anabaptism and Catholicism it is often agreed today that it is not correct to simply interpret the Anabaptist movements as the left wing of a scale where Catholicism is on the right and Lutheranism and Calvinism in the middle. (However, it could be questioned how meaningful a comparison between such broad and diverse phenomena as Anabaptism and medieval and sixteenth century Catholicism is.) Weaver writes that "Anabaptists stood to the left of the reformers on ecclesiology, sacraments, and political and social outlook, but to the right on certain doctrinal issues such as affirmation of free will and insistence on righteous personal living."[63]

If one widens the comparison to the whole Believers' Church tradition, the relation becomes even more complex, although the later churches obviously more clearly grew up on Protestant soil. One might still in theological terms see part of this heritage as closer to Catholicism than to Protestantism. In the form it takes in the theology of Hauerwas, this can be seen in the following: his emphasis on the visibility of the church and its character as a disciplined community in contrast to the strong individualism in much of Protestantism, parts of the Free Church included; the centrality of sanctification against the strong emphasis on justification by faith (in Lutheran interpretation); the Bible as read in the Christian community against a simple *Sola Scriptura* principle; and his strong emphasis on the eucharist and on liturgy (here together with Lutheranism) against spiritualism and ra-

---

[59]*The Radical Wesley*, 123. See further ibid., 109-124. On the differences between Radical Reformation and Methodist theology, on the one hand, and Catholic and Reformation theology, on the other, see Finger, *Christian Theology*, vol. 2, 225-245. Durnbaugh discusses Methodism as one type of Free Church Pietism in *The Believers' Church*, 130-145. See also Westin, *Den kristna friförsamlingen*, esp. 222-226.

[60]Snyder, *The Radical Wesley*, 117f.

[61]Ibid., 114.

[62]"Characterizing Perfection", 262 n. 27.

[63]Weaver, *Becoming Anabaptist*, 20. See also e.g. Klaasen, *Anabaptism: Neither Catholic nor Protestant*, Goertz, *Die Täufer*, 149f, and McClendon, "Balthasar Hubmaier, Catholic Anabaptist".

tionalism. Radical Reformation should thus not be understood as Radical Protestant.[64] Instead, when Hauerwas is described as a Radical Reformation theologian
the broad sense I have given this designation and his ecumenical or catholic intention should be remembered.

e) Contemporary Radical Reformation Theology and Political Theology

Contemporary Radical Reformation theology is thus *one* way of doing theology out of the faith-practice of the complex tradition or family of traditions I
have described. But I do not think it is exaggerating to say that, in the theological
community, Hauerwas and Yoder are its most influential representatives today,
especially concerning the issues of church and world.[65]

That I qualify this Radical Reformation theology as "contemporary" denotes
that it is a theology formed as much in a twentieth century ecclesial, social and
intellectual world as political theology is. These two types of theologies also have
much in common, for example the stress on the practical nature of Christian faith,
the social and political nature of salvation, the Bible as a critical subversive
memory, a strong eschatological perspective, the critique of society and the established church, the necessity of a post-Constantinian or post-Christendom
church, and the visibility of the church in the form of committed grass roots or
base communities as signs of the kingdom of God.

In this the increasing importance given by political theology to the base communities as context and bearers of the Christian faith and practice is crucial. As
such it can be interpreted as a further example of the recurring phenomenon of the
Radical Reformation.[66] When Metz writes that "the Christian church is a com-

---

[64]Although both Yoder and Hauerwas are best interpreted as "neither Catholic nor Protestant" one difference between them could be described in terms of Yoder being more Protestant and Hauerwas more
Catholic. Cf. *US* 152 n. 9. Another apparent difference is caused by the fact that Hauerwas' immediate
context is now mainline (or old-line) Protestantism, while Yoder's is Mennonitism. So while Hauerwas'
critical front has been liberal Protestantism (and Catholicism), Yoder's front has been more double,
both the ecumenical churches and the partly much more conservative Mennonite churches. This has
made him more amenable to self-confessed "progressive" theologies than Hauerwas has been, although
their substantial positions are close.

[65]Especially Yoder's influence has been remarkable. "Almost singlehandedly, Yoder has caused the
theological world to take seriously the Anabaptist ecclesiology and social ethic." (Webber and Clapp,
People of the Truth, 133.) Philip Wogaman considers this tradition to be one of four principal
"'generating centers' of Christian political thought" (*Christian Perspectives on Politics*, 31) in current
North American theology. His label for it is "Christian pacifist and anarchist perspectives", chosen because of the central role of peace and because of the primacy of church over state. The others are
"Christian liberationist perspectives", "Neoconservative Christian perspectives", and "Mainstream liberal Christian perspectives".

[66]The base community movements are widely described as one contemporary example of Radical
Reformation or Believers' Church ecclesiology. See e.g. *OHD* 115, Durnbaugh, "Characteristics", 30f
and McClendon, "Balthasar Hubmaier", 33. Guillermo Cook, in his large work on the Latin American
so-called base ecclesial communities, *The Expectation of the Poor*, develops this view extensively
discussing similarities in social and political context, theology and polity in his treatment of movements
such as the early church, Montanism, Donatism, various monastic communities, Anabaptism, Congre-

munity of the wholehearted discipleship of Jesus which gathers around the eucharist to remember and narrate its story",[67] it could just as well have been written by Hauerwas.

Yet, as stated above, these developments in political theology have led to severe tensions in its theological project, as I will try to show in the case of Moltmann,[68] and I will suggest that Radical Reformation theology shows what a more consistent unfolding of the consequences of the newer developments in political theology could look like. I will, moreover, suggest that Radical Reformation theology has also certain advantages in analytical power and applicability. This raises the question how such a thesis might be argued and leads us to the next chapter.

---

gationalism, Presbyterianism, Pietism and Methodism. See ibid., 173-199. In the book *Freedom and Discipleship* (ed. by Schipani) several Mennonite theologians discuss liberation theology, with responses from liberation theologians. Here also this theme is clear. It should, however, be remembered that liberation theology and the base community movements originally were separate phenomena, although they emerged in similar times and circumstances, so that it is not correct to describe the original roots of either in terms of the other. See Cook, *Poor*, 61-68, Hewitt, *Base Christian Communities and Social Change in Brazil*, 13-27, and McGovern, *Liberation Theology and Its Critics*, 199-201 for accounts of the emergence of the base communities. For a theological reflection from a liberation theologian, see Boff, *Church*. It is, however, interesting to find the criticism directed to them as in themselves being politically ineffective, and that they therefore are urged to collaborate more with political parties and movements. This criticism (reported and supported by McGovern, *Liberation Theology*, 212) is interesting, because it is the same criticism that is directed against Hauerwas and Yoder. On this issue the conclusion of Hewitt's empirical study is that social change "is far more subtle, far more indirect than the more optimistic (and especially liberationist) visions of the groups have suggested." (*Base Christian Communities*, 84. See further ibid., 81-90.) Cf. also Martin, *Tongues of Fire* and Stoll, *Is Latin America Turning Protestant*, who both argue that evangelical Protestantism and especially Pentecostalism is not only a much larger phenomenon, but also probably more important for the future transformation of both Latin American Christianity and society than the base communities and liberation theology. Cook, in a review article on these two books, says that according to recent studies large numbers of members of Catholic base communities are joining Pentecostal churches. See "The Evangelical Groundswell in Latin America", 1175. Hewitt also says that the groups are decreasing in numbers and influence (*Base Christian Communities*, 91-105).

[67]"Suchbewegungen nach einem neuen Gemeindebild", 155.

[68]I cannot develop it here, but I think there are similar developments and concomitant tensions in Metz' theology as in Moltmann's, even if there are many important differences between them. See e.g. his later works, such as *The Emergent Church, Followers of Christ* and his contributions to Kaufmann and Metz, *Zukunftsfähigkeit*. Cf. also Wiedenhofer's account of the development of political theology (and especially Metz) in "Politische Theologie". On the subject of changes in Latin American liberation theology, see Sigismund, *Liberation Theology at the Crossroads*, 176-182 and McGovern, *Liberation Theology*, 132-135.

Chapter 2

Reflections on Method

> Nearly all methodological debate is useless, because nearly all methodological debate is reducible to the formula: You should not be doing your job; you should be doing mine.
>
> J. G. A. Pocock[1]

> preoccupation with method is like clearing your throat: it can go on for only so long before you lose your audience.
>
> Jeffrey Stout[2]

This book discusses the mutual relation and relative adequacy of two contemporary theological traditions and the forms of ecclesial practice they are related to. I do not only describe and compare these two theologies, I also perform a modest argument about coherence, faithfulness and applicability. In substantial terms this book could thus with George Lindbeck's words be described as a contribution to the discussion to how in our context "life is to be lived and reality construed in the light of God's character as an agent as this is depicted in the stories of Israel and Jesus."[3] One advantage with this characterization is that it is a good description of what both Moltmann and Hauerwas want to do.[4] In this chapter I will discuss how this task can be accomplished with reference to a way of understanding theology that, in somewhat different forms, has become common in the international literature.[5]

I do, however, think that this sort of methodological preface has limited value. Methodological self-consciousness is valuable, but methodological competence has more to do with the skill learned through practice than with any knowledge of general principles. Therefore, there is more than a little truth in Jeffrey Stout's recommendation that a "theology that hopes to converse on moral and other topics in a pluralistic setting like ours had better dispense with the quest for a

---

[1]"Political Ideas as Historical Events", 139.

[2]*Ethics after Babel*, 163.

[3]Lindbeck, *The Nature of Doctrine*, 121.

[4]To put it differently, as an exercise in what in Lund is now called systematic theology, its main task is "to contribute to an interpretation of the teaching of Christianity that elucidates what Christian faith can involve in the current ecclesial, social and cultural situation." If "practice" is included in or added to "Christian faith", this recent Swedish semi-official description of the task of systematic theology is also a good description of what I am doing in this book. The citation is from Jeffner, Lønning, Jørgensen, "Sakkunnigutlåtande rörande professuren i systematisk teologi vid Lunds universitet", 1f. This is almost wholly reproduced in Frostin, "Systematisk teologi i ett pluralistiskt samhälle", 156f.

[5]In my understanding of the subject-matter and method of systematic theology, I am especially indebted to Fiorenza, *Foundational Theology*, Gregersen, *Teologi og kultur*, idem, "How to Cope with Pluralism in Dogmatics", Lindbeck, *The Nature of Doctrine*, Murphy, *Theology in the Age of Scientific Reasoning*, and Thiemann, *Revelation and Theology*. Though not having identical positions, they all affirm something like the nonfoundational and holistic approach to theological argumentation that I in the following describe.

method. There is no method for good argument and conversation save being conversant—that is, being well versed in one's own tradition and on speaking terms with others."[6] Furthermore, methods are relative to the tasks pursued, which makes discussions of general methods of lesser importance. A further reason for scepticism about the value of this chapter is the notorious lack of agreement on methodological issues. However, if it can help explain what I am doing, and in light of the fact that theological method for decades has been the dominating and most controversial issue in especially Swedish theology, the following reflections might be of some value. However, since this is not a treatise in theological method, I will only be able to describe my position, not extensively argue for it. For further argumentation the reader has to go to the literature referred to.

1. A Nonfoundational and Holistic Account of Justification

My approach is nonfoundational and assumes a holistic account of justification.[7] This needs some explanation. Foundational[8] epistemologies have dominated Western thought for centuries, but have in the second half of this century been severely criticized,[9] although the older habits of thought still have much power

---

[6]Stout, *Ethics after Babel*, 165. Cf. also James Gustafson's comments on this preoccupation with method in theology and ethics. There might, he says, be good reasons for that, especially given the current academic situation for these disciplines, but he also points to the oddness of the idea that "one had to resolve the methods of science before one engaged in any scientific investigation, as if the correction of method did not take place in the process of dealing with the substance of the problems under investigation." Furthermore, "[n]o one has established that an investigator does better science as a result of his knowledge of the philosophy of science, though self-criticism of one's method and procedure is a merit." (*Theology and Ethics*, 64. See further ibid., 62-76.)

[7]For the following, see from theological and philosophy of religion perspectives, in addition to the works mentioned in n. 5, Placher, *Unapologetic Theology*, McClendon and Smith, *Understanding Religious Convictions*, Mitchell, *The Justification of Religious Belief*, Wolterstorff, *Reason within the Bounds of Religion*, and the works mentioned below in n. 17, and from more general philosophical and moral philosophical perspectives Bernstein, *Beyond Objectivism and Relativism*, Dancy, *An Introduction to Contemporary Epistemology*, MacIntyre, *Whose Justice? Which Rationality?*, idem, *Three Rival Versions of Moral Enquiry*, Putnam, *Reason, Truth and History*, Rorty, *Philosophy and the Mirror of Nature*, Rajchman and West (eds.), *Post-Analytic Philosophy*, Stout, *Ethics after Babel*, and Taylor, *The Sources of the Self.* I have here basically limited myself to the Anglo-American traditions of philosophy and theology (the Danish theologian Gregersen is an exception). One reason for that is that these traditions are most relevant to the Swedish discussion which is so formed by analytical philosophy. I have furthermore, for my purposes, not found it worthwhile to relate myself to the German (e.g. Gadamer and Habermas) and French (e.g. Foucault and Derrida) discussions. For anyone interested in these relations, I recommend Placher, *Unapologetic Theology*, 74-104 and Bernstein's above mentioned book (where he tries to show an increasing convergence between Continental and Anglo-American post-empirical philosophy) as well as Bernstein's recent *The New Constellation.*

[8]In Swedish, following a common German usage, foundationalism is sometimes confusingly translated as "fundamentalism". E.g. in *Kommunikativt handlande*, 15 Habermas talks about "Kant's fundamentalism".

[9]"On all fronts foundationalism is in bad shape. It seems to me that there is nothing to do but give it up for mortally ill and learn to live in its absence." (Wolterstorff, *Reason*, 56.) "Although there are still some rearguard skirmishes, I think we can say, using James's phrase, that the 'choice' between founda-

over thought and institutions.[10] There are different versions of foundationalism, but for our purposes the following simplification might be enough. Foundationalism divides our beliefs in two types: beliefs that need the support from other beliefs and beliefs that are self-evident or irrefutable. For the former beliefs to be rational, they should in some way be based upon the foundation of self-evident or irrefutable beliefs. This can take both empiricist and rationalist forms. In the former case the basic beliefs are justified empirically, in the latter by transcendental deduction or conceptual analysis. This has in popular terms often boiled down to the idea that rational knowledge consists of observation plus logic and made the idea of the certain method central, with the consequence that whatever cannot be in such a way methodized (like values and religious beliefs) is considered to be outside rational knowledge.

The objections to this view are many. There is the difficulty to specify basic beliefs as well as to specify the relation between these basic beliefs and the theory they are supposed to support. However, the perhaps most influential argument is Quine's claim in his celebrated essay "Two Dogmas of Empiricism"[11] that "[o]ur statements about the external world face the tribunal of sense experience not individually but only as a corporate body."[12] Empirical statements, as other statements, do not have meaning separate from the whole web of belief in which they are inserted. The view that isolated statements are in some way equivalent to or represent simple facts in the world, and that they therefore can be directly verified or falsified by experience, is thus not tenable. Quine's often quoted web-metaphor is quite telling:

> The totality of our so-called knowledge or beliefs . . . is a man-made fabric which impinges on experience only along the edges. . . . A conflict with experience at the periphery occasions adjustments in the interior of the field. . . . But the total field is so underdetermined

Quine's argument

---

tionalism and non-foundationalism is no longer a 'live option;' it is a 'dead option.'"(Bernstein, *Philosophical Profiles*, 91.) And "with the qualifications now needed to evade criticism there is no longer any point in holding a foundationalist view of knowledge." (Murphy, *Theology*, 8 n. 10.)
[10]MacIntyre has aptly described the current mentality in the academic world in the following way: the "moral and intellectual *weltanschauung*" that is built on foundationalistic assumptions has been undermined "in such a way as to make it no longer rationally defensible, yet left it in place in the university community as a set of no longer quite held, not to be explicitly articulated, background presuppositions, a set of almost but not quite believed propositions still informing both the academic curriculum and modes of teaching and enquiry in a number of significant ways". (*Three Rival Versions*, 229.) Mary Midgley writes similarly on logical-positivist thinking. "Academics have indeed long ceased to defend its confusions, but it is still powerful. Though its logic was quickly exposed, its general message was never refuted in a manner understandable to the heart." ("Strange Contest", 47.) A further reason for its strength is its role as what Michael Mulkey in *The Sociology of Science*, 62-78 calls an occupational ideology that legitimates the status and authority of science or the academic world.
[11]*From a Logical Point of View*, 20-46.
[12]Ibid., 41.

by its boundary conditions, experience, that there is much latitude of choice as to what statements to reevaluate in the light of any single contrary experience.[13]

There is then no clear-cut methodical way to verify or falsify individual statements, but neither is any statement in principle immune to revision.

There is a further argument that, in effect, is even more damaging. No one has yet succeeded in formulating a foundationalist account that has found general support. This lack makes such accounts practically useless for arguing contested knowledge claims to people who either believe in contending foundationalist accounts or deny foundationalism itself. Why base often less contested substantial claims on much more controversial epistemological theories? As Don Herzog says, "successful foundational justifications are philosopher's pet unicorns; we have yet to see one."[14]

This has been confirmed in the philosophy of science. For a long time this discipline was dominated by logical positivists and (later) neopositivists who tried to develop a logic of science in terms of verification or falsification. These approaches have broken down, both because of internal incoherence and because historical studies have shown that science does not follow these rules, and that if they were strictly followed this would hinder scientific progress. Most familiar are the work of people like Michael Polanyi, Thomas Kuhn, Imre Lakatos and Paul Feyerabend.[15] It is well known that Kuhn describes the development of science in terms of the development of paradigms, and Lakatos in terms of research programs. In an accepted paradigm or research program the basic convictions and theories are assumed, and therefore not continuously tested. The continuing work instead consists of, against the background of the accepted web of beliefs, developing the paradigm and of solving puzzles that arise. When a paradigm's problem-solving capacity decreases, the anomalies increase, and if an alternative paradigm is available, a paradigm shift occurs. But there is no direct logical road from one paradigm to another. The basic difference between Kuhn and Lakatos is that the latter argued that the criterion of empirical progress can be used for choosing one research program over another, but not even that is a clear-cut criterion that can give immediate result.[16]

The perhaps most common alternative to foundationalism is holistic types of justification.[17] This means that there is no foundation or starting-point for argu-

---

[13]Ibid., 42-43.

[14]*Without Foundations*, 225.

[15]See e.g. Polanyi, *Personal Knowledge*, Kuhn, *The Structure of Scientific Revolutions*, Lakatos, *The Methodology of Scientific Research Programmes*, and Feyerabend, *Against Method*.

[16]Murphy's book is an ambitious attempt to make the Lakatosian program relevant for theology. Lindbeck and Mitchell are examples of theologians that in this respect tend in a Kuhnian direction.

[17]The works in systematic theology I mentioned in n. 5 all defend some form of holism. For a somewhat different response to the collapse of classical foundationalism, see Plantinga and Wolterstorff (eds.), *Faith and Rationality*, Plantinga, "Coherentism and the Evidentialist Objection to Belief in God", Clark, *Return to Reason*. For some critical remarks to this approach, see Murphy, *Theology*, 192-195. Also relevant to this discussion is Alston, *Epistemic Justification*, esp. 17-78.

mentation, but that disputed beliefs are justified by appeals to currently undisputed beliefs. Disputed beliefs cannot be settled through reference to an unquestionable set of beliefs (comparison of beliefs with facts), but only through reference to other parts of the web of belief, because there is no theory or language independent relation to something called "reality". Francis Schüssler Fiorenza can therefore write "that a discipline is rational not because it has a foundation, but because it is a self-correcting enterprise that examines all claims, all relevant background theories—even though not all at once."[18]

2. Nonfoundational Theology

For theology this means that, as Ronald Thiemann writes, "justification of Christian belief is specific to the Christian faith, community, and tradition." He continues

> that for all its variety of expression, its quarrels and disagreements, Christianity *is* a tradition. By tradition I mean that Christianity is 'an historically extended, socially embodied argument . . . an argument precisely in part about the goods which constitute that tradition.' 'The Christian faith' is that set of beliefs and practices which in their social and historical reality provide the context for arguments about which beliefs and practices ought so to function.[19]

Christianity can thus be seen as an interpretative community conveying past experiences and a language in which new experiences can be interpreted.[20] Arguments for specific beliefs and practices are consequently made in terms of this tradition, that is in terms of common beliefs and practices. Political theology and Radical Reformation theology are thus participators in this historically ongoing argument about how in our context life is to be lived and how reality is to be construed in the light of the Christian faith. They do not stand above the tradition, but argue in terms of it. The same is thus true for me doing this investigation. This means that instead of starting the argument with some universal principles or criteria that every rational person should accept, one starts from shared convictions. As Thiemann writes: "In order for rational argument to occur between proponents of theologically diverse positions, one simply needs some set of common beliefs from which to begin the process of persuasion. The more extensive the set of beliefs held in common the broader the range of agreement is likely to be."[21]

The concern of this study is practical—one might describe it as a study in Christian political theory. The issue is how the church's political claims should be

---

[18]Fiorenza, *Foundational Theology*, 287.

[19]Thiemann, *Revelation and Theology*, 72f. The internal quotation is from MacIntyre, *After Virtue*, 207.

[20]It is in such terms Soskice contends that referential claims are made. See *Metaphor and Religious Language*, 142-161. Cf. also Murphy, *Theology*, 130-173.

[21]Thiemann, *Revelation and Theology*, 69.

understood and practised. Its type of argumentation can therefore fruitfully be compared to arguments in political theory. On this Michael Walzer (criticizing John Rawls' *A Theory of Justice*) says the following:

> Even if they are committed to impartiality, the question most likely to arise in the minds of the members of a political community is not, What would rational individuals choose under universalizing conditions of such-and-such a sort. But rather, What would individuals like us choose, who are situated as we are, who share a culture and are determined to go on sharing it? And this is a question that is readily transformed into, What choices have we already made in the course of our common life? What understandings do we (really) share?[22]

The question for the theologian then is how the community called the church, sharing these particular convictions, living with these particular practices and moral traditions, should deal with this or that issue.

Conversely, new insights, knowledge or experience might also lead to revisions in formerly assumed beliefs and practices. If the Christian tradition is understood as an ongoing argument, it is revisable. Furthermore, if it deals with the whole of reality, as Moltmann and Hauerwas claim, it will always interact with other claims to knowledge, which it has to interpret and assimilate in some way. How that should be done is one of the issues between Moltmann and Hauerwas, but neither of them defends a notion of theology as wholly separate from other fields of knowledge or from other moral institutions and communities.

In our case Moltmann and Hauerwas share many beliefs that I in the following will treat as premises for further argument. This includes a trinitarian construal of the Christian faith, the centrality of the story of Jesus Christ, the intrinsically eschatological nature of Christian faith, its public and political nature, the centrality of the church as a concrete community, and a theological ethics. Not everyone, of course, accepts all or any of these premises, but as this book concerns a discussion between Moltmann and Hauerwas I will assume them.

3. Criteria Used

Which types of more concrete criteria can then be used? Even if there are no easily formalizable criteria, in a more loose sense several criteria are suggested in the literature I have been using. Niels Henrik Gregersen mentions inner logical consistency, coherence and Christian authenticity (the latter includes the proposal's relation to Scripture, the theological tradition and contemporary theology and its reception in the Christian communities);[23] Thiemann talks about the criteria of intelligibility, Christian aptness, and warranted assertability;[24] and Lindbeck about faithfulness, applicability and intelligibility.[25]

---

[22]*Spheres of Justice*, 5.
[23]*Teologi og kultur*, 227-239 and "Pluralism".
[24]Thiemann, *Revelation and Theology*, 92.
[25]Lindbeck, *The Nature of Doctrine*, 112-138.

It is obviously impossible to use these criteria in an exhaustive way. Limitations in ambition have to be made. First there is the issue of *consistency* and *coherence*. They are not only prerequisites for intelligible communication, but also helpful for clarifying the structures of and discussing the relation between these two theologies. While the question of the coherence of these theological programs has a prominent place in this investigation, it should however be remembered that Christianity is not first of all an intellectual system, but "a complex, various, loosely held, and yet really discernible community".[26] A problem with the metaphor "web of belief" is that it easily leads to the idea of theology as a sort of conceptual system that is independent of the concrete beliefs, practices, rituals, and institutions of the Christian church. Theology then becomes a general study of the concept "God", about its meaning and possible reference. Such a view of theology might be common, but is alien to the way Moltmann and Hauerwas see the theological task. For them theology is primarily a practical discipline closely related to the actual life of the church as a critical reflection on its faith-practice. Yet, this faith-practice raises, as we will see, issues of consistency and coherence in very direct and practical ways.

Christian authenticity, aptness or *faithfulness* concern their theologies' relation to Scripture and the general Christian tradition.[27] This criterion is crucial for these two theologies. Yet I will not make an independent analysis of their use of the Bible and tradition. There are several reasons for this, besides the inherent problems and the lack of space and time for such an investigation. First, there is (a growing) general agreement between Hauerwas and Moltmann, especially on the issues we deal with. This agreement in the use of Scripture is thus part of the set of background beliefs that functions as premises for the argument. This consensus can be used both for internal criticism and for mutual argumentation. I will for example suggest that it is not difficult to defend central aspects of Hauerwas' theology in terms of how Moltmann reads the Bible. Second, Moltmann's and (especially) Hauerwas' understandings of Scripture are notably seldom criticized. The criticisms are usually directed at a more general theological level or at the political inadequacy or unfeasibility of their theologies. Third, the biblical case has been well made by others. Most important is probably the work of Yoder and Lohfink, but I will in later chapters give also other examples.[28]

---

[26]Frei, *Types of Christian Theology*, 12, cf. 19f.

[27]On this Gregersen says that any theology which wants to identify itself as Christian must be able to show its relation to Scripture. It is not a question of strict deducibility, but "there must exist structural similarities" ("Pluralism", 134) between Scripture and theological proposals. Again this cannot be a neutral or independent criterion, both because the interpretation of the Bible is in itself a contested issue and because different Christian communities construe Scripture differently. The interpretation of Scripture, as other arguments, so to say, occurs inside the web of belief and practices the tradition in question constitutes. See Kelsey, *The Uses of Scripture in Recent Theology*.

[28]In relation to the classical theological traditions I will basically not do more than describe their own perspectives and arguments. It is also impossible to discuss their relations to all the various modern

The criterion of *applicability* concerns "how relevant or practical they are in concrete situations"[29] or, to put it differently, the ability of these two theologies to "guide praxis".[30] This criterion is crucial for both Moltmann and Hauerwas as well as for the purpose of this book. The political hermeneutics that Moltmann has developed is a sort of criterion of applicability and Hauerwas often argues for the intrinsically practical nature of Christian convictions and their justification. This criterion is thus internal to the theological programs at hand. That is to say that applicability has to be judged in relation to the basic convictions of respective theologies and therefore by their own standards.

This opens up large issues and I cannot deal with them all. There are however three considerations that I will keep in mind. I will, first, consider how their respective theologies work as tools for interpreting existing society. Second, I will determine how practical and relevant these theological proposals are in guiding and assessing Christian social and political practice. Third, I will discuss how ecclesially sustainable these proposals are; including already present or presumed consequences in churches following these proposals. I do not believe in strict sociological prediction (for reasons I will later provide), but there is a place for informed speculation on practical matters.

I will do this partly through extensive exposition and discussion of their interpretations of modern society and church life and their concomitant constructive recommendations, and partly through sociological inquiry. I will use tools and insights from other disciplines like sociology, political science, political and moral theory. What I have already said makes it clear, however, that I do not consider the more empirical disciplines as providing certain and unproblematic "facts" to which theology (or any other discipline) just has to bow. In sociology, for example, empirical knowledge is as theory bound as in any other discipline. Current sociology works from a great variety of perspectives, uses many different theories and methods, and consequently also displays much variety in how modern society is interpreted. There is therefore no simple way of using sociology (and other social sciences) and I cannot therefore say more than that I have used sociological tools and results that I have found fruitful, illuminating and persuasive.

Furthermore, my use of sociology is theoretically low key and is primarily used as contemporary social history. This approach reflects my primary need, but is also a consequence of my scepticism regarding the idea that there exist some social laws or general principles to which historical and social reality can be reduced, so that history becomes applied sociology or that religion can be reduced to its social base. Social life and social change are contingent. This does not deny that we can discern general patterns and lines of development, but there is, or so

---

theological proposals. I primarily limit myself to the two proposals they themselves represent. The "reception criterion" is also basically left outside this work.

[29]Lindbeck, *The Nature of Doctrine*, 124.

[30]Fiorenza, *Foundational Theology*, 307.

it can be argued, no necessity in these developments.[31] I will later, especially in chapters 11, 14 and 15, provide some arguments for this view.

Such an interpretation of sociology is not without importance for the sorts of theological projects that Moltmann and Hauerwas represent, because both of them argue the contingency of social life and that the Christian church represents an alternative perspective of reality as well as an alternative social order. These interpretations are thus not compatible with just any sociology. The question then becomes how persuasive and fruitful their social theologies are in this respect.

The mentioned criteria rarely give wholly decisive results. Arguments on the level of choice between theological programs are seldom conclusive in themselves. "There is no instant rationality in science or theology".[32] Fiorenza writes that this type of argument is "similar to practical and prudential judgements insofar as it is not based on the manifest evidence of one criterion or foundation, but rather on a multiplicity of diverse factors that must be continually re-evaluated and reinterpreted."[33] Most of my argument consists of descriptions of Moltmann and Hauerwas, and the argument depends first of all on the persuasiveness of these descriptions. Furthermore the conclusions one should draw from their common convictions are also more a question of practical judgement than strict logic. If my description of severe incoherence in Moltmann's theology is accepted, there might yet be other ways of resolving this than the one I will suggest. To use the language of philosophy of science, one might say that because theological traditions or programs take time to develop, they should not be given up too easily. Problems of coherence or applicability are not necessarily in themselves sufficient reasons for giving up a program. They could be corrected, or if no immediate solution is found they could be left aside for the time being because one judges the program in general as promising or progressive. Too many inherent problems will however in the long run make a program or tradition increasingly untenable. Yet, a program seldom dissolves only because of internal problems. A more promising alternative is also needed. That is what I suggest in this case. I will try to describe the theological politics of Hauerwas as a positive alternative to Moltmann's political theology.

---

[31]"It is supposed . . . that historiography gathers particular evidence, which is then dealt with by social science in a more universal fashion. Yet something like the converse is the case: there can only be a 'science' of particular, relatively stable formal systems, whereas history is the royal discipline which contemplates the transitions of systems, and so alone approaches, although in a sceptical spirit, the question of the human as such, human society as such." (Milbank, *Theology and Social Theory*, 259f.) The best general discussion about the relations between theology and social theory is found in Milbank's book, which we will return to later on.

[32]Murphy, *Theology*, 207.

[33]Fiorenza, *Foundational Theology*, 310.

4. On the Content of the Book

The rest of the book is divided into two main parts (followed by a conclusion). In Part Two I will discuss "the impasse of political theology" as we see it in the theology of Moltmann. I will in chapters three to five take up his understanding of the theological task, give an outline of his theological perspective, and describe his ecclesiology. The presentation and discussion will be oriented towards the issues of this book. This means, for example, that I will not in the chapter about his basic theology address all the various controversial issues that his theology raises, for example his trinitarian account, just as I will not in any detail discuss, for instance, Hauerwas' theory of virtue. In chapter six, which is crucial, I will deal with Moltmann's attempt to mediate Christianity and the Enlightenment tradition and the severe problems to which this leads. Chapter seven will in more detail treat one specific political and ethical issue: violence and peace. I have chosen this issue because it is central for and extensively discussed by both Moltmann and Hauerwas. It can therefore help us clarify the consequences, strengths and weaknesses of these two theological approaches. The final chapter in Part Two will discuss the social sources of political theology in the Christian parts of the so-called new social movements and the consequences this has. The perspective in chapters six and seven will be mainly the ones of theology and political theory, while it in chapter eight primarily will be sociological.

The third part of this book will present the theological politics of Hauerwas as a possibly better alternative than Moltmann's political theology. It is not only generally, I will contend, more coherent, it also more consistently follows up a central part of Moltmann's own theology. Granted the adequacy of these common convictions, Hauerwas can better integrate them in his theology than Moltmann is able to do. Furthermore, the problems in Moltmann's theology can persuasively be explained in terms of Hauerwas' theology. The move from political theology to theological politics is thus, or so I will argue, partly indicated in Moltmann's own theology. I will make this argument through a description of Hauerwas' theological politics that parallels the one of Moltmann and at the same time try to show its advantages. It is, however, not only more coherent, it has, I will suggest, certain advantages on the level of applicability. It has more powerful interpretative tools, its account of the church's life is more realistic and practical, and, as a consequence, it can better deal with the challenges to the church that modernity (and an emerging postmodern culture) poses.

Parts Two and Three are, however, not entirely parallel, because my primary interest is argument, not comparison. There is no separate chapter on Hauerwas' theological method, because these matters are in his case better dealt with in other chapters. Then there are two additional chapters. Chapter 11 on sectarianism deals extensively with the most common objection to Hauerwas' theology, and chapter 15 deals with the main worry which in its turn is related to that objection that Moltmann has with Radical Reformation theology. In chapter 16, finally, I will draw the argument together, partly through an explicit return to the provided criteria. These criteria determine the inquiry in the intervening chapters, but I will not explicitly discuss them until the last chapter.

My interest is therefore more systematic than genetic. I will not systematically treat from whom they got this and that idea or how their theological programs have developed. Besides the fact that these issues are not my primary interest, they have already been addressed by others.[34] Such issues will thus only be dealt with when they are helpful for the overall thesis.

Both these two theological programs have developed extensively during the years. Development is often a sign of strength, but it is not always so. Positive development can have to do with new insights, a working out of the logic of one's project, application to new areas, dealing with inadequacies and problems in the program, and so on. We find this sort of development in both Moltmann and Hauerwas. In these cases I will basically assume the most recent form of their theologies, without making any systematic analysis of the way toward this position, more than when it is helpful for describing and discussing their current positions. Part of the changes of Moltmann's theology is also inherent in his mediating project. As the context changes, his mediating theology also has to change. In the case of Moltmann this leads to serious problems. This will lead us to ask critical questions also about his mediating project and method. An analysis of this type of change and the reasons for the problems will consequently have a central place in a systematic investigation of this sort.

5. On the Broad Scope of the Book

What I have said shows that this will be a rather wide ranging inquiry, touching not only different areas inside theology, but also sociology, political theory, moral philosophy, and so on. This comes in certain conflict with the common academic ideals of specialization and avoidance of broader generalizations, both results of making methodological rigour primary. Obviously my knowledge of the various disciplines I use is limited and uneven. Furthermore space limitations make extensive discussion of many issues impossible. Either one is silent or one has to make certain generalizations and unguarded statements. I do not, however, know any other interesting way of doing this type of investigation. It is the nature of systematic theology, like political theory, to be wide ranging and generaliz-

---

[34]For Moltmann, see esp. Meeks, *Origins of the Theology of Hope* and Bauckham, *Moltmann*. On Hauerwas, see Richardson, "Christian Community and Ethics", 19-79 and Hütter, *Evangelische Ethik als kirchliches Zeugnis*. Here could also Lindquist, "The Church as a Christian Community of Hope: A Comparative Study of Moltmann and Hauerwas Using a Cultural-Linguistic Style of Thinking" be mentioned. This is the only larger study on Moltmann and Hauerwas. It has, however, not been to much help for my project.

ing—assuming it is something more than history of ideas or conceptual analysis. Furthermore, the nature of the theologies of Moltmann and Hauerwas make this wide ranging approach necessary, because that is the way they work. It is thus the subject studied and not disciplinary borders that determines which tools should be used.

Although it is a very often deplored and criticized tendency, the academic world continues in the direction of increasing professionalization and specialization leading to sharp borders between disciplines, escalating internal specialization and obsession with method. The historian Håkan Arvidsson thinks that this not only is a legacy of the positivist ideals of the scientist as a value-free observer which during the postwar years conquered the human and social sciences, but also has to do with the institutional form of the universities with its inbuilt narrow instrumental rationality. He further says that the methodological demands of complete reading and documentation make strict limitations necessary, with the effect that discussions of broader issues of general significance become impossible. "Putting it in a slightly exaggerated way, the result is that everything of broader interest is unscientific, and everything that is scientific is uninteresting. This in its turn has as a consequence that the voice of science becomes silent in the public conversation."[35] This system thus encourages a type of academic work that concentrates on methodological perfection and criticism, while it discourages interest in larger questions, creativity and constructiveness—that is, it is not too congenial to the type of work that Hauerwas and Moltmann represent, who —whatever else may be said about them—not only are interested in deeply significant matters and involved in public conversation, but also are extremely creative and constructive to the price of a certain methodological imperfectionism.[36] Hauerwas says with his characteristic forthrightness, and I think Moltmann would concur:

> I simply am not interested in 'careful' theology if that means avoiding the risk of writing about Christian convictions and practices as if they do not matter. Indeed, I believe that

---

[35]"Tystnaden i Sverige och vad den möjligen kan bero på", 48. "Science" ("vetenskap", cf. the German "Wissenschaft") is here, of course, used in the broad European sense.

[36]Smith's and Sahlin's discussion about the creative and noncreative researcher in "Forskaren och vetenskapsidealen" is enlightening, thinking about the work of Hauerwas and Moltmann in the context of traditional academic life. While methodological certainty ("prefer a well-turned meaninglessness to an unwieldily made innovation" [p. 58]), preoccupation with small and safe research problems, fear of the unexpected, characterize the noncreative researcher, enthusiasm for the surprising, and the original, tolerance for the obscure, but perhaps profound, theoretical risky boldness, along with a difficulty in interesting themselves for things unrelated to their own perspectives, characterize the latter. They further think that our university system and scientific ideals strongly favour the former. To this it might be said that it is people like Moltmann and Hauerwas that keeps disciplines like theology, philosophy, political theory going and give the rest of us something to do.

many of the disciplinary divisions characteristic of contemporary university and seminary curricula are but excuses for intellectual laziness or cowardice, or both.[37]

Furthermore, by avoiding larger issues one also avoids asking questions about the basic assumptions, the large amount of tacit knowledge only assumed, that determines one's perspective and the theories and methods one uses.[38] A crucial part of important intellectual work is just the questioning of common assumptions and the construction of new perspectives.

Finally, the professionalization of intellectual work also risks to separate and abstract the discipline from the practical activities which are its base. The discipline creates its own community with its own language, creating its own problems and questions, in which requirements of methodological rigour and spurious foundationalist ideas of objectivity play an important role, tend to draw the discipline further and further away from what it supposedly deals with.[39] Both Moltmann and Hauerwas are theologians that try to avoid these consequences of professionalization in their attempt to work as Christian theologians in close connection with practised Christian faith. And it is time to leave these already too long methodological reflections and go over to substantial discussions of their theological projects.

---

[37]*US* 7. Cf. the historians Rolf Torstendahl's and Thorsten Nybom's criticism of recent historical work for being "more inclined to search for the 'safe and sometimes trivial truths' than ready to risk the 'fruitful mistakes', which interpretations of structural processes and broad generalizations about social systems and epochal changes always will involve." (*Historievetenskap som teori, praktik, ideologi*, 8.) In this sense I am more interested in risking "fruitful mistakes" that might contribute to the ongoing theological conversation than in methodological perfection.

[38]What Basil Mitchell says about philosophers is also true for theologians. "If philosophers always confine themselves to small-scale manageable problems of the sort that can be handled with full analytical rigour they are exposed, by their very concentration, to the risk of allowing fundamental assumptions to go uncriticized and even, perhaps, unnoticed." (*Morality*, vii.)

[39]Cf. e.g. Elshtain's criticism of the professionalized discourse of "International Relations" in *Women and War*, 86-91, MacIntyre's of philosophy ("the conception of philosophy as essentially a semi-technical, quasi-scientific, autonomous enquiry to be conducted by professionalized specialists is in the end barren. There is indeed in philosophy a large and legitimate place for technicality, but only in so far as it serves the ends of a type of enquiry in which what is at stake is of crucial importance to everyone and not only to academic philosophers. The attempted professionalization of serious and systematic thinking has had a disastrous effect upon our culture." [*Whose Justice?*, x.]) and Gunnell's of political theory ("Arguments by John Rawls and others about justice or other 'political' concepts are seldom related to real political circumstances and events. They are so far removed from actual political discourse that only the faith and isolation of political theorists explain their acceptance as 'political' arguments. Because they belong to another realm of discourse, they have about as much hope of guiding politics as metaethics has for influencing the practice of morals." ["In Search of the Political Object", 38.]).

Part Two

The Impasse of Political Theology

Chapter 3

Mediating the Christian Message to the Modern World

Political theology is a way of doing theology. It is not a theology of the political, a theology dealing with one part of the Christian theology, but a way of understanding the theological task as a whole. It is often said that Moltmann's main contributions are his development of a political hermeneutics and his substantial practice of this hermeneutics.[1] In the introduction I, however, said that the inherent problems with political theology have to do with the basic conception of its political hermeneutics. In this chapter I intend to explicate the basic structures of this understanding of the theological task. The problems with this way of doing theology will in the subsequent chapters increasingly become clear through the description and analysis of Moltmann's substantial use of it. However, I will already in this chapter begin by pointing to some inherent unclarities and problems in the very construction of a political hermeneutics. Furthermore, Moltmann has himself pointed to limitations in the political hermeneutics and tried to find ways to complement and correct his earlier formulations. Yet, these new elements do not easily fit into the political hermeneutics, but tend to break it apart. One reason for this is that his theological methods are also strongly contextual and as the context or his understanding of it changes, not only his theology changes but also his understanding of the methods theologians should use.

1. Making Present

In the most general terms the following quotation summarizes well Moltmann's view of the theological task.

---

[1] "The greatest achievement of Moltmann's theology has been to open up hermeneutical structures for relating biblical faith to the modern world." (Bauckham, *Moltmann*, 140.) "Moltmann's greatest and probably lasting achievement, in my opinion, has been in the area of theological hermeneutics, the area where his work has focused." (Hunsinger, "The Crucified God and the Political Theology of Violence", 395.)

Christian theology has the task of relating the Christian tradition and message critically and therapeutically to this modern situation, for only in that way can it communicate the tradition of Christian faith, love and hope. This 'mediation' calls for both adaptation and contradiction. Theology must accept the changed circumstances of the world in order to change these in its turn towards peace, justice and the life of creation.[2]

He describes here the task as one of mediation of the tradition to the modern world. Theology must be able to show the relevance of the Christian faith to the current situation. This is the apologetic task. But the question of relevance is not only and not primarily a theoretical matter. His apologetics is not one of trying to theoretically justify the Christian doctrines. Instead he tries to show the practical relevance of Christian faith to the struggles for justice, peace, and the integrity of creation. The context for his theology thus is the political sphere and he describes his theology as a political theology.

Moltmann has himself portrayed the crisis of relevance for Christian faith which became especially critical during the 1960s as the immediate social context for the rise of this understanding of theology.[3] He describes how church and theology in many people's eyes had lost contact with the scientific, social and political reality. Students of theology as well as priests and pastors abandoned theology for the seemingly more relevant and practical subjects of sociology and psychology or went directly into political work. Church and theology tried to answer this in new ways through relating to this social and political reality and through working in solidarity with the new social movements. Moltmann has strongly supported this. But his concern was, and is, that Christians take part in these struggles *as Christians*, that the Christian identity is maintained. "Solidarity with others in meaningful actions loses its creative character if one no longer wishes to be anything different from others."[4] But he strongly stresses that the question of identity should be asked not in the abstract, but just in the active struggle for freedom and justice. Otherwise the protection of Christian identity easily ends up in only rigid orthodoxy and legalistic morality. This latter sort of defence of identity leads, Moltmann concludes, to the marginalization of the church. It becomes a sect that loses its social significance and therefore also, through passive assimilation, just that identity it wants to preserve.

In other words, the task of theology is not just preservation, but *making present* "the historical recollection of Christ and the tradition of the Gospel".[5] This

---

[2]*ThT* 94 (102).

[3]*CG* 7-31 (12-32), *EH* 1-4 (13-17).

[4]*CG* 16 (21). "Only when they have the courage to be and to act different from others can they be for others (Bonhoeffer) and mean something to others." (*EH* 3 [16].)

[5]*ThT* viii-ix (8). "In historical terms, any Christian theology is a 'mediating theology' whether or not it is aware of the fact, since it mediates the Christian message that has been handed down in such a way that it falls within the horizons of the understanding of the people of a particular time. Mediation between the Christian tradition and the culture of the present is the most important task of theology."

process of "making present" involves, according to Moltmann, two different but necessary aspects: 1) adaptation and translation, and 2) contradiction and opposition. To make Christian faith at all understandable it has to be adapted or translated to the thought forms of the contemporary culture. However, he thinks this is especially problematic in our time, because of the tradition-critical and relativistic character of modern thought. Therefore it is necessary to defend Christian faith against the doubt of modern thought. But that is not enough. Theology must also be able to display the culture-critical and therapeutic relevance of Christian faith. From this it follows that the task never can be one of only adaptation. The Gospel radically questions a world that causes so much suffering and oppression. "The saving and liberating potential of the historical recollection of Christ is not just manifested in 'modernism'; it first becomes evident through participation in the history of suffering in the present, by taking the side of the victims of the 'modern world'."[6] So theology for Moltmann is not just a theoretical enterprise. Theology takes part in the struggle for freedom and justice against oppression and suffering and cannot avoid taking sides. Therefore he can write the following about his own early books: "In them I wanted so say something specific in a particular cultural, theological and political situation, and took sides. They were written from the time and for the time, and are thus to be understood as contextual theology, set within the conflict of contemporary life."[7] As a theologian he thus wants to take part in the movements of the time and write in dialogue and conflict with the purpose of making "a contribution to the healing of everything in church, culture and creation."[8]

His theology can thus be described as a mediating or correlational theology. He wants to mediate the Christian tradition and the modern world. This mediation, however, is theoretically low key and informal, not systematic. He does not subsume the two poles under some superstructure that can provide the language, tools and/or criteria for the mediation. One does therefore not find in his writings any systematic specification of criteria for making or for judging these mediations. His theology is thus basically non-foundational. He sees theology as a partner in the ongoing and often sharply conflictual conversation of the Western civilization, or more correctly, in his view, of the slowly coming-to-be world civiliza-

---

(*ThT* 53 [59].) For the following, see *ThT* viii-x (8f), 53f (59f). The German word that is translated "making present" is *Vergegenwärtigung*, which he sees as an equivalent to *aggiornamento* (p. ix [8]).
[6]*ThT* ix (9).
[7]*HTG* 173f (230). He talks here about the two early main books *TH* and *CG*, but it is to a large extent also true for his theology as a whole. He says in another context that "theology for me has never been a neutral scientific study or an objective doctrine, but an existential experience, which must be personally suffered, digested and understood." ("Foreword" to Bauckham, *Moltmann*, vii.) For grasping how Moltmann understands his own work both *HTG* 165-182 (219-240) and the mentioned "Foreword" are helpful.
[8]"Foreword" to Bauckham, *Moltmann*, viii. See also *HTG* 176-180 (233-238).

tion. In this conversation he tries to make theology appealing by showing its therapeutic relevance to modern society.

I think one can rightly say that the genius of Moltmann as theologian, and the most important reason for his theology's great impact, is his ability to make a creative use of classical Christian language in his attempt to show the relevance of Christian faith to the social and political movements (or at least to the Christians who sympathize with them) which have dominated radical political thought and action during the last three decades. He reconstructs Christian doctrines, but without surrendering classical trinitarian Christian faith. Instead, he finds the basic sources for formulating a relevant theology in the biblical language and the Christian tradition themselves.[9]

2. Political Hermeneutics

His most comprehensive discussions of the task and methods of theology concern what he calls the therapeutic role of theology. This is the heart of his political theology and hermeneutics. This hermeneutics is called political because it regards politics as "the inclusive horizon of the life of mankind".[10] He contrasts this with earlier theology's cosmological focus. The reason that politics has become the inclusive horizon is the fact that the world no longer is just an expression of the rhythms of nature, but is more clearly than before a human project. Society is seen as a human and historical project of realizing the future kingdom of freedom. Central characteristics of this modern project are secularization, a concentration on the future and thereby strong criticism of traditions and institutions. The ground for Moltmann's basically positive appraisal is the emancipatory interest he sees behind these developments and attitudes. In his understanding the modern world and its self-understanding are based on freedom movements. And while today the main threats against humanity are created by humanity, it is through politics that the future can be changed. This makes the political horizon the necessary frame for theology.[11]

---

[9]Cf. Bauckham, *Moltmann*, 140f. Here it might be helpful to see how he compares his own way of doing theology with a cultural theologian such as Harvey Cox, who "theologizes" cultural trends and who basically has gone through the same shifts as Moltmann. The context for the following comment is a discussion of Cox' way of talking about Jesus as clown in *Feast of Fools*. "I think highly of him. He's a theologian of culture, and he sees what there is in culture and tries to interpret it. As a European Protestant theologian, I am more absorbed by the Bible and I try to extract what corresponds to biblical testimony. I would be reluctant to apply to Christ a title like 'clown' or fool. . . . Basically, I think the same as Harvey Cox. Nevertheless, I believe that what we think doesn't all have to be projected in a new image of Christ. From the true story of Jesus we can extract figures and titles much more profound than a clownish figure." ("A Conversation with Jürgen Moltmann", 126.)

[10]*RRF* 98 (*PdT* 139).

[11]*TH* 230-238 (210-217), *RRF* 83-86, 93-97 (*PdT* 128-130, 135-138), *OHD* 97-100 (*PTPE* 152-155), *ThT* 18f, 23-26 (27, 31-33).

These are constitutive ideas for the origin of political theology, but increasingly they have come in a certain tension with Moltmann's later ecological understanding and the consequent questioning of the primacy of history. But it does not seem to have led him to any drastic changes in his later explications of his political hermeneutics. In this section I basically use material from the 1980s, although earlier texts are also used.

What is said above demonstrates that Moltmann, in his understanding of the modern world, stands in the so called left-Hegelian tradition.[12] This becomes also evident in his defence of the primacy of practical reason. For a key element of the political hermeneutics is the adoption of the functional Marxist criticism of religion, which is not concerned with the being and truth of religion as such, but with its social function. In modernity rationality is, according to Moltmann, primarily understood not as correspondence but as effectiveness. Reason has an instrumental character. In other words, praxis becomes a criterion of truth. Reason and knowledge are means for the historical project of bringing about a more humane world.[13]

The consequence for theology then is that it has to analyse and test the psychological, social and political implications of its doctrines, concepts and symbols, as well as of the institutional form of the church and of the moral shape of Christian life. The aim is to clarify the transformative intentions of Christian beliefs in the contemporary society. The task is thus not only critical and descriptive, but participatory. The objective is to contribute to liberating social change. Moltmann theologically warrants this approach in terms of his theology of hope, which he describes as the origin of political theology.[14] The Bible is understood "as witness of God's promissory history and the human history of hope. The interest which guides its knowledge is an interest in the power of the future and how this is revealed in God's promises and stirred in human hope."[15]

If the theological reflection does participate in the struggle for change, theory and praxis have to be held together. Instead of giving either theory or praxis primacy, Moltmann wants a dialectical relationship. Christian hope motivates to liberating action. But this action has to be analysed and criticized in the light of the Gospel, just as the theology has to be analysed and tested in light of its political function. Theory and praxis "mutually drive each other forward."[16]

With this praxis he does not refer to any praxis, but to a *Christian* praxis that has a twofold *Sitz im Leben*: the church of Christ and the poor and oppressed. To know Christ presupposes discipleship, what he calls christopraxis, and this leads the Church to the poor and oppressed. From this follows that theology must par-

---

[12]Cf. McCarthy, "Philosophical Foundations of Political Theology", 28.
[13]*RRF* 97f (*PdT* 139), 138-140, *OHD* 98 (153), *ThT* 92f (100f).
[14]*OHD* 100 (155).
[15]*OHD* 105 (159).
[16]*OHD* 109 (*PTPE* 161).

ticipate in their struggle for freedom and justice and learn to see reality from the underside of history, from the perspective of the poor and oppressed.[17]

To summarize so far: political theology, according to Moltmann, is not a theology about the political, and it does not want to politicize theology. The purpose is instead to analyse and reconstruct theology as a whole in the light of its political functions. So for Moltmann political theology is a fundamental theological or a hermeneutical category. Every theology has conscious or unconscious political functions. Political theology aims to clarify and critically analyse these functions. "It does not want to politicize the church, but it does want to christianize church politics and the political involvement of Christians. It therefore takes up the modern functional criticism of religion and urges movement from the orthodoxy of faith to the orthopraxis of discipleship of Christ."[18]

So the "political theology designates the field, the milieu, the environment, and the medium in which Christian theology should be articulated",[19] but the content of theology is not derived from the situation. The *text*, so to say, is the history that the Old and New Testaments witness to, which culminates in Jesus Christ. Thus all theological discourse must be defensible in terms of this history. In this sense, Moltmann's theology moves from the particular, i.e., the history of Israel and Jesus, to the universal, i.e., the interpretation of reality in general. This is possible because the eschatological horizon of the Christian faith implies that this particular history anticipates the future of the whole creation. This means that he is critical of a theology that begins with general concepts about God or human existence.[20] However, this particular history must be formulated in relation to the actual historical, political and cultural *context* and be translated into a contemporary understandable idiom.[21] The question of salvation, he says, changes through time and Christian theology has to be formulated in relation to the contemporary form of this question. However, the salvation that the Christian faith talks about is not just any salvation, but the salvation of Christ as witnessed to in biblical history. So this salvation has to be shown to be therapeutically relevant to the modern hopes of salvation.[22]

He does not, however, in any detail discuss how this hermeneutical process takes place. One common criticism against Moltmann is the seemingly arbitrariness of his theological constructions.[23] What he actually seems to do, and more

---

[17] *WJC* 42f, 39 (60f, 56f), *CPS* 121-132 (141-152).

[18] *OHD* 99 (*PTPE* 153f).

[19] *EH* 102f.

[20] *TH* 140-43 (126-129).

[21] *EH* 44f (65), *RRF* 203f (*UZ* 150f).

[22] *WJC* 38f, 43-46 (56f, 62-64). Another way he uses to say this is to distinguish between a hermeneutics of origins and a hermeneutics of effects. See *WJC* 43f (62).

[23] One finds this worry even in such Moltmann-sympathetic theologians as Bauckham and Hunsinger. The former says that "elements of undisciplined speculation seem increasingly common" ("Jürgen Moltmann", 308f). Hunsinger goes further: "It is dismaying to watch Moltmann pursue his theology without any serious methodological reflection. He seems to proceed by sheer intuition, and in this book

clearly so in his later writings, is to take up themes from the biblical and Christian traditions as well as from modern thought and science, and try to merge this material in a both faithful and relevant imaginative synthesis. In this process, he says, fantasy plays a vital role. "Theology always includes the imagination, fantasy for God and his kingdom."[24] Therefore he can describe his theology as "risky", "experimental" and written as contributions to an ongoing theological dialogue.[25] The critics however are concerned about how this process is disciplined, how others are able to follow and argue with his not seldom very daring and speculative suggestions.[26] He has not yet given much of an answer to these worries.[27]

3. Doxological Theology

Political theology works, as seen, with an instrumental concept of reason. Truth is realized in praxis. But Moltmann himself early recognized the limits of this understanding in three different, albeit related, contexts. Firstly, he became at the end of the 1960s, like the culture in general, increasingly critical of the modern utilitarian morality that also characterized the revolutionary movements and his own theology. As a result he tried to complement the ethical orientation of the political theology with a theological aesthetics which gives play, celebration and beauty a major role. Theology must then be understood not just as the theory of praxis, but also as doxology, pure theory, which worships God in a free play of words and pictures.[28]

Secondly, he could not defend his extensive elaboration of the doctrine of the Trinity in purely practical terms, although it is far from lacking practical relevance in his theology. However, Christian life, he says, is not just action, but also gratitude, joy and worship. "Faith lives in meditation and prayer as well as in practice. Without the *vita contemplativa* the *vita activa* quickly becomes debased into activism, falling a victim to the pragmatism of the modern meritocratic society

---

[that is *TKG*] more than ever before the result is a kind of methodological mishmash." (Review of Moltmann, *The Trinity and the Kingdom*, 129, see further ibid., 129-131 for examples.) Cf. also Härle and Herms, "Deutschsprachige protestantische Dogmatik nach 1945", 57-71, Link, "Schöpfung im messianischen Licht", 84f, and Ritschl, "Die vier Reiche der 'drei göttlichen Subjekte'", 464f. The title of Niewiadomski's book *Die Zweideutigkeit von Gott und Welt in J. Moltmanns Theologien* is also telling.
[24]*GIC* 4 (19). See also *GIC* 2-4 (17-19) and "Zum Gespräch mit Christian Link", 93.
[25]"Foreword" to Bauckham, *Moltmann*, viii.
[26]The most problematic books from this perspective seem to be *TKG* and *GIC*.
[27]For an attempt to find a consistent method in Moltmann's approach, see Schweitzer, "The Consistency of Jürgen Moltmann's Theology". It does not, however, answer the sort of questions this book raises.
[28]*TJ* is the primary expression of this view. For the above, see esp. p. 49 (33f).

which judges by performance."[29] He describes how one through meditation and contemplation opens oneself to God and thereby experiences a joy in the fellowship with God that more deeply changes oneself than is possible through a life only directed to action. In contrast to the power-oriented pragmatic understanding, knowledge in this perspective is seen more as wonder and participation in the life of others than as power. "Here knowing does not transform the counterpart into the property of the knower . . . On the contrary, he is transformed through sympathy, becoming a participator in what he perceives."[30] In this view meditation and worship is crucial for keeping liberating praxis from degenerating into a legalistic activism.

Thirdly, also in light of the ecological crisis he thinks it essential again to take up the premodern concept of reason as "the organ of perception and participation".[31] He tries to do this especially in *God in Creation*, as he here questions the view that history is primary and instead argues that nature is the more comprehensive category. It is therefore important to criticize an exclusively analytic, objectivizing and instrumental concept of knowledge. Instead he contends that a more poetic, meditative, holistic and participatory concept is required. "We no longer desire to know in order to dominate, or analyse and reduce in order to reconstruct. Our purpose is now to perceive in order to participate, and to enter into mutual relationships of the living things."[32]

An obvious question is how the earlier described, praxis-oriented concept of knowledge and truth is related to this poetic, holistic and participatory concept. I will, after having exemplified how his mediating program is concretely used, return to this issue.

4. The Mediation Practised

We have seen that Moltmann endeavours to write theology as a participant in contemporary events and movements as a contribution to the struggle for freedom and justice. He wants to write a contextualized and side taking theology. In this section we will see how this program has affected his main works. My description here will mainly be limited to following how he himself has described it. This task is not so difficult as he often comments on his own work. In other words, I am in the following concerned with the context, and not primarily with the text. Following Moltmann through three decades of contextual theology gives some

---

[29]*TKG* 7 (23). He asks also if "truth, which under certain given circumstances is incapable of realization, therefore [is] to be despised and thrown away simply because of that? Is the truth which God himself is, so 'practicable' that people have to 'realize God', 'put God into practice'? Is the doctrine of the Trinity a practical truth?" (*TKG* 6 [22].) Another factor behind this language is his increasing appreciation of mysticism and meditation. See *EG* 55-80 (46-71), esp. 57-61 (48-51).
[30]*TKG* 9 (25).
[31]*GIC* 2 (17). So also *ThT* 93f (101).
[32]*GIC* 3 (18).

perspective on the strengths, risks and consequences of this way of doing theology.

a) Theology of Hope

His first main work was *Theology of Hope* which was published 1964 in
German. When he a few years later reviews the context of this book he mentions
three historical situations or factors.[33] The immediate situation was the spirit of
the 1960s with its "new sensibility for an open future"[34] formed by the technological developments and a belief in almost unlimited possibilities. And he is well
aware that the general mood of the 1960s contributed to his book's great success
and impact. He mentions the era of Kennedy, the Civil Rights Movement, the
Prague Spring, the Second Vatican Council, the World Council of Churches conference in Uppsala 1968, and the Christian-Marxist dialogue.[35]

The second factor he mentions is the modern history of freedom related to the
modern future directed consciousness. Moltmann argues that the church has often
failed to understand the true nature of this shift, and has not seen that the criticism
of traditions and institutions has been made in the hope of freedom for the new.
Christian theology has for centuries been embedded in an antique more static understanding of reality which now has vanished. History, as a human-made and
future-directed reality, has replaced nature as the primary horizon.[36] For Moltmann the choice was clear. Either the church will vanish together with this older
conception or it has to free itself from it. Trying to sustain a premodern theology
forces Christianity into a ghetto situation and makes it unintelligible and irrelevant
for modern society.[37]

> The Christian mission has no cause to enter into an alliance with romanticist nihilism
> against the revolutionary progressiveness of the modern age and to present its own tradi-
> tion as a haven of traditionalism for a contemporary world now grown uncertain and
> weary of hoping. The emancipation of reason and society from their historic past is upheld
> in modern times by a millenarian enthusiasm. To this present world Christian proclamation
> must give an answer concerning its hope in the future of the crucified one (I Peter 3.15) by
> conveying to the godless justification and hope of resurrection. We cannot turn our backs
> on the open horizons of modern history and return to perpetual orders and everlasting tra-
> ditions, but we must take these horizons up into the eschatological horizon of the resur-
> rection and thereby disclose to modern history its true historic character.[38]

---

[33] *EH* 187 (8).
[34] *EH* 44 (64).
[35] *EH* 44 (64), *UZ* 11f.
[36] *TH* 230-238 (210-218), *OHD* 99f (*PTPE* 154f).
[37] "If God is not spoken of in relation to man's experience of himself and his world, then theology
withdraws into a ghetto and the reality with which man has to do is abandoned to godlessness." (*TH* 89
[79], cf. 180-182 [163-165]).
[38] *TH* 303 (279).

He could therefore describe secularization as a realization and transcending of the hopes of Christianity by the modern messianic pathos for the emancipation of reason and the whole society from the chains of tradition.

If these two factors constitute the context, the third is the text: "the originating events of the Bible's promissory history which has called Judaism and Christianity into being and which must determine their life."[39] It is this history of promise he attempts to mediate to the modern experience of the world as interpreted especially by the tradition from Hegel and Marx. In Moltmann's case this tradition was above all represented by the Marxist philosopher Ernst Bloch. Moltmann even describes his own theology of hope as a parallel to Bloch's philosophy of hope. Bloch gives him a set of categories and concepts for translating the biblical language into a modern understanding of reality.[40]

b) The Crucified God

Eight years later in 1972, his second main work *The Crucified God* is published. Here not hope, but the cross is the determining base and criteria. If God in the former book was the power of future, God is now experienced in suffering. God involves himself in the suffering of history and carries the history forward through suffering love. Moltmann himself wants to see the two books as not contradictory, but as complementary. Both try to see the whole from one focal point.[41] But this change of focus is not part of a preformed theological program, but is provoked by a change in the modes of the time, i. e., in the context. He says that when he wrote *Theology of Hope* he expected radical changes in church and society.[42] But these optimistic expectations quickly transformed into severe disappointments: the end of the Prague Spring and the Civil Rights Movement in USA, and setbacks in the developments in both the Catholic and Protestant

---

[39] *EH* 187 (8).

[40] *UZ* 10, *EG* 11 ("Der Gott, auf den ich hoffe", 273f). The use of Bloch is much more extensive than the few explicit references may indicate. For examples, see Bauckham, *Moltmann*, 10. On Moltmann and Bloch, see e.g. Matic, *Jürgen Moltmanns Theologie in Auseinandersetzung mit Ernst Bloch*, Spencer, "Marx, Bloch and Moltmann", O'Collins, "The Principle and Theology of Hope", and Bauckham, *Moltmann*, 7-14. Interestingly enough, although *TH* is by far the most Blochian, Bloch is actually mentioned much more often in several of his later books. In *TH* Hegel is the most often mentioned author—a not unimportant observation. On Moltmann and Hegel, see Meeks, *Origins of the Theology of Hope*, 34-38. Bauckham summarizes the Hegelian influence by saying that the Hegelian inheritance "was to be the key to Moltmann's development of an eschatology based on the contradiction of the cross and resurrection of Jesus." (*Moltmann*, 6.)

[41] *CG* 4f (10f), *HTG* 173 (230), "Foreword" to Bauckham, *Moltmann*, ix. In "Antwort auf die Kritik an 'Der gekreuzigte Gott'", 168, where he also defends himself along the same lines, he expresses some doubt about the degree of consistency.

[42] "When I wrote *Theology of Hope* I was nursing a certain enthusiasm and a short-term hope that the changes I desired were going to happen soon" ("Conversation", 123).

churches.[43] In this situation he finds help in the theology of the cross, just as it had helped him during the years after the World War II.

> The theology of the cross which was meaningful for us then, and gave us firm ground beneath our feet, came to my mind again when the movements of hope in the 1960s met stiffer resistance and stronger opponents than they could stand, and many abandoned their hope, either to adapt themselves, half resigned, to the usual course of events, or to withdraw into themselves in total resignation. . . . the centre of my hope and resistance once again became that which, after all, is the driving force of all attempts to open up new horizons in society and the church: the cross of Christ.[44]

The philosophical climate in Germany also changes. Bloch's influence decreases. It is now instead the Frankfurt school with Adorno and Horkheimer and their "negative dialectics" and "critical theory" who, he says, becomes his primary philosophical dialogue partner.[45] As the theology of hope functioned as a theological parallel to the philosophy of hope of Bloch, he now describes the theology of the cross as a Christian parallel to critical theory. The crucified Christ demystifies oppressing ideologies in church and society.[46]

c) The Church in the Power of the Spirit

Already in 1975 the next larger work from Moltmann's hand is published: *The Church in the Power of the Spirit*. This book lacks the clear focus of the two earlier and has more the character of an ordinary systematic treatise on the church,[47] although the content is radical, if seen in the light of his ecclesial context. The background he mentions for this book, in earlier form delivered as lectures for the first time already 1966,[48] is again the crisis of relevance in the 1960s for the West German churches. Both the traditions and the institutions of the church were radically questioned. He found in this challenge not only a crisis but a chance for renewal:

> Either the Protestant church would continue the course that had led to the crisis, from a state church to a people's church, and from a people's church to a church for the people which offered them pastoral care, and from that to the organized religion of this soci-

---

[43]Another factor that, he says, led to second thoughts, was (when lecturing in USA) his discovery how easily his theology of hope could be used as a defence of the activistic and optimistic American lifestyle. See "Conversation", 124 and his stern "Response to the Opening Presentations" (from a conference on hope in New York 1971).

[44]*CG* 2 (7f).

[45]*CG* 5 (10).

[46]"Christian theology cannot be a pure theory of God, but must become a *critical theory of God*. . . . Thus because of its subject, the theology of the cross, right down to its method and practice, can only be polemical, dialectical, antithetical and critical theory." (*CG* 69 [71f].) Cf. Bauckham, *Moltmann*, 66f, and, for a general discussion on the context of *CG*, ibid., 53-58 .

[47]*HTG* 175 (232).

[48]*CPS* xiv (12).

ety—or it would renew itself through forces from below and became a community church of the people of God in the people.[49]

It is, he says, experiences of concrete church life all over the world (his experience as pastor included) which have led him in this direction. He mentions the Korean church, the charismatic and independent African churches, the base communities of Latin America, the American free churches as well as movements inside both the Protestant and Catholic churches in Europe.[50]

d) The Trinity and the Kingdom of God

The next major work, *The Trinity and the Kingdom of God* from 1980, signifies an interesting shift. I have shown that social movements and situations in church and society rather than the academic theology itself have constituted the most important horizon for his theological reflection.[51] He admits, however, difficulties.[52] Since movements come and go, theological work that relates itself closely to these movements can be rather ephemeral. Another difficulty is that it is not easy for an individual theologian to be involved in all these movements. This became clear for him during the 1970s. He felt at home in the radical movements that originated in the decade before and in the related movement of political theology. But during the 1970s this type of theology was increasingly concretized into different contexts of struggle for liberation; he mentions black theology, Latin American liberation theology and feminist theology. Moltmann is neither black, poor or woman. He discovered the limitations of his own experience. He writes that this experience of not being able to be fully involved was at first very painful for him. But he continues that it also helped him to see more clearly the risks involved with too much concentration on the context instead of on the text.[53] There is also a value in a "productive disengagement"[54] from the movements. With this he means that he continues to concern himself with the issues of these movements, but not as if they immediately concerned him personally. His personal experience and involvement has by necessity limits, but through being in dialogue with the Christian tradition, with other theologians and with different movements he thinks that he as a white, European, male theologian may transcend his own experiential context and be able to give voice to the oppressed.

---

[49]*HTG* 174f (231f). See further *HTG* 174-176 (231-233) and *CPS* xiii-xvii (11-14).

[50]*CPS* xv (12f), *HTG* 175 (232).

[51]Here one might also mention his reaction to the religious renaissance of the 1970s, which leads to a new appreciation of the mystical tradition. See *EG* and more generally "The Challenge of Religion in the '80s."

[52]For the following, see *HTG* 179f (237f) and *TKG* xiif (12f).

[53]This is, as we have seen, not the first time he discusses this risk. The search for Christian identity has always been important in his theology. (Cf. e.g. *EH* 3 [16].) But his comment here might be interpreted as a mild criticism of his own performance in this respect.

[54]*HTG* 180 (237).

"Behind all this is the conviction that, humanly speaking, truth is to be found in unhindered dialogue."[55]

He explains that this discovery is a basic reason for him not to continue with his earlier method of seeing the whole of theology from one focus and instead start writing systematic theology in more classical form. He conceived of a five (later changed to a six) volume contribution to theology that would deal with the classical theological issues of which the book on the Trinity is the first volume.[56] When he discusses the contexts in which these books are developed he mentions three.[57] The first is the theological tradition, the second the contemporary ecumenical fellowship, and the third is the dialogue with Judaism.

In other words, to a greater extent than in the earlier works the context here is the theological tradition and the contemporary theological discussion, and not so much the immediate political movements. This does not mean that the book is politically irrelevant. Especially in the last part of the book the importance of the doctrine of the Trinity for our understanding of freedom and democracy for church and politics is delineated.[58]

This admitted difference from earlier books should however not be overemphasized. For a theology of mediation there are two poles, tradition and situation, and the starting point for the reflection can be either of them. It might also be said, in terms of his political theology and hermeneutics, that the elaboration of his doctrine of the Trinity is made in awareness of specific social and political interests, especially freedom and democracy.

e) God in Creation

If the nature of the social movements central to Moltmann during the 1970s necessarily forced him to a certain dissociation, the situation is again changed during the following decade. Now the ecological movement and the peace movement become the two most important social movements for Moltmann. In these social movements, just as in the revolutionary movements in Europe of the 1960s, Moltmann can involve himself directly. They concern himself in a way that, for example, the feminist movement does not. Much of Moltmann's writings during the 1980s have also dealt with the issues of ecology and peace, so even his two main works from this time: *God in Creation* from 1985 and *The Way of Jesus Christ* from 1989. He continues his systematic project, but in a sense these two books are more like *Theology of Hope* and *The Crucified God* in that the imme-

---

[55]*TKG* xiii (12).

[56]"What are important to me are not the immediate, short-term questions, but the longterm problems of theology, because the big theological decisions have longterm results for good or ill." ("Foreword" to Bauckham, *Moltmann*, x.) Until now *TKG*, *GIC*, *WJC*, and *SL* (not part of the original plan) have been published. The two remaining will deal with eschatology and theological method.

[57]*TKG* xiii-xv (13-15).

[58]*TKG* 191-222 (207-239). He also shows the relevance of this doctrine to the issues raised by feminist theology. See *TKG* 162-166 (179-183).

diate political context here is more present and more clearly determines the questions he discusses and how his theology is developed than is the case in *The Trinity and the Kingdom of God*. But if these two books are similar to his first two main works in their common explicit *context*-dependence, the later books are partly strikingly different in *content* from the two earlier. The reason is the change of context.

This is most obvious in *God in Creation*. The starting point is the ecological crisis, which Moltmann argues will develop into a global catastrophe if drastic changes are not made. This crisis has its origin in the industrial state which has developed in a culture formed by Christianity. One legitimation for this development has been based, Moltmann thinks, on a misunderstanding of the Genesis creation stories. So the ecological crisis and the historical responsibility of Christian faith constitute the necessary context for a reconstruction of the doctrine of creation. He thus formulates his basic question in the following way: "How must the Christian belief in creation be interpreted and reformulated, if it is no longer to be itself one factor in the ecological crisis and the destruction of nature, but is instead to become a ferment working towards the peace with nature which we seek?"[59] With this he does not want to adapt the doctrine to the new ecological interest. The Christian doctrine of creation has its own language, question and visions, but it can today only be heard in relation to the modern ecological awareness.[60]

This has lead him to rather drastic changes in his understanding of reality. If he in *Theology of Hope* strongly emphasized the basically historical character of reality, he is now deeply critical against the way modern theology has made nature a part of history and understood reality in primarily historical terms. Instead history has to be understood in terms of creation.[61] This change has several important consequences, not the least for the understanding of the relation between God and the world, although the strong continuities in his trinitarian, christological and eschatological perspective should not be forgotten. It is however a bit strange that he does not more clearly acknowledge these changes and that his recent sharp criticism against modern theology[62] hits his own earlier theology more than most others.[63] It is, to use Moltmann's language, the changed context which

---

[59]*GIC* 21 (35). The subtitle to the book is accordingly *An Ecological Doctrine of Creation*.

[60]*GIC* 20-23 (34-36).

[61]French writes that "[r]ead against Moltmann's earlier works, this book displays a grand reversal of theological direction and sensibility, a seismic shift from a focus on history, eschatology, and 'openness to the future' to one on nature, creation, and respect for 'dwelling' within the present." ("Returning to Creation", 79.) See also Del Colle, "God in Creation".

[62]*GIC* 29-32 (43-47). Cf. also *CJF* 14f, 61f, 75, 95f (26f, 82f, 98, 121f).

[63]The nearest he in *GIC* comes to such an acknowledgement is a short footnote about *TH*. See pp. 31 and 325 n. 24 (45). A bit more is said in *HTG* 170 (242): "In 1964 the 'ecological crisis' had not yet penetrated my consciousness. At that time we were more terrorized by the horrors of history and fascinated by its possibilities." But he does not discuss how to relate these two books to each other. French comments: "It is disturbing that Moltmann fails to acknowledge how his earlier eschatological

has led him to read the text differently. The belief in technology and progress and the revolutionary expectations of the 1960s have been replaced by the recognition that humanity is on its way to destroying nature. But the radical, almost apocalyptic, language he uses for describing the two situations is however the same.[64]

f) The Way of Jesus Christ

The other great movement in the 1980s is the peace movement. The question of peace is central in *The Way of Jesus Christ*, even if also other pressing issues are taken up, including above all the ecological crisis and poverty. In other words, he follows the WCC call for a "covenant for justice, peace and the preservation of creation".[65] This is for him a question of entering soteriologically and therapeutically into the actual situation of the contemporary world[66] and it leads him to develop his christology in relation to some crucial questions. *"Who really is Christ for the poor of the Third World?" "Who really is Christ for us today, threatened as we are by the nuclear inferno?" "Who really is Christ for dying nature and ourselves today?"*[67] I will deal with this book extensively in following chapters. For now it is enough to say that the way he discusses the question of Jesus and violence and the use of violence as a political instrument in the context of the peace movement is as different from how he discussed it in the context of revolutionary movements as his ecological doctrine of creation is from his early eschatological theology.[68]

---

program constitutes one of the most thoroughgoing and influential attacks on creation and nature in the name of eschatology and 'history' seen in modern theology. If Moltmann is right now, he was wrong then." ("Returning to Creation", 78.)

[64]In 1968 he could write following: "If there are no major wars, the United States and the European countries will be faced with a long revolutionary march through the outmoded, authoritarian structures of their societies. The 'good old days' are gone. Now the future is our heaven or our hell and the present is something like a purgatory." (*RRF* xvi.) "We live in a revolutionary situation. In the future we shall experience history more and more as revolution. We can be responsible for the future of man only in a revolutionary way. . . . The new revolutionary situation has brought Christianity into a deep crisis of identity. Christians and the churches will rediscover their true self-consciousness only if they overcome their own religious alienation and their own hindrance to the free self-realization of man." (*RRF* 130, 132.) In 1985 he writes: "What we call the environmental crisis is not merely a crisis in the natural environment of human beings. It is nothing less than a crisis in human beings themselves. It is a crisis of life on this planet, a crisis so comprehensive and so irreversible that it can not unjustly be described as apocalyptic. It is not a temporary crisis. As far as we can judge, it is the beginning of a life and death struggle for creation on this earth." (*GIC* xi [11].)

[65]*WJC* 68 (87). The official English version has "integrity" instead of "preservation". The dialogue with Judaism is another important part of the context for this book.

[66]*WJC* 39 (56).

[67]*WJC* 65, 67, 68 (84, 87, 87).

[68]*SL* (published in German 1991, i.e., only two years after *WJC*) does not in this sense go beyond *WJC*. One note from another post-1989 text could however be mentioned. In light of the democratic revolutions in Europe 1989, he thinks that the WCC program has to be extended to include freedom to self-

5. Tensions in Moltmann's Political Hermeneutics

The impact of Moltmann's theology shows that many Christians find his theology highly relevant for their concerns. Yet, the foregoing description of the deliberate contextual dependence of Moltmann's theology also leads to serious questions. He wants to write critical theology, but one might ask if it is critical enough. In the light of his later theology he made severe mistakes in his early celebration of history and the human ability to control nature and history. In his interest to be relevant and meaningful for "progressive" people of the 1960s he failed to use the resources in Christian faith to criticize the understanding of history, nature, and human power that legitimates the misuse of nature. He not only failed to criticize, he actively supported that understanding, both positively through the way he formulated his eschatological theology and negatively through criticizing theological accounts that could be used in a critical way. This further raises the question whether his recent radical development of an ecological doctrine of creation perhaps will be seen to have similar problems.

Furthermore, his later poetic, holistic and participatory concept of truth seems to come in tension with the more instrumental praxis concept inherent in his political hermeneutics. He says that these conceptions are complementary, but he does not say much about *how* they complement each other. As it is they tend to exist independently of one another. Although he often uses the later conception to criticize the former, giving the impression of some tension between them, the later approach is most often simply added to the earlier, without this being modified. However, this development at least shows that his theological method is also contextual. The instrumental theory-praxis model is an expression of the optimistic modernity's belief in its own ability to control and form history through politics. The later holistic and participatory model expresses a pre- or postmodern more humble attitude towards nature and history, which questions the place instrumental reason has in the modern civilization.

Besides these problems there are the inherent problems with the theory-praxis language and the unclarities of Moltmann's use of it.[69] One can sometimes interpret Moltmann as if he does not mean anything more with the unity of theory and praxis than that theology is a theoretical reflection on the faith that is lived (and already theorized) in the Christian church. Theology is then a practical discipline

---

determination. "Thus: In the name of freedom—for justice, peace and the preservation of creation." ("Theologie im demokratischen Aufbruch Europas", 39.)

[69]For historical discussions, see Lobkowicz, *Theory and Practice* and Lobkowicz' short but sharply pointed article "On the History of Theory and Praxis" and Bernstein, *Praxis and Action*. For a shorter account, see e.g. Lane, *Foundations for a Social Theology*, 32-55. On Moltmann, cf. Berdesinski, *Die Praxis*, esp. 17-19, Geertsema, *Van boven naar voren*, 202-309, esp. 292-309, and Vroom, *De Schrift alleen?*, 157-181.

dealing with the common life and thinking of the church, and not a theoretical reflection abstracted from the concrete practices and beliefs of the Christian community. This is both a coherent and a plausible understanding of the theological
task.

However, he goes further and connects his use of this language to especially
the Marxist tradition,[70] although he also says that this conception is characteristic
of modernity in general. Though the use of the theory-praxis language in the
Marxist tradition is anything but clear,[71] it is against this background that one
should understand the idea of praxis as the criterion of truth. Theology is tested in
terms of its effects: Is it liberating or oppressive? To this method objections can
be made. First, there is Moltmann's own objection against reducing reason to instrumental reason. Second, this seems to make the incorrect assumption that what
is liberating or oppressive is self-evident. Marxism describes history as one general movement through different stages to the coming communist kingdom of freedom. In every stage there is some central collective actor that carries the movement forward. In the capitalist stage the proletariat has this role. Its interests
therefore objectively correspond to the interests of the whole of humanity. To be
on the side of the proletariat, embodied in the party, is then to be on the side of
the progressive history that leads to liberation. The active transformation of the
world and the understanding of the world become one dialectic process in which
the contradictions between fact and value, will and prediction, necessity and freedom dissolve.[72]

In such terms the saying that praxis is the criterion of truth might be understandable, even if not plausible.[73] Although strongly influenced by Marxism,
though first of all by the more esoteric Marxism of Ernst Bloch, Moltmann has
never been a Marxist and never accepted the specific Marxist understanding of
history. Rather than using a specific social and historical theory, he instead
merely reasoned inside the general climate that the New Left of the 1960s, so

---

[70]See the references in n. 13 above. The same is true for Latin American liberation theology that has
made this conception even more central than Moltmann has. About the distinction I make between a
more general understanding of the unity between theory and praxis and the more specific Marxist one,
cf. Kasper, "Die Theologie der Befreiung aus europäischer Perspektive", 85f and Milbank, *Theology
and Social Theory*, 249-252. Generally on Moltmann and Marxism, see Chapman, "Jürgen Moltmann
and the Christian Dialogue with Marxism".

[71]Lobkowicz writes: "There is certainly no philosophical tradition in which so much was and is said
about theory and praxis as in the Marxist—and in which, at the same time, it remains so radically
unclear what theory and praxis actually are." ("Praxis", 24.) Cf. also the telling title of Bubner's
Theorie und Praxis—eine nachhegelsche Abstraktion.

[72]These ideas have in the history of Marxism been drawn in very different directions. My interest here is
only to give a general picture that might help us understand Moltmann. For the history and various
developments of Marxist thought, see Kolakowski, *Main Current of Marxism*. For some pertinent
comments on our issue, see vol. 3, 297-300.

[73]For criticism, see e.g. (besides Kolakowski) Castoriadis, *L'institution imaginaire de la société*, Giddens, *A Contemporary Critique of Historical Materialism*, and idem, *The Nation-State and Violence*.

strongly influenced by Marxism, created.[74] He developed a theology that showed parallels and was relevant to this general mood of thinking, for the purpose of helping Christians and Marxists to cooperate in the struggle for a new society. In such terms one might say that in Moltmann's theology the Christian eschatology takes the place of the Marxist metanarrative, the poor and oppressed takes the place of the proletariat, and "the orthopraxis of discipleship of Christ"[75] takes the place of the praxis of the party. This means that Christian theological reflection takes place inside the commitment to the poor and oppressed and the struggle for justice and freedom; that is, inside the commitment to the coming kingdom of God. In the "translation" process, however, the idea of praxis as criterion of truth diminishes in intelligibility. Marxist analysis was built on a specific understanding of the functioning of capitalism, which for instance gave the proletariat and not the poor in general its crucial role, and which explained the "necessary" movement forward to socialism and communism. In Moltmann's theology it is God's promises to the poor and oppressed (a much more indeterminate category than the proletariat of the Marxist theory) that give the impetus to side with the progressive movements.[76] But without some type of metahistory, like Marxism, there is no self-evident way of identifying the progressive forces. There are seldom just two alternatives, though Moltmann often writes as if this were the case. Furthermore, if one does not accept that the contradictions of capitalism by necessity lead to socialism, the direction of social change is a moral and political issue, and not simply a question of the results of social science, as also Moltmann (most often at least) would agree. As Fiorenza argues, even the very "experience of oppression is not only an immediate experience but also results from the conflict between cultural values and present experience."[77]

This means moreover that it does not help to refer to some hermeneutical privilege of the poor, an idea which seems to be a theological use of the mentioned Marxist class theory. This theory is in itself problematic. And if one separates it from the general Marxist understanding of history, while still interpreting it strictly as a sort of foundationalist praxis theory, it becomes even less comprehensible. More loosely, without these foundationalist ambitions, it is more sensible. Fiorenza, after having criticized this idea, writes that

> a more moderate and modified approach would acknowledge that by opting for the oppressed one gains an insight into ideological distortions of the dominant culture. But it

---

[74]He even says that the Christian-Marxist dialogue "was the starting point for European 'political theology'" (*SL* 329 n. 31 [153]). Cf. e.g. his discussions of Marx and Marxism in *RRF* 74-76, 93-97 (*PdT* 202-204, 135-138), *HP* 190-193 (*PdT* 261-264), *UZ* 26-44, *TJ* 65-75 (51-63), and *Man*, 47-59 (73-89). I will later return to the issue of Moltmann's relation to Marxism and socialism.

[75]*OHD* 99 (*PTPE* 154).

[76]"If we find in the Bible the written promises of freedom and in proclamation the mission of this freedom, then it is the peculiar responsibility of a historical hermeneutic to outline the means and the methods of practical liberation." (*RRF* 98 [*PdT* 139].)

[77]*Foundational Theology*, 309.

would at the same time appeal to the tradition to uncover those values in conflict with contemporary ideologies, and it would recognize that truth cannot be localized within one class, but must be seen in relation to a plurality of subjects and traditions.[78]

The conclusion of this is therefore that there cannot be a praxis without theory, which Moltmann also recognizes when he says that theory and praxis "mutually drive each other forward".[79] If theory and praxis cannot be separated there is no meaning in saying that praxis is the *criterion* of truth. Neither can one identify modern functional criticism of religion with "the orthopraxis of discipleship of Christ",[80] because in the latter Jesus Christ is the criterion for Christian praxis, and it is not self-evident that this praxis of discipleship is identical with some current understanding of emancipatory praxis. In a later chapter, we will actually see that there are deep tensions between the very conception of Christian discipleship, as explicated by Moltmann, and modern emancipatory traditions. Furthermore, there are different traditions which all claim to be progressive and emancipatory. Just as Marxism can describe socialism as the next step after capitalism, can liberalism describe the historical movement towards modern democratic capitalism as the final metahistory, in which socialism was only a reactionary and romantic moment. One can also, instead of correlating Christianity to some other metahistory, understand the church as representing a contrast society that does not develop out of modernity, but is an alternative to it. We will in the next chapter see that Moltmann takes this road, but does so without reflecting on the consequences that this might have for his theological method.

---

[78]Ibid., 309.
[79]*OHD* 107 (*PTPE* 161).
[80]As Moltmann does in *OHD* 99 (*PTPE* 154).

Chapter 4

Messianic Theology

In this chapter I will give an overview of Moltmann's basic theology. The previous chapter has dealt with method and context and this will deal with content. Moltmann is a systematic theologian who writes classical dogmatic theology. He describes his own theology as "messianic theology". This is also the overall title of his later more systematic "contribution to theology". The notion "messianic theology" indicates both the eschatological character of his theology and its centre in the history of Jesus Christ. His eschatological and trinitarian theology is a christocentric theology. Its centre is the history of Jesus Christ. Because of this I have found it appropriate, in this chapter, to concentrate primarily, but not exclusively, on two of his main works: his first main book *Theology of Hope* and the recent *The Way of Jesus Christ*.[1] Through taking up these two books, and shortly discussing the development between them, I will be able to show both the origin of Moltmann's political theology and the way to, and the content of, his full-blown mature position. In *Theology of Hope* he develops an eschatological theology that, although in changed and revised forms, is present throughout all his later work and becomes the source of his political theology. *The Way of Jesus Christ* is not only the most important statement of his christology,[2] it also takes up and synthesizes themes from all his earlier works, and helps clarify the development from *Theology of Hope* to *The Way of Jesus Christ*. A further reason that makes this book especially significant for this project, is that the development of his theology in the direction of Radical Reformation theology is more evident here than at any time before. In addition, it contains the most developed ethical dimension of any of his main books.

My treatment of Moltmann in this chapter will be primarily descriptive and analytical, but not critical, not because I think that there are no problems here, but rather that this is not the focus of my examination and argument. Furthermore there are dozens of works that deal with such questions. My focus is on the relation between church and world, and the purpose of this chapter is to give the theological basis for the following. I will, however, return to some basic problems in his theology in the light of the further discussion.

---

[1] In the next chapter I will extensively review a third of his main works, namely *CPS*.

[2] In relation to *CG*, his first christological work, *WJC* is both more comprehensive and more systematic.

1. Promise and Mission

The Theology of Hope is one of the most influential theological works written during the second half of the twentieth century.[3] With this book Moltmann not only wanted to make Christian faith relevant to the modern future-directed consciousness, but also to show how this consciousness is an outgrowth of Christian faith itself. Beginning from the particular history of Jesus Christ, his death and resurrection, as seen against the background of the history of promise in the Old Testament, he tries to develop a universally relevant theology of promise and hope. His starting point is thus not a general phenomenology of hope or human existence or a general idea of God, but the biblical revelation, from which he wants to address the modern interests of freedom, future and change. To do this his book includes a broad discussion of the biblical bases of an eschatological theology, a critical discussion of alternative theological conceptions (especially the ones of Karl Barth, Rudolf Bultmann, and Wolfhart Pannenberg), and a critical mediation of this theology to the modern philosophical discourse on history.

Modernity understands the world to be future-directed and transformable. Humanity must strive to realize its hope of a just and peaceful world. The basic and connected biblical categories that Moltmann explores in order to be able to "take these horizons up into the eschatological horizon of the resurrection"[4], that is to mediate these central ideas of modernity and Christian faith, are, in Bauckham's words, "an understanding of divine revelation as *promise* and an understanding of history as *mission*."[5]

According to Moltmann it is closer to a true biblical understanding to see God revealed in an "apocalypse of the promised future" than in an "epiphany of the eternal present".[6] The latter he sees as the Greek view which early was absorbed into Christian theology. It means that God is regarded as the immanent ground of reality that transcends this world's changeableness, struggles and sufferings. But with this philosophical frame it is impossible to do justice to the biblical account. Moltmann demonstrates that the faith of Israel begins as a nomadic religion where God is perceived as journeying with the people. This God is a God of promises, promises that open up a future into which the people may enter in obedience. He further shows how this faith survives and develops in the transition to a settled agricultural life and how the confrontation with the surrounding epiphany religions adapted this faith to farming life.

---

[3]For Moltmann's own view of the effects of the book, see his preface from 1977 in the German edition, pp. 6f.

[4]*TH* 303 (279).

[5]Bauckham, *Moltmann*, 24. For a good discussion of the language of promise, see Morse, *The Logic of Promise in Moltmann's Theology.*

[6]*TH* 57 (49f).

A promise talks about something which yet is not and thus opens the future. Promises of God have their ground not in history itself, but in God and in God's faithfulness. This is important for Moltmann, because it means, first, that the promised future cannot be deduced from reality as it is. God's promise talks about something that is not, which means that it stands in contradiction with the given reality. Second, as the promises are based on God's faithfulness, there is no need to make them into rigid schemes. There is place for surprises. He also emphasizes that the promises transcend their historical fulfilments and point to further fulfilments. This creates a history of promise. One example is how the Exodus tradition is reapplied during the time of the exile. In this way the tradition, or the memory, functions as a promise that questions the present reality. God's promises open up a realm of freedom, but the people have to respond in obedience. To participate in the promises they have to go in the direction the promises lead. In light of this, Moltmann can describe the covenant "as a history-making event which opens up specific possibilities of history".[7] Furthermore, it is just this experience of God as the God of promise which, he claims, results in the fact that reality is experienced as history.

Moltmann finds the same basic pattern in the prophetic and apocalyptic writings. But what also happens here is a *universalization* and an *intensification* of the promises. They concern the whole of humanity, and the whole of existence, death included. The importance of apocalyptics is, therefore, that not only humanity but the whole cosmos is drawn into God's eschatological history. Apocalyptic becomes

> the beginning of an eschatological cosmology or an eschatological ontology for which being becomes historic and the cosmos opens itself to the apocalyptic process. This historifying of the world in the category of the universal eschatological future is of tremendous importance for theology, for indeed it makes eschatology the universal horizon of all theology as such.[8]

Moltmann develops his understanding of Jesus Christ against the background of this understanding of revelation. It helps him to take seriously the apocalyptic structure of the New Testament faith and its connection of God with the future. In the light of the further development of Moltmann's christology, it is, however, significant that he here wholly concentrates on the death and resurrection of Jesus Christ, while the life and preaching of Jesus does not play any role.[9]

The crucial event for Moltmann is the resurrection of Jesus. Because it is the Old Testament God of promises who raises Jesus Christ from death, the resurrection can be seen as God's confirmation and validation (*In-kraft-setzung*)[10] of the

---

[7]*TH* 121 (109).
[8]*TH* 137 (124).
[9]Cf. also Phillips, "The Use of Scripture in Liberation Theologies", 276-284 which shows his strong Pauline focus in his use of Scripture in his early work.
[10]*TH* 147 (132).

promises of the eschatological new creation. They are "made true in Christ—and made true wholly, unbreakable, for ever and for all."[11] In addition, it is the cruci- fied who is raised from the dead, which for Moltmann means that the promises are freed from Israel and the law and therefore become unconditional and univer- sal grace for the godless.

This validation of the promises of a new creation in the resurrection of Jesus Christ gives people strength and courage to live and act against the oppression and suffering of the world. The God who promises a just world is by this promise always questioning the world as it is. Evil and suffering will be overcome. The future is open, and people are invited to enter this future. Moltmann takes up Paul's language of baptism to clarify this. Believers participate through baptism in the death of Christ, which means that communion with Christ is suffering com- munion with the crucified. But in hope they also participate in the resurrection of Christ through obedient discipleship. This discipleship, which concerns life here and now, exists in the horizon of the coming kingdom. It criticizes what is in terms of what is promised. This means that eschatology, thus understood, does not make history meaningless. Just the opposite, it is the hope which is the driv- ing force of history. So Moltmann can write that eschatology "keeps history moving by its criticism and hope"[12] and that "the resurrection has set in motion an eschatologically determined process of history, whose goal is the annihilation of death in the victory of the life of the resurrection, and which ends in that right- eousness in which God receives in all things his due and the creature thereby finds its salvation."[13] It is this eschatological understanding of reality, implying openness for radically new possibilities, that determines the mission of the church and makes it a transformative force in the world.

It is also this understanding that makes it possible for Christian faith to posi- tively meet the modern future-oriented consciousness. Society is seen as human- made and therefore as something that can be changed and formed according to will. The utopia of the good society, and not a past golden age, becomes the point of departure for criticism of present reality. According to Moltmann, this mood is not only congruent with Christianity, but it has its basic source in Judeo-Christian messianism. He especially refers to "a *sense of mission*, a belief in a history that is meaningful and a faith in the great task of mankind"[14] that characterizes much of the thinking of the nineteenth century. The liberation of reason and society from tradition, while deplored by many Christians, is a result of just this modern messianic passion that grows from the Christian hope for a new creation.

Therefore Moltmann can argue that it is this sense of mission that gives the context in which Christian talk about God and humankind can be meaningful. We meet God in the promise of a new future and therefore in the mission this promise

---

[11]*TH* 147 (132f).
[12]*TH* 165 (149).
[13]*TH* 163 (148).
[14]*TH* 262 (240).

gives birth to.[15] Likewise, the nature and possibilities of the humankind are understood in terms of its vocation. The transforming mission

> seeks for that which is really, objectively possible in this world, in order to grasp it and realize it in the direction of the promised future of the righteousness, the life and the kingdom of God. . . . To the eye of mission, not only man is open to the future, full of all kinds of possibilities, but the world, too, is a container full of future and of boundless possibilities for good and evil.[16]

He is anxious, however, to dissociate this Christian eschatology from a general belief in progress. The possibilities he talks about are not immanent in history, but are based on the resurrection of Christ. This means that theology does not derive its understanding of possibilities from a study of reality as it is. The task of theology is instead to explore "the inner *tendency* of the resurrection event, asking what rightly can and must be expected from the risen and exalted Lord".[17] The Christian hope is consequently not empty, but is defined by Christ. As it concerns new creation, it is also full of surprises. Moreover, the study of eschatology is closely connected with the concrete mission task. Moltmann does not want to formulate a theory of universal history,[18] but to make people conscious of the contradictions between the present and God's promises and direct them to the possibilities that these promises open. Christian knowledge of God consequently cannot be divorced from a practical active hope for the future.

2. Developments and Modifications

As indicated in the previous chapter, much has happened in Moltmann's theology since *Theology of Hope*. I will not discuss the degree of change here or how much this change is a consistent development of this book. But before taking up his more recent christological thought I will briefly identify a few of the more important developments.

One question *Theology of Hope* arouses concerns the content of the promises of God. If one is to act in light of these promises for the future, the content of the promises must be important. But Moltmann tended to avoid this question by referring to the radical newness of God's act that makes it impossible for us to know the future. He therefore only talked in very general terms of justice, life and freedom, to point to the fact that God's salvation concerns the whole reality. The

---

[15]It is in this context he, following Bloch, can say that God has "future as his essential nature" (*TH* 16 [12]), a statement he no longer upholds. See *WJC* 321 (345).

[16]*TH* 288 (266).

[17]*TH* 194 (176). With "tendency", a concept adopted from Bloch, he means that which "mediates between the real, objective possibilities and the subjective decisions, and to that extent places the historical 'facts' within the stream of the historical process and sets the subjective decisions of the historical observer within this same process." (*TH* 243 [222].)

[18]We will later see that he comes close to doing just this.

result is that any course of action or any movement that claims freedom or justice as its aim might be defended in terms of this theology.

It is also difficult to know what he means with his radical disassociation of Christian eschatology from a general belief in progress and with his idea that the possibilities he talks about are not immanent in history, but should be understood as new creation. He actually uses these ideas for mediating one form of *revolutionary* belief in progress (in contrast to a more linear liberal evolutionism) with the Christian faith. But revolutionary changes also use immanent possibilities, which Moltmann recognizes when he talks about finding what is possible in the direction of the hoped for future. Maybe he only wants to say that there are no immutable divine orders, and that the hope of the coming kingdom of God leads to criticism of what is, and thereby to work for change. If so, this is a strange way of saying this. If he wants to say something more I am unsure what that might be.[19]

Moltmann, partially accepting the criticism of the overly formal (and therefore in practice ethically and politically empty) nature of his eschatology, later writes that "this general trend of theology and practice towards eschatological hope . . . is not something that can be taken back. But it must be made more profound if it is not to become the superficial sanctioning by religion of an officially optimistic society, sworn to economic growth and political and cultural expansion."[20] We therefore in *The Crucified God* find attempts to elaborate clearer christological criteria for Christian life and action. The emphasis here is not only on God's promise of a new creation, but on God's suffering solidarity with the victims of the world. The stress is consequently more clearly put on a political praxis in solidarity with the poor and oppressed and their interests and not just on change in general. In the last chapter, moreover, he tries to identify various "ways toward political liberation of man". Yet, except in the critique of political religion in terms of his theology of the cross,[21] the substantial connections to the christology he developed in the book are not easy to see.[22]

---

[19]The 1960s was also a time with strong belief in social planning and Moltmann discusses the relation between hope and planning in *HP* 179-199 (251-268), but it does not make his view on this issue clearer for me. Cf. also his later essay "Hope and Development" in *FC* 49-58 (59-67) where the hoped or wished for future is contrasted with the calculable future. The result is the following: "Social policy only emerges when sociological, economic and purely scientific extrapolations are linked with ethical anticipations. It does not emerge purely from the calculable and extrapolated future, or solely from ethical maxims and desires, but only from the linking of what we know and can do with what we hope for and desire." (*FC* 56 [65].)

[20]*CG* 256 (244). But cf. Norman Young's comment to this admission: "it [the theology of hope] has been used far more by those at the opposite end of the political spectrum, and in view of its rather doctrinaire application by some theologians of revolution Moltmann might have added, 'nor to become an indiscriminate endorsement of every movement pledged to overthrow existing economic and political structures'." (*Creator, Creation and Faith*, 155.)

[21]*CG* 321-329 (298-305).

[22]Cf. Forrester, *Theology and Politics*, 152.

Another result of his concentration on the cross is a much more developed trinitarian structure of his theology. The trinitarian history of God, and not eschatology, now becomes the widest framework for his whole theology. Here he is part of the general renaissance of trinitarian thinking in modern theology from Barth and Rahner to Jüngel, Pannenberg, Kasper and others. His full blown, although not final, formulation is found in *The Trinity and the Kingdom of God*. What should be stressed is how he explicates his trinitarian doctrine from the history of Jesus, that is through the narrative of the relations between the Father, the Son and the Spirit. In these terms he formulates what he calls a social doctrine of the Trinity, which I cannot describe better briefly than Bauckham has done in the following concise account.

> It understands the trinitarian God as three divine subjects in mutual loving relationship, and God's relationship to the world as a reciprocal relationship in which God in his love for the world not only affects the world but is also affected by it. He relates to the world as Trinity, experiencing the world within his own trinitarian experience, and so his changing experience of the world is also a changing experience of himself.[23]

So the history of the world is taken up in God's trinitarian history, the goal of which is to unite everything in God. Also this book ends with an ethical and political chapter, now better integrated with the earlier trinitarian discourse than was the case in *The Crucified God*.

This trinitarian account helps him, in *God in Creation*, to formulate an ecological doctrine of the creation where the world not only dwells in God, but where God as Spirit dwells in the world. His book on creation is a very rich one, although maybe also his most speculative. Here it should only be stressed that his doctrine of creation, in accordance with his overall theological project, is eschatological and trinitarian, which means that it is christological and pneumatological. It is thus not something that could be explicated separately from the whole eschatological trinitarian account. For his theological anthropology this, for example, means that he interprets the *imago Dei* in messianic terms. "The restoration or new creation of the likeness to God comes about in the fellowship of believers with Christ: since he is the messianic *imago Dei*, believers become *imago Christi*, and through this enter upon the path which will make them *gloria Dei* on earth."[24] This makes discipleship a crucial category for understanding the Christian life and Christian ethics. This later becomes fully developed in *The Way of Jesus Christ*.[25]

Finally, one more consequence of his more explicit trinitarian theology should be mentioned. It enables him, as we will see in the next chapter on the church, to

[23]"Jürgen Moltmann", 303.

[24]*GIC* 226 (232),

[25]Moltmann's theology of creation is thus very different from that specific sort of Lutheran theology of creation that dominates Scandinavian theology. For an attack on Moltmann from this perspective, see Lønning, "Die Schöpfungstheologie Jürgen Moltmanns".

understand pneumatology as mediating the eschatological possibilities to the world, which means that these possibilities are not so exclusively related to the Word as in *Theology of Hope*. The result is that the presence of God and the Kingdom in people's hopes and struggles outside the church can be more clearly understood.

3. Christology in Messianic Dimensions

The Way of Jesus Christ is a good example of Moltmann's outstanding ability to explore the relevant meaning of biblical faith. Its scope is broader than most other comparable works and as all of Moltmann's main books it is extremely rich in ideas and its uses of traditional notions are not seldom breathtaking.[26] Moltmann argues, as was seen in the previous chapter, that christology has to be constantly reformulated in relation to people's changing questions of salvation. In this book Moltmann concentrates on poverty, the nuclear threat and the ecological crisis. Two other influential factors are the Jewish-Christian dialogue and feminist theology.[27]

That Moltmann's theology has not lost the early eschatological focus is clear already from the subtitle: "Christology in messianic dimensions". This title also alludes to his attempt to write "Christology in the Jewish-Christian dialogue".[28] Actually the continuity with Old Testament faith is even more manifest here than in *Theology of Hope*. He sees the presuppositions of christology in the messianic promises of the Old Testament, and the task of Christianity is to pervade the world with this messianic hope.[29] He argues that already in the Old Testament faith a dialectic between historical-prophetic messianism and an apocalyptic-transcendent Son of Man-expectation develops. "Messianism is the historical side of apocalyptic, and apocalyptic is the transcendent side of messianism."[30] This leads him to distinguish "between the messianic future *in* history, or at the end of history, and the eschatological future of this whole history"[31] and consequently between the carriers of the messianic hope and humanity as a whole. In other words, the messianic dimension is taken up into the apocalyptic and the eschatological without being dissolved. He therefore attempts to interpret christology in the light of the trinitarian and eschatological history of God with the world, a history that includes both humanity and nature. By eschatological he thus refers to "the com-

---

[26] I furthermore agree with the leading Moltmann-scholar Richard Bauckham's judgement that "this book is Moltmann's finest since *The Crucified God*" ("Moltmann's Messianic Christology", 519). It is better argued and not so speculative as the two first volumes of his "contribution to theology".
[27] *WJC* 63-72, xvif (83-91, 14f).
[28] *WJC* 28 (45). For a discussion of *WJC* that particularly concentrates on—and celebrates—this aspect, see Klappert, "Christologie in messianischen Dimensionen".
[29] *WJC* 1-3 (17-19).
[30] *WJC* 16 (34).
[31] *WJC* 21 (38).

ing redemption of the world" and by eschatological history he means "the history which is aligned towards this future through God's calling and election, his promise and his covenant, and which is experienced and effected in the context of that future."[32] The book itself is built up and narrated as a history where the messianic is taken up into the apocalyptic and eschatological, from the messianic sending of Christ through his apocalyptic suffering and eschatological resurrection to the cosmic Christ.

This means that he tries to go beyond both the classical cosmological and the modern historical and anthropological christologies. He criticizes the latter, which he describes as Jesuology, for being the civil religion of modern society, ministering "to its educated and ruling classes, but not to its victims."[33] Presupposed is the privatization of religion that reduces salvation to the existential and individual sphere of life. He tries, against this, to integrate the earlier cosmological and historical approaches into an eschatological and cosmological frame, and thereby formulate, what he calls a postmodern christology.[34]

A crucial difference from *Theology of Hope* and *The Crucified God* is that the work and teaching of Jesus here has an important role, in contrast to the earlier concentration on his cross and resurrection. The longest part of the book, entitled "The messianic mission of Christ", deals with his birth, baptism, preaching and healing. Yet, his perspective is not that of the search for the historical Jesus. He follows instead the Gospels themselves and understands Jesus in the light of his resurrection and his presence now in the Spirit. The Jesus of the Gospels is not dead, but living and present. "He is raised and present in the Spirit, not only as the one crucified, but also as the one baptized, as the healer, the preacher on the mount, the friend of sinners and tax-collectors, and the one whom the women accompanied to the moment of his death."[35] This means that there is and must be a congruence between our experience of his presence in the Spirit and the Gospel's memory of his life. Jesus is not only now present in the Spirit, but his whole life was from the beginning lived in the power of the creative Spirit, and Moltmann therefore, in continuity with the Old Testament messianic hope, understands the life of Jesus in terms of a Spirit christology. His whole being is from the beginning "the warp and the weft of the Spirit",[36] whom Moltmann contends we have to call the divine mother of Christ.[37]

Jesus proclaimed the gospel of the kingdom of God. Seen against the background of the Old Testament, Moltmann interprets it as "the gospel of the liberation of the people".[38] In Jesus Christ, in his preaching, healings and expelling of

---

[32] *WJC* 70 (90).
[33] *WJC* 63 (82).
[34] *WJC* xvi (13).
[35] *WJC* 76 (95).
[36] *WJC* 86 (106: "sein ganzes Dasein geistgewirkt ist").
[37] *WJC* 73-78 (92-97).
[38] *WJC* 96 (116).

demons, the messianic time as the immanence of the eschatological new creation has come. In other words, the gospel "does not bring new teaching; it brings a new reality."[39]

The significant place Moltmann here gives to the messianic mission of Jesus has important consequences for his theology. While the resurrection of Christ in *Theology of Hope* was understood as only a divine confirmation of the promise of a new creation in general, which was an important reason for the formal and abstract character of his early ethics, it is here the confirmation of the actual life and message of Jesus. This enables him to give concrete content to the hope and therefore to the Christian praxis. The saying that the hope is defined by Christ which was not concretely explicated in *Theology of Hope*, can now be fully fleshed out. He can therefore also integrate christology and ethics in a way he was unable to do even in *The Crucified God*. We have seen that this is a climax of a continuous development of his theology, a working out of the logic of his early position. It should also be noted that the way he formulates himself is strongly influenced by the works of John Howard Yoder and Gerhard Lohfink.

For this reason, we find, under the title "The messianic way of life",[40] one of his most extensive and significant accounts of Christian ethics. He, first of all, strongly defends the existence and necessity of a specifically Christian ethics.

> If there is no specifically Christian ethic, then the acknowledgement of Christ is itself called in question; for then Jesus' message cannot have been ethically meant, in the sense of making a public ethical claim. It was then either purely religious, and hence non-political; or wholly apocalyptic, and hence without relevance for changes in the world itself; or confined to personal life, and hence without any relation to the public conditions in which personal life is lived. But can Jesus then still be called the messiah in a sense that is in any way relevant?[41]

The public nature of Jesus' messiahship is central for Moltmann's whole theology, and that means also the public nature of his specific ethic. The *solus Christus* applies then, according to Moltmann, also to ethics. Moreover, christology and christopraxis are inseparable. One learns to know Christ through following him. "If praxis acquires this cognitive relevance in a holistic christology, then Christian ethics cannot be anything except ethical christology."[42]

If Christian ethics is a discipleship ethics,[43] then it is an ethics for the community that follows Jesus. It makes universal claims, is proclaimed for everyone, and is aimed at the salvation of all, but it cannot be separated from Christ, from the eschatological horizon, and from the community of the disciples. He stresses es-

---

[39] *WJC* 97-99 (117-119). The citation is from p. 99 (119).

[40] *WJC* 116 (136). For the following discussion of ethics, see *WJC* 116-127 (136-148).

[41] *WJC* 117 (137).

[42] *WJC* 119 (139).

[43] "Christian ethics are not asked merely for good or better solutions to general problems. They are asked how far the way of Jesus is to be taken seriously." (*WJC* 118 [138].)

see Radical
Reformation - *Anabaptist*
theology

Messianic Theology

like the
sermon on
the mount

71

pecially that Christian ethics is not an ethics just for individuals, but is always a community ethics. Only then does it make sense and become liveable. This understanding is the context in which Moltmann expounds the Sermon on the Mount, which he sees as a messianic interpretation of the Torah for all people. This is also the background of his description of the messianic community as a contrast society, which offers a concrete and liveable alternative to existing societal systems (we will return to this in the next chapter). At this point in the book he especially concentrates on the witness of the messianic community to peace.[44]

The ethical normativeness of Jesus, the community character of the Christian ethics, the eschatological horizon and the centrality given to living out the messianic peace, all show the increasing convergence between Moltmann's political theology and Radical Reformation theology, which Moltmann explicitly recognizes.[45] Yet, it makes the questions I raised at the end of the previous chapter even more pressing. Does not a perspective like this break apart his political theology and hermeneutics? This will be a crucial issue for my continuing investigation of Moltmann's theology in coming chapters.

The next part of *The Way of Jesus Christ* has the title "The Apocalyptic sufferings of Christ." As this title indicates, Moltmann interprets the suffering and death of Jesus Christ at the cross in an apocalyptic frame. Apocalyptic in the form of the message about the kingdom of God talks about the coming of the new creation, and since that new creation has already begun in Christ, the end-time struggle between the new creation and the old system has also begun in his life and in his followers. His suffering is then no private suffering, but apocalyptic suffering for the world. Furthermore, if the resurrection is understood "as the anticipation of the general resurrection", then his death has to be interpreted as the anticipation of the universal death. He continues:

> As an anticipation of the universal death, Golgotha is the anticipation of the end of this world and the beginning of a world that is new. It is the anticipation of the divine judgement out of which the kingdom of righteousness and justice proceeds. What has already happened to Christ is representative of what will happen to everybody: it is a happening *pars pro toto*. Consequently he has suffered vicariously what threatens everyone. But if he has suffered vicariously what threatens everyone, then through his representation he liberates everyone from this threat, and throws open to them the future of the new creation.[46]

Soteriologically Moltmann further develops the consequences of the death and resurrection of Christ in the Pauline terms of God's righteousness, which he understands as God's creative power creating new life—the beginning of the new creation. This means that forgiveness of sin is only one component of salvation. Others that he mentions are liberation from the power of sin, reconciliation with

Liberation
Theology

---

[44] *WJC* 127-136 (148-157).
[45] *WJC* 118 (138). He says that the only recent German theologian who has taken up the theme of discipleship is Bonhoeffer (*WJC* 357 n. 66 [118]).
[46] *WJC* 155 (176).

God, new life in righteousness, inheritance in the new creation, and the struggling participation for that new world already now. So justifying faith is to be understood as the beginning of the way to the new creation. Justification is therefore a wider concept than reconciliation, because it denotes not only restoration of the covenant but also transformation and new creation.[47]

The death and resurrection of Christ established his lordship also over the dead. He became present with them, as their "brother and deliverer".[48] For Moltmann this means the triumph of justice over injustice and violence. Oppressors and murderers do not definitively triumph over their victims. God's justice, not death, has the last word. This also points to the communion of the living and the dead and the importance for a society to be aware of the relationship between the generations.[49]

As seen, Moltmann interprets the resurrection as a divine confirmation of Jesus and the life and message which brought him to death, and as the triumph of God's justice and the beginning of the new creation. The concept of resurrection points to the continuity between the mortal and the resurrected life. In the same way, Moltmann understands new creation, not as a different world, but as this world redeemed. Further, the resurrection of Christ is the beginning of a process. This event "in the Spirit determines the present, because it opens up the future of life."[50] It is through the experiences of this process that one learns to know the resurrected Christ. It is a question of "participating through the Spirit in *the process of resurrection*."[51]

In *Theology of Hope* Moltmann's interest was almost entirely on how the resurrection opened the world for God's future. Since then he has, as seen, become aware of the ecological crisis and sees how reality as primarily history has contributed to this crisis. In his later works he therefore tries to place "human history ecologically in the framework of nature."[52] For christology this means that "modern historical christology must be, not abolished, but gathered up into an ecological christology".[53] Consequently he does not only consider the relations between resurrection and history, but also between resurrection and nature. The fact of Christ's *bodily* resurrection (as well as *bodily* suffering and death) thus becomes prominent. From that he derives the resurrection of nature and an account of the *rights* of nature.[54] This has, Moltmann argues, important corollaries for human praxis. First, the hope of a bodily resurrection means the abolishment of the hostility between soul and body. The repression of the body is replaced by

---

[47]*WJC* 183-189 (205-211).
[48]*WJC* 189 (211).
[49]*WJC* 189-192 (211-215).
[50]*WJC* 241 (264).
[51]*WJC* 240 (263).
[52]*WJC* xvi (13). Cf. 274f (297f).
[53]*WJC* 247 (270).
[54]*WJC* 252-256 (276-279).

a new spontaneous harmony. Second, he emphasizes the unity of the different stages of personhood from the embryo to the old age and that the hope of resurrection includes all these stages. The consequence is a critical view of the praxis of abortion. Third, from the fact that bodily existence is also social existence he criticizes the principle of competition that rewards effective people at the expense of the weak. Fourth, because human beings are also "generation beings", he finds it necessary to think in terms of a contract between the generations, so that our generation does not destroy the possibilities for coming generations. Fifth, in the light of the hope of the resurrection of the body, and of nature, theology can explicate the relation between human culture and nature in covenantal terms.[55] Again we see how the formal eschatological account of the early Moltmann, has been replaced by an ethically substantial account.

Moltmann's wish to develop an ecological christology makes him also open for taking up the cosmological christology of the New Testament. This has, he contends, its epistemological basis in the resurrection of Christ. He tries to explicate this theme through interpreting "Christ's mediation in creation in three separate strands or movements: 1. Christ as the ground of the creation of all things (*creatio originalis*); 2. Christ as the moving power in the evolution of creation (*creatio continua*); and 3. Christ as the redeemer of the whole creation process (*creatio nova*)."[56]

Moltmann here discusses both God's immanent dwelling and ongoing creative activity in the world through the Word and Spirit and the eschatological redemption of the creation. Doing this he sharply distinguishes between teleology and eschatology. The new creation or the kingdom of God does not grow teleologically out of the history of evolution, but is only possible eschatologically. Evolution means selection, but in the new creation even the victims of evolution are taken up. In that sense, Moltmann argues, the "movement of *redemption* . . . runs counter to evolution"[57]—it comes from the future. Criticizing the use of evolutionary theory for justifying modern aggressive attitudes and manipulation of nature, Moltmann consequently writes: "It is not at the supreme points of evolution that Christ is present. He is present in nature's weakest creatures, who are the first victims of developed human societies."[58] Finally, he argues that the practical significance of a cosmic christology is that it can become the basis for a new way of living with nature and a basis for developing an ethics of reconciliation as well as an ethics of rights for nature.[59]

The last part of the book deals with the parousia. This theme is not frequently discussed in modern theology, but Moltmann contends that christology becomes

---

[55] *WJC* 259-273 (282-296).
[56] *WJC* 286 (310).
[57] *WJC* 303 (327).
[58] *WJC* 306 (330). See further *WJC* 287-305 (311-329).
[59] *WJC* 305-312 (329-336).

incomprehensible without this actual fulfilment of the eschatological hope.[60] This hope has great significance for the church's life. Moltmann thinks it is no accident that the church gave up its hope of parousia when it became integrated in the Roman society.

> People who are trying to fit into the world and to gain its recognition are bound to dispense with hope for the messianic kingdom which will change and renew everything. . . . But for people who embark on a true conversion which takes them out of what they are, present hope for the coming of Christ and his kingdom is important. They need this sustaining staff of hope, in order to free themselves from the present and to confront it freely (1 Cor. 7.31).[61]

This hope decisively forms the life of the Christian community, as the New Testament paranesis shows. It calls it to lead a life that in the power of the Spirit anticipates the coming new creation and points to the fundamental place the patience of hope has in the Christian life. These are all themes that, as we will see, are central in the Radical Reformation tradition.

The account in this chapter of Moltmann's theology provides the theological background to the specific form of Christian political criticism that political theology constitutes. But it provides also a background for understanding Moltmann's move from an ethically abstract eschatological theology in the direction of Radical Reformation theology, with a more substantial account of Christian ethics closely allied to a specific form of ecclesiology. To Moltmann's ecclesiology we therefore now turn.

---

[60]"It is the keystone supporting the whole of christology, and this also makes it the key to the understanding of the history of Christ." (*WJC* 316 [340].)
[61]*WJC* 313f (337).

Chapter 5

The Church in the Liberation History of God

In the previous chapter we noticed the way Moltmann in his christology and ethics has moved closer to a Radical Reformation position, and how this grew out of his earlier theology. There is one area in which his explicit affinity with the Radical tradition was early evident, namely in his ecclesiology. He has even written that "the future of the church of Christ lies in principle on this [left] wing of the Reformation because the widely unknown and uninhabited land of 'the congregation' is found here."[1] He thinks that this way of going on from the reformation of doctrine to the reformation of life and the forming of free congregations was only a logical consequence of the Reformation message. But there are differences. If he in his description of the life and ministry of the church is close to much Radical Reformation theology, there are not surprisingly significant differences in how the relation between church and world, and therefore the basic framework in which one sees the mission of the church, is understood.

The issues of church and world and of the church's political mission will take a prominent place in this chapter. Yet, the account will be kept quite general. In the following chapters I will show how Moltmann actually interprets modern society, including which issues he discusses and what recommendations he makes for particular Christian political and social practices. The purpose of this chapter is to give the background for these coming chapters. Furthermore, the later chapters will give ample opportunity to analyse and discuss his views. I will therefore in this chapter minimize my own comments.

1. The Messianic Vocation

Moltmann unfolds his ecclesiology in the framework of the history of the triune God with the world. The goal of this history is the uniting of humanity and creation with the Father and the Son in the Spirit. The history of the kingdom of God is nothing else than this process of liberation and unification. The church is part of the mission of the Spirit in the world. It is one moment in the continuing process of the liberation of the creation and the consequent glorification of God.[2]

It is against this background Moltmann formulates his messianic ecclesiology.[3] That the church understands itself in messianic terms means that all it is and does must be justified by the messianic future defined by Christ. The church

---

[1] *OC* 117 (142f). Cf. also *OHD* 140f, 142f (*PTPE* 83f, 86). He describes himself "as a 'free-church person' in the midst of a *Volkskirche*" ("The Challenge of Religion in the '80s", 110).
[2] *CPS* 50-65 (66-82).
[3] The subtitle of *CPS*, which is his main ecclesiological work, is "A Contribution to Messianic Ecclesiology". A shorter, more popular account is found in *OC*.

is the anticipation of the kingdom of God in history and is therefore "the people of the kingdom of God".[4] The Gospel is the breakthrough of the messianic future into the present which creates new possibilities and calls people out of this present captivity to new freedom. Moltmann consequently can designate the church an Exodus community,[5] the vanguard of the new humanity[6] and "the beginning of the reconciled cosmos which has arrived at peace."[7] As the church of Christ it participates in his death and resurrection which leads to "conflict with the society in which it lives, and evokes conflicts between the powers of the past and the forces of the future, between oppression and liberation."[8]

In *The Way of Jesus Christ* he has also taken up Gerhard Lohfink's description of the church as a "contrast society".[9] "The community of Jesus which lives and acts messianically in the sense described, practices the great alternative to the world's present system. It is a 'contrast society', and through its existence it calls in question the systems of violence and injustice."[10] The church that follows this way will thus "offer a public alternative to the ethics of the world."[11] This alternative is the beginning of the universal future God promises, i. e., of the coming world. Consequently the church should not be understood as non-world, but as that part of the world that already has turned to that future and freedom which is on its way. "It is the community of the liberated, the community of those who are making a new beginning, the community of those who hope. Their fellowship serves to spread the call of freedom in the world and, as new fellowship, should itself be the social form of hope."[12] From this messianic perspective it follows that the church is an instrument for the spreading of the kingdom of God. The growth of the church as an institution is not a goal in itself. The essential is that the creation is liberated, that people come to peace with each other, that freedom and justice are established. And this occurs also outside the church.[13]

If Moltmann answers the question *what* the church is with the concept of the people of the coming kingdom, he distinguishes this question from the question *where* the church is found. Instead of following tradition and describing the signs of the church, he starts from the promises of Christ's presence. He finds three such categories. Christ has promised to be present 1) in the believing community, 2) in 'the least of the brethren', and 3) in the parousia. Concerning the first group he refers to Christ's promises of presence in the apostolic proclamation, in bap-

---

[4]*CPS* 196 (221), cf. 289 (316).
[5]He says that "the initial form of God's coming rule is the gathering and exodus of the people from slavery." (*CPS* 78 [96].) "Exodus Church" is the title of the last chapter of *TH*.
[6]*CPS* 196 (221).
[7]*WJC* 285 (308).
[8]*CPS* 83 (101).
[9]See Lohfink, *Jesus and Community*, idem, *Wem gilt die Bergpredigt?*, and *WJC* 116-136 (136-157).
[10]*WJC* 122 (142). See also ibid., 125 (146).
[11]*WJC* 126 (147).
[12]*CPS* 85 (103). See further *CPS* 83-85 (101-103).
[13]*CPS* 11, 64f, 153f (24, 81f, 174f).

tism and the Lord's Supper, and in the fellowship of the believers. The second category refers to the promises of Matthew 25:31-46. If the church is present where Christ is present, it follows that the church exists both manifestly in the community of the believers and latently in the community of the poor. These two communities are united when the manifest church is present with the poor, hungry and imprisoned. The important question is then not, concludes Moltmann, how people outside it relate themselves to the church, but how the church relates itself to the presence of Christ among the poor.[14] He has later reformulated the same idea in terms of how Jesus proclaimed the gospel. To the poor, it is proclaimed unconditionally. They are not called to the kingdom, as it already belongs to them, a truth that gives their life true dignity. To the rich, the message of liberation, on the contrary, includes the call to conversion and discipleship. From this follows that the new messianic people consist of the converted together with the poor.[15] The practical consequence for the life and mission of the church is that

> this mission should neither bring the people again into the church nor the church into the people, but rather discover the church *of* the people and live the brotherhood of Jesus in the brotherhood of the 'least of these.' This happens best in and through basic communities and groups which live intensively with the gospel and their neighbors and which come together in prayer and in the breaking of bread.[16]

It is not too easy to know how this should be understood in practical terms. First there is the problem with the abstract use of the category "poor" that goes through the whole of his writings. Poverty and oppression are relative terms and it is not possible simply to divide humanity into two groups, rich and poor, oppressors and oppressed. The same person can, depending on the relation focused on, be oppressed and oppressor or poor and rich at the same time. For example an economically poor and oppressed man may be an oppressor of his wife and part of an ethnic group that is both rich and oppressive in relation to some other ethnic group. Upper class women can similarly see themselves as oppressed because of their sex, while other people see them very differently. Moltmann seldom reflects on such complexities or on the possibility of conflicts between different emancipatory interests.[17] This makes it difficult to talk about one basically unitary progressive history of liberation in the way Moltmann tends to do.

In the light of this, and in the light of Christian history and contemporary Christian existence, is not the idea that discipleship is not for the poor odd? Is not the common life of following Jesus Christ a beginning of a new life and salvation

---

[14]*CPS* 121-132 (141-152).Tripole has in a comprehensive discussion of the exegetical debate on this text in Matthew questioned the exegetical foundations of Moltmann's identification of the least of Christ's brethren with the poor in general. His conclusion is that Matthew has in view Christian missionaries. See Tripole, "A Church for the Poor and the World". Bauckham, *Moltmann,* 159f n. 4 concurs.
[15]*WJC* 99-104 (119-124). See also *HC* 24f (*DHRG* 25-27) and *CPS* 78-80 (96-98)..
[16]*OC* 110 (133).
[17]He recognizes these types of conflicts in *FC* 100f (107f), but this does not help explain the question we asked.

also for the poor? That the Gospel is presented differently for different people is one thing, but to make the sort of sharp contrasts Moltmann makes is another, which makes it very difficult to understand in practical church terms what he might possibly mean.

2. The Historical Shape of the Church

If the church is the messianic people of the coming kingdom then it must bear witness already through its way of life. The church's organization, its structures and life speak before proclamation and sacraments do. Hence, Moltmann can never consider questions of church order as inessential.[18] This does not mean that he defends some unchanging church law or denies that the church in its institutional life is dependent on the society and the time it lives. But if the church is a people that anticipates the future of God, this must take concrete form.[19]

Moltmann has also extensively discussed both the historical forms of the church and the way he thinks the contemporary church should live. In the context of the German people's church (*Volkskirche*) his proposals are radical. The reactions to and discussions of his ecclesiology have, perhaps as a result, been meagre—in conspicuous contrast to the rest of his theology.[20]

Already in his way of describing church history he shows close affinity to the Radical Reformation understanding. Thus he points to the fateful consequences of the so-called 'Constantinian turn'.[21] As Christianity became the state religion of the Roman empire it acquired the functions of civil religion, i. e., it became society's administrator of the system of religious meaning. The church now had a similar organizational structure as the civil society. The result was that the visible Christian communities were replaced by geographical division, with the consequences that the offices of bishop and priest became part of the power structures of the empire and that priesthood and laity were sharply separated from each other. Faith was then practised primarily as participation in church arrangements. Evangelization was replaced by forced christianizing, and the fellowship in the church by fellowship with the church. Its community acts became official sacramental acts. Moltmann does not think that the Reformation succeeded in changing these patterns. Although a different ecclesiology was formulated, it did not have

---

[18]*CPS* 291 (318).

[19]"As the church of Christ, the congregation with all its own powers has to realize the social, political and cultural potentialities of a particular period in a way that is in accordance with the cause it maintains; so that through its physical and public profile as well people will be confronted with the freedom of Christ and will be invited to the messianic kingdom." (*CPS* 290 [317].)

[20]Bauckham thinks this has to do with the radical way Moltmann questions the actual forms of much, and especially European and German, church life, his belief in reform from below, and the fact that he transcends the academic boundaries between systematic and practical theology. (*Moltmann,* 114.)

[21]Cf. Ruhbach (ed.), *Die Kirche angesichts der konstantinischen Wende*. The reference to Constantine is not to be taken too literally. This process had started before him and continued to develop after him. He is more a symbol for the changed relation between church and society, than a concise turning point.

much impact. The new national churches continued to function as political and civil religion.[22] The established situation of the church as here described is then what is meant by the term "Constantinianism", which has almost acquired the status of a technical term, and is used both by Moltmann and Hauerwas.

If Moltmann is critical of the Constantinian tradition, he is more positive, but not uncritical, towards the so-called sectarian reform movements that arose in protest against these developments in the church. He distinguishes between two types: reforming and prophetic sects. The former exalt the early church and protest the alliance between church and state. This type tends to emphasize the direct relation with Christ and a discipleship ethics, where the Sermon on the Mount often is central. The prophetic sects, on the other hand, do not look backwards, but see themselves, led by new prophets, as vanguards of the kingdom of God. These sects have since the Enlightenment become so common that their form tends to be seen as the most characteristic expression of modern Christianity.[23]

The Anabaptists of the sixteenth century are one example of what Moltmann calls reforming sects. He mentions them often in positive terms, but he seldom discusses them extensively. One exception is a discussion of the pacifist challenge of this tradition.[24] He is generally positive, but he thinks they exaggerate the distinction between church and world. He is worried that they forget that the world is God's creation in which God continues to be active, and that they end up denying the world instead of criticizing it in the light of the kingdom of God. They risk becoming more interested in *faithful* discipleship in itself than in a *political* discipleship directed towards social change.

In light of this, it is not surprising that he is positive to Thomas Müntzer, who, as Moltmann describes it, struggled for divine justice in all spheres of life and who used violence in the struggle against the oppression. Moltmann regards him as a liberation theologian of the sixteenth century and his theology of the liberation of the oppressed as a necessary consequence of the Reformation doctrine of the justification of the sinners. The basic problem Moltmann sees with Müntzer is that he was better as a theologian than as a military strategist. If he had been able to combine theology and military strategy as effectively as Oliver Cromwell in seventeenth century England was able to do, Moltmann envisions, he might have succeeded.[25]

The importance of the Radical Reformation, according to Moltmann, is then that it followed up the reformation of doctrine with the reformation of life and church organization. This congregational tradition and practice (with its political breakthrough in the Puritan revolution), together with European humanism (de-

---

[22]*HC* 39f (*OMM* 165f), *CPS* 224, 317-320 (250, 344-346), *OHD* 136f, 156f (*PTPE* 80f, 97f), *OC* 120f (146f), *WJC* 135f (156f), "Christian Theology and Political Religion", 47-52 ("Die Politik der Nachfolge Christi gegen Christliche Milleniumspolitk", 24-27).

[23]*CPS* 318-322 (346-348).

[24]*OHD* 113-131 (*PTPE* 180-192). See also *WJC* 118 (138).

[25]"Thomas Müntzer".

fending the freedom and rights of the individual), Moltmann contends, laid the groundwork for later democratic development. The right to start independent churches leads to the idea of voluntary religion and to the forming of popular and free base communities, which in its turn influences political development. "The free churches' understanding of religion has had immense political consequences; the right of the community became the underlying tenet of basic democracy in the Anglo-Saxon world, particularly in North America."[26] He further argues that national churches as such never contribute to democracy. "State churches and people's churches never create a climate friendly toward democracy—this is true in the Federal Republic of Germany too—because they never renounce their claim to dominate the religion and morality of men and women."[27]

3. Criticism of the Practices of the National Churches

This view of the Reformation thus entails a sharply critical stance towards the practice of the established and national churches that have dominated European Christianity until today.[28] Moltmann points to the double form of these type of churches, where the large world open church lives together with different communities living in a consistent discipleship (for example the monasteries). The Reformation intended to break with this double form. There are not two sorts of Christian existence. Every Christian is supposed to live the life of discipleship and Christian fellowship in daily life. But this vision failed, argues Moltmann, because the rejection of monasticism was not followed by a rejection of the territorial church system. It was only the Anabaptists who took the congregational principle seriously. The results of the Reformation were therefore further secularization rather than a deepening of the Christian life *and* a stronger dependence on society and its authorities. The first real attempt to renew the established church was the Pietistic revival movements.[29]

Because an established people's church is an integrated part of the social system, it accepts the system's basic values and aims as given. Therefore it will necessarily compromise with the state and accommodate to general opinion.[30] Moltmann is accordingly critical of modern attempts to revive a sort of double strategy inside the national churches, which aims to both preserve the openness of the people's church and to simultaneously form committed core-groups who can help the church to find new ways. Moltmann thinks the result will be a new hier-

---

[26]*OHD* 140 (*PTPE* 84). See further *OHD* 140f, 142f (*PTPE* 83f, 86). This does not mean that he is uncritical of the free church tradition. See e.g. *PPL* 160f.

[27]"Religion and Politics in Germany and in German-American Relations", 100. So also "Die Zukunft der Aufklärung und des Christentums", 77.

[28]He is also deeply critical of the ecclesial development in Germany after World War II. See *PTPE* 11-33, esp. 17-21, "Religion and Politics in Germany", and "Religion and State in Germany".

[29]*CPS* 322-324 (348-351), *OC* 122 (148f).

[30]*CPS* 325f (351f)

archy between elite and mass. Moreover, the silent majority will often stall new initiatives of the more committed. The result will be nothing else but a service church *for* the people.[31] Furthermore, he is convinced that the post-Constantinian and pluralistic situation in the West will force the established churches into some form of Free Church and Congregational practice.[32] Moltmann therefore says that his purpose with *The Church in the Power of the Spirit* was

> to point away from the pastoral church, that looks after the people, to the people's own communal church among the people. I do not believe that there is any other way in which the church can proclaim the gospel responsibly, theologically speaking, or can celebrate the Lord's supper, baptize with the sign of the new beginning, and live in the friendship of Jesus.[33]

4. The Congregational Principle

What then is the church Moltmann hopes for like? In answering this question I will only briefly mention some of the characteristics and features which are relevant to my study. As seen previously, Moltmann stresses the lack of community in the territorially organized people's church. This lack of community he considers fatal since the church is by nature a gathering (*ekklesia*). The forming of and the life in a community are necessary requirements for the life of the Christian church.[34] Just as important is the voluntary membership. Faith and discipleship must be personally affirmed. A consequence is that he is sharply critical of the practice of infant baptism, which he regards as the base for the people's church, the civil religion and the idea of a Christian society. This means that a reform of the practice of baptism must be an essential part of church reform. Moltmann interprets baptism "as *incorporation into the Christian calling to discipleship and service.*"[35] It testifies to the new identity given in Christ and thus to the freedom from all other loyalties that the incorporation into the history of the kingdom of God entails.[36]

---

[31]*CPS* 333 (358f). For a recent example of the type of view Moltmann criticizes, see the booklet from the German Evangelical Church *Christsein gestalten*.

[32]"But the increasing independence of modern people in moral and political questions, and in religious ones as well, is going to mean that, in the Federal Republic as well, the churches will become congregational churches instead of people's churches, and they will increasingly take over elements from the free churches. If the churches cannot make this change themselves, they will be forced to make it, sooner or later, by the slow moment toward a renunciation of official church affiliation. We can already see this change of structure in the local churches themselves: church attendance is declining, but participation in the Lord's Supper is growing. The quantity of Christian life is diminishing; the quality is increasing. Voluntary participation and involvement are taking the place of passive membership." ("Religion and Politics in Germany", 100.)

[33]*CPS* xvi (13).

[34]*CPS* 334 (360).

[35]*HC* 50 (*OMM* 177 is slighly different).

[36]*CPS* 226-242, 314 (252-268, 340), *HC* 40f, 46-51 (*OMM* 166f, 174-178), *OC* 124f (151f). We find in these texts his analyses and criticisms of the common arguments for infant baptism, as well as his on

If the church is to be a community, the local churches must be small, not larger than it is possible to know everyone. This has not only practical but also theological significance. Only in such a community can one concretely experience the love of God. A large hierarchical church, on the other hand, witnesses to God as the heavenly omnipotence.[37] Related to this is his stress on the local congregation and its responsibility. The church is primarily the local gathered congregation, and it is important that it is given freedom and space for action.[38] This does not, however, prevent him from seeing the value of forms that express the universal unity of the church and mediate common action.[39]

Against this background it is not surprising that he describes the inner functions of the congregation in charismatic terms. The Spirit has given the whole congregation and every individual tasks and gifts. Consequently "the whole people becomes the subject of the history of freedom".[40] The mass of believers is not subordinated to a chosen group of clergy and prophets. He does not, however, understand this in democratic terms, because the church is subordinate to Christ and because the presence of the Spirit should not be understood pantheistically. The Spirit gives various gifts to various persons, though these gifts are all functions of the common mission of the church.[41]

Moltmann's congregational understanding of the church is summarized in the concept of "friendship". The church is a community of friends.[42] He prefers the concept of "friendship" over "brotherhood" for two reasons. First, "brotherhood" has, even if not intended, sexist implications. Second, brotherhood entails a relationship that is not chosen, while friendship is voluntary. Moltmann thinks that this stress on freedom—the friend is the one who is loved in freedom—best expresses the liberating relation to God and the power-free and classless society the Christian hope points to. The concept of friendship must however be qualified by the life of Jesus, for the friendship he demonstrates is open. It is not just a friendship among the like, but is open for the despised and unrighteous.

In addition he defends the public nature of this friendship, in contrast to modern privatized and emotionalized understandings. He writes that "Christian

---

the New Testament based description of baptism in terms of calling, and practical suggestions for a congenial practice of baptism.

[37] *OC* 125 (152), *CPS* 325 (351), *HC* 40 (*OMM* 166).

[38] "Let us make the congregation strong. The large supra-congregational organizations of the churches often relieve the congregations of independence and responsibility. But in the last analysis, in the times of contempt and persecution, the church stands or falls with the gathered congregation and with no one else. The individual who comes alone to church and returns home alone is powerless. He or she suffers from inner doubt and remains a pawn in the hands of first this and then that power. Only in the gathered congregation does the believer become ready for action and capable of resistance." (*OC* 125f [153].)

[39] See *CPS* 343-345, 310f (369-371, 337f), and *OC* 125 (152f).

[40] *CPS* 302 (328). See also *OC* 108-112 (130-136) and *PPL* 163f.

[41] *CPS* 305f (331f) and *SL* 180-197 (195-210).

[42] *CPS* 314-317 (341-344). See further *CPS* 114-121 (134-141) and *OC* 50-63, 120 (51-70, 145f).

friendship cannot be lived in the inner circle of one's equals but only in open affection and public respect for other people."[43] This understanding of friendship leads to a critical stance towards all forms of closed church life. For example, the risk in the Pietistic movements is that they in their stress on separation from the world "cut the gospel off from the very world to which it seeks to proclaim liberation".[44] Service to and openness for the world are essential parts of the congregational practice Moltmann defends,[45] but at the same time he wants to distinguish between the qualified openness of the kingdom of God and the unqualified openness of the people's church. The openness Jesus Christ showed was an openness that required commitment, while the organized people's religion leads to "an *institutionalized absence of commitment.*"[46]

Moltmann's affinity with the Radical Reformation is also visible in his descriptions of the church in terms of contrast to and as an alternative to the existing social and political systems. This is, as seen, most strongly manifested in *The Way of Jesus Christ*, but can also be found in his earlier writings. The church should be an historical representation of the coming eschatological order of peace and freedom.[47] To describe the church as a community of friends means that it is not only constituted by preaching and sacraments, but concerns the whole of life. "The community of brethren proclaims the kingdom of God through its way of life, which provides an alternative to the life of the world surrounding it."[48] The church should not only be a place where people can hear the Gospel, but also a place where people can experience it.

5. The Social and Political Mission of the Church

The mission of the church should be understood in terms of God's liberation of the creation. In relation to other religions, world views and ideologies Moltmann mentions two aims for this mission. The first is to "awaken faith, to baptize, to found churches and to form a new life under the lordship of Christ."[49] The second is the change of the atmosphere of life, of thinking and practice. This is done

---

[43]*CPS* 120 (140).

[44]*CPS* 225 (251). Cf. *OC* 62 (69).

[45]*CPS* 242 (268).

[46]*PPL* 159. Such a people's religion can, however, also have a free church form. Cf. *PPL* 160f.

[47]*CPS* 291-293 (318-320). Cf. also following comments already in *TH* 324 (299) about the church as an exodus community. "If the God who called them to life should expect of them something other than what modern industrial society expects and requires of them, then Christians must venture an exodus and regard their social roles as a new Babylonian exile. Only where they appear in society as a group which is not wholly adaptable and in the case of which modern integration of everything else fails to succeed, do they enter into a conflict-laden, but fruitful partnership with this society. Only where their resistance shows them to be a group that is incapable of being assimilated or of 'making the grade', can they communicate their own hope to this society." And in *CG* 17 (22) he says that Christians will be aliens in any society.

[48]*CPS* 316 (342). See further *CPS* 314-317 (341-344).

[49]*CPS* 152 (173).

through dialogue with people of other religions and ideologies. He describes this as to "'infect' people, whatever their religion, with the spirit of hope, love and responsibility for the world."[50] Moltmann affirms both these aims, but he has almost nothing to say about the first. He rather seems to de-emphasize it, when he writes: "Its aim is not to spread the Christian religion or to implant the church; it is to liberate the people for the exodus in the name of the coming kingdom."[51] However this should be interpreted, his own major interest is clearly the second aim.[52]

As seen, he is highly critical of the privatization of the Christian faith in modern society.[53] This privatization has been, contends Moltmann, legitimated by Luther's doctrine of the two kingdoms. This doctrine has often, moreover, been turned into an ideology that blesses a positivistic reason that prevents the church from being a critical force in society. He thinks the Nazi-years clearly showed the inability of this doctrine to give a base for resistance and to withstand this sort of abuse of it. Theologically, this doctrine, he argues, is built on an apocalyptic eschatology that stresses the ongoing struggle between the kingdom of God and the kingdom of the devil, but that does not make sufficient allowance for the victory over the devil in the death and resurrection of Jesus. He also finds the closely related Lutheran concept of the law unclear. He summarizes his criticism in following words: "Basically, it is a theology of history but not a foundation of Christian ethics. It serves to sharpen the conscience; that is its strength. It brings into Christian ethics a realism which reckons with the given facts. But it does not motivate world-transforming hope. That is its weakness."[54]

He is more positive to the Barthian doctrine of the lordship of Christ, though he thinks it can too easily be misused in a clericalistic direction. Furthermore, its language about the church as an example for the society presupposes a church that does not exist. "The actual church, with its feudal constitution, its anachronistic symbols and rites, and its outdated language is in most cases less like the forerunner of the civil community than it is the taillight of cultural development."[55] In theological terms he thinks that Barth does not make sufficient allowance for the fact that the lordship of Christ is the lordship of the Crucified that rules through weakness.[56]

Despite this criticism, his idea of anticipating the kingdom of God through corresponding to Christ in social and political actions is explicitly a development

---

[50]*CPS* 152 (173f).

[51]CPS 84 (103). Bauckham is critical of the distinction Moltmann makes in this quote and does not think Moltmann's theology makes it necessary. See *Moltmann*, 136f. Cf. further n. 13 above.

[52]*CPS* 150-163 (171-185), cf. 21-24 (7-11).

[53]See *TH* 304-324 (280-299) for a critical discussion of the function of religion in modern society.

[54]*OHD* 76 (*PTPE* 136). See further *OHD* 61-77, 104, 108, 114-118 (124-136, 158, 162, 182-184), *CG* 318f (294f), and *FC* 50-52 (60f).

[55]*OHD* 92 (*PTPE* 149). He talks in the German version about the German established church, which could partly explain his criticism of an idea that he, as we have seen, himself often seems to use.

[56]See further *OHD* 79-96, 104f, 108 (*PTPE* 137-151, 158f, 162), and *CG* 319-321 (295-298).

of the Barthian theology. To this is added his language of political discipleship, which is taken up and developed from the religious orders and the Radical Reformation tradition. One might say that these two categories—anticipating the kingdom of God in political discipleship—summarize quite well Moltmann's understanding of the church's political mission.

This means that he is not interested in developing a Christian theory about the state or the society. Neither does he want to see Christian faith as the base or the unifying force of society.[57] His decisive, but not only, reason for that position is "the fact that Christ was judged in the name of the Pax Romana as a Jewish Messiah-pretender and died on a Roman Cross."[58] That Jesus was killed in the name of political religion and raised by God as the crucified makes political metaphysics or a general Christian political doctrine impossible. He is further critical of the idea that Christ already is Lord over the political order, which would make a christocratic ethics for society possible. This criticism is based on his eschatological christology—the kingdom of Christ is not yet established. He here makes an important distinction between the kingdom of Christ and the lordship of Christ. "The kingdom of Christ is neither politically present nor present in the church. It is pure messianic future. The lordship of Christ, however, is present. It reaches historically as far as people become obedient and follow Christ so that they may take their cross upon themselves."[59] The conclusion of this is that it is impossible to formulate a Christian politics for the civil community or a Christian ethics on which society and state can be built. What, on the other hand, should be done, is to formulate a Christian ethics for Christian activity in the political sphere. It is this Moltmann names political discipleship. "Christocratic ethics can only be discipleship ethics. It is ethics for Christians, but not Christian ethics for the state. It is political ethics of the Christian community but not Christian politics of the civil community."[60] The political actions of the church and Christians must reflect the lordship of Christ, and this lordship "does not resemble that of a *king* but is the lordship of the crucified one, who conquers not through great power but through weakness and rules through his vicarious suffering on the Cross."[61] Consequently any triumphalism, "ecclesiasticizing" or search for direct political power for the church are made impossible.[62]

This discipleship means that the church and Christians must seek "to correspond to Christ in political and social acts". In doing so they anticipate the kingdom of God or mediate the kingdom in history. He writes that the world "is the

---

[57]Cf. his criticism in *PTPE* 21-25 of the proposals of Pannenberg and Rendtorff. For his critical attitude towards "civil religion", see "Christian Theology and Political Religion" ("Politik der Nachfolge"), "The Cross and Civil Religion" (*PTPE* 34-69), and *PTPE* 70-78.

[58]"Christian Theology", 52 ("Politik der Nachfolge", 28).

[59]Ibid., 56 (30).

[60]*OHD* 95 (*PTPE* 151).

[61]*OHD* 94 (*PTPE* 150).

[62]*CPS* 167f (190).

battleground and the construction site for the kingdom, which comes from God himself."[63] He further describes these mediations as sacramental, because the anticipative actions in the Spirit make the kingdom of God present in history. God is in a hidden, sacramental way present when people are fed, given dignity and freedom, or when they live in peace with nature.[64] He summarizes his basic ethical view as follows:

> To act ethically in a Christian sense means to participate in God's history in the midst of our own history, to integrate ourselves into the comprehensive process of God's liberation of the world, and to discover our own role in this according to our own calling and abilities. A messianically oriented ethics makes people into co-operators for the kingdom of God. It assumes that the kingdom of God is already here in concrete, if hidden, form. Christian ethics integrates suffering and ailing people into God's history with this world; it is fulfilled by the hope of the completion of God's history in the world by God himself.[65]

One question this account raises is how to reconcile his statements that the kingdom of Christ is pure future and that the kingdom of God is present already, though in a hidden way.[66] One key is to observe the different contexts for these two statements. The first concerns tendencies to identify political empires with the kingdom of God and nations with the people of God, as well as attempts to develop a theological legitimation of the state and a Christian politics for the state.[67] The motive behind his sacramental language, on the other hand, is his wish to stress the material character of God's presence and activity and the concrete human participation in God's liberation of the world. God's presence is actually experienced when the oppressed are liberated and democracy is established. These anticipations, however, are not identical with the kingdom of God, but point beyond themselves to an always fuller presence of God and to the final eschatological fulfilment when God will be all in all. In other words, he wants to avoid both an idealistically understood Christian ethics and an ideological fixation on already attained social and political results. Political movements, ends and results are relativized and the future is always kept open.

The context of the church's life is God's ongoing liberation of the world. The church is one, but not the only, moment in the work of the Spirit. Because it is the mission of the Son and the Spirit Moltmann finds it natural that the Spirit also works through people and movements outside the church. Consequently, the church cannot make absolute claims for itself. The church is not the only place

---

[63]Both citations are from *OHD* 109 (*PTPE* 162).

[64]"Thus, real history becomes the sacrament of Christian ethics. Christian praxis celebrates and completes the presence of God in history." (*OHD* 109 [*PTPE* 163; the German text has "die verborgene Gegenwart Gottes"].) See also *CG* 335-338 (312-315).

[65]*OHD* 111 (*PTPE* 164; the German text is slightly different). Generally he describes his ethics as "christologically founded, eschatologically oriented, and pneumatologically implemented." (*OHD* 109 [*PTPE* 162].)

[66]Cf. Bauckham, *Moltmann*, 45.

[67]"Christian Theology", 56 ("Politik der Nachfolge", 30), *OHD* 95 (*PTPE* 151).

where the Spirit is active. Rather, the question is for the church to place itself
where the activity of the Spirit is seen; that is, where people experience liberation
and justice, where peace among people and with nature is established. Christians
thus have to work together with other people taking part in the liberating activity
of the Spirit of God. Moltmann finds this way of thinking more important today
than ever, because we live in a world that by necessity has a common future.
Humanity survives together or not at all. This makes him sharply critical of all
particularistic thinking. Christians can contribute, but do not have all the answers.[68]

Expressed in another way, this means that Christianity (he here talks about
Christianity instead of church, because he wants to stress that major responsibility
is given to Christians in their secular professions) relates itself to institutions and
processes in society and tries to understand which processes and tendencies correspond to Christ and the kingdom of God.[69] The processes he mentions are the
economic, the political, and the cultural, and the tendencies Christians should
follow are liberation from economic exploitation of human beings and nature,
political liberation from oppression, and cultural liberation from racism and sexism, as well as the recognition of the human dignity of the handicapped. He expresses this positively as symbiosis, human rights, and identity.[70]

Another, and for Moltmann the most common, way of describing the struggle
for liberation and his holistic concept of salvation is in terms of the basic and related dimensions of life in which the struggle takes place. He talks about the struggle for economic justice, human rights and freedom, human solidarity, ecological
balance, and meaning and hope in personal life. He stresses that these dimensions
are interrelated, and thus the struggle for liberation has to be fought on several
levels at the same time.[71]

To conclude, I think that Moltmann's discussions of the relation between
church and world tend to draw in different directions. Moltmann understands the
church (or, as he sometimes says, Christianity) as a subject for political action.
Christians are not a party that seeks its own power, but a people that struggles for
the liberation of the oppressed and the preservation of nature. He therefore
stresses that the church is one moment in the liberating history of God, a history
seen in the ongoing political and social liberating processes and movements. It is
then the task of the church to discern where the Spirit of God is active and place
itself there. Consequently, Christians have to take part in political conflicts. The
church cannot be neutral or a third force, but must take sides in accordance with

---

[68]*CPS* 64f, 153f, 164, 192 (81f, 174f, 187, 216).

[69]He uses the language of ordering processes instead of the classical language of secular orders, which
he thinks reflects an older more static society. See *CPS* 163f (186f), also *HP* 112-118 (160-165). For a
general and critical discussion of these issues in Moltmann and Brunner, see Schuurman, *Creation,
Eschaton, and Ethics.*

[70]*CPS* 163-189 (186-214).

[71]See e.g. *CG* 329-335 (306-312), *FC* 109-114 (116-120), and *OHD* 110 (*PTPE* 163f).

how it understands the activity of the Spirit in history. It can then work both as a catalyst and as a corrective factor in the movements it works together with. Here the general political processes set the agenda. This perspective tends to be rather optimistic about the general political processes of the society and less so about the church's own life. He has for example sometimes expressed himself critically of the idea of the church as a model, because "in practice it only becomes free with the society in which it lives."[72]

On the other hand he can also talk about the church as a contrast society that presents the world with concrete alternatives, a view that seems to imply that the church in some way sets its own agenda out of its own faith and practice. Then the theological and ethical reflection concerns more what should be done than which side the church should be on. This perspective, which is more optimistic about the church and less about society, is more strongly emphasised in his later writings, and is combined with his development of a more substantial Christian ecclesial ethics. Saying this, it should be noted that the texts used in this chapter for presenting his views of the church's political mission mainly represent a time (roughly from the 1970s up to the early 1980s) in which he still talked about political discipleship abstracted from a concrete explication of the life and message of Jesus Christ. It is, however, this earlier perspective that has dominated his political thinking and basically still does so, although increasingly modified, as we will see in the coming chapters.[73]

---

[72]*CG* 320 (297).

[73]It might be appropriate here to comment on some very odd features of Mary Brink's recent analysis of Moltmann's ecclesiology in her dissertation "The Ecclesiological Dimensions of Jurgen Moltmann's Theology". To test Moltmann's proposals "against lived Christian practice" (p. 6) she compares his work with the ones of Gutierrez and Boff. This seems more like comparing theory with theory, but may be an expression of the almost canonical status Latin American liberation theology has in certain North American and European theological circles. According to Brink, the subject for Moltmann's theology is himself and his personal experience of being a prisoner of war, while the subject of liberation theology is the base communities (pp. 248, 287f). This makes Moltmann's ecclesiology highly individualistic and idealistic, and he seems therefore unable to conceive of the possibility of a *corporate* praxis of socially and politically transformative discipleship. This situation is aggravated by, so she says, his Lutheran theology (on her description of Moltmann as Lutheran, see above n. 38 in chapter one) and the absence of anything like base communities in Europe (pp. 269-273, 275-277). Although one can agree that there is a certain abstract character to his ecclesiology and a lack of reflection on how the sort of contrast society he talks about can be formed and sustained, most of Brink's criticisms are rather absurd, as I hope my exposition has shown. Brink writes as if the Latin American base community movements are something wholly new and unique. Yet, the roots of Moltmann's ecclesiology is not just his own personal biography, but both the established churches in Germany and the history and contemporary existence (in many and various forms) of the Free Church and base community practices both in the First and the Third World. It should also not be forgotten that he for five years worked as pastor in a local church. See *CPS* xv (12f).

Chapter 6

The Enlightenment Heritage
and the Struggle for Freedom and Justice

After having described central characteristics of Moltmann's theology and method, I will in the remaining chapters of this part discuss his understanding of the modern Western society and the church's life and practice in the specific social, cultural and political reality of modernity. The development of Moltmann's theology can be described as a complex interplay between the working out of the inner logic of his theology and the modifications and new starts which changes in context cause. New contexts give him occasions not only to take up new themes, but also to further develop themes that earlier were in the background or were underdeveloped.

Moltmann's political theology was formed in the Barthian tradition of Reformed theology and in the heritage of the Confessing Church. The outer context of the emergence of political theology were the challenges of modernity: secularization, science, revolution and the thereby implied beliefs in progress and politics. He wanted to show the meaningfulness and therapeutic relevance of the Christian faith to this modern world.

In this light political theology is a positive Christian reception of modernity. Through showing the centrality of history, future and freedom in Christian faith it tries positively to meet the modern criticism of tradition and morality, its stress on history as the process of human realization of freedom and its depiction of personal life in terms of self-realization. However, this reception of modernity stands in an uneasy relationship with central parts of his theology. This has become clearer through the modifications caused by his increasingly more critical stance towards modernity. Yet, Moltmann seldom recognizes the radicality of some of these shifts and tensions.[1] Instead it seems that he develops different lines of thought for different questions. The result is that apparently contradictory ideas coexist, sometimes even in different chapters of the same book. In this chapter I will, against the background of his theology of freedom, especially discuss, first, the relation between his ecclesial discipleship ethics and his description of the Christian life in terms of self-realization; second, the tensions in his theology of power, which are caused by its heterogeneous sources in Christian power critique, modernity's Prometheanism, and the "green" criticism of modernity; and, third, the relation between a human rights discourse based on the Christian faith and a

---

[1] We have noticed his comments on his new ecological awareness and we will in a later chapter encounter his discussion about political violence and pacifism. Though sometimes recognizing the problems he has not really worked out consistent solutions or seen all the problems his different commitments lead to.

claimed self-evident universal rights discourse, as well as the tension between his discipleship ethics and his rights ethics. I will also, finally, discuss how this whole approach works itself out in Moltmann's advocacy of democratic socialism in peace with nature. In all this we will observe both severe tensions in his project of mediation of modernity and Christianity and tensions in his understanding of the modern world as such, for example between his socialism and his later ecological awareness.

1. A Theology of Freedom

a) The Vision of Freedom Contra the Authoritarian Principle

How to understand and judge modernity is controversial not just in the church, but also in our culture in general. According to Moltmann there are two main self-interpretations of the modern bourgeois age: "the vision of freedom" and "the authoritarian principle".[2] The former, which is the actual foundation of modern society, understands the American and the French revolutions as well as the Industrial revolution as the beginning of a radically new society where freedom, equality and the idea of universal human rights are basic; a shift from the old, feudal society into a new egalitarian, achievement-oriented society, with political democracy, religious freedom and a secular state.

According to Moltmann, this leads to a basic change in the understanding of the nature of reality. Instead of thinking about reality in terms of a cosmic order, reality is now understood as history. The subject of this history is humanity, an idea which in this story implies a strong belief in progress. This progress is principally perceived in terms of emancipation—emancipation from nature, from authority, from oppression. Because freedom and equality are universal rights, they must continuously be used critically against their particular applications. The liberals worked for political democracy and economic freedom, the socialists against the new bourgeois class for economic democracy, and feminists against a patriarchal culture for equality between men and women. So understood this interpretation of modernity can be seen as a secularized messianic hope for building the kingdom of God on earth.

Another related consequence of modernity is its criticism of traditions and its strong secularizing tendency. Science and rationality are seen as being in conflict with moral traditions and religions, which one has to be liberated from to be able to rationally and consciously form the future society. Religion therefore loses its public role, and is removed to the private sphere.

This criticism of religion and tradition has led to a wholly different interpretation of modernity, which Moltmann describes as the conservative idea of the authoritarian principle. In this interpretation, as Moltmann describes it, the mod-

---

[2]*TH* 210-217 (230-238), *ThT* 1-8 (11-17), "Revolution, Religion and the Future", *SL* 105-109 (117-121). As these references show, this theme is present throughout Moltmann's writings.

ern age is depicted in apocalyptic terms. Evil powers threaten the basic order of life. Revolution, democracy, secularism, liberalism and socialism are all results of a sick society. Revolution is not just an attack against human authority, but also against the order of God and leads to atheism and political and moral anarchy. The conservative alternative is "God, king (the state), country" or "God, family, country". This, Moltmann claims, is the ideology of the counterrevolution. The main churches long followed this interpretation of modernity, with the result that they have been against democracy, liberalism, socialism, scientific-technological rationality and cultural freedom.

According to Moltmann, the church has two basic options: to accept either the progressive or the conservative interpretation. He does not consider the possibility of other options, but places the church before a sharp either-or. This is a typical Moltmannian rhetorical strategy and as usual his own choice is clear. The very description of the alternatives forecloses the choice. He considers the church's choice of the conservative option a tragedy that can only end in failure. The reason is that the church thereby allies itself with a society that is inevitably past. If the church wants to be something more than a marginal and irrelevant sect, it must be able to show the relevance of the Christian faith to modernity.[3] His acceptance of this necessity is furthermore not reluctant. His basic attitude to the "modern spirit" is affirmative, though not uncritical. His criticism, which steadily has increased in strength, is a criticism from inside, a part of the ongoing argument about modernity and its failures to live up to its own professions to freedom and equality. But still, it is modernity that through its self-definition sets the stage for theology.

b) History as the Progressive Struggle for Freedom

According to Moltmann the modern world has arisen from liberation movements and is still understood in terms of freedom. He describes western history as a history of the struggle for freedom. He even says that "freedom is the meaning of each individual life history and of our entire world history."[4] Therefore modern theology becomes *by necessity* a theology of freedom.[5] We find thus again that the direction of theology is decisively determined by its context, although it is then formulated in terms of its own language.

In order to be able to mediate Christianity and the modern vision of freedom, he tries to show that there is a close inner connection. He does this through de-

---

[3] *TH* 303 (279), *CPS* 37f (53f), *OHD* 99f (*PTPE* 154f).
[4] *HIG* 62 (*MRF* 87). *HIG* 55-69 is a somewhat longer version of *MRF* 81-95.
[5] *ThT* 24 (32). Concerning the "necessity", cf. Frei's statement in a discussion of *Theology of Hope*: "In post-Kantian German theology, there is always some sort of material affirmation concerning human being and its connection with wider reality that forms the necessary presupposition for Christian theology and for making Christian affirmations meaningful." Reflecting on the difficulties many have to accept these "necessary" frameworks, he says: "Where does it say that the gentile must become a Jew before he becomes a Christian?" (Review of Moltmann, *The Theology of Hope*, 269, 271.)

monstrating that Christianity is a fundamental source of this progressive liberating history, which he in an early text tries to demonstrate through writing a history of freedom from the Greeks to modernity.[6] The basic contours of this reading of history seem to be assumed in his later more systematic expositions of freedom. He has also, for the period from the Reformation onward, recently partly restated and developed this history.[7] His account has an unmistakable Hegelian stamp, not only because freedom is made the key to world history, but also in its dialectic character.[8] He describes this history in terms of different stages that dialectically correct and complement each other. The first stage he names "Freedom out of Christ". In Jesus Christ and the early church arose a new kind of human being liberated from the orders of the cosmos for a life of free decisions. It was a liberation from "the idolatry of nature, of fate, and of political power."[9] Theologically he bases this in Israel's experience of Exodus and the Christian's experience of the resurrection of Jesus Christ.[10] But this liberation movement developed into the Constantinian effort to make the world Christian, which made the church captive of the imperial state. Therefore the second stage was the church's struggle for autonomy, which was won in the Middle Ages. This made clear that the kingdom of God on earth is not embodied in the empire but in the church. The price though was the clericalization of the church.

The third stage in the story Moltmann tells is the Reformation. In the gospel of justifying grace every Christian is given freedom. And because this freedom is based on the crucified Christ every Christian also becomes a servant of his or her fellow human beings. In the congregation the common priesthood of all believers is declared against clerical privilege. The Reformation also has its perversions. Because of its failure to develop congregational churches and an understanding of the Christian life in terms of discipleship it tended to legitimize national religion and the power of the nobles.

This use of the Reformation was broken first by the West European Calvinist reformation and then further developed in the Anglo-American Free Church tradition. In his earlier text he said that the weakness of this tradition was that it concentrated on the freedom of the Christian. Only with the American and French revolutions was the concept of freedom universalized. It was also for the first time understood in secular terms. Everyone is born free and has the right to

---

[6]*RRF* 63-82 (*PdT* 189-211).

[7]"Is Protestantism the 'Religion of Freedom'?" (this is basically the same as "Protestantismus als 'Religion der Freiheit'"). When in the following account nothing else is said, I follow the text mentioned in the previous note.

[8]Cf. Ritter, *Metaphysik und Politik*, 183-233. On the Hegelian character of German Neo-Marxism, see Bubner, *Modern German Philosophy*, 154-218. Bubner writes: "The constant references back to Hegelian categories in fact keep the Marxist doctrine alive." (Ibid., 156.)

[9]*RRF* 71 (*PdT* 199). He would today express these ideas somewhat differently, I suppose.

[10]For later accounts of this, see also *FC* 105-109 (113-116), *HIG* 57-60 (*MRF* 83-85), and *SL* 99-105 (111-117).

choose one's own life as far as it does not hurt anybody else.[11] In the later text[12] he differentiates between the anticlerical and therefore secularist French Enlightenment, the Protestant but anti-state church and therefore religiously privatizing German Enlightenment, and the English-American Enlightenment that "was Protestant-dominated, non-conformist, free church, and very religious".[13] In this light he describes denominations like the Quakers, the Baptists and the Methodists as "[t]he Christianity of the Enlightenment".[14] They were, so to say, forerunners of the modern world.[15] For the Enlightenment as well as for Protestantism it is, he continues, the freedom of the individual that is in the centre; over against the state freedom of religion, over against the church freedom of conscience and the right to form free congregations from below, and over against the Bible and traditions the freedom of belief. This stress on the dignity of the human person and on individual human rights "became the foundation of liberal democracy."[16]

The Enlightenment also led to severe disappointments: the disillusionment with the results of the French revolution, the misery of capitalism and Christian legitimation of liberal individualism. Therefore a new stage developed: socialism and the struggle for freedom from economic slavery and for a society where everyone's free development in community is guaranteed. This freedom movement was, however, perverted into Stalinism.[17] This, he thought, "will certainly become the motor of post-Marxist revolutions."[18] In the late 1960s he saw promising notes in "the liberal socialism in the Polish Marxists Adam Schaff and Leszew Kolakowski".[19] In church terms he later describes the Ecumenical movement as

---

[11]"The free development of the humane in every single person is the presupposition of the humanization of society." (*RRF* 73f [201].)

[12]"Protestantism", 37-41 ("Protestantismus", 18-22). So also "Die Zukunft der Aufklärung und des Christentums", 73. Cf. *SL* 116 (129).

[13]"Protestantism", 37 ("Protestantismus", 18).

[14]Ibid., 37 (19). "In England and USA, Free Church Protestantism became the religious basis for liberal democracy." ("Einführung" to *Religion der Freiheit*, 8.) See also *OHD* 140f, 155-158 (*PTPE* 83f, 96-99), *PTPE* 20. He describes this tradition as a pneumatological complement to the christocentric theologies of the Reformation. See *SL* 116 (129).

[15]Continental Protestantism and Roman Catholicism were much later (the time of Enlightenment and 1960s respectively), and the Orthodox churches have still to meet this challenge. See *ThT* 56 (62).

[16]"Protestantism", 40 ("Protestantismus", 22). See further ibid., 38-41 (20-22) and "Einführung" to *Religion der Freiheit*, where he also says that the feminist movement and feminist theology have roots in American Free Church Protestantism (p. 8). Because of the subject of this book a remark on this description of the Free Church tradition cannot be avoided. This description (as much else in this reading of history) is too unnuanced and consequently too easily conflated to liberal individualism. His description is partly more true of the strong individualistic and privatizing form established Protestantism (e.g. in Germany) took especially in the nineteenth century, than of central strands of the Free Church tradition with its strong sense of community, discipleship and authority of the Bible.

[17]In another context, he wrote that "a new social freedom was introduced into the world by the socialist revolution only to be shortly denied by Stalin and the bureaucratization of the Russian revolution." (*RRF* 28.) Cf. also *ThT* 1, 6 (11, 15).

[18]*RRF* 75 (*PdT* 202).

[19]*RRF* 76. (*PdT* 203-205 n. 24-25 contains a longer version of this claim). Kolakowski has of course gone a long way since then. See his *Main Currents of Marxism*.

expressing the same social view of freedom, stressing the catholicity of the church and its solidarity with the suffering and the oppressed.[20]

Moltmann presents this history as steps "toward the universal and eschatological hope of freedom for the whole suffering creation, which is the Christian hope for the salvation of the body."[21] He therefore wants to see these different forms of freedom movements integrated. Each new stage must take up the earlier traditions and develop them, not discard them. One reason for the perversion of socialism was, for example, that it did not positively take up the heritage of liberal democracy.

Much could be said concerning this reading of history. I will here only make a few further comments. First, it is radically Eurocentric. He tells his story from the perspective of Western modernity and the rest of the world becomes part of this universal history of freedom through making this history, with its specific understanding of the human destiny, its ethics and its politics, their own. Modernity has thus the same normative role for other cultures and religions as it has for Christianity in his mediating project. He has in another context criticized theories of universal history for being Eurocentric. They, he charges, "thereby serve—consciously or unconsciously—the hegemony of the European culture."[22] It is hard to understand how Moltmann himself can avoid this charge.

Second, the supersedure of socialism over liberalism has for Moltmann always been an almost self-evident axiom. The actual development of socialism did hardly turn out the way Moltmann's dialectic account presupposes, it mainly denied, but did not take up liberal democracy. The revolutions of 1989, furthermore, were not post-Marxist, but liberal. So if one insists on telling the form of dialectic history that Moltmann has attempted, socialism might just as well be described as a reactionary disruption of the history of freedom. How Moltmann, in the terms of his analysis, would answer this is not clear, more than making democratic socialism into an ethical ideal rather than the next "necessary" stage in history.

Third, can history and the church's relation to it plausibly be written in this way? Is history not much more filled with plurality, (non-dialectical) breaks and discontinuities, than Moltmann allows for, even granted that his rather crude account could be filled out? Furthermore, Moltmann himself seems often to deny the possibility of this type of synthesizing universal history. He has repeatedly criticized Richard Rothe, Ernst Troeltsch and at present Trutz Rendtorff for their integration of Christianity and modernity. In *Theology of Hope* he does it from the perspective of his eschatology. "If . . . the promise of the future of Christ arises from the resurrection of the one who was crucified, then the promise enters into such a contradiction to reality that this contradiction cannot be classified

---

[20]"Protestantism", 41-44 ("Protestantismus", 23-27).

[21]*RRF* 74 (no exact correspondence exists in the German version).

[22]*PTPE* 22f. From this perspective, his remark about Gutierrez' *A Theology of Liberation* that "Gutierrez presents the process of liberation in Latin America as the continuation and culmination of the European history of freedom" ("On Latin American Liberation Theology", 59) is interesting.

within a general dialectic of history such as can be deduced from other processes."[23] In the *Crucified God* it is the cross of Christ that breaks apart all such
syntheses. Against the idea of an integrating theory of Christianity, the theology
of the cross leads to the idea of theology as "a critical theory of God"[24] that is
based on a critical and liberating practice.[25] One might further ask how to reconcile his historical account with the contrast he in *The Way of Jesus Christ* makes
between teleology and eschatology, and the conviction that Christ is found not at
the edge of the evolution, but with its victims?[26] Finally the idea of the church as
a contrast society also seems to point to a more disruptive, discontinuous and plu-
ral understanding of history.

Moltmann describes the theology of Rendtorff (who also, following Hegel,
understands Christianity as the religion of freedom) as a mediating theology,
which is critical of the self-isolation of the church, and which interprets the Enlightenment and secularization as outgrowths and realizations of Christianity.[27]
This has remarkable similarities with Moltmann's own theology. The difference
between these two mediating projects seems to lie in the difference between
Rendtorff's liberal and Moltmann's socialist understanding of modernity. Rendtorff's theology becomes an affirmative theology of the liberal society, while
Moltmann's sees his own theology as a theology of a critical and liberating practice in the direction of democratic socialism. The similarities are then a sign of the
close affinity between liberalism and socialism—both being nineteenth century
children of the Enlightenment. Though Moltmann and Rendtorff represent opposing poles in German theology, they have a common mediating purpose, which
gives their theologies a certain structural similarity.[28] Moltmann uses his eschatology, his theology of the cross and his ecclesiology, all which seem to make integrating programs impossible, to mediate Christianity, not with modernity as it is,
but with the critical and future-oriented moment inside modernity. He is, in other
words, mediating Christianity and Neomarxism[29] and the critical culture of Western societies generally. His theology is a critical theory trying to take the dialectic
of the Enlightenment and its prehistory seriously. Put differently, the world critical character of Christianity becomes a mediating principle to the critical culture
of modernity. Yet, the question is, if his theology really makes it possible for him

---

[23]*TH* 226 (206).
[24]*CG* 69 (71).
[25]*CG* 67-73 (69-75) .
[26]See above p. 73.
[27]See, in addition to the above mentioned texts, also *PTPE* 22-24, *HTG* 140-142 (191-193), and (on
Rothe, but followed by Rendtorff) *CPS* 45-47 (61-64),
[28]For a discussion of Rendtorff's position in the context of political theology and German ecclesiology
and in relation to Moltmann, see Weth, *"Barmen" als Herausforderung der Kirche*, esp. 54-65, 128-
147. Cf. also Metz' comments on the similarity between Moltmann and Rendtorff in *Faith in History
and Society*, 157f. Of Rendtorff's many books the recent *Theologie in der Moderne* can be mentioned.
[29]The *RRF* text that outlined the history of freedom grew out of the Christian-Marxist dialogue.

to consistently work out this program. We will later repeatedly encounter the difficulties into which this leads him.

That Moltmann sees a deep historical and systematic continuity between the Christian faith and the Enlightenment is also clear from the way in which he describes Christian chiliasm as the background to the Enlightenment belief in progress and the coming humane world.[30] He says that when this chiliastic tradition was constricted in the church, it went into the sects. He especially mentions Joachim of Fiore's theology of three historical stages, which was influential in the sectarian wings of the church and then lived on in the Enlightenment's talk about the modern age as a qualitatively new age in which the human race has become mature enough to form history according to reason.[31] The emancipation of reason from tradition is, he says, based precisely on "the eschatological, messianic passion of the 'modern age'." This is also the ground for his statement that "'[s]ecularization was no apostasy from the traditions and ordinances of Christianity, but meant in the first instance that Christian expectations were realized in the field of world history, and then that Christian hopes were outstripped by millenarianism."[32] He further says that political theology grew out of the theologies of secularization that theologians like Dietrich Bonhoeffer, Friedrich Gogarten and Harvey Cox developed, especially the ideas of the worldliness or historicity of the world and of the primacy of praxis.[33] Though critical of secularism, he thus accepts secularization as a basically positive development that the Christian faith must constructively meet by its own hope based on the resurrection of the crucified Christ. In other words, he tries to mediate Christian hope to the modern utopian consciousness. Christian hope stimulates creative thinking about the possibilities for radical changes in the direction of a more humane (more free) society. For the Christian the world is full of possibilities given by God. This is, according to Moltmann, a more realistic attitude than that which is normally called "realism", because it takes into account the movements in natural and social reality, and therefore the possibilities for change.[34]

c) A Trinitarian Doctrine of Freedom

In more systematic terms he talks about different (historically developed) dimensions of the concept of freedom. He differentiates among freedom understood

---

[30]*TH* 261-265, 291-303 (240-243, 268-279), *Man*, 28-30 (47-50).

[31]*TKG* 202-209 (221-226).

[32]Both citations are from *TH* 294 (271).

[33]*ThT* 16-19 (24-27). This is also clear in the case of Metz. See *Theology of the World*, 19f, where he writes: "The secularity of the world, as it has emerged in the modern process of secularization . . . has fundamentally, though not in its individual historical forms, arisen not against Christianity but through it. It is originally a Christian event and hence testifies in our world situation to the power of the 'hour of Christ' at work within history."

[34]*TH* 25f, 32-36 (20f, 27-30).

as rule, community, and project.[35] Freedom as rule denotes the mastering of the natural and human environment. The ruler is free, the subject is not. This means that other people are seen as competitors, as limiting one's own freedom. He especially relates this concept of freedom to questions of power and property. In modern Western society this understanding lives on in middle-class liberalism.

A second definition, which he relates to Hegel and Marx, is freedom understood as community. He writes that

> the truth of freedom is love. It is only in love that human freedom arrives at its truth. I am free and feel myself to be truly free when I am respected and recognized by others and when I for my part respect and recognize them. I become truly free when I open my life for other people and share with them, and when other people open their lives for me and share them with me.[36]

This freedom breaks down barriers and creates unity, which necessarily, he says, entails struggle against oppression, with the purpose of creating true community.[37]

He also points to a third dimension: freedom as "project", as "creative initiative". Freedom is to transcend the present in the direction of the future in thought and practice, it "is the creative passion for the possible."[38]

He tries theologically to justify this understanding of freedom through a trinitarian doctrine of freedom, in which each member of the Trinity expresses different stages or experiences in the movement of freedom. In the kingdom of the Father, God is Creator and Lord, and one experiences freedom in service of him. In being dependent on God, one is free from all other powers. In the kingdom of the Son, the servants have become children of the Father, which means free access to God and being bound together with all other children of God. In the kingdom of the Spirit, finally, servanthood and childhood are transformed into friendship, which means sharing the rule of God. He sees these three dimensions as both strata and a trend in the experience of freedom, i. e., that these three strata are both parts of each experience of freedom, and that they express a process of maturity.[39]

We thus find that, just as his history of freedom is an attempt to integrate Christian and Enlightenment understandings, his systematic account of freedom is constructed in a way that makes it open for the Enlightenment ideas of autonomy, both seen (in the version advocated by Moltmann) as personal self-realization and

---

[35]See esp. *HIG* 55-69 (*MRF* 81-95), *TKG* 213-218 (230-235), and *SL* 117-120 (130-133).

[36]*TKG* 216 (233).

[37]In *SL* 118 (131) he describes this as communicative freedom. Cf. Huber, who in *Folgen christlicher Freiheit*, 113-127 elaborates this concept.

[38]The citations are from *TKG* 216f (234). "Thus, we strain with passion toward the future, and in this yearning our reason is transformed into productive imagination. We dream the messianic dream of a new, whole, totally lived life. We explore the possibilities of the future in order to fulfill this dream of life." (*HIG* 66 [*MRF* 92].)

[39]*TKG* 218-222 (236-239).

globally as humanity being the subject of history striving to "attain their unhinde-red humanity."[40] First, when he criticizes the liberal view of freedom as rule, he associates this especially with property, but not with the idea of autonomy, which he defends. Second, in his account of freedom as community it is first of all a question of accepting and being accepted as one is, not of being formed through the community. Third, in describing freedom as a project, freedom is understood as the striving for the future realization of humanity. Fourth, in his trinitarian doct-rine of freedom the concept of friendship with God is the "highest" dimension. The importance of this is that, in Moltmann's interpretation, it makes it possible to redefine the relation between God and humanity in non-hierarchical terms.

He is thus able to read the Christian history, in the light of the Enlightenment doctrine of the primacy of freedom, as a history of freedom movements, but also modernity as a secularized version of the Christian messianic hope. There is in this sense a direct continuity between the Christian tradition and modernity. He thus attempts to establish simultaneously the modern legitimacy of Christianity and the Christian legitimacy of modernity. The fact that the great hopes and promises of the Enlightenment often have turned into their opposites, gives him at the same time ample opportunity to show the therapeutic relevance of faith and church.

d) Towards a Postmodern Theology

However, his criticism of modernity has increased so much that he in the late 1980s has talked about the need for a change of paradigm, for reaching a post-modern perspective.[41] He even sometimes describes his own later theology as "postmodern".[42] From this outlook he identifies modernity as "the human project of technological scientific civilization."[43] It is characterized by seeing the human being as an individual subject of understanding and will, the reification of the natural environment, and power over nature. Postmodernity then, Moltmann con-tends, sees freedom as community, replaces thought of domination and control with mutuality and partnership, and sees the goal of history as "[b]eing at home with and holding a balance with nature".[44]

---

[40]"Latin American", 62. The concept of autonomy has played a central role in Enlightenment and post-Enlightenment thought and especially in German philosophy and theology. But it has been used in several different ways and in relation to different issues. For Kant moral autonomy refers to the grounding of morality in the necessary and universal law of reason. This is not the view usually es-poused by Moltmann. He instead sees autonomy as being able to realize one's inner potential without external restrictions. On these and further uses of the concept of autonomy and its importance for modern theology, see Hill, "Autonomy of Moral Agents", Amelung, "Autonomie", Macken, *The Autonomy Theme in the* Church Dogmatics, 1-21, Kasper, *Theology and Church*, 32-72, and Gunton, *Enlightenment and Alienation*, 55-107.
[41]*HTG* 140-142 (191-193). But cf. "Revolution", 49 (32).
[42]*WJC* xvi (13),
[43]*HTG* 141 (192).
[44]*HTG* 142 (193).

The idea of postmodernity is notoriously ambiguous and controversial. Molt-mann's description is formed out of what he thinks necessary for the survival of humanity and nature. More interesting than this definition, however, is the criticism of modernity it involves, including its vision of freedom. We thus again encounter a development in Moltmann's theology that seems to come in tension with the origin of political theology as explicitly a theology of modernity. One could consequently understand this as a more radical break than the one Molt-mann sees between bourgeois modern theology and political theology. Most of twentieth century theology has, he maintains, been a theology for the privatized religion of the bourgeois society (Bultmann, Tillich, Rahner). Political theology should in contrast be understood as post-bourgeois theology. The contrast here, however, is not between modernity and postmodernity, but between an imperfect bourgeois modernity and the hope of the fulfilments of the promises of modernity.[45] This theme still forms much of his later work, although the inner contradictions of modernity now are painted in stronger colours than in his earlier theology.[46] Yet, at other times, he seems to envision the need for a more radical break with the modern paradigm.[47] However his criticism of modernity is expressed or viewed, it has led him to take up parts of the Christian tradition that earlier played little role in his theology. The tensions this leads to will be the theme of the following sections. We will begin with a discussion of his attempts to integrate the modern ideas of personal autonomy and self-realization, and how these attempts relate to the church as a community of discipleship.

2. A Committed Church in an Individualistic Culture

Moltmann has, concerning the future of the church, written that "[o]nly voluntary and determined groups, made up of people who are prepared to become 'strangers in their own country,' can operate against the prevailing interests and the pressure of self-interested parties."[48] We have seen how he in his later work has formulated an eschatologically oriented ecclesial discipleship ethics. This means an ethics that will stand in contrast to the prevailing ethics in the current society, offering a concrete alternative.

One might think that there is some tension, not to say contradiction, between this discipleship ethics and the modern ideals of autonomy and self-realization. But Moltmann seems not to think so, as he is a strong defender of both. He finds it wholly adequate to describe the individual Christian life in terms of actualizing

---

[45]Cf. the section title "Political theology and imperfect (*unvollendete*) modernity" in *ThT* 87 (94).

[46]*ThT*, "Revolution", *OHD* 97-100 (*PTPE* 152-155). This contrast has also determined much of Metz' theology. See e.g. *The Emergent Church* and "Political Theology".

[47]*WJC* 46-72 (64-91), *HTG* 140-142 (191-193).

[48]"The Challenge of Religion in the '80s", 111.

oneself, of realizing one's essence, and is also highly critical of Christian criticisms of the ideas of autonomy and self-realization.[49]

a) Liberation to Autonomy and Self-Realization

One way he theologically develops this view is through the doctrine of the justification of the godless. This justification liberates people to a new life. They do not need to create themselves, but can live out the new life in the Spirit. This life is characterized by spontaneity and playfulness. "A life which is worthy of the gospel, however, liberates us to be ourselves and fills us with the powers of the Spirit. We are enabled to give ourselves up and trust ourselves to the leading of the Spirit. Then we are able to accept ourselves just as we are, with our possibilities and limitations, and thereby gain a new spontaneity."[50] It is interesting to note how he combines 'giving oneself up' with 'being ourselves'. Classical biblical language is here mediated to the modern language of self-realization.

This goes together with a strong criticism of thinking in terms of self-control, of controlling natural urges, and of ecclesial discipline concerning personal life.[51] Therefore he also finds the Pauline language in Romans 6 of changing dominions from sin to Christ unfortunate. Christ's lordship should be understood not as lordship but as brotherhood and friendship. The language of "new obedience in faith" is (explicitly) reinterpreted to mean not obedience at all, but life characterized by freedom, fantasy and love.[52] Christians do not experience God as Lord, but as Friend.[53] In another context he says that "God wants us as 'autonomous human beings'" and that "[w]e should look for the Spirit where human beings become autonomous agents of their own life and take the initiative for themselves".[54]

We find these themes throughout the Moltmann corpus. His later major books furthermore all have long sections criticizing the body critical and repressive attitudes of Western philosophy and theology.[55] Against this he contends that the Spirit in the Jewish and the Christian traditions is "the life-force of created be-

---

[49]*OHD* 10 ("Christlicher Glaube und Menschenrechte", 24f).

[50]*OC* 38 (34). Similarly *CPS* 280 (307). In these two books he talks about the Christian life in terms of a messianic or a new lifestyle. See *CPS* 275-288 (302-315) and *OC* 37-49 (32-50). He refers also to Luther's rejection of the third use of the law as a way to preserve this spontaneity (*CPS* 395 n. 129 [307]).

[51]*CPS* 277 (304), *OC* 38 (33f), and the texts mentioned in following footnotes.

[52]*TJ* 67f (53-55). Cf. also *CG* 303-307 (281-285). In a context discussing the Christian contribution to revolution he writes the following: "Marxism speaks of the transformation of work into free spontaneity. This is the transition from the 'kingdom of necessity' into the 'kingdom of freedom.' This idea has a long history and is also alive in Christianity. Here it means the liberation from the law of works by faith, which brings forth the free fruits of love. . . . What does faith mean other than already here and now in the midst of the kingdom of poverty and necessity to begin realizing the future of freedom, love, and play?" (*RRF* 147.)

[53]*OC* 57 (62).

[54]*HIG* 122.

[55]*GIC* 244-275 (248-278), *WJC* 259-267 (282-290), *CJF* 71-79 (94-104), *GHH* 4-6 (16-19), *SL* 83-98 (95-110). *GHH* 60f (80f) gives a personal background to these views.

ings" and "of the resurrection"[56] that enhances the vitality of the created life. The Pauline language of the conflict between spirit and flesh should be understood in an apocalyptic framework as "the conflict between the Spirit's drive for life and sin's death drive."[57] When the church transformed this apocalyptic into a time-eternity dualism, this conflict was, in turn, transformed into a body-soul dualism that has formed Christian spirituality and morality since then.[58] Against this, Moltmann's account leads to the idea of spirituality as the liberation and vitalization of the created life and the perichoretic unity between soul and body. He contrasts the dominion of the soul over the body, the sublimation of the urges and needs of the body and the moral repression of life with "the gathering up of the body regimented through self-control into the spontaneous body of love".[59] This should not be understood in only individualistic terms, because this spontaneous life is lived out not in isolation, but in "union with others in sensuous mutuality and community."[60] True humanity is realized only in community. In another context he talks about how the "autonomous subjectivity" only can be realized "in the free community . . . without above and below."[61]

This sort of language and the conception of life it entails has increasingly, in different forms, become the dominating moral language in the modern Western culture.[62] We will in chapter eight further discuss the social roots of this understanding of life. It is a crucial part of the critical modern culture to which Moltmann wants to mediate the Christian faith. In terms of intellectual history his view is a complex amalgam of biblical and Christian (especially Lutheran[63]) tradition interpreted in the light of Marxist or Neomarxist thought,[64] German philosophies of life and its various off-springs,[65] feminist theology,[66] Freudian psychoanalysis[67]

---

[56]*SL* 84 (96).

[57]*SL* 89 (101).

[58]*SL* 89-93 (101-106).

[59]*WJC* 260 (283). He writes further about the replacing of "the techniques for repressing and sublimating the 'drives' by the spontaneous passion of love, in which body and soul, unconscious desires and conscious will are attuned in a single harmonious configuration." (*WJC* 261 [284].) So also *SL* 95 (108).

[60]*WJC* 260 (283).

[61]*HIG* 122.

[62]See e.g. Bell, *The Contradictions of Capitalism*, Bellah et. al., *Habits of the Heart*, Berger, *Facing Up to Modernity*, 23-34, Lasch, *The Culture of Narcissism*, Lyttkens, *Den disciplinerade människan*, Rieff, *The Triumph of the Therapeutic*, and Sennett, *The Fall of Public Man*.

[63]On the relation between Lutheran theology and these modern understandings, see Lindbeck, "Modernity and Luther's Understanding of the Freedom of the Christian". On Moltmann and Luther in this concern, see Gunnemann, *The Moral Meaning of Revolution*, 218.

[64]This is found throughout his work. See for examples n. 52 above and *FC* 98 (106). On this Romantic motif in Marxism, see Kolakowski, *Main Currents of Marxism*, vol. 1, 409-412.

[65]*SL* xiii, 85f (12, 96-98). The "philosophy of life" was a movement of thought during late nineteenth and early twentieth century associated with people like Dilthey, Nietzsche, Bergson, and Simmel. The common theme was criticism of the repression of life through social conventions, prevailing moralities and intellectualism. Instead the authentic, the dynamic, the creative, the immediate was stressed. "The moral instrumentalization of life was to be replaced by life's free intensification, by way of its creative

and humanistic psychology. In popular culture the latter has been most important, and one psychologist which in this respect is often referred to by Moltmann is Norman O. Brown.[68] Don Browning names Brown's position "instinctual romanticism"[69], and sees it as one radical form of the extremely influential, not least in Christian circles, humanistic psychologies.[70]

The liberated life Moltmann depicts seems thus to be a life in community freed from inner and outer pressure. It is lived in harmony between mind and body, and between people. He describes it as a spontaneous and playful realization of ourselves, of living according to nature.[71] This sounds as what Browning has called the "culture of joy", by which he means

> an image of the good life which sees it consisting primarily of a rather uncomplicated matter of giving expression to and actualizing the innate human potentials that everyone has. These potentials are seen primarily as positive, benign, creative, and socially constructive. Through a simple process of discovering one's own potentials and expressing them, individual fulfillment can be experienced and social harmony achieved.[72]

Moltmann sees this conception of life as a "rebellion against the disciplinary measures of modern civilization"[73] and the industrial society. An alternative interpretation, which I will develop further in chapter eight, sees it as much a result of modern technological and capitalist society as a reaction to it. This society entails criticism of moral traditions and communal authority and a hope for an abundant life. Yet it is also a society in deep tension with itself, as it requires both disciplined work *and* hedonistic, consumer-oriented lifestyles. In addition, it is the

---

expression." (*SL* 85 [97].) This philosophy was taken up for instance in existentialism, in philosophical anthropology (e.g. Plessner and Gehlen, whose works Moltmann has used from his earlier writings on to today), in Neomarxism and Critical Theory, and in Freud's psychoanalysis. One can find similar ideas today in various "alternative movements". Another line of influence went into fascism and nazism, which is a reason why the actual explicit conception of "philosophy of life" went into oblivion. See Schnädelbach, *Philosophie in Deutschland 1831-1933*, 172-196. Cf. Tillich, *Perspectives on 19th and 20th Century Protestant Theology*, 191-207 who also discusses its medieval theological prehistory.

[66]*SL* xiii (12).

[67]*CG* 291-316 (268-292), *FC* 98, 104 (106, 111).

[68]See e.g. *HP* 48 n. 28 (53), *WJC* 260 n. 60 (283), and *SL* 86 n. 7, 91 n. 21, 95 n. 32 (98, 103, 107). For a more critical note on Brown, see *CG* 294 (271). See Brown's books *Life against Death* and *Love's Body*. On Brown cf. Bell, *The Winding Passage*, 292-297.

[69]*Religious Thought and the Modern Psychologies*, 62.

[70]Another form of humanistic psychology that has been influential on Moltmann is the Gestalt therapy of Pearls and others. See *GIC* 353 n. 40 (262). On humanistic psychology, see Browning, *Religious Thought*, 61-93 and Wallach and Wallach, *Psychology's Sanction for Selfishness*. On the strong influence it has had in pastoral care, see Holifield, *A History of Pastoral Care in America*, 259-356.

[71]*CJF* 79 (102).

[72]*Religious Thought*, 65.

[73]*CJF* 79 (103).

modern material affluence that has created the condition for a development of an "instinctual romanticism".[74] Christopher Lasch writes:

> As the new elite discards the outlook of the old bourgeoisie, it identifies itself not with the work ethic and the responsibilities of wealth but with an ethic of leisure, hedonism, and self-fulfilment. . . . it has replaced character building with permissiveness, the cure of souls with the cure of the psyche, blind justice with therapeutic justice, philosophy with social science, personal authority with an equally irrational authority of professional experts.[75]

In an affluent consumer society, an ethos of freedom, spontaneity and joy (life without effort) thus becomes central, but at the same time a life of sharing, sacrifice and service becomes more difficult to sustain.

We have seen that an "oppression-liberation" model permeates Moltmann's theology. It is also in place here. The language of repression, alienation, self-realization and authenticity seems to assume a set of natural needs and capacities that have been suppressed by social, cultural and moral forces and therefore need to be liberated. When liberated from repression the "natural" life can be realized. As Moltmann says: "We will again be able to 'live in accord with nature' if we transcend the individual and social repressions of our body by the consciousness and will of the soul and come into a living harmony with ourselves and one another."[76] In this conception the ideas of self-control, morality and ecclesial discipline are consequently seen as suppressive forces.

b) Discipleship, Autonomy and Self-Realization

This raises the question about the compatibility between the conceptions behind the language of autonomy, self-realization and spontaneity, on the one hand, and the language of discipleship, on the other. Moltmann can say that "[t]o follow Jesus always means to deny oneself and to take 'his cross' on oneself." Jesus' calling of disciples meant "an unparalleled claim to authority on his part."[77] More generally he maintains the existence of a specific Christian ethics, the way of Jesus Christ. The church has to follow this way in opposition to the way of the world. This discipleship ethics is furthermore the ethics of the messianic community. It is possible only as a community ethics, as the ethics of a church which is a contrast society.

---

[74]For a discussion of other possible social conditions, see Berger, *Facing up to Modernity*, 23-34. He writes that "[i]nstitutionalized psychologism, as derived directly or indirectly from the psychoanalytical movement, constitute an admirably designed response to the needs of this particular sociohistorical situation" (p. 32).

[75]*The Culture of Narcissism*, 221. Philip Rieff describes it as "a revolution of the rich by which they have lowered the pressure of inherited communal purpose upon themselves." (*Triumph*, 240.)

[76]*CJF* 79 (103). This means to live "in agreement with the laws and rhythms of the earth-system" and "of our own bodies." (*CJF* 71 [94].)

[77]Both citations are from *CG* 54 (55f).

To follow means to go after. Christians are called to follow the way of Jesus.[78] It is not imitation, but it implies following one way instead of other ways. The question is then not only liberation from oppression, but of following the way of Jesus. It is thus difficult to see how discipleship can be understood in terms of autonomy and self-realization.[79] Neither can it be described as liberation from morality in general, because the issues are *which* morality and *how* people are morally formed. Furthermore, if it is a community ethics, it implies a common way. One can agree that in the way of Jesus there is space for much diversity, but it cannot contain *any* form of diversity. There is much space outside, or many ways beside, the way of Jesus Christ.

One can find certain support for this criticism of the use of the language of alienation and self-realization also from some of Moltmann's more general accounts of human life. He argues that "[h]uman life is necessarily life in community".[80] It is formed through an interplay between the genetically given structures and the historical, social, cultural and moral environment, which also implies a similar interplay in the inner life.[81] Human beings are thus formed also through the social and political history they are part of.[82] Furthermore, both individuals and communities can be seen as systems open to the future. Moltmann can therefore say that human actions have an anticipatory character that is influenced by the expectations and hopes one has.[83]

The outcome of this seems to be that there exists no potential self that can be abstracted from this identity-forming process which includes genetic structures and the historical, social, cultural and moral environment. The contexts we live in and the moral languages we use for construing reality form our experience. If our subjectivity is shaped by the cultural language we live in, liberation is not a question of being emancipated from internal and external repression, but of learning and living with a true language. Developing individuality is not a question of just "letting be", of realizing some given potential, but of being so formed through learning a language and a set of practices that the life one considers good becomes a possibility.[84] If this is right, it is in this context misleading to use the language of oppression and liberation, as it leads us to see all forms of social shaping

---

[78]Cf. Dykstra's description of Christian discipleship: "To be a disciple is to be an adherent of the way of Christ. It is to be a follower of his, and to have one's life formed through the strenuous discipline of going where he went, looking at things the way he did, trusting as he trusted, making ourselves vulnerable as he was vulnerable." (*Vision and Character*, 90.)

[79]Cf. Metz, who in *The Emergent Church*, 4 contrasts the messianic virtue of discipleship and the bourgeois value of autonomy.

[80]*GIC* 266 (269).

[81]*GIC* 258-262 (261-265).

[82]*SL* 161f (176).

[83]*GIC* 264-266 (267-269).

[84]Moltmann seems to recognize this in *GIC* 261 (265).

as repressive of the true spontaneous individuality.[85] How we experience our needs is dependent on the social and cultural context we live in and the language we use. The consequence is that what we think are our needs could be questioned. Every need is not automatically legitimate. In discussing the norm of health, Moltmann concurs that this is the case, as "health is a norm which changes with history and is conditioned by society."[86] We have to question, he says, if the language of health used in a culture of work and joy is able to form a Christian life open for suffering and passion, without this being seen as unhealthy. If he takes this seriously, it seems that he cannot use the deceptive language of self-realization and spontaneity in the way he does. It presupposes a false understanding of the identity formation process, which cannot be accommodated to his just-described way of understanding health, of how human identity is formed, or the centrality of discipleship in his account of the Christian life.

In this light, Moltmann's talk about the church as a contrast society carrying a contrast ethics is important, for it seems to imply that being Christian is to be incorporated and formed by a specific community, with its own specific history, practices and eschatological hope. The church thus constitutes the space that makes this different life a possibility. It does not come spontaneously from the taking away of repression. If life in discipleship means "(a) preparedness to be estranged from society ('the world'); (b) readiness to suffer for the sake of the kingdom of God; (c) openness to the imaginative creativity of a love that seeks to liberate the world" or if it "commits us to non-violence",[87] it is dependent on a moral and practical formation of life in the light of Christian convictions.

One reason why Moltmann can so easily avoid these questions is that he keeps his account on a highly abstract level and he paints a very harmonious picture of the ideal formation of both individual life and community. He often talks as if the socialization process could take place without pressure. Indeed, it is difficult to see what meaning he can give the concept of "socialization",[88] if we become truly liberated through transcending all forms of psychological and social pressure. Furthermore, if everyone lived out one's self there would supposedly be no conflicts of interest, but true social harmony would emerge. This view assumes the ideal of a harmonious world that functions so that what is to my advantage never comes in conflict with other people's interests and therefore explains why he does not see any contradiction between his "expressive individualism"[89] and his likewise strong community conception. This is further helped by the fact that

---

[85]This criticism of the language of spontaneity is, of course, not against spontaneity in general, but against understanding spontaneity as a basic moral principle. Our spontaneity is also something that is formed or given a content in different ways.

[86]*CG* 314 (291). So also *EH* 164 (184f) and *GIC* 270-275 (273-278).

[87]*HC* 132f.

[88]It is a concept he uses, see *CPS* 306 (333) and the German version of *GIC* 267 (270).

[89]For this expression, see below n. 91.

he sees the function of the good community as primarily recognizing and accepting the individual as he or she is.

It is difficult to imagine what this would be. For utopians, from Marx (with his free association of free individuals in which the free development of individual human beings is the ground for the free development of all[90]) to Norman O. Brown, the idea of a harmonious society presupposes a world of abundance. In a society beyond scarcity no conflicts exist. Moltmann says that the social structures must be changed so that there will be objective possibilities for developing one's true self. The structures must be humanized. We remember that his criticism of liberal individualism concerns the need of a more communal relationship to property and power.[91] Yet for Moltmann, and especially for the later "green" Moltmann, creating a world of total abundance is no possibility.[92] But he seems reluctant to abandon some of the political and psychological views which presuppose this sort of utopianism, although so much in his theology points away from it. His explicit solution appears instead to be the Holy Spirit. Our spontaneity is the form the Spirit takes in the individual life, which could explain why our different spontaneities end up in a grand social harmony.[93]

A further reason why Moltmann does not see any problem in the relation between his ecclesial discipleship ethics and the therapeutic moral language of self-realization is likely that both can be so construed that they seem to fit his basic language of freedom understood in terms of oppression/liberation. Both can be interpreted as struggles for freedom, the only difference being that they concern different spheres of life. And the latter fact points to an additional reason. The matters that Moltmann discusses in terms of discipleship are of a public/political nature: they are peace, social justice and ecological questions; while the language of spontaneous freedom is used concerning the private/personal life.[94] This explains the co-existence of a defence of personal autonomy and a strongly moralistic attitude to political questions. In the area of political opinion and practice, he defends the possibility and desirability of a common Christian understanding and of ecclesial discipline, while his stress in the sphere of personal life is on indivi-

---

[90]Moltmann now describes this view as "entirely in the spirit of liberalism" (*SL* 251 [263]).

[91]He does not, however, see total abolition of property as possible or desirable. See *TKG* 217 (235). In the light of his criticism of liberal individualism the distinctions Robert Bellah and his team in *Habits of the Heart* make between four different types of individualism in the American tradition—biblical, republican, utilitarian and expressive—(see pp. 27-51, 333f, 336 for definitions) are helpful for understanding Moltmann. Understood in these terms Moltmann can be said to, in his discussions of the personal life, mainly side with the expressive type criticizing the other three strands. When he himself talks about individualism, it is the utilitarian version he most often thinks of. This differentiating of several types of individualism clarifies why he can be said to defend a rather extreme sort of individualism in spite of his intense critique of individualism.

[92]For a general criticism of Marx along this line, see *Man*, 47-59 (73-89). See below p. 127.

[93]*WJC* 263-273 (286-296) and *GIC* 98-103 (110-115).

[94]See e.g. *WJC*, in which the language of discipleship is used when discussing peace (pp. 116-136 [136-157]) and the language of spontaneous self-realization is used when talking about personal life in general (pp. 259-267 [282-290]).

duality, spontaneity, autonomy and against outer and inner pressure. Yet it is difficult to imagine a discipline that is not experienced as some form of pressure.[95]

This discussion of the various, seemingly contradictory elements of Moltmann's understanding of the Christian life might also throw a different light on Paul's language about change of lordship, which we found that Moltmann was not satisfied with. If one instead of accepting the idea of emancipation to autonomy and self-realization, understands the formation of one's identity and practical life as socially and morally shaped in contingent ways, Paul's language about change of lordship can be construed as a change of way. This entails becoming part of the body of Christ, of the church. Part of what this means is learning to see and describe reality and life in a Christian way, something that is learned in the community. Furthermore, if one accepts Moltmann's eschatological account of the conflict between Spirit and flesh, the conflict is still there and concerns the whole of life, including the bodily life. The new life is not spontaneous, it does not come just through the taking away of restraints and repressions, but is a question of being rightly formed. Self-control, for Paul a fruit of the Spirit (Gal. 5:23), but for Moltmann one of the worst vices of the Western civilization,[96] could then be understood in the light of this struggle and of the goal towards which the Christian strives. It is not asceticism for the sake of asceticism, but a self-control that is needed for making resistance against the powers of this world. Would not self-control be important in a consumer society? If the Christian life, with Moltmann, is understood to be an alternative to the dominating ethos, it requires a community to be sustainable. The Christian way of understanding reality and the Christian practice do not live spontaneously, but must be nurtured in alternative communities.[97] This requires some form of personal (self-control) and ecclesial discipline. If Moltmann's hope of a new radical ecological ethos, in contrast to the modern work and consumer ethos, is to be fulfilled something like the committed, disciplined communities he describes in the opening quote of this section seem to be needed. Only such communities have the strength and imagination

---

[95]He does not discuss the issue of ecclesial discipline much, but in a discussion of Paul Schneider he writes: "Church discipline brings God's commandments and God's promise into practical daily life. God must be obeyed more than any other powers. Without discipline there is no genuine Christian discipleship. And Paul Schneider learnt that church discipline is necessary not merely in the sphere of personal morality, but in the sphere of politics too." (*WJC* 200 [222].) In the case of Moltmann, and in much of modern Christianity, the last sentence could be turned around. He has exemplified what political church discipline might concern (in *GHH* 22f [37f] he mentions apartheid, nuclear deterrence and the world economic system), but has not much to say on the personal sphere—neither on what nor how it should be exercised. See also *EH* 143-146 (160-163).

[96]Though often discussing self-control, he never discusses how to understand Paul's use of it. Oddly enough, when he once quotes Paul's list of the nine fruits of the Spirit, he excludes the last one, that is self-control, from the quotation. See *SL* 176 (190). He describes the early Methodist understanding of sanctification with its emphasis on self-control as in part an expression of the early industrial society, but the way it was developed entailed also a transcending of this society leading to social and political transformations. See *SL* 164-171 (179-185).

[97]Cf. Berger and Luckmann, *The Social Construction of Reality*.

needed for creating and sustaining alternative social practices and forms of life.[98] But it seems that his therapeutic account of human life both theoretically and practically undermines any form of discipleship ethics.[99]

The confusion at the roots of Moltmann's understanding of the Christian life thus has several sources: the inherent tensions and implausibility of the therapeutic account in itself, the tensions between Christian and modern therapeutic understandings, his tendency to develop different models for different spheres of life, which in turn are affected by his type of distinction between private and public. If he would question therapeutic moral language, he would question some of the most sacred convictions and practices in modern society, including those segments he himself most strongly supports. He would, it seems, have to challenge crucial parts of the Enlightenment tradition itself, especially the construing of the alternatives as the vision of freedom and the authoritarian principle. That is to say, it would shake his whole mediating project. It seems to me that he, concerning the issues of this section, has to choose between a stronger Christian critique of modernity or develop a stronger revisionist account of Christian theology, or some combination of both.[100]

3. The Crucified God and the Power of Humanity

Behind making politics the primary horizon for theological thinking is an assumption about humankind's power to consciously form the future. Because history is created through politics, humanity is the subject of history. Enlightenment thinkers saw the concept of God as a foe to human freedom and dignity. Their dream was instead that mature humanity could itself create a free, just, and peaceful world. I will treat this theme through discussing the question of power in Moltmann's theology. I will not deal only with the relation between the power of God and the power of humankind, but also with the closely connected question about how he theologically discusses the use of power in church and society.

a) A Theological Critique of Power

Moltmann has dealt extensively with the question of God and power, as he thinks that much of the church's failures derive from a faulty understanding of God's power. He has both tried to answer the contrast modern thinkers have seen between God and human freedom in general, and the way God has been used in

---

[98]See his comments on 'the arcane discipline' as the source behind the power of Bonhoeffer's resistance in *WJC* 201 (223). Cf. also Gunnemann, *Revolution*, 217f.

[99]Cf. Hunter's discussion of evangelical literature in *American Evangelicalism*, 91-99, where he shows how the increasing use of a therapeutic language has lead to radical changes in the understanding of the Christian life.

[100]Furthermore, if he wants to keep the main lines of his therapeutic moral language, it does not only require a critique and revision of his ecclesial discipleship theology, but also a more adequate and plausible formulation of this position itself. I doubt that is possible.

political religion to legitimate political power. Concerning the first aspect, we have already seen how he argues that the relation between God and human beings should not be understood in terms of domination and subordination, but in terms of covenant and friendship.

Second, a crucial interest in Moltmann's theological project has been to develop theological resources for a critique of political religion.[101] We find this first in his eschatological emphasis on the God of promise and hope, who does not legitimate the existing order, but promises a new social order. We find it also in his trinitarian understanding of God. Christian political religion has been monotheistic. This monotheistic understanding of the all-powerful Lord and possessor of the world has sanctioned both the political order as well as a hierarchical ecclesiastical order. He talks about political and clerical monotheism. Against this he formulates a trinitarian theology that "binds the God-concept to the fate of the crucified and resurrected Jesus. In principle this makes it impossible to use this concept of God for the legitimation of political dominance."[102] Then there is the theme about the God of the poor. The kingdom belongs to the poor and suffering, and the Christian community lives therefore at "the edges of society",[103] which means that this God can never be identified with the powerful. He also points to the universal character of the Christian faith, which makes it impossible to use Christian faith rightly for legitimating particular national powers. All this makes the Christian faith a faith of resistance.

Just as the relation between God and humankind should not be construed in terms of domination, the same ought to be true of all human relations. What true lordship is, Moltmann says, is learned through the life of Jesus. "True dominion does not consist of enslaving others but in becoming a servant of others; not in the exercise of power, but in the exercise of love; not in being served but in freely serving; not in sacrificing the subjugated but in self-sacrifice."[104] This service, it should be stressed, is a service that leads to freedom, not to dependence. The ultimate hope is the abolition of every rule, authority and power and the establishment of the "dominion-free brotherhood".[105]

This obviously has important ecclesiological consequences, as "[i]n the Spirit that new community comes into being which is without privileges and subjection, the community of the free."[106] The church must live in a way that reflects this promise of freedom from dominion, and it must also, in relation to the surrounding world, deny itself all political power. Politically it means that "[i]n this

---

[101]For the following, see "The Cross and Civil Religion" (*PTPE* 34-69), *CG* 321-329 (298-305), *TKG* 191-222 (207-239), and "Christian Theology and Political Religion" ("Die Politik der Nachfolge Christi gegen Christliche Milleniumspolitk" is a slightly shorter version of the same article).

[102]"Christian Theology", 54 (this passage is not in the German article).

[103]Ibid., 55 (29).

[104]*CPS* 103 (122).

[105]*CPS* 104 (123).

[106]*TKG* 211 (228).

'crooked generation' the hoped-for conquest of the structure of lordship and servitude is achieved in no other way than through the social and political form of a voluntary self-surrender on behalf of the liberation of those who are oppressed at any given time",[107] i.e., through the struggle for political and economic freedom and justice.

In the later work of Moltmann this understanding of power has become even more relevant because of the ecological crisis. The modern civilization is characterized by a will for power, which manifests itself in science, technology and economy. Partly responsible for this, Moltmann thinks, is the image of God as pure power, which was particularly developed at the time of the Renaissance.[108] Against this he develops a trinitarian account of God as a community of love that through the Spirit indwells the creation.

b) The Power of Humanity

So far the drift of his argument seems quite clear. The above depicts a sort of strong anti-power theology. Both God's power and power relationships in church and politics are reinterpreted in terms of service and community. We said earlier, however, that modernity's critique of power has gone together with a strong belief in humankind's own power to consciously shape the future. As already hinted at, we find this theme also in Moltmann's writings.[109] Actually Moltmann's theology seems to demonstrate some of the most conspicuous celebrations of the search for power to be found in modern theology. This is especially so in his earlier writings, in which he praised the modern project and the humankind's new found ability to control nature and history and create the future it wants. His Enlightenment rhetoric at this time was exceedingly strong. In a text from 1968 he quotes Kant's famous words that "Enlightenment is man's *exodus* from his self-incurred tutelage" and then continues on to say that "[f]or the first time men and peoples throughout the earth are entering into one, common world history. For the first time they no longer have to endure history unconsciously but must consciously create and control history." Humanity not only can control its own history, but likewise has now even the unprecedented means for "consciously controlling the evolution of nature".[110] The theology of hope teaches us "that the world can be changed and that nothing has to remain as it has been."[111] It is mod-

---

[107]*CPS* 104 (123). See further *CPS* 89-93, 115f (108-112, 134f).

[108]*CJF* 53-55 (73-75).

[109]See above p. 82 n. 40.

[110]Both citations are from *RRF* 26 (*UZ* 118). Without expressing himself in such strong words, we find a similar celebration of "the modern process of the objectification of nature" in Metz' early theology. See *Theology of the World*, 37f.

[111]*RRF* 132.

ern science which, if used for the liberation of humanity, has given the human race these titanic powers.[112]

Though Moltmann's theology has undergone some dramatic changes since these statements were made, he still talks about the necessity that humanity, as one united subject, should create in a relatively short time a wholly new civilization.[113] This is mandatory if humanity shall be able to survive the nuclear and ecological threats. The basic difference between the early and the later Moltmann is that the optimism that celebrated the power of humanity has been sobered. The first question now is just surviving. But if peace and survival come through the creation of a just world, the difference is not especially marked. Although the tone has changed, he still puts his hope in a politics that can control the centre of the (world) society and its development. A dramatic shift has, however, occurred in his understanding of the relation between humanity and nature.

The quotations above throw special light on his discussion of the nature of sin in *Theology of Hope*. Here he characterizes the description of sin as primarily pride, i.e., wanting to be as God, as being one-sided. Without denying the element of pride, he instead stresses the sin of despair and hopelessness. "Temptation then consists not so much in the titanic desire to be as God, but in weakness, timidity, weariness, not wanting to be what God requires of us."[114]

A closely related issue is his understanding of the use of political power. We saw above that his hope is a world characterized by non-domination, and that this is achieved through voluntary self-surrender on behalf of the oppressed. One might have expected that this would have radical consequences for his views of the use of power in the political struggle, that he would be sceptical against mak-

---

[112]"The sciences are being recalled to their truly human possibilities and promises. They are to be enlisted for the realization of humanity. They can no longer be the slaves of a society which misses its genuinely human opportunities." (*RRF* 131.) "Scientific knowledge, then, is a means to the self-liberation of man from obdurate dependence only when it is employed in responsibility for a more human future." (*RRF* 132.) See also *HP* 159 (235).

[113]*CJF* 21f (36), *WJC* 66 (86).

[114]*TH* 22 (18). See further *TH* 22-26 (18-21). In *FC* 122 (129) he describes "sin and slavery as the self-closing of open systems against their own time and their own potentialities." Cf. also his statement about the early Christian view of sin and freedom: "The past was considered to be the power of sin; the future, the dynamics of grace; and the present, the time of decision." (*RRF* 71 [*PdT* 199].) Connected to this is the idea that the problem of the evil today is understood primarily as a political phenomenon. (*RRF* 99-101 [*PdT* 140f], *Man*, 22f [38f].) The corollary is the modern tendency to see the evil as a problem to be solved, rather than as force or mystery that pervades the existence. The basic task becomes therefore to give the political power to people of good will. A more classical Christian view is less optimistic. All human action is permeated with sin. We do not even see reality correctly, with the result that all political programs are highly ambiguous. A more humble attitude towards the human power follows. There are statements, especially in his later writings, that could be interpreted in this direction. See *PTPE* 112f, *OHD* 30f (*PTPE* 175), and *WJC* 184f (206f). As yet, a more humble view of the ability of politics has not resulted. Cf. the critique of Shaw, "Beyond Political Theology", 52-54 ("The Achilles heel of Moltmann's political theology is his failure to understand the radical character of sin." [p. 52]) and Gilkey, *Reaping the Whirlwind*, 230-231, 406-407. See also more generally Dykstra, *Vision and Character*, 42-50.

ing the direct struggle for political power central and instead argue for alternative political practices. But that is not the case. Again his statements from the 1960s are most straightforward. "It is fully clear that the transformation of the conditions of power will come only through the use of power and the assumption of authority."[115] This can also mean the use of revolutionary violence. His theology has been an attempt to analyse, understand and help the church to take sides in the political and cultural struggle for the control over the processes of social change. He has not questioned that it is the (main?) task of the church to take part in this power struggle. Instead it has been a leading concern of his that church and theology shall not become marginalized from this political struggle and therefore lose their influence, that is, power. What he has questioned, however, is that the church should search for power for itself.

c) Moltmann's Conception of Power Questioned

To summarize Moltmann's beliefs on divine and human power is not easy. His position is highly complex. But if understood from the perspective of his attempt to mediate Christianity and modernity a rather clear logic is apparent. We see this, first, if we relate his affirmation of the Enlightenment celebration of human power over history with his understanding of the non-power of God. Second, his acceptance of the primacy of politics corresponds similarly with his affirmation of the non-power of the church.

Much criticism has been directed against this view. George Hunsinger says that in Moltmann's account God's lordship "has been evacuated of content" and "sentimentalized" to "mere friendship", while humanity on the other side is inflated. "Can we really believe that this essentially impoverished, tragic and self-humiliated deity is finally going to sway the future after all?"[116] Moltmann has countered a similar criticism through referring to the idea of covenant. However, the covenant between God and Israel was not between equal partners, even though "it entails mutual loyalty and commitment."[117] The covenant language, nevertheless, ought at least to lead to criticism of his often-used idea of humanity as the subject of history. We also find this in a recent text, where he instead says that history is formed in the interaction between God and humanity.[118] Still, not only the biblical language of covenant, but also the language of discipleship goes

---

[115]*RRF* 143.

[116]All citations are from his review of Moltmann, *The Trinity and the Kingdom*, 136. Stephen Sykes asks if one reason for the Moltmannian type of non-power theology is the church's loss of societal power. "The theological celebration of powerlessness, based on what appears to be a misunderstanding of Paul's theology of the cross, has an altogether too suspicious air of *post factum* justification for loss of political influence." (*The Identity of Christianity*, 75.)

[117]For the criticism, see Conyears, *God, Hope and History*, 187-202, and for Moltmann's answer (including the citation), see his "Foreword" to this book, p. viii.

[118]*WJC* 245 (268).

beyond the equal sharing of rule, just as the Christian eschatological hope seems to do.

Moltmann's recent questioning of the language of humanity as the subject of history arose together with his increasing criticism of modernity's will to power, with its disastrous consequences for nature and society.[119] This makes his position even more complicated. When discussing the ecological question, he stresses the necessity of a change in the basic values of the Western society away from the will to power, which he thinks was influenced by the theological idea of God as pure power. The theological base for this change is the conception of God as a triune community. The political outcome is the building of a decentralized society that is in a state of equilibrium. Yet it seems that this does not basically change his fundamental confidence in the ability of politics, and therefore the power of humanity, to shape the future. He maintains that the radical ecological reforms he envisions are "technically quite possible if there is the political will."[120] Supposedly the main and the more difficult task seems to be to give the power to people of good will, people who see the necessity of new basic values and of radical reform. The implementation of this total reformation of society is, on the contrary, described as a relatively simple technical matter. It is on this immense power of humanity that the survival of the creation hinges.

A final problematic factor is his elaboration of the concept of power itself. For Moltmann power tends to be equalized to domination, especially when he talks about power in the church and the already existing power in society. His hope is also for a dominion-free church and the dominion-free society, although he recognizes the necessity of power for reaching this stage. Moltmann's account makes it difficult to realistically depict how power actually works in church and society. Power becomes simply something bad. But it is, of course, impossible to have any form of human community and institution without power relations. The question therefore is how to understand different forms of power and how it works. But Moltmann's monolithic concept makes such analysis difficult. Sykes, discussing the use of power in the church, writes concerning Moltmann's understanding that "[a] more realistic appraisal of power would suggest that no church order is free of the dominating impulse, and that harmony can exist only in the presence of consent to a form of government, whatever that government is."[121]

As I have already said, I think there are resources in Moltmann's theology that could be used for a more adequate account of power in the relation between God and humankind, as well as in church and society, but he has either not satisfactorily developed them or curbed their critical force. In this respect, particularly

---

[119]In relation to the text referred to in the former note, see *WJC* 246 (269).

[120]*CJF* 14 (26). Where the ET has "quite", the German original has "durchaus", i. e. "completely" or "totally". Cf. also his comment that "[t]ogether, in solidarity, we are strong enough to shape our destiny." (*CJF* 9 [20].)

[121]Sykes, *The Identity of Christianity*, 297 n. 61. See further ibid., 51-77 and idem, "The Dialectic of Community and Structure". Cf. the similar analysis by Gunnemann, *Revolution*, 210f, 218-220.

his trinitarian theology, his theology of the cross, his discipleship ethics, and his ecclesiology could be further elaborated. The problem is that these themes, in the interest of mediating Christianity and modernity, have been used more frequently to depowerize the concept of God, the church, and the existing political powers, than to rethink the concept and use of power generally. Just as troublesome is the other side of this, that his theology actually has been justifying modernity's pretensions of an almost unlimited power, an attitude which, from the perspective of Moltmann's later writings, can be said to have strongly contributed to the situation he now deplores. But he has still not satisfactorily dealt with the ambiguities in his own theology of power that underwrite these attitudes. In other words, his discussion of power is a further example of the problematic nature of his mediating project.

4. The Rights of Humanity and Nature

Another important manifestation of his integration of Christianity and the Enlightenment tradition is the central place the notion of human rights has in his theology.[122] As Moltmann also includes the rights of nature in his account one should more exactly talk about rights in general instead of the more limited notion of human rights. Through an account of rights Moltmann thinks he both can relate his political theology to secular politics and translate this theological project into concrete political proposals.

> I believe, the further knowledge, development, and advancement of human rights has become the framework of ecumenical politics and ethics. Liberation, development, passive and active resistance, the overcoming of racism, economic aid to developing countries, nuclear reactors, and the building up of a sustainable society are discussed today within the framework of human rights. For church guidelines on political and social matters gain their universal significance only through reference to human rights. Through its relationship to human rights the church becomes the church for the world.[123]

To say that the church's political proposals only gain universal significance through the concept of human rights seems to be an overstatement, as he also uses other types of languages. But the central importance rights have in his theological project is not in doubt, and he maintains that all forms of particular ethics (for example the Sermon on the Mount) have to be subordinated to this universal

---

[122]For Moltmann's main general treatments of human rights, see *IGMEB* 32-48, *EH* 147-157 (164-176), *CPS* 176-182 (199-206), *MRF* 13-35, *OHD* 3-58 (3-18 = "Christlicher Glaube und Menschenrechte", 19-35 = *PTPE* 166-179, 37-58 = "Der Sinn der Arbeit"—in the following I will only give page and not article references to these German texts), *WJC* 307-312 (332-336), and "Human Rights, the Rights of Humanity and the Rights of Nature". (There is another article written together with Elisabeth Giesser which has the same German title "Menschenrechte, Rechte der Menschheit und Rechte der Natur". It is basically only a shorter version of the former, but with a different introduction.)
[123]*OHD* 7 (21), cf. *EH* 147f (165).

rights ethics. Not to accept this, he says, would make Christians (or anyone else) "enemies of the human race."[124]

a) A Theology of Rights

Human rights-thinking has become central in moral, political and legal discourse in the post-World War II era. It has become a sort of international moral language used in all areas of life from marriage to relations between states. Although resisted for a long time by established European Protestantism and Roman Catholicism, it has now not only been accepted but celebrated by much of contemporary Christianity.[125] Though exploding in the recent decades, the idea has had a much longer history. Early preparatory formulations are found already in English seventeenth century declarations of rights, but the first developed declarations of what we today mean with human rights came through the American and French revolutions. Moltmann, however, is convinced that the development of this human rights tradition is a result "of the process of the Christianization of societies and states."[126] He refers to how the idea that all individual human beings share one common humanity has its source in Greek, Hebrew and Christian traditions. God created humanity in God's own image and it has a common eschatological destiny. From this it follows that humans are bearers of rights and duties and that the state exists for the sake of humans. However, the consequences of this were only taken partially and gradually. Especially important for modern development were, according to Moltmann, the Puritans, who on the basis of the doctrine of the covenant formulated the idea of political contract, demanded freedom of religion, conscience, assembly and press, as well as civil liberties. Moltmann finds here a trajectory of "secularization, desacralization and democratization of political rule"[127] that the church should follow further.[128]

In his own exposition Moltmann bases the human rights on the doctrine of the creation of humanity in the image of God, but he develops this doctrine in more historical and eschatological terms than the tradition usually has done. In doing

---

[124]"Human Rights", 134 (173).

[125]For, besides Moltmann, general and positive accounts from a theological perspective, see e.g. the following quite different works: Holleman, *The Human Rights Movement*, Hollenbach, *Claims in Conflict*, Huber and Tödt, *Menschenrechte*, and Stackhouse, *Creeds, Society and Human Rights*.

[126]*EH* 152 (170). This view, and Moltmann's attempt to ground the human rights theologically, has been criticized by the Lutheran theologians Wolfgang Huber and Heinz Eduard Tödt on the ground that the human rights tradition, though in various ways influenced by the Christian tradition, was much more a secular development (usually opposed by the church) than Moltmann allows (*Menschenrechte* 66f, 124-130). Moltmann answers that this is true for the continental Lutheran churches, but not for the Western Reformed tradition that directly partook in the development of the human and civil rights tradition. See *OHD* 12f (27-29), "Streit um Menschenrechte". Stackhouse, *Creeds* strongly supports Moltmann on this.

[127]*CPS* 179 (201).

[128]*EH* 148-150 (165-168), *CPS* 201f (178f). For a much more elaborated defence of this view, see Stackhouse, *Creeds*, 26-80.

this his argument revolves around the concepts of liberation, covenant, and the claim of God, as these express the experiences both of Israel and the early church. Israel was liberated from slavery in Egypt and entered into a covenant with God, which regulated the rights and duties of the liberated community. In the New Testament Jesus Christ liberates humans from law, sin, and death, and establishes a new covenant with the people of God. He, as the visible image of God, opens the way for humanity "toward the realization of their human destiny as the image of God in the world." In other words, the particular history and experiences of Israel and church presuppose the original destiny to which God as Creator has created the whole humanity. "In the 'image of God' concept, the divine claim upon human beings is expressed. Human rights to life, freedom, community, and self-determination mirror God's claim upon persons, because in all their relationships in life . . . they are destined to reflect the image of God."[129] This entails that the rights and duties are, so to say, descriptions of what it is to be truly human. It is also important to note how his emphasis on the claim of God shows why rights and duties are indivisible. One cannot have the rights without the duties.[130] Yet he says very little about duties. He mentions the duty of resistance and the duty to work for liberation of people whose individual rights are denied, but not much more.[131]

He has recently extended his account to include nature. Christ died and was raised also for the reconciliation and resurrection of the nature. This grounds a cosmological community of law that makes it possible to talk about the rights of nature—of the earth, animals and plants.[132]

He furthermore derives specific rights theologically. From the fact that not the king, but humans in general are seen as the image of God, follows: the idea that the state exists for the sake of human individuals; the right to democracy in all areas of life; equality under the law; and the right to and duty of resistance. From the conviction that humans *in community* are the image of God follows the social rights to a just society. From the created right to rule over the earth follows, first, the "basic economic right to a just share in life, nourishment, work, shelter, and personal possession",[133] and, second, the earth's "rights" over against humanity. And as created for the realization of the kingdom of God, present generations have duties in relation to the future generations' right to a just share.[134]

These considerations also reveal his stand in the contemporary debate on rights. Though rights language has become dominant in the modern world, there

---

[129]Both citations are from *OHD* 22 (168).
[130]*OHD* 21-23 (167-169). It is a recurring theme of Glendon's *Rights Talk* that while the European tradition more stresses both rights and responsibilities, the latter have little place in the American tradition.
[131]*CPS* 180 (203f), *MRF* 22.
[132]See esp. *WJC* 252-256, 270-273, 305-312 (275-279, 294-296, 329-336) and "Human Rights", 130-133 (171f).
[133]*OHD* 27 (172).
[134]*OHD* 23-29 (169-174). See also the slightly different account in *CPS* 202-205 (179-181).

is much controversy between different theories and uses of rights language. One such controversy has concerned the relations between individual and social rights. Moltmann sees them as only different aspects developed and emphasized in different situations. The North Atlantic liberal stress on individual rights has its background in the struggle against fascism. The socialist states' highlighting of social rights evolved in the struggle against capitalism and class rule. In the same way has the Third World in its struggle against imperialism come to emphasize the right to existence and self-determination.[135] All these different emphases are valid, but not in isolation. Individual and social rights go together, without any priority. The same is true for human rights in relation the rights of humanity, the economic rights in relation to the rights of nature, and the rights of humanity in relation to the rights of the earth.[136] In this way Moltmann develops rights ethics into a comprehensive moral-political program.[137]

Moltmann's account of rights is thus wholly theologically based. Yet, the significance of rights language for Moltmann is that it helps the church translate its proposals into a universal moral and political language. Because it is universal it helps people from different cultures and religions to work together politically for peace, justice and nature. He claims that the rights, when once stated, are immediate and self-evident truths.[138] His argument seems to be that the rights historically have developed in particular traditions, but once formulated and clarified they are seen as tradition-independent and self-evident. This means that rights language as the universal and basic moral language has priority over all particular traditions. The latter ones may creatively contribute to the further development of rights language, but they are never allowed to contradict it.[139] One reason for this

---

[135]*OHD* 19f (166), "Human Rights", 121f (165f). He says that "the peoples of the Third World, who are seeking their path to freedom from colonial dependence, cultural alienation, and political suppression" have different priorities than in the West. "In these countries the interest in freedom of the press or in the right to strike is understandably slight. The right to life and to the means which make continued living possible stands in the forefront." (*OHD* 6 [19f].) This is odd, as one would rather think that the right to strike and freedom of the press are important just in the struggle for better life and more justice, although the leaders of these countries may not think so. For a strong defence of a view similar to the one Moltmann seems to express here, see Holleman's rather amazing book *The Human Rights Movement*. He uses Reinhold Niebuhr for basically defending the view of human rights espoused by, among others, Brezhnev, Andropov, Chernenko, Castro, and different African and Latin American leaders, against dissenters like Sakharov, human rights organizations like Amnesty, and the Helsinki declaration. The way he tends to identify the "people" and their leaders is remarkable. Generally, however, Moltmann does not subscribe to the view of Holleman, but at the price of less consistency.

[136]"Human Rights", *OHD* 33-35 (177-179).

[137]Cf. Bauckham's comment: "I think one could almost say that human rights come to play the kind of role in Moltmann's political theology that Marxism plays in the liberation theology of Latin America." ("Moltmann's Political Theology", 12.)

[138]He says that rights in a substantive sense are universal ideas (like mathematics) that, once stated, "leuchten allen Menschen unmittelbar ein". This is the German original. ET is weaker: "seem plausible and convincing simply on their own account". ("Human Rights", 120 [165].) This idea of self-evidence is contradicted by his critique of the idea of "natural rights" in *Man*, 71-75 (106-111).

[139]"Human Rights", 121, 133f (165, 172f).

is the priority and universality of truth.[140] Yet Moltmann's most common argument is that the survival of the humankind depends on the maintenance of the rights of humanity and of nature. It is not clear how these two arguments are related, if truth is not identified with the interest of the survival of humankind. In this context that might be the most plausible interpretation.

This is, of course, a version of the Enlightenment view. The only way seen to overcome religious strife was finding the universal truth above all particular convictions. Positive religion could be accepted as far as it coincided with reason.[141] So what Moltmann in effect is saying is that the Christian faith and ethics can be followed only as long as they are not contradicting the universal truth of the ethos of modernity and that their truth has to be defended at the bar of modern universal reason. The same is, of course, true for all other cultures and religions. Here is another example of the assumed universal normativeness of modernity.

b) The Status of the Theological Derivation of Rights Language

This whole account raises several critical questions. If the rights are self-evident the Christian legitimation of rights seems superfluous. Christianity has been one source of its development, but one can seemingly reach the same conclusions through other ways. Moreover, when they are stated he claims they are self-evident and do not need any further argumentation. What, then, is the practical value of his theological account? To this several complementary answers could be given. One is that it inside the church shows the Christian legitimacy of rights language. Another is its apologetic function of showing the compatibility between Christianity and modern rights thinking. A third is that it might contribute to the further development of the common rights language.

What, then, is the status of the derivation of a rights account from a theological description of reality? On the surface, it seems that his rights account is dependent on and becomes intelligible in terms of specific Christian convictions about God, creation and redemption. Yet, this cannot be Moltmann's view, because the rights are intelligible abstracted from any theological convictions. The belief that humanity is created in the image of God and that this destiny is realized through following Jesus Christ then does not make any practical difference.

He claims that the rights are self-evident. Now there are many different and conflicting accounts of rights. Moltmann's own account is very wide-ranging. To claim self-evidence for his account is surely not credible. It would be hotly contested from several different directions. Most philosophical attempts to develop some universal account of rights try to make them independent of specific views of the good life. Rights belong to human beings as such, independent of their circumstances and beliefs. If they were not, they could not, it is argued, be said to

---

[140]Ibid., 133 (172f).
[141]Cf. for some interesting comments on this Stout, *Ethics after Babel*, 79-81 and Thiemann, "Gotthold Ephraim Lessing".

be universal. Such theories thus become thin and formal. However, one main criticism of rights theories is that they are impossible to formulate separately from specific historically developed social contexts and moral beliefs.[142] Moltmann could avoid this criticism, because as he develops his rights account, it is embedded in a theological account of the divine aim for creation. The price would, however, be the loss of the claim to universal self-evidence. This is a price he does not seem prepared to pay, but he cannot have it both ways.

The problems with his account become even more acute when we come to the issue about how to relate his claims for a Christian ecclesial discipleship ethics to his claim that rights language is the universal moral language to which all other moral languages have to be subordinated. His theology is a theology based on God's particular history with Israel and Jesus Christ, and he explicitly defends a specific Christian ethics. This Christian ethics makes a universal claim, but that is an eschatological claim argued in specifically intra-Christian terms. It is an ethics that has to be followed even when it (as has often been the case) comes into conflict with the dominating existing ethos of the world.[143] It has to take priority because, Christians claim, it is the truth, public truth. We have already quoted him saying that "[i]f there is no specifically Christian ethic, then the acknowledgement of Christ is itself called in question; for then Jesus' message cannot have been ethically meant, in the sense of making a public ethical claim."[144]

The compatibility of these two seemingly contrasting views cannot be argued simply through asserting that Christian discipleship ethics and rights ethics are basically congruent.[145] Even if they are congruent, which is not self-evident, his two argumentative strategies are irreconcilable. Both cannot claim absolute primacy. Furthermore, the logic of Christian discipleship language that talks about suffering love and love for one's enemies seems to be different from an ethics of rights. A more modest rights account might be subordinated to and determined by Christian convictions. But Moltmann's strong claims make the opposite the only allowable strategy.

---

[142]See e.g. MacIntyre, *After Virtue*, 60-75, Sandel, *Liberalism and the Limits of Justice*, and Shapiro, *The Evolution of Rights in Liberal Theory*. MacIntyre says that instead of seeing rights as self-evident and universal truths ("there are no self-evident truths"), we have to understand that they "presuppose . . . the existence of a socially established set of rules." (*After Virtue*, 65.) MacIntyre, Sandel and Shapiro are all very critical of modern rights discourse.

[143]So latest and most emphatically in *WJC* 116-119, 125f (136-139, 146f).

[144]*WJC* 117 (137).

[145]To be sure, that Moltmann in fact appears to believe this is probably part of the reason why he does not seem to see any problem here. This would mean either that his argument of the priority of the ethics of rights over Christian (and Jewish, Muslim, Buddhist, and so on) ethics, is not to be taken seriously, but only as a polite tribute to the inter-religious dialogue, or that the ethics of the world religions all go in the direction of the universal rights tradition, and what does not has to be discarded. Cf. his "Is 'Pluralistic Theology' Useful for the Dialogue of World Religions?", 155f with Milbank, "The End of Dialogue". See also Stackhouse, *Creeds*.

One consequence is that the specifically Christian ethics becomes a sort of personal superstructure on top of a universal general ethics.[146] The particular Christian tradition cannot make, so he seems to argue, the sort of universal truth claims that the rights ethics can (though he claims the opposite in other contexts). The result is just that sort of privatization of Christian faith and practice that his whole theology and his use of human rights language are supposed to counter.

So again we see the dilemmas of his variety of mediating strategy. Both his type of Christian ethics and the rights language have their own inherent logics that more or less inevitably draw his arguments in different directions. Putting rights in the centre of Christian ethics almost unavoidably transforms the latter. What creates the confusion is that he does not always draw these consequences.

c) The Political Use of Rights Language

Disregarding these problems, one could also question the political usefulness of his understanding of rights, except as political rhetoric. As we have seen, Moltmann seems to make all sorts of political questions to rights questions. In that he is in agreement with the general development in especially the Western world. Politics has increasingly become a contest between different claims to rights. Whatever the successfulness of philosophical theories of rights, the actual practised rhetoric of rights in moral and political discourse often seems arbitrary, without any means of adjucating the conflicts. There are little resources in Moltmann's account to discipline this use and to adjudicate different rights claims. He seems rather to contribute to the inflation of rights discourse, as he includes almost anything he thinks is necessary and good under the heading of rights. What is the difference between what Moltmann thinks people ought to have and inalienable rights? As Michael Walzer has said:

> The effort to produce a complete account of justice or a defense of equality by multiplying rights soon makes a farce of what it multiplies. To say of whatever we think people ought to have that they have a right to have it is not to say very much. Men and women do indeed have rights beyond life and liberty, but these do not follow from our common humanity; they follow from shared conceptions of social goods; they are local and particular in character.[147]

But this local and particular character of rights, their embeddedness in substantial accounts of social goods, is what Moltmann wants to transcend, because "[h]uman rights are by definition rights which man as man has towards the state—man meaning every human being . . . They are rights that are integral to man's being

---

[146]Cf. *OHD* 31f (*PTPE* 176f).

[147]*Spheres of Justice*, xv. Glendon, *Rights Talk* likewise criticizes and gives many examples of this inflationary use of rights language.

man."[148] This makes it difficult to understand the practical argumentative and political value of his proposals.

This also raises questions about how to go from rights to practical politics. Moltmann asserts that rights are not ideals but "legal and political aids on the road to man's becoming man and the unification of mankind."[149] When the account of rights, as in Moltmann's case, seems to be the same as a description of the just society, the practical realization of rights becomes identical with the building of the just society.[150] But the question is how to practically realize the rights. It is easier to start to implement the so-called negative rights (freedom of press, religion, etc.) than to form a society in which everyone is guaranteed fulfilling work of his own choice or to create a democratic world economy. Moltmann avoids such problems because of the high level of abstraction in his account.

Besides the right to resistance (which we will return to in a later chapter) the only right he has dealt with somewhat more extensively is the right to work. On this he maintains that the right to work and the right to free choice of work imply each other.[151] What can this mean in practice? A possible answer might be that the state ensures everyone a guaranteed income (independent of work) and just the work any individual prefers. The second part seems again to presuppose a society beyond scarcity.[152] In the absence of such a society, it is hard to understand what it means that the right to work, as defined by Moltmann, is not a political ideal but a legal aid.

When politics in this way is reduced to a question of rights and when one makes the sort of universal claims for rights language that Moltmann does, politics acquires an absolutist character that tends to destroy political discourse. As Mary Ann Glendon says: "Our rights talk, in its absoluteness, promotes unrealistic expectations, heightens social conflict, and inhibits dialogue that might lead toward consensus, accommodation, or at least the discovery of common ground."[153] In other words, how practically useful is it to translate almost everything into rights language? There might be good answers to such questions, but

---

[148]*CPS* 179 (202).

[149]*CPS* 181 (205).

[150]"The rights of persons can only be developed in a just society, and a just society can only be developed on the ground of the rights of the person." (*OHD* 26 [171].)

[151]*OHD* 54 (78f), "Human Rights", 125 (168).

[152]He actually says that the problem with the modern political system is that "opportunities, professions and jobs are in principle kept scarce, the result is a struggle of all against all, since 'there is never enough for everyone'." (*CJF* 9 [20].) He also writes: "When all regularly recurring work processes can basically be carried out by computer, the development and proliferation of free, responsible, 'creative' activities will be not only a possibility, but also an urgent necessity." (*OHD* 54f [79].) His practical suggestions in *CJF*—shortening work hours, just renumeration and human organization, job training, sabbatical years, recognition and payment for "housework and work with children and old people in families" (pp. 10f [21f])—are not so far reaching, but are therefore also no solution to the problem of implementation of the "right to work" as described by Moltmann. For a critique of the idea of the "right to work", see Elster, "Is There (or Should There Be) a Right to Work?".

[153]Glendon, *Rights Talk*, 14.

Moltmann has not begun to answer them, or even shown awareness of the problems.

One way out of some of these difficulties could be to more clearly historicize his argument.[154] Then one could argue that the rights ethos has slowly developed inspired by Greek, Hebrew, Christian, Enlightenment, and other sources, without defending any form of universal self-evidence. Further, one might say, that in a radical, pluralistic society without any genuine common moral community, this ethos is the best we have for living together. And instead of arguing in terms of a common humanity, one might defend particular conceptions of rights relative to different spheres of human life and shared concepts of common goods. Practically usable notions of common goods have to be widely agreed about, which means that they have to be put on a rather low level and not built on any grand vision of the perfect society. More particular substantive ethics (for example a Christian discipleship ethics) might exist alongside the "thinner" rights ethics, because our relations include more than contract and exchange relations. Jon Gunnemann talks about the former as "morality-in-place" and the latter as "morality-out-of-place". The former is the basic matter of our ordinary moral life, while the latter is important because of our pluralism. It helps us deal with our disputes without killing each other. "The increased use of the language of human rights corresponds to an increase in interaction among differing groups of people and cultures, to a general increase in the scale of human association, and to the complexity and differentiation implicit in that scale."[155] However, particular ethical perspectives might contribute to the further development of the shared concepts of social goods to the extent that they reach general agreement.

This is a more modest view than the one Moltmann maintains, but it is a view that is more easy to defend. It is not without its theoretical and practical problems. It implies a relativization and a depolitization of the Christian discipleship ethics that leads to a sort of two level account of Christian ethics that Moltmann would be uncomfortable with. However, if he thinks it is politically necessary to give a central role to rights language, this seems to be a more credible and workable view. An alternative would be to more radically criticize the rights language from the direction of the Christian ethics and therefore subordinate it to substantive Christian convictions. This is, as we will see the way Hauerwas goes, but with Moltmann's primary interest directed towards national and international politics this would hardly be attractive for him.

---

[154]For the following, see Gunnemann, "Human Rights and Modernity". See also Stout, *Ethics after Babel*, esp. 225f and Walzer, *Spheres of Justice*.
[155]"Human Rights and Modernity", 173.

5. Capitalism and Democratic Socialism

Political theology emerged out of the turbulence of the 1960s and Christian engagement with the radical, mainly socialist and Marxist, movements in the First and the Third Worlds. It was not just a response to modernity in general, but to the socialist version of modernity, with its criticism of the Western capitalist world. This made socialism an integral part of political theology. Though a discussion occurred on different interpretations of socialism and Marxism and on different ways to socialism, socialism as such has almost never been questioned. In the final section of this chapter I will take up Moltmann's contributions to this discussion. It is at the same time an answer to the questions of how he describes modern society and what sort of future society the church ought to work for.

a) Capitalist Society

Moltmann is an anticapitalist thinker. He places capitalism on a par with racism and sexism. Furthermore, it is the combination with capitalism that makes racism and sexism so dangerous.[156] What then does Moltmann understand with the word capitalism? This is not easy to answer. He often mentions capitalism, but seldom discusses it. He has two slightly longer accounts, but they are still very short.[157] What he seems to emphasize is that capitalism is a system where power is built on the possession of capital. This capital in turn comes from work and mainly from other people's work and hence the opposition between capital and work. Inevitably this leads to poverty for large groups in the rich countries themselves,[158] but especially to poverty in the Third World.

But capitalism alienates also the privileged classes. The bourgeois idolatry of vocation, work, achievement, success and property leads to a modern form of work righteousness. He follows C. B. McPherson and talks about it as a "possessive individualism" where social security is based on private property, instead of on community. Capitalism furthermore destroys community, because the riches that give security are built on the exploitation of the working class and competition with other members of their own class, resulting in continuous war with both the oppressed class and their own class.

Another deeply problematic characteristic of the capitalistic economy that he points to is its autonomy from ethics and politics. Earlier, economy was discussed in moral and political philosophy, but now economy is seen as an autonomous reality with its own laws. And in economics the human being is only perceived as producer and consumer, which means that the *homo economicus* is an abstraction. Life is much more, but this has no place in economic decision making. Yet,

---

[156]*MRF* 63-72.
[157]*CPS* 168-173 (191-195), *MRF* 68-72.
[158]*WJC* 65f (85).

Moltmann maintains that in reality the modern economy is not autonomous but is built on a special ethos. Its most basic characteristic is the will to power[159] and the consequence is growth as an overriding value. He contrasts this modern growth economy with earlier economies where the ideas of equilibrium and limits were central. Capitalism cannot exist without unlimited growth, expansion and conquest. But unlimited growth is impossible in a world of limited resources. This makes the capitalist system in the long run impossible. "If the idols of growth, expansion and exploitation remain a part of economics, then a global destruction can be seen ahead that will make all human economics alike impossible."[160] It should be added, that this stress on limits was not part of Moltmann's early criticisms of the capitalist system. In the 1960s he instead, in a Marxist way, pointed to the unequal development between technical possibilities and the constricting social, political and economic systems. "The existing political, social, and legal ways of organizing production and distribution of products are no longer capable of progressive and equitable exploitation of new technical possibilities." So, he continues, "the future as the fullness of possibilities comes into conflict with the constricting institutions of the present."[161]

b) The Exploitation of the Third World

The result of the existing economic world order is, according to Moltmann, not only an increasing gap between rich and poor countries, but also the actual creation and continuing increase of the poverty in the Third World. The reason is that the poor countries have paid and still pay the cost of the economic growth of the industrial countries. And the injustices in the world system are getting worse and worse.[162] Of course it is controversial to argue that the wealth of the rich countries is built mainly on exploitation of the rest of the world. He does not discuss and explain much how this happens. Earlier it was a question of direct colonialism and slavery. Nowadays the colonial system lives on in the structures of the world market system. To explain this he seems to accept the dependence theory, which

> demonstrates that the overall development of the world always benefits the centres and conurbations of power, while the poor are increasingly marginalized. As a result of the division of work in the world economy, mono-cultures are being forcibly created in those

---

[159]"Capitalism is the unlimited, permanent intensification of power and thus also the unceasing struggle for dominion. The aggression, which it releases, to be able to build its world, must—if one follows the aggression-agony-thesis—have its source in a bottomless agony, which it presupposes and spreads." (*MRF* 71f.)

[160]*CPS* 172 (195).

[161]*RRF* 130 and 131. See further *RRF* 130-132.

[162]This is a theme that goes through most of Moltmann's writings. See e.g. *RRF* 130, *UZ* 50-52, *EH* 180f (204f), *CG* 330 (306f), *CPS* 175 (197), *PTPE* 11, 15f, and *WJC* 64-66 (83-85).

countries for the world market, and as a result of this the indigenous subsistence-economies are being destroyed.[163]

c) The Ecological Crisis

Another clear sign that Western civilization is basically flawed is for Moltmann the ecological crisis. This was not, as we have already noted, part of his writings in the 1960s, which were characterized by a strong faith in technological progress, but has become increasingly important from the early seventies and is now together with peace his most common political theme.[164] The ecological crisis also makes it clear that the problem is not only capitalism, but industrialism and the scientific-technological civilization itself. But behind this civilization stands the same societal value system as behind capitalism: the will to power. Contrasting modern civilizations with earlier ones based on equilibrium, he writes: "It is only modern civilizations which, for the first time, have set their sights on development, expansion and conquest. The acquisition of power, the increase of power, and the securing of power: these together with 'the pursuit of happiness', may be termed the values that actually prevail in modern civilizations."[165] The scientific method itself is formed by these values: the goal of natural science is power over nature, which also determines its methodological principles.

d) The Socialist Vision

What then is Moltmann's counter vision? He tells us first that biblically everything is ultimately the property of God. Therefore an autonomous economics is impossible. This will inevitably lead to a break with the driving powers of modern economy. "They will choose the path that leads away from the ruthless satisfaction of demands, to community; away from the struggle for existence, to peace in existence; away from the will to supremacy, to solidarity with others and with nature."[166] Most importantly, social justice must have priority over economic growth. Internationally this will mean renunciation of further growth for the rich nations for the sake of economic development in the poor nations. He calls this socialism—socialism in human relations and in relation to nature.[167] Again he does not say anything about what a non-growth economy would be like and how to achieve it. Neither does he discuss how the introduction of a non-growth economy in the First World would lead to economic growth in the Third World.

---

[163]*ThT* 20 (28). Cf. *RRF* 130, *EH* 180 (205).
[164]*GiC* 23-29 (36-43), *CJF* 4f , 13-15, 51-55 (14f, 25-28, 70-75), *WJC* 67f (87).
[165]*GiC* 26 (40).
[166]*CPS* 174 (196).
[167]*CPS* 173-176 (195-198). In another context he defends his version of socialism—which he calls personal socialism or social personalism—on the basis of his social doctrine of the Trinity. This, he maintains, eliminates the antitheses between personalism and socialism. See *TKG* 199f (216f).

In another context he describes socialism as "economic co-determination and control of economic power by the producers." And further: "If and in so far as socialism in this sense means the satisfaction of material need and social justice in a material democracy, socialism is the symbol for the liberation of men from the vicious circle of poverty."[168] It is noteworthy that he describes "socialism" as a symbol[169] for liberation from poverty and for social justice. It seems to indicate that he considers socialism to be more a moral ideal or vision than as a concrete form of economic and political organization of society. The neo-Marxism to which Moltmann has related tends likewise to be more a critique of ideology than a socio-economic theory.[170] We have noted that the early Moltmann sometimes talked in terms of the forces of production outgrowing the organization of production, which creates a revolutionary situation.[171] Nowadays Moltmann makes changes in the basic value structures primary.[172] If the early Moltmann related his hope to the possibilities the technological revolution of the industrial world created, the later Moltmann (usually) thinks more in terms of the moral necessity of limits and preservation, and of creating a society of equilibrium. The primary need is thus a moral revolution. If so read, he has travelled a long way from his early Marxist socialism to this moral socialism. He has, however, never consistently worked out the relations between these two types of socialism nor the relations between either type of socialism and his later "green" thoughts.

He concludes one of his longer and harsher disputes with capitalism by saying that "the so-called actually existing socialism provides no alternative, because its ethos of achievement and its will to power are not different."[173] This has become even more evident in connection with the ecological crisis, which shows that the basic problem is in the industrial system itself and behind that in the basic value system that upholds and reinforces the scientific-technological civilization in which both capitalism and socialism are participators.[174] He thinks Marx's failure to distinguish clearly between capitalism and industrialism was a basic source of the disappointments in the developments of the socialist societies. The dehumanization that is a result of the industrial system, and even less so the destruction of

---

[168]*CG* 132 (309).

[169]For his use of the concept of "symbol" in this context, see *CG* 337 (314).

[170]Bubner, *Modern German Philosophy*, 173. Moltmann can express himself very harshly against Marxism as a scientific theory of society. As such it is "a betrayal of the original dialectic of the historical process of communication between man and nature discovered by Marx" and therefore "an enemy of both history and of man" (*HP* 211 [279]).

[171]So e.g. in *RRF* 130-132.

[172]*GIC* 23-32 (36-47). I will discuss this further in chapter 15.

[173]*MRF* 72.

[174]*GIC* 28, 40-45 (42, 54-59), *WJC* 67f (87). On the enormous extent of the ecological destruction in the former socialist countries, see e.g. Hedlund, *Östeuropas kris*. In 1985 Moltmann thought that in terms pollution of the environment the two systems were neutral (*GIC* 28 [42]). In this he was wrong.

nature, are not eliminated through the removal of capitalist property relationships.[175]

More generally he thinks that the Marxist account of alienation is so general and so romantic that it becomes practically unusable, even if it is theoretically attractive. The counter picture becomes the total human being which lives in complete harmony with itself, with other people and with nature. This, Moltmann concludes, "would be infinite man", the "elimination . . . of human infinitude."[176] And it is dangerous to build politics on such a basis. We have, however, seen that Moltmann's himself sometimes seems to come close to this view.

His most common criticism, though, was the lack of democracy in the existing socialist states.[177] He said that the Eastern European states appear like "Prussian military socialism or feudal bureaucratic socialism".[178] Economic and political democracy are dependent on each other. Neither socialism without democracy nor democracy without socialism is possible. Especially in the Western democracies it is unimaginable that people would be ready to give up the sort of democratic rights they already have attained.[179] And he is critical of the common Leftist description of parliamentary democracy as just formal democracy.[180]

He therefore celebrated the revolutions of Eastern Europe in 1989. He does not see these as the end of socialism, only as the end of the politically, ideologically and economically centralized socialism, included the system of planned economy. In its place he puts his hope in a decentralized federal democracy giving a large place to personal initiatives. How this system should be economically organized, he does not say, but he continues his critique of capitalism in the name of the victims of the free market. Interestingly enough he now finds a foundation to this critique in the Roman Catholic encyclical tradition.[181]

So the sort of socialism he actually envisions is a completely new world order built on a new set of basic values that can help to build a world society that is at peace with nature and is characterized by the satisfaction of material needs and social justice. If this is to be made possible, he thinks that it is indispensable with a democratic world government.[182] All sorts of particular interests must be subordinated to the interests of the whole world. In other contexts he argues for the

---

[175]*Man*, 54 (82f).

[176]*Man*, 55 (84). See further *Man*, 47-59 (73-89). Another longer discussion of Marxism is found in *UZ* 26-44.

[177]*CG* 332f, 335 (309f, 312f), "Latin American", 61f, *OHD* 174 (*IGMEB* 73), *HIG* 66f.

[178]"Latin American", 61.

[179]He seems to think that under special circumstances a transitional Leftist dictatorship for the sake of building democratic socialism may be defensible. He seems able to imagine such circumstances only in the Third World, not in Western democracies. See ibid., 62.

[180]*Man*, 101f (147f).

[181]"Die Christenheit und das Neue Europa", 86f.

[182]Explicitly so in *EH* 174f (197f). We find the same idea in e.g. *CJF* 21f (36), where he writes (on p. 22) concerning the threat of nuclear annihilation that "the survival of humankind is conceivable only if the nations organize themselves into a collective subject of action for survival." (I have made a change in the translation, as it wrongly has "object" instead of "subject".) See also *WJC* 66 (86).

necessity of real participatory democracy on all levels and in all areas of societal life. Each individual must have equal part in political and economic responsibility. To this decentralization of power, he has lately added the need for a much larger independence for regions and local communities—a sort of federalism.[183] This is what Moltmann would consider a concrete—i. e. a practically feasible—utopia.[184]

e) Political Theology as Social Criticism

In the following comments I will not at any length discuss his analysis of the modern world, nor his proposals, though there is much to be said at that level. I will instead concentrate on the basic character of his analysis and proposals, and the function it has in theology and Christian practice.

The starting point for Moltmann is the actual conflict between capitalism and socialism. We saw earlier how he described socialism as the next step beyond liberal capitalism in the universal history of freedom. It is the political form of the hope of a society in which poverty is overcome and individual self-realization can be fulfilled in communal solidarity. In this light, the current capitalist society, characterized by poverty for the many, class war and competition, egoism and lack of solidarity, and the exploitation of nature, is found wanting and on par with racism and sexism.

His description of the two alternatives, capitalism and socialism, really pre-empts theological reflection.[185] For Moltmann it is so obvious on what side the church should stand in the political struggle that the theological reflection is more or less superfluous and therefore tends to become thin and superficial.[186] Further-more, because of the abstract and general character of his theological analysis, he becomes wholly dependent on the terms of analysis given in the social critique he supports.

These terms of analysis are in a general sense Marxist/socialist. He does not develop any theory on the relation between theology and political, social and economic theory. He uses what he needs for the moment in a rather eclectic way, although presupposing a general socialist perspective. The same is true for his vi-

---

[183]*CG* 332f (309f), *DHRG* 40, *CJF* 9f, 14, 101 (20f, 26, 127f), "Has Modern Society any Future?", 59 (37), "Christenheit", 86, *SL* 251f (264f). He writes: "If the project of human history is to survive, civilization must be decentralized." (*CJF* 101 [128].)

[184]Following Bloch, he describes concrete (in contrast to abstract) utopias as "dealing with objectively real possibilities". See *Man*, 41-45 (65-70). The quotation is from p. 42 (66). Cf. Kolakowski's critical discussion of Bloch's concept of "concrete utopia" in *Main Currents of Marxism*, vol. 3, 431-436.

[185]His discussion of the issue of the exploitation of nature has the same character.

[186]For what a more substantial Moltmannian theological critique of the political economy might look like, see Meeks, *God the Economist*. Although both theologically and politically going in the same direction as Moltmann, he is less confident than him concerning the question about the relation between capitalism and socialism. He seems to want to go beyond both, though it is difficult to know the relation between his theological critique and concrete policy. On the decisive influence of Moltmann on the work of Meeks, see Meeks, "Political Theology and Political Economy", esp. pp. 446f.

sion of the future society and the way to this society.[187] His extensive theological critique and construction have more the function of mediating Christianity and socialism, of criticizing Christian theology that supports economic and political domination, and of positively constructing a liberating theology, than of actually formulating a theological critique of modern society or reflecting on alternatives.

Moltmann's discussions of political questions are sweeping, and black and white. The stress is on commitment to the struggle for social justice and liberation, not on nuanced discussions of policy alternatives. In answer to this it might be said that he writes as a theologian, not as an economist. This might have been an adequate answer if Moltmann did not make the sort of far reaching claims he does. He clearly defines what Christians can and cannot support, and does not give much space for being critical of his general direction.[188]

Though heavily influenced by Marxism and though his social analysis has a sort of general Marxist form,[189] he is also sharply critical of Marxism and actual existing socialism. He says that Marx' failure to rightly distinguish between industrialism and capitalism, his romantic anthropology and the utopian vision this implies, his criticism of parliamentary democracy, and his idea of a centrally planned economy have had disastrous consequences. He further argues that so-

---

[187]Moltmann and Metz were for a long time often criticized by Latin American liberation theologians for not more systematically including social science (which usually meant Marxism) and (because of a faulty eschatological account) for not strongly enough committing themselves to socialism. See the different criticisms in Alves, *A Theology of Human Hope*, 55-68, Gutierrez, *A Theology of Liberation*, 217f, Miguez Bonino, *Doing Theology in a Revolutionary Situation*, 80, 144-150, and Segundo, "Capitalism Versus Socialism", 245-249. Moltmann's long answer is found in "Latin American". He finds the criticism unfounded, and has difficulties seeing any substantive development beyond European political theology in Latin American theology. In this judgement he is supported by Dorrien, *Reconstructing the Common Good*, 88 and Schillebeeckx, *Christ*, 761f. Moltmann's article is interesting, because it is an (in his corpus rare) example of critical reflection directed towards positions close to his own. It is also interesting to see that he in his early writings discussed with academic sociology and tried to reflect on the relations between theology and sociology. Soon, however, the ideological self-understandings of the new social movements and their uses of social theory (for Moltmann for a long time especially Marxism) became the primary dialogue partners and he did therefore not systematically continue the direct dialogue with sociology. See for his early discussions of sociology *HP* 101-154 (149-173, 212-231). These texts, originally published 1960 and 1961, also mirror his belief, common in the beginning of the 1960s, that ideology was about to disappear. See *HP* 138 (220). For a general discussion of the relation between theology and social theory in Moltmann, see Boone, "The Concept of Political Majesty in the Thought of Reinhold Niebuhr and Jürgen Moltmann", 202-205, 209-222.

[188]In an interview from 1984 he even proposes that the churches "proclaim the *status confessionis* in respect to the unjust world economic system" (*GHH* 22 [37f]), just as churches have done in respect to apartheid and nuclear deterrence. This would mean that support for the economic system would be equivalent with denying Christ and being outside salvation. Cf. *Bekennende Kirche wagen* and "Bekennende Kirche werden."

[189]In a lecture from 1966 (published 1970) he said: "Marxism is the first and in many respects still most convincing formulation of the direction of this progress of history in the conditions of the early industrial alienation of human beings: a) through its Promethean pathos for the humanization of nature, history and society, b) through its dialectical energy of revolutionizing social evils, political oppression and economic slavery, c) through its mediation of hope for the human kingdom of humankind with the real possibilities of the industrial world." (*UZ* 28.)

cialism is just one variant of the scientific-technological civilization with its will to power. Together these criticisms seem to add up to a rather devastating criticism of socialism, including many of the socialist revolutionary movements he has supported through the years. Yet he has seldom used this type of critique to ask critical questions about these movements and theories, either in the West or the Third World.[190] If, as Moltmann (together with most observers today) seems to think, socialism as actually practised have been a failure on all levels—political, social, economic and cultural—and if they have created oppression, poverty and ecological exploitation on a scale never known before,[191] hard critical questions ought to be asked in the name of the poor and oppressed. One might therefore expect a higher degree of cautiousness about claims of revolutionary changes. If the cause of these failures is not just the lack of democracy, but has to do with the economic system and socialist theory as such, as Moltmann seems to believe, then it is not enough to say that he supports a different sort of socialism. He ought at least to indicate the sort of institutional arrangements he supports and why there are good reasons to believe that these changes will not end up in the same failures as earlier attempts.[192]

---

[190]He later criticized the radical movements of the 1960s for being elitist. Even if the necessity of a revolution was there and possible alternatives were present, there was no real subject for the revolution. The "revolutionary theories found no basis in the people and therefore remained without a subject." ("Latin American", 61.) The important point for us is that he wrote this 1976, not in the 1960s. At that time he was an ardent advocate of revolution. (See e.g. *UZ* 27 and *RRF* 130-132.) His theology did not provide the critical tools that would have helped him to a more critical reflection.

[191]For general discussions, see e.g. Eberstadt, *The Poverty of Communism,* Ellul, *Changer de révolution,* and Hedlund, *Östeuropas kris.* Particularly the first decades after the revolutions, with their plans of totally reshaping the societies, have been extremely ruthless. I do not just think about the oppression against opposition, but the direct results of the economic policy. The collectivization in Soviet 1929-1934 (see Heller and Nekrich, *Utopia in Power,* 232-244) and the "Great Leap" 1958-1959 in China (see Godement, "La tournamente du vent communiste (1955-1965)", 42-55) directly caused starvation catastrophes of gigantic proportions. No one knows the exact numbers of people who died in the famine in China during the years after the "Great Leap". Godement writes (p. 51): "The Great Leap resulted in between 15 and 30 millions dead, and a total demographic deficit of more than 50 million people." Salisbury reports Chinese estimations from 30 to 46 millions (*The New Emperors,* 166)! Cf. the population statistics in Bianco, "Croissance démographique et politique antinataliste", 125. (One can compare the 55 millions dead in the World War II.) For a very interesting analysis of socialist inspired politics in Africa, see Hydén, *No Shortcuts to Progress.*

[192]For reflections on such issues, see e.g. Nove, *The Economics of Feasible Socialism,* Elster and Moene (eds.), *Alternatives to Capitalism,* and Bowles and Gintis, *Democracy and Capitalism.* Especially important is Nove, as his book includes both a full scale and devastating critique of existing socialist theory and practice and reflections on what an economically feasible socialism could be. That is, he explains very well why the Communist systems have worked so badly. He also thinks that Marxist economic theory, because of its specific assumptions, simply ignored the problems any socialist economy has to deal with, and therefore is wholly irrelevant and misleading. Because Marx described the socialist society simply through contrasting it with capitalism, it is an obstacle, not a help, for reflecting on a possible socialism. See ibid., 58-60. Bowles and Gintis are interesting in relation to Moltmann, because they, like him, try to combine the radical democratic tradition, liberal social theory and Marxism. They also, like him, make a radicalization of the language of rights central for their politics. Their criticism of the neo-Marxist tradition (p. 215 n. 21) is also relevant concerning Moltmann. I have here

One question the description of his vision of the future society especially raises is how to relate decentralization and participatory democracy with the necessity of a strong centralized world government. He seems to avoid the problem through relating his proposals to different issues. The former becomes important when he discusses ecology and national economy, the latter when he discusses peace and (one would think, although he does not clearly say so) international economy.

Similar hard questions have to be asked about the world system. The so-called dependency theory he uses has little support anywhere today. Many, including socialists, would argue that its explanatory power is slight and that following its proposals of lesser integration in the world economy would worsen the plight of the poor in the Third World.[193] Even if Moltmann is right, he has to give some reasons for his views. As it now is, he writes as if his views were self-evident for all people of good will. But even if one agrees that there is much injustice in the current world order, neither the explanation of this nor the proposals for change follow automatically. Although we are not dealing with it here, the same type of questions could also be directed towards his discussion of ecology.

One root of these problems in Moltmann's political theology (which he shares with other forms of political theology and liberation theology) is his theology of freedom and power. We have seen the importance of the oppression/liberation model in Moltmann's theology. In his early thought he developed it in terms of a dialectic of the negation of the negative, and that model of thought still characterizes Moltmann's theology, irrespective of the terminology he uses. Although he has later in more positive terms formulated his vision of the future society, this is still so imprecise and abstract that it does not make much difference for his general approach. We cannot, he said, directly know the future of freedom, because we have not experienced it. But when we hope for and seek this future freedom, we experience, in the contrast to this hope, the suffering and oppression of the present situation. He expresses it theoretically in the following way: "the positive, the new, the future which we seek can be historically circumscribed in the pro-

---

mentioned books that positively, but critically, discuss the possibility of socialism. There are of course also many works that go further in criticism. To take just two interesting examples of analysis and challenge that a socialism of Moltmann's type has to meet, see Dunn, *The Politics of Socialism*, and Berger, *The Capitalist Revolution*.

[193] Even inside liberation theology this theory has been criticized. Gutierrez writes following in the introduction to the 1988 edition of *A Theology of Liberation* (p. xxiv): "It is clear . . . that the theory of dependence, which was so extensively used in the early years of our encounter with the Latin American world, is now an inadequate tool, because it does not take sufficient account of the internal dynamics of each country or of the vast dimensions of the world of the poor." So also Moll, "Liberating Liberation Theology". For further criticism, see e.g. Nove, *Feasible Socialism*, 183-195, Berger, *The Capitalist Revolution*, 115-139, and Hydén, *No Shortcuts to Progress*, 203-207. For an overview of theories and strategies of development, see de Vylder, "Utvecklingsteorier och utvecklingsstrategier igår och idag".

cess of the negation of the negative."[194] The future is thus not defined beforehand, but grows out of the negation of the negative present. Put differently, it grows out of the struggle against the causes of the suffering and oppression.[195] A complementary idea is that the negative is understood as "the definite estrangements of man from his true essence and his future."[196] Through the struggle against the forces of oppression, humankind can take steps toward the realization of its humanity.

This approach might help him to identify oppression and, as a consequence, liberation, but it does not help him concretize what is possible, discuss potential consequences of different policy alternatives or discriminate between various desirable options. Because liberation, the realization of the true humanity, comes from the negation of the negative, that is from successful struggle against and the removal of repressions, the concentration is put on the struggle against the negative, while little place is given to reflection on different possibilities, and even less to critical questions to movements and policies claiming to be progressive and liberating. Furthermore, because this freedom history is described as a universal history leading the whole humanity in the direction of the kingdom of freedom, the political forces tend to be reduced to two basic groups: the reactionaries and the progressives, or as Moltmann says "the 'Party of Anxiety' and the 'Party of Hope'"; and the political choice is consequently reduced to the issue "on which side we stand".[197] Yet, the dialectic of this history, where each liberating step also includes its own distortions, makes it necessary to go on criticizing and transcending every new actualization of freedom. That is a reason why Moltmann strongly supports revolutionary movements, but is much more cautious to postrevolutionary situations.[198] However, it seems important to be able to ask critical questions beforehand.

He defends this view theologically in terms of the eschatological dialectic of cross and resurrection.[199] Generally, his eschatology functions as a critical theory that delegitimizes the present for the sake of the hoped for just, free and peaceful future. Because God has opened the future, everything can be changed.[200] Against this background any dissatisfaction with the present society easily translates into uncritical affirmation of utopian political programs promising a new society. In other words, his eschatological theology underwrites total criticism of what is and does not lead us to see limits of what is socially and politically possible and does

---

[194]*RRF* 30.

[195]*RRF* 29-31.

[196]*RRF* 38.

[197]Both citations are from *RRF* 132.

[198]I suppose this is a reason for the frustration of liberation theologians mentioned above. Although the difference is not too big (they also talk about the necessity of a *different* socialism), the latter have tended to be somewhat less critical of actually existing socialism.

[199]*RRF* 33-35.

[200]Cf. now *CJF* 95 (121f), where he sees the religious roots of industrial society in the religions of hope; that is, the Abrahamic religions.

not give us criteria for testing revolutionary politics.[201] John Dunn has character-ized "the central flaw" in the revolutionary socialist tradition "as lying in a persis-tent readiness to allow intensity of moral distaste for a present state of affairs to excuse a weakening in the determination to understand (or even to reflect seri-ously upon) the causal properties of the future social order with which it is hoped to supplant the present."[202] I think that this is also a good characterization of Moltmann's political theology, including his discussions on the future ecological society.

The situation does not become better when to this is added a strong belief in the human power to determine or open the future for its true realization, because such beliefs do not nourish humble attitudes toward the possibilities of politics and reflections on the limits of the possible. The historical socialist experience is an example. The final aim of socialism was to create a society without political power. The primary means to this end, however, has been a strict centralizing of the state power. Behind this was a strong version of the modern assumption about the humankind's power over history. As Moltmann himself says,[203] socialism has its origin in a Promethean faith in the ability of the human race to form history and create a world of abundance. The utopian character of the hoped-for socialist society, including its economic system, becomes, as we earlier noted, meaningful only against the background of this faith in humankind's possibilities to use tech-nology for creating the unlimited affluence that would make all conflicts super-fluous and therefore create complete freedom. This is today usually ignored. Without this the socialist vision is much more difficult to sustain.[204] Related to this utopian hope is the fact that the question of power has been one of the weak-est parts of socialist political and social thinking.[205] This lack of adequate analysis of power, violence, the nation-state and surveillance has had well-known and dreadful results. In spite of his sometimes evident scepticism, and his criticism of actually existing socialism, it is this sort of utopian consciousness Moltmann mostly has been underwriting.

Helmut Harder once wrote that for Moltmann "the determining norm for Christian ethics is not the way of Jesus Christ but rather a messianic vision which

---

[201]This is one of the most common criticisms of the theology of hope. See e.g. Boone, "Political Maje-sty", 241-254, 273-286, Cornelison, *The Christian Realism of Reinhold Niebuhr and the Political Theology of Jürgen Moltmann in Dialogue*, 192f, Gunnemann, *Revolution*, 220-222, and Gustafson, *Theology and Ethics*, 43-48.

[202]*Western Political Theory in the Face of the Future*, 97.

[203]*TH* 24 (19f), *UZ* 28, *Man*, 47-59 (73-89), *HIG* 56 (*MRF* 82), *CJF* 92f (118f).

[204]Nove, *Feasible Socialism*, 15-20, 58-60.

[205]Giddens writes that "the lack of a satisfactory treatment of power, including the use of violence by individuals, collectivities and states, runs like a red thread . . . through the writings of Marx and of Marxists subsequently. The importance of this points both backwards and forwards: backwards in the direction of the inadequacies of historical materialism as an account of societal development; forwards to the anticipation of socialism. . . . But this is the century of Stalin and the Gulag. No socialist can afford to ignore this very basic 'absence' in Marxist thought." (*A Contemporary Critique of Historical Materialism*, 244.) Similarly Ellul in *The Betrayal of the West*, 131f.

is impassioned by a zeal for the messianic kingdom of God rather than by the way of Jesus. And we are left to our own ethical decisions when it comes to choosing the means of achieving the end."[206] In his answer to Harder, Moltmann agreed that he had "not yet sufficiently integrated the meaning of the earthly Jesus as the messianic prophet".[207] We later find him doing just this in *The Way of Jesus Christ*, which means going from the ethically formal and abstract eschatology of his early theology to a specifically Christian ethics. However, he has yet to work out the implications of this shift for the church's relation to the world's politics of power. We have to remember that political theology emerged as a positive Christian response towards the modern utopian and rationalist political project, and many of the assumptions behind this project still function as more or less taken for granted background beliefs in Moltmann's theology, although in increasing tension with later developments of his theology.

If political theology is going to be able to transcend the current crisis of Marxism and the forms of socialism that have dominated in the twentieth century, it seems to me that it has to undergo a radical self-critique and extensive revisions. One might, for example, ask what would be the consequence if Moltmann consistently thought through the idea of socialism as a morally based alternative, rather than seeing it as the "necessary" consequence of the inner contradictions of capitalism and/or the result of the dialectical history of freedom. His positive reception of the Catholic social teaching implies the same moral approach. The oppression/liberation model as developed by Moltmann seems to suspend the need for ethical analysis beyond making "spontaneous" freedom the norm, which is one explanation for the absence of ethical analysis in his early theology. What should be expected of the church, he then said, was not "verbose sermons on morality" or claims to "transcendent wisdom",[208] but commitment to the oppressed and thereby commitment to the (autonomous) revolutionary way to the future universal freedom. Structurally it is not so different from the liberal defence of the promises of the autonomous capitalist economy.

His later ethical approach could be interpreted as neither expecting the emergence of socialism as a spontaneous result of liberation from oppression, nor as seeing the positive formation of socialism and its content as spontaneous or self-evident. What the hoped-for socialism is, has then to be explicated through substantial and contingent interpretations of freedom, peace and justice, because what freedom, peace and justice are is not self-evident. In addition, the ethical reflection cannot be restricted to the question on which side one should be, but must also deal with how to work for a new society.[209]

---

[206]"Response to Moltmann's 'Political Theology and Political Hermeneutics'", 32f.
[207]"A Response to the Responses", 52.
[208]*RRF* 140f.
[209]Cf. his comment about the need of an ethics for political theology in *PTPE* 9f, which he both in this book and in later ones has tried to meet. Two recent attempts to formulate a liberationist ethics is

In this respect his theologically based critique of power could be significant, if he more consistently turned it towards a critique of the Promethean assumptions of the modern (including socialist) rationalist political project. His decentralist and federalist ideas and to that correlated ideas of working for change from below might be seen in this light, and could contribute to a critique of the grand centralized revolutionary projects.[210]

Finally, the correlate to his claim of a specific Christian ethics is his understanding of the church as a contrast society. It represents a public alternative. It is thus, it seems, more than a moment in a universal freedom history. If he worked through the implications of this understanding of the church, a different approach to the world politics could be the result. In his early theology the decisive change had to come through a world revolution, through taking control over the processes of social change. Attempts to small scale changes could then be interpreted as hindering the revolution and as anyhow impossible. The idea of the church as a contrast society implies that it is both possible and desirable to form alternative practices without first changing the whole world system.

Kammer, *Ethics and Liberation* and Miguez Bonino, *Towards a Christian Political Ethics*. None of them is especially helpful for drawing out the consequences of Moltmann's later development.
[210]Concerning the Third World, cf. his comment that "church aid and development agencies have shown themselves especially effective, because the churches are already in place and share the life of the people." ("Christenheit", 87.)

Chapter 7

War, Revolution and Non-Violence

In this chapter I will take up a particular issue at more depth. The purpose is to clarify with a specific case example how Moltmann's political theology works and therefore at the same time illustrate the problems with the project of political theology we have repeatedly encountered. Because Moltmann (and also Hauerwas) has discussed the set of issues that war, revolution and non-violence raises more extensively than any other moral and political question and because he has done that throughout his writing career, it is an especially appropriate area for analysis and discussion.

The following quotation is a good starting point for understanding Moltmann's theological reflections about violence.

> I had to sacrifice five years of my life in meaningless service to arms and a criminal war, without my consent—indeed against my will. When I returned home after the war and could finally get out of my uniform and throw it away, I swore two things to myself. First, war never again (*nie wieder Krieg*), never again to bear arms; better to be shot than to have to shoot again! And secondly, never to tolerate a dictator again, never again to allow a tyrant to come to power, and in extremity to be prepared to *murder a tyrant*, just as German officers on July 20, 1944, had attempted to kill Hitler, and as Dietrich Bonhoeffer had also wanted.[1]

As this quotation demonstrates Moltmann's position concerning violence is deeply formed by his experiences during the Nazi period and the World War II. The double attitude he expresses—never again to bear arms in war and never accept a tyrant, even if that will mean that the tyrant must be killed—goes through all his writings until today. Changed context has, however, led to significant shifts in emphasis and in how he motivates his positions.

1. The Right to Resistance and Revolution

We shall in this and the following two sections begin with a few texts from the 1960s and the beginning of the 1970s. At this time the revolutionary movements of the Third World and the increasing revolutionary consciousness in the West were at the centre of Moltmann's interest. He was fully convinced that even the industrial world now was at the brink of radical revolutionary changes. That made it necessary for the churches to find its own place and identity in these radical changes.[2] This raised also the question of the use of violence.

---

[1]"Commentary on 'to Bear Arms'", 48.
[2]*RRF* xvi, 130, 132.

He takes up this question in a lecture in 1968 at The World Student Christian Federation.[3] His answer is unmistakable. "The problem of violence and nonviolence is an illusionary problem. There is only the question of the justified and unjustified use of force and the question of whether the means are proportionate to the ends."[4] It is, Moltmann argues, usually the powerful that most strongly speak in favour of nonviolence, while it is people without any other means of power that defend the use of revolutionary violence. And the only way to social change is through the taking of the political power. To the question of the criterion for when and how much violence can be used, he answers that any use of violence must be justified in terms of the human aims of the revolution. "The criterion for action is the measure of possible transformation. We need skilled judgement to bring together the opponent, the means, and the end in such a creative tension that the hoped-for effect will come to fruition."[5]

Yet, he sees the risk, even if he is basically optimistic, that the use of violence may destroy the aims of the revolution and make the post-revolutionary situation critical. The means have therefore to be carefully evaluated and the use of violence must be as limited as possible. He thinks that Christians in the revolutionary movements here can make a significant contribution in counteracting the tendencies to legalism, self-righteousness and black-mailing of the enemy that are present in every revolution. Though deeply committed they need not take themselves and their cause too seriously because of their Christian hope. Instead they may be able to dance and laugh in the midst of the revolution.[6]

It is evident that Moltmann has developed the right to murder tyrants into the right to revolution against a tyrannical social and political system. Furthermore, his definition of a tyrannical system was so broad that it included the Western Europe of the 1960s. He found the situation here such that a revolution was necessary. His most important reason for this was the West's exploitation of the Third World. In a radio speech of 1969[7] he said that the world faces a hunger catastrophe that will kill many more than all previous wars together, although it is known how to defeat hunger. Only anachronistic economic, political and cultural institutions both of the Third and the Industrial World block the necessary changes. The question of violence then becomes a question of time. Is there time for peaceful but slower means of change when people starve? He is nevertheless at this time doubtful about the value of revolutionary violence in highly industrial

---

[3]"God in Revolution" in *RRF* 129-147.
[4]*RRF* 143.
[5]*RRF* 143.
[6]"Christians will be strange birds in the revolution. Perhaps they are something like the fools of revolution. They are deeply committed to it and laugh about it *because* they are the forerunners of a yet greater revolution, in which God will abolish even greater oppositions than any human revolution can envision." (*RRF* 146.) He elaborates this theme in *TJ*.
[7]"Gewalt und Liebe" in *UZ* 45-55.

societies and points to other possible means as worker and consumer strikes and consciousness raising.

He concludes his speech with some reflections on the relation between love and violence. As love is directed towards the freedom and happiness of the other, and is dependent on political and social structures, it cannot be limited to the personal level. Consequently, revolutionary violence may be a necessary work of love, which means that the wish to preserve one's innocence (by not using violence) must be subordinated to the love for the other. Following Bonhoeffer, he contends that love must be understood as transmoral and as ready to carry the guilt of revolutionary violence for the sake of the other. But it follows also, he says here, that one cannot speak of a just revolution.

In the article "Racism and the Right to Resist"[8] from 1971 he discusses the right and the duty to resist in relation to the situation in South Africa. As racism is closely connected to the economic and political structures the change of attitudes must go together with a redistribution of power. But as the whites have refused any sharing of their power and have met the nonviolent struggle of ANC with violence, the ANC now sees use of violence as necessary. Moltmann concurs and writes: "Nonviolence in the solution of social and political problems is only possible in areas where power is more or less absent and these are rare on this earth. However, the principle of nonviolence can provide desirable criteria on which to base political action involving the use of force."[9]

In this article we also find one of the few treatments of the nonviolence of Jesus in his early writings. As this theme will have a very prominent role in Moltmann's later theology, his discussion here is of great interest. At this time Moltmann describes the nonviolence of Jesus as an eschatological hope.

> The concept of nonviolence belongs to the eschatological remembrance of faith in Jesus. The hoped for kingdom of God is the kingdom of brotherhood without violence and in this sense "anarchy" (Berdyaev). This explains the Christian's deep horror of violence already in the present. He does not want to be master of any slaves or the slave of any master and will do his best to create and extend spheres of communication that are free of domination. He will also give preference to nonviolent methods in political disputes. In the domain of politics, however, it is a question of power, distribution of power, and participation in the exercise of power.[10]

The eschatological hope of a world without violence becomes in the face of the necessary use of violence a transcendental ideal that always questions the necessity of every use of violence and challenges to use as little violence as possible.

But he maintains that the starting point can never be a principle of nonviolence, but only the hope of a world free of violence. Every use of violence must

---

[8]*EH* 131-146 (145-163). The rest of this section refers to this article.
[9]*EH* 136 (152).
[10]*EH* 136f (152).

be justified in view of this hope. Consequently, the basic issue is not the one of violence or nonviolence, but the criteria that determine the use of power. He differentiates between justified violence, which he calls power, and naked unjustified violence. The former is ultimately justified in terms of the human rights.

This makes resistance against oppression legitimate. He finds support in the Christian tradition of justified resistance to tyranny, which has its origin in the old Germanic legal tradition and was taken up into the natural law tradition of the medieval church.[11] Also in Protestant theology the right and the duty of resistance have been defended.[12] His conclusion is that "[i]n the case of obvious and proven tyranny, there is theological backing, based on Christianity, for the right and obligation to resist." The obvious question then becomes how to determine when this condition is reached. As an answer he mentions three criteria. "Tyranny is proven where there is: (1) continuous violation of law; (2) violation of the constitution; and (3) violation of human rights which is itself legalized by laws and constitutions."[13] Active resistance in such situations must be described as legitimate use of justified political power. On the other hand, the resistance must also justify itself through restoring of legality or of the constitution, or through the making of a new just constitution. In other words, legitimate resistance, violence included if necessary, is nothing else than the legitimate exercise of state power. Consequently, if one does not have any problem with associating with normal government activity there cannot be any problem of conscience here.

What Moltmann appears to be doing here is espousing a sort of theory of the just revolution. He does not follow the classical criteria for just war, but his account has a similar intention.[14] Especially notable is the absence of the criteria for proper conduct in war (*jus in bello*), for example the distinction between citizens and soldiers, which are difficult to keep in a guerrilla war. There are obviously many difficulties with his account. But I will only make one note. The criteria for legitimate resistance he uses might seem to refer to a limited cleaning up of a corrupted political system (restoring legality). Yet he uses it for legitimating a revolutionary ideology that has considerably more far-reaching aims, namely rebuilding the whole societal system from top to bottom. In the 1960s Moltmann used these criteria for defending the legitimacy of a revolution that would remake the whole world system. With the wide-ranging account of rights he maintains, it is actually difficult to find any legitimate present government and political system. It would have been helpful if he had given examples of illegitimate revolutions, but his interest has always been to defend the legitimacy of existing ones, with the result that he has never dealt with this issue. In this light one might say that even if his reasoning has the character of some form of just revolution, it tends in prac-

---

[11]Otherwise, he is critical of the natural law tradition. See *Man*, 71-75 (106-111).

[12]He mentions Luther, Barth and Eivind Berggrav.

[13]Both citations are from *EH* 140 (157).

[14]Cf. *OHD* 119f (*PTPE* 184f) for Moltmann's account of the criteria of just war and a passing remark on "a doctrine of the 'just liberation struggle'".

tice to come closer to Crusade-thinking, where war is justified in terms of its good cause and its basis in the claimed will of "the people".[15]

2. The Impossibility of War in a Nuclear Age

The question of violence is raised not only by the issue of revolution, but also by the question of international war. Moltmann is convinced that modern and especially nuclear weapons have made war an impossibility. The threat against the survival of humanity makes all conflicts relative and a common responsibility for the future of our one world necessary.[16] He strongly maintains that every particular interest, national or other, must be subordinated to the search for a common future, as we survive together or not at all.[17] Because of the power and scope of the modern military, economic and technical means of power he thinks the system of sovereign national states has become obsolete. The only solution he sees is a world government.[18] The way towards that is long, but he contends that transitional forms are already possible. He does not say what this could mean concretely, but the idea is to make national foreign politics into world domestic politics. All decisions must be judged in view of how they promote the world peace and the interests of the world community as a whole.

What then is the contribution of the church to this process? It describes itself as a testimony to and anticipator of the coming world-wide shalom. Consequently it has to manifest this peace in its own existence. Moltmann gives three examples.[19] It must first give up all claims to absoluteness and instead live in open dialogue and cooperation with people of other faiths.[20] It must further demonstrate its own unity. Finally, it must free itself from national, racial and class dependencies. The ecumenical work is thus of great importance for the world peace.

He points also to the more direct political work of the churches. As peace is not just absence of open violence, but goes together with justice, the church has to promote social justice and work against racism and the destruction of nature to help establish peace.[21]

---

[15]Cf. Yoder, *Christian Attitudes to War, Peace, and Revolution*, 513f.

[16]For this section, see *EH* 172-185 (194-212). "Versöhnung und Befreiung" contains basically the same material.

[17]He writes that "the future can no longer be the continuation of our national, cultural, and religious pasts; it must be something new. On this threshold of history, the alternative is simple: united we stand, divided we fall." (*EH* 173f [196].) So also *UZ* 48.

[18]*EH* 174 (197).

[19]*EH* 176-180 (200-204).

[20]"Every claim to absoluteness is an obstacle to this peace. Every refusal to cooperate is a threat to peace." (*EH* 177 [200].)

[21]"Christians, in my opinion, have the task of working with the oppressed to reduce anxiety, hysteria, and violence, of achieving first economic and then political freedom, and finally of creating a climate of trust in the vicious circle of mistrust and fear. The large churches, in my opinion, have the task of paving the way for political peace agreements. They can often succeed at this because they are *nongo-*

To summarize, Moltmann claims that instead of seeing the issue of violence or nonviolence as central, one should talk about the just or unjust use of power in the struggle for justice and freedom for the poor and oppressed. "It is not the idealistic principle of nonviolence that is consonant with the gospel, but the responsible action of love."[22] Revolutionary violence becomes thus an often necessary possibility. On the other hand, modern weapons have made international war impossible, as it would be the same as the destruction of the human race.

3. The Theology of the Cross and Political Violence

The most notable fact in Moltmann's early treatment of the issue of violence is the absence of any relation, not only to the preaching and history of Jesus (which anyhow played a marginal role in Moltmann's early theology), but to his theology of the cross. Even in *The Crucified God* the life, death and resurrection of Jesus function primarily as a formal, but not material, principle in his social ethics.[23] As George Hunsinger writes, the cross "formally indicates those with whom the Church must identify, but not the material content of that identification. The cross functions on a noetic level by leading to a critical theory, but not on a somatic level by leading to a critical practice."[24] Put differently, the theology of the cross tells us that Christians should identify with the poor and oppressed, but says nothing about *how* this should be done. Although he wants to show the relevance of the theology of the cross to all areas of life, the cross is hardly mentioned in relation to the use of violence. Hunsinger describes the consequences of a theology of the cross, as he sees it, in the following way. "The very love that finds the suffering of others intolerable is the love that accepts suffering rather than inflicting it, in the hope that suffering will become redemptive."[25] But instead of taking this road, Moltmann takes up the natural law tradition to justify his view of violence and argues generally in terms of effectiveness. How he is able to re-

---

vernmental international organizations. And political settlements need such preparations." (*EH* 182 [207].)

[22]*EH* 143 (160).

[23]We find in *CG* the same stance towards the problem of violence as in the articles mentioned above. He writes for instance the following about the attitude of Jesus (pp. 140 [134]): "The main theme of his polemic was not the practical question whether resistance should be non-violent or violent, but the fundamental question of the righteousness which was demanded by God." One might, however, ask if his account of the difference between Jesus and the Zealots in *CG* 136-145 (129-138) should not have had more consequences for his understanding of revolution.

[24]"The Crucified God and the Political Theology of Violence", 393f. Earl Shaw similarly writes that "the logic of his theology of the crucified God would seem to endorse a nonviolent strategy. If the cross is the paradigm for the moral act, the violence of justice is overcome on the cross by suffering love, as one who accepts rather than inflicts suffering." ("Beyond Political Theology", 56.)

[25]"Crucified God", 393.

concile this with his theology in general is difficult to see, as many of his commentators have recognized.[26]

4. A New Moment—The Sermon on the Mount

During the 1980s the questions of war, violence and nonviolence again become central in the writings of Moltmann.[27] The primary context is, however, no longer the issue of revolution, but instead the growing peace movement, which is very strong especially in the German churches, and its opposition against the nuclear arms race.[28] His double basic stance is intact, but we find one large and significant shift. His general opposition to war and his argument for a unilateral nuclear disarmament is now based on the life of Jesus and especially on the Sermon on the Mount. Together with this is made a positive, if qualified, evaluation of the Radical Reformation tradition in the so-called peace churches with their explicit pacifism.[29]

In a text from 1982[30] he discusses different alternative positions in relation to nuclear armament. He discards the doctrine of "the just nuclear war" because we cannot be assured that a nuclear war can be kept limited.[31] He is also critical of the doctrine of "just nuclear armament" for several reasons. First, if only deterrence, but no use is allowed, the deterrence does not work. Second, this strategy leads, in practice, to further armament to keep the balance. Third, the result is that the society becomes directed towards armament and that the resources needed for the Third World increasingly are used for weapons.[32] The most reasonable alternative then, so Moltmann argues together with the peace movement, is (even unilateral) disarmament and a "life without armaments".[33]

That makes the peace practice of the Anabaptists relevant for modern Christians. But he differentiates between a personal and a political decision to live without armaments. The Anabaptists prioritized faithful discipleship over the responsibility for the world and did not advocate their own peace practice as a

---

[26]In addition to Hunsinger and Shaw (n. 24 above), see the discussions of Young, *Creator, Creation and Faith* 162f, Gunnemann, *The Moral Meaning of Revolution*, 210f, Finger, "Response to 'Following Christ in an Age of Nuclear War'", Dorrien, *Reconstructing the Common Good*, 89-96, and Wiebe, "Revolution as an Issue in Theology".

[27]The most significant material from this period is found in *OHD* 113-131 (*PTPE* 180-191), *WJC* 127-136 (148-157), and *CJF* 16-50 (29-69). The latter text is a compilation of several earlier articles. These three texts contain much overlapping material.

[28]See Wasmuth, "Die Entstehung und Entwicklung der Friedensbewegungen der achtziger Jahre".

[29]See e.g. *PTPE* 10, *OHD* 113-131 (*PTPE* 180-191), "A Response to the Responses", *WJC* 116-136 (136-157), "Vorwort" to Yoder, *Die Politik Jesu*, and "Vorwort" to Arnold, *Salz und Licht*.

[30]"Discipleship of Christ in an Age of Nuclear War" in *OHD* 113-131 (*PTPE* 180-191). This text, which is published in several only slightly different forms, was issued for the first time 1982. See also *PPL* 47-63 (61-79).

[31]*OHD* 120f (*PTPE* 185).

[32]"Religion and Politics in Germany and in German-American Relations", 105.

[33]*OHD* 123 (*PTPE* 187), see further *OHD* 121-123 (186f).

model for non-Christians to follow, i. e. they did not make it into a political demand. The other possibility, which Moltmann prefers, implies that "Christians
and non-Christians who want to end the arms race can deny themselves and seek
to make their readiness to live without armaments a political injunction for all
human beings of their nation."[34] They then do not only take a personal risk, but
also a social and political one, because others may suffer the possible consequences. The question becomes: is this a risk we can take?

Moltmann's answer to this question is significant, as it clearly reveals his new
way of justifying his position. He writes: "Up to now both sides of this issue have
made their calculations as if neither Christ nor the Sermon on the Mount had existed. With Christ, however, there comes into the calculation a factor which sus-
pends the whole process and changes everything: It is the *reality of God* which
actually supports us all."[35] The Christian, in other words, interprets reality in a
different, and arguably truer, way than the so-called "realist politicians". But Jesus does not only help people interpret the world differently; through him a new
reality and therefore new possibilities emerge.[36] This perspective is further elaborated in later writings. He says that in Jesus the *shalom* of God has begun, and is
now experienced in the Spirit.[37] He can also describe Jesus as the Wisdom mes-
siah that brings creation the peace which inaugurates a new situation.[38] Finally, he
elaborates this Christian peace witness as an ecclesiological ethics. It is not an
ethics for individuals as such, but for the Christian church. It is made possible in
the context of the convictions, hopes and practices of the church, as a community
of disciples of Jesus Christ. As such it offers the world "a real and livable alternative to the systems existing in the world",[39] and in this sense makes universal
claims.[40]

With this conviction Moltmann develops Jesus' message of loving one's
enemies as a message relevant for international politics.[41] If one meets the enemy
with love, the vicious circle of violence and retribution is broken, which means
that something new is created, a new situation arises. The love for one's enemy is
thus not a passive attitude, but "the creative and intelligent overcoming of en-

---

[34]*OHD* 124 (*PTPE* 188).

[35]*OHD* 125 (*PTPE* 189).

[36]*WJC* 99 (119).

[37]In the following I complement the mentioned text with other material from the 1980s. One development is his use of the Old Testament concept *shalom* as background and context for the preaching of the
kingdom of God of Jesus. See "Peace the Fruit of Justice", 111-114 (76-78) and *CJF* 38f (56).

[38]*WJC* 127-129 (148-150).

[39]*WJC* 135 (156).

[40]*WJC* 116-136 (136-157).

[41]In this Moltmann takes part in the intensive debate on the Sermon on the Mount in the early 1980s in
Germany. The year 1981 was proclaimed as "the year of the Sermon on the Mount" and the Sermon
was widely discussed in the public debate, and provoked even to public expositions from the President
and the Prime Minister. See "Einführung" to *Nachfolge und Bergpredigt*, 9 and "Religion and Politics
in Germany", 107. Cf. *Ohne Rüstung leben*.

mity."[42] Moltmann sees it as a creative love that corresponds to the love of God that sustains the world.[43] The first issue, in this perspective, is not my own security, but how I can take responsibility for my enemy, and how the enmity can be removed. Moltmann asks, for instance, "What helps the Russian people to gain peace more, our further armament or our disarmament?"[44] The creative love that is based on the freedom God gives liberates us from anxiety and helps us love our enemies, and therefore leads to a new way of understanding national security. This perspective makes the idea of living without armaments possible for Moltmann.[45]

In the light of this understanding and against the background of the mass destruction character of modern weapons the conclusion for Moltmann is plain: all war (as well as the bare possession of nuclear weapons) must be described as sin. "The modern military means of mass destruction have changed war so much that the real nature of war is revealed now before everyone's eyes. We have reached the point, therefore, where we must go back and say that all war is irresponsible, is sin, and there can be no justification of it."[46]

What then is, in Moltmann's perspective, the political role and task of the church in this context?[47] Peace is an essential part of the church's existence, something it demonstrates in its own life and in its political service. It must for example try to overcome the friend-foe thinking that lies behind and distorts the security policy. It can further help people see the real dangers, for instance the connections between East-West, North-South conflicts and the ecological crisis, and become a voice for the oppressed peoples. To be a peace church, furthermore, it has to become a free church, free from the state.[48]

5. Love for One's Enemies and Revolutionary Violence

Since Moltmann's pacifism concerning international war is now motivated by the Sermon on the Mount, one might have expected that this should have led him to a general pacifism. His theological and ethical argumentation seems clearly to

---

[42]*CJF* 43 (61).

[43]"God's perfection is his limitless ability for suffering, his almightiness is his patient suffering for and with all things. God's uniqueness is his inexhaustible creative power of love." (*OHD* 127 [*PTPE* 190].)

[44]*OHD* 127 (*PTPE* 190). The German version has "zur Freiheit im Frieden".

[45]"To the degree that the risk of the vulnerable, defenseless but creative life becomes conscious to us, the more free and patient we become. Only the unknown and the repressed make us really anxious. In this sense I am personally willing and ready to live without armaments." (*OHD* 127 [*PTPE* 190; the last sentence is not in the German version].)

[46]*OHD* 129 (there is no exact correspondence in the German version in *PTPE*).

[47]The tenor of his direct political suggestions in the early 1980s is exemplified in following quotation. "We therefore demand immediate and binding arms talks among the great powers. We advocate a European disarmament in the area of conventional arms and the agreed-upon building up of cooperation in Europe and Asia, in particular in the area of economic justice." (*OHD* 129f [*PTPE* 191].)

[48]*OHD* 130f (*PTPE* 191f). See also *CJF* 47-50 (66-69).

point in that direction and there is not much in his main texts on peace from this period that contradicts that impression. He also explicitly affirms pacifism, without qualification,[49] and points to how non-violence can overcome oppressive and violent systems, as seen in recent bloodless revolutions against military dictatorships and against the Communist regimes in Eastern Europe, even if it also can lead to martyrdom. Suffering can however, he says, have liberating power.[50]

Yet this pacifism is not a general pacifism, although it often sounds like that. It seems to concern only international warfare, but not violence on "lower" levels, especially revolutionary violence. In the only longer text from the 1980s that primarily deals with the latter issue. he has no doubts about the legitimacy for a Nicaraguan Pentecostal pastor to personally take part in the Sandinists' violent struggle against the Somoza regime.[51] His arguments, based on some form of natural law theory and the decisive "will of the people",[52] are exactly the same as in the 1960s and 1970s. The sort of arguments he uses when discussing the peace issue is totally absent here. He also expresses sympathy with the German conscientious objectors that were ready to use weapons in defence of the Sandinista revolution against the Contras.[53]

He mentions this apparent contradiction several times, but has no solution to it. In an answer to the criticisms from some Mennonite theologians he writes that he cannot avoid this double position, although it embarrasses him. He does not defend the doctrine of just war, but "there are situations in life which one must resist and become guilty, in order to save human lives."[54] In another discussion he says that peace theology and liberation theology reflect different contexts and experiences, and that a way of integrating these two theologies with each other has yet to be found.[55] Generally, however, he has now greater respect and hope for

---

[49]"I believe that so-called pacifism is no longer an illusion or utopia. Pacifism is the only *realism* of life left to us in this apocalyptic situation of threatened world annihilation. Pacifists are the realists of life, not merely voices of utopia." (*OHD* 131. This paragraph is not in the German version.) Cf. also his statement that "[w]ithout the Sermon on the Mount there is neither any humane government, nor any humane revolt against injustice and exploitation." (*PPL* 59 [74].)

[50]*CJF* 44f (62-64), "Die Christenheit und das Neue Europa", "Theologie im demokratischen Aufbruch Europas", 30f.

[51]"Commentary" (1983). He writes also that "I admire and support the liberation movements in the Third World, which oppose racist and military dictators" (p. 49) and he would personally be prepared take part in such a resistance himself. Cf. also *OHD* 119f (*PTPE* 184f).

[52]"Commentary'", 52. How to determine the will of the people is not a question that he discusses.

[53]He mentions this dilemma in "Einführung" to *Friedenstheologie – Befreiungstheologie* 10f, without explicitly giving his own opinion. He did that however in an interview with the author in Tübingen 1988.

[54]For the criticism, see *Dialogue Sequel to Jürgen Moltmann's 'Following Jesus Christ in the World Today'*. His answer to this question is found on pp. 60f (the citation is from p. 61).

[55]"Einführung" to *Friedenstheologie – Befreiungstheologie*. In "Einführung" to *Annahme und Widerstand* Moltmann says that following Jesus means learning to combine the right to resistance with the love for one's enemies, which, he says, is only possible through non-violent means (p. 11). Here he sounds like a pacifist. The context for this discussion is the struggle of the European peace movement,

non-violence in the political struggle and shows much more sympathy for pacifist understandings than in his earlier writings.

It is not easy to make sense of his general position, more than as a strongly contextualized theology, where arguments are developed according to contextual needs. To defend nuclear, but not general pacifism, is arguably both a sensible and consistent position. But when he not only says that nuclear armaments have made wars between nuclear powers impossible (and seemingly all international warfare), but also tries to defend this position with the help of the Sermon on the Mount, his argument breaks down. For why is the logic of the Sermon on the Mount valid in relations between nations, but not in the same way in conflicts on lower levels? His answer seems to be that modern mass destruction weapons have made international warfare impossible and love for one's enemies a necessity. In other words, it is not the inherent logic of the Sermon on the Mount that is convincing, but the fact that there is no alternative in international politics.[56] If it is true that the reality of God and God's action in Jesus Christ "changes everything", why is this not also true for national conflicts and revolutionary violence? Which historical fact represents the most basic change, Jesus Christ or nuclear weapons?[57] Moltmann tends to give the impression that the latter is the most decisive, and that his use of the Sermon on the Mount is primarily strategic. Both the peace movement and the revolutionary movements are on the "good side" and whatever arguments that support these not easily reconcilable positions are legitimate.

His position would be more persuasive if he had confined himself to say simply that nuclear weapons have made wars between nuclear powers impossible, and not tried to support this position through Christian pacifist arguments, which imply much more. The problem with that, however, is that these theological arguments, however strategic they may seem, in fact grow out of the centre of his theology. Indeed they seem intrinsic to his position, as several commentators noted concerning his early theology, and much more so in his later theology. So a more positive interpretation might be that the peace movement of the 1980s created a fertile context for following up the logic of his own theology. We have seen that his whole theology, and not just his reflections on this question, have moved in the same direction. However, he has not yet consistently elaborated (or hesitated to do so) the consequences of this theological development.

---

not revolutionary wars. In *PPL* 28-37 (39-50), in a sermon developing his peace theology, he talks about sometimes unavoidable violence, but expresses also strong doubts on what it can accomplish.

[56]"I would claim that no politics of survival in the nuclear age can go against the Sermon on the Mount. One can 'do politics' with the Sermon on the Mount, but only the politics of peace." (*CJF* 44 [62].)

[57]"Since Hiroshima 'the bomb' has changed the world at a stroke, but Christian theology is only slowly becoming aware of the new situation in which all its traditional concepts for dealing with power, terror and war have become antiquated." (*CJF* 19 [33].) But one cannot say that the pacifist understanding he uses is new.

His hesitancy has to do partly with the seeming impossibility of wholly giving up the means of violence, and partly with his commitment to revolutionary movements. I think it would be (at least before 1989) almost impossible for him to take a more critical view of the sort of revolutionary thinking that was constitutive of the original conception of political theology and that played an important role in socialist politics and liberation theology. I think it is significant that when he discusses the revolution in Nicaragua, the type of theological analysis we otherwise find during the 1980s is absent and that he instead falls back into the type of reasoning he developed in the 1960s. It might be possible to argue, also from his new perspective, that in some extreme situations violence can seem unavoidable, but we have seen that concerning revolutionary violence he is ready to go far beyond that. It is furthermore difficult to see the qualitative difference between usually justified revolutionary civil wars and never(?) justified international wars. He wants Germany to live without armaments. What if Germany becomes occupied, is it then legitimate to violently struggle against the occupying power? Was a military defence against the Contras legitimate but not against, say, Honduras? If one starts asking this sort of questions, the position of Moltmann (and many others) seems genuinely confusing. It is difficult to find a consistent position beyond just war and pacifism, and Moltmann's attempt is no more persuasive than any other.

Finally, the basic tension in his theology is also clear in regard to another problem that we have earlier encountered. As in his early writings on war and peace he continues to argue that nuclear weapons have made it necessary for the nations to see themselves as part of one common history and organize themselves accordingly. All particular interests and all politics must be subordinated to the general interest of a just peace and a common ethics for humanity that makes survival and life together into the absolute values that relativizes all other interests and values. To attain this Moltmann turns to the categorical imperative as the absolute principle.[58] Here we again encounter the tensions and difficulties that appeared in our discussion of his understanding of human rights. Is it so obvious that this Kantianism is easily compatible with his *solus Christus* ethics?

One can summarize by saying that his discussions of violence and peace show how he tries to mediate a commitment to social movements with a commitment to Christianity. His political and theological analysis and recommendations presuppose the existence of two opposing sides—the progressive side of justice, freedom and peace against the reactionary side of injustice, oppression and war. The therapeutic aspect of his theology is directed to this situation, the apologetic to the progressive side, and the critical to the "other" side. As the situations are described, commitment to the movements that claim to struggle for justice, freedom and peace comes first. Their descriptions and recommendations of action are made the starting point for the reflection. Moltmann's aim in relation to these

---

[58]*CJF* 46f (64-66).

movements and Christians active in them is then to show the support Christianity gives. The critical aspect towards one's own side is almost non-existent. Although he, for example, gives some criteria for judging the justice of revolutionary violence, he does not give concrete examples of a critical use of these criteria. Furthermore, though the theological arguments he uses for defending revolutionary movements and the peace movement respectively seem to exclude each other, he is so convinced of the righteousness of the movements they support, that he can continue with both types of arguments without letting them seriously modify each other. In this sense his theology is not critical, but motivating and supportive.

A complementary and more positive reading of his developing theology of peace is as an example of the general development of his theology in the direction of an ecclesial discipleship ethics. The peace movement here became an occasion for him to develop what was already implicit in his theology. He is, however, hesitant to draw the full consequences of this shift, or does not see them, because of his strongly apologetic approach to theology and his commitments to the social movements.

Chapter 8

Political Theology and the New Social Movements

We have seen that Moltmann consistently during his theological career has related himself to what has been called the new social movements, such as the New Left, the feminist movement, the ecology movement and the peace movement. He has tried to show the relevance of Christianity for first the Christians (but also, of course, for others) in these movements and tried to motivate church people to participate in them.[1] As he himself states: "Political Theology is no purely academic theology, but a theology which draws upon the expectations and experiences of initiative groups and movements of the people in Europe."[2] In this chapter I will argue that the close affiliation of political theology to the new social movements is one reason for the severe substantial tensions we have found inherent in the theology of Moltmann and that he fails to see this because he misunderstands the social and political nature of these movements and their place in modern society. So in this chapter I am only doing what political theology has said we should do: for the purpose of christianizing theology ask questions about its social and political contexts and functions. These could be different than the stated.

1. Self-Description

If we ask how he theologically articulates the close relationship between his political theology and these social movements, we do not find any systematically worked-out answer beyond general discussions of theology's relation to social groups and conflicts. Moreover, in light of the claims of political theology one might expect some sustained reflection about these movements in terms of social and political theory. But we do not find this, with some interesting exceptions. Moltmann seldom discusses these movements from some distance, but sees them, political reality, and the church from an internal and basically uncritical perspective. His more distanced and critical reflections usually come during the times of decline of specific movements.

A first model he uses, we have seen, is the claim that Christian practice and theology should have a twofold *Sitz im Leben*: the church of Christ and the poor and oppressed. Political theology participates in the struggle of the poor and op-

---

[1] Political theology "wants to motivate Christians to participate in those movements and to put their own visions into action." ("Political Theology and Liberation Theology", 212.)

[2] Ibid., 213.

pressed for freedom and justice, and is justified by this participation. It attempts to be the voice of the victims.[3]

Another model of thought we have met is the description of history as an ongoing process of liberation led by the Spirit of God. The church has to read history to see the direction of the historical work of the Spirit so that it can side with it. There are two basic social and political forces: the progressive and the reactionary. The church must become part of the progressive movements of modernity to avoid become a marginal sect.

The second model can be related to the first through saying that God is working for the liberation of the poor and oppressed and for suppressed nature. The progress of history and the liberation of the poor are thus identified. We have seen that this can be understood as a generalization or vulgarization of Marxist class theory in which the poor and oppressed in general take the place of the universal class of the proletariat.

Negatively this is expressed in his emphatic denial that political theology is a theology of the middle class. For Moltmann the middle class is a central part of the oppressive system. He thus says that political theology "is not a 'progressive,' liberal theology for the already entrenched middle class, but rather a political and socio-critical theology of the victims of and in the First World" and that it "has always had a critical stance over and against the self-justification of the dominant groups in society."[4]

In the absence of a Marxist, or some similar, identification of the victims with the progressive forces, there is a tension between being a theology of the progressive forces and being a theology of the victims. The quote above demonstrates this ambiguity as also liberal middle class theology can be called "progressive". In this chapter I will suggest that the former self-understanding, being a theology of the progressive forces, has more support than the latter. The social base of political theology is one of the most privileged, affluent, secure and powerful sectors of the social elite in the Western society. It can still be a voice *for* the oppressed, but it is not directly a voice *of* the oppressed.[5] The perspective is not directly the one of the oppressed, but the one of a social elite. There are theologians, whose theological and political concerns are similar to Moltmann's, who admit this. Sallie McFague, for example, writes that her sort of "liberation theology" is "written out of and to the social context of those who control the re-

---

[3]"Political Theology has always attempted to speak for the victims of violence, to become the public voice of those without voice . . . It concerns itself primarily . . . with the liberation of victims and a critique of the victimizer." (Ibid., 214.)

[4]Ibid., 205 and 214. Cf. 213, where he contrasts political theology to the liberal middle class theology of Pannenberg and Küng.

[5]However, Moltmann sometimes defines the victims so widely (the workers, "the (potential) victims of a nuclear war" and women) that the great majority of the population in the Western world is included. See ibid., 214.

sources—the money and power—necessary to liberate life. It is admittedly, therefore, middle-class and mainstream."[6]

The argument for this conclusion is simple: the primary base, both inside and outside the church, for the new social movements comes from the highly educated and rapidly growing upper middle class of especially the post-war generations. My argument is not reductionistic. I do not argue that Moltmann's theology is socially derived and explainable only in terms of class. Rather, it is Moltmann's own explicit project to mediate, for both apologetic and therapeutic reasons, Christian theology and the new social movements. The only addition my analysis gives to Moltmann's own description of political theology is a sociological portrayal of the social groups that constitute the base for these movements inside and outside the church. Yet, that addition is not inconsequential.

For much of political theology to say that a theology is allied with middle class segments is to automatically disqualify it. This is the reason for Moltmann's vigorous denial that political theology has close relations to the middle class. That is not a position I defend in this chapter. I do not argue that political theology and the social movements are wrong because of their relations to specific social elites. But I think this ought to lead to a more critical and discriminating relationship between political theology and these movements. He cannot defend various positions only by claiming that they represent the perspective or the interests of the oppressed, but he has to argue these positions theologically, sociologically, and politically on their own merits.

2. The Western Church in the Post-War Period

In this and the next part of the chapter I will use various sociological studies and especially three groups of material. I will first describe certain developments in German and American Christianity in the postwar period. There are several reasons for the inclusion of American studies already in this chapter. First, I am not only interested in the immediate context for Moltmann, but also in the wider development, reception and prospects of political theology in the Western world. Second, Germany and America represent two cases of general tendencies and developments that are present in this region.[7] Studies of the North American situation can therefore illuminate also the German development and vice versa. Third, this gives a background for the discussion in Part Three of this book. The second group of material I will use discusses social change in terms of culture and class and their interrelation. The third group contains studies directly dealing with the new social movements. In the latter part of this chapter, after this long sociologi-

---

[6]*Models of God*, xiv.
[7]This is not to deny the many important differences that also exist, because of differing historical, cultural, and church circumstances. The church landscape in Germany, with two large established churches, is, for instance, markedly different from the denominational system in United States.

cal detour, we will return to the theology of Moltmann and see how these studies can throw light on the nature and inherent tensions of political theology.

a) Germany

Moltmann describes the 1960s as a time of "growing crisis of relevance and credibility" after a period in the postwar years in which "the churches and theology fed undisturbed upon their own resources". Among students and especially students of theology a growing feeling arose "that a church which simply continued its previous form and ideology was in process of losing contact with the scientific, social and political reality of the world around it, and in many respects had already lost it."[8] For many, the result was that they left theology and the church for sociology and psychology or political and social work. Inside the church this crisis, moreover, created an increasingly sharp polarization between traditional and progressive groups. This is the context for the emergence of political theology.

One recent synthesis of studies done about this period in German Christianity is Karl Gabriel's *Christentum zwischen Tradition und Postmoderne.*[9] He describes how in the latter part of the 1960s and in the beginning of the 1970s a major change took place in German society and church life, just as in the Western world in general. Gabriel's thesis is that the modernization process took a long step forward during this time. What happened here was the break down of the former social gestalt of modern Christianity in what he calls the bourgeois-modern industrial society. This society was characterised by a symbiotic relation between an industrial sector and an agricultural-craft sector. In the latter sector the method of production and the way of life were traditional, and the bourgeois-modern industrial society was therefore also an amalgam of tradition and modernity. This created the social space for a similar amalgam of tradition and modernity in the church. In addition, the church was the major institution that came out least compromised from the Nazi period and met large general public confidence after the war. The 1950s and the early 1960s were therefore a very strong period for the German churches and they had also forceful political influence.[10]

However, between 1968-1973 the number of regular churchgoers was reduced with a third. The church also lost much of its moral and political influence. A

---

[8]All the citations in this paragraph come from *CG* 8 (12f).

[9]Gabriel uses material on and discusses both Catholicism and Protestantism, although the detailed case studies concern the Catholic church. For my limited purposes this is no large problem. See further Hach, *Gesellschaft und Religion in der Bundesrepublik Deutschland*, Kaufmann, Kerber and Zulehner, *Ethos und Religion bei Führungskräften*, Kerber (ed.), *Säkularisierung und Wertewandel*, and Köcher, "Religiös in einer säkularisierten Welt". Inglehart, *Culture Shift in Advanced Industrial Society*, esp. 177-211, and Pettersson, *Bakom dubbla lås* include also much material on European and German religious life.

[10]On this, see Spotts, *The Churches and Politics in Germany*. Spotts writes (p. x): "The immediate postwar years saw the German churches at their most influential since the Reformation."

value change took place inside and outside the church. One reason the change came so quickly during this time was, according to Gabriel, the disappearance of the traditional agricultural-craft sector. The whole population was integrated into one wage-labour market. The result was that the social space for the mix of tradition and modernity that characterized the form of Christianity in bourgeois-modern industrial society disappeared. The whole society was detraditionalized. Other important factors (besides the further development of structural and functional differentiation of society that generally characterizes modernity) were the development of the welfare state, the increasing social mobility, the education explosion, and media and mass culture.

For the Christian religion, one result was a radicalization of religious individualism. Already the bourgeois-modern form of Christianity, especially Protestantism, was individualized and subjectivized, now this was much more accentuated. This goes together with a strong deinstitutionalization of religion. The church as institution loses in legitimacy. It is the educational and media elites that especially criticize the Christian tradition and institutions. Part of the theological community and the educated elites inside the church strongly support this criticism. Christianity also increasingly loses its religious monopoly, which contributes to the pluralist tendency. The religious-churchly socialization of beliefs and norms reaches only a minority. The social control mechanisms of the church also lose their power. All this contributes to a strong individualization and pluralization of Christianity.

This in its turn leads to an increasing polarization and differentiation inside the churches. In the Catholic church Gabriel distinguishes five different sectors. The development in Protestantism is similar. 1) A fundamentalist sector that tries to restore classic Catholicism. 2) A sector of explicit and "institution-near" Christians, characterized both by active church practice and growing claims of autonomy concerning personal life. 3) The largest sector is characterized by a diffuse and undetermined catholicity. He talks about a sort of individualistic folk religion. 4) A sector that partly overlaps with the other consists of people working in various church organizations. 5) Finally, there is the movement-sector. Political theology represents this tendency, as does the Charismatic movement. He describes them as innovative reactions to the modernization process. They take up much in modernity and its value changes, relate this in a creative way to the Christian tradition, and create new community forms and expect a conscious and reflexive faith practised in daily life.

From this, Gabriel identifies three major tendencies in the contemporary churches. The first is the fundamentalist reaction, like the evangelical movement in America. The second is an alternative and base community form of Christianity. Gabriel thinks that the movement-sector, because of its innovative capacities, will have an important function in the future, but it will, like fundamentalism, never be more than a marginal phenomenon in modern society. Trying to reform the whole church according to this model would make the church into a small sect. The third tendency, which Gabriel thinks is the major and the only possible as a general strategy, is what he calls pluriform Christianity. The church should, in a non-authoritative way, serve the divers religious needs of people in these various sectors. He can therefore also talk about a critical conversion of the church towards the distanced and diffuse folk religiosity.

b) The United States

The development of Christianity in America has been rather similar. A comparable work to Gabriel's is Robert Wuthnow's *The Restructuring of American Religion*, although giving more historical detail and being theoretically more modest, with the result that the portrayal given is more complex than Gabriel's theoretically neat account.[11] Also for the American churches the 1950s was a time of progress, stability and relative unity, the 1960s a time of upheaval, partial decline and increased polarization, and the post-1973 period a time of consolidation and continuing polarization.

The most significant factor behind the upheaval in the 1960s is, according to Wuthnow, the explosion of higher education. This in its turn is correlated to a change in world economy. "From the laissez-faire, decentralized, firm-oriented capitalism of the nineteenth century, the U.S. economy has shifted increasingly toward a regulated, centralized, state-sponsored form of production in which technology and information become crucial to sustained economic growth."[12] One part of this is the massive increase in the social importance of state sponsored higher education. This has led to

> a growing sector of the occupational structure which depends heavily on highly specialized training and which works mainly with science, advanced technology, education, and information processing. Described in some of the literature as a 'new class,' this sector is not so much a distinct class as it is a differentiated class fraction whose values and interests differ sharply both from the less privileged and from less educated members of the social elite. . . . a kind of vertical cleavage has developed which cuts through many traditional communities and modes of social differentiation, including both gender differences and ethnicity.[13]

This situation has created an environment that has led to the increasingly sharp polarization between so-called liberals and conservatives in American politics and church life. This cleavage goes right through the different religious bodies and has become more important for self-identification than denominational differences. Although both sides have highly educated elites, the liberal side is more integrated in the knowledge sector than the conservative side is. Education has become a

---

[11] For other important works I have found useful, see Finke and Stark, *The Churching of America, 1776-1990*, Roof and McKinney, *American Mainline Religion*, Hunter's two books *American Evangelicalism* and *Evangelicalism*, and Wuthnow, *The Struggle for America's Soul*.
[12] Wuthnow, *Restructuring*, 320.
[13] Ibid., 316.

primary base for social stratification and cultural cleavage both outside and inside the churches.[14]

One trend was both defection and lower commitment to organized religion among the young and better educated. Another was that the college-educated parts of the churches together with parts of the also well-educated clergy became the base for a new social activism.[15] Here the civil rights movement and the Vietnam war were very important.

He also tells the story about the consolidation and growth of the evangelical community in the postwar period, a certain left-wing turn among parts of the younger evangelical elite in the 1960s, the upsurge of a new elite in the 1970s that became the base of the New Religious Right. This latter elite was not part of the evangelical establishment, was usually from the South, was lesser educated, had its roots primarily among Pentecostals and Baptists, and had its base in religious television and new megachurches.

To this he adds another factor. The Watergate Scandal, the Supreme Court decision 1973 about free abortion, and an emerging, widespread questioning about the strict border between private and public in the general culture, made morality a central issue in the public debate. Wuthnow thinks that this was important for opening the way to a new religious political activism based on morality. However, evangelicalism and the Religious Right are far from identical. The cleavage goes right through the evangelical movement and it is only a minority that identifies itself with the organizations of the Religious Right. Most are in the middle. Moreover, the Religious Right is even less identical with the broader conservative wing of American Christianity, but only a right wing part of it.

The result of this polarization is the existence of two versions of civil religion.[16] On one side there is the conservative version with the motto "One Nation Under God" who believes that America has been founded on Judaeo-Christian values and has a specific God-given calling in the world. Therefore it is important to defend and restore these religious values as the base for the American society. Against this the liberal version advocating "With Liberty and Justice for All" is more universalistic in its language, and talks more about human rights, international justice, the nuclear threat and peace, and ecology than about a specific Judaeo-Christian tradition, and wants to see the powerful America enlisted for these aims. The role of Christian faith is here basically motivating.

Wuthnow does not reduce this conflict to only a social and political conflict. Specific social, economic and political developments create the environment or the field for the internal dynamic of the development and various adaptations of the churches. It does not create them. James Davison Hunter, in his large work

---

[14]For an interesting discussion about why education has these effects, see his *The Struggle for America's Soul*, 142-157. He finds little support for the idea that it reflects an inherent conflict between science and religion or that higher education in itself has these effects.

[16]Wuthnow, *Restructuring*, 244-257.

Culture Wars, says that although it has political manifestations and social characteristics, "the conflict is prepolitical and it precedes class. What ultimately explains the realignment in America's public culture are *allegiances to different formulations and sources of moral authority*."[17] What Hunter calls the orthodox
commit themselves "to an external, definable, and transcendent source of authority."[18] This can take the form of revealed Scriptures and/or, also among secular-
ists on the orthodox side, of a natural law and high view of the given social order.
On the progressive side, authority is based especially on critical rational discourse
and on personal experience.[19] The outcome of this is that the two sides live and
talk within two different moral vocabularies, two "deeply rooted and fundamentally different understandings of being and purpose."[20] This explains the intermin-
able character of the debates. Hunter's conclusion is that today it is not Jesus, nor
Luther or Calvin, but the Enlightenment that represents the most important division. "The politically relevant world-historical event, in other words, is now the
secular Enlightenment of the eighteenth century and its philosophical aftermath."[21] It is, he continues, not a question of being wholly pro-modern or antimodern, but a matter of priority. Most people place themselves somewhere in
between. Hunter has also shown how much modernity, with its subjectivizing and
individualizing forces, strongly forms evangelicalism.[22] But he still thinks that the
relation to the Enlightenment and its aftermath is the crucial point of division. We
have seen that this is also Moltmann's understanding.

3. Cultural Change, "Class" Struggle and the New Social Movements

The cultural changes and struggles inside the church are also found in society
at large. That is not surprising when we remember that the majority of the population in Germany and United States also are church members. Class theories that
concentrate on the struggle for control over the forces of production, as Marxism
does, cannot explain most of the sorts of political, social and cultural conflicts
that are central for Moltmann. It is not a conflict between proletariat and bourgeoisie, and even less between poor and rich in general. Other descriptions have
to be found. I shall here take up two partly overlapping conceptualizations of
these developments that further throw light on the developments Gabriel and
Wuthnow describe and which they have also partly used, namely the idea of a
growing culture-shift from Materialist towards Postmaterialist values and the
"New Class" theory. Both theories have been widely used for understanding the

---

[17]*Culture Wars*, 118.
[18]Ibid., 120.
[19]Ibid., 120-127.
[20]Ibid., 131. "The alliances, rather, reflect the *institutionalization and politicization of two fundamentally different cultural systems*." (Ibid., 128.)
[21]Ibid., 132.
[22]See his books *American Evangelicalism* and *Evangelicalism*.

development of religion in the Western world as well as the new social movements. I have several serious reservations for these two theories, but they are helpful in highlighting certain important developments and in generating valuable empirical information.

a) The Postmaterialist Thesis

Ronald Inglehart argues that a general cultural shift is slowly occurring in the modern world related to the emergence of a post-industrial society.[23] "The values of Western publics have been shifting from an overwhelming emphasis on material well-being and physical security toward greater emphasis on the quality of life."[24] This has made self-realization, autonomy, and belonging more important than economic and physical security. An important reason for this change, according to Inglehart, is that the post-World War II generations have grown up in relative physical and economic security and therefore take peace, security and prosperity for granted. This has made the classically class-based conflicts less important, while cultural conflicts between Materialist and Postmaterialist interests have increased in importance. The latter group tends to have its background in families with higher socio-economic status, is younger, more well-educated, has more high status occupations and is politically more interested and easily mobilized than the population in general. They are still a minority, but a rapidly growing minority, especially among the elites. Inglehart even says that "by 1981 . . . Postmaterialist values were predominant among most of the elite groups in West Germany".[25]

It is in these groups the new social movements have their core constituency. "Though the pure Postmaterialist type constitutes only one-eighth of the public, they consistently furnish an absolute majority of the movements' activists."[26] Inglehart further claims that the old Left-Right polarization was basically a class-based conflict about economy, the new Postmaterialist-Materialist polarization concerns non-economic values. This strains and transforms the old Left-Right

---

[23]See esp. his two books *The Silent Revolution* and *Culture Shift in Advanced Industrial Society*, of which I have mainly been using the latter more recent book. A summary and discussion of much of the material around Inglehart's work and an application of Swedish material is found in Pettersson, *Bakom dubbla lås*. Cf. also idem, "Välfärd, värderingsförändringar och folkrörelseengagemang".

[24]*The Silent Revolution*, 3.

[25]*Culture Shift*, 323. That Inglehart has strong sympathies with Postmaterialist values forms his way of describing it. Other studies describe this development rather differently, although the substantial content is not so different. One example is an in-depth study of German elites, Kaufmann, Kerber and Zulehner, *Ethos und Religion*, which talks about the emergence of what it calls "opportunism" and the decline of both Judeo-Christian and Enlightenment-humanist views. This "opportunism" is characterized by a strong "I-centred" attitude, search for success, a materialist-hedonist attitude that highly values free time, material welfare and pleasure (pp. 281f). They explicitly contrast this to the Postmaterialist thesis, but the contrast becomes so strong only because of a very one-sided description of the Postmaterialist ethos (pp. 282f).

[26]*Culture Shift*, 380.

scale. The old Left was Materialist in Inglehart's sense and was positive to economic growth and technological progress. The new Left is ambivalent or negative
to both, and instead stresses issues like peace, the environment, women and gay
rights. Because the existing party system reflects the old divide, this creates severe tensions. Since the Left is identified with change, Postmaterialists tend to see
themselves as Left, but are often in conflict with the traditional Left. They have
become highly influential in some left wing (in America "liberal") parties, but if
these parties follow the Postmaterialist agenda too closely they risk losing their
traditional constituency and the general public, where the Postmaterialists are still
in minority. The emergence of new social movements is thus, Inglehart maintains,
one sign of the difficulty of introducing the New Politics of Postmaterialism into
the political system.[27]

This also, argues Inglehart, explains the decline of Marxism. When economic
issues are losing its prominence Marxism loses its explaining power. In the early
phase of the emergence of Postmaterialism, the student movement of the 1960s,
Marxism was still the primary language of protest and social change. As Inglehart
writes: "When Postmaterialism first emerged as a significant political force in the
1960s, its proponents tended to express themselves in Marxist slogans, which
were then the standard rhetoric of protest in Western Europe."[28] But already at
that time there were deep tensions for example around the issue of the role of the
state, where for many the concentration of power in the state became not a solution, but a problem. The role of Marxism has then drastically declined in the new
movements, just as the Communist parties have lost much of their support among
the young and the Postmaterialists.

b) The New Class Theory

This value change, which has moved the centre of political conflict into the
cultural sphere, has led several theorists to develop the so-called New Class theory.[29] Inglehart has explicitly connected the New Class with the rise of Postma-

---

[27]"Except in the very general sense that the Left (then as now) constitutes the side of the political spectrum that is seeking social change, the traditional and contemporary meanings of 'Left' are very different; the Old Left viewed both economic growth and technological progress as fundamentally good and
progressive; the New Left is suspicious of both. The Old Left has a working-class social base; the New
Left has a predominantly middle-class base." (Ibid., 375.)

[28]Ibid., 263.

[29]See e.g. Bourdieu, *Distinction*, Bruce-Briggs (ed.), *The New Class?*, Gouldner, *The Future of the
Intellectuals and the Rise of the New Class*, Hargrove, *The Emerging New Class,* and the recent Kellner and Heuberger (eds.), *Hidden Technocrats*. On the history of the theory, see Heuberger, "The New
Class". For its use in the sociology of religion, see, in addition to Hargrove, e.g. Berger, "American
Religion", idem, "The Class Struggle in American Religion", idem, "Different Gospels", idem, "Ethics
and the Present Class Struggle", Gay, *With Liberty and Justice for Whom?,* Hunter, *American Evangelicalism*, 102-119, idem, "The New Class and the Young Evangelicals", Roof and McKinney, *American Mainline Religion*, 115f, and Wuthnow, *The Struggle for America's Soul*, 60-62.

terialism.[30] The idea is that the major class conflict in a post-industrial society is not between proletariat and bourgeoisie, but between two middle classes, the old middle class consisting of the business community and its affiliates dealing with the production of material goods and the New Class consisting, to use a definition of Peter Berger, "of people whose occupations deal with the production and distribution of symbolic knowledge." He continues to say that "[t]hese are the people employed in the educational system, the communications media, the vast counselling and guidance networks, and the bureaucratic agencies planning for the putative nonmaterial needs of the society".[31] In the post-industrial society the number of people working in these sectors has grown dramatically, which has drastically changed the class-structure.[32]

This theory has been espoused both by Leftist and conservative theorists. For the former it has been a way reconstructing the Marxist class theory in a post-industrial setting, where this class can be seen as the carrier of the possibilities of a new society that formerly the working class had. Alain Touraine, for example, has seen in these groups the real possibility of opposition to technocracy and bureaucracy. This opposition will not come from the workers, who are too integrated in the industrial economy. Only the New Class has the resources and ability to oppose and participate directly in the centres of modern societies and has therefore the potential to take control over the processes of social change.[33]

Alvin Gouldner similarly points to the culture of the New Class as a culture of *critical* discourse. Such a discourse, primarily cultivated at the universities, tries to be universalistic and situation-free. This commitment to rational public discourse can lead to a commitment to good argument in all sorts of public concerns, which can temper the self-interest of the New Class, and make it a positive, even if flawed, force in modern society. He thus describes it as "Flawed Universal Class".[34]

---

[30]*Culture Shift*, 331f. "I suggest that the rise of Postmaterialism and its subsequent penetration of technocratic and professional elites has been a major factor behind the emergence of the new class, for this group is distinctive not only in its occupational and educational characteristics, but also in its values—and the ideology attributed to the new class reflects Postmaterialist values rather closely" (p. 332).

[31]Berger, *The Capitalist Revolution*, 66f.

[32]See e.g. Bell, *The Coming of Post-Industrial Society*, esp. 165-265, and Touraine, *La Société post-industrielle*, esp. 41-118, for two quite different accounts which both show this.

[33]Touraine, *La Société post-industrielle*, 41-118.

[34]*New Class*, 7. "The New Class is the most progressive force in modern society and is the center of whatever human emancipation is possible in the foreseeable future. It has no motives to curtail the forces of production and no wish to develop them solely in terms of their profitability. The New Class possesses the scientific knowledge and technical skills on which the future of modern forces of production depend. At the same time, members of the New Class also manifest an increasing sensitivity to the ecological 'side effects' or distant diseconomies of continuing development. The New Class, further, is a center of opposition to almost all forms of censorship, thus embodying a universal societal interest in a kind of rationality broader than that invested in technology." (Ibid., 83.) However, the New Class is also elitist and "bears the seeds of a new domination." (Ibid., 85.)

Peter Berger gives an example of a conservative description when he writes, that the New Class has, first, "an interest in having privilege based on educational credentials" in which they have an advantage, and, second, an interest "in the expansion of the welfare state, which, of course, is that part of government in which this class finds employment and subsidization."[35] Because of their stake in the expansion of the welfare state, they have a vested interest in the criticism of society which can legitimize demands for government interventions and are therefore politically drawn to the Left. Like the early bourgeoisie they rhetorically identify their own interests with the underprivileged and with the general welfare of the society.[36] Because of their power in the media, they have an obvious advantage in forming public opinion—or the image of public opinion, which is not the same thing.[37] Their interests in welfare and redistributive programs mean that this elite can form alliances with underprivileged groups. At the same time, they often come into conflict with the industrial working class, especially with the labour unions, which tend to have very different interests.[38] One example is in relation to ecological questions.

Recent studies have, however, modified this picture.[39] Instead of an all out war between the business class and the New Class we find increasingly "a mutual cultural exchange"[40] in which the market economy absorbs many of the impulses of the New Class, from environmentalism and feminism to, and above all, the stress on self-realization. Hansfried Kellner and Frank W. Heuberger have, for example, shown the strong influence of Postmaterialist New Class values in German business consulting. Values often mentioned in this context are the "individual's quest for an 'unfolded' personality", "self-realization, autonomy, and authenticity", "emotional well-being, and intimacy", "the rights of private over public life", the "search for 'meaning'", "spontaneity" and "creativity and fantasy".[41] A "vaguely emancipatory rhetoric"[42] is used, and stress is put on "the whole person" and the importance of "participation".[43] Their overall description of the function of such consultants, often trained in social and psychological sciences, is that "they are one of the prime mediators between the functional logic of rationalization and the social demands posed to industry in our contemporary

---

[35]*The Capitalist Revolution*, 69.

[36]Ibid., 70; idem, "Ethics", 9-11.

[37]For examples about how the media elite can form images of general opinion which are in their own interest, but in radical variance with what seems to be the actual opinion, see Westerståhl and Johansson, *Bilden av Sverige*.

[38]According to Hargrove, *The Emerging New Class*, 67, it is the working class families which today are the primary inheritors of the bourgeois ethos.

[39]On this, see Kellner and Heuberger, *Hidden Technocrats*. For Berger's reflections on this modification, which he recognizes, see his and Kellner's contribution to this book, titled "Life-style Engineering".

[40]Berger and Kellner, "Life-style Engineering", 19.

[41]"Modernizing Work", 57.

[42]Ibid., 73.

[43]Ibid., 63. This picture is in agreement with the studies of Inglehart and Kaufmann et. al.

situation."[44] James Davison Hunter and Tracy Fassenden similarly writes that "bourgeois culture is in decline because it is no longer an adequate stimulus to contemporary capitalism. . . . If this is correct, then it is to the knowledge sector . . . that we must look to see how a newer moral order—one that greases the wheels of postmodern capitalism—takes shape."[45]

Against this background it is understandable that Inglehart does not accept the idea that the 1980s were mainly characterized by a conservative reaction. Quite the opposite. The adherence to Postmaterialist values continued to grow among the young and the more educated, including those in industry. Inglehart in fact says that the "yuppies" (young professionals), which often have been described as a sign of a conservative development in the 1980s, are one of the strongest Postmaterialist segments of all.[46] However, what has changed is that increased state planning and control no longer are seen as obviously progressive and therefore also a somewhat more positive view of the market has evolved. The reasons for this, he thinks, are that "the welfare state has begun to reach a point of diminishing returns",[47] that high tech society needs initiative and creativity, and the general cultural change in the direction of Postmaterialist values emphasizing quality of life and autonomy. Clearly conservative movements, like the Moral Majority, he sees more as reactions to the trends than as forming them.[48]

What this shows is that the conflict does not so much concern material interests but culture. The main opposition to the New Class does not come from the elites of the business class, but from the lower middle and working classes. The New Class is highly educated (and education is strongly dominated by the New Class) and tends, we have noted, increasingly in the direction of Postmaterialist values. Craig Gay thinks that opposition from the lower middle and working classes "is perhaps best explained by the fact that these groups are simply less secularized than members of the New Class and so are less receptive to the secular social symbols the New Class has generated."[49] This furthermore explains why "the conflict has been most heated between a highly secularized symbolic knowledge elite and a coalition of conservative religious believers upset that their symbolic understanding of social reality has been undermined by that of this elite."[50] To this can be added Inglehart's comment that religious attitudes are much deeper, more coherent and stable than the more ephemeral political atti-

---

[44]Ibid., 80. It should also be said that they are rather critical of this development and "the technocratization of the life-word" (p. 80) this amounts to.

[45]"The New Class as Capitalist Class", 187.

[46]See *Culture Shift*, 320f. Berger and Kellner comments: "The phenomenon of the so-called 'yuppies' . . . nicely illustrates this marriage of 'soft' values and hard cash." ("Life-style Engineering", 19.)

[47]Inglehart, *Culture Shift*, 9.

[48]Ibid., 7-12.

[49]Gay, *With Liberty and Justice for Whom?*, 191.

[50]Ibid., 192. See further ibid., 190-193.

tudes, because the former are socialized early and are sustained through frequent religious activity, while political activity is sporadic.[51]

One of the weaknesses of the designation "New Class" is that it gives the impression that the conflict it wants to explain is primarily a conflict about scarce economic resources. We have seen that this is not the case. It is more a cultural conflict. Furthermore, one cannot simply explain the nature of the cultural development in class terms or in terms of prosperity and security. There is no necessity in the nature of the Postmaterialist development Inglehart describes.[52] It has deep historical roots, which is to say that it could be different. This is a reason why, for example, Daniel Bell, while agreeing with the general description, early criticized the concept of New Class.[53] In the more recent literature this seems to be a more general trend.

c) The New Social Movements

How can one then in this light understand the new social movements? I will not here take up all the possible answers, but will concentrate on theorists that assign these movements a crucial and positive role in social development, which therefore might be congenial with political theology.[54] Of recent social theorists maybe nobody has given them such a monumental role as Alan Touraine, who builds on the account of the new class we already met above.[55] He is a Postmarxist thinker that, like Moltmann, talks in terms of grand historical projects, humanity as the subject of history, the major conflict being between oppressors and oppressed over the control of the processes of history, and sees social movements as the heart of this conflictual progressive process.[56] He therefore writes: "The social movement is the organized collective behaviour of a class actor struggling against his class adversary for the social control of historicity in a concrete community."[57] In every society there is a central conflict between the dominating and the dominated over the control of the social processes. In capitalist industrial society the major conflict was between labour and capital, which made the worker's movement the central agent. This conflict is, however, no longer the central one.

---

[51]Inglehart, *Culture Shift*, 182.

[52]Inglehart recognizes this. See ibid., 152f.

[53]Bell, "The New Class".

[54]There is an overwhelming amount of material on the "new social movements". See e.g. Brand, *Neue soziale Bewegungen*, Dalton and Kuechler (eds.), *Challenging the Political Order*, Eyerman and Jamison, *Social Movements*, Inglehart, *Culture Shift*, 371-392, Melluci, *Nomader i nuet*, Roth and Rucht (eds.), *Neue soziale Bewegungen in der Bundesrepublik Deutschland*, Touraine, *The Voice and the Eye*, and Wasmuth (ed.), *Alternativen zur Alten Politik*.

[55]He has developed his ideas in many books, but see esp. *Voice*. For a good, secondary account of Touraine's social thought, see Österberg, *Metasociology*, 235-249.

[56]He starts *Voice* with following words: "Men make their own history: social life is produced by cultural achievements and social conflicts, and at the heart of society burns the fire of social movements" (p. 1). "In our type of society, social movements are more than ever the principal agents of history" (p. 9).

[57]Ibid., 77.

Touraine calls the emerging post-industrial society the programmed society. Here control over information and communication is central, which has made the conflict between technocracy and the rest of the population the central conflict. The struggles concern liberation from the various technocratic apparatus in the name of self-management. In the workers' movement the central agents were not the most exploited workers, but the most qualified workers. In the same way, "it is a fraction of the *professionals* who perform"[58] this central role in programmed society in alliance with wider more exploited groups. Touraine's work has then been an analysis of the new social movements for the purpose of determining if any of them might take the role the workers' movement once had.[59]

Ron Eyerman and Andrew Jamison have written one of the more important theoretical studies on the new social movements. Like Touraine they have much sympathy with them and give them an important role in modern society, though they are more modest in their evaluation than Touraine and his grand socio-historical search for the agent of a new society.[60] They are also personally involved in these movements and describe themselves as "partisan" theorists.[61] This has made them critical of the reductive approach of much sociological study of these movements.[62] They instead develop a cognitive approach that takes the movements' own terms seriously and interpret them as a sort of cognitive praxis and place them in a political and historical context. In this light they describe the social movements in the following way: "Social movements are thus best conceived of as temporary public spaces, as moments of collective creation that provide societies with ideas, identities, and even ideals."[63] In challenging established politics they "offer the possibility of new projects, new ways of viewing the world and of organizing social life".[64] This also means that they challenge evolutionist

---

[58]Ibid., 22.

[59]When writing this book, he seemed to see the ecological and especially the anti-nuclear movements as the most promising candidates. See ibid., 24. This also means that socialism has lost its crucial role. "Socialism, which used to be a social movement, has become above all a political force, to the point of sometimes being no more than a doctrine widely propagated by the university *establishment* in France and certain third world countries; it no longer represents the aim of the major social struggles." (Ibid., 13, cf. 80.) Cf. also his reflections about Christian populism as a step towards a full-fledged social movement that might apply to political theology (ibid., 20, cf. also ibid., 78f).

[60]Cf. also Alberto Melucci's claim, against Touraine, that the idea of a central collective agent leading the historical process now is untenable. In the modern complex society there are many different conflictual dimensions that cannot be put into one basic conflict. See *Nomader i nuet*, 33-36.

[61]*Social Movements*, 8.

[62]In much American sociology, knowledge and identity is often seen as nonempirical and therefore outside the area for sociological study. The result is "that knowledge becomes disembodied; it is relegated to a largely marginal, ephemeral or superstructural level of reality, and not to the centrality of movement identity formation where we contend it belongs. The identity of the movement becomes disinterested, stripped of its driving ideas, its cognitive meaning." (Ibid., 46.) In much European sociology, on the other side, the cognitive identities of the movements gets lost in a socio-historical approach that places them in a general theory of history or social change. See ibid., 46f.

[63]Ibid., 4. See further ibid., 2-4.

[64]Ibid., 149.

modernization theories that describe history as a basically linear path of differentiation and rationalization. Their cognitive approach opens for more contingency
and new possibilities.

Eyerman and Jamison contend, like most others, that the New Left had its
roots in the expansion of the public sector and especially the higher education
during the postwar decades. At the centre "was a general quest for 'liberation'",
what they call "a liberation cosmology",[65] very much influenced by existential
and humanistic psychology and Third World prophets. This general liberation
cosmology in the New Left opened up for more specialized and limited liberation
movements, such as environmentalism and feminism.[66] This movement period
starting in the 1960s "had by the end of the 1980s, largely been incorporated into
established politics, in the guise of green parties, mainstream public interest organizations, women's studies departments, environmental bureaucracies, etc. . . .
the cognitive praxis of the new social movements has been 'transferred' into more
established forums: the mass media, the academy, the marketplace".[67] In this perspective social movements are carriers of specific and limited cultural projects
that are partly diffused into society and taken up in the established institutions.[68]

4. Political Theology in its Social Context

a) Political Theology as a Postmaterialist Transformation of Christian Theology

It is, of course, not surprising that Moltmann's theology shows a strong affinity with the aims of the new social movements, from their criticism of capitalism
to their struggles for the natural environment, peace and women's rights. It is part
of his project. More interesting is the large extent to which he takes up and identifies political theology with the whole world-view and morality of the Postmaterialist or New Class fraction of the upper middle class. This reflects his general
apologetic interest. He wants to formulate Christian theology in a way that makes
sense to these culturally highly influential elites as he meets them in the university. These groups' increasing indifference to the church and Christian theology
was, he tells us, one of the central motives behind the emergence of political theology. He wanted to develop a theology that at the same time would be relevant to
their world-view and interests and preserve the Christian identity.

Moltmann's description of the rise of political theology is similar to the accounts given by Gabriel, Wuthnow and others of the social, political and cultural
changes that sharply accelerated during the 1960s. Moltmann describes political

---

[65]Ibid., 90.

[66]"Both feminism and environmentalism are inconceivable without the student movement of the 1960s.
Their reconceptualizations of nature and gender, and of social relations more generally, were impossible
without the articulation of a more fundamental belief in liberation. The 1960s opened the space for later
movements to fill with specific meanings." (Ibid., 91.)

[67]Ibid., 92.

[68]Cf. also Melluci, *Nomader i nuet*, who in this respect has a similar perspective.

theology as a way of mediating modernity, with its future-oriented and secularizing forces, with Christianity. He therefore sees one's position to the Enlightenment as providing a basic division in modern Western society and church life. His description of two main interpretations of modernity, the progressive vision of freedom and the conservative authoritarian principle, corresponds to Wuthnow's two versions of civil religion. The version Wuthnow gives the label "With Liberty and Justice for All" is in its political content identical with Moltmann's project.

Moltmann, like the Postmaterialist/New Class fraction, makes liberation and justice the central categories of his theology. The theology of hope is a Christian version of what Eyerman and Jamison calls "a liberation cosmology". Behind the formation of political theology lies a positive reception of secularization read as humanity becoming subject of its own history. Moltmann thus describes history as a continuous history of freedom movements, through which different forms of oppression are overcome, restrictions upon autonomy are taken away, so that a "natural" and "spontaneous" freedom can be realized. The role of the church in this process is to be a critical and messianic force for freedom.

Because humanity is the subject of history and society, politics, understood as the struggle for control over the processes of social change, becomes the basic horizon for theology. He therefore also shares the rationalistic attitudes of these groups to life and politics, where social and personal questions tend to be seen as "problems" to which "solutions" are to be found. This together with the growth of the state reinforce the belief in the power of politics. His actual political beliefs have also followed the major tendencies of the Postmaterialist/New Class fraction and like them he appeals to the welfare of the people, to the interests of the poor and the underprivileged to justify his political program. We thus find in his writings a development from an early strong faith in economic and technological growth to his later criticism of growth and technology.

This model of liberation from restrictions to a "spontaneous" freedom is also his basic model for understanding personal life. Like Postmaterialists he is deeply influenced by humanistic and existential psychology. The language of self-realization and autonomy therefore dominates his account. It is revealing that most of Kellner's and Heuberger's description of the Postmaterialist values of current German business consulting could just as well have been a description of Moltmann's understanding of the Christian life. Especially noteworthy is that we find the same contrast between a tolerant attitude that affirms different lifestyles at the level of personal life and an activist and absolutist attitude to public affairs that one finds in much of Postmaterialism. The other side of this is his thoroughly critical attitude to what he considers bourgeois culture and church life and Christian traditionalism.[69] Even his sympathy for a Free Church ecclesiology has affinity with the new social movements and their Postmaterialist supporters, as "these

---

[69]See above and also his comments on the integration theologies of Pannenberg and Rendtorff and on the very different evangelicals in *PTPE* 21-26.

groups prefer a decentralized, open, and democratic structure" in accordance with their participatory ideals.[70]

Also important are the sort of questions which are *not* part of his agenda. As we might expect, these include issues like family policy and sexuality. The centrality and even sacredness of individual freedom and autonomy in Postmaterialist thought is expressed in the development of a permissive and individualistic "situation ethics" often described in anti-bourgeois terms.[71] Inglehart writes that "Postmaterialists are far more permissive than Materialists in their attitudes toward abortion, divorce, extramarital affairs, prostitution, and euthanasia"[72] as well as towards homosexuality. Moltmann's general account of the good human life and his strong criticism of church discipline concerning the personal life point in this direction, but he does not directly support such views. The fact that he is silent rather than directly supporting more liberal and permissive views, may indicate some hesitancy or personally more traditional views. I do not know. The important point is that he does not make them part of his agenda. The typical context for the word "family" in Moltmann's writings is instead the reactionary agenda of "God, family and country". The impression he gives, through leaving these topics outside his political agenda, is that they, like generally questions of lifestyle, are part of the private sphere where the church has to leave freedom to the individual.[73]

The only major question where he seems to come in direct and explicit conflict with the Postmaterialist strata is abortion. This issue has only a minor place in his writings, but he has dealt with it a few times. He wrote 1971, together with Eberhard Jüngel, Ernst Käsemann and Dietrich Rössler, during the German debate about abortion, a piece against free abortion.[74] Three other similar texts argue, if I understand them correctly, that life is constituted through its personal and societal affirmation and acceptance. This argument can be turned both ways, but he seems to assume a restrictive attitude to abortion.[75] However, he hopes that the issue will disappear "through progress in family planning"![76] This hope of solving the moral problem through technical inventions might be a good indication of

---

[70]Dalton, Kuechler, and Bürklin, "The Challenge of New Movements", 13.

[71]Pettersson, *Bakom dubbla lås*, 139f, 144, Kaufmann, Kerber and Zulehner, *Ethos und Religion*, 281f. For a further discussion of emotivism as embodied in modern culture, see MacIntyre, *After Virtue*, 1-34.

[72]Inglehart, *Culture Shift*, 195.

[73]There are in his later writings comments which, if developed, could be interpreted as going in another direction. But these comments are weak compared to his celebrations of autonomy and self-affirmation, and he does not seem to reflect on the connections between this and the individualism he deplores. Generally it mirrors changing attitudes to the family in parts of recent radical social criticism. Cf. e.g. *CJF* 95 (121) and *SL* 236-239 (249-252).

[74]"Abtreibung oder Annahme des Kindes". But in a conversation with the author in 1988 he said he would not have written this today. It is not that he personally is positive to abortion, but that he thinks it is a question that only women should decide.

[75]*EH* 164-167 (185-188), *FC* 141-145 (149-153), and *DHRG* 82-84.

[76]*FC* 145 (153).

New Class rationalism. But finally in *The Way of Jesus Christ* he seems to clearly take a stand against abortion.

> Each temporal Gestalt [of the human person] has the same dignity in God's sight, and hence the same rights before human beings. Every devaluation of the foetus, the embryo and the fertilized ovum compared with life that is already born and adult is the beginning of a rejection and a dehumanization of human beings. Hope for the resurrection of the body does not permit any such death sentence to be passed on life.[77]

Which social and political consequence, if any, he thinks one should draw from this rather strong language he does not say.[78]

This chapter does consequently not support Moltmann's idea of political theology as a theology grown out of a church in direct relation with the poor and oppressed. Political theology is better described as a Postmaterialist transformation of Christian theology. It has its main support in the Postmaterialist upper middle class strata and promotes the same values and policies. It can be seen as an apologetic attempt to mediate Christian faith to these strata, which dominate the cultural sphere.

This analysis could also give content to Moltmann's claim that political theology is a post-bourgeois theology, but not in the way he himself seems to think. It can be described as post-bourgeois in the sense that it represents the emergence to prominence of new types of elites in the post-industrial society. If Moltmann recognizes this, theories like the ones of Gouldner or Touraine ought to be attractive in a theological approach that justifies its theology in terms of being on the side of the progressive forces.

We have seen that Moltmann denies that political theology has its primary base in the middle class. He then thinks in terms of a semi-Marxist interpretation and does not discuss the type of interpretation I have given. But he explicitly supports my analysis of the New Left movement in his book *Man* from 1971. Here he describes the New Left as one example of a recurring form of romantic criticism of the industrial civilization. It has its social base in the bourgeoisie.

> They come only rarely from the poorer layers of the proletariat, and generally from the middle and higher levels of the bourgeoisie, that is, from a generation which has not known unemployment and homelessness for itself. It is an antibourgeois rebellion of the bourgeois, and it is perhaps the first movement which is not immediately economically conditioned, but only morally motivated.[79]

---

[77] *WJC* 268 (291).
[78] *WJC* 267f (290f). If his view is the one he gave in the interview mentioned above (that is one year before *WJC* was published) his conflict with supporters of free abortion is in practice not very intense.
[79] *Man*, 34 (54f). See further *Man*, 31-37 (50-59).

Here we find most of the motives we earlier have encountered: romantic protest movements,[80] a conflict in the higher middle class, its base in secure and affluent circumstances, and its moral motivation.

Moreover, he describes the Rightist movements of "God, family and fatherland" as being an unrealistic reaction against the rationalizing developments of modernity, having its social base in "the insecure layers of the population" and appearing in times of "inflation, unemployment, and social readjustments".[81]

This understanding of conservatism is common in Moltmann. The description of the New Left, however, stands in a marked contrast to his earlier celebration of the central potential role this movement could have in the Western part of the world revolution and to his later descriptions of the various social movements that in different ways came out of the New Left. That he describes it in such distanced terms may reflect that this book was written during the decline of the New Left and in the aftermath of the disappointments of the late 1960s.

b) Contrast Society or Postmaterialist Church?

The close alliance with the new social movements and the general Postmaterialist/New Class fraction is also a reason behind the deep substantial tensions and ironies built into the theology of Moltmann that we have repeatedly encountered. These tensions have to do, first, with conflicts between central themes in the Christian tradition and modernity that Moltmann fails to successfully mediate and, second, with inherent tensions and contradictions in modernity itself that the new social movements themselves often exemplify.

A first question this account raises is how the church can be both a contrast society and a "progressive" Postmaterialist church. Is there no tension between the desire of political theology "to 'christianize' the political existence of the churches and of individual Christians according to the standard set for the disciples of Christ in the Sermon on the Mount"[82] *and* to mediate the Christian tradition to the world-views and practices of the Postmaterialist elites? It is in this light difficult to see the sharp opposition that he describes between middle class "progressive liberal theology" and his own likewise middle class Postmaterialist theology, or between "old" and "new" political theology. When Moltmann in *The Crucified God* discusses the double crisis of relevance and identity, he writes:

> When a Christian community feels obliged to empty itself in certain social and political actions, it must take care that its traditional religious and political identity is not exchanged for a new religious and political identity, but must sustain its non-identity. Otherwise a

---

[80]The view that the social movements primarily should be understood as a recurring form of middle class radicalism has especially been espoused by Karl-Werner Brand. See e.g. his "Cyclical Aspects of New Social Movements".

[81]*Man*, 38 (61). See further *Man*, 37-39 (59-61).

[82]"Political Theology", 208.

church which, seeking for an identity and not preserving its distinctiveness, plunges into a social and political movement, once again becomes the 'religion of society'.[83]

He goes on to say that even a progressive political religion is confronted by the cross of Christ. This cross should enable "people to criticize and to stand back from the partial historical realities and movements which they have idolized and made absolute."[84] Moreover, in a recent article he states: "The subject for the new political theology is the Christian existence in its *difference* from the general bourgeois existence, and the church in its *difference* from society and state."[85]

Of what does this *difference* consist? The question here concerns not the difference to the bourgeoisie, but to the progressive movements with which political theology symphatizes. What difference does the Christian confession make? It is difficult to see that it makes any substantial *political* difference. We have seen that he in the 1960s explicitly denied that it could make a political difference. The Christian contribution was reduced to the *motivational* level. He has since then increasingly stressed the newness and the difference of the Christian practice. Yet, we have seen how difficult it is to specify any substantial ethical and political difference between Moltmann and the movements he has supported and supports.

From such general statements as the one given above one could expect a more critical and selective relation to the social movements. However, two factors hamper the development of a more critical attitude: his understanding of politics and his apologetic interest. The political base for Moltmann is the current struggle by the social movements for the control over the processes of social change, not the church as an independent entity. He therefore lacks the social space and distance that make criticism and "productive disengagement"[86] possible. When the question of Christian identity can only be authentically asked by a church already committed to the struggle of the progressive social movements, the possibility of radical substantial criticism is preempted.

This is reinforced by the strongly apologetic mode of Moltmann's theology, which puts the critical potential in the background in the interest of showing the relevance of Christian theology to the modern world and the world-view and interests of the Postmaterialist segment in general and the social movements in particular. If the distance would be too large, church and theology would, he contends, be marginalized. Put differently, for the church to avoid being marginalized it has to ally itself with the progressive forces; that is, the currently culturally dominating elites.[87] Moltmann contends that while the "old" political theology of

---

[83]*CG* 17 (21).

[84]*CG* 17 (22).

[85]"Covenant oder Leviathan?", 316 (my emphasis).

[86]Cf. above p. 53.

[87]"One could speculate, then, that the tendencies toward political polarization among religious elites represent relatively distinct strategies for regaining the center. . . . For the theologically progressive, political liberalism and even radicalism represent the effort to form alliances with those who currently oc-

Carl Schmitt is affirmative and legitimating, the "new" political theology is criti-cal. Furthermore, the historical subject in the latter is the church, while in the former it is states, revolutions, and counterrevolutions.[88] However, one can de-scribe Moltmann's political theology as affirmative of Postmaterialism and the new social movements and as seeing these movements as the primary subjects. It is Christian participation in these movements that forms the base for political theology. Because Moltmann ignores or does not see the nature of the social strata that political theology allies itself with, it is difficult for him to even start answering these questions.[89]

c) The Capitalist Base of Postmaterialism

Political theology is an anti-capitalist theology. From the beginning it was, however, strongly oriented towards technological and economic growth. A so-cialist organization of society could liberate the productive forces to a more rapid growth than outdated capitalist structures could. This entrance into a society of abundance would make a more fully free and human life possible. In contrast, the later Moltmann is an anti-growth thinker, for whom one of the problems of capi-talism is that it seems to require a growing economy.

We have, however, seen that there is much to be said for the view that a suc-cessful capitalism and industrial growth have created the conditions for the sort of

---

cupy the centers of cultural power in advance societies, the strata of secular cultural elites. For the theologically orthodox (and especially the evangelicals), political conservatism and even reactionism represent the effort to challenge the legitimacy of the center—to fundamentally transform the center of cultural power." (Hunter and Hawdon, "Religious Elites in Advanced Capitalism", 53f.)

[88]"Christian Theology and Political Religion", 43 ("Die Politik der Nachfolge Christi gegen Christliche Milleniumspolitk", 20). Carl Schmitt was a famous conservative scholar in constitutional law that used the concept of "political theology" during the 1920s. This has been called the "old" political theology, in contrast to the "new" political theology of Metz and Moltmann. The substantial political positions of Metz and Moltmann are, of course, vastly different from Schmitt's. Cf. Schmitt's book *Politische Theologie* and also *PTPE* 77f and "Covenant oder Leviathan?", 311-314.

[89]One illuminating illustration of this tension in Moltmann's theology is the different ways in which he can describe the prehistory of political theology in twentieth century European theology. In *ThT*, originally published as two long essays for an Italian encyclopaedia, he describes modern theology as a mediating project between the Christian tradition and the modern world. The end product of this history is his own political theology. Most remarkable in this narrative is the absence of Karl Barth, who is only mentioned in passing (see *ThT* 37, 77, 79 [44, 84, 86]). The great figures are instead people like Bultmann, Rahner, Tillich and (more implicitly) Moltmann himself. It is, of course, in itself astonishing that one can write a history of European modern theology and leave Barth outside. It is even more astonishing for a post-Barthian theologian like Moltmann, whose own theology is inconceivable without the influence of Barth. The reason may be that Barth cannot easily be fitted into the mediating model that frames Moltmann's narrative. Barth's theology can be described as an attempt to break out of the mediating approach of liberal Protestantism. In a recent article, Moltmann's interest is instead to discon-nect political theology from liberal theology, which he describes as "the theology of the middle class" ("Political Theology", 213). Here Barth becomes crucial. "Political Theology, however, has its roots in the anti-bourgeois theology of Karl Barth and in the resistance experience of the Confessing Church." (Ibid., 213f.) So also in *PTPE* 26f.

Postmaterialist individualism Moltmann defends,[90] as well as the Postmaterialist New Politics he espouses. Its base is the affluence and security that capitalism and the welfare state (which is built on the resources created by capitalism) have created. On the other hand, modern individualism was also a prerequisite for the development of capitalism. Daniel Bell writes that capitalism and this culture "shared a common source, the ideas of liberty and liberation, whose embodiments were 'rugged individualism' in economic affairs and the 'unrestrained self' in culture."[91] However, the calculating and methodical attitudes of the bourgeois came in conflict with modernist stress on spontaneity and self-expression. Bell says that this anti-bourgeois culture slowly has won autonomy from the techno-economic structure and the bourgeois world-view and moral and now penetrates most areas of life. He writes that "[t]he traditional bourgeois organization of life—its rationalism and sobriety—now has few defenders in the culture, nor does it have any established system of cultural meanings or stylistic forms with any intellectual or cultural respectability."[92] The ascetic side, the bourgeois character structure, has eroded, and the modernist culture has become the dominating legitimation of social life. Instead of character, one now talks about lifestyle. What is important to see, however, is that the modernist culture, with its critique of tradition, was one factor in the rise of capitalism, and that capitalism, on the other hand, has given the economic and social space for the modernist culture, with its stress on self-realization and autonomy. Bell can therefore say that "[t]he breakup of the traditional bourgeois value system, in fact was brought about by the bourgeois economic system—by the free market".[93] And we have seen how capitalism now tries to accommodate this change.

We have, moreover, seen that Moltmann himself says that conservative and traditionalist opposition has its base in the insecurity the changes industrial society, unemployment and inflation create in the lower social strata. This produces a dilemma for Moltmann's recent anti-growth thinking. Although Inglehart is very sympathetic towards Postmaterialist values and developments, he thinks that they, taken for themselves, are self-defeating. He contends that:

> carried to an extreme, Postmaterialism can be equally self-defeating. The antiindustrial outlook of some of the movement's ideologues could lead to neglect of the economic base on which Postmaterialism ultimately depends. In the long run, a new synthesis of Materialist and Postmaterialist orientations will almost certainly emerge, through sheer functional necessity.[94]

---

[90]Cf. *CJF* 95 (121).
[91]*The Cultural Contradictions of Capitalism*, xxiii.
[92]Ibid., 53.
[93]Ibid., 55. On this tension, see also Berger, *The Capitalist Revolution*, 90-114.
[94]*Culture Shift*, 334.

This is again an example of the problems an inadequate self-understanding lead to. His questioning of capitalism ought to lead him to a more radical analysis of the modern culture than his apologetic approach allows.

d) The Congregation and Postmaterialist Individualism

Another tension we have met is the one between the individualizing and deinstitutionalizing trends that Moltmann strongly affirms and his likewise strong interest in the formation of committed local congregations or base communities as expressions of the church as a contrast society. Another way of saying this is to contrast his celebration of religious and moral autonomy with his sharp criticism of the increasing privatization of Christian faith and life. He does not appear to recognize that these from a sociological perspective are two sides of the same thing. Moltmann puts part of his hope on the political initiative groups related to the new social movements. These are, however, short-lived and dependent on external political circumstances and developments. The church cannot, as he recognizes, build only on them.[95] Moreover, Gabriel has argued that the base community model cannot, in modern society, be anything more than a marginal phenomenon. For him the individualizing and deinstitutionalizing forces leave only one realistic option for the church as a whole: to become the church of a pluralistic and diffuse folk religion. Moltmann sharply criticizes this conception of the church, but he celebrates processes that seem to make some such strategy inevitable. The problem for him is that the elite strata he makes central are the most post-Christian and individualized. They have not reversed, but radicalized the processes of subjectivization and individualization that characterize bourgeois Christianity. The liberation of the self is thus seen as standing in contrast to loyalty to the church as community and institution. In other words, how is it possible to sustain the sort of common political discipleship he describes on the basis of the radical expressive individualism he also affirms?

If the sort of church Moltmann espouses should be possible to sustain in a modern individualistic consumer society, it requires, or so it seems, a degree of commitment and institutionalization that he may be unwilling to consider. If not, his theology may be reduced to an apologetic legitimation of the process of secularization in the upper middle class portions of Western Protestantism. It may not, in effect, say more than that a Postmaterialist can, without change, be a good Christian. So understood this theology will be no more than a transitional phenomenon. However, the heart of his theology points in a different direction.

e) Progressive or Different?

Progressive—reactionary dualism is central for Moltmann's thinking. This assumes either that history has a definite direction or that there exists a specific self-

---

[95]*SL* 241-243 (254f).

evident value perspective. Moltmann, like many others, often combines these two assumptions. History is a history of liberation in the direction of the kingdom of freedom. There is seldom for him any doubt about which side is the progressive one.[96] If the church fails to side with the progressive forces it condemns itself to irrelevancy and marginality. The Postmaterialist or New Class segment that Moltmann thinks the church should ally itself with is the culturally dominant segment of modern society. Although in a conflictual symbiosis with the social strata related to economic and technical production, it seems to have the power to determine the cultural development of the near future. He can hardly argue that their perspective is privileged because they represent the oppressed, nor because they see the world from the underside of history. If they should be given a privileged position it should be because of their superior education and their claim to be bearers of a universal critical discourse and perhaps also because of the security and confidence prosperity and social status create. Put differently and more provocatively, they are privileged because they are so positioned that they better than other groups can see the world from above.[97]

Against this stands, or so it seems, his account of the church as a contrast society and its correlate the ecclesial discipleship ethics. A Postmaterialist will likely be uneasy with the very words "ecclesial" and "discipleship". Although it might be interpreted as the avant-garde of the progressive forces, his actual account points in a different direction.

This latter path, of course, is the one Radical Reformation theology takes. For it, to use Moltmann's formulation, the church and the Christian existence in their *difference* from society, state and dominant culture should be the subject for Christian theology. The third part of this book will show what a more consistent elaboration of this claim might look like and the consequences it can have.

---

[96]In relation to this strongly dualistic approach one of the oddest features of his theology is his strong and often repeated criticism of friend/foe schemes, although his own work so strongly is characterized by friend/foe dualism. One can see this in the very dualism between progressive and reactionary forces, in his hard criticism of Christian traditionalism, in his anti-Capitalism, in his anti-bourgeois view, in his anti-anti-Communism, and so on. He writes in "Christian Theology", 43, 47 ("Nachfolge Christi", 20, 23f) that friend/foe thinking is one characteristic of political religion.

[97]It is hardly an accident that especially Catholic political theology so strongly identifies itself with Habermas' project. He may be the premier defender of the Enlightenment project, with its claim to a universal rationality. For Habermas the Postmaterialist transformation of values and the new social movements are hopeful signs in this project. Habermas himself also generally interprets the new social movements in the way I have done above. He argues that the central conflicts and the primary protest potential today is found not "in domains of material reproduction" but "in domains of cultural reproduction, social integration, and socialization". He follows Inglehart in seeing this as "an expression of the 'silent revolution' in values and attitudes" and describes the conflict in class terms as I do. Thus "the 'old politics' is more strongly supported by employers, workers, and middle-class tradesman, whereas the new politics finds stronger support in the new middle classes, among the younger generation, and in groups with more formal education." All the citations come from Habermas, *The Theory of Communicative Action*, vol. 2, 392. See further ibid., 391-396.

Part Three

Towards a Theological Politics: Contemporary Radical Reformation Theology as an Alternative

Chapter 9

The God of Jesus Christ and Salvation

Part Two on the political theology of Moltmann has tried to demonstrate that severe tensions are built into the project of political theology. They have to do, first, with the conflict between what one could call the political theology and the Radical Reformation strands of his theology, and, second, with inherent tensions inside the project of political hermeneutics (that is, a tension inside the political theology strand) that partly reflects inherent conflicts in the project of modernity. These tensions, which express themselves in various ways, tend to draw his theology in different directions. Consequently there may be more than one way out of this dilemma. One possibility could be to draw the consequences of a starting point in a liberating praxis more consistently, developing what could be called a radical constructivist approach, in which Christian symbols are formulated and changed according to some emancipatory interest or criteria.[1] In Moltmann' case the commitment to the new social movements could explicitly be made primary. A less radical option would be to develop his correlational approach in a more consistently revisionist direction. This could lead to a more critical and revisionist attitude both towards Christianity and the social movements (as well as to mod-

---

[1]Cf. Kaufman, *The Theological Imagination*. He says that "instead of *theological claims* about some extraworldly or ultimate 'salvation' being made the criterion of what we should believe and practice in this world, I am proposing that what is necessary or required to build a humane order in this world should be made the criterion for assessing our theological beliefs and for determining the character of the theological task. Theology is done by living human beings in this present world, and it should serve their lives and aspirations." (Ibid., 182f.) See also McFague, *Models of God*. McFague distinguishes her own "metaphorical" or "heuristic" theology from Kaufman's constructivism, but her position is still close to Kaufman's.

ernity in general), which might contribute to a formulation of a more coherent theology.[2]

I will not discuss the likelihood of a successful realization of these options, except for a few reflections in chapter 16. My exposition in Part Two has disclosed some of the problems these approaches encounter. It should, however, be clear that the price of taking one of these routes would be high for a theology of Moltmann's type, whose strength to a large extent lies in the critical potential of the classical Christian tradition. The revisions required would be of such a large scale that it would change the nature of his whole substantial theology.[3] Furthermore Moltmann has, as seen, little sympathy with such strategies.

However, the suggestion made in this book is that a more promising way forward for Moltmann would be for him to develop more consistently the Radical Reformation strand of his theology. What makes this suggestion particularly interesting is that this is the direction Moltmann himself increasingly has taken, partly "forced" by the logic of his theological convictions. If his political hermeneutics points in the constructivist or revisionist direction, his substantial theology and ecclesiology points in the direction of Hauerwas' theological politics. Part Three of this book will therefore, in a continuing discussion of the political theology of Moltmann, present what the alternative provided by a Radical Reformation theology could be like. So one way of reading the following is to see it as an attempt to work out the implications of a central strand in Moltmann's theology. The conclusion of this could, of course, be twofold. It might seem as a fruitful way forward, or one might find the outcome, for whatever reasons, unacceptable and it would therefore show either the need for a radical revision of Moltmann's substantial theology or the hopeless nature of his theological project as a whole.

1. Theology as Ecclesial Discourse

Moltmann is a systematic theologian who sees ethics as part of systematic theology and who therefore writes extensively on ethics.[4] All of his theology has a practical dimension, even though the bulk of his writings does not deal with specific ethical questions. Hauerwas' academic discipline is theological ethics, but he thinks of himself as a theologian. He writes that "I understand myself as a theologian and my work as theology proper. I have accepted the current academic designation of 'ethics' only because as a theologian I am convinced that the intel-

---

[2]David Tracy's critique of political (and liberation) theology in *The Blessed Rage of Order*, 30f, 242-246 is an example of the demand for a more revisionist direction, i. e. that it develops a more critical and revisionist attitude to the Christian tradition. He thinks that it is too influenced by neo-orthodox theology.

[3]This is not made clear in the work of Tracy, because he avoids the hard questions through keeping his account on a very high level of abstraction, just like much of political theology besides Moltmann has done.

[4]It is doubtful to which extent this is an adequate description of the work of the early Moltmann.

ligibility and truthfulness of Christian convictions reside in their practical force."[5] He thus does not accept the today often strict separation between theology and ethics. Ethics is an intrinsic part of theology, because "Christian theology is concerned with which theological convictions should be central to Christian life, and how these convictions might be properly entertained as truthful."[6] Theology is a practical activity, which has to do with how Christian convictions construe reality. The question about their meaning and truth is, he therefore argues, not primarily answered through their relations to ontological schemes, but "by asking how through our language and character they form and display our practical affairs".[7] Ethics is consequently not something that follows theology. On the contrary theological assertions are intrinsically also ethical assertions, because they construe reality in a specific way, and the first task of ethics is to learn to see the world rightly.[8] He can therefore also say that "[t]he task of Christian ethics . . . is simply the task of theology itself—namely to help the churches share their stories truthfully."[9] Theology is thus an activity that analyses and develops the linguistic skills that help the church to understand and do better what it does.[10] In other words, theology is an activity in the service of the concrete people of God and not a form of autonomous philosophical analysis.[11] Its starting point is the discourse and practices of the church through the centuries. In this sense theology is subordinate to the primary activity of the Christian church.[12] The active subject of theology cannot be autonomous individuals. Theologians are not independent "thinkers" analysing the concept of "God" in abstraction from the use of the word "God" in the church. Such views of theology are, he claims, a product of the Enlightenment idea that thought can be separated from its social and political context.[13]

This does not mean that Hauerwas thinks of theology as isolated from other intellectual enterprises. First of all, he has no sympathy with the common view in

---

[5]*CC* 1.

[6]*TT* 8. He writes in another context: "Our task as theologians remains what it has always been—namely, to exploit the considerable resources embodied in particular Christian convictions which sustain our ability to be a community faithful to our belief that we are creatures of a graceful God. If we do that we may well discover that we are speaking to more than just our fellow Christians, for others as a result may well find we have something interesting to say." (*AN* 44.) See also *PK* xvi, 54f, and *CCL* xviii.

[7]*TT* 9.

[8]"Christian ethics offers the means for exploring the meaning, relation, and truthfulness of Christian convictions. That is not to say that Christian convictions are proven meaningful or true by showing their ethical implications; rather they are both true and ethical in that they force us to a true understanding of ourselves and our existence." (*CC* 90.)

[9]*CET* 125.

[10]*CET* 123, *RA* 97.

[11]*CET* 110, 115.

[12]Theology is "rooted in the practices that constitute the church as a community across time." ("Why *Resident Aliens* Struck a Chord", 424.)

[13]"Why *Resident Aliens*", 420f.

Protestant theology since the nineteenth century that faith is "arational", that is, a special category separate from theoretical knowledge. He thinks that faith is rational and is knowledge, although he questions foundationalist accounts of knowledge and rationality. He has also often said that the question about how Christian convictions can be claimed to be true or false has been of central importance for him.[14]

Second, he also, like Moltmann, disregards disciplinary borders. In his conception there is no "purely theological" dimension. He says himself that much of his work "is a strange mixture of theology, social and political theory, and what might be called high-culture journalism."[15] His interest is not the discipline of theological ethics, but what is helpful for the life of the church. His footnotes are a running commentary on recent writings in philosophy, political theory, sociology, history and so on. From one perspective he is very much part of and in dialogue with the developments of intellectual life in America during the last decades. From another he is, as we will see, very different. He uses all sorts of material, but selectively and for the purposes of his own theological concerns.

He is, again like Moltmann, also sceptical of the very idea of "systematic theology" understood as an autonomous theoretical system of beliefs.[16] He does not want to develop a general Christian theory or a total theological system. His reflections are purposively more piecemeal.[17] This does not mean that he is not a systematic or consistent thinker. As with any major "thinker" writing over a longer time, there are tensions between different parts of his theological program, though there are more problems in his theoretical apparatus than in his substantive convictions. Although he has developed and clarified his "position", which has meant some major changes, there is a basic continuity between his early and his latest writings. However, he does not write general systematic treatises, but usually reflects on specific issues of a practical or theoretical nature. His favourite format is the essay. Recently he has also begun to write theology in the form of sermons.[18]

This creates a difficulty for a project like this one. If I make a system out of his writings I will misconstrue him. His way of writing theology as reflections on

---

[14]*TT* 1, 8-10, *CC* 10, 90, 96, *PK* 15, *AN* 5, "Faith in the Republic", 479 n. 16.

[15]*AC* 19. So also *US* 7f.

[16]*AC* 19. Cf. also *AC* 13f and 182 n. 14.

[17]This is one of his questions concerning Milbank's attempt "to supply a counter-narrative to that of liberalism. Does he reproduce exactly the violence of liberalism by trying to write such grand narrative . . . Obviously in my own work I have tried to chip-away at liberalism one piece at a time. Milbank, however, may be right that you can only counter a totalizing narrative with another narrative that is equally totalizing, but I fear in the process the Gospel cannot help but appear as but another 'system' or 'theory'." ("Creation, Contingency, and Truthful Non-Violence", 15 n. 7. So also "The Church's One Foundation Is Jesus Christ Her Lord", 35 n. 3.)

[18]So e.g. *US*. These are actually preached sermons. He can say: "I think the exhibits contain my best theology, which means that the form and content of theology and sermons are integrally related." (*US* 8.) *PtS* consists of sermons by William Willimon and commentaries by Hauerwas.

specific questions is impossible to do justice to. It cannot be summarized. But to be able to compare Hauerwas with Moltmann I have to systematize his thought to a limited extent, but without transforming it into an independent system. The reader should, however, be aware that the format of a book like this makes it much easier to do justice to Moltmann's type of theology than to Hauerwas'.

This difficulty becomes especially acute here, because Hauerwas discusses the type of theological questions which are the subject of this chapter mainly when dealing with various ethical issues. Even if his general position is clear, it has to be 'distilled' from discussions that often primarily deal with other issues. Consequently, we frequently lack a more sustained elaboration and defence of his positions. We find, however, a marked difference between his earlier and his later writings, in that they have become steadily more explicitly theological (in contrast to an earlier, stronger methodological concentration). The result is that this chapter is much easier to write today than ten or even five years ago.

A common way of describing Hauerwas' thought is to take some formal theoretical concepts he uses and make them into a general framework into which his theology can be fitted. One could thus start with his early work on character and virtue, and show how this led him to see the significance of the concept of vision, later more or less substituted by that of narrative, for understanding the ethical process, and how this in its turn forced him to develop an account of the community that carries these narratives. This is not wholly wrong. It partly expresses the way Hauerwas' work has developed as is evident from the titles of his earlier books: *Character and the Christian Life*, *Vision and Virtue*, and *A Community of Character*. But to describe Hauerwas in this way is today a mistake. The reason is that the path Hauerwas' theology has taken him has transformed these formal categories. If earlier he began by trying to supply a phenomenology of moral experience that could do justice to Christian ethics, he now begins with the practices and discourses of the Christian church. As we will see, this means that he is not interested in a virtue theory in general, but in Christian virtue; he talks more about the Christian story or stories than about the narrative character of the self; and it is the church, not community as such, that has a central role in his theology. This is also expressed in the titles of his later books, like *The Peaceable Kingdom*, *Against the Nations*, *Suffering Presence*, *Christian Existence Today*, and *Resident Aliens*. Some of these titles also show that he does not suffer from any false or true modesty!

He likewise, in contrast to many other theologians, seems purposely to avoid using general categories like postmodern, postliberal, pragmatist, communitarian, neo-Aristotelian, and so on, for describing his own position, though all of them might have some relevance, and others sometimes use them for describing him. In contrast, he finds it, as we saw in the first chapter, more meaningful to define himself in relation to ecclesial traditions like Catholic, Methodist or Mennonite.

In my exposition I will therefore concentrate on his substantial theology and let the more methodological considerations grow out of this. There is therefore not any independent chapter on Hauerwas' theological and ethical methods. Instead this sort of topics will be dealt with at appropriate places throughout the coming chapters.

2. Trinitarian Theology

In general terms, the theological positions of Moltmann and Hauerwas are relatively similar, and have, as we have seen, become more so through the development of Moltmann's theology. Both defend a sort of eschatologically oriented trinitarian theology. I do not thereby imply that Moltmann and Hauerwas agree in detail, but only that their general positions point in similar directions.

Hauerwas' theology is thus trinitarian. "God" is not a concept or a principle immediately available for philosophical reflection, but, he claims, more like a proper name of an agent in a story. This means that God and God's salvation are not knowable abstracted from history as mediated through the traditions of Israel and the church. This knowledge is from the beginning practical. It is knowledge directly connected with these particular communities' lives with God. One learns to know God through being part of this embodied narrative.

Christians believe that the pivotal centre of this narrative is the life, death and resurrection of Jesus, but understood in continuity with the history of Israel. They share Israel's conviction that "a series of events in her history was decisive for God's relation to mankind"[19] and that the task God had given them was to walk the way of the Lord. Therefore Hauerwas can write that the early Christians in the life and destiny of Jesus

> had found a continuation of Israel's vocation to imitate God and thus in a decisive way to depict God's kingdom for the world. Jesus' life was seen as the recapitulation of the life of Israel and thus presented the very life of God in the world. By learning to imitate Jesus, to follow in his way, the early Christians believed they were learning to imitate God, who would have them be heirs of the kingdom.[20]

Christians thus learn to know God and God's way with the world by following Jesus Christ. This common discipleship, as the continuation of the life of Jesus Christ, is made possible by, and is the concrete form of, the presence of the Holy Spirit. Hauerwas' explicit use of pneumatological language is meagre, but it is implicit in his ecclesiological account. He would, I think, strengthen his theology if he developed it in more explicitly pneumatological terms.[21]

---

[19]*PK* 77.
[20]*PK* 78.
[21]Cf. Hütter's criticism of Hauerwas and positive suggestions in *Evangelische Ethik als kirchliches Zeugnis*, 149.

One criticism against the central place given to Jesus is that it is in tension with the trinitarian belief in God as Creator.[22] This is a strange criticism as the doctrine of the Trinity by definition is christocentric in the sense that the doctrine of God cannot be separated from the history of Jesus. As Moltmann shows, the doctrine of the Trinity is a theological interpretation of the history of Jesus. This does not mean that the concept or the history of God is limited to the history of Jesus, but that God as the Creator or the creation cannot be understood independently of the whole trinitarian history from the creation to the consummation of the kingdom of God with its centre in the history of Jesus Christ. The alternative would be to start with some form of independent philosophical theism that is complemented or modified christologically into a trinitarian doctrine,[23] a way of constructing the doctrine of God that has been severely criticized in the modern renaissance of the doctrine of the Trinity.[24] Following Michael Buckley, Hauerwas argues (again like Moltmann) that the modern atheism, as well as the modern "problem of evil", has its origin in just this philosophical theism with its specific understandings of divine omnipotence.[25] Put differently and related to the practical nature of theology, Hauerwas' point is that we do not know who God is "abstracted from our knowledge of God which is dependent on our living in faithful continuity with those historic communities we call Israel and the church", which means "that we do not even know what it means to call God good separate from learning what it means to be a creature and redeemed through the cross and resurrection of Jesus of Nazareth."[26] The doctrine of creation is therefore for Hauerwas, as for Moltmann, part of the whole trinitarian narrative and must be understood christologically and eschatologically. The creation must be explicated in the light of the salvation in Jesus Christ and the consummation of the whole creation.

> For the church finds in Jesus not simply the restorer of a lost creation known separately from Jesus himself, but rather in Jesus the church discovers the very nature of the created order. In short, in Christ we know that creation was not an act in and for itself, but an act

---

[22]Cf. e.g. Gustafson, "The Sectarian Temptation", 84f, 92f, and idem, "A Response to Critics", 191, 196. See also Gustafson's comments on Yoder in *Theology and Ethics*, 74f. Cf. the blunt statement of Miscamble that "[d]octrines of creation and incarnation . . . have no place" in Hauerwas theology ("Sectarian Passivism?", 71). Robert Jenson describes this charge as "bizarre" ("The Hauerwas Project", 292).

[23]One might, of course, stop with a "pure" theism like older and modern deists, or like Gustafson himself (a fact that makes his criticism of Hauerwas peculiar).

[24]On modern trinitarian thought, see (besides Moltmann) e.g. Gunton, *The Promise of Trinitarian Theology*, Jüngel, *God as the Mystery of the World*, Kasper, *The God of Jesus Christ*, and Pannenberg, *Systematic Theology*, vol. 1. This tradition of thought is very much influenced by Barth. For a very different approach, see Macquarrie, *In Search of Deity*.

[25]*NS* 39-41, Buckley, *At the Origins of Modern Atheism*.

[26]"On God", 204f.

carried out for a purpose. . . . The original creation is aimed at a new creation, the creation of a community of all flesh that glorifies God.[27]

The God at work in creation is the trinitarian God.

For Hauerwas this does not mean the denial of all forms of natural theology,[28] for God is of course active in the whole of reality, but that cannot be seen rightly separate from the trinitarian perspective and from being initiated into the story of God. He can thus write that

> once one begins within the rationality of Christian claims about God as trinity, we can then indicate how the very finite character of existence is a witness to God. But the witness is not just to God's existence, but to a very particular kind of God that we have learned to name through the very means that God has made available to us—that is, through the on-going practices of a community who has learned what it means to be a creature and redeemed.[29]

This makes him critical of making "creation" synonymous with "nature", an approach which he thinks can too easily be combined with implicit deism, nature romanticism and a survivalist ethic. To talk about the world as creation means seeing it as in bondage and longing for redemption, a conception which he thinks entails understandings and practices at variance with nature romanticism and survivalism.[30]

The direct question in this debate usually concerns the cluster of issues that traditionally has been related to the notion of natural law, a view that bases ethics in a philosophical and/or scientific account of human nature or the whole reality, and theologically defends that in terms of God as Creator. Hauerwas generally, on several grounds, denies the possibility of such a law, but his basic theological argument is that a trinitarian doctrine of God as Creator should not be used "to underwrite an autonomous realm of morality separate from Christ's lordship."[31] Even if the trinitarian story of God is larger than the story of Jesus Christ itself, there must be a basic continuity. Consequently, one cannot develop a creation ethics that is in opposition to the way of Jesus.[32]

He is similarly critical of the common idea that "incarnation" signifies God's affirmation of the human, if that "human" is defined separately from Jesus Christ. He affirms the claim that to be Christian is to be truly human, but he denies that we know what it is to be human on the basis of our desires or an independent philosophical account. Put differently, one cannot "start with the human to de-

---

[27]"Chief End", 207.

[28]We will in chapter 12 see that he does not accept the common division between revealed and natural knowledge of God, because he does not understand revelation as an epistemological category. See *PK* 64-71.

[29]"On God", 205.

[30]"Chief End", 202-205. It would be interesting to discuss this in relation to Moltmann's development of these themes in *GIC*, but that is outside the scope of this work.

[31]*CET* 17.

[32]*AN* 201f n. 10. For a short summary of his criticism of the idea of a natural law, see *PK* 63f.

termine what it means to be a disciple of Christ."[33] It should be the other way around. In one of the few places Hauerwas mentions Moltmann, he following Moltmann, argues that restoration to the image of God occurs through fellowship with Christ, who is the messianic image of God.[34] The image of God is thus for Hauerwas and Moltmann a christological and eschatological notion as much as a creational.[35] Again Hauerwas does not deny all talk of natural morality or that all social life requires, for example, trust and honesty, but he does think that trust and honesty cannot be separated from the various communal and narrative contexts in which they are embedded and made into self-explanatory "universal" notions. He further thinks that a qualified form of natural law assumptions is part of Christian ethics. He writes that "'natural law' really names those moral convictions that have been tested by the experience of the Christian community and have been judged essential for sustaining its common life."[36] Experience is an integral part of any Christian ethics, but it is not some assumed fictional "universal" experience, but the experience of discipleship of Jesus. Part of the life of discipleship, he however argues, is openness to challenges from others.[37]

All this leads to many questions, some of which will be dealt with in further chapters. Our concern now has been to show the nature of his trinitarian theology and how he answers the charge that the central place of Jesus downplays the doctrine of creation.[38] The way he does this is strongly supported by the much more elaborated trinitarian theology of Moltmann. This defence of Hauerwas does, however, not necessarily suggest that his actual explication of his trinitarian doctrine of creation is always satisfying, but this is a question that has to be dealt

---

[33]*PK* 58.

[34]"Chief End", 205f. See *GIC* 226 (232).

[35]*PK* 55-59, *CC* 48f.

[36]*PK* 120.

[37]See further *PK* 59, 64-71, 103, 116-121, *TT* 57-70, and "On Developing Hopeful Virtues", 112.

[38]In the contemporary Swedish context it is especially Gustaf Wingren who is known for affirming what he calls creation theology. In view of how he usually describes the alternatives it might be important to see that the difference between him and a theology like Hauerwas' is not that the former in contrast to the latter emphasizes that the Christian life is the ordinary life directed to the needs of the neighbour and not some separate religious life. Hauerwas theology is as much directed towards ordinary life as Wingren's. Rather, the difference is, first, that Hauerwas denies that moral life is self-interpretative, and, second, that he sees the church as an actual people and not as an institution that is specialized in proclaiming the forgiveness of God. Concerning the first issue, it is not clear how Wingren is able to deal with moral disagreement and conflict. Although he was professor in theological ethics he seldom in his writings deals with specific issues. Instead, his approach seems to fit rather well the dominating utilitarian ethos of Sweden, although the later Wingren is deeply critical of the current policy of Sweden and the Western world generally. Wingren discusses these issues in most of his books. For a shorter, ethically-oriented account, see "Reformationens och lutherdomens ethos". For a very different historical and systematic interpretation of the theology of creation in Reformation and modern theology, see Link, *Schöpfung*.

with in terms of individual issues, and not as a general charge that he lacks an (adequate) doctrine of creation.[39]

3. Jesus, the Kingdom of God and the Politics of Salvation

The story of Jesus, Hauerwas argues, is the story of the kingdom of God. Jesus did not proclaim himself, but the kingdom of God.[40] He thinks, however, that the early church was right in seeing this kingdom, the rule of God, in the life, death and resurrection of Jesus Christ. The kingdom of God is an eschatological concept. Hauerwas relates this to Israel's way of seeing reality as a story, a drama with a beginning and an end. This end is revealed and has already begun in the life, death and resurrection of Jesus, and therefore people find their true destiny and learn to know God through following him. The life and destiny of Jesus Christ shows that God does not rule through coercion, but through forgiveness and mercy, and that therefore a life of forgiveness and love for one's enemies is a real possibility. Hauerwas thus sees the possibility of the new life as based in the coming of the kingdom in Jesus Christ. He can consequently argue that the idea that, for example, the Sermon on the Mount is an impossible ideal fails to understand the eschatological context of the teaching of Jesus.[41] The Sermon on the Mount is a possibility because the kingdom of God has begun in the midst of history through Jesus Christ, and this makes the existence of a people of followers possible. This is salvation.

His account of salvation is thus historical and social. Answering the question what salvation is, he says that "Jesus saves us from sin and death. Yet sin and death are embodied in a history that requires an alternative history if our salvation is to be anything more than a vague hope. The name we give the social manifestation that makes that history present is *church*."[42] He is consequently sharply critical of individualistic and ahistorical accounts of salvation, whether they are about saving individuals from sin, giving meaning to life, or giving a new self-understanding.[43] "[S]alvation is God's work to restore all creation to the Lordship of Christ,"[44] and it is historically and socially mediated. Grace is not an unavoid-

---

[39]For examples of accounts close to Hauerwas, which try to more systematically explicate creational and general trinitarian perspectives on the moral life, see Jones, *Transformed Judgment*, McClendon, *Systematic Theology: Ethics*, esp. 77-155, Milbank, *Theology and Social Theory*, 380-438, and Spjuth, *Creation, Contingency and Divine Presence*.

[40]On the following, see esp. *CC* 44-46, *PK* 76-91, *AN* 107-121, *RA* 86-92, *US* 63-72, and "Epilogue", 159-163.

[41]"To be sure, Jesus' demand that we forgive our enemies challenges our normal assumptions about what is possible, but that is exactly what it is meant to do. We are not to accept the world with its hate and resentments as a given, but to recognize that we live in a new age which makes possible a new way of life." (*PK* 85.)

[42]"Epilogue", 163. See further *CET* 47-54, *RA* 49-68, and *AC* 23-44.

[43]"Epilogue", 162, *RA* 59.

[44]*AC* 37.

able ontological condition (like Tillich's "you are accepted"), but historically mediated and embodied through a specific people.[45] It is thus not surprising that he, especially in contrast to much Protestant theology, stresses the close continuity between Israel, Jesus and the church, as well as the central importance of the continuous, if often painful, relationship between Israel and the church.[46]

So, according to Hauerwas, salvation is that God creates a people that is bearer of the new life that Jesus Christ made possible. This understanding of the social and political nature of salvation and the ecclesiology this implies is at the heart of Hauerwas' theology. Here we have a decisive point of both continuity and discontinuity in relation to political theology that we will explicate and discuss in the rest of this book. Hauerwas' view is well summarized in the following quotation: "Christianity is mostly a matter of politics—politics as defined by the gospel. The call to be part of the gospel is a joyful call to be adopted by an alien people, to join a countercultural phenomenon, a new *polis* called the church."[47] There is in history an alternative narrative, a different politics, embodied in a concrete people's social practices. Being Christian is to be initiated into this embodied narrative through baptism, whereby one's own life becomes included "in the drama of God's redemption of his creation."[48] He can therefore describe the church as the concrete form of Christ's continuing presence through the Spirit.[49]

This historical and dramatic understanding of salvation also makes him critical of ahistoric and individualistic theories of atonement. Following Denny Weaver, he argues that such theories are correlative to the changed socio-political situation of the church when it became the imperial religion, while the earlier language of grand drama and victory was meaningful when the church was a people in conflict with the world.[50] For Hauerwas the whole life, death, and resurrection of Jesus are part of God's establishment of his rule, i. e., of the kingdom of God. This world, he says, is ruled by powers that derive their strength from our fear and

---

[45] *US* 73-83, *PK* 27.

[46] *PK* 76-87, *AN* 61-90, *US* 140-148. His stress on Jesus' Jewish context and the social character of the salvation Jesus and the early church proclaimed (and these two elements are closely connected) find support in the way the NT is read in much recent NT-scholarship. One can mention e.g. Johnson, "The Social Dimension of *Soteria* in Luke-Acts and Paul", Lohfink, *Jesus and Community*, idem, *Wem gilt die Bergpredigt?*, idem, "Jesus und die Kirche", idem, "Die Not der Exegese mit der Reich-Gottes-Verkündigung Jesu", Meyer, *The Aims of Jesus*, Roloff, *Die Kirche im Neuen Testament*, Wiebe, *Messianic Ethics*, and Wright, *The New Testament and the People of God*. Cf. the overviews in Wiebe, 51-54, and Holmberg, "En historisk vändning i forskningen om Jesus". In addition, see Yoder, *The Politics of Jesus*. This implies also a decisively theological and communal character of "NT ethics". In addition to Lohfink, Yoder, and Wiebe, see Meeks, *The Moral World of the First Christians*, Schrage, *Ethik des Neuen Testament*, and Verhey, *The Great Reversal*. We have seen that Moltmann in *WJC* goes in the same direction.

[47] *RA* 30.

[48] *CET* 52.

[49] *CET* 52f, 59f.

[50] *AC* 36f, Weaver, "Atonement for the NonConstantinian Church". See also *PtS* 39 and *AC* 168 n. 21.

who offer us security in exchange for truth.[51] But by letting the story of Jesus become the central story of their lives, Christians become able to see through these false claims and descriptions of reality, because they see in the death and resurrection of Jesus that, what seemed like powerlessness was in fact the victory of truth over falsehood and violence. It shows that God's rule in the world and his dealing with evil is not by coercion, but by suffering love, forgiveness and mercy. Through God's confirmation of Jesus' life and death by his raising of him from the dead, Christians know that a life of forgiveness and peace is an actual reality, because this is how God deals with the world.[52] Consequently, Hauerwas does not "believe that Jesus simply exemplifies a way of life for us to follow. On the contrary, without the ontological change occasioned through Christ's resurrection, there would be no possibility of living as he did."[53] I think this should be understood in terms of an historical ontology, that God in history creates the possibility for this life.

What has been said above demonstrates again that Hauerwas (and that is of course a cardinal point for Radical Reformation theology), like the later Moltmann, makes the life and teaching of Jesus, and not only the cross and resurrection, theologically decisive. He is therefore critical of christological accounts that fail to take the life and teaching of Jesus as well as its eschatological context seriously. By claiming that the history of Jesus is part of the very definition of God, he defends a "high christology", but he is suspicious of talking about Jesus Christ only in terms of substances and divine and human natures, if one thereby supposes that one can define his reality separately from his history. That too easily gives the impression that the whole of his life before the Passion was more or less accidental without deeper significance for the real point of his existence, regardless of whether this is understood abstractly as incarnation or atonement. But we do not know, he contends, who God is, or what the truly human is, or the concrete content of salvation, separately from the whole history and destiny of Jesus.[54]

Furthermore, to learn to know Jesus is not a purely theoretical matter and cannot be separated from being his disciple. He writes that "[t]he form of the Gospels as stories of a life are meant not only to display that life, but to train us to

---

[51]"I still find Rauschenbusch's account of the forces that put Jesus to death—religious bigotry, graft and political power, corruption of justice, mob spirit and action, militarism, racial sin in class contempt—one of the most compelling account of the kind of powers Jesus exposed and redeemed." (*CC* 238 n. 57.)

[52]*PK* 76-91, *CC* 50, "Epilogue", 159-163.

[53]"Epilogue", 162. "Because we have confidence that God has raised this crucified man, we believe that forgiveness and love are alternatives to the coercion the world thinks necessary for existence. Thus, our true nature, our true end, is revealed in the story of this man in whose life, we believe, is to be found the truth." (*PK* 87.)

[54]*CET* 17. "That God was peculiarly at work in Jesus there is, for us, no doubt. How that work is to be explained is quite another matter—Jesus, very God and very man, is not a bad place to start." (*CET* 17.)

situate our lives in relation to that life. For it was assumed by the churches that gave us the Gospels that we cannot know who Jesus is and what he stands for without learning to be his followers."[55] This discipleship is a communal discipleship. It presupposes the memory and the social context of the church, and it concerns its common life. There cannot by definition be any private discipleship, because salvation is about God's creation of a new polity. Consequently, christology and social significance cannot be separated. But he thinks that most classical and modern christology has been formulated without concern for the social shape of Jesus' work.[56]

Even to put the question as "the relationship between christology and social ethics or politics" is, he contends, problematic. "The question presupposes that the meaning and truth of commitment to Jesus can be determined apart from his social significance. In contrast I will argue that what it means for Jesus to be worthy of our worship is explicable only in terms of his social significance . . . a christology which is not a social ethic is deficient."[57]

This view makes Hauerwas critical of the way the concept of the "kingdom of God" in modern Christian ethical thought has often been used as an ethical ideal or a program for social change. The problems with this view, according to Hauerwas, are several.[58] First of all, it disregards the eschatological nature of the kingdom. The kingdom of God is not a human utopian project, but is a reality established by God. This does not mean that it is only future. The church trusts "that the kingdom was present in Jesus, is present in the church by the power of the Holy Spirit, and will be fully manifest in the second coming."[59]

Secondly, it also abstracts the ethical ideals from the community it presupposes. The kingdom of God is not an ahistorical ideal, nor another name for the world political processes, but is first of all manifested in a people called out from the nations. Put differently, it is historically and socially embodied in the community of the Christian church, even though God's reign is wider than the church and even though the church often has been and is unfaithful. He writes: "Without the kingdom ideal, the church loses its identity-forming hope; without the church, the kingdom ideal loses its concrete character. Once abstracted from the community it presumes the kingdom ideal can be used to underwrite any conception of the just society."[60]

---

[55]*PK* 74.

[56]He directs this criticism even against the best modern christological works, like the ones of Pannenberg, Rahner, Kasper, and Barth. One of the few exceptions he finds is Jon Sobrino's *Christology at the Crossroads*. See *CC* 233 n. 4.

[57]*CC* 37.

[58]On this, see esp. *AN* 107-121.

[59]*AN* 116.

[60]*AN* 112f. "The kingdom does not start with nature, with the notion that the perfection implicit in creation be reformed by divine assistance; rather, the kingdom starts as the hope of a people called by God, which for Christians is defined by the life and death of the crucified Christ. The universal scope of the

Thirdly, it often reduces the kingdom of God to supposedly self-interpreting ethical ideals like love and justice and thereby fails to see that it is first of all the history of Jesus that defines the content of the kingdom, because it is through this life we have learned to know how God acts in the world.[61]

4. Towards a Theological Politics

The language of the kingdom implies a politics, but a politics of a very specific sort, determined by the history of Jesus. To be a disciple, to be a Christian, is therefore to be part of this politics. This makes Hauerwas deeply critical of the modern privatizing of faith, as well as of the very distinction between private and public, which lies behind modern theology's reduction of the Christian faith to a spiritual or religious dimension of one or other sort.[62] In this respect, he is sympathetic to the concerns of political theology.

> The proponents of "political theology" are therefore right to claim that the meaning and truth of the Christian convictions cannot be separated from their political implications. They are wrong, however, to associate "politics" only with questions of social change. Rather the "political" question crucial to the church is what kind of community the church must be to be faithful to the narratives central to Christian convictions.[63]

Moltmann and political theology make politics the basic horizon for Christian theology and practice. Hauerwas can be said to agree, but their understandings of the political horizon differ. For Moltmann the politics of the national and world communities, and more precisely power over the national (or a future world) state, has priority. His concern is the participation of Christians in this political struggle. Hauerwas, on the other hand, sees the church, the called people of God, as the primary locus for a new politics.[64] The church as an alternative *polis* or

---

kingdom is rooted in the universal scope of God's reign. What we can know of this God and his kingdom is always given through the history of Israel filtered through the light of Jesus' cross." (*AN* 115.)

[61]"Scripturally there seems to be no good grounds to associate the kingdom of God with any form of political organization and/or to assume that it is best characterized by any one set of ethical ideals such as love and justice. As a platitude it may be unobjectionable to claim that God's kingdom must surely be one of love and justice, but that does little to help one understand what is the meaning and content of love and justice. Indeed, when the content of such ideals is spelled out . . . we begin to suspect that the language of the kingdom is being used to underwrite ethical commitments and political strategies that were determined prior to the claims about the centrality of the kingdom for Christian ethics." (*AN* 111. See further *CC* 44-51.)

[62]*CC* 121, *PK* 96f.

[63]*CC* 2.

[64]See also Yoder, *The Christian Witness to the State*, 17f. Cf. the definition of politics by the political scientist Clarke Cochran. This definition has much in common, although it is not identical, with Hauerwas' view. It also clarifies the different uses of this word by Moltmann and Hauerwas. "I understand politics as participation in the comprehensive ordering of the life of a group or institution. Politics is collective debate and decision making about the common good of a whole. In this sense, politics is a

civitas is thus carrier of a specifically theological politics; that is a politics determined by the new reality of the kingdom of God as seen in the life and destiny of Jesus. He therefore understands the politics of the world, and relates to it, in the light of this new politics.

If we continue to use the language of church and world, Moltmann makes God's activity in the world, understood as the political struggle for emancipation, the horizon in which the church's theology and practice are interpreted, while Hauerwas makes the church's story the "counter story" that interprets the world's politics. In this difference we find the most decisive parting of ways between Moltmann's political theology and Hauerwas' theological politics.

Entailed in Hauerwas making the church the primary locus of politics is not only a change of political horizon, but also a different understanding of the nature of politics. Hauerwas writes that "genuine politics" is the "conversation necessary for a people to discover the goods they have in common".[65] This view, embedded in his theological convictions, has important implications. First, there is something called common goods, and this something has a public nature. It is not arbitrary, but can be reasoned about. Second, violence is not politics with other means or, even less, the essence of politics, but destroys politics, because it destroys the conversation. Third, this makes reflections on the sort of people, the communal structures and institutions, and the forms of authority that can sustain this sort of politics crucial for Hauerwas.

For Moltmann the hope is for a world free from dominion and authority, which seems to imply the end of politics. But the means for reaching this state, according to a prominent line of thought in Moltmann's theology, are political struggle for the power over the state and the processes of social change. Politics as a means for assuming power becomes thus a central concern for Moltmann. Violence is therefore also a form of politics. Politics becomes more a struggle against oppression than a positive conversation about the sort of society we want. Moltmann seems to presuppose that the latter is self-evident or a technical matter which comes by itself when oppression has been overcome and the good forces

---

necessary and legitimate part of the life of all groups and institutions. I distinguish this from politics in the strict sense. Politics in this latter sense is participation in the ordering of an entire society. As such, it always involves the disposition of instruments of power and force. Politics in this sense is public. But so is politics in groups and institutions smaller than the society as a whole. What is objectionable is the tendency of politics in the strict sense to swallow up other politics." (*Religion in Public and Private Life*, 52.) To this one can add that the church, as both Hauerwas and Moltmann understand it, is larger than any national society, although it historically and today, because of its divisions, often has failed in its international witness. This transnational character is, for Hauerwas, one of the most positive sides of the Roman Catholic church, and it also, for both Moltmann and Hauerwas, makes the ecumenical movement important.

[65]"Epilogue", 179.

have taken the power.[66] That politics so understood is made the primary field for theology has important consequences.

We have, however, also found another line of thought in Moltmann. When he describes the church as a contrast society, with its specific and public ecclesial ethics of discipleship centring on the practice of peace, he goes far in the direction of Hauerwas. This similarity is based on a further (though partial) theological unity, which this chapter has given ample evidence of. We find it in their eschatological and trinitarian theology, based on the history of Israel and Jesus Christ, which for both leads to a social and political understanding of salvation and to an account of the common Christian life in terms of following Jesus Christ. There is much difference in how they explicate these common themes, but there is enough agreement for making an interesting argument.

To conclude, Hauerwas' work can thus be understood as an attempt to reflect on the meaning and consequences of the alternative politics which Christians are called to embody. He can thus follow Milbank who describes "theology as itself a social science, and the queen of the sciences for the inhabitants of the *altera civitas*, on pilgrimage through this temporary world."[67] There can be a theology as a social theory because there is a distinctive form of Christian discourse and practice, because there is a contrast society. This gives theology a specific perspective.[68] Hauerwas therefore describes part of his theological project as an attempt to redescribe reality, and in his case especially the American society, in Christian terms.[69] In this sense theology has its base in ecclesiology.[70]

---

[66]Moltmann can explicitly define politics in Weberian terms, making force the final definition of politics. "A political association of people is an association for rule, which is able to enforce its decisions with the threat of physical compulsion." (*CPS* 176 [199].) However, this force has to be legitimated in terms of democracy and human rights. See *CPS* 176-182 (199-206). Exactly how he relates political action, radical democracy and his universal and all embracing theory of rights is an interesting question to which I have no clear answer. Because his rights account does not seem to give any place for the possibility of radical political disagreement, it seems only to reinforce the idea of politics as a struggle of power between good and evil forces. One can also find statements that question the Weberian understanding of politics. See e.g. his "Foreword" to Cornelison, *The Christian Realism of Reinhold Niebuhr and the Political Theology of Jürgen Moltmann in Dialogue*, iv-v.

[67]Milbank, *Theology and Social Theory*, 380 and Hauerwas, "Christian Ethics in America", 4.

[68]Milbank says that "Christian sociology is distinctive simply because it explicates, and adopts the vantage point of, a distinct society, the Church" (*Theology and Social Theory*, 381).

[69]"Christian Ethics in America", 26.

[70]Hütter thus says that Hauerwas' ecclesial ethics has its base in the third article of faith. "The aim is to understand evangelical ethics as ecclesial discourse-practice, which is given with the contingent realities of the congregation, where its authentic 'Sitz im Leben' is found and it has as its subject witness to the Gospel in all the situations of life." (*Evangelische Ethik*, p. vii.)

Chapter 10

The Church as the Manifestation of the Kingdom

In the preceding chapter we found that Hauerwas explicates his understanding of salvation in unmistakable ecclesial terms. Salvation means that God creates a people as the social manifestation of the new alternative history determined by the kingdom of God that has come in Jesus Christ. Therefore the church is from the beginning a political reality; in the words Moltmann uses, a contrast society. This chapter will deal with the consequences of this ecclesiology regarding the life of the church, its use of the Bible, its social and political practice, and its relation to the world (including the politics of the nation-state). Moltmann identifies his own ecclesiology primarily with the Radical Reformation tradition and Hauerwas and Moltmann thus have much in common. Yet, their divergent understandings of the locus and the nature of politics lead to important differences.

1. The Marks of the Church

The connotations of the word "church" can be very different. For some, ministry and hierarchy are the primary connotations. For others "church" is first of all a local group of people. Such differing practical contexts (and the given examples are just two among several) for the term "church" cause much confusion and misunderstanding.[1] To understand Hauerwas one has to see that for him the Christian church is a real people that exists in definite historical and institutional forms. There is no invisible church or some universal entity that is more real than the actual existing people with their history, institutions and practices. Neither is the church primarily the institution with its ministers and sacraments, but the people that the institutional forms and the ministers serve.[2] This gives the local congregation a role that is different from many traditional ecclesiologies. This also makes any static, timeless view of the church impossible. The church is a historical and in relation to new social contexts changing phenomenon. It is a living tradition that constantly is arguing about how to live faithfully to Jesus Christ. The Christian story about God (the interpretation of which in itself is contested) is the critical norm that constantly questions the actual practice, keeping the discussion going and thereby keeping the tradition alive. If faithfulness is the aim, unfaithfulness is always a possibility. Obviously, for Hauerwas the failures of the historical and contemporary church are as evident as its faithfulness. However,

---

[1] *CET* 111f.

[2] *PK* 107, "Epilogue", 153, *CET* 111f, "Why *Resident Aliens* Struck a Cord", 424. As often with such issues Hauerwas does not get into any extended discussion with the Christian traditions concerning the distinction between visible and invisible church. On this, see e.g. Weber, *Foundations of Dogmatics*, vol. 2, 540-547.

what constitutes failure is in his view a contested issue. This also is part of the ongoing argument about the nature and consequences of the coming of the kingdom in Jesus Christ. So the church can be seen as the continuation of the biblical story and as the place where this story makes itself known.

> What it means to be Christian, therefore, is that we are a people who affirm that we have come to find our true destiny only by locating our lives within the story of God. The church is the lively argument, extended over centuries and occasioned by the stories of God's calling of Israel and of the life and death of Jesus Christ, to which we are invited to contribute by learning to live faithful to those stories. It is the astounding claim of Christians that through this particular man's story, we discover our true selves and thus are made part of God's very life. We become part of God's story by finding our lives within that story.[3]

Being a real people, the church is dependent on specific means for its continuing existence. Discussing this, Hauerwas refers in a traditional way to the "marks" of the church,[4] which he describes as the means that God has given the messianic pilgrim people[5] for sustaining its life as "resident aliens". The marks he mentions are baptism and eucharist, preaching and the holy life. Through baptism people are initiated into the Christian story and "[t]he eucharist is the eschatological meal of God's continuing presence that makes possible a peaceable people."[6] The Christian story is, so to say, enacted through baptism and eucharist. Furthermore, they are *political* rituals, as they form the identity of the Christian people and help them see how the kingdom of God is present in the world. Preaching, on the one hand, forms a people to live with the story and to be challenged by it, and, on the other hand, witnesses to those who do not know the story.

The final mark he mentions is the call to be a holy people, that is, "a people who are capable of maintaining the life of charity, hospitality, and justice". This makes "mutual upbuilding and correction" essential. Here his Radical Reformation and Methodist theology is visible as this is a theme usually not stressed in some other traditions. The importance of this theme is made clear by his remark that "the church is finally known by the character of the people who constitute it, and if we lack that character, the world rightly draws the conclusion that the God we worship is in fact a false God."[7] He closely connects this holiness with the sacramental life, because through eating the meal together Christians learn the forgiveness that helps them live together in love and justice.[8]

---

[3] *CET* 102. "The church is where the stories of Israel and Jesus are told, enacted, and heard, and it is our conviction that as a Christian people there is literally nothing more important we can do." (*PK* 99f.)
[4] *PK* 106-111.
[5] Cf. *VV* 240 n. 41.
[6] *PK* 108.
[7] All citations in this paragraph are from *PK* 109.
[8] Cf. 1 Cor. 11:17-26.

Hauerwas gives the sacraments, and especially the eucharistic life of the church,[9] a central place. This reflects the "high-church" dimension of his theology. However, his explicit sacramental theology is very sketchy and this creates some problems. Like much contemporary theology he wants to integrate the sacraments in the liturgical and social life of the church, but he does not say much about what this might actually mean for the *practice* of the eucharist. Neither does he discuss how contemporary eucharist practices reflect theological convictions and a history that might be in conflict with his own theological politics. He tends to write about the eucharist as if its practice and meaning were self-evident. Here Moltmann and Yoder are more helpful and their discussions of this subject could be useful for a development of Hauerwas' sacramental views in a direction that is consistent with his general theological perspective.[10]

The early church had no concept of sacrament in the later sense. Its development is an outworking of the movement away from the Jewish character of Christianity, the depolitization and individualization of the understanding of salvation, the relative loss of the eschatological character of the Christian faith, and its development into an imperial religion that Hauerwas criticizes. This development was heightened in the conflict between church and state in the medieval time, where the church increasingly developed into a separated sacramental sphere. This in its turn contributed to the secularization of the world. Certain practices, separated from their liturgical, social, political and everyday context, became centred religious rites with specific powers.

Recent theology has again tried to integrate these practices into a wider theological, ecclesial, liturgical and political context. This has also entailed a different use of the word sacrament. Walter Kasper, following the Second Vatican Council, talks of Jesus Christ as "the primal sacrament"; the "church as the universal saving sacrament of Jesus Christ"; and the "individual sacraments as an unfolding of the sacramental structure of the church".[11] This could also be an appropriate way to describe Hauerwas' understanding.

Moltmann similarly tries to develop a trinitarian concept of sacrament. The church is an expression of the eschatological work of Christ through the Spirit in the world. In this pneumatological context both Christ and the church can be described as sacraments, and the practices usually described as sacraments can, he thinks, be more adequately understood. "In the eschatological gift of the Holy Spirit 'word and sacrament', 'ministries and charismata' become comprehensible as the revelations and powers of Christ and his future. As the emblematic revelations of Christ they are the messianic mediations of salvation."[12] In this perspective "proclamation, baptism, the Lord's Supper, worship, prayer, acts of blessing

---

[9] Cf. "Faith in the Republic", 524 and *CET* 118-121.

[10] On the following, see *CPS* 197-288 (222-315), Yoder, "Sacrament as Social Process", idem, "The Lord's Supper in Historical Perspective", and, in addition, Kasper, *Theology and Church*, 111-128.

[11] Kasper, *Theology and Church*, 119, 121, 122.

[12] *CPS* 205 (231).

and the way in which individual and fellowship live" are all seen as "means of salvation" or "mediations and powers of the Holy Spirit"[13] together with the gifts and ministries of the church. Yoder similarly talks of baptism and the breaking of bread together with "fraternal admonition", the "universality of charisma" and "the Spirit's freedom in the meeting"[14] as social and political practices that constitute the church as community. They are ordinary, everyday practices that do not stand for something else, but in themselves are what they stand for. "It is that bread *is* daily sustenance. Bread eaten together *is* economic sharing. Not merely symbolically, but in actual fact".[15] He contrasts this view both to Zwinglian and "sacramentalist" views.[16]

Both for Moltmann and Yoder this requires not only a different theological understanding of the "sacraments", but also and more importantly a different practice. To take the case of the eucharist, Moltmann stresses, for example, the integration of the eucharist in the worship service and wishes that the sharing of "experiences and problems of everyday life"[17] becomes part of its celebration. He would also like the eucharist to be celebrated as part of an ordinary meal.[18]

2. A Community of Virtue

a) Discipleship

This call to be a holy people makes discipleship and mutual upbuilding crucial in Hauerwas' account. It also throws interesting light on his relation to the political theology of Moltmann. We have previously found severe tensions in Moltmann's depiction of the Christian life between his "expressive individualism" (stressing spontaneity, autonomy and self-realization) and his account of an ecclesial discipleship. We will see that Hauerwas is deeply critical of the former and develops one possible version of the latter.

According to Hauerwas, becoming Christian is to become part of the church. "It is by faith . . . that we become joined with the body of Christ, which involves our participation and emersion in the daily practices of the Christian church: prayer, worship, admonition, feeding the hungry, caring for the sick, etc. So we are transformed over time to participate in God's life."[19] The church is a com-

---

[13]*CPS* 198 (223).

[14]"Sacrament as Social Process", 34f. In *The Priestly Kingdom*, 93 he relates this perspective to the Roman Catholic understanding of the sacramentality of the church.

[15]"Sacrament as Social Process", 37.

[16]Cf. also Berkhof, *Christian Faith*, 345-392.

[17]*CPS* 259 (285).

[18]*CPS* 259f (285f). In difference to Yoder he seems still to separate the actual eucharist from the meal although eaten at the same time. It is difficult to understand why. For a concrete discussion how such a meal could be celebrated, see Eller, *In Place of Sacraments*, 79-144. See also idem, *Proclaim Good Tidings*.

[19]"Virtue Christianly Considered", 20. "We are 'in Christ' insofar as we are part of that community pledged to be faithful to this life as the initiator of the kingdom of peace." (*PK* 93.)

munity that is called to witness to the peaceable kingdom in common discipleship of Jesus Christ. To be a disciple therefore is to be part of the new *polis* that has the Gospels as constitution.[20] As a life of discipleship, Christian life thus concerns the formation, or rather the transformation, of people through the tradition-formed community called the church.[21]

Seeing the Christian life in terms of discipleship shows that it is not something spontaneous, something that comes "naturally". Neither is its content "self-evident", in the sense that sufficient intellectual effort would make it available for anyone. Instead, Hauerwas contends, Christian life has to be learned and therefore requires training.[22] He compares it to how we learn a craft, play a musical instrument or learn a language (which in themselves are also moral practices). Initiation into a craft is learning through apprenticeship. Learning a craft includes not only learning a set of skills, but also learning the language related to those skills, a language that "embodies the history of the craft".[23] In other words, one has to be initiated into a tradition carried by a community, and one is initiated by masters. Describing the moral process in this way underscores that the important issue is not only what to do, but also how to do it. This is learned through example and training. Being moral is being formed in certain ways, learning to see, describe, desire and act rightly.[24] Being thus comes before doing. This leads Hauerwas to talk about the importance of "saints", by which he means "personal examples of the Christian faith".[25] They function as "central paradigmatic examples"[26] recognized by the Christian tradition.

This also explains the important role examples and stories present in Hauerwas' writings. Theological reflection on such examples is one important function for Christian ethics. And one prominent form of Hauerwasian writing is therefore to retell and comment such stories. This should not be understood as a pedagogical technique, but as an essential form of ethical reflection. He has, to name some examples, (beside biblical stories[27]) used a scene from C. S. Lewis' *Silver Chair* for reflecting on the "new morality";[28] discussed self-deception with the help of Albert Speer's autobiography;[29] described his understanding of social ethics using

---

[20]*CC* 46-51, *AN* 116.

[21]"To become a disciple is not a matter of a new or changed self-understanding, but rather to become part of a different community with a different set of practices." (*AC* 107.)

[22]On the following, see e.g. *AC* 93-111, *RA* 93-111, and "Honor in the University".

[23]*AC* 101.

[24]"Living morally is not simply holding the right principles; it involves nothing less than learning to desire the right things rightly." (*CET* 103.)

[25]*RA* 103. See also *CET* 104, *US* 99-104, "The Church and/as God's Non-Violent Imagination", "Why Resident Aliens", 424, and "What Could It Mean For the Church To Be Christ's Body?".

[26]*CET* 71.

[27]Besides the general biblical "master plot" which is behind most of what he writes, he until rather recently seldom used specific biblical stories for his reflections. But see e.g. *TT* 135-139, *CC* 46-49, *PK* 78-81, *AN* 55f, *CET* 47-54, *RA* 130-140, and *US*.

[28]*VV* 93-110,

[29]*TT* 82-98.

Richard Adams' story of rabbits in *Watership Down*;[30] discussed hope and power through Robert Bolt's play about Thomas More;[31] discussed honour with one of Anthony Trollope's novels;[32] and reflected on truthfulness and forgiveness through Anne Tyler's *Saint Maybe*.[33] His book *Naming the Silences* consists to a large part of a retelling of the stories about ill and dying children and in *Resident Aliens* stories from ordinary church life have a crucial role.[34]

He also stresses, as we will see later in more detail, that this conception of Christian formation should not be understood as restricting. Instead it is a question of learning things that otherwise would not have been a possibility. It increases the options I have, just as training and discipline in a craft or in learning to play a musical instrument creates a freedom that was not there without the training.

However, this understanding of Christian discipleship does require, Hauerwas contends, developed ecclesial practices of discipline, forgiveness and reconciliation. Sin can be confronted without destroying the community because of specific practices of forgiveness and reconciliation. Without a radical practice of forgiveness a community that confesses the existence of common goods would be dangerous.[35]

Forgiveness is consequently a crucial category of Radical Reformation theology. However, it is important to see the close connection Hauerwas makes between God's forgiveness and the practices of mutual forgiveness and reconciliation in the church. God's forgiveness forms a people of peace, because forgiveness creates the space that makes peacefulness possible, which in its turn involves the ongoing practice of mutual forgiveness and reconciliation. In this perspective being *forgiven* thus comes before being *forgiving*. He notes that it is more difficult to accept forgiveness than to give it. It is so because to accept forgiveness means giving up the control of one's own life and consequently to trust someone else. In the classical Christian way he says that it is through accepting the forgiveness of God one can receive the capacity to give up this control and acknowledge that one's life also is in other hands. Christians must therefore be a people that risk trusting others and not fear the new, the different, and the surprising. As a forgiven people it can accept its own history without denials and distortions. Consequently, they do not need to fear that others will reveal or destroy the illusions they live with. Hauerwas thinks that it is precisely such fear that creates aggression and violence.

---

[30]*CC* 9-35. The recent "The Church and/as God's Non-Violent Imagination" also uses this story.

[31]*CET* 199-219.

[32]*DFF* 58-79.

[33]*DFF* 80-88.

[34]This is a result of it being cowritten with a minister, William Willimon.

[35]*CET* 89-97, *DFF* 80-88. For other discussions of various aspects of this theme that enlightens Hauerwas' approach, see Yoder, "Binding and Loosing", Jeschke, *Disciplining the Brother*, McClendon, *Systematic Theology: Ethics*, 209-239, and Cartwright, "Practices, Politics, and Performance", 298-413.

This love that is characteristic of God's kingdom is possible only for a forgiven people—a people who have learned not to fear one another. For love is the nonviolent apprehension of the other as other. But to see the other as other is frightening, because to the extent others are other they challenge my way of being. Only when my self—my character—has been formed by God's love, do I know I have no reason to fear the other.[36]

Forgiveness is thus crucial for the conception of peace that is at the heart of Radical Reformation theology.

b) Virtue

This conception of the Christian life forms the background of Hauerwas' use of virtue language. He is well known, and for a long time principally known, as the most influential theological protagonist for the recent renaissance of so-called virtue ethics.[37] It is outside the scope of this work to discuss his conception in any detail. However, it is not correct to describe his ethics just as virtue ethics, because there is no virtue ethics as such.[38] His ethics is a Christian or an ecclesial ethics, and his interest is therefore Christian virtue. Human existence is intrinsically historical. "As humans we cannot be anything we wish, but, as the virtues show, our nature demands that we wish to be more than our nature."[39] The consequence is, as history shows, that there is much diversity between different virtue accounts.[40] Just stressing the importance of virtue in general is not necessarily positive, the important question is which virtue. Furthermore, although he has

---

[36]*PK* 91. See further *PK* 87-91 and 142-144.

[37]This goes through most of his writings. For more sustained theoretical discussions, see e.g. *CCL*, *VV* 48-67, *TT* 40-56, *CC* 111-152, *PK* 102-106, *CET* 191-197, "Virtue", "Happiness, the Life of Virtue and Friendship", "Virtue Christianly Considered", and "The Difference of Virtue and the Difference It Makes". For other recent examples, see from a Lutheran perspective Meilander, *The Theory and Practice of Virtue*, and from Roman Catholic perspective, Cessario, *The Moral Virtues and Theological Ethics* and Wadell, *The Primacy of Love*. In philosophy, MacIntyre's *After Virtue* is especially well known. For general overviews of the explosion of interest in the role of virtues, see Spohn, "The Return of Virtue Ethics" and Yearley, "Recent Work on Virtue". Yearley, writing in 1990, says that "what only ten years ago was a cottage industry threatens to become an industrial giant." (Ibid., 1.) It should be noted that most of Hauerwas' writings on virtue is from the "cottage industry period", that is, it predates 1980, although he has written quite a lot since then.

[38]He contends "that there is no virtue theory in general. Rather the characterizations of the virtues, their content, how they interrelate, will differ from one community and tradition to another." ("The Difference of Virtue", 260.) This does not hinder him to think that Christian theology has much to learn from other accounts. Concerning virtue that first of all means Aristotle. The exposition of Aristotle, and Thomas Aquinas' Christian transformation of Aristotle's account, thus plays a central role for Hauerwas' reflection. Cf. the discussion between Quinn and Hauerwas in Quinn, "Is Athens Revived Jerusalem Denied?" and Hauerwas, "Athens May Be a Long Way From Jerusalem But Prussia is Even Further".

[39]*CC* 123.

[40]For a short display of this diversity, see *CC* 121-123.

found it helpful to explicate the content of the life of discipleship in terms of virtue, he thinks there are also other possibilities for Christian ethics.[41]

Hauerwas' account of the virtues is thus not derived from a general conception of the human nature or the human good, but from the Christian story and the understanding of the life it depicts. This life he describes in terms of a journey that requires certain virtues. So understood, the virtues are not self-referential, but should be seen as "skills for a people who are trying to be faithful to a journey they believe to be crucial for God's dealing with the world."[42] The virtues thus cannot be displayed in the abstract and in general terms as applicable for everyone everywhere at any time. They are instead connected to the Christian community and its story of Jesus Christ. In that sense they are a politics, but a politics dependent on Jesus Christ.[43] This does not mean that he denies that there is much overlap. Every community requires virtues like trust, hope and love to be sustained. He can therefore even describe the traditional "theological virtues" (faith, hope and love) as in a sense "natural". But he also says: "For Christians, the sense of what it is in which they have faith, in which they hope, and the kind of love that must be displayed among them derives from the tradition that molds their community."[44]

He does not develop a precisely defined *telos*, a well-rounded description of the *telos* of the human nature. His use of the metaphor "journey" is meant to suggest that people on this journey do not have exact knowledge as to where the journey will lead.[45]

For the *telos* in fact is a narrative, and the good is not so much a clearly defined 'end' as it is a sense of the journey on which that community finds itself. In political terms it means that the conversation of community is not *about* some good still to be realized, but the

---

[41]On the relation between discipleship and virtue, see his "Happiness", 28f and "Athens", 60. See also "Virtue Christianly Considered", 4. For some partly critical comments by Yoder on the use of virtue language, see his *Nevertheless*, 130-132.

[42]"Happiness", 29.

[43]"Virtue Christianly Considered", 9 and "The Difference of Virtue", 250.

[44]*PK* 103. This means that Christians cannot just take over e.g. the antique Greek understanding of the virtuous life. Because the Christian story has a different *telos* than the Greek ones, their respective understandings of virtue are very different. Although Hauerwas has drawn extensively on Aristotle, he does not think that Christians can build their understanding of virtue and the virtues on his account, because Christianity is an inauguration of a new *telos*. He seems to accept Milbank's characterization of the Greek tradition as basically heroic—there is in the end (even for Aristotle) no other *telos* than conflict. ("Virtue Christianly Considered", 9-21 and Milbank, *Theology and Social Theory*, 326-379. See also "The Difference of Virtue".) The Christian *caritas*, on the other hand, "sees the person of virtue as essentially standing in mutuality with God and with her fellow humans." ("Virtue Christianly Considered", 13.) Therefore, for the Christian, peace, as more than just absence of conflict, is more basic than conflict. In this stress on the discontinuity between the Greek and the Christian tradition he seems to differ from MacIntyre. (Ibid., 8-21.)

[45]So "in the journey of faith, we have no clear idea of what our end will be except that it shall be, in some form, true and complete friendship with God." (*RA* 61.)

conversation *is* the good insofar as it is through the conversation that the community keeps faithful to the narrative.[46]

The character of the Christian narrative thus forms how the virtues are described and which are the most central. Hauerwas has not given any lists of virtues, but he has stressed especially the importance of *hope* and *patience* for a people on the way "between the ages" that remembers and tells "the story of a crucified savior."[47] Patience is needed for the church to be able to live as a peaceable people in a violent world. Without patience the Christian hope is in danger of turning into fanaticism or, as failed optimism, into cynicism and despair. As a patient people the church does not lose hope in God and God's promises to use its faithfulness. He further says that this hope in God both helps the church to see reality as it is and as it could be and therefore forces the church to look for alternatives to a reliance on violence and power.[48] This illustrates his claim that to be able to witness to the peaceable kingdom the church "must be a particular kind of people formed by a particular set of virtues."[49] It is in this sense that he describes the church as a community of virtue.

It should be noted that my account here reflects the views found in the later writings of Hauerwas. His earlier writings are more problematic. He has always defended a position similar to the one I have described, but his writings did not all the time adequately work it out. His discussions about virtue and character and his theology were not sufficiently integrated. One example is his essay "The Virtues and Our Communities: Human Nature as History".[50] This is not only a basically philosophical account of virtue, he also seems to derive the virtues hope and patience from a phenomenology of the historical nature of human existence.[51] In contrast to this a central theme in much of his later writings is the difference a Christian faith-practice makes not only to the individual virtues, but also to the very understanding of virtue as such. However, here more work needs to be done, particularly regarding specific Christian virtues.

---

[46]*PK* 119.

[47]*PK* 103.

[48]On hope and patience, see esp. *CC* 127f, *PK* 103-106, and *CET* 199-219.

[49]*AN* 118. See also *PK* 102f and *RA* 61.

[50]*CC* 111-128.

[51]For similar criticism, see Jones, *Transformed Judgement*, 15-19 and Ramsey, "A Question (or Two) for Stanley Hauerwas", esp. 33-45. Cf. also Van Gerwen's early dissertation, which tries to describe Hauerwas' ethics through starting in the general concepts and phenomenology that it builds on, though Van Gerwen knows this is against Hauerwas' intentions. He writes: "It is my intuition that Hauerwas, while not intending to propose a general system or 'foundation' of ethics, has in fact produced a very good one. . . . As a Roman Catholic I am prepared to recognize in Hauerwas' ethical concepts the phenomenological equivalent of a natural law ethic or an ethic of the human." ("The Church in the Theological Ethics of Stanley Hauerwas", 2f.)

c) Virtue and Justification by Faith

A common criticism of the use of virtue language is that it comes in conflict with the Christian understanding of grace and the doctrine of the justification by faith.[52] We find this criticism also in Moltmann. We have seen that he argues his view of spontaneous self-realization in terms of the doctrine of justification by faith, and he does it in explicit contrast to the use of virtue language.[53] Moltmann's criticism, especially directed against Aristotle and Marx, is the traditional Protestant charge that the doctrine of virtue implies that humans create themselves. The Christian view is instead that God makes the sinners righteous independent of their works. They are constituted as persons by the accepting love of God. When they do not need to create themselves through works they become liberated to free, spontaneous and joyful works. The new life is not forced, but comes from within as fruit on a tree. Only, he continues, the structures of society have to be changed so that objective possibilities for the new life are given.

Hauerwas answers this both through questioning the Lutheran understanding of justification and through showing how the Christian life is understood to be a gift. First of all, he questions making concepts such as "justification" and "sanctification" primary. They are better understood as rules for telling and living the Christian story rightly. "'Sanctification' is but a way of reminding us of the kind of journey we must undertake if we are to make the story of Jesus our story. 'Justification' is but a reminder of the character of that story—namely, what God has done for us by providing us with a path to follow."[54] Furthermore, the traditional, too individualistic Lutheran interpretation tends to miss the social, eschatological and practical nature of God's righteousness and saving work.[55]

Furthermore this new life is not created by ourselves, but is a gift, in the sense that it is formed through our being initiated into a narrative that we have not created. He can thus say that our character

> comes not by constant effort to realize an ideal, but rather character is our discovery that we can look back on our lives and, by God's forgiveness, claim them as our own. Character, in other words, is that continuity of self that makes possible retrospective acknow-

---

[52]For a Lutheran criticism of Hauerwas along this score that still is sympathetic towards the idea of a virtue ethics, see Zinger, "Are Grace and Virtue Compatible?"

[53]*TJ* 65-75 (51-63).

[54]*PK* 94. His use of the language of justification and sanctification in *CCL* 179-233 he therefore now thinks was less helpful. See his later comments on this in *CCL* xxviii-xxxi.

[55]In his reinterpretation of Paul, which I think could be expressed much more clearly, he has partly drawn on recent Pauline scholarship. He refers to such works as Sanders, *Paul and Palestinian Judaism*, Beker, *Paul the Apostle*, idem, *Paul's Apocalyptic Gospel*, and Hays, *Echoes of Scripture in the Letters of Paul*. See *CC* 240 n. 10, 245f n. 58, "On Developing Hopeful Virtues", 111, and *AC* 37f. For further discussion of these issues, see the classical work of Stendahl in *Paulus bland judar och hedningar* and the more recent work of Dunn in *Jesus, Paul and the Law*, "The Justice of God", and *Romans*. See also the use of these new perspectives in Yoder, *The Politics of Jesus*, 215-232 and Finger, *Christian Theology*, vol. 2, 165-195.

ledgement that our lives have been made more than we could acknowledge at any one time.[56]

Also Moltmann himself is usually otherwise critical of the common Lutheran understanding of the doctrine of justification.[57] It bases, he says, the doctrine one-sidedly on the cross, which makes justification essentially a question of forgiveness. When it is also based on the resurrection of Christ, it also means new life in righteousness, a new creation. Generally he interprets it as God's creative and rectifying justice. In relation to Hauerwas the following words are pertinent.

> Because the raising of Christ shows this added value and surplus over against his death, the justification of sinners initiates a process of exuberant intensification: justification – sanctification – glorification (Rom. 8.30). Justifying faith is not yet the goal and end of Christ's history. For every individual believer it is no more than the beginning of a way that leads to the new creation of the world and to the justification of God.[58]

This comes close to the view of Hauerwas, and also to his own discipleship ethics. One difference is the explicit ecclesial explication in Hauerwas. Moltmann develops a strongly political interpretation of the doctrine, but again in terms of his specific understanding of politics. God's righteousness creates justice on different levels and makes people hunger and thirst, and therefore work for justice in the world. We will later see why Hauerwas finds this way of talking about justice to be too abstract. Similarly, Hauerwas would also find Moltmann's discussion of sanctification abstract, because it does not relate to how people actually are formed or transformed. It is not bodily enough! Moltmann can write that

> believers are not merely the passive objects of divine sanctification. . . . As determining subjects of their own lives in the covenant with God, they take the beginning of life in re-birth, or regeneration, seriously, using the enlightened eyes of their understanding, the liberated powers of their will, and the assurance of their hearts. They lead a 'special' life, because instead of living according to the ethics of their own society, they increasingly already live according to the law of God's kingdom, Jesus' Sermon on the Mount. Sanctification is *the discipleship of Jesus* and means coming to life in God's Spirit. In this new life one can develop distinctive features too. An inward holiness can grow. But it doesn't develop from the habit of good deeds. It springs from the goodness of the person who is loved by God and already sanctified.[59]

In the last sentences he sounds again remarkably Lutheran. What makes this so abstract, from Hauerwas' point of view, is thus the lack of reflection about how

---

[56]"On Developing Hopeful Virtues", 114. See also "Virtue Christianly Considered", 9 and *PK* 42f.

[57]For some major discussions of justification, see *TH* 203-208 (185-189), *FC* 149-171 (156-179), *WJC* 181-196 (203-219), and *SL* 123-143, 149 (136-157, 163). *HTG* 44-56 (74-89) is an only very slightly different version of the *SL*-text. Why is the same text published in two books in the same year by the same publisher?

[58]*WJC* 186f (208).

[59]*SL* 175 (189).

this is socially and psychologically mediated. It is this Hauerwas tries to provide through his account of the virtuous life.

3. "The Politics of the Bible"[60]

For Hauerwas, it is the church as a community of virtue that gives the context for the Christian use of the Bible.[61] To put it differently, its authority and interpretation are political questions. "The authority of Scripture derives its intelligibility from the existence of a community that knows its life depends on faithful remembering of God's care or his creation through the calling of Israel and the life of Jesus."[62] In this section we will take up what this means.

a) The Bible, the Church, and the Narrative Character of Christian Convictions

In the foregoing, "story" and "narrative" have been frequently occurring words. Hauerwas is also often described as one of the most influential proponents of narrative in theology.[63] But it is misleading to describe Hauerwas' theology as a narrative theology or to make the concept of narrative as such central. It is the biblical narrative in its relation to the continuous history of the church that is of interest for Hauerwas, not the narrative category in itself.[64]

How Hauerwas uses narrative and the issues this raises could, just like virtue, be the subject of a book. I will here only give a short outline.[65] He once points to three claims that the concept of narrative helpfully explicates and interrelates. "First, narrative formally displays our existence and that of the world as creatures—as *contingent* beings." If the world and the history are contingent then nar-

---

[60] *US* 13.

[61] His most extended discussions of the Christian use of the Bible are found in *CC* 53-71 and *US* 13-44.

[62] *CC* 53.

[63] Paul Nelson describes Hauerwas as "the most significant and influential exponent of narrative among contemporary Christian ethicists" and he sees narrative "as the dominant and controlling term" in Hauerwas' ethical conception. See *Narrative and Morality*, 109, 111 for these quotes, and further pp. 109-151. Jerry Gentry likewise describes Hauerwas and McClendon under the label "narrative ethics" in "Narrative Ethics and Economic Justice". For overviews of uses of narrative in theology, see, in addition to Nelson, Goldberg, *Theology and Narrative* (specifically on Hauerwas, see pp. 173-178) and Stroup, *The Promise of Narrative Theology*. Hauerwas and Jones have edited a reader, *Why Narrative?*, that includes many texts that have been important in the renaissance of narrative. For understanding Hauerwas' use of narrative and its developments, Hütter's account in *Evangelische Ethik als kirchliches Zeugnis*, 132-151 is, as usual, the best. See also Heeley, "The Ethical Methodology of Stanley Hauerwas", 102-145.

[64] "Hence, it is a mistake to assume that my emphasis on narrative is the central focus of my position . . . Narrative is but a concept that helps clarify the interrelation between the various themes I have sought to develop in the attempt to give a constructive account of the Christian moral life." (*PK* xxv.) He also says that he for a long time tried to avoid use the language of narrative and story because of the faddish and lose nature of much talk of narrative. But his own position forced him to use it in developing his account of character. See *CCL* xx-xxi and *PK* xxv.

[65] This theme is found throughout Hauerwas' writings, but see esp. *VV* 68-89, *TT* 15-39, 71-81, *CC passim*, *PK* 24-34, 116-134, *CET* 25-65, *RA* 53-60, and "Why the Truth Demands Truthfulness".

ration is the most basic way of describing it. "Second, narrative is the characteristic form of our awareness of ourselves as *historical* beings who must give an
account of the purposive relation between temporally discrete realities." Because
of the historical nature of the self, we understand ourselves as a story, which in its
turn is given its coherence through the larger communally carried stories we live
with. "Third, God has revealed himself narratively in the history of Israel and in
the life of Jesus."[66] He says that the grammar of "God" is not like the grammar of
a concept or a universal, but like a proper name. We learn to know God through
God's history with Israel and Jesus Christ. It is the claim of Christianity that we
learn to know ourselves and the world through locating our own and the world's
stories in the story of God.[67] He also thinks one can see Scripture "as one long,
'loosely structured non-fiction novel' that has subplots that at some points appear
minor but later turn out to be central."[68] One advantage of this way of seeing the
Bible is, according to Hauerwas, that it releases theology from trying to show the
unity of Scripture or from building on putatively central biblical concepts and
doctrines. He instead thinks that this "open" character of the narratives of Scripture makes the Bible more truthful and therefore more helpful for the church. It
also shows that how the story is told is a political and moral issue, which is to say
that it cannot be separated from the life of the church.

Crucial for Hauerwas is that this narrative does not only "render the character
of God" but also "in so doing renders us to be the kind of people appropriate to
that character."[69] The story about God is not a "text" that creates its own textual
world. Rather, it is carried by the communities of Israel and the church. The
church is the continuation of the story, the "recapitulation" of the life of Jesus.[70]
He thus says that "the story is not self-referential but rather creates a people capable of being the continuation of the narrative by witnessing to the world that all
creation is ordered to God's good end."[71] Or to use Milbank's words, for Hauerwas "Bible-Church constitute a single, dynamic 'inhabited' narrative", which is
"the God-given possibility of a 'different' history".[72] So the church in the telling
of the story is the story told. Letting one's life be part of this narrative is letting it
be part of the church.[73]

If narration is the most basic way of talking about God and the world, it follows that doctrines or other non-narrative modes of discourse are secondary.
Hauerwas says that doctrines should be understood as providing an "outline of
the story" and as tools "meant to help us tell the story better." He even goes fur-

---

[66]These three citations are from *PK* 28f. Cf. Milbank, *Theology and Social Theory*, 259-277.
[67]*PK* 24-29, *TT* 76-79.
[68]*CC* 67. The internal quote is from Kelsey, *The Uses of Scripture in Recent Theology*, 48. Kelsey,
whose book has been influential on Hauerwas, is here discussing Barth's use of Scripture.
[69]*CC* 67.
[70]*PK* 29.
[71]*CET* 61.
[72]"Critical Study", 213.
[73]*CET* 54 and *PK* 33.

ther and points to the importance of liturgy. "Because the Christian story is an enacted story, liturgy is probably a much more important resource than are doctrines or creeds for helping us to hear, tell, and live the story of God."[74]

Hauerwas of course recognizes that the church is not the only community Christians participate in. The Christian story (or stories) is therefore not the only story they live with. There is much truth outside the church and the stories it tells. But from the Christian convictions about the contingency of reality and the intrinsic relation between community and narrative it follows that there is no standpoint outside history, no place above our various narrative accounts of reality, no story of stories. For the Christian the issue is instead how the Christian

> stories help provide the means for recognizing and critically appropriating other stories that claim our lives. For it is true that we always find ourselves enmeshed in many histories—of our families, of Texas, America, European civilization, and so on—each of which is constituted by many interrelated and confusing story lines. The moral task consists in acquiring the skills, i.e., the character, which enable us to negotiate these many kinds and levels of narrative in a truthful manner.[75]

Saying this also reminds us that, for Hauerwas, Christianity is not an independent set of beliefs, but a medium through which one sees reality or a set of skills for living the Christian life. Through being ingrafted into the Christian story and learning specific practices, Christians see the world in a new way. Because one acts in the world one sees, one therefore will also live differently.[76]

Hauerwas has increasingly stressed this intrinsic relation between church and narrative. In his earlier writings he sometimes wrote more abstractly about narrative or failed to adequately interrelate his discussions of church and narrative.[77] In

---

[74]All the citations in this paragraph come from *PK* 26. On the importance of liturgy, see also *CC* 240 n. 9 and *CET* 106-110, 124f.

[75]*CC* 96. See also *CET* 64f n. 17. In *AN* 1, 3 Hauerwas uses Lindbeck's language of "absorbing the universe into the biblical world" (Lindbeck, *The Nature of Doctrine*, 135). Lindbeck further says: "Intratextual theology redescribes reality within the scriptural framework rather than translating Scripture into extrascriptural categories. It is the text, so to speak, which absorbs the world, rather than the world the text." (Ibid., 118. See further ibid., 112-138.) On this conception, see Marshall, "Absorbing the World". Hauerwas is, however, critical of Lindbeck's emphasis on the text as such, although Lindbeck has moved in the direction of a more ecclesial account. See *US* 155 n. 7.

[76]Thus "religion is not primarily a set of presuppositions to be believed or disbelieved, but a set of skills that one employs in living. Such skills are acquired by learning the stories of Israel and Jesus well enough not only to interpret the world, but to do so in specifically Christian terms." ("Embarrassed by God's Presence", 98. This general use of the word "religion" is also something he increasingly has become doubtful about. Cf. e.g. *PtS* 15 n. 9 where he questions if the category "religion" is intelligible.) See also *PK* 29f and "The Church and/as God's Non-Violent Imagination".

[77]See e.g. "The Self as Story" in *VV* 68-89 where he starts in a "phenomenology of moral experience" (p. 69) and "Story and Theology" in *TT* 71-81 where he analyses how stories as such function and, among other things, claims that the meaning of stories is in the stories themselves. In both these texts the church plays almost no role. But when we come to *CC* it is very different. He now constantly stresses the necessary interrelation of rendering God and rendering community and that the biblical narratives become intelligible as Christian Scripture only in the context of the church. But even in this book and sometimes afterwards, there is still some ambiguity. This use of narrative in his early writings is also a

his later writings it is the church that is in the foreground, while the language of narrative is placed in the background.[78] What should be stressed is that the construal of the biblical narrative and one's growing into it should be understood ecclesially.

b) The Church as an Interpretative Community

Following Stanley Fish,[79] Hauerwas argues that it is wrong to see the text's meaning as objectively inherent in the text. But neither is the reader the source of the meaning. Instead the text exists and is understood in the context of interpretative communities with specific interpretative interests.[80] The church is the interpretative community for the Bible as Scripture.

On one level this is only a working out of a nonfoundationalist perspective. Naive empiricism is as untenable in exegesis as in other enquiries. One cannot test an interpretation against the text, understood as an independent uninterpreted object. The position is not, of course, that there is nothing out there, but that what we perceive is always shaped by our interpretative acts.

But more important is the political nature of the reading of the Bible. The church does not look for some abstract "meaning" as such, "meaning" as a property inherent in texts, but for how the Bible is used by God for the upbuilding of the church. The reading is determined by this purpose. That the Bible is not an "objective text" is seen already in its canonical nature. He points to how, for example, the letters of Paul change when they become part of the church's Scripture. Paul's intention is then no longer privileged, although Hauerwas does think that study of "authorial intention" can be useful. There is therefore not one way of construing Scripture inherent in the texts themselves. The question is inevitably political.[81]

Nicholas Lash has compared the church's use of the Bible with the practical interpretation of musical and dramatic texts. To perform a symphony or *Hamlet* is to interpret texts. Likewise, "the fundamental form of the Christian interpretation of scripture is, in the concrete, the life, activity and organization of the Christian community, and that Christian practice consists . . . in the performance or enact-

---

parallel to the above mentioned abstract use of "virtue" in these books. Thiemann in *Revelation and Theology*, 83, 175f and Nelson, *Narrative and Morality*, 112f have pointed to this ambiguity, but have, I think, misconstrued it. In Thiemann's terms, the question concerns whether the importance of narrative for theology should be based on the narrative form of Scripture or on the narrative quality of experience. In his answer, Hauerwas argues that if one starts with the intrinsic relation between Bible and church, one does not need to choose. See *CET* 58-61. Milbank, discussing Nelson's criticism, agrees that this opposition is a mistake. See his review of Nelson, *Narrative and Morality*, 393-395.

[78]See his self-criticism in *US* 18 n. 5. Cf. also *CET* 54-62.
[79]For the following, see *US* 19-21, 36f. By Fish, see *Is There a Text in This Class?* and *Doing What Comes Naturally*. On Fish, cf. Moore, *Literary Criticism and the Gospel*, 108-130.
[80]On interpretative interests, see Fowl, "The Ethics of Interpretation".
[81]*US* 20, 151 n. 2, *CC* 64-66.

ment of the biblical text: in its 'active reinterpretation'."[82] This is a good way of describing Hauerwas' view. Therefore the context for the Christian use of the Bible is the liturgy and the preaching in the service of the common discipleship.[83]

Just as a symphony requires an audience that has been trained so that it is able to hear it, the Bible requires a community that is trained and lives in such a way that the Bible becomes intelligible.[84] For example, Christian idolatry of the family, and lack of a Christian account of singleness, make texts like Luke 14:25-33 unintelligible. Furthermore, without practices of non-violence and reconciliation the church does not know what to do with the Sermon on the Mount.[85] This is only another way of saying that a right use of Scripture requires training, and is part of the life of discipleship. Therefore, the use of Scripture should also be understood as learning a craft under the initiation of masters.[86]

Hauerwas writes: "The church is that community pledged constantly to work out and test the implications of the story of God, as known through Israel and Jesus Christ, for its common life as well as the life of the world."[87] To understand this form of communal rationality, it is, he says, more important to understand how communities work than how ideas work.[88] He describes it as an ongoing process of discernment that is dependent on the various gifts and virtues of the community. Following Yoder, he mentions as examples "agents of direction", "agents of memory", "agents of linguistic self-consciousness", and "agents of order and due process".[89] Experts in the modern sense, like biblical critics or ethicists, have no privileged place in this process. Often other gifts and skills are more important.[90] Hauerwas' view entails that many good readings are possible, that new situations and challenges, as well as the internal richness of the Bible, will spark new readings.[91] He denies that this makes interpretations arbitrary. The

---

[82]*Theology on the Way to Emmaus*, 90. See further ibid., 75-92. Cf. also Meeks, "A Hermeneutics of Social Embodiment".

[83]On preaching, see *PtS*.

[84]"That story requires the formation of a corresponding community which has learned to live in a way that makes it possible for them to hear that story." (*CET* 101.)

[85]*US* 42f, 117-125. So also *RA* 128.

[86]On this, see esp. *CET* 101-110.

[87]*PK* 131f.

[88]"Practical reason is not a disembodied process based on abstract principles but the process of a community in which every member has a role to play. Such a process does not disdain the importance of logical rigor for aiding in their deliberation, but logic cannot be a substitute for the actual process of discernment." (*CET* 73.) He is here (*CET* 72-74) following Yoder's discussion of "The Hermeneutics of Peoplehood" in *The Priestly Kingdom*, 15-45. See further *CET* 67-87, *PK* 130-134, and *CC* 54.

[89]*CET* 73f. See Yoder, *The Priestly Kingdom*, 28-34.

[90]"Moral reflection and reason is the activity of a whole community. Often some of that community's best 'casuists' may not even be those who manifest the strongest rational skills. Those with intuitive gifts may simply 'know' better than they can say what the gospel requires of us. The church must be a community of discourse so that the moral significance of such people is not lost because we fear the prophet." (*PK* 134.) On this, see also "The Church and/as God's Non-Violent Imagination".

[91]*US* 36f, 39-42, *CC* 61, 63, On preaching he writes: "It is not as if preaching explicates the same invariant meaning of the text, applying it to different circumstances, but rather that preaching helps us

readings are formed by the church as an interpretative community with specific interpretative strategies and interests that constrain what is possible and relevant to say.[92]

c) Sola Scriptura, Protestant Individualism and Liberalism

Although this might sound radical, Hauerwas thinks that this represents the views of the Roman Catholic church,[93] the Orthodox reading of the Bible[94] and the practice of the gathered community in the Radical Reformation tradition.[95] They all, in various ways (we will later say, more various than Hauerwas tends to recognize), interpret Scripture in the context of the church as interpretative communities. On the other hand, he is critical of the Protestant principle of *sola scriptura* so far as it is used to separate church and Bible, text and interpretation, discipleship and reading. He does not think this use necessarily follows from this principle, it could be read as a church-internal tool, but historically and today it has had, he thinks, that effect.[96] As such the principle reflects the desire to find a certain method, a foundation for theology and church outside the contingencies of history. It is, however, Hauerwas' claim that there is no way in which the Bible can function unmediated. It functions through its concrete and various uses in the church.[97]

---

see that what is at stake is not the question of the 'meaning of Scripture,' but the usefulness of Scripture, given the good ends of Christian community." (*US* 37.)

[92] *US* 20f, 36f. I think his position would be stronger if he added something like Milbank's perspective on narrating. Like Hauerwas, Milbank wants to banish the idea of "meanings" and he describes reading texts as renarrating them. "Yet it is not arbitrary in the sense that one can repeat a text in just any fashion, although one can indeed do so in any number of fashions. The text, if we are attentive, forms a loose and complex knot of resistance, but we do not first of all register this resistance and position it precisely (explanation), and then pass on to the more freewheeling tasks of the spirit. On the contrary, we register this resistance in any number of ways. We may place the pressure here or there, complicate the knot here, undo it a little there—yet, infuriatingly perhaps, we cannot undo the knot altogether (a final deconstruction is endlessly postponed). Always we feel the resistance, although this is from elsewhere, and we cannot precisely place it, for it belongs, ultimately, to a whole wider network of resistances and counter-resistances, which we ourselves, by our intervention, are further adjusting and altering." (*Theology and Social Theory*, 267.) Cf. also Hays, *Echoes of Scripture*, esp. 178-192.

[93] *US* 21-24.

[94] *US* 24f. For a longer account along this line, see Cartwright, "Practices, Politics, and Performance", 190-297.

[95] *US* 158 n. 10, *CC* 54, *CET* 67-87, Cartwright, "Practices, Politics, and Performance", 298-413.

[96] *PK* 98, *US* 27f and 152 n. 17-18. On the Reformation roots of this principle he writes: "The Reformers were rightly concerned that the Scripture act as a judge on the Church. *Sola scriptura* was, no doubt, an important form of protest against many of the normal readings that had so captured the imagination of the Church at the time of the Reformation. The problem now is not how *sola scriptura* was used by the Reformers but how it is used by us." (*US* 27.)

[97] "God certainly uses Scripture to call the Church to faithfulness, but such a call always comes in the form of some in the Church reminding others in the Church how to live as Christians—no 'text' can be substituted for the people of God." (*US* 28.)

Historically the *sola scriptura*-principle was important in the emergence of the liberal society and there is a close relationship between this principle and modern individualism. Both fundamentalism and the historical critical method reflect, Hauerwas contends, the politics of the modern liberal society. Both approaches assume that the Bible should be read as a text immediately available for anyone separate from the practices of the church and from training in discipleship. Thus the nineteenth century fundamentalists saw their way of reading the Bible as a form of Baconian science, the systematization of facts and the general principles to which they pointed. The clear meaning of the text was there open for anyone to see. This view thus corresponded to American religious individualism, distrust of authority and the primacy of the individual conscience. The Bible became the possession of individual citizens. In practice, however, as Hauerwas' argues, the primary community was the United States as a Protestant nation. The result was that the Bible became part of nationalistic ideologies.[98]

The same individualistic assumption is, Hauerwas continues, behind biblical criticism. It also assumes that the text as such has a meaning that is available for anyone, although training in historical and linguistic skills is necessary. The mediation of the church can only distort the meaning.

> Accordingly, fundamentalism and biblical criticism are Enlightenment ideologies in the service of the fictive agent of the Enlightenment—namely the rational individual—who believes that truth in general (and particularly the truth of the Christian faith) can be known without initiation into a community that requires transformation of the self.[99]

He thus thinks that a theological education that primarily teaches historical-critical methods is inadequate for the church. He is not against historical-critical readings as such. They can be valuable in giving new readings, and he himself uses, as we have noted, historical-critical studies. But he refuses to grant them any privileged place for the church's use of the Bible.[100]

He is for the same reason critical of much current literary and hermeneutical theory. It often continues the same putatively apolitical project. "Indeed I suspect that hermeneutics becomes the preoccupation of theology when the text of Scripture is divorced from particular practices of the Church that make it make sense in

---

[98] *US* 31f. On this, see Hatch and Noll (eds.), *The Bible in America*.

[99] *US* 35.

[100] *RA* 161-164, *US* 23. On the relationship between the emergence of political liberalism and historical critical study and the aporias this have created for modern biblical study, see Levenson, *The Hebrew Bible, the Old Testament and Historical Criticism*, 106-126. "For historical criticism is the form of biblical studies that corresponds to the classical liberal political ideal. . . . Like citizens in the classical liberal state, scholars practising historical criticism of the Bible are expected to eliminate or minimize their communal loyalties, to see them as legitimately operative only within associations that are private, nonscholarly, and altogether voluntary." (Ibid., 118.) Levenson, like Milbank in *Theology and Social Theory*, 17-20, claims that historical criticism, as pioneered by Hobbes and Spinoza, was part of the process of subordinating the church under the state and to remove religious convictions to the private sphere. See also Fowl and Jones, *Reading in Communion*, 14-21.

the first place."[101] In the absence of such practices hermeneutical skills cannot make the Bible relevant.

d) Hermeneutics and Politics

The way Hauerwas relates the Bible to the church illuminates the different paths Hauerwas and Moltmann take. We have seen that one way Moltmann describes the theological task is in terms of a correlation between text/tradition and context/situation. From Hauerwas' perspective this is misleading because it seems to suggest, firstly, that we have two poles which we from the outside can relate to each other in different ways, and, secondly, that there is some abstract essence or kernel of Christianity that has to be formulated in different cultural contexts. But if Christianity is about the formation of an alternative people, a contrast society, as Hauerwas and Moltmann maintain, Christianity is nothing separate from its social and cultural form. Christianity is not a set of abstract ideas about God and humanity, but a people. It changes and develops, but not through correlation of some essence with some independent "culture", but through critically negotiating new situations, knowledge and challenges both inside and outside the church.[102]

In Moltmann's correlation model, *theology* is the bridge between the Christian tradition and the modern world. It is the task of theology to mediate or translate this tradition so that it becomes meaningful for modern people in their struggle for justice and freedom. In Hauerwas' conception it is not theology but the *church* that has this role. "The church is the bridge where scripture and people meet."[103] It is the life of the church that makes Christian faith intelligible both for people inside and outside the church. The hermeneutical problem is thus more a political than an intellectual problem. It is the lack of faithful church life that makes much of the Bible and the Christian tradition unintelligible.[104] Moltmann's ecclesial discipleship ethics in *The Way of Jesus Christ* comes close to this view, in contrast to the correlation model he otherwise often uses.

Moltmann's political hermeneutics also seems to come closer to Hauerwas' understanding. Both stress the political context and interests behind the interpretation of the Bible. Here instead the issue between them is "Which politics?" For Hauerwas it is the politics of the church; for Moltmann it is the politics of a putative global community. While for Hauerwas the "Bible-church"-narrative is primary, Moltmann makes a universal history of freedom the basic context. The conflict between Hauerwas' view and Moltmann's political hermeneutics (but not Moltmann's ecclesial ethics) concerns thus how the politics that makes the Bible intelligible and determines the interpretative interests is construed.[105] Hauerwas'

---

[101] *US* 18. So also *CC* 54, *CET* 40f, 55, *RA* 171.
[102] *RA* 21, "Athens", 60.
[103] *RA* 129.
[104] *RA* 128f.
[105] *CC* 53.

conclusion would be that the way Moltmann subsumes the Bible and the church under a universal (a false claim, Hauerwas would say) history of freedom makes the Bible into an "ideology for a politics quite different from the politics of the Church."[106]

Moreover, he says that the very question about how to relate the Bible to ethics or politics reflects the church's captivity to an alien politics. It presumes the politics of the world as something given, be it the liberal politics of United States or some revolutionary socialist politics, and then asks how the Bible can be relevant to this politics. It is this giveness that the church questions.[107]

e) Ecclesial Hermeneutics and Ministry

This account raises one intricate question for Hauerwas. We have seen that he points to the similarity between Roman Catholic, Orthodox and Radical Reformation practices of reading the Bible in the context of the church in contrast to a more individualistic understanding in much of Protestantism (including many parts of the Radical Reformation heritage). Although there are general similarities, the actual practices in these traditions are very different. The radical tradition's "hermeneutics of peoplehood" is not the same as the magisterium and the ordained clergy in the Roman Catholic church. Hauerwas uses variants of both models, but does not discuss the tension to which this leads. Yoder's account of ecclesial hermeneutics assumes a "charismatic" view of the functioning of the church, where there is no distinction between an ordained ministry and an unordained laity. When Hauerwas discusses this communal hermeneutical process, he follows Yoder and elaborates his view in "charismatic" terms. Instead of a mono-pastoral approach, we thus find a multiplicity of gifts and tasks, which makes the whole church participating in the exercise of practical reason. They do not participate as an undifferentiated mass, but in accordance with their different "gifts" and "ministries". There is, in this view, a clear and recognized leadership, but this leadership takes various forms and is exercised by different people, in contrast to a mono-pastoral pattern.[108] Yoder thus writes: "Instead of being dismayed by the idea of the concept of ministry being vaguely diffused through the laity *as a whole*, why not conceive of *specific* ministries being assigned to all members *specifically*, so that what is done away with is not the specialized ministry, but the undifferentiated laity? This option is not seen and then discarded for good reason; it is simply not noticed"[109] Moltmann also has a similar view.[110] But this

---

[106]*US* 15. Cf. also Fowl, "The Ethics of Interpretation", 391-398.

[107]*US* 39. Following Cartwright, "Practices, Politics, and Performance", 31-68, he writes about Reinhold Niebuhr: "If you want, as does Niebuhr, to privilege the realist discourse of liberal democratic politics in the name of sin, then as a matter of fact Scripture, and of course Jesus, is relevant only as the impossible possibility." (*US* 156 n. 2.)

[108]On this see esp. Yoder's *The Fullness of Christ* and *The Priestly Kingdom*, 15-34.

[109]*The Fullness of Christ*, 46f.

[110]See *CPS* 289-314 (316-340).

understanding seems absent from the rest of Hauerwas' writings on church-life and ministry, included *some* of his discussions about the Bible and the church. Instead he usually works with an ordinary ministry-laity distinction,[111] though following the general Protestant tradition of the common priesthood.[112]

It is thus a question not only of coherence, but of the practical viability of his ecclesial hermeneutics. The issue is not the necessity of authority and power, but how specific practices of power and authority are best formed. Yoder writes: "The alternative to arbitrary individualism is not established authority but an authority in which the individual participates and to which he or she consents."[113] This seems close to Hauerwas' understanding of authority, as we will later see, but it is not identical with how the Roman magisterium works. Hauerwas, in an article co-written with Robert Wilken, actually criticizes John Paul II along this line.[114] More generally, one would also like to see his answer to the biblical, theological, historical and political challenge Yoder provides in his *The Fullness of Christ* and Moltmann provides in *The Church in the Power of the Spirit.*

4. "The Church is a Social Ethic"[115]

The church is, Hauerwas contends, an alternative community, a new *polis* that carries an alternative story and practice—or, to follow Moltmann, a contrast society with a contrast story and practice. The major challenge for the church is therefore not how to make some old texts and an antique system of beliefs meaningful and relevant for the belief systems of the modern world. The challenge is instead political—how to live as community in the light of the story of Jesus Christ in the context the church finds itself.[116] "The gospel is a political gospel. Christians are engaged in politics, but it is a politics of the kingdom that reveals the insufficiency of all politics based on coercion and falsehood and finds the true source of power in servanthood rather than dominion."[117]

If this is true, what does it mean for the common life of the church? That is the issue Hauerwas deals with. This is the background of his characteristic statement that the church does not have a social ethic, it *is* a social ethic.[118] It means that it is not the primary task for the church to form social strategies for the state (either this is for the people currently at power or for possible future power holders). The church is called to witness to the new reality that is the kingdom of God—a reality that makes the beginning of new social and political life a possibility. For the

---

[111]Cf. e.g. *CET* 133-148, esp. 133-137, and *RA* 112-143.

[112]See *RA* 112-114 and *SP* 59 n. 24.

[113]*The Priestly Kingdom*, 24.

[114]"Protestants and the Pope". Cf. also "What Could It Mean", 12f.

[115]*PK* 99.

[116]*RA* 30.

[117]*PK* 102.

[118]*RA* 43, *CC* 40, *PK* 99, *AN* 74f, *CET* 101, 111f.

church to assume the understanding of power and politics dominant in a world that does not by itself know this new reality is thus to give up this witness and to let its politics be determined by an understanding of reality that is foreign to the kingdom of God.

a) Church and World

What does this then mean for Hauerwas' understanding of the relation between church and world?[119] First it has to be seen that the concept "world" is here a theological construct—it says something about existence from a Christian perspective. Put differently, church and world are relational concepts. "World" has no meaning in itself, separate from the church; just as "church" has no meaning separate from the world. It is therefore Hauerwas can say that the world only knows that it is world in relation to the church as a separate people.[120] In biblical terms he relates himself to the double Johannine concept of the world as both that order that is in opposition to God and therefore under God's judgement and the world as created, loved and redeemed by God. This doubleness implies for Hauerwas that the world's opposition to God is not ontological, it is not inherent, but has an historical and contingent character. He does not give much help in answering all the classical questions that this raises. His point is instead that the difference between church and world is not a distinction "between realms of reality, between orders of creation and redemption, between nature and supernature", but "between agents",[121] some of whom confess Jesus Christ as Lord and others who do not. The church is a people who want to follow Jesus Christ; this is the basic distinction. But to the extent the church and the Christians are not faithful, the world is also in the church and in the individual Christian. Both church and world are under the judgement of God.[122]

Because the world is God's world, the church furthermore is not "anti-world, but rather an attempt to show what the world is meant to be as God's good creation."[123] The world is in principle redeemed, and the church is the first fruits of this redemption. This thus gives hope that the world can change. If sin is not inherent (that is, ontological) in the world, violence, for example, is not an absolute necessity. It is the task of the church to witness to the peace that is a real possibility. So although Hauerwas can be rather pessimistic about the possibilities of current liberal society, this is not a basic pessimism. Instead, he does not want to

---

[119]On the following, see primarily *PK* 100-102, 166 n. 3, but see also *CC* 247 n. 8.
[120]*CC* 91, *PK* 100.
[121]*PK* 101.
[122]"Those of us who attempt to live faithful to that Kingdom are acutely aware how deeply our lives remain held to and by the world. But this cannot be an excuse for acting as if there were no difference between us and the world. For if we use our sin to deny our peculiar task as Christians and as members of the church, we are unfaithful both to the Kingdom and to ourselves—and most importantly to the world itself." (*CET* 102.)
[123]*PK* 100.

set limits on what is possible. His sort of historicist convictions is relevant here. States and societies can take, and have taken, many different forms, and he does not preclude what is possible, though he does not want to develop utopian blue-prints for the ideal society.[124] This might also further clarify that the separateness of the church is *for the sake of* the world. He thinks that "the church serves the world by giving the world the means to see itself truthfully"[125] and when it, often in very small ways, shows possible alternatives. Furthermore, the contingent, manifold and non-homogenous forms societies and states take make it impossible to describe the church's relation to the world in static and ahistorical terms. For Hauerwas this means that his discussions primarily deal with the church in, what he calls, a liberal society.[126]

How does he theologically base the co-operation between Christians and non-Christians? His answer is in terms of the faith in God's salvation of the world and of the conviction that the kingdom of God is larger than the church. "As the church we have no right to determine the boundaries of God's kingdom, for it is our happy task to acknowledge God's power to make his kingdom present in the most surprising places and ways."[127] He does not develop a doctrine on how this occurs, but it is through being trained in the story and the practices of the church that Christians obtain the interpretative skills for seeing the presence of the king-dom of God in "others", at the same time as the church from these "others" can learn both about its own unfaithfulness and better ways to be faithful to Jesus Christ. Like Moltmann he can also say that the success of the kingdom cannot be assumed to depend on the success of the church, but that the mission of the church should be measured in terms of how it serves the kingdom of God.[128] His theoretical reflection on this whole issue is however not very developed and leaves much unsaid.

b) "The Interpretative Power of the Christian Story"[129]

It is crucial for understanding the position of Hauerwas to see the importance he gives to the interpretative task. The social and political questions the church (as well as the individual) confronts are, he contends, not self-evident and given, but intimately dependent on the sort of community it is, the stories it tells, its so-cial location, and the social practices it lives. The same is, of course, true for other communities, even the wider national communities. The Christian interpre-tations are not superimposed on some "bare reality" all can agree on, because

---

[124]"Thus the world, when it is true to its nature as God's redeemed subject, can be ordered and gover-ned without resort to violence." (*PK* 166 n. 3.) See further *PK* 166 n. 19, *AN* 196, and "Epilogue", 176f.
[125]*PK* 101f.
[126]Cf. *PK* 1f.
[127]*PK* 101. See also *CC* 93, 106, *AN* 114-119.
[128]*AN* 90 n. 39.
[129]*CC* 89.

there is, he argues, no bare reality, but only a socially and historically constituted reality. That is why Christians should not uncritically accept dominant situation descriptions, because these trade on stories and practices that might be in conflict with Christian convictions. He thus does not accept the idea that the social sciences provide the facts and theology the values. This is because he sees the fact-value distinction in itself as untenable and because this distinction necessarily privileges the facts as common public truth, while values become more or less subjective opinions.[130] Also the social sciences are dependent on the sort of society (with its moral traditions and practices) they exist in—that is in our case the sort of modern liberal society that Hauerwas' books constantly deal with.[131] Which issues are discussed and how they are described depend on matters taken for granted and therefore not discussed. How the church understands and deals with the handicapped, with abortion or with peace should thus be determined by basic Christian convictions and practices.

The intellectual developments hinted at in chapter 2, with the breakdown of foundationalism and the concomitant questioning of the sharp dualisms between objective and subjective, fact and value,[132] which in its turn has contributed to the return of normative moral and political theory,[133] makes Hauerwas' position more

---

[130]Cf. Beiner's criticism of the "reductive notion of 'values'". He writes: "what it suggests is that value originates not in what is admirable or worthy of being cherished in the world, but in the idiosyncrasies of our own inner life. It is an intrinsically subjectivizing vocabulary." Consequently, the "discourse of values, intended to be neutral, is already predisposed toward a particular way of experiencing and thinking about moral and political phenomena." (*What's the Matter with Liberalism?*, 40f.)

[131]*AC* 142, *CET* 130 n. 15, 189 n. 30, "Creation, Contingency, and Truthful Non-Violence".

[132]See much of the literature mentioned in chapter 2. Hilary Putnam, who has extensively discussed these issues in his many books, says: "if 'values' seem a bit suspect from a narrowly scientific point of view, they have, at the very least, a lot of 'companions in the guilt': justification, coherence, simplicity, reference, truth, and so on, all exhibit the *same* problems that goodness and kindness do, from an epistemological point of view. None of them is reducible to physical notions; none of them is governed by syntactically precise rules. Rather than give up all of them (which would be to abandon the ideas of thinking and talking), and rather than do what we are doing, which is to reject some—the ones which do not fit in with a narrow instrumentalist conception of rationality which itself lacks all intellectual justification—we should recognize that *all* values, including the cognitive ones, derive their authority from our idea of human flourishing and our idea of reason. These two ideas are interconnected: our image of an ideal theoretical intelligence is simply a *part* of our ideal of total human flourishing, and makes no sense wrenched out of the total ideal, as Plato and Aristotle saw. . . . I claim, in short, that without *values* we would not have a *world*. Instrumentalism, although it denies it, is itself a value system, albeit a sick one." (*Realism with a Human Face*, 141.)

[133]For a systematic theologian to read discussions about the fate and future of political theory (which has a similar place in departments of political science as systematic theology has in departments of theology) gives a strong feeling of *déjà vu*. As example the book *What Should Political Theory Be Now?* (ed. by John Nelson), which includes major contributions from many leading American political theorists, could be read. The attacks on political theory and philosophy during the years after the war for being "unscientific" was based on a positivist methodology including a strong fact-value distinction. This led to retreats into intellectual history and an excessive concern for epistemology. Changes in the general cultural and philosophical climate has since then led to the renewal of the discipline (Shapiro talks about "the veritable explosion of first-order political theorizing" during the last some twenty years [*Political Criticism*, 4]), although there is much controversy on how to go on. There is still a mutual

intelligible. This perspective has become increasingly common also in the social sciences. Sociology seems to be one of the disciplines that today most openly recognizes that both perspective and method are theory and value dependent and rooted in the social and political context in which they exist.[134] Of the social sciences economics seems closest to the natural sciences and has made the strongest claims for predictive competence. Several studies, however, have shown the inadequacy of this self-understanding. Donald McCloskey has sharply criticized, what he calls, the modernist view of the economic discipline and its predictive claims, and argued the irreducibly metaphorical, narrative, rhetorical and ethical character of economics. It is therefore, he concludes, best understood as social history.[135] Even more interesting, for our purpose, is Robert Nelson's highly praised *Reaching for Heaven on Earth: The Theological Meaning of Economics*. As the subtitle shows, Nelson, who himself is an economist, analyses classical and modern economic theory as theology.[136] He tries

> to show not only that modern economic thinking is a secularization of the Judeo-Christian tradition in a general sense, but that it recreates many specific theological controversies of the Western religious heritage. Modern economic theologies have been a radical departure from earlier faiths in outward form, but far less in theological content.[137]

It is these theologies that, according to Nelson, give economists their authority in modern society. The claims of economics to be a predictive science like physics he thinks are spurious and have basically a symbolic and legitimating function. What I have said in a few sentences Nelson develops through expositions of

---

suspicion between so-called political science and political theory and a lot of discussion both about the object of its study and the identity of the discipline; is it epistemology, intellectual history, conceptual analysis, normative theory, normative policy analysis, or what? If this book reflects the current trends the dominant tendency is away from metatheory, history, and conceptual analysis, towards concern for substantial normative theory. This includes antifoundationalism (including the claim that there exists no essential difference between the truth claims of a political theorist and a politician), stress on the necessary connections between theory and political practice, and the importance of the embedding of theory in substantive claims.

[134]See, for some very different examples, Bernstein, *Beyond Objectivism and Relativism*, 44-49, 171-239, Beronius, *Genealogi och sociologi*, Bertilsson, *Slaget om det moderna*, Giddens, *Social Theory and Modern Sociology*, 52-59, Milbank, *Theology and Social Theory*, Vidich and Lyman, *American Sociology*, Himmelstrand, "Den sociologiska analysen av Sverige", 13-16, and Dahlström, "Moderniseringens gränser, samhällsvetenskapens självreflexion".

[135]See his books *The Rhetoric of Economics* and *If You're So Smart*. See also Mirowski, *Against Mechanism* and Weintraub, *Stabilizing Dynamics*. For a sharp criticism of such views and a defence of the view that scientific knowledge requires prediction, see Rosenberg, *Economics*. However, because he persuasively shows that economics is a failure as a predictive science, he suggests that it is better understood as applied mathematics!

[136]"In describing economics as a 'theology,' I am using the term in the sense that economic theology offers a set of principles and understandings that give meaning to, define a purpose for, and significantly frame the perception of human existence." (*Reaching for Heaven on Earth*, xxv.)

[137]Ibid., 23.

classical philosophers and theologians and, above all, modern economists, from Adam Smith and Karl Marx to John Meynard Keynes, Paul Samuelson, Milton Friedman, James Buchanan, and many others.[138]

This shows one of the deepest and most consequential contrasts between Hauerwas' theological politics and Moltmann's political theology. Hauerwas stresses the interpretative power of the Christian story. Therefore, the focus of his works is, on the one hand, upon which kind of community the church must be to be able to truthfully tell the Christian story, and, on the other hand, upon how the church should interpret the modern world in the light of this story and the practices it entails. For this reason his books consist to a large degree of "thick" social and political analysis. He is *as theologian* a shrewd interpreter of the modern world. Moltmann, on the other hand, is very short on political interpretation and analysis. He takes both the descriptions current in the movements he supports and their suggested political solutions for granted. At this level he is unoriginal. He does not say that the interpretations are neutral. It is the commitment to the struggle of the social movements concerned with justice and peace that forms the interpretative context. In this sense the interpretative work seems to be pre-theological. The theological problem for him is thus not social and political interpretation, but theological reconstruction in the light of the given political interpretations. The question that primarily concerns him is how a theology that is relevant to these interpretations can be formulated. For Moltmann the "situation" is there as an independent factor, to which the Christian tradition has to be related in one or another way. For Hauerwas the "situation description" is in itself a theological and political task. He therefore spends much time in seeking to understand how to better ask the questions or describe the issues, how the issues can be redescribed in the light of Christian faith.

In Moltmann's case the political conflicts in society give the church its agenda. The church must take side. Expressed theologically, the church must see what the Spirit is doing in the world and take part in it. For Hauerwas the church has its own agenda, and should therefore not just choose sides in the contemporary conflicts.[139] The latter leads Christians to uncritically acquiesce to assumptions foreign to Christian faith and practice, which makes them unable to radically challenge the modern polity. This is one reason why the independence of the church is so politically significant for Hauerwas. It provides "the space and time necessary for developing skills of interpretation and discrimination sufficient to help us recognize the possibilities and limits of our society."[140]

---

[138]Similarly, see Milbank, *Theology and Social Theory*, 27-48 on "political economy as theodicy and agonistics". Cf. also Powell, *The Moral Tradition of American Constitutionalism*, who offers an interpretation of the American constitutional tradition that is informed by the work of Hauerwas and Yoder.

[139]*PK* 100, *VV* 245.

[140]*CC* 74.

c) The Lack of Control

Hauerwas' questioning of making the control over the state and the processes of social change primary is also dependent on his understanding of the way God works in history. Like Moltmann he makes cross and resurrection central. God does not govern the world through superior raw force but through suffering love. This explains why peace and non-violence have such crucial role in Radical Reformation theology. He points further to the temptation narratives where Jesus rejects the devil's offer of dominion over the world. Hauerwas' comment is: "God's kingdom, it seems, will not have peace through coercion. Peace will come only through the worship of the one God who chooses to rule the world through the power of love, which the world can only perceive as weakness."[141] In another context he refers to Jesus' concern for the poor and the weak as a sign of how God deals with history through the weak.[142] The task of the church is to witness to and to be faithful to this God. It thus cannot search justice through coercive power. It does not attempt to control history.

This has important ethical and political implications. He thinks that the social place and context for the church's social ethics are not the people who think they have power, not the government and other power elites, nor the people who want to be future power holders, but a church that does not search to control history. The truth about reality is, he contends, better seen by those who know that they lack the control.[143] They have fewer illusions. That is why the existence of the poor, oppressed, and marginalized tell us more about the way society functions than varying social theories that make claims about how society works and how it should be governed.[144] In Hauerwas' perspective it can thus be a political resource if the church lives in some form of marginalization from the society's central power structures in solidarity with people who in different ways live in the periphery in relation to these structures. It makes it more capable to see rightly and to develop its social and political imagination.[145] He further asserts that precisely the fact that one does not think in terms of controlling history strengthens the imaginative ability, because it gives space for moral acts and social experiments that otherwise easily are judged unrealistic and ineffective. This is especially important when non-violence is given such a central role. The church has to show that violence and force are not the only means available for obtaining justice.[146]

---

[141]*PK* 79.

[142]*TT* 135-139, esp. 138.

[143]"Christian social ethics, therefore is not best written from the perspective of the Secretary of the State or the President, but from those who are subject to such people." (*PK* 106.)

[144]Cf. "Work as Co-Creation", 54.

[145]*PK* 102-106.

[146]*PK* 105. One effect of the minority and politically and culturally outsider position of Radical Reformation theology is seen in the fact that a significant part of the arguing style of theologians such as

Hauerwas therefore points to the significance of giving society real alternatives or options. Even the pluralistic West lives with strong conventions that seldom are questioned, even though theoretically it is known that there have been and are societies that do not accept these conventions. It is both possible and common to scientifically describe such alternatives, without seeing them as "real options". With the expression "real options" is meant "the ability of people to change their convictions so that they can live within and retain their hold on reality while making rational comparisons between the new option and their present outlook and then acknowledge their transition to the new option in the light of such comparisons."[147] One way for the church to serve the world is thus to be a people that confronts the societies and cultures it lives in with such "real options"—alternative ways of understanding and forming our common life. It is as an identifiable people living in the midst of society telling its own stories and living with its own social forms that it might have this function. Without such an alternative *polis* or contrast society there cannot exist any *real* options.[148] This can express itself in their alternative stories and practices, and in varying social experiments, in that one "pioneer those institutions and practices that wider society has not learned as forms of justice. . . . The church, therefore must act as a paradigmatic community in the hope of providing some indication of what the world can be but is not."[149] He also recognizes that the process also happens in the reverse—that the church learns from others better ways of forming its life.

So understood, "living out of control" does not, as it is often thought, entail uninterest in "effectiveness". This issue has several levels.[150] First of all, although his own language sometimes may have been open to this misunderstanding, he questions the contrast frequently made between faithfulness and effectiveness; or, as it is regularly stated, moral purity against responsible use of power.[151] So described it is, he says, a false alternative. He does not think that Christians should be uninterested in results. On the other hand, people defending effectiveness are interested in effectiveness for some purpose. Consequently, the issue is not faithfulness versus effectiveness, but of giving priority of one principle over another. To say that the church must qualify some of its convictions in order to influence

---

Hauerwas and Yoder is extensive analyses of the implicit (and therefore usually unaccounted for) assumptions at the base of the explicit arguments of theological and political views. As outsiders that question some of the basic assumptions of the current Western social order, not seldom accepted by all major theological and political forces, this is necessary for making their proposals intelligible. This is also one explanation for the extraordinary constructive and innovative character of their theological work, which has, despite their outsider position, made them so influential in modern theology.

[147]*CC* 103.

[148]*CC* 101-108.

[149]*TT* 142.

[150]*RA* 46f, "Epilogue", 180, "On God", 207f. See also Yoder, *The Priestly Kingdom*, 96-99 and 140.

[151]See e.g. Miscamble, "Sectarian Passivism?", 74, Gustafson, "The Sectarian Temptation", 88, and Heeley, "Ethical Methodology", 277.

society, is to say that influencing society is more important than these other convictions. Furthermore, there is no effectiveness as such, only effectiveness in relation to what one wants to attain. The church should not be interested in influence as such, but in influencing society in a specific direction. Therefore, means and ends cannot be separated.[152] *Bonhoeffer ~ ajze?*

The word "responsibility" must similarly be specifically determined. One cannot be responsible in general, but only responsible for something, for a nation-state, an institution, an enterprise, and so on, and the content of the responsibility is also open to interpretation. In Radical Reformation theology the primary responsibility is to the kingdom of God and the church, which qualifies and shapes other responsibilities. To put it differently, "the issue is not whether the Christian is to be responsible or not, but rather what form that responsibility is to take in the light of God's action in Jesus Christ."[153] As Yoder says:

> The strong emotional appeal of the word *responsibility* and the extreme pejorative ring of the epithet *irresponsible* have avoided the need for precise definition of the virtue in question. Rigorous analysis of the function the term discharges in the ethical argument of the Niebuhrian school would probably confirm that there is no more exact meaning than that *responsibility signifies a commitment to consider the survival, the interest, or the power of one's own nation, state, or class as taking priority over the survival, interest or power of other persons or groups, of all of humanity, of the "enemy," or of the church.* If it does *not* mean this, the concept of responsibility cannot prove what it is being used to prove in current debate. If it *does* mean this, it is clearly questionable at two points: a) the priority of state over church; b) the priority of oneself and one's own group over others or the "enemy," as the locus both of value and of decision. This basic egotism of the responsibility argument is clothed as a form of altruism.[154]

It is Hauerwas' claim that a responsibility shaped by basic Christian convictions is the best way the church can take its responsibility for the world. In this chapter we have already met several arguments to that effect. In the following chapters I will, from different perspectives, present additional arguments. One could add that the minority status of the church also determines the character of responsibility. A dissident minority cannot act as if it is the majority or as if it controls the political centres, but as a minority it has unique strengths that it should cultivate.

Finally, that the church's first responsibility is to the kingdom of God implies, Hauerwas contends, that the church's practice should mirror the way God acts in the world, as it has learned to know it through Jesus Christ. So living, the church, it believes, is true to reality. This means that "cross and resurrection must be

---

[152]He thus says that "those of us committed to nonviolence want to be effective as we want to live in societies in a way that our nonviolence makes it possible for all people, Christian and nonChristian, to live as non-violently as possible. What we must see is that we simply cannot think about effectiveness—faithfulness, control, and lack of control—in the abstract." ("On God", 207.)

[153]*VV* 214.

[154]*The Christian Witness to the State*, 36 n. 1.

more determinative for our explication of history than cause and effect".[155] The difficulty, and one central challenge for theology, he says, is how this reading of history can be done in a compelling way.

d) *"Politics as Gesture"*[156]

This also illuminates the social and political significance he gives to the small acts, the everyday life and local existence of churches and Christians. This can easily be overlooked, because of the normal connotations of the word "politics" as having to do with competition over the control over the central power structures and the processes of social change. In such a context the language of the church as a *polis* and a contrast society, easily takes the connotations from politics understood in modern rationalist and utopian forms. The church becomes then a representative of a utopian ideal and an agent for realizing this ideal. This is the notion of politics that dominates political theology. The theological politics of Hauerwas is not just different in that it makes the church the locus for its politics, it also, as already noted, understands the nature of politics differently. The church's politics that Hauerwas talks about concerns the common life of the community, the small acts that fill life, but are often seen as politically irrelevant. Hauerwas, however, contends that it is through these small acts and gestures that people communicate, form and embody their world. It is through them a people of virtue is formed that has the ability to imagine and live out alternatives. The kingdom of God is present in these gestures.[157] Such a "Politics as Gesture" are, he thinks, politically more significant than power struggles and large scale social strategies.[158]

This perspective also determines the way Hauerwas does theology and ethics. He does not want to describe an ideal church, nor develop from the ordinariness of the church a separate systematic theology or ethical system. Instead,

> it is the task of those committed to the theological enterprise to develop the linguistic skills that can help congregations understand better the common but no less theologically signifi-

---

[155]"On God", 208.

[156]*CET* 106.

[157]"We must be a community with the patience, amid the division and the hatreds of this world, to take the time to nurture friendships, to serve the neighbor, and to give and receive the thousand small acts of care which ultimately are the heart blood of the kingdom. That we must take the time to help the neighbor in need, no matter how insignificant that neighbor or his or her need is from the perspective of the world, is but a sign that we recognize that we are called not to make history come out right but to be faithful to the kind of care we have seen revealed in God's kingdom." (*CET* 105.)

[158]"Nothing in life is more important than gestures, as gestures embody as well as sustain the valuable and significant. Through gestures we create and form our worlds. Through gestures we make contact with one another and share common tasks. Through gestures we communicate and learn from each other the limits of our world. In this sense, the church is but God's gesture on behalf of the world to create a space and time in which we might have a foretaste of the Kingdom." (*CET* 106.) See further on this *CET* 101-110 and *RA* 67.

cant activities which constitute their lives. . . . e.g., pray, baptize, eat meals, rejoice at the birth of a child, grieve at illness and death, reroof church buildings, and so on.[159]

Theology and ethics should thus "help us see the significance of the everyday and the sacredness of the ordinary . . . those ordinary tasks are the most determinative *political* challenge to our culture."[160] Part of his writings therefore deals with such concrete events.[161] This furthermore underscores the importance of the ordinary saints for Christian ethics, because they give material for ethical reflection. He thinks that one reason for the poverty he sees in much Christian ethics has to do with the fact that ethicists tend to make denominational and social justice committees rather than local churches their primary context for theological work.[162] One consequence is that they get caught in the politics of modernity and fail to see and understand the riches of ordinary church life.[163] This way of valuing the ordinary and concrete everyday life of the local church (or base community) ought to be amenable to one stream of political theology, but because the dominant line tends to value the local church according to its contribution to the political struggle of the world and because of the dominance of an utopian consciousness this perspective tends to be suppressed at the theological level.[164]

e) The Church as a "Tactic"

Another misunderstanding to which the language of the church as a *polis* and a contrast society might lead, is that the church is seen as a wholly independent agent or as a separate space. Another metaphor he uses is the church as a colony and Christians as resident aliens. "The church is a colony, an island of one culture in the middle of another. In baptism our citizenship is transferred from one dominion to another, and we become, in whatever culture we find ourselves, resident aliens."[165] This language, as he recognizes, also has its shortcomings if it leads to a defensive view of the church as a well-defined place or position that has to be cultivated and defended. Because the church is used by God for the salvation of the world it will have an offensive relation to the world—"against the world, for the world".[166] In a recent text he explicates this with the help of Michel

---

[159]*CET* 123f.

[160]"Why *Resident Aliens*", 424.

[161]*CET* 111-131 is an especially instructive example. Also notable is *RA*.

[162]*CET* 129 n. 11.

[163]"Why *Resident Aliens* Struck a Chord", 424.

[164]From this perspective he can also defend "charity" and speak about "the politics of charity" (*TT* 132-143). Charity does not require that all injustice is taken away, but that one meets the needs of the neighbour when one is confronted with it. One has the time to be as inefficient as Mother Teresa because one knows that God's kingdom comes through such acts. On this, see also *CET* 105f.

[165]*RA* 12.

[166]*RA* 51. See further *RA* 51f.

de Certeau's distinction between strategies and tactics.[167] In the words of de Certeau a *strategy* is

> the calculation (or manipulation) of power relationships that becomes possible as soon as a subject with will and power (a business, an army, a city, a scientific institution) can be isolated. It postulates a *place* that can be delimited as its *own* and serve as the base from which relations with an *exteriority* composed of targets or threats (customers or competitors, enemies, the country surrounding the city, objectives and objects of research, etc.) can be managed.[168]

Having a place gives a certain freedom in relation to varying circumstances and possibilities for planned future expansions as well as the possibility to make other forces into observable, measurable and therefore controllable objects. The precondition of such knowledge is then the described power over a place.

In contrast to this, de Certeau describes a *tactic* as "a calculated action determined by the absence of a proper locus. No delimitation of an exteriority, then, provides it with the condition necessary for autonomy. The space of a tactic is the space of the other. Thus it must play on and with a terrain imposed on it and organized by the law of a foreign power."[169] The consequence is that it cannot plan general strategies, but has to take advantage of favourable situations and possibilities. "In short, a tactic is an art of the weak."[170]

Following this distinction, Hauerwas describes the church as a tactic. It exists on alien space and must act on this alien space determined by an other. It has to use the language, resources, and tools that are at hand, but not wholly determined and controlled by the church. It does not have the independent space and power from which it could plan a general strategy for controlling social change or general intellectual life. This lack of independent space also makes withdrawal impossible, as it lacks a place to which it could withdraw. It is thus in this situation the church has to live both on the practical and theoretical plane. Hauerwas can therefore not write a general theory of society. This is also the reason for his suspicion of the idea of systematic theology in a strict sense. It presupposes the strategic and hegemonic power for which the church should not have searched.[171]

5. The Constantinian Heritage

Hauerwas thinks that much of the perspective and specific resources described above was lost when Christianity became a state religion in the Roman empire. Since then the specific Christian universality has been seen as embodied in the Western civilization or the state, and not in the church. That makes a crucial

---

[167]*AC* 16-19 and de Certeau, *The Practice of Everyday Life*, 34-39.
[168]de Certeau, *Practice* 35f.
[169]Ibid., 36f.
[170]Ibid., 37.
[171]*AC* 19, 182 n. 14.

difference. Because he thinks the social form of the church is intrinsically connected to its theology, he (like Moltmann) sees the so-called Constantinian shift as theologically and politically decisive and fateful.[172] He thinks that most modern Christian social ethics are still determined by habits of thought and practices that were shaped through this shift. We will also see that although Hauerwas' understanding of this change seems similar to Moltmann's, his analysis suggests that political theology has failed to free itself consistently from these habits of thought.

The Constantinian shift means that the church changes from being a minority to becoming the imperial religion of, with time, almost everyone. Not to be Christian thus required great conviction. This led to the creation of the doctrine of the invisible church as the true believers or the elect still were considered a small minority. The church thus no longer signified an identifiable people, but came to mean primarily the hierarchy and sacramental institution, with the consequence that faith and Christian life primarily were understood in inward terms.

This radically changes the understanding of ethics. When the church still was a minority it could assume resources not generally available. Yoder (whom Hauerwas follows) mentions things like "personal commitment, regeneration, the guidance of the Holy Spirit, the consolation and encouragement of the brotherhood, training in a discipleship life-style."[173] However, when the church consists of everyone, and its role is seen as civilizational religion keeping society together, ethical discourse is assumed to be directly applicable to anyone, irrespective of whether these resources are present or not. The consequence is that a minimalistic ethics (theologically often legitimated in some form of natural law terms) is accepted, which is complemented with "evangelical counsels" for a motivated spiritual elite. As civilizational religion providing the empire with a common ethos, Christianity did not require conversion and membership in a counter culture, but "became that set of beliefs which explains why the way things are is the way things were meant to be for any right-thinking person, converted or not."[174] The radical ethic of the early Christian church did not think of itself as a civilizational ethos separate from an identifiable Christian people. But now the question—in relation to, for example, money and violence—becomes "What would happen if everyone did it?" Hauerwas (following Yoder) thinks that a more adequate question is "What if nobody else acted like a Christian and we did?"[175]

Furthermore, it is now assumed that Christian faith should be able to give moral support and advice to the ruler, which makes the ruler the paradigm for social ethics. The crucial question becomes what the ruler and the state should do

---

[172]On the following, see esp. *CET* 180-184 (where he follows Yoder, *The Priestly Kingdom*, 135-147), *AN* 74-78, and *NS* 55f, 38f. See also Yoder, *Christian Attitudes to War, Peace, and Revolution*, 39-54. For description and reflection on "Constantinianism" from an Orthodox perspective, see Guroian, *Incarnate Love*, esp. 83-85, 119-124, 147-150.

[173]*The Priestly Kingdom* 139.

[174]*NS* 55.

[175]*CET* 182, quoting Yoder, *The Priestly Kingdom*, 139.

with its power. Because the agenda and interest of the empire and the ruler are taken for granted the New Testament is, as we earlier noted, seen as irrelevant for social ethics. The church is thus no more a political alternative, but fulfils instead moral and religious functions in the given political order. The church hierarchy becomes a part of the power structure itself, and understands Christianity and history from that perspective.

Behind this Hauerwas sees a crucial shift in the understanding of history and eschatology. It is at this point that the difference between Hauerwas and Moltmann becomes clear. For the earlier minority church the provident rule of God over the world was a question of faith, while the reality of the Christian church could be concretely experienced. After Constantine the true church was invisible, but the provident rule of God could be concretely and visibly experienced in the emperor and the Roman empire. Therefore it becomes important for the church to strengthen the empire. The interests of the church and the empire coincide. That tends to make effectiveness for the empire a central test for moral discourse.

> Once the course of history is thought to be empirically discernible and the prosperity of our regime the measure of the good, efficacy becomes a decisive test for the moral rightness of our action. Self-sacrifice that is not tied to some long term account of result becomes irrational. This is particularly important in assessing the validity of violence and the Christian's participation in war.[176]

In practice it tends to be assumed that God is on the side of the winners of history, and from that it follows easily that it is the winners that are good. Hauerwas admits that the kingdom of God is about God's rule over the world and that Christians claim the Christian story as the true story and the Christian polity as the true polity. This makes theocracy in one form or another a constant and dangerous temptation. He says that "by taking up Rome's project, Christians were attempting to further the kingdom through the power of this world: an understandable but disastrous strategy that confused the politics of salvation with the idea that in the name of God Christians must rule."[177] It is his claim that this basic strategy has dominated the main churches since then and therefore determined their moral logic.

Like Moltmann, he considers the Reformation, in this respect, as a further step in this direction, because it replaced the cosmopolitanism of medieval Christendom with the supremacy of the nation-state. The churches, thus, became important ideologists for the building up of these nation-states, including their wars against each other.[178] If the Enlightenment broke this close relation between church and state, "the moral identification of Christians with the state remained

---

[176]*CET* 182.
[177]*AC* 39. He also thinks that the theologically necessary incorporation of the continuing history of the Jewish people into the history which the church tells of itself makes the Constantinian assumptions impossible and requires another social form of the church. See *AN* 74-78.
[178]See also his "Athens", 61f.

strong."[179] Moltmann's Germany, Hauerwas' America, and my own Sweden are all illustrative and, in their different ways, instructive examples of this.

On American theology he writes: "In effect, from Rauschenbusch to the present Christian social ethics has had one agenda: to show why American democracy possesses distinctive religious status. The primary subject of Christian ethics in America has been America."[180] The context for Christian social ethical reflection is thus the national community and particularly the state. In one way or another the church is supposed to help the democratic system to work. This he thinks is as true of the New Christian Right, the neoconservatives, various strands of political or liberation theology as of main stream liberalism. "Everybody" and "the ruler" are still the paradigms for reflection, a fact which tends to make the story of Jesus politically irrelevant and in an increasingly secular society forces Christians to translate their convictions into a secular language. And "once such a translation is accomplished, it becomes very unclear why the theological idiom is needed at all."[181] He describes the changes from Social Gospel, through Reinhold Niebuhr to current theological ethical thought as dependent on the increasingly secular context. The Social Gospel movement could assume a semi-Christian culture and therefore use an explicitly Christian language (somewhat like what Latin American liberation theology can do today) in a way that more recent Western theology cannot. What, however, is assumed by almost everyone is that Christian ethics and politics is concerned with devising positions and then asking or pressing (often through the mobilization of "public opinion") the government to support these. The state is thus the main actor, the subject from which basic social change is expected, while the church becomes a pressure group.[182] It is assumed that the church has power to form opinion and is one of the basic power groups of the political game. Hauerwas, on the other hand, does not assume this power, because he expects the church to be in more radical opposition to the power system. In his view, the church is therefore more like a dissenter phenomenon, i. e., not an established and accepted participant of the game.[183]

This makes it obvious why Hauerwas does not think that the sort of political theology that Moltmann represents has succeeded in overcoming Constantinian-

---

[179]*CET* 182.
[180]*CET* 177. This thesis is developed in *AN* 23-50. See also *AN* 10 and "Faith in the Republic", 507.
[181]*AN* 38.
[182]*RA* 70, 81. They "begin with the Constantinian assumption that there is no way for the gospel to be present in our world without asking the world to support our convictions through its own social and political institutionalization. The result is the gospel transformed into civil religion." (*RA* 81.)
[183]On this modern Constantinianism and its consequences for theology, especially in its American form, see e.g. *AN* 23-50, *CET* 171-190, *RA* 30-48, and *AC* 45-92. Cf. his comment that Reinhold "Niebuhr became the most, and perhaps the last, influential Protestant public theologian in America. He achieved this status, however, exactly because he provided the theological justification to support the liberal ideology of the rising political elite, whose self-interest was commensurate with making the United States a world power." (*DFF* 141.) See further on Niebuhr *AN* 29-33, *DFF* 91-106, and "The Irony of American Christianity".

ism, although the latter also claims to be a post-Constantinian theologian and one growing line of his theology clearly points in that direction. The crucial difference is again their differing placement of Christian politics, which is connected with their different eschatologies. For Moltmann the "secular" political history is the locus for the interpretation of the work of God's Spirit. He seems confident about our capability to know the forces of good, a task that is simplified by his general dualistic reading of history as a struggle between good and evil, oppressed and oppressors. At least in his early work, which was formative for political theology, he was sure that the good forces would win and that the church had to line up with the winning side of modernity and revolution if it should have a place in the future society. His confidence nowadays is somewhat muted—his language stresses the necessity of the way he supports for our survival rather than its sure victory. Furthermore, he tends to believe that the political relevance of church and theology is determined in terms of the agenda and interests of the political forces he supports. And the locus for the struggle is the state or the coming international superstate. That seems to be the primary context for his social ethical thinking, which also explains the central role consequentialism has had in his political and moral discourse. That he is critical of the present social and political system, and therefore works for an alternative order thus does not make his approach less Constantinian in Hauerwas' understanding. I do not know how Moltmann would answer this in these terms, but generally he would worry that Hauerwas' Radical Reformation theology risks abandoning the world to itself. We have already begun to see how Hauerwas answers this and much of the rest of this book will, from different angles, discuss this issue.

6. Church, State and Public Policy

a) Church and State

The primary context and the starting point for Christian social ethics are thus, according to Hauerwas, the church. It is in principle an ethics for all, but in the sense that everyone does not yet affirm the lordship of Christ it is only an ethics for the people of God. Above all, it is therefore not an ethics for the state, for how the world should be governed. He does not believe there is a specific Christian theory about the state or about the best form of government. The state can take, and has historically taken, many forms. The modern nation-state is something quite different from earlier forms of the phenomenon called the state, and it is not the church's task to defend this (or some other historical or hypothetical) form of the state, as a necessity for human life.[184] Neither does he know how "the state" could evolve in the future. What he discusses is therefore the state he knows, the liberal state of the Western world and first of all his own American state. But he

---

[184]"Epilogue", 175.

is also open to new forms of political organization, which may or may not be subject to the same type of criticism.[185]

Theologically he can in traditional terms describe the role of the state as an agency for the balancing of essentially destructive forces, protect the good and hinder the evil forces, which gives the church a place for its task.[186] The task of the state should thus not be mixed with the one of the church. The state cannot witness to the kingdom of God. The church should consequently not demand of the state more than what encompasses its limited task. But the church should be faithful to the kingdom of God and not see as its role to give religious legitimation to the state, or to formulate its ethic so that the state can make it its own. Furthermore, his understanding of the church as a people called to witness to an alternative political order makes it impossible to develop a neat, systematic relation between church and state, as many theologies with other understandings of church and salvation, where church and state have well defined separate but complementary tasks. If Hauerwas is right there will always be tensions, although in varying degrees.[187]

Hauerwas does however think that the above given theological account of the state, even if correct, does not give much guidance about how Christians should relate to actual existing states. Even more important, neither theological nor other theories about how the state ought to be ordered or function keep it limited. "No state will keep itself limited, no constitution or ideology is sufficient to that task, unless there is a body of people separated from the nation that is willing to say 'No' to the state's claims on their loyalties."[188] The Christian church as a com-

---

[185]"As a pacifist, I . . . believe I am called to be of service to the neighbor, and in particular the enemy-neighbor. But I do not assume the state as such is a special creature of God provided for that service. . . . I simply believe that the state—which can take the form of any group that provides order, from Augustine's robber bands to North Carolina to the United States of America—exists. I do not need a theory about its existence or its penchant for making war. Rather what I need is a community schooled with skills provided by a truthful account of the world to give up the power to interpret the perversities and possibilities of the states that come and go." ("Epilogue", 175f.) See further "Epilogue", 175-177 and *CC* 109f. For an extended account of the development of the modern nation-state that confirms Hauerwas' views, see Giddens, *The Nation-State and Violence*. For a shorter summary, see idem, *Social Theory and Modern Sociology*, 166-182.

[186]"Epilogue", 159f. "The characteristic of Christ's reign is that evil, which still certainly exists, is now made to serve God's purposes in spite of itself. Thus vengeance, instead of creating chaos, is harnessed through the state to preserve order and to give room for the work of the church. Vengeance is not made good, but it is made subservient to God's purposes as an anticipation of the ultimate defeat of sin." (Ibid., 160.) In this he follows Yoder, *The Original Revolution*, 52-84. Cf. also Yoder's *Christian Witness*.

[187]"The Kingship of Christ", 126.

[188]*AN* 123. He says in another context that "I have used Barmen as a test case for my thinking about Christian social ethics. For example, I have long thought the crucial question facing any theological position is whether it provides us with the skill to discern (as well as respond faithfully to) the challenge of Hitler." ("On Learning Simplicity in an Ambiguous Age", 43.) The German church to a large extent lacked both the skills of discerning and of appropriate response and we will in a later chapter see that it is Hauerwas' argument that the church also has largely failed to discern the (very different) nature of the liberal state.

munity of virtue distinguishable from the larger society should have both the possibility and the moral courage that is required to say "No" to the state and enough distance to the state to be capable to see through its ideological legitimations.

His conviction of the contingent nature of states and societies has as consequence that it is not possible to discuss in the abstract how Christians should relate to and work in state and society. Such a discussion is relevant only in relationship to specific societies. As a result, the answers to these questions will change from society to society. Furthermore, the choice is not between general involvement or withdrawal from cultural, economic or political life, but "the question is how to relate discriminatingly both to the cultures and the corresponding political forms in which Christians find themselves."[189] The state's use of violence is one such limit. However, he does not accept the view that violence is the essence of the state.

b) The Church and Public Policy

We have seen that Hauerwas holds that "the most important political service the church does for any society is to be a community capable of developing people of virtue"[190], and that it as such might be able to cherish alternative views and to develop and experiment with new social institutions and practices. It is this that he thinks can give the church a meaningful base for public declarations, because it positions "the church in a manner such that the church can serve society imaginatively by not being captured by societal options or corresponding governmental policy."[191] Without such a "position", declarations become abstract and nothing but part of the current power struggles.[192]

As has been said, he does not think the church should require that the state should act as if it was a church. Consequently, when the church speaks to the state, it can use criteria determined by the task of the state. One might for example use the language the state uses for legitimating itself as a critical tool against the state.[193] This also indicates that he is not against the search for a common lan-

---

[189]"Will the Real Sectarian Stand Up", 87. See also "Epilogue", 167-181, *CET* 11-16, *TT* 10, and *DFF* 116-135. He stresses that the Anabaptists of the sixteenth century did not withdraw themselves from society, but that they were forced to withdraw because their societies did not accept the challenge to the political system they were. Later on, though, they tended to make a virtue out of the necessity. See "The Sermon on the Mount, Just War and the Quest for Peace", 39 and "Real Sectarian", 91.

[190]*CET* 13.

[191]"Real Sectarian", 90.

[192]Cf. e.g. "Epilogue", 152f.

[193]*TT* 141, *CC* 253f n. 39, "Epilogue", 177. This have led some to talk about the "necessity" of two moralities. See Koontz, "Mennonites and the State", Eller, *The Promise* 79-98, idem, *Christian Anarchy*, and Ellul, *To Will and to Do*, 73-110. The problem with this, from Hauerwas' perspective, is that it might give a too static view of (and even ontological status to) the morality of the state and a too neat division between the ethics of the church and the state. To this might be added that Ellul's strongly dialectic approach is less open for this criticism than Eller's more non-dialectical "Ellulianism". On these issues, see also Yoder, *Christian Witness*.

guage with people outside the church. His criticism of the talk about common language is directed against foundationalist understandings and therefore of systematically basing the Christian language on other languages, not against, on a more *ad hoc* basis, trying to make oneself understandable. The types of languages that at specific times and places dominate public life are historically formed and changeable and might as well be renewed by the Christian language as in other ways.[194]

He has himself written reports at the request of government ethics committees concerning experiments on children and *in-vitro* fertilization.[195] It is instructive to see how he argues. I will only describe here the form of his arguments, not its substance, as this is beyond the scope of this chapter.[196] If we start with the text on *in-vitro* fertilization, two things should be noted: the theological and the political nature of his argumentation. This means that he "does not pretend to speak from principles that are or should be shared by everyone in our society."[197] This is not only a result of his theological position, but also of his claim that modern society lacks the sort of coherence that would make that possible.

The place of theology in his argument does not mean that he argues directly from the Bible or from specific theological beliefs. At the centre of his discussion is instead the question of the relation between the use of *in-vitro* fertilization and the sort of community the church should be. He thus writes that "for the Christian the question of the use or non-use of *in-vitro* fertilization will be determined primarily by whether such a procedure is appropriate to our understanding of what kind of community we should be and in particular what kind of attitudes about parenting we should foster."[198] In this sense, it is a political question. He therefore describes and discusses this issue in the context of Christian understandings and practices of parenting. But he also makes a social analysis of the difficulties a liberal society has when dealing with such issues.

The text on experimentation on children similarly tries to show the embeddedness of the most often used moral language of rights and autonomy in liberal society, the sort of common life it entails, and the difficulties that follow from it. To help to see this he uses certain religious communities as contrast examples. The first text concludes with some advice to Christians and recommendations for public policy (not exactly the same). In the second he confesses that because of the situation in modern society and the moral languages it uses he does not know what to recommend, although he follows up with some tentative suggestions.

---

[194]"Real Sectarian", 93.

[195]They now constitute chapters 7 and 8 in *SP*. David Schmidt has studied the argumentation of the latter one in the light of Hauerwas' overall position in his dissertation "Theological Ethics and Public Policy". (The dissertation also deals with Paul Ramsey's corresponding text.)

[196]However, see p. 292 below.

[197]*SP* 142.

[198]*SP* 143.

What we find here then is, first, the stress on description that we encountered above, and the close relation between description and the beliefs, practices and institutions with which we live. He analyses what comes before the point where much other ethical reflection starts. Second, his ethical reflection is inherently political, in the sense that it points to the social and political nature of the issues discussed. Third, his discussion is theological and political in that it makes the Christian faith-practice crucial for the argument. One could here use Moltmann's language of contrast society. The church becomes a contrast society and is the base for a contrast ethics. Hauerwas does not recommend the government to directly make his Christian ethic into public policy. But his descriptions and analysis may help to see liberal society from other perspectives, help people to see where the problems and issues are and which social contexts different proposals presuppose or require. These texts are then contributions to the ongoing conversation in society. They do not give final answers or knock down arguments or proposals that in themselves could be made into public policy tomorrow, but seen as contributions to a conversation, they are part of a public discussion, and their theological character does not make them less public or less consequential.

David Schmidt, following Richard Rorty, compares two different types of philosophical (and therefore also theological) thought: systematic and edifying. The systematic tries to conform all public thought to one universal and prior standard. The edifying type by contrast "seeks to perpetuate a *conversation* marked by a generous respect for differences among views. Adopting the pragmatic and empirical mood of the descriptive sciences, the edifying philosopher opposes the way epistemology seeks to confine 'public' discourse to a strictly circumscribed range of utterances." In such a perspective, Schmidt concludes, Hauerwas' "edifying" discourse should be seen as public.[199]

Neither should Moltmann have any basic problem with Hauerwas' approach. Moltmann's own approach is also distinctively theological. The political nature of Hauerwas' discussion furthermore should be amenable to political theology. Ironically, Moltmann's discussions are usually more abstractly theological in nature. He tends to draw political consequences more directly from theological beliefs and does not frequently discuss the embeddedness of these beliefs in certain practices and institutions. If we stay with examples from so-called "medical ethics", which also Moltmann has dealt with, this becomes clear. When he in *The Way of Jesus Christ* discusses the praxis "bound up with hope for 'the resurrection of the dead and the life of the world to come'"[200] he addresses questions like

---

[199]See "Public Policy", 202-208. The citation is from p. 205. He also argues that Hauerwas' pacifism and the place he gives to the stranger further help strengthen the public character of his theological discourse. See esp. ibid., 172-190. (We will return to this theme in chapter 12.) Schmidt's conclusion is that "Ramsey and Hauerwas each meet Toulmin's requirements for an 'ethics of argument,' which calls for cooperative dialogue and mutual learning, evidenced by a willingness to give reasons for one's claims and to listen seriously to the reasons of others" (p. 188).

[200]*WJC* 263 (286). See further *WJC* 263-273 (286-296).

abortion and euthanasia. Here he draws direct practical consequences from theological beliefs without any political and social analysis. In the much earlier text
"Ethics and Biomedical Progress"[201] the opposite is the case. This text is more
political in its argumentation, but also much less theological. The central moral
categories here seem to be "self-liberation" and "power over nature", but he does
not show how he derives them theologically. In both texts the church as a community is absent. For Hauerwas it is the reality of the church, the contrast society
of Moltmann, that integrates theological and political analysis to a theological
politics. We find partly this integration when Moltmann discusses peace in *The
Way of Jesus Christ*, but until now this book has been an exception. The result is
that the discourse of political theology tends to be either abstractly theological or
only "secular".

---

[201]*FC* 131-148 (140-156). It was originally written for a symposium 1971.

Chapter 11

The Genealogy of the Charge of Sectarianism

The wholly dominating criticism directed against Hauerwas is that his position is sectarian. This is almost always, more or less by definition, considered a deeply deficient position. Though this criticism is common, it is usually not carefully developed, even if the basic content is clear.

First of all, his emphasis on ecclesial identity and integrity and his criticism of mainline social ethics is said to lead to a withdrawal from public responsibility. James Gustafson, for example, has written that "[i]n Hauerwas's case . . . this means that Christian morality is not based on a concern to be responsible participants in the ambiguities of public choices. It is rather based on its fidelity of the biblical narratives, and particularly to the gospel narratives."[1] Christianity becomes isolated and its participation in public life becomes severely limited. Philip Wogaman goes even further and says that it is impossible "to escape doing whatever the state is doing", because "the state represents society acting as a whole".[2] So because the state by definition is "we", we share the responsibility for managing it rightly. To confuse matters, other critics, who recognize that Hauerwas does not say that the church should be silent in the public sphere and that he himself is not, argues that he thereby is inconsistent. He ought to be silent. Paul Nelson is one example when he writes that if "Hauerwas were to be consistent, he would relinquish the possibility of advising (however generally) on matters of public policy. As a theologian, an interpreter of the Christian narrative, he simply would have nothing of relevance to contribute."[3]

This is intrinsically related to a second charge, namely that his approach keeps Christian faith and language separate from public language and accountability, with the result that Christian faith becomes unintelligible in a world where few are trained in the Christian language.[4]

Third, this approach is seen as sociologically impossible, because the church is only one of the communities that shape the life and thought of modern Christians. This makes the claims Hauerwas makes for the church indefensible.[5] Some

---

[1]Gustafson, "The Sectarian Temptation", 88. So also Miscamble, "Sectarian Passivism?", Nelson, *Narrative and Morality*, 130-139, Heeley, "The Ethical Methodology of Stanley Hauerwas", 277, Neuhaus, "Challenging the Culture", and Christoffersen, "Etikk for fremtiden?", 30.

[2]Wogaman, *Christian Perspectives on Politics*, 136.

[3]Nelson, *Narrative and Morality*, 138.

[4]Gustafson, "The Sectarian Temptation", 92, 94, Glebe-Møller, *Den teologiske ellipse*, 70-82, Holland, "The Problems and Prospects of a 'Sectarian Ethic'", 165-167.

[5]Gustafson, "The Sectarian Temptation", 90f, Wogaman, *Christian Perspectives on Politics*, 135-137, Heeley, "Ethical Methodology", 277, Nelson, *Narrative and Morality*, 137, Christoffersen, "Etikk for fremtiden?", 30, Weston, "The Invisible Church".

critics furthermore maintain that the church cannot itself form a different social life without prior changes in the structures and institutions of the whole society.[6]

Finally, these charges are, as we have already seen, usually theologically backed up by the criticism that Hauerwas lacks a doctrine of creation and that his theology is excessively christocentric. Making Jesus and the Christian story central in the way Hauerwas does, makes, claims Gustafson, the Christian God into a tribal god and not the Creator of the whole world.[7]

This criticism for sectarianism is thus wide ranging, and affects the heart of Hauerwas' theology. In chapter nine we saw how Hauerwas (with strong support from Moltmann) deals with the last charge. I have in the previous chapter started to deal with the other three criticisms and will continue to discuss them in the rest of the book. This section will tackle the issue from another direction. One might describe it as a genealogical analysis of the sect language. I will discuss its theological and sociological origin and development, disclose and critically analyse its inherent social, political and theological assumptions, and discuss its conceptual coherence. I will do that primarily through discussions, first, of Ernst Troeltsch's church-sect typology and its background in Max Weber's sociology, and, second, of H. Richard Niebuhr's influential development of this typology in *Christ and Culture*.

The relation between political theology and these charges is ambiguous. Moltmann's explicit criticism of Radical Reformation theology is that it tends to not develop a political discipleship and therefore risks abandoning its political responsibility. Yet, he affirms the centrality of Jesus for ethics and politics, describes the church as a contrast society, and partly identifies himself with the Christian tradition that often is described as sectarian. David Tracy can therefore describe political theology, Moltmann and Metz included, as a retrieval and reformulation of the sect model.[8] Moltmann is also open to much of the same criticism that is directed at Hauerwas.[9] This ambiguity reflects the basic tension we have discovered in Moltmann's theology, and this chapter thus helps to clarify this tension and the relation between Hauerwas and Moltmann.

---

[6]Kammer, *Ethics and Liberation*, 190 n. 7.

[7]Gustafson, "The Sectarian Temptation", 93, Heeley, "Ethical Methodology", 27, Miscamble, "Sectarian Passivism?", 71, Wogaman, *Christian Perspectives on Politics*, 111-113, 137-140. In the case of Gustafson it should be said that he can describe this position in less polemical terms. One could mention his discussion of Yoder's theology in *Theology and Ethics*, 74f. He says that "all constructive theology in the Christian tradition needs to be defined to some extent in relation to this radical option. . . . it represents the sharpest challenge to any theology and theological ethics that desires to claim some backing from the particularities of the Christian tradition while moving in quite another direction. There are historical warrants for this radical position in the early Christian church; there are biblical warrants for it; there are sociological and moral warrants for it. The theology and ethics of the radical Protestant tradition cannot be as easily dismissed as most theologians believe" (p. 75). See also Gustafson, *Protestant and Roman Catholic Ethics*, 66f.

[8]*The Analogical Imagination*, 76f.

[9]Cf. Gustafson's very sharp criticism of Moltmann in *Theology and Ethics*, 43-48. See also Wogaman, *Christian Perspectives on Politics*, 53-71.

In addition to this clarification, the principal reason for this chapter is that sect language to such a great degree determines how Hauerwas and other Radical Reformation theologians are read. The categories of church and sect or the more developed categories of Niebuhr seem so deeply embedded in especially American theology that they control almost all understanding of these issues.[10] That makes it difficult for theologians like Yoder and Hauerwas, who questions the adequacy of these categories, to be understood. If my reading of Hauerwas' position is somewhat correct, the descriptions that we find in critics like Gustafson and Miscamble are severely distorted.[11] The categories they use not only tend to assume what should be argued, they also distort the description. The aim of this chapter is thus both to show why these common categories make it so difficult to understand what Hauerwas means with "church as *polis*", and to show the questionable character of the assumptions behind these categories.

1. The Background in Theology

In theology "sect" usually has referred to any group of believers that deviate from the majority or the "orthodox" norm in doctrine, practice or leadership. The politically established churches in Europe have until recently referred to every non-established church as a sect. This traditional polemical and apologetic use of the word has given it a pejorative sense, which strongly colours the current use of it. This use has to be differentiated from the sociological use of the concept, but in practice, at least when theologians use it, the older pejorative theological sense tends to be combined with a modern sociological sense. It is also problematic that the opposite to "sect" is "church", which is Christianity's name for itself in its institutional form, and therefore is a word with positive connotations, in contrast to the negative sense of "sect". Yet if we look to the actual content that is given to these concepts in the sociological tradition, these connotations are far less obvious. Hardly any of Hauerwas' critics would like to be associated with "church" as it is there described, while some of the characteristics of the "sect" are more agreeable today. But this fact is seldom taken note of when Radical Reformation-theology is criticized for being sectarian. Still, it must be the sociological sense that is intended, as the theological hardly makes sense today, because it assumes one politically established church. Neither is Hauerwas sectarian in the sense that he denies the Christian legitimacy of all (or most) churches except his own. His theology is not intended for a special movement or ecclesial group, but for the catholic or ecumenical church. The criticism is therefore not that he is sectarian in relation to the catholic church, but in relation to the "world", that is, the cultures and societies in which the church lives, and then especially in relation to the na-

---

[10] In much of European theology the alternatives to established national churches are simply ignored.

[11] Cf. also Hauerwas' own answers to Gustafson's and Miscamble's criticisms, *CET* 3-18 and "Will the Real Sectarian Stand Up".

tion-state and the cultural and political elites. The issue is thus once again whether the politics of the church or the politics of the world (in practice, the nation-state) should have primacy.[12]

2. The Sociological Tradition from Weber and Troeltsch

The sociological use of the concept "sect" can be traced back to Max Weber[13] and Ernst Troeltsch. Especially the latter's more directly theologically related analyses have been extremely influential, and have in large part formed the perspective and the vocabulary for the continuing discussion of these issues.[14] He interpreted church history in terms of a typology of "church", "sect" and "mysticism", where particularly the opposition and dialectic between church and sect are constitutive of the church's historical and social development. The type "church" refers to the established type of organization that is conservative, accepts secular order, dominates the masses, has universal claims, and therefore uses (and becomes used by) the state and the ruling classes to sustain and expand its domination and to stabilize and determine the social order. Theologically, redemption through the atoning death of Christ, objectively mediated through the ministry and the sacraments, is given the central place.

The sects, on the other hand, are comparatively smaller, and stress both a more personal and a more communal faith and practice. They are connected with the lower, or at least oppositional, classes, and do not try to dominate the world, but work from below and defend egalitarian views and practices. Separation from the world is stressed, as well as religious freedom and voluntary membership. Theologically, they put the lordship of Christ and discipleship, and therefore also the life and message of Jesus in the centre. Furthermore, while the "church" tends to identify itself with the kingdom of God, the kingdom in sectarian thought is more eschatologically understood.

Troeltsch argues "that both types are a logical result of the Gospel, and only conjointly do they exhaust the whole range of its sociological influence".[15] The sect starts from the teaching and life of Jesus, and the church starts in the Exalted Christ and Redeemer. In the first centuries, the church vacillated between sect and church-type and it is first with the political establishment of the church and its developed hierarchical and sacramental theology, that we get clearly separated

---

[12]If the word "sect" traditionally signified "a challenge to the unity of the Church", it today "means those who refuse to 'act responsibly' for building a just society." (*US* 154 n. 2) So also Jenson, "The Hauerwas Project", 292.

[13]See e.g. "The Protestant Sects and the Spirit of Capitalism", *Economy and Society*, vol. 3, 1204-1210, and (for concrete discussions of Pietism, Methodism and Baptism) *The Protestant Ethic and the Spirit of Capitalism*, 128-154.

[14]For the following, see Troeltsch, *The Social Teaching of the Christian Churches*, 328-343 and *passim*

[15]Ibid., 340f.

sects. The fully developed church-type cannot exist without the aid of state coercion.

The church-type is thus another name for the Constantinianism that both Moltmann and Hauerwas renounce. Their theology and social thought are obviously closer to the sectarian type. This is the reason that Hauerwas in his early work himself used the church-sect typology, and could describe his own sympathies as with the sectarian type, without considering it as a pejorative designation.[16]

On the other hand, as said, few of even the harshest critics of sectarianism would today defend something close to the pure church-type as a normative position. The reason is that one of the causes of the changes that have formed the modern world, with its religious freedom, political democracy, human rights, and economic creativity is, or so Troeltsch (following Weber) argues, sectarian Christianity (Anabaptists, Baptists, Pietists, and Methodists) through its alliance with and reconstruction of Calvinism, and he seems to see the sectarian part as more important than the Calvinist.[17] This, which he calls, "Ascetic Protestantism" has had a social and political vitality and importance to which there is little resemblance in the more church-type Catholic and Lutheran churches. We have seen that this is also Moltmann's view.[18] Troeltsch moreover says that the sect-impulse, which had an important place in medieval Christianity, was within the Roman Catholic church after the Reformation increasingly stamped out. He thinks this helps explain the loss of vitality in the Catholic church.[19]

One reason for this role of the sects, he says, is their social location in the lower classes and social minorities. Because the societal elites, who benefit from the social order, are conservative, they do not contribute to much social and religious creativity. Instead, "it is the lower classes which do the really creative work, forming communities on a genuine religious basis. They alone unite imagination and simplicity of feeling with a non-reflective habit of mind, a primitive energy, and an urgent sense of need."[20] Without this, "no religious movement can live."[21]

---

[16]Another reason was, of course, his training in the Niebuhrian tradition. For examples of his use of sect-language, see "The Ethicist as Theologian ", 411, "The Future of Christian Social Ethics", 129f, *VV* 214, and *TT* 215 n. 5. This has led Robert Richardson to criticize Hauerwas for this use of 'sectarian', because he recognizes that the way this concept is ordinarily used does not suit Hauerwas' position. See "Christian Community and Ethics", 384-388. For his discussion of Hauerwas in the direct context of Troeltsch's typology, see ibid., 296-302. Richardson oddly enough has failed to see that Hauerwas no longer uses this terminology for describing his own position, both because of its connotations and because it presupposes theological and political assumptions he does not accept. The later Hauerwas therefore emphatically denies that his position is sectarian. See e.g. *AN* 7, *CET* 1-18, 113, *RA* 39-43, 155f, *AC* 16-19, and "Real Sectarian?".

[17]In addition to *Social Teaching*, see also his *Protestantism and Progress*, esp. 36-38, 52, 57, 60, 67-69, 74-78, 88.

[18]He does not, however, accept Weber's analysis of the relation between Calvinism and capitalism. See *EH* 119-130 (131-144).

[19]Troeltsch, *Social Teaching*, 700-703.

[20]Ibid., 44.

With time, to survive, they have to fuse with the high culture form of religious life and thought. But the point is, without these sectarian movements there would not be any Christianity to begin with, and neither would the Christian contributions to the modern world have been what they have been. Jesus, his disciples, and even Paul were examples of this naive, but necessary religious life. The origin of Christianity as well as its various great renewal movements have thus been of this sectarian character. The "superior" church-type is then dependent on these sectarian movements, and lacks itself creative strength, and works mostly conservatively in alliance with whatever social system it happens to live in.

So we have the interesting paradox that the so-called sectarianism of Hauerwas is seen as a deficient position because it marginalizes the church and makes it politically and socially impotent, while the reason the subject of sectarianism has been such a central occupation for sociologists from Weber and Troeltsch to our day is the exceptional political and social influence the sectarian forms of Christianity have had in the Western society.[22] While the church-type's main social function is described as integrative, legitimating and conservative, the sect-type has often functioned creatively and "progressively", even if (or because) their aim has not been to directly transform the world. Indeed, according to Troeltsch, the "non-aggressive" (this is Troeltsch's language) and the least obviously political sects have been more important than the more "aggressive" sects (in Troeltsch's time represented by Christian Socialism) that more directly aimed at the transformation of society.[23]

Troeltsch's typology has been very influential, but it has also been criticized for being too narrow and too dependent on the established church system of Europe, and therefore not able to explain, for example, the situation of America. It has consequently been amplified in various ways, the most important being the concept of "denomination" as a middle form between sect and church and typical of modern pluralist society.[24] The denomination does not have the universalist and absolutist claims of the church, but is more accepting of and integrated in the social order than the sect, and therefore also internally more tolerant and accepting of diversity, even if it tends to reflect the class-structure of society more than both the universal church and the egalitarian sect. In Hauerwas' perspective a significant deficiency of the denominational form is that it, unlike both church and sect (if these categories are used), lacks a space (like hierarchy, sacraments, dogmas, *and* independent ecclesial, moral and intellectual life respectively) free

---

[21]Ibid., 45.

[22]One very recent example is David Martin's *Tongues of Fire*. For a recent general sociological account of sectarianism, see Wilson, *Religious Sects*.

[23]Troeltsch, *Social Teaching*, 802-820.

[24]On this and generally on the discussion after Troeltsch, see Robertson, *The Sociological Interpretation of Religion*, 112-149.

from domination by the prevalent surrounding culture and therefore tends to be more easily accommodated.[25]

Today even European established churches have a denominational character, and Anthony Battaglia has therefore argued that in our pluralist post-churchly culture, which also philosophically increasingly is characterized by historicist and non-foundationalist understandings, the alternative is not between church and sect, but between revised forms of sectarian and denominational theologies, in his article represented by theologians like David Burrell, Hauerwas and George Lindbeck on the former side and David Tracy, James Gustafson and Francis Schüssler Fiorenza on the latter.[26]

Although Troeltsch showed the social importance and theological legitimacy of the sectarian position, he thought "that the Church-type is obviously superior",[27] because of its preservation of the message of divine grace and its ability to foster a national and popular religion that can include very different ways of life and degrees of maturity and therefore also directly form or influence the ethos of the society.[28] Not surprisingly, he likewise thought a radically revised form of national church as the way for the future.[29] Yet what has been said above suggests that Troeltsch can be read in a different way and that the conclusions he draws from the story he tells are not evident, but say as much about his own theological, sociological and political commitments as about anything else.

However, Hauerwas does not just interpret this history differently, he questions the very assumptions behind the construction of the Troeltschian typology.[30] Above all, he questions Troeltsch's thesis that the message of Jesus, as well as of early Christianity, was purely religious and therefore lacking any social ethic.[31] Troeltsch thinks so, Hauerwas says, because a social ethic for him "provides the means to rule and control society."[32] It is an ethic "relevant to the needs of an empire".[33] Troeltsch therefore describes issues like how the church is organized and how Christians live their everyday lives as purely religious.[34] This purely religious message must consequently be complemented by a natural law account, otherwise it will remain socially irrelevant. Thus "natural law functions ideologi-

---

[25]*CET* 113 following Gilkey, *How the Church Can Minister to the World Without Losing Itself,* 19f.

[26]Battaglia, "'Sect' or 'Denomination'?".

[27]Troeltsch, *Social Teaching,* 1007.

[28]He says also that "it cannot be denied that this does mean a modification of Christian thought in order to bring it down to the average level, to the level of practical possibility; and it is a principle of far-reaching adjustment and compromize." (Ibid., 1007)

[29]Ibid., 1006-1013.

[30]For his direct comments on Troeltsch in this connection, see *CC* 38f, "Ethics", 163, and "Christian Ethics in America", 29-32.

[31]See Troeltsch, *Social Teaching* 39-89 (esp. 39f, 43, 50). This was also, Hauerwas says, "epistemologically wedded to an ahistorical and asocial account of religious knowledge." ("Christian Ethics in America", 31.)

[32]*CC* 38.

[33]*CC* 39.

[34]Cf. Troeltsch, *Social Teaching,* 39.

cally to justify the assumption that Christians have a responsibility to fulfill the demands of the state and institutions associated with it."[35] Hauerwas therefore concludes that Troeltsch's account, because of the way it is set up, is written from the perspective of the church-type.

Hauerwas argues against Troeltsch that the story of Jesus is social and political from the beginning. It is in itself a social ethic. The social is not something added to the religious. This is a modern dualism that he thinks is foreign to Jesus and the early church.[36] It is important to note that he is not defending some sphere or dimension of religion that is separate from or irreducible to the social, but that the social and the religious cannot be separated from each other. He is therefore positive towards Troeltsch's concern to describe the faith of Christians in relation to their practices and social context. His criticism relates only to Troeltsch's separation of the social from the religious as finally separate dimensions.[37]

John Milbank has in *Theology and Social Theory* more extensively developed this criticism against Weber and Troeltsch and the whole modern tradition of sociology, and particularly the sociology of religion.[38] He recognizes that Weber was concerned, over against positivism and Marxism, to give a determinative place to substantive value rational goals beside instrumental rationality. However, Weber assumed that only means-ends rationality can be directly and objectively studied, because what is outside the factual realm of "economic rationality, formal bureaucracy, and Machiavellian politics" . . . "belong to the 'irreal' realm of valuation, and . . . exist primarily as hidden, subjective forces."[39] Milbank therefore contends that the consequence is that Weber is only able to discuss substantive value rational goals negatively as deviations from instrumental rationality. It is this view, and not empirical results, that Milbank thinks give categories such as 'charisma', 'routinization' and 'traditional authority' the important role in Weber's sociology of religion they have.

> Any religious pattern of valuation which semi-permanently distorts the operation of pure means-end rationality cannot be acknowledged as a factual presence in terms of its symbolic ordering of the world; instead it can only be registered as an inertia, as a mechanical

---

[35] *TT* 214 n. 5.

[36] See also Friesen, "Normative Factors in Troeltsch's Typology of Religious Association" and (from a very different perspective much closer to Troeltsch's) Pannenberg, *Ethics*, 109-111 for criticisms of this dualistic understanding.

[37] It is noteworthy that the leading sociologist of early Christianity Wayne Meeks singles out MacIntyre, Yoder, and Hauerwas and their understanding of the inseparable social embodiment of the faith as having affinity with his own socio-cultural approach. See his "Understanding Early Christian Ethics", 6. Hauerwas, on his side, comments positively on the "social world" methodology of Meeks and others in *CET* 130f n. 19. Cf. however also Milbank, *Theology and Social Theory*, 111-121.

[38] For the following, see esp. pp. 75-143.

[39] Milbank, *Theology and Social Theory*, 84.

persistence of the effect of response to charisma, after the original charisma has passed away.[40]

In this way the essence of religion is understood as extra-social, while organization and doctrine, which are socially explained, are seen as secondary phenomena. Furthermore, religion as organization can only survive if it accommodates itself to the 'rational' self-interest that *always* and *everywhere*, Weber contends, is the essence of the public realm. Machiavellian assumptions are thus intrinsic to Weber's sociology. But Milbank questions these *a priori* distinctions between political, economic, and religious spheres, and argues that social differentiation is "not the outworking of rationality itself," but "a contingent historical event (albeit both immensely widespread and persistent) in western history."[41] The emergence of separate political and economic spheres is a recent phenomenon ("[o]nce, there was no 'secular'"[42]), which Milbank traces in the first part of his book,[43] and can only be narrated and not made into general sociological "explanations". If this dualism between the "religious" and the "social" in Weber's (and Troeltsch's) sociology is questioned, one can no longer talk about a final social base for religion, because "there is nothing 'social' it could be reduced to."[44]

From this synchronic factor in Weber's sociology, Milbank goes on to discuss a complementary diachronic element, "which has as its main theme the emergence of formal-instrumental rationality."[45] This Weber and Troeltsch describe not as a contingent construction in the Western history, but as an always latent phenomenon. Modernity was latent in the Jewish and the Christian faith from the beginning. So what they describe is how in the Western civilization instrumental reason is slowly emancipated from various sorts of constrictions. As a result other cultures are defined in terms of what they lack; i. e., why the emancipation of instrumental reason did not occur in them. Milbank instead sees modernity as a particular cultural formation that could have been otherwise. For Hauerwas the church represents precisely a different way of ordering social life. It is not premodern or postmodern, concepts that tend to assume one necessary history, it is an alternative. But Weber's and Troeltsch's way of describing history as the emergence of formal-instrumental rationality makes such a possibility invisible.

> Thus Troeltsch and Weber fail to see individualism, voluntarism, fideism, and Kantian ethicization as contingent *changes* in Christian doctrine and ethos, but project these things back into the beginnings of Christianity and even the Old Testament. The history of the

---

[40]Ibid., 84f. He continues: "No doubt, of course, religions do undergo something like a 'routinization of charisma' (it did not take sociology to observe this) but it is not metaphysically inevitable in the way Weber makes it. Neither does it make sense to reduce all tradition to *stasis*, and even less to suppose a primal charisma arising before and apart from regular symbolic patternings."

[41]Ibid., 89.

[42]Ibid., 9.

[43]Ibid., 9-48.

[44]Ibid., 92.

[45]Ibid., 92.

west is turned into the always coming-to-be of liberal protestantism or its secular aftermath, and this means precisely the always-coming-to-be of Weber's and Troeltsch's methodology, their instrument of investigation.[46]

The detailed way Weber and Troeltsch argued their case in terms of polytheism and magic, Roman law, Ancient Judaism, and the origin and history of Christianity is today, Milbank says, altogether questionable, but this what Milbank calls "the liberal protestant metanarrative"[47] is still dominant both in sociology and theology. Recent sociology of religion[48] also continues to assume the separation of an unreducible religious universal dimension from its particular historical expressions. The latter are socially explained and mainly understood as integrative. The particular content itself is dealt with as arbitrary and not formative. This explains why one can talk about religion in general.[49]

> At the level of private experience, the content of religion is universal, and concerns a permanent dimension of human being. At the level of the cultural sub-systems it is plural and diverse, reflecting various arbitrary symbolic conventions. But at the level of 'society' as a whole, of civil religion, it is once again universal, because *at this level only*, symbolic arbitrariness is a cipher for something real, namely, an organic whole . . .,[50]

that is, the self-regulating society. This is nothing else than making modern liberal society and its self-description universally normative—liberalism as the inevitable end of history—why Milbank can describe modern sociology of religion as "a secular policing" that excludes religion from public life.[51] The claim is that only social science can understand society with its sub-systems as a whole. In the words of the sociologist Margareta Bertilsson: "Sociology is the theology of the secularized society!"[52]

> What is refused here is the idea that religion might enter into the most basic level of the symbolic organization of society . . . such that one would be unable to abstract a 'society'

---

[46]Ibid., 93.

[47]Ibid., 92.

[48]Milbank mentions people like Geertz, Berger, Luckmann, Bellah, and Luhmann, who all in different ways follow Parsons. See ibid., 106.

[49]Ibid., 104.

[50]Ibid., 109.

[51]Ibid., 109. Cf. *DFF* chapter 4. In a text originally from 1961 Moltmann similarly says: "Sociology is always a reflection of that society in which and from which it is derived, even when it attempts to be positivistic and free of value judgements. . . . In this way, the sociology of religion shows how society sees the church, in what roles it understands the church and how it 'defines' the church." (*HP* 130 [212].)

[52]*Slaget om det moderna*, 97. This book can be read as a confirmation of Milbank's analysis, even if Milbank goes further. Another interesting work that gives support to Milbank is Vidich and Lyman, *American Sociology*. In a wider context, not specifically discussing sociology, Charles Taylor makes in his *Sources of the Self* a somewhat similar argument as Milbank when he questions the idea of secularization as simply "the removal of obstacles to enlightenment" (p. 316) and instead describes the emergence of modernity in terms of contingent cultural mutations (see esp. pp. 305-320).

[53]Milbank, *Theology and Social Theory*, 109.

behind and beneath 'religion'. If this were the case, then it would become impossible to 'account for' religions in terms of 'other' social phenomena. One would only be able to narrate religions, with varying degrees of favour or disfavour . . .[53]

Christian theology should not, Milbank says, accept this sociological account, but much of it has. The charge of sectarianism can paradoxically be understood as precisely a policing of Christianity.[54] The church should participate in public life, but only on terms set by the currently dominant polity and culture. The particular Christian symbolic universe and practice should be kept outside the public sphere. Theologically this can be argued in terms of the provident work of the Creator or the historical work of the Spirit, where the point is that God in society or history itself provides the norms for social and political life. However it is done, the results tend to be the same. The liberal society (in our modern Western context) and its self-understanding becomes the norm for Christian social responsibility. The effect is the marginalization and privatization of Christian faith and practice.

A theological politics of Hauerwas' type denies the way liberal societies encompass religion. It denies the liberal description of Christianity and therefore also the liberal understanding of the church's relation to the "wider society", and it maintains the public and political nature of the church. But because it does not accept the role religion has been given in the current liberal order, it is described as sectarian. Furthermore, Christianity also, Hauerwas argues, comes in substantial conflict with the Machiavellian assumptions in modern sociological and political theory. He does not question their partial descriptive power, but he does question that all social life can be so understood. Even more importantly, in the name of Christian peace and virtue he denies that these assumptions are ontologically basic and necessary. Alternative forms of social life are possible and the church should be such an alternative. A problem with the Weberian account, as with liberalism generally, is that it cannot imagine any alternative to self-interest and struggle for power, only ways to make the struggle more fair.[55]

Milbank's extremely dense account, of which I have been able to give only a short outline, thus shows that the emergence of the sociology of religion that developed the church-sect language is imbued with sociological and theological assumptions that are questionable and in basic conflict with the theology of Hauerwas. An interesting question is how far Hauerwas' critics accept these assumptions. The problem is that most of them simply take the sect-language for granted, so it is impossible to know how they would qualify it.

Milbank also shows how Catholic political theology and liberation theology, most clearly in its earlier forms, assume and continue this "liberal protestant

---

[53]Milbank, *Theology and Social Theory*, 109.
[54]See the chapter "The Democratic Policing of Christianity" in *DFF*.
[55]*PK* 9.

metanarrative",[56] although in a socialist form, and we have seen that this is also true for Moltmann. We see this in his history of freedom, in his Weberian view of politics, in his early view of ethics, and in the idea that the world gives the church its agenda. But it is also clear how the Radical Reformation strand of his theology, in all these respects, goes in an entirely different direction.[57]

3. The Christ—Culture Typology of Niebuhr

There is one other book about the church's relation to the world that has decisively determined the continuing discussion, but which also raises some similar issues as Troeltsch's account does. It is H. Richard Niebuhr's book *Church and Culture* (which is deeply influenced by Troeltsch) with its five part typology: Christ against culture, Christ of culture, Christ above culture, Christ and culture in paradox, and Christ the transformer of culture.[58] People who describe Hauerwas as sectarian would also see him as an example of the Christ against culture-type. Niebuhr himself puts Protestant sectarianism, with the Mennonites as the most pure example, in this category.[59] Even granted the adequacy of the typology, this categorization could be questioned. Charles Scriven argues in his book *The Transformer of Culture* that the Radical Reformation position is best understood in terms of Christ the transformer of culture, the position Niebuhr himself clearly prefers (even if he does not explicitly say so). The paradox-position may also be possible. It is similarly difficult to know how to place Moltmann. The way Niebuhr describes the Christ of culture-type (for example Rauschenbusch[60]) seems to be the closest. With Troeltsch's description of the aggressive sects in mind, the Christ against culture is also possible, although the transformer-type may be closest to Moltmann's intention.[61]

---

[56]Milbank, *Theology and Social Theory*, 206-255 and idem, "On Baseless Suspicion". See e.g. Metz, *Theology of the World* and Gutierrez, *A Theology of Liberation*.

[57]Cf. also his early criticism of Troeltsch and others in *HP* 56-98 (57-92), which may be read as a groping attempt to question and overcome the "liberal protestant metanarrative".

[58]He sees his book in part as a supplement and a correction to Troeltsch's *Social Teaching*. See *Christ and Culture*, xii.

[59]Ibid., 56. For a sociological rejection of this description of the Mennonites, see Redekop, *Mennonite Society*, 114f. On Hauerwas, cf. Van Gerwen, "The Church in the Theological Ethics of Stanley Hauerwas", 162-168, Richardson, "Christian Community and Ethics", 302-306, and Neuhaus, *The Catholic Moment*, 18.

[60]Cf. also Hütter's interesting article on Rauschenbusch and Yoder "The Church: Midwife of History or Witness of the Eschaton", where the former is described as "a prefiguration of modern political theology" (p. 48).

[61]Gregory Scott describes Moltmann's position as a combination of Christ above culture and Christ the transformer, with stress on the latter. He also finds elements of Christ of culture, but nothing of Christ against culture. See "A Comparison of the Political Thought of Jacques Ellul and Jurgen Moltmann", 182-196. Scott's extensive use of Niebuhr's typology is not to its advantage, but that may say more about Scott than the typology. He even succeeds, through reading Barth's description of Schleiermacher as Niebuhr's description of Barth, making Barth into one of the classical examples of Christ of culture!

There are, however, deep problems in the assumptions behind the very construction of the typology around the poles of Christ and culture.[62] The Jesus of Niebuhr is a radical moralist that preaches the incomparable value of the transcendent in relation to any concern for culture, who therefore "points away from the many values of man's social life to the One who alone is good".[63] Culture, on the other hand, denotes the "total process" and the "total result" of human activity, "the 'artificial, secondary environment' which man superimposes on the natural."[64] So constructed the typology deals with how the absolute and transcendent ideals of Jesus Christ can be related to the social reality of culture, for it is obviously impossible to live without culture. We have here the same dualism we found in Weber and Troeltsch, and which Hauerwas' theological politics questions. According to Niebuhr's definition of culture, there is not, and cannot possibly be, any acultural Jesus or message of Jesus. Niebuhr describes the Christ against culture as the type closest to Jesus (whose message is described as against culture), but he contends at the same time that this position is impossible, because one cannot live and communicate without culture. It consequently was also impossible for Jesus. This very construction of the argument around two separate poles, Christ and culture, is thus one crucial deficiency in his argument. Yoder writes that *Christ + culture + false dichotomy*

> Niebuhr has so defined his terms as to make it clear from the outset that Jesus must be *by definition* inadequate. To do this, Niebuhr has excised from his picture of Jesus precisely those dimensions, clearly present in the Biblical record and in classical theology, which would have made impossible the kind of interpretation which he gives of Jesus as pointing away from the realm of culture, and thereby as needing the corrective of a more balanced position.[65]

To be able to use Niebuhr's categories, Scriven therefore finds it necessary to redefine Niebuhr's concept of culture, and talks instead about the "*prevailing culture*", or in other words "*the dominant way of life*".[66] The conflict is not between Christ and culture *per se*, but between an alternative culture and the domi-

---

Chopp formulates a sixth model for situating political and liberation theologies, "Christ liberating culture" (*The Praxis of Suffering*, 118-133).

[62]For the following, see esp. Yoder, "How Richard Niebuhr Reasons", but also Scriven, *The Transformer of Culture*. For Hauerwas own critique of Niebuhr's book, see *RA* 39-43, "Real Sectarian", 87, and "Ethics", 163f. His general assessment is "that few books have been a greater hindrance to an accurate assessment of our situation than *Christ and Culture*" (*RA* 40). He also says that Niebuhr mixes descriptive and normative arguments, and that the whole book is so constructed that the normative superiority of the Christ as transformer-type is shown.

[63]Niebuhr, *Christ and Culture*, 28.

[64]Ibid., 32.

[65]Yoder, "How Richard Niebuhr Reasons", 30.

[66]Scriven, *The Transformer of Culture* 45. See further ibid., 38-48, and Yoder, "How Richard Niebuhr Reasons", 31f. Scriven writes that "the very idea of "Christ against culture" is logically impossible given the definitions of the terms" (p. 44).

nant culture. The gospel of the kingdom of God represents not a transcendent ideal that points away from culture, but alternative social and cultural practices. As Yoder says:

> The tension will not be between a global reality called 'culture' on one side and an absolute spiritual distance called 'Christ' on the other side, but rather between a group of people defined by a commitment to Christ seeking cultural expression of that commitment and a group of other people expressing culturally values which are independent of such a confession.[67]

It is therefore Scriven can contend that the radical position is best understood in terms of Christ the transformer, because the alternative community leads to transformations of the wider cultures it lives in. He even argues that the very theology of Niebuhr himself leads in this direction. The essential question is *how* the church transforms the world.

Another often mentioned weakness in Niebuhr's account is his monolithic concept of culture. Culture is dealt with as a global unity, so when the representatives for the Christ against culture-type withdraw from some parts, but partake in and use other parts, which they always do, they are seen as inconsistent. But culture is better seen as "an indefinite congeries of powerful practices, spread over time and space, so that any number of these practices may impinge upon believers in a variety of ways, while our witness to them will necessarily take a corresponding variety of forms."[68] Consequently, Hauerwas does not think that his position leads to withdrawal, but instead to a discriminating attitude and practice, which means different relations to different parts of culture or society and to different societies. In his own words, "the form of our participation will vary given the nature of the societies in which we find ourselves."[69] This is also related to the third charge above, that the church is only one of the many communities Christians participate in. Hauerwas, of course, agrees, but again the question is *how* they participate.

> What is required for Christians is not withdrawal but a sense of selective service and the ability to set priorities. This means that at times and in some circumstances Christians will find it impossible to participate in government, in aspects of the economy, or in the educational system. Yet such determinations can only be made by developing the skills of discrimination fostered in and through the church.[70]

This readiness to partial withdrawal, moreover, ought to be true for any serious theological or moral position. It is difficult, and the way many churches functions today and their lack of any sense of disciplined community, make it even more

---

[67]Yoder, "How Richard Niebuhr Reasons", 47.
[68]McClendon, *Systematic Theology: Ethics*, 231. See also Yoder, "How Richard Niebuhr Reasons" 27f and Scriven, *The Transformer of Culture*, 43-48, 60-64.
[69]*CET* 14. See also *CET* 121f and "Real Sectarian", 87.
[70]*CET* 15f.

difficult. One need only think of the churches roles in Hitler's Germany or in communist states, to take extreme examples. It is Hauerwas contention that there is reason for dissent also in Western democracies and he asks how to form Christians ready to say "No" and form alternative ways of life. Most of his critics have not even started to ask the question.

4. The Church Telling a Counter History

With this long discourse on "sectarianism" I have wanted to elucidate the built-in assumptions in the vocabulary and the perspective used in this common criticism of Radical Reformation theology. We have seen that this language presupposes the normativeness of specific understandings of church and politics, in short, of Constantinianism and liberalism. The very word "sect" has historically been used by politically established churches for denying the Christian legitimacy of various reform and renewal movements inside or outside their own institutional borders. The same use has continued even in societies, like the American, without formally established churches but with (in the American case) a semi-formal Protestant establishment. Most modern social ethics has its origin in this type of established churches that take some form of hegemonic cultural and political role for granted, even if this in a modern secular and pluralist context takes other forms. The close relationship with the political and cultural elite and with the nation-state as primary actor is not questioned. One has to add the further fact that theologians often have the university as their daily life context, an institution deeply embedded in the elite culture and the nation-state (in European countries like Sweden, the state even has had monopoly on university education and research).

We have also seen that the sociological use of the term, which is not intended as pejorative, is part of liberal societies' self-understanding, and that the categories used for understanding the role of religion in society presuppose the normativeness of liberal society and ideology and the concomitant marginalization of religion in public life. In other words, the very phenomena and their accompanying ideologies that Hauerwas has so consistently attacked in modern church and society, Constantinianism and liberalism, are intrinsic to the vocabulary used for discussing the adequacy of Hauerwas' position. What we find in the writings of Hauerwas, Yoder, and Milbank are attempts both to undermine this story and to tell a different one. But the critics seem not to recognize this. This may explain why they have hardly begun to meet the criticism Hauerwas and others direct against their own perspectives or tried to show what is wrong with the counter history told. Furthermore, the assumptions intrinsic to the language and models used for criticizing Radical Reformation theology are not clearly amenable to some of the theological positions defended. How many of the critics we have mentioned would accept the assumptions on religion behind the sect and church-language in Weber and Troeltsch? Would not these assumptions undermine their own theological perspectives as well?

In this context it is interesting that political theologies like Moltmann's seldom are criticized or described as sectarian. In Troeltsch's terms they are a modern variant of aggressive sects. They are deeply critical of the capitalist form of liberal social order and they are no less utopian than Radical Reformation theology, given the latter's arguably greater realism on what is possible. But they are not called sectarian. I suppose it is so because they have allied themselves with more or less oppositional elite groups of modern society, as Troeltsch said they had to do to survive, and they are therefore less critical, but also more hopeful of immediate radical social changes directly managed by them.

We have also seen that one can plausibly read Weber's and Troeltsch's accounts as showing that Christianity may have been more important for social change when it has been itself without calculative political intentions, than it has been when it directly tried to form public policy. The objection that the inadequacy of what they call the sectarian position is shown in the fact that its influence has been mediated through other more established groups is not valid for several reasons. First, there would not have been anything to mediate without the "sectarian" and non-calculative practice in which the minority position was intrinsic. There are values of the minority position which are lost if it is given up. Second, the alternative strategy of the more church-type churches has, according to Troeltsch's account, in terms of social creativity not been impressive. Third, the objection assumes falsely that history is in decisive ways determined by state policy. In practice the possibilities of state policy to determine society in a constructive way is severely limited by factors it cannot control (its destructive ability however is considerably greater, the most extreme example being war). That is not only true of earlier states (our way of putting the question is very modern), but also of modern ones. Yet one way of opening up new possibilities is through the imagination, social practices and virtues of dissenting minorities. In chapter 15 I will at more length develop and explain these points.

Being a minority and not in control means that one cannot determine how one's influence is woven into history. However, if the abilities to intentionally control society and social change by political means are limited, this is true for any position. In so far as modernity is part of the legacy of the Radical Reformation tradition, this legacy is, from its perspective, highly ambiguous. The role of capitalism is the most obvious example, but we will later also discuss the ambiguous forms of the secular development of the languages of freedom, justice and rights. Yet we should also remember that Hauerwas, in criticism of MacIntyre's overstated criticism of the Enlightenment, can see "the Enlightenment as a secularization of the genuinely new (to the ancients, that is) Christian vision of a community at peace."[71] One of several reasons for the secularization were the re-

---

[71] "Virtue Christianly Considered", 18. See also *DFF* 198 n. 30.

ligious wars after the Reformation, where the main-line Constantinian churches, because of their Constantinianism (i. e., their church-type strategy), failed to meet the challenges of diversity and violence. In the case of the Protestant churches they instead became providers of ideological legitimation for the developing nation-states.[72]

I have in this chapter given examples of how Troeltsch's own account gives material to read the history of the church's relation to the society in a rather different way than the one he himself took. If these alternative readings can be upheld, then the whole construction of Troeltsch's liberal metanarrative would be questioned, and a counter history would be asked for, which discards the basically liberal categories with which Troeltsch works.[73] Milbank says that

> the Christological-ecclesial narrative *arises*, in the first place, not simply as an 'identification' of the divine, but also as a 'reading' and a critique-through-practice of all historical human community up to that point. . . . For theology to surrender this claim, to allow that other discourses—'the social sciences'—carry out yet more fundamental readings, would therefore amount to a denial of theological truth. The *logic* of Christianity involves the claim that the 'interruption' of history by Christ and his bride, the Church, is the most fundamental of events, interpreting all other events. And it is *most especially* a social event, able to interpret other social formations, because it compares them with its own new social practice.[74]

Because the church, for Milbank as for Hauerwas, is the continuation of this narrative, it is a story still enacted and continuously reinterpreted. It becomes also, in their accounts, a deeply self-critical narrative because this history to a large extent tells the story of a tragic failure.[75] Such an alternative history, based in the life of the church, would discard with, among other things, the dualism between public rationality and basically arbitrary and subjective religious forces, and with the division of society into private will contra a Machiavellian political sphere. It further questions the split between a universal religious dimension and its particular and subjective historical expressions. What Troeltsch describes as naive, primitive historical expressions of early Christianity, from the preaching of Jesus to the theological interpretations of his death and resurrection, are of course the basis for the theologies of Hauerwas and Moltmann and their various readings of history.[76] The following two chapters will give examples of Hauerwas' attempt to redescribe the world in a Christian way.

---

[72]The Swedish Lutheran church is one of the most striking examples of this. See for a recent account, Petrén, *Kyrka och makt*.

[73]*AC* 150.

[74]Milbank, *Theology and Social Theory*, 387f. On the question *how* this counter history should be told, Hauerwas expresses some hesitation to Milbank's grand narrative. See above p. 177 n. 17.

[75]Milbank, *Theology and Social Theory*, 388, 432f.

[76]In this Gustafson is of course similar to Troeltsch. Cf. his *Theology and Ethics*, 97f, 229f.

Chapter 12

The Church and Liberal Society

The foregoing chapters have shown that Hauerwas' theological politics takes a very different road from Moltmann's political theology, but also follows up one central line in Moltmann's project. The consequences of this become clear in their divergent discussion of church and modernity. We have seen how Moltmann tries to give Christian legitimacy to modernity and at the same time show the relevance of Christian faith for the Enlightenment project. This strategy is, according to Moltmann, necessary if the church is not to become irrelevant to modern society. He does this through describing modernity as one step in God's history of liberation of the world, which then implies the necessity to show the compatibility of the central values of modernity with Christian faith and the ability of Christianity to work critically and therapeutically to further this work of liberation against its own distortions.

Hauerwas' strategy is vastly different. The idea that Christian faith has to be mediated or translated for the modern age if the church should avoid becoming marginalized and lose its influence is for Hauerwas just another example of how Constantinian habits of thought still control the imagination of theologians who think of themselves as anti-Constantinian. If for Moltmann the problem is how to make the Christian message relevant and influential in the struggle for the control of the processes of social change, and therefore of formulating a more relevant theology, the question for Hauerwas is how to form a church faithful to the way of the gospel or, to use the title of one of Moltmann's books, the way of Jesus Christ.[1] The church has its own way, and should not identify itself with either radical, liberal or conservative agendas. This does not mean that the church isolates itself from the world, or that it does not learn from the world. The most important thing for the church is not that it has the right set of convictions, but that it is a people created by the life, death and resurrection of Jesus Christ. As a people with its own story, it can develop the skills for a discriminating relation to and interpretation of the world.

In this chapter we will see how this works out in his interpretation of modernity, which according to Hauerwas has its main expression in the Western liberal society. He does not develop a sort of well-rounded theory of modernity and even less a theoretical alternative, but he tries to show the inherent tensions that characterize the structures, institutions and theories of liberalism and its conflicts with church and Christian faith and how the church can witness to different possibilities.

---

[1]Cf. *RA* 23f.

The next section is intended as an introductory summary of his overall charac-terization of liberalism that should help to place the following more specific sec-tions. The state and the market are the two dominating institutions of a liberal society and they will be the subject of the second section. Liberalism has created its own forms of moral language, and the third and the longest section will thus deal with Hauerwas' critique of liberal moral and political theory and his con-structive alternative. This is followed by a section where I in more detail compare his approach with two prominent, but very different forms of liberal theory. Free-dom and justice are the two chief liberal values, and they will be given one sec-tion each. Finally, I will draw the chapter together by means of a discussion of the manifold and complex relation that exist between Christianity and liberalism.

1. Liberalism as the Principal Ideology of Modernity

Hauerwas and Moltmann describe, understand and appraise modernity and the Enlightenment tradition in notably different ways. On a first reading one could however easily miss this radical difference, especially if one, like Moltmann, in-terprets contemporary political and cultural reality in terms of radical versus con-servative. It is the American society that is at the centre of Hauerwas' analysis. The basic categories he uses for describing this society are "liberal" and "liberalism". However, for him liberalism is not only the dominant ideology of the American society, but also the political theory *par excellence* of modernity in general.[2] This means that he uses the concept "liberalism" in a wider sense than has been usual especially in Europe, but also in ordinary political discourse in America (as distinguished from political theory). A further complication is the fact that the word "liberal" is used somewhat differently in America compared to Europe. In America liberalism is primarily understood in contradiction to conser-vatism, which means that the more liberal one is, the more left one is. In Europe, on the other hand, liberal is mainly used in contrast to socialism, which makes it closer to the sense of American conservatism.[3] In more recent times, however, both socialism and European conservatism have increasingly lost its more social-

---

[2]John Gray, whose *Liberalism* gives a good first overview of liberalism, writes: "Liberalism . . . is the political theory of modernity. Its postulates are the most distinctive features of modern life—the autonomous individual with his concern for liberty and privacy, the growth of wealth and the steady stream of invention and innovation, the machinery of government which is at once indispensable to civil life and a standing threat to it—and its intellectual outlook is one that could have originated in its fullness only in the post-traditional society of Europe after the dissolution of medieval Christendom." (Ibid., 82.) Alan Wolfe similarly writes: "Liberal principles now have a near monopoly among political theorists of modernity." (*Whose Keeper?*, 108.)

[3]It has to be remembered that because classical European conservatism emerged in reaction to early modernity and in defence of the *ancien régime* it had a more reserved attitude against capitalism. This has never been true of American conservatism, because America was from the "beginning" a bourgeois society. See Berger, "Capitalism and the Disorders of Modernity" and Nisbet, *Conservatism*.

ist respective conservative features and become variations of a basically liberal polity. This is true at both the practical and the theoretical levels.[4]

This latter development supports Hauerwas' contention that liberalism is the primary political theory of modernity. This becomes even clearer, when we see the intrinsic connection Hauerwas makes between liberalism and the Enlightenment project.

> In the most general terms I understand liberalism to be that impulse deriving from the Enlightenment project to free all people from the chains of their historical particularity in the name of freedom. As an epistemological position liberalism is the attempt to defend a foundationalism in order to free reason from being determined by any particularistic tradition. Politically liberalism makes the individual the supreme unit of society, thus making the political task the securing of cooperation between arbitrary units of desire. While there is no strict logical entailment between these forms of liberalism I think it can be said they often are interrelated.[5]

In institutional terms the "liberal project" is associated with "an allegedly limited state in service to a social and economic order based on exchange relations."[6] One part of this project was thus to emancipate people from the historical particularity of their traditions and communities, which politically meant that the two basic units in modern societies are the individual on the one hand and the state on the other.[7] A central part of the political struggle in modernity has therefore concerned the relation between the individual and the state. The main political scale is construed around these poles. On one side the rights of the individual and the free market are emphasized, and on the other the social rights and actions of the government towards greater social justice. Hauerwas stresses the intrinsic connection between the emphasis on freedom and emancipation on the one hand and the strong state on the other. Freedom, which stands at the centre of the Enlightenment, is basically understood in an individualistic sense.[8] The autonomy and independence of the individual in reaction against traditional communities and tradition in general are therefore a central article of faith. The other side of this is

---

[4] An illustration to the liberal triumph over conservatism. In Swedish radio I heard one prominent member of the Swedish conservative party ("the Moderates") say that his conservatism could only be expressed as a private preference, while any legitimate public policy has to be liberal.

[5] *AN* 18. In an earlier text he writes: "It is, of course, true that liberalism is an extremely complex phenomenon that is not easily characterized even by the most sophisticated forms of political theory. I associate liberalism, however, with the political philosophy of Rawls and Nozick, the political science of Dahl, and the economics of neo-capitalism. There often appear to be deep disagreements between the advocates of liberalism in America, but such disagreements are finally arguments between brothers." (*CC* 289 n. 8.) Cf. Placher, who describes liberalism as that "broader tradition, beginning with the Enlightenment, of those, often suspicious of tradition, who believe that society should not try to find a common vision of the good toward which we could work together. Rather, they accept that we will always have different religious and ethical ideals, and we are socially united only in procedures that preserve our rights to pursue those different ideals without interference." (*Unapologetic Theology*, 75.)

[6] "Can Aristotle Be a Liberal?", 677.

[7] "Marriage and the Family", 4.

[8] *PK* 6-10.

the necessity of a powerful bureaucratic state capable of keeping all these individual interests together.[9]

A natural corollary is an ethical language dominated by the categories of freedom and justice. The subject of ethical thinking is the autonomous individual, free from social roles, traditions, and particular communities, constructing for him/herself moral meaning. Justice is the principle through which people's different needs and wants are made compatible with each other. All this leads to a strong emphasis on rights.[10] A consequence is the way the distinction between a private sphere (where different personal goods, which cannot be publicly argued about, can be pursued) and a public sphere (where no common good exists, but only rules for just distribution) is made.[11] By necessity religion as a tradition and community bound practice is removed to the private sphere. Religion is consequently associated more with personal taste than with public truth.[12]

From this follows also the common assumption that society does not need people who are just in order to have a just polity. The accepted notion is instead "that politics is about the distribution of desires, irrespective of the content of those desires, and any consideration of the development of virtuous people as a political issue seems an inexcusable intrusion into our personal liberty."[13]

Understood in this way, it is not so surprising that Hauerwas stresses the commonality between liberalism and socialism and that he can describe most forms of Western socialism as forms of liberalism.[14] Liberalism and socialism are different versions of the same Enlightenment project that stresses freedom and justice, universal scientific rationality and progress.[15] In libertarian forms of libe-

---

[9]*CC* 78, "Faith in the Republic", 496.

[10]*AC* 45-68, "Marriage and the Family", 4.

[11]Michael Sandel writes: "While we may be thickly-constituted selves in private, we must be wholly unencumbered selves in public, and it is there that the primacy of justice prevail." (*Liberalism and the Limits of Justice*, 182.)

[12]*AC* 69-92.

[13]*CC* 73.

[14]Michael Walzer says "that liberalism is, among other things, the American version of social democracy." ("Retrospective", 197.) The leading liberal theorist John Rawls says in *A Theory of Justice*, 271 that his theory in principle is neutral in relation to capitalist and socialist economic systems.

[15]*AN* 123f, *AC* 61f, "Faith in the Republic", 497. Cf. MacIntyre's conclusion "that Marxism's moral defects and failures arise from the extent to which it, like liberal individualism, embodies the *ethos* of the distinctively modern and modernizing world" (*After Virtue*, viii). He find this not surprising as "[s]ecreted within Marxism from the outset is a certain radical individualism", a fact which helps explain why Marxists always have "fallen back into relatively straightforward versions of Kantianism or utilitarianism" (ibid., 243) when forced to take clear moral stances. Peter Berger, from another direction, agrees: "The socialist program is based on all the standard cognitive assumptions of modernity—history as progress (an idea which must be understood as a secularization of biblical eschatology), the perfectibility of man, scientific reason as the great liberator from illusion, and man's ability to overcome all or nearly all of his afflictions by taking rational control of his destiny. In these assumptions, socialism, like liberalism, is the child of the Enlightenment. Unlike liberalism, however, socialism has also successfully incorporated the themes that have arisen in protest of discontents of modernity, notably the theme of renewed community." Discussing socialism in relation to counter-modern currents, he continues further on: "The genius of socialism, though, is that its secularized eschatology incorporates

ralism individual freedom and market are stressed, while in egalitarian forms of liberalism and socialism more stress is put on justice and state led social engineering.[16]

Swedish social democracy is one example of how socialism can be interpreted as a form of liberalism as Hauerwas describes it. We see it in its acceptance of what in Sweden is called "value nihilism", of the idea of scientific social planning, of bargaining as the method for reaching consensus, and of the crucial role of the (politically regulated) market. The socialist vision has a community motive, but in practice community has tended to be identified with the welfare state as the large caring community.[17]

It should also be noted that Hauerwas does not believe that the American society is consistently liberal, but he thinks it is slowly becoming more and more so. Furthermore, he suggests that the success of liberalism is partly a result of the fact that it has been able to live "on social structures and habits it did not create and in fact over time undermines."[18] The liberal vision works as a sort of self-fulfilling prophecy slowly destroying the non-liberal elements, because of the difficulty of imagining an alternative public philosophy.

So understood it is clear that the main features of Moltmann's political vision is part of the liberal project, although this project comes in certain conflict with some of his central theological convictions. In the rest of this chapter I will develop Hauerwas' critique of liberalism on more specific issues and at the same time try to relate this to the differences and convergences between his theological politics and Moltmann's political theology.

---

in addition the central aspirations of modernity—a new rational order, abolition of material want and social inequality, and complete liberation of the individual. Socialism, in other words, promises all the blessings of modernity and the liquidation of its costs, including, most importantly, the cost of alienation." (*Facing Up to Modernity*, 60, 61.)

[16]In discussing the socialist criticism of the liberal individual ethos, Sullivan says that "[o]n the Left . . . often, as in most Marxist arguments, there is still a strong commitment to the Enlightenment idea of progress as a continuing extension of instrumental control over social relations." (*Reconstructing Public Philosophy*, 16.) He also writes that "[t]he logical goal of liberal rationality is a scientific social engineering that will be able to bring about a perfect adjustment of needs and wants." (Ibid., 26.)

[17]"Although the ideology of social democracy (or welfare liberalism) has often included affirmations of community, its operative ethos has been, in important ways, anti-communitarian. This slant stems mainly from the welfare liberal's commitment to rational organization and general rules—in a word, to bureaucracy." (Selznick, *The Moral Commonwealth*, 512.) Exemplifying with Sweden Selznick also writes: "The programs of the welfare state are mainly designed to serve individual needs. Guided by principles of equality and personal autonomy, they display only passing concern for the integrity and well-being of groups and institutions, that is, for the spontaneous arrangements of civil society. As government moves in to supplement (and replace) private ordering, the fabric of community is weakened." (Ibid., 512, cf. n. 59.) For a short overview of the Swedish case, see Lyttkens, *Politikens klichéer och människans ansikte*, 25-46. See further Hirdman, *Att lägga livet till rätta*, Wolfe, *Whose Keeper?*, and, for the philosophical underwriting of this conception, Källström, *Den gode nihilisten*, and Nordin, *Från Hägerström till Hedenius.*

[18]*AN* 18.

2. Market Economy and the Liberal State

The state and the market are dominant institutions of the liberal society and therefore also in Hauerwas' analysis of liberal society. Particularly because of the central role of non-violence in Radical Reformation thought, Hauerwas has discussed the Christians relations to the state, including the liberal state, rather extensively. One the other hand, his discussions of how Christians and the church should understand and relate to the economic dimension of life, including work, are more meagre, although he often stresses how the modern market system forms human life. There can be several reasons for this. One may simply be that he cannot do everything and he, of course, still has time to develop his often very suggestive comments. A more important reason may be the weakness of the church in this area, and theology is dependent on the practices of the church. This in its turn has to do with the little space for freedom the economic system gives.

What he has written, however, illustrates clearly the differences between Moltmann and himself. In Moltmann's political thought the crucial issue has been the choice between capitalism and socialism. His hope has been the coming of a democratic socialist system, the content of which is not too clear, but in the most general terms seems to be a combination of a radicalized liberal political system with a socialist economy. This is not the approach of Hauerwas. The church neither chooses between theories or provides its own general theory. Such strategies assume both a perspective from above and a position of current or future control that the church does not have. A second reason is his scepticism towards such general theories and their claims to knowledge. A third reason is that both capitalist and socialist theories to a large extent build on the same questionable assumptions and social and economic structures.[19]

Hauerwas' approach is more modest. Instead of starting in a general theory, he starts with the assumption that the economic system should serve moral and social purposes—especially making possible the support of families and the raising of children. In this context he can, for example, talk about the just wage, of which a central aspect is the possibility of supporting a family. "The just wage, so to speak, is not an economic theory, but rather a moral challenge to any theory or system in that it reminds us what we should be about. While it involves no uto-

---

[19]"Work as Co-Creation", 51-54 and "In Praise of *Centesimus Annus*", 418. These are the two most helpful texts for understanding Hauerwas' general perspective on economy and work. Both deals with encyclicals by John Paul II. The first, which has the subtitle "A Critique of A Remarkably Bad Idea", is a very critical discussion of *Laborem Exercens*. The second is a much more positive treatment of *Centesimus Annus*. Against the interpretation of the latter encyclical as first of all a support of market economies, Hauerwas reads it as primarily a theological document that subordinates economic life to a theologically informed view of human life, and therefore sees it as critical both of socialism and liberalism. On this reading, see Nortcott, "Preston and Hauerwas on *Centesimus Annus*". For a discussion and use of Hauerwas' and McClendon's ethics for reflection on economic justice, see Gentry's dissertation "Narrative Ethics and Economic Justice".

pian ideal of a harmonious or egalitarian economic system, it stands as a simple reminder that any system must at least deal with these matters."[20] Another question that should be asked to any economic system is the sort of people they form.[21] Moreover, the church's best resource for its reflection on the economic life is not economic theories but "the actual experience of Christian men and women who must find ways to negotiate the extraordinarily complex economic systems in which we find ourselves caught."[22]

The contrast between Hauerwas and Moltmann may be illuminated by Robert Nelson's discussion of modern economic theory as theology, which we shortly met in chapter 10.[23] A central belief, Nelson says, in modern economic theology has been that material scarcity and the competition this leads to is the basic cause of evil and human sinfulness. Consequently, the solution to the economic problem will bring salvation. And humanity has the power to eliminate scarcity through scientific knowledge of the economic laws and technological development. This belief is behind both socialist and market doctrines in their many variations and is the basis for the authority of the economists in modern societies.

We have seen that Moltmann share this belief, at least in his early writings. Although he now (as many others, which Nelson also shows) questions the blessings of economic progress, his thought is still formed by what Nelson calls the progressive faith that the right and good ordering of society is only a *technical* problem if people of good will have the power. One can therefore read Moltmann's political theology as an attempt to mediate Christian theology and one type of modern economic theology. In this mediation it is the latter that gives the agenda and the political substance.

Hauerwas, on the other hand, not only questions the claims of economics to be able to predict and control the future (and in chapter 15 we will see that there are good reasons for this scepticism), he also questions the belief that the problem of human sin and evil can be solved by technological and economic progress. He does not think that the market, bureaucracy, and technology can supersede moral training and communal practices. He can, for example, say that "we can only free ourselves from the coercion of the market when we are morally trained not to think of ourselves as deserving whatever we desire, or perhaps more accurately, when we learn to desire the right things rightly."[24] What is required, then, is not a new theory, but communities of care and virtue.[25]

He is therefore also deeply critical of the type of far-reaching conclusions about a radical reconstruction of society Moltmann draws from a theology of

---

20"Work as Co-Creation", 53.
21"*Centesimus Annus*", 420.
22"Work as Co-Creation", 56.
23See *Reaching for Heaven on Earth*. Cf. p. 214 above.
24*CC* 251 n. 33.
25"Work as Co-Creation".

work.[26] In contrast to Moltmann, Hauerwas does not see work as primarily a self-fulfilling activity, but a means of survival and service to others. This is what work is for most people and the idea of elimination of all unfulfilling work is wholly utopian. "Attributing greater significance to work risks making it demonic as work then becomes an idolatrous activity through which we try to secure and guarantee our significance, to make 'our mark' on history."[27] This relativizing of work also enhances the significance of the non-work parts of our life.

In light of what is said, it is not surprising that he is very critical of the way the market increasingly subordinates "everything to issues of economic rationality"[28] and how human relations more and more are seen and treated as exchange or contractual relationships.[29] Because the economy should serve human purposes outside the economy, Christians should not accept the idea of an independent economic realm determined by its own laws, and consequently neither the idea of economics as a science that is independent of ethics and politics. He is for the same reason also sceptical of the common description of society as consisting of different realms, such as culture, politics and economy, both because it might be interpreted as a defence of the autonomy of the economy and because it fails to take account of how the economic rationality in a capitalist society tends to invade all areas of life.[30] This is also his most common criticism of neoconservatives that call for a return to traditional values and republican virtues, and at the same time ask for the strengthening of the capitalist economy and the supremacy of the freedom of the individual (and often the former as an undergirding of the latter). They fail to see, he argues, that the actual relationship is the opposite, how the capitalist economy and the freedom of the individual as the supreme value undermine the sort of traditional values they defend, and they become upset when people use their freedom to undercut these values.[31]

The questions to Hauerwas are then what his questioning of the primacy and autonomy of the economy might mean in practice on the personal, the ecclesial and the societal levels? How is or could the church witness to alternative practices? Hauerwas has so far said little in answer to such questions. In a similar way he can talk about the determining influence of technology in modern society

---

[26]His longest discussion of work in general, on which this paragraph builds, is his very critical discussion of *Laborem Exercens*, whose arguments have some parallels to Moltmann's theology of work, in "Work as Co-Creation". Cf. the discussions of Ellul in *Ethique de la liberté*, vol. 3, 258-283 and "Le travail".

[27]"Work as Co-Creation", 48.

[28]"*Centesimus Annus*", 425.

[29]He writes that "liberalism, and the way it works, in effect makes a claim that the economic model of human relationships should become paradigmatic for all relationships. In other words, all relationships become fundamentally exchange relationships; that is, I do something, and I get something back. What that does is to make *manipulation* the heartblood of all relationships." ("Marriage and the Family", 5.) See also "Medical Care for the Poor" for a critique of "market justice" in the area of medical care.

[30]*AC* 184 n. 9, "*Centesimus Annus*", 418f, *PtS* 26.

[31]*CET* 195f, *AN* 18, 124f, *AC* 184 n. 9.

where the technological development has been taken out of the wider ethical and political context.[32] But concerning such issues we find even less discussion. Because of the all-encompassing nature of modern economy and technology for everyday life, these questions are quite impossible to avoid and ought to be a central issue for the sort of Christian ethics Hauerwas defends.

His critique of the role of the market does not lead him to ask for a strengthening of the state. Instead he is deeply wary and sceptical of the state in general, and the modern state in particular, the liberal state included. He can even say that "[t]oday, the new universal religion that demands subservience is not really Marxism or capitalism but the entity both of these ideologies serve so well—the omnipotent state."[33] According to Hauerwas, we have seen, most Christian ethics (as well as theology in general) is formulated within the context of the nation-state. Central tasks in this project have been to develop theological justifications of the American liberal democratic system or to make the battle for democracy against other systems (i. e., for a long time for USA against the former Soviet Union) a chief task of the church.[34] In this pursuit the nation-state system is usually taken for granted, something Hauerwas thinks Christians should question.

> We live in a mad existence where some people kill other people for abstract and unworthy entities called nations. The church's first task is not to make the nation-state system work, but rather to remind us that the nation, especially as we know it today, is not an ontological necessity for human living. The church, as an international society, is a sign that God, not nations, rule this world.[35]

Instead of developing a Christian theory of the state, he thus wants to question the deep assumptions that adapt Christian morality to the needs of the nation-state and wants instead to help the Christian community to develop the skills necessary to keep the state limited and to live truthfully in the nations where they are placed. We will in the next chapter return to this whole issue of church, nation-state and violence.

From this does not follow that he sees no significant differences between different states and political systems or between democratic and totalitarian systems. Although he is much more critical of American (both domestic and foreign) policy than most American theologians, this does not prevent him from being more positive to the American society than to, for example, the former Soviet society.[36]

---

[32]"*Centesimus Annus*", 423, "Work as Co-Creation", 47.
[33]*RA* 42.
[34]He quotes Yoder who writes that if Christian "claim for democracy the status of a social institution *sui generis*, we shall inflate ourselves and destroy our neighbors through the demonic demands of the claims we make for our system and we shall pollute our Christian faith by making of it a civil religion. If, on the other hand, we protect ourselves from the Constantinianism of that view of democracy, we may find the realistic liberty to foster and celebrate relative democratization as one of the prophetic ministries of a servant people in a world we do not control." (*The Priestly Kingdom*, 165f, *CET* 183f.)
[35]*CC* 109f.
[36]*AN* 123, "On Learning Simplicity in an Ambiguous Age", 43, *CET* 13.

Furthermore, just because of his views on politics and violence he thinks the church ought to strive for a more open society.

> Once one disavows the use of violence, it means one has a high stake in developing political processes through which agreement is reached without the necessity of coercion. As Christians, we, of course, want to make our societies as open as possible to the voice of dissent, exactly because we believe so profoundly in the necessity of politics—politics understood as the discussion of peoples necessary to discover the goods they have in common.[37]

From such a perspective he can thus give a positive description of democracy as "a system of social relations and institutions to encourage the discussion necessary for the articulation of the good a people can share in common."[38] Yet, his problem with modern liberal states and societies is that this is not the way they function and he doubts that such an understanding of democracy is a practical possibility given current liberal structures and convictions.[39]

3. The Institution of Morality in Liberalism

Modernity and the liberal tradition have also developed their own types of moral and political philosophy. Hauerwas has formulated his own perspective through a continuous critical dialogue with these traditions. In chapter ten I outlined his basic understanding of ecclesial ethics. Here I will try to sharpen its contour through taking up his analysis and criticism of the liberal tradition. This section will concentrate on the *form* of its ethical reflection. I will later take up the two central values of liberalism, justice and freedom, although form and content are, as we will see, dependent on each other. The issues dealt with in this section are extremely complex. There are many, often very different and contradictory, forms of liberal political and moral theories of high sophistication. In the 1970s John Rawls and Robert Nozick were the two towering figures of liberal political and moral philosophy and in Hauerwas' earlier formative writings, his criticism of liberalism usually included Nozick and (especially) Rawls. The increasing criticism liberalism has met has both led to modifications of existing liberal theories and to the emergence of a bewildering variety of different, often incompatible, types of liberal philosophies.[40] In addition, there is the problem of the relation between these theories and the actually used moral languages in liberal

---

[37]"Will the Real Sectarian Stand Up", 91.

[38]*CET* 195. The state cannot and should not form virtuous people, but "a good state can exist as a correlative of a good society where coercion is at a minimum precisely because people are virtuous." ("Real Sectarian", 90.) Cf. also *CC* 13f, *AN* 7, and *CET* 185, 194.

[39]He writes that the problem with American democracy "is simply the American people who believe, after two centuries of instruction, that at least in the realm of politics their task is to pursue their own interests. We are finding it hard to restrict that lesson to 'politics,' since nowadays people increasingly live it out in church and family." (*DFF* 105.)

[40]See e.g. Rosenblum (ed.), *Liberalism and the Moral Life.*

societies. My intention is obviously not to make any exhaustive discussion of the relation between Radical Reformation theology and liberal moral and political theory. The aim is more modest: to describe (and also that briefly) Hauerwas' understanding and criticism of modern moral theory and thereby clarify his own position and relate this to political theology.

Political theology stands in a complex relation to the liberal moral tradition. In substantial terms it is one Christian form of the left-wing of this project at the same time as it tries to challenge the privatization of Christianity inherent in the liberal project. We have seen that this creates severe tensions that draw political theology in different directions.

a) The Emergence and Nature of Modern Moral Languages and Theories

The moral languages and theories of liberal society are closely related to the basic structures, processes and life forms of this society. One factor is the differentiation of society, that tends to divide economy, politics, law, religion and morality into separate and autonomous spheres and discourses. Economy, for example, is seen as following its own laws that cannot be subordinated to morality. Another factor is the increasing pluralism that has made a common and coherent ethical discourse difficult. Historically important were the wars of religion after the Reformation that created a longing for a common morality independent of controversial religious convictions. A further factor is the increasing naturalism and strong belief in science in post-Enlightenment thought, which has either called for a scientific rationalization of moral and political discourse or denied its rationality altogether.

This differentiation of discourses, the pluralism (or, as Hauerwas prefers, the fragmentation) concerning the goods of life, and the search for an objective and universal morality able to form peaceful and cooperative societies, have thus transformed and created the distinct form of modern ethics. One can even say, that it is this situation that has made morality into a clearly demarcated sphere, which in its turn has created the modern subject called ethics.

Against this background Hauerwas points to two "dominant characteristics of recent ethical theory:"

> (1) the stress on freedom, autonomy, and choice as the essence of the moral life; and (2) the attempt to secure a foundation for the moral life unfettered by the contingencies of our histories and communities. . . . these are closely related insofar as it is assumed that freedom depends on finding the means to disentangle ourselves from our own engagements.[41]

---

[41]*PK* 6f. Hauerwas and MacIntyre have edited a book titled *Revisions*, which contains important essays critical of this standard account. The works of, among others, MacIntyre, Taylor and Williams, mentioned later in this chapter, are also helpful for understanding Hauerwas. Another very interesting book is Shaffer, *American Lawyers and their Communities*. Shaffer is a prominent legal scholar who has written much on legal ethics and who is highly influenced by Hauerwas.

The first point stresses that we create our morality, puts the actual desiring rather than what it is we desire at the centre, and sees freedom as always being open and keeping our options open. A critical edge is consequently directed against community and tradition. At the social level, being responsible is thus "to pursue our desires fairly—that is, in a manner that does not impinge on anyone else's freedom." The common good in this conception "turns out to be the sum of our individual desires."[42]

The second element is the attempt to find a foundation for the ethical project that is free from contingency, that is, free from specific historical communities and traditions. Only so, it is claimed, can ethical judgements have universal validity. A universal ethics must be able to abstract from specific conceptions of the good life and remain neutral in relation to them. One crucial consequence of this has been the privatization of religious convictions. Because they are community and tradition related and not based on reason as such, they are said to be outside the realm of public reason. Religious arguments can therefore not be part of the public political discourse.[43]

Hauerwas contends that this wish for a neutral and universal ethics has given modern ethics a very different appearance from older ethics. Traditionally ethics concerned itself with how to live the good life. Modern ethics tries to abstract from issues of the good life, because of the pluralism and particularity of conceptions of the good life and because of its search for an impersonal rationality. It deals instead with the question of the right, with universally and objectively valid principles of obligation that are independent of specific preferences concerning the good life. Thus the so-called "moral point of view" concerns what anyone as a rational person should be committed to do independent of his or her social roles and convictions about the good life.[44]

The other side of this foundationalist aim is ethical scepticism. Foundationalist theories are developed to meet scepticism, just as scepticism is a result of the perceived failures of foundationalism. During a large part of the twentieth century various non-cognitive, emotivist or value nihilist theories (the designations have been many) have dominated moral philosophy, and in general culture we have seen the increasing predominance of relativistic and subjectivistic understandings of the moral life.

b) Ecclesial Ethics Contra the Institution of Morality

We saw in chapter ten that Hauerwas' conception of ethics is very different. Contra the modern ideal of individual autonomy he upholds the practice of communal discipleship and the formation of the churches as virtuous communities.

---

[42]Both citations are from *PK* 9.
[43]*PK* 2-15.
[44]*TT* 16-18. "This logical feature has been associated with such titles as the categorical imperative, the ideal observer, universalizability or more recently, the original position." (Ibid., 17.)

This also means that he defends a specifically Christian ethic built on Christian convictions and practices. He is therefore critical of the "moral point of view" and the search for non-contingent ahistorical foundations. This latter project is not only, he argues, a failure in itself, it has also privatized Christian convictions and denied them their public nature. As even liberal thinkers increasingly concede, liberalism is not neutral, but supports specific understandings of life that not seldom, according to Hauerwas, are in conflict with Christianity, exclude it from the public arena, and change it in ways that Christians should not consider good.

We have seen that Moltmann develops an ecclesial account that stresses the church's community character and describes it as a contrast society which, through a common discipleship, witnesses to an alternative social and political practice. Yet, what is lacking in his work is an account of how such communities are formed and sustained. His actual depiction of the Christian life as liberation to spontaneous self-realization was seen to be incoherent and implausible and it, furthermore, does not give resources for reflection upon the formation the church. What is lacking in Moltmann's political theology is what Hauerwas tries to provide through his account of the virtuous community. The problem for Moltmann is that such an account comes in conflict with central parts of the liberal project that political theology has made essential to its own program.

Hauerwas' ethics is regularly described as a virtue ethics. This is then often understood as a parallel method of ethical deliberation to deontological and utilitarian approaches. But this is to misunderstand him. Rather, he is questioning the very idea of morality as a specific realm; that is, he wants "to challenge the assumption that there is a special sphere of morality characterized by the language of obligation—a sphere in which we are 'moral agents' only to the extent we have certain duties to act or refrain from acting (or perhaps one main duty, such as to maximize happiness)."[45] This is, as we have seen, related to the differentiation of society into separate spheres with their different logics of discourse; the dominance of an idea of rationality that puts issues of the good outside the public discourse and therefore reduces ethical discourse to neutral, often procedural, principles; and an understanding of freedom that centres on personal choice and autonomy, which likewise has the consequence that ethics is reduced to procedural rules of fairness, while the substantial content of life is a question of personal preference that is outside moral discourse.

In one of his discussions of this, Hauerwas uses Bernard Williams' distinction between "morality" and "ethics". Williams lets "morality" refer to the differentiated discourse that deals with moral obligation. "Ethics" is instead defined by Socrates' question "How should one live".[46] Ethics is thus a much broader con-

---

[45]"Virtue Christianly Considered", 2.
[46]Ibid., 1-5 and Williams, *Ethics and the Limits of Philosophy*, esp. chapters one and ten. For a similar descriptions of the "institution of morality", see *TT* 205 n. 8 and *AC* 27-31. But cf. his different use of this distinction in the early *VV* 82-89, which includes a defence of the realm of morality. See also Taylor, *Sources of the Self*, 53-90.

cept that deals with the whole of life and not specific obligations and duties. In this sense Christian ethics is nothing else than the question of Christian discipleship. The first question then becomes who we are, not what we should do. Who we are determines what we should do. This further explains why he claims that Christian ethics is theology. "'Christian ethics' is Christian theology in so far as reflections about whom God would have us be (the explicitly theological form of Socrates question) are intrinsically tied to reflections about redemption, the identity of Jesus, creation, the Church, the eschaton, and so on."[47] The rather recent invention of Christian ethics[48] as a distinct discipline is then understood in the light of the invention of what Williams calls "the peculiar institution" of morality.[49]

Liberal societies are characterized by a strong cleavage between public and private, though there is much controversy about how to make this distinction and where to draw the border. One form this takes is to put issues of the "right" on the public side, and questions about the "good life" and how this is formed on the private. Hauerwas' conception implies a deep criticism of this way of splitting private and public from each other. "The idea that some significant distinction can be drawn between public and private reflects a political theory that assumes the political realm is not dependent on people of virtue."[50] In this view politics is primarily about interests and power, or about scientific social planning, and a political morality (so far that is believed in at all) only concerns rules of fairness. In contrast, Hauerwas argues that every society trains people in specific virtues. The question is which virtues and how this is done.[51] Liberal societies specifically foster procedural virtues such as tolerance, sincerity, and fairness. These public virtues are seen as separate from more substantial virtues, which cannot be socially supported, as that would threaten personal freedom. In other words, they can only have personal, but not public and political significance. But it is not only the state that should abstain from the social formation of virtues, but also, it is increasingly thought, family, churches and associations of various sorts. Here we have the radically individualistic view of the good life that characterizes Moltmann's thought and that tends to reduce his account of communal discipleship to liberal political practice.

---

[47]"Virtue Christianly Considered", 3.

[48]*PK* 50-54, *AN* 26-29.

[49]Williams, *Ethics*, 174.

[50]*CET* 191. For the following, see *CET* 191-197.

[51]"No society and corresponding government can avoid training people to have virtue. That is not even a very interesting observation, since it is obvious. The virtues are not something we choose to have or not to have. The only interesting questions have to do with which virtues we acquire, how they are acquired, and what they tell us about the kind of social order in which we exist." (*CET* 192.)

This is a view, Hauerwas maintains, the church ought not to accept. The church should foster virtue. As *polis* it should help people live virtuous lives. And it ought to encourage conversation about what Christian life is about. In this way it can witness to an alternative to making force central and to the increasing legalization of modern society. He says that

> if the church, which after all is a public institution, can be the kind of community that manifests the political significance of virtue, then the church may well have a political function not often realized. Moreover, to be such a community is not to withdraw from 'society' but rather to stand within our society making present what would otherwise be absent.[52]

Christian ethics is, according to Hauerwas, an ethics for friends, for people sharing an ongoing tradition, arguing together about what following Jesus Christ means. In contrast, the described modern moral traditions try to develop an ethics for moral strangers. This is an ethics that should help people without any common moral tradition and with various and arbitrary preferences about how life should be lived to cooperate.[53] Although theories of political liberalism often claim that their moral theory only applies to the political sphere, in practice this understanding increasingly takes over all of society and tends to make any form of social support of common goods difficult to argue and sustain.

Against these ethical models which start with the individual, either it is the abstract rational individual subject of Kantian versions or the self-realizing individual of more Romantic versions, Radical Reformation theology defends a communal form of ethical rationality. It is communal in several senses. First, it takes its starting point in the self-understanding of the community. What it and its individual members should do is dependent on what it is or should be. Second, how its common life is formed determines how situations are described and which possibilities are open. Third, the actions of individuals affect others, not only in terms of benefit and harm, but also in terms of how the church understands life and reality, and therefore the future life of the Christian community. Fourth, the actual process of moral deliberation is communal. It is not a theoretical reflection by abstract individuals on general principles, but a structured process of ecclesial discussion formed by the gifts and ministries of the church. He can thus describe the church as a "community of moral discourse".[54] This ecclesial locus for Chris-

---

[52]*CET* 195. This is of course related to his questioning of the view that politics is primarily about interests, distribution, and power. Instead he defends a "richer" conception, which argues that the "basic task of any polity is to offer its people a sense of participation in an adventure. For finally what we seek is not power, or security, or equality, or even dignity, but a sense of worth gained from participation and contribution to a common adventure. Indeed, our 'dignity' derives exactly from our sense of having played a part in such a story." (*CC* 13.)

[53]In the modern liberal society "[m]orally and politically, we act as though we are members of no community, share no goods, and have no common history. Thus, the challenge is to provide a theory of how moral 'objectivity' can be achieved in such a society." (*CC* 120.) So also *TT* 17.

[54]*PK* 131. On this theme, see esp. *PK* 130-134 and *CET* 67-87.

tian ethics shows again why he does not accept any sharp distinction between private and public and why all Christian ethics are also social ethics.[55]

In contrast liberal ethics is, Hauerwas maintains, the outgrowth of a community and tradition that wants to deny that it is a contingent community with a specific history and tradition. But in this denial it misunderstands itself, for liberalism also tells its stories that make their claims intelligible. It is not one, but rather several different stories, whose plots, according to Hauerwas, usually involve a history of liberation from oppressive communities and traditions and especially the history of the liberation of reason. Important subplots then are the emergence of science, of the free individual, of human rights and of the hope of the creation of a society of justice and peace. Comte and Hegel give classical examples and Moltmann gives a more recent one.[56] On the personal level exist corresponding stories of liberation from community and tradition to individual maturity and autonomy that create the context for much modern ethical thought, either in their rationalist or subjectivist forms. "The goal of this ethic is to detach the individual from his or her tradition, parents, stories, community, and history, and thereby allow him or her to stand alone, to decide, to chose, and to act alone."[57] Hauerwas thus argues that moral principles are only abstractions that depend on the stories they presuppose. The problem with modern accounts is that they deny these connections.[58]

A central component of the "institution of morality", where the contrast to an ethics of discipleship becomes very clear, and which grows out of this history of the liberation of reason, is its narrow concentration on obligations, and (in the interest of finding a rational and neutral ethical method) the reduction of ethics to one basic principle (such as universalization or maximization of happiness).[59] A consequence of this, which Hauerwas is deeply critical of, is that one concentrates on moral quandaries. The subject-matter of ethics is therefore "problems", those situations that we do not immediately know how to morally handle. Ethics becomes a question of how to rationally deal with these situations, a sort of "rational science that evaluates alternative solutions."[60] This assumes, Hauerwas

---

[55]"All Christian ethics are social ethics because all our ethics presuppose a social, communal, political starting point—the church." (*RA* 81.)

[56]"The plot was given in capsule by August Comte: first came religion in the form of stories, then philosophy in the form of metaphysical analysis, and then science with its exact methods. The story he tells in outline is set within another elaborated by Hegel, to show us how each of these ages supplanted the other as a refinement in the progressive development of reason. So stories are prescientific, according to the story legitimizing the age which calls itself scientific." (*TT* 25.)

[57]*RA* 79.

[58]*TT* 25-27, *CC* 99-101, *RA* 79f, 98-101.

[59]*PK* 22.

[60]*TT* 18. "Ethics becomes a branch of decision theory. Like many of the so-called policy sciences ethics becomes committed to those descriptions of the moral life that will prove relevant to its mode of analysis, that is, one which sees the moral life consisting of dilemmas open to rational 'solutions.'" (*TT* 18.) He has discussed this theme extensively in several of his books, but see e.g. *VV* 11-89, *TT* 15-39, and *PK* 17-34, 116-134.

contends, that moral judgements can be made apart from the history, convictions, and interests of the person or the group confronted with the situation. It also assumes that the situations we confront are simply out there as bare facts. We have seen that Hauerwas find these assumptions false.

In any description "facts" and "values" or "descriptive" and "prescriptive" components are inevitably and inescapably entangled. Following Julius Kovesi[61] he argues that this becomes clear when we see that moral notions (such as "murder", "abortion", "cruel") "describe only as we have purposes for such descriptions", which means that they "do not merely describe our activity; they also form it."[62] As purpose dependent notions they are embedded in and therefore affected by specific narratives. This explains why moral (as well as many other sorts of) controversies are so difficult to resolve. The conflicts cannot be reduced to relations between moral principles and facts, because one's perception is formed by different narratives.

He has for example, tried to show that the reason why the debate on abortion usually does not lead anywhere is that the opposing parties tell different stories (about the place of children, sexuality, and so on) with the consequence that the notion "abortion" is embedded in different conceptual worlds.[63] He compares this debate to "an argument between a member of the PLO and an Israeli about whether an attack on a village is unjustified terrorism. They both know the same 'facts' but the issue turns on the story each holds, and within which those 'facts' are known."[64] The facts cannot be disentangled from these different stories.

This is to say that the questions of which quandaries one encounters and how one describes them are related to the sort of person one is, the sort of community one lives in, and the way one's life is construed.[65] The ethical reflection is not done from some impersonal standpoint, but from where and who one is. This determines what will count as moral considerations, with the consequence that moral reasoning in this understanding is a much wider and more complex process than in the modern standard accounts of moral rationality.

Another way of describing Hauerwas' criticism of the modern rationalistic models of moral reasoning is that in their attempts to ground morality in rationality they fail "to deal adequately with the formation of a moral self"[66] and there-

---

[61]*Moral Notions.* See Hauerwas' use of Kovesi's analysis in *VV* 11-29 and *TT* 21-23. See further Hütter, *Evangelische Ethik als kirchliches Zeugnis*, 116-123 and Jones, *Transformed Judgment*, 20-72 (on Kovesi esp. 46-54).

[62]*TT* 21.

[63]*CC* 212-229.

[64]*TT* 22.

[65]He writes: "the kind of quandaries we confront depend on the kind of people we are and the way we have learned to construe the world through our language, habits, and feelings. If it is true that I can act only in the world I see and that my seeing is a matter of learning to say, it is equally the case that my 'saying' requires sustained habits that form my emotions and passions, teaching me to feel one way rather than another." (*PK* 117.)

[66]*TT* 20.

fore develop a deficient understanding of the nature of moral reasoning. One analogy he uses for explicating this failure is the difference between an artist and a critic. In Hauerwas' perspective the moral life is best seen like an artist practising and developing his skills. Most modern ethics, on the other hand, functions more like a critic making judgement on the finished work of the artist. The skills and procedures required for these two activities are obviously very different. In the one case the central issue is the moral formation of the agent, in the other it is the search for objective principles of judgement for the outside observer.[67] Hauerwas' argument is that because the latter approach, the "moral point of view", does not deal with the agent's moral formation it fails not only to account for the skills needed for living the moral life, but also for describing and understanding. These are not separate procedures. It is important to remember that for Hauerwas these skills are not only of an intellectual, but also of a moral nature. To see rightly requires for example trust, courage and hope. Self-deception and illusion are important ways for defending ourselves from uncomfortable truths about ourselves, other people or social contexts we live in. To face this, courage, trust and hope are needed.[68] The conflict with the "moral point of view" is here clear and explicit.

> Such discipleship can only appear heteronomous from the moral point of view, since the paradigm cannot be reduced to, or determined by, principles known prior to imitation. For the Christian, morality is not chosen and then confirmed by the example of others; instead, we learn what the moral life entails by imitating another. This is intrinsic to the nature of Christian convictions, for the Christian life requires a transformation of the self that can be accomplished only through direction from a master. The problem lies not in knowing *what* we must do, but *how* we are to do it. And the how is learned only by watching and following.[69]

To this is connected a further failure Hauerwas sees in most modern moral theory, namely its sharp separation between reason and affection and the consequent need of suppression of the affections when making moral judgements. This presupposes that the affections are some form of irrational force that must be controlled. The mirror image of this view is the one that makes the passions the ground for the moral life, which Moltmann sometimes seems to hold. The good life is realized when it is liberated from the restrictions of reason and morality. This view likewise separates beliefs and emotions. Hauerwas does not accept this separation nor the idea of the emotions as an irrational force that either is controlled or liberated. On the contrary, the affections are inseparable from our beliefs,

---

[67]*VV* 157f. He here follows Stuart Hampshire, who in "Fallacies in Moral Philosophy", 52-54 has developed this analogy.
[68]*PK* 43f.
[69]*CC* 131.

the way we see reality. This implies that the affections are narratively formed and also that the Christian life involves the right formation of our affections.[70]

c) Beyond Objectivism and Relativism

Hauerwas denies that this conception of moral rationality, as it is often thought, leads to relativism, subjectivism or scepticism. Modern moral philosophy (that is true, though somewhat differently, both in the Enlightenment and in the recent revival of normative ethics) arose in answer to scepticism or in a milieu of scepticism. One therefore still accepted that issues concerning the good of life were outside public and rational discourse. What was being searched for were the basic principles of justice which could be argued independently of any conception of the good. Furthermore, this was reinforced by the concept of freedom where questions about the good life were seen as questions of personal choice only limited by the procedural rules of fairness. Similarly, the subjectivist, relativist or emotivist understandings of morality were nurtured by failures to develop convincing foundationalist moral accounts.

Hauerwas questions the neutrality claim of liberalism and thinks issues of the good life should be open for public discussion and persuasion. The idea of neutrality has been developed in various ways, but however construed, Hauerwas is deeply critical of this doctrine. A first objection follows from his general rejection of foundationalist accounts. There is no tradition-independent rationality. Questions of right cannot be wholly separated from questions about the good life. Second, attempts to make this separation lead to the failures discussed above in understanding the actual moral process. Third, through proscribing which sorts of argument are allowed in public discourse it, instead of being neutral, privatizes and/or excludes alternative views and practices from the public sphere. The public truth claims of the Christian church (as well as of other traditions outside the mainstream) are denied. Fourth, the consequence is that far from being neutral, it underwrites a view of reality and an account of freedom, justice and happiness which not only are outgrowths of modern liberal society, but also in several ways stand in contradiction to Jewish and Christian faith and practice. But the claims of the liberal state to being neutral and limited conceal this situation, and make it more difficult to see its imperialistic claims[71]

---

[70]*CC* 123-125, *TT* 23f. He says that "the virtues are a unique blend of 'nature' and 'reason,' since our passions do not so much need control as they need direction." (*CC* 124.) Paul Lauritzen develops this understanding, using the work of Hauerwas, in "Emotion and Religious Ethics". Hauerwas thinks his early work was deficient in this concern. See *CCL* xxiv. See also Roberts, "What an Emotion Is", Nussbaum, "Narrative Emotions", and Jones, *Transformed Judgment*, 67f.

[71]MacIntyre writes that the liberal principles "impose a particular conception of the good life, of practical reasoning, and of justice upon those who willingly or unwillingly accept the liberal procedures and the liberal terms of debate. The overriding good of liberalism is no more and no less than the continued sustenance of the liberal social and political order. . . . liberal theory is best understood, not at all as an attempt to find a rationality independent of tradition, but as itself the articulation of an historically developed and developing set of social institutions and forms of activity, that is, as the voice

This critique of the idea of neutrality and the claim that liberalism is a tradition among other traditions have become common in recent political and moral theory, increasingly also among liberals, although there are radically different views on what the implications of this recognition are.[72] For Hauerwas, however, there is no way to avoid discussing substantial issues of the good life. The question is not if, but how it is done. Hauerwas' account of this is dependent on his understanding of the Christian faith. It is his contention that any starting point outside our history is impossible for all ethical thought. All ethics is narrative-dependent. This is particularly manifest for Christian ethics. The reason is its starting point in history, in God's history with Israel, Jesus Christ and the church; that is, in an embodied narrative. This means that the question if theology or anthropology should be the starting point for Christian ethics is a false question. There is no starting point abstracted from the ongoing faith-practice of the church. "For Christian ethics begins in a community that carries the story of the God who wills us to participate in a kingdom established in and through Jesus of Nazareth."[73]

Hauerwas closely relates this storied character of human existence and God's salvation inherent in the Christian account to the necessity of witness and to non-violence. The gospel is not a "general truth", a description of the unavoidable nature of human existence that anyone will recognize on reflection, but a message about God's salvation through the church made possible by Jesus Christ. The gospel can therefore only be presented through the witness of a community that tells and embodies this narrative, and not by philosophical arguments abstracted from this embodied story.[74] The church cannot prove the truth of its story or the fallacy of alternatives, nor can it (or anyone else) provide a general argument that *a priori* defeats relativism. What it can do is to provide an alternative narrative carried by an alternative community and thereby give others what he calls "real options".

Hauerwas connects this stress on witness to the inherent non-violent character of the gospel. The church can only witness to its truth, not force people to follow

---

of a tradition." (*Whose Justice? Which Rationality?*, 345.) For Hauerwas' discussion of these issues, see e.g. *CET* 240f and *AC* 69-92, 133-152.

[72]MacIntyre talks about the tradition bound character of rationality and moral convictions, Taylor about the inescapability of frameworks and strong evaluations, and explicit liberals, such as Galston and Stout agree. The later Rawls and Rorty also accept the contingent nature of liberal polity, but still want to keep e.g. religion outside public discourse. In addition to books by MacIntyre, Taylor and Stout mentioned in n. 7 in chapter two above, see also MacIntyre, *After Virtue*, idem, "Objectivity in Morality and Objectivity in Science", idem, "Epistemological Crises, Dramatic Narrative and the Philosophy of Science", Taylor, *Philosophy and the Human Sciences*, idem, *Explanation and Practical Reason*, idem, *Multiculturalism and "The Politics of Recognition"*, idem, "Overcoming Epistemology", Galston, *Liberal Purposes*, Rawls, *Political Liberalism*, Rorty, *Contingency, Irony, and Solidarity,* and idem, *Objectivity, Relativism, and Truth.*

[73]*PK* 62.

[74]Of course, inside this witness of a specific community there is a place for arguments in a general and non-foundational sense in the confrontation with other communities and stories.

it. It can consequently also explain disagreement, as non-Christians are people who do not know or do not follow Jesus Christ. In contrast, the assumption that there exist some universal standpoint and rationality leads easily to the perception of the opponent as irrational or less enlightened. There is only a short step from such assumptions to the use of coercion to force people to see their error when they do not see it by themselves. This is also one of his criticism against a Christian use of natural law theories.[75]

He does not think this makes discussion impossible nor that it leads to arbitrariness. He is very critical of describing the choice as being between objectivity and truth on the one side and arbitrary power and relativism on the other. The absence of an ahistorical and tradition-independent rationality does not make the giving of reasons impossible or unnecessary. But one has to start in the middle, start where one is in the middle of history with the particular convictions and practices with which oneself and others live. He writes that "the way forward is through the appreciation of particular communities which are committed to finding as much shared understanding as possible on particular issues. If such communities do not in fact exist, then no amount of philosophical reflection on practical reason will be of much use."[76] He does believe that we can expect many points of contacts, common experiences, shared understandings and overlaps between traditions, but there is no way to find out where and how before the actual confrontations and conversations begin. "What is required is not theory but actual engagement with other people in hopes of securing and finding common commitments."[77] Agreement is something that one discovers. There is no need for a theory that explains it beforehand. Above all, his view is consequently not compatible with theories of rationality that *a priori* exclude certain types of reasons from the conversation.[78]

He theologically elaborates this theme through the importance of hospitality and openness to the stranger. We have said that the church as a God-forgiven

---

[75]"The universal presumptions of natural law make it more difficult to accept the very existence of those who do not agree with us; such differences in principle should not exist." (*PK* 61.) On this sense of witness, see *CC* 105, *PK* xvii, 14f, 61, *RA* 101f, *AC* 133-152 (esp. 148-152), and "Creation, Contingency, and Truthful Non-Violence. Cf. the similar comment by the economist Donald McCloskey: "Believing, mistakenly, that operationalism and objectivity and statistical significance are enough to end all dispute, the economist assumes that his opponent is dishonest when he does not concede the point at issue, or that he is motivated by some ideological passion and by self-interest, or that he is simply stupid. It fits the modernist split of fact and value to attribute all disagreements to political differences, since facts are alleged to be, unlike values, impossible to dispute. . . . The claims of an overblown methodology of science serve merely to spoil the conversation." (*The Rhetoric of Economics*, 184.)

[76]*CET* 84. In another context he says: "Our conviction that the God whom we worship is in fact the God of all creation does not give us the warrant to assume that others must already share our faith and/or moral presumption, but only to hope that if we manifest in our own social life some of the marks of what it means to be a new people, others will be converted to the reality of his kingdom." (*AN* 77.)

[77]"Real Sectarian", 93. See further *PK* 60, *CC* 106.

[78]On this, see further Placher, *Unapologetic Theology*, 104-122 and Walzer, "A Critique of Philosophical Conversation".

people at peace with itself does not need to fear challenges of the other. The stranger, who can come in many forms, including the children growing up inside the community, can through its questions and challenges help the church to understand itself better and see through its self-deceptions and illusions. It thus can result in new insights and changes in the tradition. "Hospitality is part of their holiness, as they have learned to welcome the stranger as the very presence of God."[79]

From this perspective, the church should expect to learn from other traditions and from the confrontations and conversations with them. He further notes the importance of the fact that the church lives in different cultures and that the alternatives it provides therefore differ in diverse contexts. Another effect of living in different cultures is that it might help the church to be more self-critical in its too-easy adaptation to one cultural context. But neither this openness to others nor his stress on the good of diversity should be construed in terms of a tolerance based on sceptical views about moral, religious or other truths or claims of the equal value of all such beliefs. He believes there is truth and falseness also in ethics, which means there is a place for confrontation and criticism, but the way this is done is all important.[80]

d) The Ethics of Political Theology and the Project of Liberalism

In an interesting way Moltmann's distinction between his political ethics of freedom and justice and his account of personal life in terms of spontaneous self-realization fits the sharp division between the public and the private spheres in liberal societies and theory. He develops a political ethics, but can give no account of how virtuous people are formed more than in terms of liberation.

In this he follows liberal moral and political theory. The Roman Catholic tradition of political theology has done this in a more systematic and explicit way than Moltmann has. This is seen in its critical, but basically affirmative, reception and use of the works of the two leading liberal theorists Jürgen Habermas[81] and John Rawls[82] in the attempt to formulate a public theology. John Rawls, whose *A Theory of Justice* more than any other book started the recent revival of political philosophy and still is the major document of liberal political philosophy, repudi-

---

[79]*PK* 146.

[80]*PK* 85, 91, 120, 142-146, *CC* 105f.

[81]See Browning and Fiorenza (eds.), *Habermas, Modernity and Public Theology*, Arens (ed.), *Habermas und die Theologie*, Peukert, *Wissenschaftstheorie – Handlungstheorie – Fundamentale Theologie*, and Arens, *Christopraxis*. For more critical theological discussions of Habermas, see Gregersen, *Teologi og kultur*,139-162 and Placher, *Unapologetic Theology*, 74-91. One might think it rather odd that Roman Catholic political theology identifies itself so much with the later Habermas ("who has recently given birth to what may strike many as a new form of academic scholasticism or a new culture industry" [Bernstein, *The New Constellation*, 45]) if one thinks of Metz' theology, but it is in continuity with his starting point in a strong affirmation of modernity. This development might further be interpreted as the academization of political theology and its inclusion in the dominant public culture.

[82]See Fiorenza, "Politische Theologie und liberale Gerechtigkeits-Konzeptionen".

ated both natural law theory and utilitarianism, and developed, on a neo-Kantian ground, a social contract theory. This endeavour was characterized by the described "moral point of view"-perspective and attempted to formulate a procedural theory of justice stressing equality and individualism. Rawls has later modified his theory in a more historicizing direction that recognizes that the theory takes its starting point in existing liberal society. He, furthermore, now describes his theory of *political* liberalism as a part of political philosophy, in contrast to moral philosophy. It is not a comprehensive philosophical and moral doctrine, but concerns only how in a pluralist society with several competing reasonable comprehensive doctrines (including both liberalism as a general moral view and religions) a just, free and stable society is possible. How and to what extent his theory has developed, however, is intensively debated in that prospering industry that Rawls interpretation now constitutes.[83]

In Germany a similar type of neo-Kantian political philosophy has been developed by Jürgen Habermas, the premier defender in contemporary philosophy of the Enlightenment tradition and the "unfinished project of modernity" against various sorts of postmodernisms.[84] Like Rawls he defends the "moral point of view", the formulation of a universal procedural theory of justice that is separate from and more fundamental than moral and religious traditions and conceptions of the good.

The case of Moltmann is more complicated. He has not systematically discussed his ethical approach or systematically related it to contemporary moral theory. Although his theology implies and he often has practised a distinctly theological ethics, he has also used non-theological ethical models. We have found both natural law, consequentialist and deontological moral arguments. That in itself is not problematic. What is problematic is the absolute claims he at various times makes for these different approaches. In his early writings we found that he could question the ethical enterprise as such. The important question was to be on the side of the revolutionary forces, not stand above it and judge it. When he ethically discussed the use of revolutionary violence he used consequentialist arguments. But increasingly this once so strong consequentialist strand has weakened and also Moltmann has begun to use Kantian or neo-Kantian types of moral argumentation. He has recently even explicitly identified one dimension of his understanding of justice with Rawls' conception in *A Theory of Justice*.[85] Although working in

---

[83]For his later view, see his *Political Liberalism*. For an overview of his original theory, his further development and the discussion and criticism it led to, see Kukathas and Pettit, *John Rawls*.

[84]For this reading of Habermas as part of the liberal project, see Placher, *Unapologetic Theology* 74-91, Poole, *Morality and Modernity*, 70-85, and Krogh, "Frontlinjer i moderne moralfilosofisk debatt". See e.g. Habermas, *Moral Consciousness and Communicative Action*, 195-215. He has himself said that "my Marxist friends are not entirely unjustified in accusing me of being a radical liberal" (*Autonomy and Solidarity*, 174).

[85]*SL* 142 and 329 n. 33 (154).

Germany Habermas has always played a minor role for Moltmann, and Habermas' later work seems wholly absent.

The most plausible interpretation of this development in Moltmann's thought (in which he parallels the development in the Left generally) has to do with his interpretation of the social and political context. His scepticism towards ethical reflection had to do with his beliefs that the revolution was close and that the struggle was between two clearly defined forces—the progressive revolutionary forces and the reactionary oppressive forces. Consequentialist arguments still reflect this basic approach and the belief that humanity can control and form history, but it has a larger place for critical reflections about the use of powerful means. His later Kantian and rights-centred approach reflects a very different situation. There is no more any clear revolutionary project, no radically new society behind the corner, and the earlier so strong belief in progress is muted. Instead we find an increasing emphasis on the fragility of the liberal democratic society, on the nuclear threat and on the endangered nature. It is now as much a question of defending something fragile and endangered as of creating something new. His recent Kantianism thus represents a more pessimistic view of history and human capability.

There is, however, one other dominant strand of Moltmannian ethical thought that has increased in strength in his recent work, namely his ecclesial discipleship ethics. This is the approach that is most consistent with his general theological project, but it goes in an entirely different direction and comes in direct conflict with the claims of both consequentialism and Neo-Kantianism, though we have failed to find any reflection whatsoever on these tensions in Moltmann's writings. Reading Hauerwas can help us see these tensions better and also understand the consequences of this development in Moltmann's thinking.

e) Hauerwas and Communitarianism

In his critique of liberal moral and political theory Hauerwas is not alone. Although the works of Rawls, Habermas and other liberals have been very influential, they have also been met with increasing dissatisfaction, from different directions. For a long time the main discussion (that is, since substantial moral philosophy returned) was between utilitarian and various forms of Neo-Kantian perspectives, where the latter slowly became predominant. Nowadays, the main conflict in especially American,[86] but also in European, moral and political theory is often described as between liberals (i. e., the Neo-Kantians) and "communitarians".[87] Other regularly used and partly overlapping labels for the latter are neo-Aristotelianism and civic republicanism. Among people frequently associated with "communitarianism" are philosophers such as Alasdair MacIntyre, Charles

---

[86]For an overview of recent intellectual life in America that might be helpful as a first orientation, see Bell, "Kulturkriege. Intellektuelle in Amerika, 1965-1990".
[87]In Sweden utilitarianism still seems to be predominant.

Taylor, Michael Sandel, and Michael Walzer, and sociologists such as Robert Bellah, Amitai Etzioni, and Philip Selznick. Few of them, however, use the label "communitarianism" themselves, and some, for example MacIntyre, would object strongly to be identified with "communitarianism".[88] They do not represent a common position, but are associated through some common themes in their critique of liberalism. It is thus misleading to put them together under the label "communitarianism" against "liberalism". It gives the false impression that they represent or defend a wholly different political and social system or a coherent alternative political ideology. Taylor argues that this debate is often confused, because ontological and advocacy issues are not separated. The former concerns "what you recognize as the factors you will invoke to account for social life", while the latter "concern the moral stand or policy one adopts".[89] The relation between these two sets of issues is complex. For example, to question the methodological individualism of much liberal philosophy does not by itself make the critics politically into anti-liberals. MacIntyre is very critical of liberalism, while Taylor, Walzer and Selznick might as well be described as a sort of liberals (or social democrats).[90]

Just as political theology increasingly has identified itself with the liberal Neo-Kantian project, it is obvious that Hauerwas has much in common with the "communitarians" and he has been described as a theological representative of "communitarianism" and one of the people most responsible for making these issues central in the theological community.[91] He was among the little group of dissenting thinkers that started to develop themes that since then have become common. He has also drawn on some of the mentioned thinkers both in his critique of liberalism and in articulating positive alternatives. But it is nonetheless clear that he is different and he also rejects this description of himself. The main source of this difference is that he makes the church and not the national community primary, and the church embodies a different story and other convictions.[92] Although

---

[88]MacIntyre has said that "I am not a communitarian" ("Nietzsche or Aristotle?", 151).

[89]Taylor, "Cross-Purposes", 159.

[90]Selznick describes his own position as "communitarian liberalism" (*The Moral Commonwealth*, xi). See also Walzer, "The Communitarian Critique of Liberalism". For MacIntyre, see e.g. *Whose Justice? Which Rationality?*, 326-348. Beiner finds a convergence between communitarian liberals and liberal communitarians, which he does not find surprising because "the protagonists . . . are good social democrats whose disagreements at the level of metaethics in no way disturbed their basic consensus on the level of policy. Here, it strikes me, MacIntyre's critique of liberalism opens up deeper possibilities of reflection than the liberalism/communitarianism debate could permit." (*What's the Matter with Liberalism?*, 20.)

[91]So e.g. in Whitmore, "Beyond Liberalism and Communitarianism in Christian Ethics".

[92]Michael Quirk associates him with the perspectives of MacIntyre, Sandel, Walzer, Taylor and Sullivan, but says also that even if he is "*aligned* with this movement", he "cannot be said to *belong* to it. His musings do not lead to the *polis* but to the church, not to *solidarité* but to *agape*." ("Beyond Sectarianism?", 79.) In his response Hauerwas agrees that this is a correct presentation ("Real Sectarian", 93-95). This major difference becomes also clear in his explicit discussions of the works of MacIntyre, Taylor and Bellah. See on MacIntyre "Virtue Christianly Considered", on Taylor "The

"communitarians" stress the importance of institutions and structures between the individual and the state more than liberals do, in the end it is in the interest of the national community they think. This is most clearly seen when it takes the form of a civic republicanism, where the contrast to Hauerwas becomes very visible. We will return to this issue in the next chapter.

To put it differently, he is, as we have seen, sceptical of all abstract talk about community, narrative and virtue. The important question is *which* community, *which* narrative and *which* virtues. There are great differences between communities and traditions. Some are more true than others. Some are false and dangerous. The search for community and tradition as such is therefore, he thinks, perilous and especially so when the community is constituted by the nation-state. He further notes that this danger is augmented by the fact that much modern longing for community is a result of the way a liberal society makes people strangers without common purposes, which can make the society more vulnerable to dangerous nationalistic movements.[93]

The outcome of this is that he, like Taylor, thinks that the very contrast between liberalism and communitarianism is built on liberal assumptions that should be overcome. "Rather, we need much thicker accounts of the different positions embraced by those two terms and the infinite variety of differences between those positions."[94] This suggestion could also be directed to Hauerwas himself, as he tends to give too unnuanced descriptions of liberal political theory.

However, the main importance for Hauerwas of so-called "communitarian" thinkers might be that they have opened a space in modern intellectual culture that makes the type of theological ethics that he represents easier to understand. One could thus argue that one of the most important effects of especially MacIntyre's *After Virtue* (the perhaps most discussed work in moral theory in the 1980s) was just that it opened the space for a wide range of earlier suppressed theological and philosophical work. Hauerwas has, however, not only used this opportunity, he has himself been one of the main actors to open this space through his work during 1970s.

To this can be added one final reflection. The problem for political theology is how to formulate a public theology in a liberal society. How can *theology* participate in the general public discourse? It is this interest that leads them to Habermas and Rawls, for whom the questions about the conditions of public discourse

---

Sources of Charles Taylor", and on Bellah "A Christian Critique of Christian America" (this is an earlier and somewhat longer version of *CET* 171-190) and "A Communitarian Lament".

[93]"Christians should have as many difficulties with most communitarian alternatives as they do with liberal alternatives." (*DFF* 157.) Communitarianism "often embodies utopian liberal fantasies". ("Christian Critique", 264.) See also "What Could It Mean For the Church To Be Christ's Body?", 9-12. This analysis and questioning of the search for community is found already in his earliest writings. See *VV* 253f, 259 n. 33. See now also esp. *RA* 77f, 100f, and "The Difference of Virtue and the Difference It Makes", 250.

[94]*DFF* 157. So also "A Communitarian Lament", 46.

in modernity stand in the centre. In contrast Radical Reformation theology asks how, in a liberal society, to form and sustain the *church*, in the form of concrete communities, as a witness to the kingdom of God. Here the church, and not something called public theology, is the bridge to the world and therefore the base for the participation of Christians in discussion with other communities and traditions. For reflection on this challenge MacIntyre and Taylor are more important conversation partners than Habermas and Rawls.

4. Neutral Liberalism, Liberalism of Virtue and Theological Politics

So far I have described Hauerwas' analysis and critique of liberal moral theory in general. To this one could object that he has not met the theories of this or that liberal theorist and in particular that his critique is formed in contrast to the liberal theories of the 1970s, and does not sufficiently face the changed and diversified nature of recent liberal theories. Although Hauerwas has in fact dealt with the continuing development of liberal theory,[95] there is by nature no general answer to this criticism as there is always another theory. Yet to give sharper contours to his position, I will in this section relate it to two recent sophisticated but very different understandings of liberal society and its moral possibilities, that in opposing ways relate themselves to the sort of criticism Hauerwas represents. The first version, formulated by Tristram Engelhardt, is a postmodern defence of a strictly neutral liberalism that puts the freedom of choice in the centre. Engelhardt accepts Hauerwas' type of description of the direction of modern liberal society and tries to meet it through developing an ethics for moral strangers. The second version, by William Galston, is critical both of this description of liberal society and of the idea of neutrality. He accepts the claim that liberalism is a substantial tradition that requires specific virtues to be sustained. He meets Hauerwas' type of challenge head on through attempting to show that liberalism *in itself* has the needed resources for forming a people with the required virtues.

a) The Neutral Liberalism of Engelhardt

The starting point for Engelhardt's argument is that "human reason is not able to provide . . . a rationally justified content-full moral vision."[96] But he also stresses the moral fragmentation, polarization and (for some) apathy that characterize modern society. The modern Western world is a world of moral strangers, which makes a coherent common substantial moral discourse impossible. There exist coherent moral communities, but not on the national level. That he describes his position as postmodern indicates that he considers the modern liberal project of morality (in its various Kantian, utilitarian and natural law forms) a failure and

---

[95]See e.g. *AC* 45-92.
[96]*Bioethics and Secular Humanism*, 1.

that we cannot avoid nihilism and relativism.[97] Against this background he tries in his book *Bioethics and Secular Humanism. The Search for a Common Morality* to discuss how the idea of a common and neutral public morality can still be articulated. He develops something he calls secular humanism as "the moral language of moral strangers".[98] The question is how moral controversies can be resolved "by peaceable negotiation".[99] The answer Engelhardt gives is, on the one hand, free and informed consent between individuals (for example between patients and physicians) and, on the other, rights to privacy in relation to the state. The result is a permissive bioethics "where everything is allowed, as long as it is done between consenting, competent adults."[100] Suicide, euthanasia, abortion, surrogate motherhood, and so on, cannot be forbidden, but neither can public funds be used without common consent. How a positive public health care policy should be fashioned, for what public funds should be used, has to be established through political procedures. This approach makes him also positive to market solutions, because "the market offers a form of pure procedural justice".[101] Generally he defends mixed (both private and public) and multiple health care systems. Specific moral communities can of course fashion their own health care systems as long they do not force it on the general population.

The secular humanism of Engelhardt is thus first of all a framework for co-operation of individuals from different moral communities. It is not a moral tradition itself. However, he also shows how it is beginning to become the first moral language of an emerging cosmopolitan segment of the population. These are people "who have shed intensely held, content-full understandings of life, health, medicine, and death that focus on moral ultimates. Their lives are constructed around instrumental goods, not ultimate moral commitments. For them, secular humanism can provide a way of giving coherent statement to their way of life."[102] He develops this latter theme in a section titled "The Yuppie as Prophet of a Secular Tradition for Health Care".[103] It is because of the importance of this secular segment that the proposal of a secular humanism receives social and political plausibility. Lacking religious and moral ultimates they "seek to make their lives rich with the goods and pleasures of this world."[104] Health becomes very

---

[97]Ibid., 102-111. His personal relation as a Roman Catholic to the position he develops is somewhat ambivalent. "I do not pretend to like all I see. The conclusions I affirm are not necessarily those I celebrate. Moreover, though faith in reason is largely lost, I have not lost the Faith." (Ibid., xvii.)

[98]Ibid., 139.

[99]Ibid., 119.

[100]Ibid., 115.

[101]Ibid., 134. "Because a free market in health care requires no particular content-full rationally justified vision of proper health care policy, only the consent of the participants, the market will always have an intellectual advantage over egalitarian health care systems that depend on a particular content-full vision of proper health care distributions." (Ibid., 135.)

[102]Ibid., 139.

[103]Ibid., 33-40.

[104]Ibid., 37.

important for them because it is a condition for human well-being understood as "preference maximization", while, for example, they have difficulty giving suffering the sort of meaning a Christian can give it.[105] In the absence of essential moral constraints, and formed and living at the centre of a technological society, they have furthermore little problem with technical interventions in life, as long as this is done with the consent of the people concerned. So Engelhardt writes: "The ethos of the cosmopolitans has become something like an international civil religion."[106] The close relation between these cosmopolitans and the emergence we earlier noted of a Postmaterialist segment or New Class-culture is obvious.

Hauerwas has discussed an earlier version of Engelhardt's proposal.[107] He finds his position "descriptively powerful", but (not surprisingly) "normatively wrong". He thinks Engelhardt is describing the direction modern society is going. One of Hauerwas' aims is therefore to discuss what the implications might be, to see if this is the way people want to live. "I suspect most accept the ethos of freedom because they continue to rely on presuppositions of past particularistic moralities that are slowly being destroyed by Engelhardt's public morality." Instead of seeing medical personal as "highly trained technocrats waiting for their customers to determine what service they wish to have performed", he describes medicine as "a moral practice constituted by intrinsic moral convictions"[108] that is sustained by the wider community's commitment to care and to be present with the ill, the suffering, the handicapped and retarded. He stresses that medicine is not only a matter of curing, but at least as much a question of taking care of people that cannot be cured. The commitment to medicine is therefore the way society sets aside some people to care for the ill and dying, and train them, not least through apprenticeship, in the tradition, skills and virtues needed for this care. He thus can write: "From this perspective one of the most overlooked aspects of our current situation is how medical schools continue to function as schools of virtue. They are among the few institutions in our society that have a coherent enough purpose that enables them to form character."[109] But he does not think this understanding of medicine in the long run can be sustained without being embedded in a larger moral framework. Though he thinks that other than Christian convictions and practices can fill this function, one important task for the church could be to be a community that stands over medicine and gives it its right proportions so it not becomes "a pseudo-salvific institution."[110] The church can also be "a re-

---

[105]Ibid., 40.
[106]Ibid., 40. He also says that "the cosmopolitans . . . are the contemporary realization of Nietzsche's 'Superman.'" (Ibid., 39.)
[107]*SP* 8-14. The article by Engelhardt he discusses is "Bioethics in Pluralist Societies".
[108]The first three citations are from *SP* 12f, and last one is from *SP* 4.
[109]*SP* 58f n. 21.
[110]*SP* 53.

source of the habits and practices necessary to sustain the care of those in pain over the long haul."[111]

When, in a society of "moral strangers" that increasingly do not have more in common than the wish to prevent illness and death, medicine lacks this sort of context, it instead, according to Hauerwas, "tries to justify its power by being what it cannot be—a science that frees us from, rather than teaches us, the limits of our bodies."[112] The relation between physicians and patients is then seen in the liberal terms of contract and autonomy. One problem with this, and therefore also with Engelhardt's argument about market justice, is that because of the nature of sickness, the relation is not voluntary and the patient is not a free and rational bargainer. Another problem is how to deal with the inevitable fallibility of physicians in relation to the impossible demands of patients. The result is seen in the ever rising levels of malpractice insurances.[113]

The issue of medical care for the incurable also raises the issue of the mentally retarded, which Hauerwas often has dealt with.[114] The basic moral issue for him is which sort of community we should be to welcome and care for the retarded. He does not think that the sort of freedom ethos maintained by Engelhardt gives any help to answer this question.[115]

Against this background he is also very critical of so-called medical ethics. Hauerwas' argument is that medicine embodies substantive moral commitments. But most medical ethics have continued to work with the abstracting traditional ethical models, and see the issues medical practice raises as only "instances of more general and universal obligations that pertain between any persons."[116] When medical personnel are trained in these ethical traditions they therefore fail to see the actual moral tradition and practices with which they already live.

b) Galston's Liberalism of Virtue

When we come to my second example of recent defences of liberalism, William Galston's *Liberal Purposes*, we will meet an approach very different from Engelhardt. Instead of like Engelhardt finding ways to uphold the idea of neutrality, he argues forcefully that liberals should abandon the idea of neutrality and instead defend liberalism in terms of a specific conception of the good.[117] The libe-

---

[111]*SP* 81.
[112]*SP* 51.
[113]*SP* 51-53 and "Medical Care".
[114]*VV* 187-194, *TT* 147-183, *SP* 157-217, *DFF* 177-186.
[115]*SP* 15f.
[116]*SP* 5.
[117]He can therefore write: "liberalism *is* a tradition, in precisely MacIntyre's sense: a historically extended, socially embodied argument about the goods that constitute a specific form of human existence." (*Liberal Purposes*, 75.) This has, he says in this book from 1991, led some to wrongly describe him as antiliberal and communitarian. See ibid., 43f. It is therefore somewhat surprising that he together with Etzioni in 1990 launched a sort of communitarian movement. See Etzioni, *The Spirit of Community*, 14-18, 251. Etzioni also calls Galston "a leading Communitarian". (Ibid., 81, 201.)

ral state neither can nor should be neutral concerning different ways of life. Instead it has formed certain institutions and practices that support the good life including certain forms of government, economic institutions and rules, and private zones.[118] This society is not sustainable in itself, but requires the nurture of a liberal culture and liberal virtues. While he points to the importance of religion for forming people, he also claims that "[l]iberalism contains *within itself* the resources it needs to declare and to defend a conception of the good and virtuous life".[119] It is impossible here to summarize this rich book. I will only say somewhat more about his views on liberal virtues, the place of religion in liberalism, and its current prospects.

Which are the virtues needed for sustaining liberal societies? Besides general virtues that are necessary for any society (courage,[120] law-abidingness, and loyalty), he first mentions independence (like many other virtues primarily engendered in the family) and tolerance needed for sustaining the individualism and the diversity so central for liberalism.[121] He then mentions virtues needed for the functioning of a market economy like a work ethic, "a capacity for moderate delay of gratification",[122] and adaptability, in addition to specific entrepreneurial and organizational virtues needed for these two basic roles. Next come the virtues needed for liberal politics. Concerning citizens this includes the capacity of discernment, first, of the rights of others, and, second, of the talent and character of political candidates. Furthermore, "liberal citizens must be moderate in their demands and self-disciplined enough to accept painful measures when they are necessary."[123] Concerning virtues of leadership it includes patience, "the capacity to forge a sense of common purpose", resistance to "the temptation to earn popularity by pandering to immoderate public demands", and "the capacity to narrow . . . the gap between popular preference and wise action."[124] Finally he also mentions two more general political virtues: publicity and "the disposition to narrow the gap . . . between principles and practices in liberal society."[125]

Although he thinks liberalism has the sustaining resources within itself, he also recognizes that in practice religion has both historically and in modern times

---

[118]"The strategy for justifying the liberal state that seeks to dispense with all specific conceptions of the good cannot succeed. Defenders of the liberal state must either accept the burden of inquiry into the human good or abandon their enterprise altogether." (*Liberal Purposes*, 301.)

[119]Ibid., 304.

[120]Courage is "the willingness to fight and even die on behalf of one's country" (ibid., 221). It is not insignificant that this is the first virtue mentioned.

[121]Ibid., 221f.

[122]Ibid., 223.

[123]Ibid., 224f.

[124]Ibid., 226.

[125]Ibid., 227. So far he has discussed the liberal virtues as means for the sustaining of the liberal society. Yet, he also discusses the virtues as ends in themselves and the tensions this creates. He here mentions "rational liberty or self-direction", "capacity to act in accordance with the precepts of duty", and "the full flowering of individuality". (Ibid., 229f.)

played an important role.[126] Early liberals, including the founders of America, took it for granted that a liberal society needed religion for forming virtuous people. It is only during recent decades that a judicial liberalism has developed which has "equated liberty with absence of all restraints".[127] This is an understanding that is not rooted in a broader public consensus, and which therefore has led to strong counter-reactions among religious and other moral traditionalists. In general terms he thinks a good case can be made both for the idea that liberalism influences social life in a society to such an extent that it can make it difficult for certain ways of life to be sustained,[128] and for the idea that liberalism and religion can be, often have been, and now are mutually supportive. It is so, because there are both areas of overlap and conflict between religion and traditionalism, on one side, and liberalism, on the other. Galston further argues that it is necessary both on a practical and a theoretical level to articulate a liberalism that can be linked to moral traditionalism. He distinguishes between *intrinsic* and *functional* traditionalism, where the latter "rests its case on asserted links between certain moral principles and public virtues or institutions needed for the successful functioning of a liberal community."[129] One example he discusses is family policy.[130] Because stable and intact two-parent families are important for the functioning of a liberal society, including the life and the future of the children, a public policy supporting such family life is desirable. He thinks this sort of substantial liberalism in fact is less biased than the now so influential "neutral" liberalism that "turns out to be far more partisan and exclusionary".[131] He further writes: "A high task of liberal statesmanship is to attend to inevitable moral conflict, not by pretending that the liberal state is neutral but, rather, by working toward the greatest possible accommodation with dissenters that is consistent with liberalism's core commitments."[132]

Galston thus agrees with much of Hauerwas' criticism of dominant liberal theory, for example its claim to neutrality and its identification of freedom as absence of restrictions. He also agrees in describing liberalism as a specific substantial tradition and in stressing the importance of fostering virtuous people for sustaining a good society. There are, of course, deep substantial differences bet-

---

[126]On the following, see ibid., 257-289.

[127]Ibid., 258.

[128]On this, see also ibid., 290-304.

[129]Ibid., 280.

[130]Ibid., 283-287.

[131]Ibid., 290.

[132]Ibid., 298. Another important book that addresses much of the critique and positive proposals of e.g. MacIntyre, but is more hopeful of present societies and parts of the liberal tradition, is Stout's *Ethics After Babel*. Cf. Hauerwas' and Kenneson's critical discussion of this book in "Flight from Foundationalism". Also relevant here is Werpehowski's "Political Liberalism and Christian Ethics", in which he starts with a sympathetic account of Hauerwas' criticism of liberalism and then tries to formulate a more positive account of liberalism in relation to Christian ethics. For Hauerwas' comments, see *AN* 21f n. 10. For an account close to Hauerwas', see Jones, "Should Christians Affirm Rawl's Justice as Fairness?".

ween the liberal and the Christian traditions as described by Galston and Hauer-was. Neither is Hauerwas close to the sort of moral traditionalism Galston descri-bes. Yet I would think that Hauerwas finds this account of liberalism more sym-pathetic than the usual ones. First of all, it acknowledges that it is a moral tradi-tion arguing about the goods people in a society have in common. This makes a public dialogue with the church possible. Christian convictions are not automati-cally excluded from public argument as by definition outside public reason. This also, as Galston contends, opens for practical compromises with dissident com-munities like the Christian church.

However, Hauerwas is more sceptical than Galston (who himself is not too optimistic) about the prospects for this sort of liberalism in current circumstances. We have seen that he argues that the ways both market and state bureaucracy work in our types of society undermine even the type of liberalism Galston de-fends. He furthermore thinks that Engelhardt's description of the dominant cul-tural forces is more correct than Galston's and (partly for that reason) the moral discourse is more fragmented than Galston allows.

Galston has a section where he discusses how well the virtues needed are en-gendered in current liberal societies and he refers to both pessimistic and opti-mistic empirical studies. His own conclusion is "that we have at least as much food for concern as for celebration."[133] Although he does not comment on it, it is notable that the optimistic studies concentrate on such typical liberal virtues as independence, democratization, tolerance, work-ethic, initiative, and scepticism, while the pessimistic ones particularly deal with the sort of political virtues Gal-ston himself defends. The latter studies contend for example that instead of fos-tering such virtues modern institutions are "executive-centered" and therefore not very open to public argument, "induce citizens to relate to one another as interest bearers and as bargainers rather than as participants in a shared process of justifi-cation"[134] and as clients to bureaucratic experts.

Furthermore, it is in the current political world hard to see much of the citi-zenship and leadership virtues that Galston describes. Modern, rights-based wel-fare state liberalism, with its specific political, economic and social structures and the political role of media, seems to undermine the sense of moderation, self-dis-cipline and duty Galston thinks necessary as well as forming a political system that cannot avoid cheap populism. Citizenship becomes a list of rights and politics is expected to be almighty and therefore all responsible. When the political sys-tem necessarily fails to fulfil these expectations a legitimation crisis follows. A sign of this is the failure—*both* in the boom years of the 1980s *and* in the depres-sion of the early 1990s—of most leading industrial countries to deal with their growing budget deficits and the severe difficulties any government, of whatever colour, has had in winning elections in times of slow or non-growing economies.

---

[133]*Liberal Purposes*, 232-237. The citation is from 237.
[134]Ibid., 234.

To this has to be added the cultural forces that seem to go in a problematic direction for Galston. He criticizes MacIntyre for failing to "see a gulf between the moral doctrines of many elites and the moral sensibilities of most ordinary citizens"[135] and therefore of describing the moral reality in liberal society as a form of emotivism, which at most is true only for the former groups. However, the social studies we have used consistently describe a movement in the direction MacIntyre and Engelhardt describe. In relation to Inglehart's thesis about Postmaterialism an interesting paradox is raised. Rapidly growing economies strengthen the sort of Postmaterialist values that Galston thinks partly undermine the liberal system, but liberalism is only thinkable, Galston maintains, over the long run, in a growing economy.

The result of all this is, one might argue, that he has not succeeded to answer the concerns that Hauerwas and others raise and therefore that the prospects of the sort of liberalism Galston defends, in current circumstances, seem increasingly feeble. Of course, there are more possible versions of liberalism than Engelhardt and Galston represent, and the most likely outcome might be something in between these two models, with prospects about which we do not know much.

What, then, is Hauerwas' solution? The not so unexpected answer is that he has no general model to offer as a solution. He can, at best, offer the church as a witness to alternatives, but he has no general theory about the good state and a viable constitution. He can give hints and suggest possible routes for further reflection, but he has no ultimate solution (nor penultimate). His theological program does not allow it. He is anyhow critical of such attempts and, finally, he simply does not know. We will in a later chapter discuss in some detail why such attempts are futile. That is not the way social change and politics actually work. What he tries to do is to understand the situation the church exists in and thereby to help it sustain a faithful witness (which in itself is difficult enough) that in various ways might help the surrounding society find some new ways. But he has no theory that tells him to where this will lead.[136]

5. Freedom—From Emancipation to Virtue

Freedom is, together with justice, the central good of modernity and stands in the centre of liberalism. There exist in modernity different understandings of freedom, but in one way or another they usually concentrate on autonomy and freedom of choice. Individuals should make their own choices, be their own laws or realize their own personal ways. Emancipation is then to be understood as liberation from anything that stands in the way of the autonomous choices of individuals so that they become free, unconstrained creators of their own lives. The same

---

[135]Ibid., 71.
[136]On this cf. *AC* 21 and "Faith in the Republic", 472f. See also Elshtain, *Public Man, Private Woman*, 300f.

is true on the social level. Humanity should be freed to create its own future. History is therefore described as a history of struggle against unfreedom and at the same time a history of increasing freedom.

a) Political Theology and Freedom as Emancipation

We have seen that liberation is also the overarching concept in Moltmann's understanding of history. He describes modern society as future-oriented, aimed at liberating both individuals and society from all sorts of constraints, so that both individuals and humankind at large can take charge over their own destinies. History is therefore described as an emancipatory process, a continuous history of freedom movements. The Enlightenment is in this view only a continuation and outbidding of the Christian history of freedom. The process of secularization can consequently in this light be understood as a process of emancipation in which humanity becomes subject of its own history.

The centrality of freedom in modernity makes it *necessary*, Moltmann argues, for modern theology to become a theology of freedom. It is necessary if the church shall be able to mediate Christian faith to modern society. We saw how he tried formulate a view of human freedom in relation to God that could overcome modern atheism, which is based on a conception of God in which God is seen as in opposition to human freedom.[137] He then tries to show the consequences of this view for the practice of freedom in relation to church, society and morality. He thus defends the compatibility between the Christian and the modern understandings of freedom and liberation through describing Christianity as the origin of and a major partaker in the *one* history of freedom.

I have earlier questioned his view of freedom. Moltmann works both on the personal and the social level with the dualism of oppression and liberation. Freedom is consequently understood as the taking away of all restrictions and the realization of a "natural" and "spontaneous" freedom. The stress is put on the removal of oppression, not on the positive formation of life and institutions. If freedom is primarily a realization of a spontaneous, natural freedom liberated from oppression there is no need for substantial positive suggestions. We have seen that he increasingly has moved away from the implications of this view and started to develop a constructive Christian ethics. Yet, he still strongly defends the idea of liberation into spontaneous self-realization when discussing the nature of the personal Christian life. This view, I have argued, is in itself incoherent, is not compatible with his ecclesial ethics of discipleship, and does not give him the resources for developing a credible account of how to form and sustain the sort of church life he defends.

---

[137]*ThT* 23f (31f).

b) Theological Politics and Freedom as Virtue

Hauerwas takes a very different road than Moltmann. But one can plausibly argue that his view can be read as an attempt to work out a concept of freedom implicit in Moltmann's ecclesial discipleship ethics. Hauerwas does not try to reconcile the modern concept of freedom with the Christian, as he thinks they are in deep tension. He furthermore contends that making liberation the overriding description of the Christian existence is a mistake. One reason is that biblically liberation is just one of the metaphors used for understanding salvation, and it is in itself not sufficiently rich to function as a comprehensive description of Christian salvation and life. More important, liberation only makes sense in relation to substantive convictions about to what we are called. Christian freedom means freedom for service, not autonomy. This implies a third reason for not using liberation as overriding concept. Because of its central place in the Enlightenment tradition the Enlightenment understanding will easily determine the Christian use.[138]

Again the consequences of their different theological and ecclesiological strategies are obvious. Moltmann wants to integrate Christianity and the Enlightenment into one overarching history of freedom—interpreted as the one story of God. This Hauerwas will not do. For Hauerwas the relation is more conflictual.[139] Furthermore, Moltmann's contention that contemporary theology *must* be a theology of freedom *because* of the central place of freedom in modernity is just the opposite of Hauerwas' argument.

This contrast might seem overdrawn in the light of Moltmann's criticism of the liberal understanding of freedom as freedom of choice and of rule and his claim that freedom is realized in community. However, Moltmann's criticism is primarily a mixture of a christianized version of the Hegelian/Marxist challenge to liberalism and of the romantic expressivist challenge to modern utilitarianism and rationalism—disputes inside the modern discourse of freedom. One might challenge the coherence of this critique (does not his view of autonomy imply freedom of choice and freedom as rule?), but, more importantly, Hauerwas disputes what these traditions have in common. In terms of Moltmann's theology, one might say that Hauerwas takes up the half of the theology which uses the language of discipleship and understands the church as a contrast society, while discarding the other half which lives on the language of emancipation and autonomy. He especially differs from the most problematic aspect of Moltmann's view, namely from the latter's "expressive individualism" or "instinctual romanticism".

---

[138]"Some Theological Reflections on Gutierrez's Use of 'Liberation' as a Theological Concept", 69-71. Parts of this article are used in *AC* 50-55. On the immediate context for this judgement, cf. Wuthnow, *The Restructuring of American Religion*, 257-264 on the role of freedom as legitimating myth in American society and religion.

[139]Cf. "On Being 'Placed' by John Milbank", 199f.

He has often sharply criticized this view.[140] Instead of using the language of emancipation and spontaneous self-realization, he talks about the Christian life in terms of discipleship and virtue. He also develops his account of freedom in these terms. He consequently can write "that freedom is a quality that derives from having a well-formed character. Put in traditional terms, only the truly good person can be the truly free person."[141] When Moltmann talks about freedom as community, the important thing to notice in relation to Hauerwas is that it is a substantially empty concept. I am free, when I can be myself, when I am accepted as I am, and when I accept others as they are. This is love, friendship and solidarity. The church should thus be an accepting, encouraging, and caring community that helps me to be myself, to freely realize my inner potential.

For Hauerwas, in contrast, the issue is to be formed rightly. Instead of seeing the free life coming from the taking away of restrictions, be they the past, traditions, or communities, he contends that freedom is given and lived through community and by being able to truthfully integrate and accept my past.[142] Freedom has no content in abstraction and for itself, it "is possible and meaningful only when it is correlated with convictions about the kind of people we ought to be, as well as the kind of institutions we ought to support."[143] In this perspective one becomes free through discipleship, through training, through learning to see reality in a specific way, and through learning to live with these descriptions. He refers to the New Testament conception of freedom to something, freedom to truth and service. Freedom is therefore "not an end in itself but rather it is the means in which it is made possible for us to serve one another. Any account of liberation in Christian ethics must be tested against this norm."[144]

From a virtue perspective, freedom is thus more a question of having a certain power that makes a truthful life possible, than having a choice. Freedom is not having all options open, but of being so formed that many options are not real alternatives. "For example, the refusal to use violence for resolving disputes, or perhaps better, the attempt to avoid persistent violent situations, becomes for some so routine they never think about it. It is simply 'who they are.' But the formation of that habit does not make it any less, but all the more, a resource of

---

[140]*VV* 250-260, *CC* 81f, 126f, 171f, *RA* 117-127, *AC* 93-111.

[141]*PK* 37.

[142]His longest account of freedom is found in *PK* 35-49. See also *PK* 6-10, *VV* 40f, 64f, 253f, *CC* 115f, 130f, 147, and "Gutierrez's Use of 'Liberation'".

[143]*SP* 14.

[144]"Gutierrez's Use of 'Liberation'", 75. On the relation between freedom and service, he writes: "The call to such service we find only in the presence of another, whose need is often the very occasion of our freedom. For it is through the need of another that the greatest hindrance of my freedom, namely my own self-absorption, is finally not so much overcome as simply rendered irrelevant." (*PK* 44.) See further "Gutierrez's Use of 'Liberation'", 69f, 75f, *CC* 130f.

and for their freedom."[145] When freedom is thus understood, the church is a place where one's life is transformed and trained so that such freedom is possible.[146]

c) Freedom, Community, Tradition and Authority

This discussion of freedom illustrates Moltmann's and Hauerwas' different theological strategies. Moltmann's mediating and apologetic interest makes the modern concept of freedom the starting point. The problem for him is how to mediate the Christian and the modern understanding so that he can defend Christianity against modern criticism and help Christians to make this mediation their own. Hauerwas' approach is not apologetical. He thinks the modern understanding is faulty and consequently points to an alternative understanding built on the church's own tradition and experience. The liberal tradition starts with the conflict between autonomy and reason on the one hand, and a conception of community, tradition and authority as inherently restricting on the other. While Moltmann usually works inside this conception, Hauerwas does not accept it.

We have seen that there is, in Hauerwas' perspective no inherent conflict between community and freedom. Like Moltmann he instead stresses the interdependence of community and freedom, but, unlike Moltmann, he sees community not only as an accepting space that liberates to self-realization, but as a place for positive transformation and formation.[147] One's freedom is enlarged through the formation of one's self that occurs through being part of the Christian community. What is decisive, however, is which sort of community, which convictions and practices it has, and therefore for which purposes it lives.

He similarly does not see an essential conflict between tradition and freedom, because freedom is learned through being initiated into a tradition. Not only to act, but also to see rightly is a question of transformation and training. Knowledge cannot be separated from discipleship and discipleship is being initiated into the Christian tradition through masters.[148]

The recent development in the understanding of knowledge as described in chapter two has put the heteronomy charge against Christian ethics in a new light. This charge was rooted in a sharp distinction between revelation, tradition and faith on the one hand, and reason and rationality on the other. However, when all

---

[145]*PK* 43.

[146]In *VV* 65 Hauerwas uses the concept of autonomy positively, which he does not do in later writings. Its meaning here is not far from his later description of freedom. But this whole essay ("Towards an Ethics of Character" originally from 1972) still gives a strange impression in light of his later work. Because the church does not play any role, his discussion has a strongly individualistic and intellectualistic tone. He is here still, as he also says (p. 61 n. 28), a sort of Kantian. For a good discussion of the concept of autonomy, see Dworkin, *The Theory and Practice of Autonomy*.

[147]He says that any community that wants to be sustained over time cannot be built only on the desire for togetherness, but must "share common purposes and loyalties. . . . no society, even very small ones, can sustain itself for the sole purpose of letting everyone 'do his own thing.'" (*VV* 254.) Said so bluntly Moltmann would surely agree, but he avoids taking the consequences.

[148]*CC* 131, *PK* 29f, *AC* 93-111.

knowledge is seen as formed, developed and tested in communal traditions of enquiry, there is no longer any abstract reason as such. When this sharp dualism, as
by Hauerwas, is discarded it does not only have consequences for the "reason
side" but also for the "revelation and faith side" of the traditional chasm.[149] For
Hauerwas revelation is not an epistemological category that refers to "super-
naturally" derived knowledge and as such functions as the foundation of theology
and ethics. Revelation, Hauerwas contends, names knowledge that is about God,
not the way of deriving that knowledge. He consequently finds the distinction
between natural and revealed knowledge about God misleading.[150] He does not
see Scripture as a set of indubitable data that could constitute a "revealed morality". He is likewise critical of attempts to develop a biblical ethics through
concentrating on specific biblical commands, basic concepts or central themes,
because commands like the Ten Commandments or the Sermon on the Mount,
and concepts like love are not self-interpreting but are only intelligible in the
context of God's history with Israel, Jesus Christ and the church. He can thus
write: "The nature of Christian ethics is determined by the fact that Christian
convictions take the form of a story, or perhaps better, a set of stories that constitute a tradition, which in turn creates and forms a community."[151] Being initiated
into this tradition, which means being initiated into the church, forms one's vision
of the world, one's desires and will, and therefore how one encounters this world.
How Christian faith helps people to see the world is thus ethically prior to rules,
laws and decisions, though these also have their important place.[152] Yet, he does
not think this places Christian ethics in another epistemological realm than other
ethics.

> Christian ethics is the disciplined activity which analyzes and imaginatively tests the images
> most appropriate to orchestrate the Christian life in accordance with the central conviction
> that the world has been redeemed by the work of Jesus Christ. Christian ethics as such is
> not in principle methodologically different from other ethics, for I suspect all accounts of
> the moral life require some appeal to the virtues, principles, and the narrative display of
> each. What makes Christian ethics Christian is not our methodology, but the content of our
> convictions.[153]

Furthermore, his approach implies, as we have seen, that also Scripture is to
be read in the interpretative community (or communities) called the church. It is
not a foundational criterion outside the ongoing life and conversation of the

---

[149]For the following, see *CC* 53-71, *PK* 64-71, and *US* 15-44.
[150]"All knowledge of God is at once natural and revelatory. But like all knowledge it depends on
analogical control. Analogies, in turn, derive their intelligibility from paradigms that draw on narratives
for their rational display. Our narratives of God's dealing with us inspire and control our attempt to test
how what we know of God helps us understand why the world is as it is". (*PK* 66.)
[151]*PK* 24.
[152]He says that "to be a Christian is not principally to obey certain commandments or rules, but to learn
to grow into the story of Jesus as the form of God's kingdom." (*PK* 30.)
[153]*PK* 69.

church. Scripture and discipleship go together, which is to say that one in the church learns skills of various sorts, including moral skills, needed for reading Scripture.

Tradition is not static, but is formed through the ongoing practices and conversations in the church in new situations about its life. We have seen that the whole church in various ways takes part in this process. In this sense, he says, the church can be said to be democratic. If discussion is the "hallmark" of the church, one should expect disagreements, conflicts and diversity, but only in a common search to be faithful to Jesus Christ.[154]

> The remarkable richness of these stories of God requires that a church be a community of discourse and interpretation that endeavors to tell these stories and form its life in accordance with them. The church, the whole body of believers, therefore cannot be limited to any one historical paradigm or contained by any one institutional form. Rather the very character of the stories of God requires a people who are willing to have their understanding of the story constantly challenged by what others have discovered in their attempt to live faithful to that tradition. For the church is able to exist and grow only through tradition, which—as the memory sustained over time by ritual and habit—sets the context and boundaries for the discussion required by the Christian stories.[155]

In initiating people into the Christian tradition the church necessarily exercises authority. No community and tradition can exist without authority.[156] One reason authority is needed is because training is necessary. This is as true of being initiated into scientific work or medical practice as of being initiated into a moral tradition. Another reason is the need for a diversity of functions and skills in a community. "By its very nature, then, authority seems to involve people's willingness to accept the judgements of another as superior to their own on the basis of that person's office and assumed skills."[157] A third reason is the existence of a plurality of means for the pursuit of the common good and the consequent need for a community to procure common action.

Authority so understood presupposes a tradition, a shared vision of the goods pursued and shared practices that embody this vision. It consequently does not demand blind obedience, but persuades and trains the apprentice to go further than even the master.[158] "What makes a master a master is that he or she knows how to go further, and especially how to direct others to go further, using what can be learned from tradition afforded by the past, so that he or she can move

---

[154]*CC* 85.

[155]*CC* 92. He can even say that "that very diversity is the necessary condition for our faithfulness" (*CC* 85) and that "[p]art of the test of the truthfulness of the church is whether it can provide a polity sufficient to sustain the differences necessary for discussion." (*CC* 96.)

[156]On authority, see esp. *TT* 195-197, *CC* 53-71, *SP* 39-62, and "Protestants and the Pope". As for this whole section *AC* 93-111 is relevant here too. Cochran, "Authority and Community" is also helpful for understanding Hauerwas' argument.

[157]*SP* 40.

[158]"We listen to the teacher and respect his authority because he speaks with greater understanding, greater wisdom, deeper experience, and more truly than do others." ("Protestants and the Pope", 84.)

toward the telos of fully perfected works."[159] Critical reflection and discussion are consequently also part of the ongoing conversation that constitutes the tradition.

In such an account of authority there is no intrinsic conflict between freedom and authority, nor between reason and authority. They instead need each other. Hauerwas can therefore write: "When a craft and a community are in good working order, discipline is quite literally a joy, as it provides one with power—and in particular a power for service—that is otherwise missing."[160] It is barely noted as discipline. But the Enlightenment understanding of knowledge as systematic doubt, the ideal of personal autonomy, and the general critique of tradition have made it extremely difficult to make a positive account of authority intelligible. However, without practices of authority and discipline not only Hauerwas' but also Moltmann's ecclesiology is impossible (as is science, law, medicine, and so on).

d) Freedom in Liberal Society

It is Hauerwas' contention that modern society lacks the sort of coherence that can make meaningful moral discussions and disagreements possible. Liberalism is conceived as an answer to this situation. But in most of its versions it makes the absence of a discussion of common goods into an ideal and stresses therefore abstract autonomy and criticism of authority and tradition as such. The result is that it thereby undermines the communities that are often said to be the base for liberal societies.

When autonomy is made central, it is, Hauerwas thinks, difficult to avoid a conflation of authority with power, and the interpretation of both as domination. The result is that social life is interpreted primarily in terms of self-interest and power struggle. Human relations thus become "forms of manipulation to maintain dominance."[161] It is therefore taken for granted that politics is struggle for power and for realizing one's own interests. The economic and political systems require self-interest as the primary public "virtue", and the dominating public philosophy legitimizes it. In contemporary social and economic science this depiction seems to be a self-evident presupposition which, until very recently, seldom has been questioned. This has been true not only of "established" economics and sociology, but also of "critical" and left-leaning thinking. (Yet it has to be said that specially after 1980 the idea that human behaviour can be plausibly reduced to self-interest has been increasingly questioned in many different disciplines—such as economics, sociology, political science, psychology and biology.[162])

---

[159]*AC* 106.
[160]*AC* 107.
[161]*SP* 56. See also *SP* 41f, 52, and *CC* 84.
[162]Etzioni, *The Moral Dimension*, Mansbridge (ed.), *Beyond Self-Interest*, Milbank, *Theology and Social Theory*, Putnam, *Making Democracy Work*, and Wolfe, *Whose Keeper?* Mansbridge, "The Rise

We see ourselves and others as but pawns engaged in elaborate games of power and self-interest. I do not mean to suggest that there has ever been a time or social order from which manipulation was absent. What is new about our present situation is that our best moral wisdom can conceive of no alternative. We seem able only to suggest ways to make the game more nearly fair.[163]

When both social and moral theory assume that self-interest is fundamental, attempts to develop alternatives are deemed non-workable.

One result of making freedom an end in itself is, Hauerwas claims, that liberal societies become increasingly legalistic, because laws become the only way of restraining self-interest.[164] When the religious and moral system, which the founders of the American system assumed would create the sort of privately virtuous people that were seen as necessary to get this bargaining system to work, is increasingly transformed by the liberal public morality ("a social order that is designed to work on the presumption that people are self-interested tends to produce that kind of people"[165]), the law is the only alternative left.

Again, Hauerwas does not think that this is the whole story of modern Western society, but that this is the direction in which this society is developing. One reason for this is that we appear not to be able to imagine an alternative.[166]

e) The Shortcomings of Moltmann's Understanding of Freedom

We have seen that Moltmann's understanding of freedom in terms of oppression/liberation, autonomy and self-realization correlates with a reduction of power to dominion. His hope is therefore for dominion-free churches and societies, which for him seems to mean communities free from all sorts of authority and power relations. It is noteworthy that in one of his discussions of autonomy, he connects this with a critique of the Christian emphasis on service, because service creates dependency and consequently "a concealed form of domination". It is only in a church "without above and below" that being with others can be reconciled with being "autonomous agents of their own life".[167] It is this view that makes his discussion of discipleship, community building and federal democracy so abstract and unreal.[168] In his attempt to avoid anything that smacks of hierarchy, authority and power he fails to give a credible account of the conditions of

---

and Fall of Self-Interest in the Explanation of Political Life" gives an overview of the recent challenges to the mainstream view.

[163]*PK* 9.

[164]*CC* 75.

[165]*CC* 79.

[166]This depiction of liberal society is found everywhere in the work of Hauerwas, but for one longer sustained account, see *CC* 72-86.

[167]The last three citations all come from *HIG* 122. So also *GHH* 13f (27f).

[168]Cf. e.g. *SL* 252 (264f).

social life, not to mention the sort of church he envisions. He raises important concerns about service, authority and power, but his account of freedom, authority and power does not give him tools for analysing *different* forms of service and power. It is this that Hauerwas tries to provide,[169] but that means he has to transcend the dichotomies inherent in the modern idea of freedom as autonomy. For when autonomy is made central it is difficult to avoid viewing all kinds of authority, discipline and power as forms of coercion.

Moltmann's account also explains the doubleness we noted in his view of politics. Because politics is about power, and power is dominion, the future society is in effect described as a society without politics, but the way to this power-free society is through the struggle for power, that is for dominion. He can give no intelligible account of how out of this process the dominion-free conditions can be created. He shares this dilemma with most radical politics. His conception of freedom seems to leave no other way open. It is also one explanation for the vacillating attitude to the possibilities of the church we noted. Hauerwas of course does not deny the pervasive nature of coercive and manipulative power in human and institutional relations, but he denies that this is their essence. The Christian faith that God rules the world assumes that peace and trust are more basic than violence and distrust.[170] This leads to the hope that alternative ways of understanding and living human life and politics are possible.[171]

6. Justice and Human Rights

The other central value in liberalism is justice and we have seen that it is closely connected to the understanding of freedom as autonomy. Hauerwas is (it should not surprise us by now) a severe critic of the central place the languages of justice and rights have in liberal society and modern theology, while Moltmann is a vigorous defender of this use. We have met Hauerwas' contention that this emphasis on justice is a result of the conditions of liberal society.

> We live in a society that assumes that there are not, nor can there be, any agreed upon accounts of what goods we ought to hold in common. Nor can we agree about the kind of people we ought to be. Any attempt to determine such goods or suggest virtues commensurate with citizenship is thought to be coercive and threatening to our freedom. In such a society justice necessarily becomes the overriding norm of social practice. For justice seems to suggest what is minimally necessary to hold such societies together in a reason-

---

[169]Cf. *CET* 145 n. 2: "The question is not power or no power, but the kind of power and how it is distributed."
[170]*CC* 110.
[171]In addition to already mentioned texts, see also *TT* 132-135, *CET* 199-219, *RA* 167-172, and "On God", 206.

able harmony. In short, justice is the name for the procedural rules necessary to secure enough fair play so that everyone will be able to pursue their private goods.[172]

Justice is used for getting a society of strangers to work, and for Christians this language, Hauerwas thinks, is popular as it appears to give them a way of working for a better society without using a Christian language. It becomes a modern substitute for natural law.

The severe difficulties that Hauerwas claims this sort of language, both in itself and for Christians, encounter is by now familiar. First of all, he questions "the assumption that we share enough to even know what justice might mean."[173] In the lack of a substantive account of what sort of people we want to be and what sort of common goods we as a community think life is about, no practical theory of justice can be developed. In a liberal consumer society he thinks this is disastrous, for when we lack substantive accounts of justice, then any desires we have are seen as legitimate. There are no common critical tools for helping us to see which desires are legitimate. This explains why most talk about justice (from right to left) in our type of society is part of the struggle for "societies that are free of constraints upon the needs of its members."[174]

He thinks this becomes clear when we consider how the language of justice is used in ordinary political (and theological) language. For there it is far from the grand theories some philosophers have tried to develop. "*Justice* has become a word people use to buttress the assertion that this or that set of circumstances is bad and needs correcting, but we seldom are given reason to know what is bad about the situation or what we ought to do about it."[175] To describe a situation as unjust is thus not very helpful in itself. The situation does not get any better by the fact that this language is often used in very contradictory ways, for example both on egalitarian and libertarian assumptions, without people noticing the contradictions. But it helps to explain, he thinks, why the language of justice does not help us to agree on very much. It is often more a tool for propaganda than for constructive public discussion of our common future.

A common way of expressing this view of justice is in terms of rights. Justice is attained, it is claimed, through securing the rights due to everyone. Hauerwas' criticism of rights language is therefore a specification of his general criticism of the liberal conception of justice. He thinks this language "tends toward individualistic accounts of society and underwrites a view of human relations as exchanges rather than cooperative endeavors."[176] Behind it stands the picture of the good society as the society of autonomous individuals left alone to realize their

---

[172]"Should Christians Talk So Much About Justice?", 14. Hauerwas has later incorporated most, but not all, of this article in the chapter "The Politics of Justice" in *AC* 45-68. My references are to the latter text, except material not included in that text.

[173]*AC* 60.

[174]*AC* 61.

[175]*AC* 46.

[176]"On the 'Right' to be Tribal", 238.

private selves and choices. Because there is no agreed upon understanding of common goods, the rights are seen as procedural rules that make possible a common life for these autonomous individuals with their different private life projects. It is thus a morality for moral strangers.

To make his position more concrete I shall briefly review his discussion of the use of language of rights in a text dealing with the question of experimentation on children.[177] He thinks that talk about the rights of children shows the way liberal society cannot avoid procedural rules instead of substantive judgements. "To employ the language of rights is to assume that children are simply one interest group among others and that they must have procedural safeguards in order to be protected from the undue advantage of other interest groups, including their parents."[178] In the absence of common beliefs about parental care of children, rights language seems to be the only alternative. This is legitimized by a moral theory that tries to abstract the individual from his or her particularities as parent, citizen or church member. In this individualistic account the family becomes an odd anomaly, something that is ethically irrelevant. The family is understood as a social contract where the members have rights against each other. Although the family clearly is not a social contract, liberal moral theory has difficulties in finding other ways of talking about it. Hauerwas' own view is that "to speak of family and child is exactly to speak of the duties of parents and children toward one another that are grounded in the concrete expectations of particular communities." But liberal ethics wants to talk about the human being as such separated from particular convictions and communities, "i. e., as if we were strangers to one another in the sense that we share no history or common purpose."[179] Behind this is also the thought that the goal of upbringing is autonomous independent individuals who alone chooses the communities they want to share and the convictions they want to have. For Hauerwas this is both an illusion and contrary to the calling of the Christian family.

This does not mean that he discards all use of the language of justice and rights. He thinks it can be used when it is dependent on more substantive moral languages. In the example given one might talk about rights, if it is determined by convictions about the parents' obligations to their children. The same is true for example in situations of misuse of power. What he is critical of is, first, its use as a *basic* moral language in abstraction from substantive accounts of moral goods, and, second, that it gives the impression that justice is primarily a question of principles and rights, and not of the sort of people we want to be.[180]

---

[177]*SP* 125-141.

[178]*SP* 125.

[179]The last two citations are both from *SP* 129.

[180]He writes that "when rights are taken to be the fundamental morality we are encouraged to take an ultimately degrading perspective on society. No real society can *exist* when its citizens' only way of relating is in terms of noninterference. The language of 'rights,' especially as it is displayed by liberal political theory, encourages us to live as if we had no common interests or beliefs. We are thus trained

For Hauerwas the church is a community of virtue, a fact that presupposes a common vision of what the church is called to.[181] In contrast, rights language makes the abstract individual as such primary, independent of the church (or any other community), which Hauerwas thinks Christians should not accept.

Moltmann exemplifies what Hauerwas criticizes when he, connecting rights language with ideas of autonomy and self-realization, says that rights language, by definition, talks about the rights the human being has as human being independent of the convictions and practices of any community. The gift of human dignity, he says, "presents them with the task of actualizing themselves, their essence".[182] This partly takes place through liberation from institutional and moral repression. In this light the struggle for social rights might be seen as the struggle for the sort of society in which each person can be free to actualize themselves. The church thus becomes a pressure group for the realization of this society. The relevant, primary moral community with respect to rights language, therefore, is not the church but the nation-state or a hoped for world-state.[183]

To this might be added the fact that although Moltmann talks about the indivisibility of rights and duties, he has very little to say about the latter, and the examples he gives are the duty of resistance and duty to work for liberation. In other words, it is a duty to create the sort of social situation that makes individual self-realization possible. A more substantive account of duty becomes difficult in the

---

to regard even our children as potential strangers from whom we need protection. But this is a formula for the disintegration of society as well as the disintegration of the moral self, as it trains us to pursue our interests as ends in themselves." (*SP* 130.) Cf. also MacIntyre, *After Virtue*, 227-237 and idem, *Whose Justice? Which Rationality?*

[181]"Such a people do not believe that everyone is free to do whatever they will, but that we are each called upon to develop our particular gifts to serve the community of faith." (*PK* 103.)

[182]*OHD* 10 (24).

[183]In the light of Moltmann's understanding of human dignity and self-realization, Peter Berger's discussion in "On the Obsolence of the Concept of Honor" of the replacement of the language of honour for the language of dignity is interesting. He argues that the typically modern manner of understanding human dignity has to do with the deinstitutionalization and the subjectivization of the human identity. (He does not, however, think that the idea of human dignity in itself is new—it is found already in Greek and Hebrew thinking. See ibid., 176.) The individual's identity and meaning is formed through the institutional web in which he or she lives. But this web is in modern society experienced as fragmented, fluid, and incohesive, which makes it much more difficult to reach stable identities, with the accompanying frantic search for identity. It is this experience which, according to Berger, makes the predominance of the concept of dignity understandable, as it "implies that identity is essentially independent of institutional roles." (Ibid., 177.) From this follows that in "a world of dignity, the individual can only discover his true identity by emancipating himself from his socially imposed roles—the latter are only masks, entangling him in illusion, 'alienation' and 'bad faith.'" (Ibid., 177.) (It is of course the opposite in a world of honour. There "the individual discovers his true identity in his roles, and to turn away from his roles is to turn away from himself—in 'false consciousness,' one is tempted to add." [Ibid., 177].) It is this solitary self that in modernity is the bearer of human dignity and inalienable rights. The close kinship between Moltmann's thinking and Berger's account is evident. In other words, we find with him the same combination of a radical romantic individualism and an account of rights.

context of his version of rights language, although not so in his ecclesial discipleship ethics.

We have also seen that Hauerwas does not share Moltmann's acceptance of the idea of a universal self-evident rights language. The human rights tradition is understandable on the basis of the structures and the stories of a liberal society.[184] Hauerwas' claim is that the failure to recognize this leads to an imperialistic attitude, which Moltmann exemplifies when he states that any opposition against the human rights tradition makes the opposers enemies of the human race.[185]

In another context he points out that the sort of arguments Moltmann uses are exactly the same arguments the Enlightenment tradition has used against the Jews. Universalistic values were used for emancipating the individual Jews, but only to the extent that they subordinated their Jewishness to the liberal society, and especially to the nation-state. This created a new sort of anti-Semitism, but now on nationalistic and racial grounds. Jewishness is accepted as a private characteristic, but Judaism understood as a people with their own identity, not subordinated to the nation-state, is another thing.[186]

7. The Complex Relation between Christianity and Liberalism

a) The Christian Heritage of Liberalism

Hauerwas' relation to liberalism is more complex than a first look might give reason to believe. It is easy to see that he is deeply critical of liberalism—most of what he says about it is critical. On the other hand, it is not difficult to find state-

---

[184]See Berger, "Honor", MacIntyre, *After Virtue*, 60-75, Shapiro, *The Evolution of Rights in Liberal Theory*, and Taylor, *Philosophy and the Human Sciences*, 187-210.

[185]Commenting on such attitudes Hauerwas writes that although rights language "at least in principle, seems to embody the highest human ideals. . . . it also facilitates the assumption that anyone who denies such rights is morally obtuse and should be 'forced' to recognize the error of his ways. Indeed, we overlook too easily how the language of 'rights,' in spite of its potential for good, contains within its logic a powerful justification of violence. Our rights language 'absolutizes the relative' in the name of a universal that is profoundly limited and limiting just to the extent that it tempts us to substitute some moral ideal for our faithfulness to God." (*PK* 61.)

[186]*AN* 61-90. The issues Hauerwas raises concerning liberal ethics in general, such as the question of moral formation, the poverization of our moral languages, and the privatization of Christian faith, are also relevant here, but I will not repeat the arguments. However, Richard Hays, in a discussion of homelessness, expresses vividly what happens when the "thick" biblical moral language is translated into the "thin" procedural rights language. He writes that "the ubiquitous appeal to a rationally-grounded notion of human rights is without warrant in Scripture. Nowhere in the New Testament is there any hint that housing—or anything else—is a 'right.' Those who fail to respond to the homeless are not castigated for violating a human right; rather, it is suggested that they have disregarded 'Moses and the prophets' (Luke 16:27-31) or that they culpably failed to recognize Jesus himself (Matt. 25:45). This last image cannot be adequately translated into the Enlightenment idiom of human rights and dignity. . . . Insofar as the church's discourse replaces these powerful images with pallid rationalistic notions of rights and equity, we as a community have lost our bearings and our identity". ("Scripture-Shaped Community", 54f.)

ments that describe the partly Christian origins of liberalism,[187] and that recognize its relative success in creating peace and limited states. He can even say that he does not mind "liberalism as political compromise".[188] Furthermore, he does not defend some preliberal society, which usually has not been more hospitable to the sort of church he envisions. Yet he never elaborates these points. The result is that his descriptions and judgements sometimes get a too one-dimensional, somewhat ahistorical and unnuanced character.

It occasionally seems as if he argues that the problem of liberal society is that it lacks a common moral tradition that could give it the context for a coherent moral and political discussion. But according to Hauerwas' non-Constantinian approach there will always be a more or less deep tension between church and world.[189] His hope, short of the eschatological consummation, is not a Christian society—even though the church in various ways has influenced and will influence the wider societies it exists in. One can therefore say that a Radical Reformation church will always be a challenge not only to liberal societies, but also to various (now hypothetical) more civic republican or communitarian types of societies in which some form of substantial public philosophy exists. Hauerwas consequently is as suspicious of many communitarian hopes as of liberalism.

He also, although never at length, points to the Christian roots of liberalism. These roots are both of a negative and a positive character. On the negative side, one can see liberalism as a response to the break-up of the church at the Reformation, the development of churches into national religions, and the subsequent religious wars, and the failure of the established churches to deal with each other non-violently. In this light liberalism emerged as an attempt to form peaceful societies of people with various convictions and practices. As Reinhard Hütter says, "a failing 'Christendom' invented liberal modernity."[190]

On the positive side one factor behind secular liberalism seems to be the actual tension between church and state built into the Western civilization. Christianity could never be wholly integrated in any society. It has always, although to different extents, been a disruptive presence that has desacralized the political power. We have also seen that he can describe the liberal vision as a secularized version of the Christian vision of peace.[191] This vision was related to Christian universalism, although to the perverted universalism of Christendom in which its messianic hope was combined with the universalism of the empire.[192] Another factor he mentions is the Reformation's affirmation (but again in an ambiguous and problematic way) of ordinary life and the consequent devaluation of the ex-

---

[187]"Faith in the Republic", 496, *CC* 99-101, *AN* 18, *AC* 70, "Virtue Christianly Considered", 18, "Real Sectarian", 93, *DFF* 197f n. 30.
[188]"Faith in the Republic", 484.
[189]Cf. "On Being 'Placed'", 199-201 and "Real Sectarian", 92-94.
[190]"The Church's Peace Beyond the 'Secular'", 114.
[191]"Virtue Christianly Considered", 18, *CC* 100f, *PK* 168f n. 17.
[192]*AN* 76f.

traordinary and of hierarchy.[193] Closer to Hauerwas, the Radical Reformation and Free Church tradition stressed the separation of church and world, questioned the idea of political religious unity, affirmed in theory and practice the right to dissent, and internally started to develop the idea of congregational decision-making through conversation.[194] Like Moltmann and many others he points out the importance of this for the development of Western democracy.[195]

In this perspective Milbank can describe liberalism as a Christian heresy.[196] And Hauerwas can say: "I think liberalism has done much good and has results from which no one would wish to back away. In particular, liberalism has been inventive in creating limitations on state power in order to encourage public co-operation for the maintenance of a good community."[197] Concerning the relation between church and state he is positive to the First Amendment of the Constitution of the United States[198] read for itself.[199] The problem, however, is that it is interpreted in the light of political liberalism and *as such* it functions in a negative way both for church and society. And he is first of all critical of "the failure of the church to hold this society to be true to its own best commitments."[200]

b) Public and Private

A central characteristic of liberalism has been to make distinctions between state and religion, public and private, and so on. We have seen that Hauerwas also defends the necessity of making distinctions. But he is critical of the way it has been done and interpreted in liberalism and in much of modern Christianity. He stresses that in a virtue ethics of his sort there is no place for the division between public and private. Yet because the notions of public and private are not self-interpreting one could well ask what he opposes. First of all, it is clear that he opposes conceptions that place religion into a private sphere strictly separate from the spheres of politics and public discourse. He also, secondly, opposes an understanding that sees Christian faith and salvation as concerning only the strictly personal and private life. Thirdly, his account of ecclesial discipleship

---

[193]*DFF* chap. 10. He here follows Taylor, *Sources of the Self*, part 3.

[194]*CC* 83-86, 254 n. 40, *CET* 72-74.

[195]*VV* 239f. See also Yoder, *The Priestly Kingdom*, 151-171 and Stackhouse, *Creeds, Society, and Human Rights*, 51-130. The importance of the Free Church tradition in this respect for the development of the Swedish democracy has been highlighted by the historian Sven Lundkvist in *Folkrörelserna i det svenska samhället 1850-1920*.

[196]Milbank, *Theology and Social Theory*, 23, 399.

[197]"Real Sectarian", 93. See also *AN* 18 and *CC* 110.

[198]"Congress shall make no law respecting an establishment of religion, or prohibiting the free exercise thereof; or abridging the freedom of speech, or of the press; or the right of the people peaceably to assemble, and to petition the Government for a redress of grievances." (Peaslee, *Constitutions of Nations*, vol. 4, 1205.)

[199]"The First Amendment could be a politically significant way for a state to acknowledge those public enterprises so essential to the public weal that they should be protected from command of the government." (*AC* 70.)

[200]*AC* 70. See also "The Kingship of Christ".

counters the idea that the determination of personal life is an entirely private matter.

But it is also clear that he affirms the separation of church and state. He in addition defends the independence of the institutions of what often is called the civil society, the informal sector or the mediating structures, from the control of the state. Put differently, he is against monolithic forms of states and societies. This also means that, although he thinks politics should concern not only procedures, but also the goods we have in common, and although he thinks the cultivation of virtue is a public matter, he does not think this should be the task of the state. "Rather, it is the function of the state to encourage those institutions and communities within society to produce people whose virtue is the resource that makes possible a non-coercive society."[201] The church, however, is called to make disciples and to form virtuous people and is therefore also called to exercise some form of ecclesial discipline. But his understanding of the church as an ongoing conversation, supported by different gifts and offices, makes the existence of diversity inside the church not only a necessity but a positive good for the life of the church.[202]

All this shows that questions that are discussed under the designation "public and private" are relevant for Hauerwas. But it also illustrates the different sorts of issues that are discussed with this conception as well as its sharply contested nature.

One especially interesting discussion of these issues is found in the book *Religion in Public and Private Life* by Clarke Cochran. It is written from the perspective of political science and takes current liberal democracy as the given context, but still comes quite close to Hauerwas' position, whose writings he frequently uses, although their different starting points leads to important differences. The book is therefore also an interesting example of dialogue between theology and political science and shows how a political scientist can find Hauerwas' writings and theology fruitful (and also give it substantial support).

Unlike Hauerwas, Cochran defends the importance of the distinction (but not the cleavage) between public and private, but he thinks that the way this distinction is conventionally used is completely incoherent. It is not only that the distinction is socially and historically constituted and therefore varies over time,[203] it is also impossible to place certain domains into the private or the public spheres. For instance, religion, family and sex, in liberal thought usually described as private, all have both private and public dimensions, depending on from which perspective they are seen. Religion, to take the central topic in Cochran's discussion, is fundamentally in itself both private and public. It does not only involve the individuals' relations with the transcendent, but is also a form of public and politi-

---

[201] *CET* 194.
[202] On the question when church discipline ought to be exercised, cf. Yoder, "Binding and Loosing", 214f.
[203] On this, see Elshtain, *Public Man, Private Woman*.

cal participation,[204] shapes character and virtue, requires a public space, and relates in various ways to "government politics". Religion consequently "inhabits the broad expanse where public and private life meet and overlap."[205] The book is therefore a discussion how the relation between the politics of the state and religion should be understood, a relation he conceptualizes as "connection through tension",[206] and which in his perspective has many dimensions and levels. We here find themes familiar from Hauerwas: the political importance of character and virtue, the place of narrative and tradition, the importance of the distinctiveness of religion, the multi-levelled relation between the languages of religious communities and the wider political discourses, to take a few examples that show the manifold relation between religion and politics.

This shows that Cochran's way of distinguishing but not separating public and private is complex and has many dimensions. Public and private do not represent fixed separate domains, but rather overlapping spheres involving different dimensions of human activities seen from different perspectives.[207] The point of this discussion is thus to say that issues dealt with through the public-private distinction cannot be avoided even in a perspective like Hauerwas'. But it might also be that discussing them in terms of public and private is less than helpful—for two reasons. First, today the conception is so closely identified with current liberalism that it can be very difficult not to let the discussion be determined by liberal understandings. Hauerwas' seemingly unqualified rejection of the language of private and public is easily read in the light of current liberal and anti-liberal discussions and consequently readily leads to misunderstandings.[208] Second, one might ask how meaningful it is to treat all these different topics under this one designation? We have seen that Hauerwas deals with them without using this language. This helps him to let his theological discourse be determined by Christian language and practice.

c) The Church Transformed by Liberalism

Although he at length has analysed and criticized modern liberal society, more important for him than criticizing liberal society "has been to offer a vision for the church (in particular, the integrity of the church) so that Christians might help negotiate the challenge of a liberal society."[209] Put differently, a main concern for

---

[204]See also Elshtain's constructive position in ibid., 298-353.
[205]Cochran, *Religion in Public and Private Life*, 43.
[206]Ibid., 150.
[207]"Private life is defined by such 'exclusionary' phenomena as the personal, shame and guilt, imperfection, and mystery and by the 'inclusionary' phenomena of integrity, trust, and intimacy. As distinctive experiences of human life, these form a tapestry of interwoven patterns defining a particular form of life. Public life has other distinct qualities. These include active participation in a common world, loyalty, trust, and narrative. The public world is closely associated with power and therefore with politics. Though the political and the public are not coextensive, they fit closely." (Ibid., 76f.)
[208]Cf. Elshtain, *Public Man, Private Woman*, 104, 217f.
[209]"Real Sectarian", 93.

him has been how the church might live and sustain a truthful life in the modern type of society so that it can witness to the kingdom of God. Consequently he is, for the sake of society, more concerned with criticizing the church's life than modern society as such.

For Hauerwas, then, it is very unfortunate that modern Christianity and theology have accepted the liberal vision to such an extent, and that theology so often sees it as its task to give theological legitimacy to the liberal project. It has been accepted, in different ways, that it is necessary to subordinate Christian convictions to the public liberal morality, although this is not construed in terms of subordination, because of the conviction that the liberal ideology of freedom and justice is a secular version of Christian understanding. The liberal democratic system is seen as fundamentally just. It keeps the state neutral and limited, and gives people the tools for creating a more just society.

One therefore fails to see, says Hauerwas, how liberalism slowly changes the life and faith of the churches themselves. A first way this is done is through the privatization of Christian convictions. Churches and theology have increasingly, though often in subtle ways, accepted the liberal relocation of religion to the private sphere. Religious truth has been separated from public truth and removed to the realm of personal "opinion". Religion is instead defended in terms of its functional value for individual and society. So we see Christianity defended because it gives meaning to personal life, reinforces traditional values or supports liberationist aspirations, not because it is true. One way this has been done in liberal society, is to point to the need for a civil religion to be a transcendent principle of criticism which can sustain the democratic system and ethos. Hauerwas points out the paradoxical situation this argument creates.

> Such a 'civil religion,' however, cannot be made up of any particularistic religious beliefs, since that would offend the necessity of religious tolerance. As a result all our more particularistic beliefs must be socially defined as 'private' and thus admitting of no social role. This situation creates a special irony, since the culture and political order that the 'civil religion' is asked to underwrite requires a disavowal of the public role of religious convictions—thus supporting the assumption that our religious opinions are just that, opinions.[210]

What happens then is that something called "faith" or "religion" in general takes priority over the actual convictions of Christian faith about reality. This is also seen in the so-called religious dialogue where liberalism functions as a meta-ideology that subsumes, relativizes and corrects all particular convictions of the different religions and at the same time creates a common language and a common ethos. What is accepted in liberal society is thus "tamed" religion, subscribed to

---

[210]*PK* 13. See also *SP* 75.

by people who do not take their own convictions too seriously, and who can sub-sume them under the interests of the liberal nation-state.[211]

The acceptance of liberalism has, secondly, led to a failure to articulate the connections between Christian convictions and Christian ethics. The attempt to separate the ethical from the religious has been a primary apologetic move to make Christianity relevant in a liberal society where this separation is one of its foundations. Hauerwas contends that the consequence of this separation of prac-tices from convictions is that both have lost their intelligibility.[212] They have lost the political context of the church as a contrast society that could make them in-telligible. Much of Hauerwas' writings are therefore attempts to show these con-nections. As seen previously, to do this he has had to challenge the moral theories of liberalism that presuppose this separation and develop alternatives.

The liberal convictions about freedom as freedom of choice and autonomy have individualized Christian faith and practice and given a legitimating language for the strongly individualizing processes of modernity. The result is, thirdly, that the church has become a consumer-oriented institution for helping people realize themselves in the way they desire (these desires are, however, strongly determi-ned by powerful social forces). It becomes "a life-style enclave and/or an um-brella institution"[213] for people of similar background and interests. When the "called church" in this way becomes the "voluntary church",[214] where the mem-bers are "consumers" of religious commodities, it becomes, he says, almost im-possible to form communities of discipleship. The language of discipleship im-plies the necessity of transformation and training of one's will and desires. It in-volves communal training and apprenticeship. But for people in a consumer soci-ety such language seems inherently authoritarian. Here basic liberal convictions support this consumer mentality. One deeply held assumption is that moral life does not require training. For Kantians what is required is rationality. For Ro-mantic thinkers, like (sometimes) Moltmann, the moral life is a sort of inner po-tential that has to be liberated so that it can be realized. In both accounts being liberated from one's communities and traditions is therefore a way to become truly moral.

> For the fundamental presumption behind democratic societies is that the consciousness of something called the *common citizen* is privileged no matter what kind of formation it may or may not have had. It is that presumption that gives rise to the very idea of ethics as an identifiable discipline within the modern university curriculum. Both Kant and the utilitari-ans assumed that the task of the ethicist was to explicate the presuppositions shared by

---

[211]*AC* 185 n. 1. Here he takes up the arguments of Milbank, "The End of Dialogue" and Surin, "A 'Politics of Speech'". On this theme, see further *PK* 12-16, *AC* 27-31, 69-92, and "The Kingship of Christ".
[212]*PK* 13, AC 23-27.
[213]*AC* 96.
[214]*AC* 94.

anyone. Ethics is the attempt at the systemization of what we all perhaps only inchoately know or which we have perhaps failed to make sufficiently explicit.[215]

In contrast a Christian ethics of discipleship sees the truthful life as being formed through being embedded in a communal tradition.[216] In a consumer-oriented society that makes freedom of choice the central value, talk of discipleship, of the epistemological importance of saints,[217] of the necessity of church and tradition seems then to restrict freedom. We have earlier seen how Hauerwas tries to answer this through an alternative account of freedom.[218]

A further consequence is that the inner political life of the church increasingly becomes a mirror of the liberal politics of the wider society. As Christian life increasingly becomes privatized and individualized, the Christian identity weakens, and common purposes and commitments decay. One result is that outside political divisions, like "conservative-liberal", become more important than the church identity. In the absence of common purposes and common language with which to discuss one's differences, procedural proceedings have become dominant and church politics becomes a power struggle between different special interest groups over the control of church bureaucracy. In such a situation, it is difficult even to imagine the possibility of alternative forms of politics.[219]

The result of all this is that the church loses its ability "to challenge the moral presuppositions of our polity and society"[220] and to form the kind of communities that could be called contrast societies. This is one of the most serious challenges for political theology. How to form and sustain such communities? How to make an intelligible account of discipleship? Of course, one could answer that political theology does not want to challenge these moral presuppositions. Part of its project is instead to accommodate Christianity to these presuppositions, to integrate the church into the liberal project. Its understanding of politics and power rather

---

[215]*AC* 97.

[216]This makes him also critical of the theories of moral development like the influential one (e.g. on Rawls and Habermas) by Kohlberg and the extensive Christian uses of them. He thinks this Kantian type of theory is what one should expect in liberal society, but that its uses for describing the Christian life are distorting, and that it like liberal ethics has an inadequate understanding of the processes of moral formation. See *CC* 129-152. He can for example write: "It is questionable, however, whether such a 'morality' is sufficient to produce good people. Martin Luther King, whom Kohlberg admires, would never have been produced nor would he have been effective if all we had was Kohlberg's sense of 'justice.' Rather Martin Luther King's vision was formed by the language of black Christianity, which gave him the power to seek 'justice' that can come only through the means of 'non-resistance.'" (*CC* 272 n. 15.)

[217]David Matzko writes: "The saint . . . is a scandal to modern morality because sainthood is a sign that every individual does not have an immediate reference to the good or the right. Sainthood is a scandal because it counters the modern moral standards of autonomy, freedom, and choice. Instead, it creates possibilities for community, apprenticeship, and veneration." ("Postmodernism, Saints and Scoundrels", 20.)

[218]See further *AC* 88, 93-111, *RA* 98-103, *CET* 195, 221-252, and *CC* 270 n. 7.

[219]Cf. Coalter, Mulder and Weeks (eds.), *The Organizational Revolution*.

[220]*CC* 73.

supports this development. Proponents of political theology have also been relatively successful in the struggle for control over many denominational and ecumenical bureaucracies, but they have in the Western world been less successful in forming local congregations. This is, however, only one side of political theology. We have seen that there is another that points in a very different direction. The difficulty is that Moltmann has not developed the sort of account that can make it credible.

So the irony with the current Christian defence of liberalism is, Hauerwas concludes, that its proponents "fail to see that the very forms of liberal tolerance they took up . . . ironically undercut the seriousness of Christian convictions that were necessary to form limited states to begin with."[221] One of the Christian roots of liberalism was dissenting churches that could say "No" to the state. However, the way liberalism, supported by Christian leaders and theologians, has transformed the churches has had as a result that "Christianity cannot any longer maintain the kinds of disciplined communities that are necessary to keep the state limited."[222] Hauerwas' critique is therefore first of all directed to Christians.

---

[221]"Faith in the Republic", 471.

[222]Ibid., 471. "What advocates of this stance often overlooked, however, in their enthusiasm for liberal society was that such a society made the internal discipline necessary to sustain a free church as an independent and socially significant presence appear arbitrary and coercive. Moreover, they failed to see that the kind of 'constitutional' democracy of the free church was radically transformed when translated into the language of liberalism." (*CC* 253 n. 37.)

Chapter 13

The Peaceful Church in a World of War

I have used the questions concerning peace and violence for an extensive and concrete explanation of how the political theology of Moltmann works. I will use the same approach to elucidate Hauerwas' Radical Reformation theology. This is particularly appropriate not only because Hauerwas has written so much on these specific issues, but also because peace is fundamental to the branch of Radical Reformation tradition (whose churches are often called the "historic peace churches") Hauerwas most closely identifies himself with.[1] As already seen, for Hauerwas peace is not only an ethical position, but it in fact determines his whole theology, both methodologically and substantially. As he says, "nonviolence is not just one implication among others that can be drawn from our Christian beliefs; it is at the very heart of our understanding of God."[2] In this chapter we will see how he discusses violence, war and peace, and how this discussion interrelates with the themes we have encountered earlier.[3] This will also further clarify the dilemmas of Moltmann's theology and to what a consistent development of Moltmann's later peace theology might lead.

1. Jesus Christ and the Ecclesial Interruption of the History of Violence

Jesus Christ inaugurated the kingdom of God, which through history is continuously (though not exclusively) manifested in the church. This means a radical interruption in the history of war and violence by an alternative history, by an alternative *polis*, or, to use the expression of John Milbank, by a new "socio-linguistic practice"[4] built on the conviction that peace is ontologically more basic than violence, because that is the way God rules the creation. That is the basic claim of the Radical Reformation theology of Hauerwas; a claim Moltmann in his later theology comes (at least) close to affirming.

---

[1] The literature here is overwhelming. For two recent examples of current work inside this tradition, see Swartley (ed.), *Essays on Peace Theology and Witness* and *The Conrad Grebel Review* 10:3, 1992.

[2] *PK* xvii.

[3] His pacifist convictions grew only slowly and reluctantly in the confrontation with the theology of Yoder. See *PK* xxiv, "Pacifism: A Form of Politics", 133-135, and *DFF* 117f. "Brought up on the thought of Reinhold Niebuhr, I simply assumed that pacifism, even if it could be justified theologically, could never sustain an intelligible social and political ethic." ("Foreword" to Friesen, *Christian Peacemaking and International Conflict*, 11.) He deals with these questions esp. in *PK, AN* chapters 6 and 8-10, *CET* chapters 4 and 14, and in "Epilogue". To this comes some further articles, of which two are mentioned in this note, and others will be mentioned below.

[4] *Theology and Social Theory*, 381.

a) The Character of Radical Reformation Pacifism

Non-violence is thus for Hauerwas not just an ethical ideal. It is instead a risk one can take because the life, death, and resurrection of Jesus show that this is the way God deals with the world, and because the kingdom of God is present.

> The reason I believe Christians have been given the permission, that is, why it is good news for us, to live without resort to violence is that by doing so we live as God lives. Therefore pacifism is not first of all a prohibition, but an affirmation that God wills to rule his creation not through violence and coercion but by love. Moreover he has called us to be part of his rule by calling us into a community that is governed by peace.[5]

This means that Christian pacifism for Hauerwas is not a general ethical position, in abstraction from Christian convictions, practices and common life, on the issue of whether or not it is allowable in some circumstances to kill or not. As he himself expresses it: "From this perspective, Christian non-violence or pacifism does not name a position; rather, it denotes a set of convictions and corresponding practices of a particular kind of people."[6] He does not try to argue his case for "everyone" separated from a specific community's convictions and practices. What is deemed possible and practical is dependent on how reality is construed and the practices available in the community in question. This changes through history, just as pacifism does. Consequently there are many different historically constituted sorts of pacifism, of which some have little in common with the sort of Christian pacifism Hauerwas describes.[7]

This means also, as we should expect by now, that he builds Christian pacifism neither on some individual biblical texts, nor on the New Testament or the Bible in general taken in separation from the church's practices. One cannot ask in the abstract if the New Testament requires pacifism, both because there is no pacifism as such and because how the church's life is constituted determines the way the Bible is read. A common question concerning the Sermon on the Mount has been whether it is applicable on an individual level alone or also on a national level. This, he claims, misunderstands the context of the Sermon, because its social and political locus is the church as a contrast society. It is a political ethics concerned with the life of the new *polis* called the church.[8] The text is read differently if the context and assumptions are the ones of some contemporary state or the international system, the abstract independent individual left to his or her own resources, or if it is a community living with the stories of the Crucified and

---

[5]"Pacifism: Some Philosophical Considerations", 99.

[6]*DFF* 120. So also "Epilogue", 162f.

[7]*DFF* 117-123. On the great variety of forms of pacifism, see Yoder's *Nevertheless*.

[8]He therefore says: "But the Sermon does not generate an ethic of non-violence, but rather demands the existence of a community of non-violence so that the world might know that as God's creatures we are meant to live peaceably with one another." ("The Sermon on the Mount, Just War and the Quest for Peace", 42.)

Resurrected Jesus Christ, trained in Christian practices such as forgiveness and reconciliation, and dependent and trusting upon the community's responsibility and care. Jesus does not describe some general "truth", for example that "love for one's enemies transforms them into friends," but a form of life that has become possible because of Jesus Christ and which is liveable not as an individual stance, but as the common life of the church. Christian pacifism and its reading of the Bible thus presuppose a christological, eschatological, and ecclesial context.[9] He therefore also contends that the early Christians did not understand themselves as pacifists, but solely as disciples of Jesus Christ. The peaceful life was an integrated part of this life of discipleship.[10]

His interrelation of the Sermon on the Mount to the whole life and destiny of Jesus also leads him to regard as false the sharp distinction some (for example Paul Ramsey following Reinhold Niebuhr) make between non-resistance and non-violent resistance. Read in isolation, the Sermon on the Mount might be seen as questioning any form of resistance. In this view the distinction between nonresistance and resistance is more important than the distinction between non-violent and violent resistance.[11] Hauerwas does not accept this distinction—for three reasons. First, it misrepresents Jesus' life and work, which was about a confrontation with the powers that enslave people. But the means of confrontation were not the means of the powers themselves. And it was precisely this refusal to use the means of the powers that made him victorious.[12] Second, he believes that one reason behind this argument is the widespread tendency to summarize the ethic of Jesus in terms of love, a love understood to be disinterested and impartial. This misses that Jesus proclaimed the kingdom of God and not a general love ethic, and even misunderstands what Christian love is.[13] Third, this view assumes an essentialistic view of the nature of state, politics, violence and non-violence that we have seen that Hauerwas opposes. Niebuhr considers all social life, by defini-

---

[9]"When the Sermon [on the Mount] is divorced from this ecclesial context it cannot help but appear as a 'law' to be applied to and by individuals. But that is contrary to fundamental presuppositions of the Sermon which is that individuals divorced from the community are incapable of living the life the Sermon depicts. To understand the Sermon as an ethic for individuals is to turn the Sermon into a new law with endless legalistic variations. The Sermon is only intelligible against the presumption that a new eschatological community has been brought into existence that makes a new way of life possible. All the so-called 'hard sayings' of the Sermon are designed to remind us that we cannot live without depending on the support and trust of others." ("The Sermon on the Mount", 39f, see also *DFF* 117-123 and "On the Ethics of War and Peace", 153.) In the text from which the quotation is taken he uses the same work of Lohfink that Moltmann uses in a similar way. See Lohfink's *Jesus and Community* (which Hauerwas uses here) and the later *Wem gilt die Bergpredigt?*

[10]"The Sermon on the Mount", 41.

[11]See Ramsey's questions to Hauerwas and Yoder in *Speak Up for Just War or Pacifism*, 115-120 (cf. also ibid., 73-76) and Niebuhr, *Moral Man and Immoral Society*, esp. 240-252. Ramsey writes (p. 74): "Nonviolence as a political or military strategy seems to me to be war (or *revolution*) by other means, under another name." He takes Gandhi and Martin Luther King as examples.

[12]"Epilogue", 177-180.

[13]"Epilogue", 177f, *US* 92-98, *VV* 111-126.

tion, coercive, which means that all participation in social and political life by necessity implies involvement in coercion.[14] The sort of Christian pacifism Hauerwas defends does not start with a theory of the essence of violence and non-violence, but with certain practices that form the community's life and lead it to interpret social life and action in certain ways. "Such a community has no stake in
the assumption that a hard-and-fast distinction can be or needs to be made between what is violent and what is not."[15] He can thus not in the abstract discuss
what Christian pacifism involves. So-called non-violent resistance should, therefore, be judged in terms of the larger network of Christian convictions and practices, and should not be defended or discarded as a whole. He similarly thinks the
same sort of discriminating analysis has to be done concerning violence, because
not all violence is the same. To take one example: because of its institutional
context and limits police power can represent a less violent form of violence. He
likewise thinks that a just war doctrine might function similarly, although the institutional context here is much weaker.[16]

b) Two Histories

Because of their convictions Christians not only interpret history in a specific
way, they also are called to embody a different history. It is therefore Hauerwas
can say that "more important than the principles used to judge war are the narratives through which we enact and interpret war."[17] Furthermore, their interpretative ability is interconnected with their practices. This is a theme we have repeatedly encountered.

In the story that Christians should tell, according to Hauerwas, Jesus Christ
and the church should not be subsumed in a narrative where the state or the
Western civilization is the primary actor.[18] The church tells another story, a story
of an ecclesial interruption, based on Jesus Christ, of the world's violent history,
of the church's attempt to witness to and live an alternative, although this history
is also a story of severe failures with tragic consequences.

To clarify this point it would have been helpful if he, in a more developed
way, had described, so to say, the genealogies of war and peace. One example of
how such a history might be told is the political scientist Jean Bethke Elshtain's
account of the discourse of war and politics from the Greeks to today as a history
of armed civic virtue and Christianity's attempt to disarm this civic virtue.[19] The
purpose with this long "excursus", which still gives only a bare outline of the
story Elshtain tells, is twofold. First, it will hopefully make Hauerwas' account of

---

[14]Niebuhr writes that "society is in a perpetual state of war" (*Moral Man and Immoral Society*, 19).
[15]*DFF* 130.
[16]Ibid., 20-28 and "Epilogue", 161f. To Ramsey, one might likewise ask what he means with nonresistance. Does it exclude e.g. non-obedience to prohibitions to preach the Gospel?
[17]"Epilogue", 165.
[18]"Creation, Contingency, and Truthful Non-Violence", 11.
[19]*Women and War*, 45-159.

how the Christian history interrupts the world's basically agonistic histories more concrete and thus more intelligible. His theology would generally benefit from more historical work in the genealogical sense. As it now is, he gives extremely suggestive genealogical comments and short-hand histories, but usually not much more.[20] My use of Elshtain does not, however, suggest that this is exactly the way Hauerwas would tell the story. He has positively used her book and they have much in common, but there are also differences in their respective commitments.[21] A second reason for choosing her account is the way she, like Hauerwas, connects the Enlightenment traditions of liberalism and socialism, the emergence of the nation-state, and modern war. This not only confirms and clarifies Hauerwas' account, but also illuminates the significance of how the history of modernity is interpreted for explicating the different turns Hauerwas' and Moltmann's theologies take.

Elshtain starts her account[22] with the assertion that "in the beginning, politics was war. . . . For the Greeks, war was a natural state and the basis of society. The Greek city-state was a community of warriors."[23] In the heroic stories, which formed expectations and practices, glory and honour understood in terms of physical courage was crucial. However, a new form of discourse on war is found in Plato and Aristotle, where the *polites* have taken the primary place from the warrior. War is for Plato "a regularized collective activity, undertaken from civic necessity"[24] for the sake of the ordered *polis*, and not for personal vengeance or honour.

From the Greeks Elshtain turns to Machiavelli (later returning to the Christian interruption). Machiavelli's wish is to revive the armed virtues of the Greek republican tradition, but he replaces the transcendent good with will. His goal is the self-sufficiency and unity of the republic, which is to be both created and defended by the disciplined and committed army of citizens. Deeply critical of the soft Christian virtues, he therefore celebrates virtues useful from the perspective of statecraft. War thus comes to symbolize solidarity. Elshtain concludes that "Machiavellian themes echo throughout the subsequent history of political discourse in the West."[25]

---

[20] In this respect, Yoder (see e.g. *Christian Attitudes to War, Peace, and Revolution*) and Milbank (*Theology and Social Theory*) are more helpful. Hauerwas' forthcoming *Christian Ethics in America* promises to be an example of what I am asking for.

[21] In "The Difference of Virtue and the Difference It Makes", 250, Hauerwas shortly uses another (shorter but similar) version of Elshtain's account in the way I do here. See also "Epilogue", 165 and "Critic's Choices for Christmas", 708 for his very positive assessments of her book.

[22] What she is doing here is not telling "a chronological history of war and politics" Her interest is instead the interconnections between narratives and the activities of politics and war, because "stories of war and politics structure individual and collective experience in ways that set the horizon for human expectations in later epochs." (*Women and War*, 48.)

[23] Ibid., 47.

[24] Ibid., 53.

[25] Ibid., 59.

Another "of the great prophets of armed civic virtue"[26] is Rousseau. For him "Christian" and "republican" stands for mutually exclusive claims and understandings of life. Christianity is dangerous, both because it espouses an ethos useful only for slaves and because it represents a particular interest against the general interest of the nation; that is, it stands between the nation and the citizen. Elshtain writes that for Rousseau "the polity must be as one; the national will must not be divided; citizens must be prepared to defend civic autonomy through force of arms; whatever puts the individual at odds with himself is a threat to '*la nation une et indivisible*'."[27] Consequently he stresses the importance of civic education for the instilling of the primacy of the nation and of military virtue.

Rousseau's ideas were important for many of the leaders of the French revolution, giving a language for the development of the nation-state, the institution of national conscription, and therefore for the emergence of modern total wars. Elshtain shows how compulsory military service was a chief factor in breaking the primacy of local and regional identities and for the forming of national identities during the nineteenth and the early twentieth centuries.[28] This is mirrored in the discourse of Hegel on the vital and necessary historic force of war. For him, Elshtain says, "[w]ar-constituted solidarity is immanent within the state form" and helps relativize "the atomized world of civil society".[29] Marx, Engels, and Lenin, and their followers could similarly talk about the inevitableness and necessity of violence and war. There are historic people destined to triumph and others destined to perish. Especially important for them, however, was the contribution of general war as paving the way for revolutionary transformations. Consequently, the virtues of revolutionary war are instilled. Lenin even treats violence as an ordinary means rather than as an extraordinary; thereby he really substitutes violence for politics. All this in the name of final peace.[30]

The technological and industrial growth of the nineteenth century combined with the resulting explosion of military capabilities was used to radically strengthen national sovereignty and the internal control of the nation-state. To this comes nationalism. She writes that

> the fusion of the nationalist idea with the nation-state apparatus is a particular historic configuration, one that remains dominant either as a political aim (for previously colonized peoples, for example) or as an extant reality to be endorsed or challenged. The nation-state now enframes, for better or for worse, the political actions and identities of the vast majority of men and women.[31]

---

[26]Ibid., 62. For Hauerwas on Rousseau, see *AN* 180-183. He has later partly criticized the way he used Rousseau in this text. See "Epilogue", 176f.
[27]Elshtain, *Women and War*, 60.
[28]Ibid., 63-66, 106-120.
[29]Ibid., 74.
[30]Ibid., 80-86.
[31]Ibid., 107f.

She thinks the World War I was pivotal both as a means to realize national identity and unity (which meant the subversion of more local identities) and to strengthen the state both in Europe and America.[32] But this war also revealed the terrible cost of the dreams of modern nationalism.

In relation to Hauerwas' claims, it is also significant that the discourse of national armed virtue is not only carried by conservative nationalists, or fascists and nazis, but in societies like the USA by the "progressive" liberals, for whom "schools and the army became the great engines of the nationalization of America."[33] The aim is Americanization, the means are the schools telling about the good wars America has fought, and the homogenizing effect of universal military conscription, and thereby the strengthening of the state. Dissent is seen as disloyalty.

Hauerwas maintains that Christianity has inaugurated an alternative history, a counter discourse and practice. Elshtain also traces the history of this alternative discourse. "Finding in the 'paths of peace' the most natural as well as the most desirable way of being, Christian pioneers exalted a pacific ontology."[34] She sees this as an interruption, as the inauguration of something new in history, a "counter politics."[35] After discussing Jesus and the early church, she claims that "[t]his sort of principled resistance to public power was something new under the sun, opening up a range of options, duties, responsibilities, dilemmas, and reassessments not available in classical antiquity, bearing implications for men and women alike."[36] How to interpret the early church's resistance to military service is controversial. Elshtain, though not herself defending pacifism, seems to agree with the scholars that maintain that pacifism was crucial to this practice, against some who think the main reason was that military service entailed idolatry.[37] However,

---

[32]Ibid., 106-108. E.g., "a *united* United States is a historic construction that most visibly comes into being as cause and consequence of American involvement in the Great War." (Ibid., 108.)

[33]Ibid., 117. She writes that "progressive and liberal opinion proved particularly susceptible to the cry for unity because of its stress on popular sovereignty, on the 'voice' of the 'people,' the notion that there must be some common civic glue to bind the nation as one." (Ibid., 119.)

[34]Ibid., 122.

[35]Ibid., 124.

[36]Ibid., 126. She refers, among others, to the two historians Roland Bainton and Peter Brock, who both claim that, in Brock's words, "[t]here is no known instance of conscientious objection to participation in war or the advocacy of such objection before the Christian era." (*Pacifism in Europe to 1914*, 3. For Bainton, see *Christian Attitudes toward War and Peace*, 53.) Brock further claims that this phenomenon is universally unique, even if ideas of non-violence have been articulated elsewhere.

[37]Hauerwas maintains the former view. After recognizing that there were several related reasons, he says that "I think there can be no doubt that the fundamental reason the early Christians had an aversion to military service . . . was their faithfulness to the example of Jesus. They simply did not believe they could be followers of Jesus and at the same time pick up arms against the enemy." ("Christianity and War", 1C.) For Yoder's discussion of this, see *Christian Attitudes*, 21-35. The modern study of this issue was initiated by Harnack's *Militia Christi* (for two good overviews and discussions of the research, see Gracie's introduction to the recent English translation of this book, and, on the most recent period, Hunter, "A Decade of Research on Early Christians and Military Service") who concluded that bloodshed was in principle rejected in early Christianity. The pacifist element was even more strongly

most would agree that Christianity in a new way gives peace primacy. The burden of proof is with those who advocate the use of violence, and not the other way around. Both the pacifist tradition and the tradition of just war not only agree on giving the burden of proof to the use of violence, but both also "evaluate social life *from the standpoint* of suffering, potential or actual victims, rather than of the triumphant, the victors."[38]

Her account continues with a positive discussion of Augustine's contribution,[39] through a discussion of the crusades, to a description of the medieval church's attempts through a long range of prohibitions to restrain the use of violence in spite of the uneasy coexistence it had to endure with the warrior codes of the political elite. Like Hauerwas and Moltmann she further sees the Reformation, especially in its Lutheran form of overpersonalization of faith, separation of public and private morality, and enhancement of secular authority, as a release of the political regimes from the constraints of the medieval church. She therefore contends that "Luther prepares the way for the political theology that underlies the emergence of the nation-state. . . . Centuries scarred by religious wars are one

---

stressed in Cadoux, *The Early Christian Attitude to War,* Bainton, *Christian Attitudes,* 53-84, and Hornus, *It Is Not Lawful For Me To Fight.* This pacifist consensus has recently been vigorously questioned in some recent studies. See Johnson, *The Quest for Peace,* 3-66, Helgeland, "Christians and the Roman Army A.D. 173-337", and Helgeland, Daly and Burns, *Christians and the Military.* Johnson argues that the probable context for understanding the first century church is their "desire to separate themselves from the world so as to live the morally pure life of the 'new age' that they expected soon to dawn" (p. 13). Later the most important motif was the question of idolatry. The most valuable aspect of Helgeland's work is the way he shows the strongly religious character of the life in the Roman army. (For sharp criticism of parts of the accounts of Johnson and Helgeland et. al., see Hunter, "Decade of Research", 87-91.) The according to Hunter "easily the best" (p. 91) of the recent studies is Swift, *The Early Fathers on War and Military Service.* Swift agrees with the earlier pacifist consensus that pacifist arguments were part of the early church's refusal to be part of the army and that the reign of Constantine involved a major shift. But he does not want to describe this shift as a reversal, because it "was made possible by earlier ambiguities and disagreements concerning the use of coercion and made necessary by the altered political circumstances in which Christians now found themselves" (p. 29). The "necessary" in this Hauerwas would not accept, neither Swift's use of Troeltsch's sect-church typology as an interpretative grid in his reading of early Christian texts. Concerning the views of Johnson and Helgeland et. al. (which are not identical), we have seen that Hauerwas neither accepts their understanding of the eschatology of the early church, nor the separation of the question of violence from the wider context of the church's relation to the world (and especially not the separation of "religious" and "ethical" concerns Helgeland works with) that their argument seems to imply. Yoder writes, commenting on Helgeland's and (an earlier version of) Johnson's arguments, that the pacifism of the early church "did not stand by itself. Christians stood in a polar relationship to the whole authority structure for every possible reason. Their rejection of the shedding of blood was just one coherent part of the polar whole." Furthermore, on practical, but not systematic, grounds "the fact of Caesar was a global fact. The idolatry, the violence, the circuses, the public abuse of minorities and enemies and feeding people to the lions for the fun of the crowd, and war, and empire, were all one package." (*Christian Attitudes,* 26f.)

[38]Elshtain, *Women and War,* 123.

[39]"Augustine's way of working things through is an exemplary alternative to the abstract, rationalist castings of much contemporary political and moral thought." (Ibid., 129.)

result of the turn."[40] She furthermore, again like Hauerwas, maintains that this crusading ethos does not disappear with the Enlightenment and the coming secularization, but reappears as the militarism of the nation-states —often strongly supported by the established national churches as well as by the not formally established American churches.

> The discourse of armed civic virtue and the ferocious excesses of holy war pursued for the state rather than for God came together in a way that fused undisguised *machtpolitik* with assumptions of state divinity, canalizing popular sentiment into collective enthusiasm for the 'state ideal' as the self-identity and definition of 'a people'; integrating whole populations into mobilized political patterns; producing young men prepared to make the 'supreme sacrifice' and young women prepared to see to it that they did.[41]

Elshtain then ends this part of her account with a discussion of what she considers to be the unhappy fate of the just war-tradition in Christian and secular thought, and then suggests that a retrieval of the thought of Augustine might be helpful.[42]

Elshtain's account gives more historical concreteness to Hauerwas' talk about the way the alternative story of the church has interrupted, but also often been integrated into, the world's history of violence. Where they differ is in Hauerwas' more critical attitude to the just war tradition (which makes him even more critical of the church's historical role since the fourth century) and in the importance he gives to the peace witness in the Radical Reformation tradition. He thinks that Christian pacifism and just war "draw on different assumptions about history and its relation to God's kingdom."[43] The latter is an ethics for states. It still makes the state the primary agent for God's providential care. Christian pacifism, on the other hand, claims that "the church is God's sign that war is not part of his providential care of the world."[44] This does not imply an automatic change of the state, but that a new *polis* living with and witnessing to an alternative history has been inaugurated, which also can, as has repeatedly been the case, lead to smaller or larger changes in the way the power of states is exercised. Consequently, if he were to tell the history of the Christian interruption he would need to tell also the history of the continued practices and failures of Christian pacifism after the Constantinian turn.[45]

Hauerwas agrees with the close connections Elshtain makes between the emergence of the modern nation-state, militarism and war, and liberal ideology. This is a major reason behind his critical stance towards liberalism, but also towards the civic republican tradition. We have seen that he, on the one hand, can

---

[40]Ibid., 136. See further on this her *Meditations on Modern Political Thought*, 5-20.

[41]*Women and War*, 137.

[42]Ibid., 149-159.

[43]*AN* 195.

[44]*AN* 197.

[45]Yoder's *Christian Attitudes* is the best example of the direction such a history would take. Because of its ahistorical and static definition of pacifism, Hauerwas is critical of the way Bainton writes this history in his classical *Christian Attitudes*. See *DFF* 118f.

describe the Enlightenment as a secularization of the Christian vision of peace and deplore the severe failings of the church to uphold its witness to peace. On the other hand, the Enlightenment and the liberal and socialist ideologies became also instrumental in the development of the modern nation-states. Their universalistic pretensions became the ideological backbone for breaking down and marginalizing all other claims to loyalty in the name of the nation-state's claim to supreme loyalty. Instead of killing in the name of religion, people were trained to kill in the name of the nation-state.[46]

Furthermore, he asks how liberalism is able to give an intelligible account of the nation-state as a geographical construct. He thinks most political philosophy simply seems to ignore territoriality, concentrating instead on placeless concepts like rights, democracy, and so on, which gives liberal political philosophy a certain air of unreality and also makes it difficult to intelligibly discuss for instance the recent events in Eastern Europe.[47] Anthony Giddens, whose work Hauerwas partly draws on, has also noted and discussed the similar peculiar absence in modern sociology and social theory (in both its socialist and liberal forms) of examinations of modern 'society' (i.e., its object of study) *as* nation-states and of the role of military institutions and violence in modern society.[48] Borders are not based on intelligible universal principles, but on historical accidents, of which war is the most important.[49]

Hauerwas' answer to the charge that his stress on the distinctiveness and primacy of the church means a retribalization in contrast to the universal claims of liberalism is thus that the (usually taken for granted and not argued) primacy of the nation-state is "the most nefarious brand of tribalism of all."[50] Giving the nation-state first loyalty is, from the Christian perspective, idolatry. He asks how Christians can kill other Christians in the name of the nation-state.[51] Because the

---

[46]He even says that "the rise of democracy went hand in hand with the rise of the violence in war. Ironically, authoritarian regimes have greater freedom to fight limited wars since they do not need to use ideals to convince a reluctant populace that they should support and fight for something from which they would receive little personal benefit. The modern scale of war, and perhaps the modern scale of weaponry, are correlative to our democratic convictions and institutions." (*AN* 148.) He is here using Michael Howard's *War and the Liberal Conscience*.

[47]*AC* 33-35, "A Communitarian Lament", 46.

[48]*The Nation-State and Violence*, 22-31. Giddens is also dissatisfied by 'right-liberal' and conservative thought. Although it discusses these issues more, "it tends to see violence and war as an inescapable part of the human condition" (p. 27) and therefore tends to neglect the novelty of the modern nation-state.

[49]On the imaginary nature of the nation and the role of nationalism in the formation of modern nation-states, see Anderson, *Imagined Communities*.

[50]*RA* 42. "Indeed, I find it odd that those who are so committed to the liberal values of the Enlightenment characterize the pacifist position as sectarian since they are usually the ones that develop justifications for Christians in one country killing Christians in another country on grounds of some value entailed by national loyalties. Surely if any position deserves the name 'sectarian' it is this, since it qualifies the unity of the church in the name of a loyalty other than that to the Kingdom of God." (*AN* 7.)

[51]*US* 63.

church for him is "global, transnational, transcultural,"[52] he consequently is critical of the idea of national churches and Christian nationalism. He therefore also agrees with Moltmann on the political importance of the ecumenical movement challenging the tribalism of the nations.[53]

The discourse carrying the so-called universalism of the Enlightenment vision has been liberalism (and its cousin socialism). Its universal claims has actually resulted in a false universalism, that has suppressed minority voices. Hauerwas, again like Elshtain, sees the educational system (besides the army) as a crucial instrument in this process. For the purpose of fostering communication and in the name of objectivity the convictions and practices of all other discourses than the one of the nation-state, including the Christian, have been marginalized and privatized. One example he mentions is how the story "the United States" is told in American schools as an objective story of peace and unity. From the perspective of native Americans, however, it more looks like a history of violence (ethnic cleansing we might say today), but the history of the natives is only told as it fits into the larger controlling history. The significance of this is clarified by his words that "the most determinative moral training we provide in schools is the history told and/or presupposed not only in courses specifically in history, but throughout the curriculum."[54] This history gives the language required for living in the American society, which explains why it is so difficult to resist it or to take alternative renderings seriously as *real* alternatives.[55] The church should be a concrete community telling and witnessing to another story. But the prize for questioning the dominant story is high, because the dominant discourse, claiming that it is unbiased and objective, determines what can be taken seriously in the public debate.

c) Virtues of a Peaceful Church

In the Hauerwasian perspective it is the life and witness of the church and not the nation-state (or the process to a coming world-state) that represents the true

---

[52]*RA* 42.

[53]"For now the ecumenical movement can be seen not just as a theological necessity, but rather as the most significant political act the church can perform for the world. . . . So the unity of the church—and we must remember that our deepest disunity is not between Catholics and Protestants, but that between classes, races, nationalities, hemispheres, etc.—becomes the prerequisite for our serving the world as God's peaceable community." ("The Sermon on the Mount", 42.)

[54]*AC* 136. See further *AC* 133-152. Cf. his similar accounts of Vietnam and black slavery in "Forgiveness and Political Community".

[55]He writes that "there is little attempt to resist the story we call the 'United States' because it contains the language necessary for us to do business. If you employed the alternative understanding of United States—as a violent process—you could not negotiate the everyday." (*AC* 141.) Cf. further his comment that we, also through our social orders and institutions, "enter into conspiracies of illusion to secure order because we rightly fear the anarchy and violence of disorder. We desire normalcy and safety even if that normalcy and safety is achieved at the expense of others. That is why there can finally be no separation of justice from truthfulness, for often demands for the former are challenges to our assumptions about the 'way things are.'" (*PK* 142.)

history of the world. To be able to sustain this witness the church has to be a community of virtue. The church should be a people offering alternative ways of dealing with conflict, of responding to violence and enemies, of dealing with tragedy, and so on. It thus must have a "spirituality of peaceableness."[56] Here we meet again one of the most significant differences between Moltmann's political theology and Hauerwas' theological politics. Moltmann concentrates on how the church can contribute to the reformation (or revolution) of the state-system (both internally and externally) that, he hopes, finally will lead to a just and peaceful world-state. According to Hauerwas the church does not offer a model for the reformation of the system of nation-states, but offers itself as an alternative.[57] The stress then is on the practices and virtues that can sustain a life in peace. "Christian non-violence, in short, does not begin with a theory or conception about violence, war, 'the state or society,' and so on, but rather with practices such as forgiveness and reconciliation."[58] Which effects on the world society it will have, if it is faithful, it does not know.

Hauerwas confronts these issues in several, complementing ways. The church's practice of *forgiveness*,[59] becomes for him especially significant. The church can be a peaceful people only as a *forgiven* people at peace with itself and its history and therefore not fearing the other. Forgiveness thus has political significance. That the church most often has relegated forgiveness to only the personal sphere is, he thinks, one of its "most glaring failures".[60] In an article discussing the place of black slavery and the Vietnam War in American history, he says that it is only as a society that faces its need to be forgiven for its involvement in Vietnam and slavery, and thus making the suffering this caused "integral to our social and personal histories",[61] that it can adequately remember and live with its past and reestablish community. In the tradition he stands, forgiveness does not, however, exclude punishment and restitution.[62] In a parallel way he thinks forgiveness is also important in the dealings inside a society for forming good polities. Because of a view of politics that stresses its character as a naked power game we do not only fail to see this, but we also "overlook the ever-present reality of forgiveness . . . how much of our life is made up of implicit promises to forgive",[63] in friendship and marriage as well as in politics.

---

[56]*PK* 135.
[57]Cf. "In Praise of *Centesimus Annus*", 417f.
[58]*DFF* 130.
[59]See above p. 195.
[60]"Forgiveness and Political Community", 16.
[61]Ibid., 16.
[62]He writes: "punishment often is a crucial gesture to guard against the trivialization of forgiveness. Genuine forgiveness is always painful and costly." (Ibid., 16.) See also *DFF* 80-88.
[63]"Forgiveness and Political Community", 15. Cf. further *US* 140-148 and "In Response: Forgiveness and Forgetting". See also Gunton, *The Actuality of Atonement*, 188-195. For a secular reflection on the political relevance of what she calls Jesus' discovery of the role of forgiveness, see Arendt, *The Human Condition*, 212-219.

We have also already seen the importance he gives to *hope* and *patience* for sustaining a life of peace in a world of oppression and violence.[64] Hope and patience are needed to face the tragedies that the convictions of Christian pacifists will entail. They will sometimes see others die unjustly, without being able to do anything. They may also create conflicts because they reveal illusions that have been basic to the current order. The Christian hope is, however, not a Stoic hope, because the kingdom of God challenges the current violent order. Neither is it built on an utopian hope that non-violence guarantees peace or that the historical processes in themselves will overcome the "folly of war". Instead, the Christian hope is in the God that "has already determined the end of history in the cross and resurrection of Jesus Christ."[65] But this does not guarantee any immediate success. Christian pacifism is not a method or an alternative strategy in which cause and effect can be calculated. In that sense it does not require an optimistic description of current realities and can in its analysis often have more in common with "realism" than with humanistic pacifism. Hope creates the space for a truthful seeing of the world. Hope, he says, is different from optimism in that the latter can exist without truth and therefore easily turns into cynicism and despair when defeated. The cynic does not look for alternatives to power. In contrast, hope "is based on truth and forces the imagination to look for alternatives. If we are unable to look for alternatives, we are forced to rely on power. Hope is therefore an alternative to reliance on power."[66] Furthermore, "hope varies inversely with the absoluteness of one's *trust* in power. Hope declines as trust in power increases, and this seems to happen because hope declines as one's sense of alternatives narrows."[67] The Christian hope based on Jesus Christ thus gives the ground for overcoming cynicism and for seeing alternatives.

This will not eliminate tragedy and the church, he says, must be able to absorb these tragedies. Furthermore, as a community in which people are trained in the habits and the practices of peace, and in the sort of communal discernment that knows when to say "No", when the state or some other power group makes demands that they should resist, it must be a community that provide courage and the possibility to say this "No". The church thus must be the sort of community that can carry the sometimes severe personal and communal consequences of its pacifist life. It therefore also "requires learning to trust in others to help me so

---

[64]See above p. 198. On the following, see *PK* 135-151.

[65]*PK* 145.

[66]*CET* 201.

[67]*CET* 202. "The words for *that* play are 'Somebody has to do it,' or 'What else are you going to do?'" (*CET* 212.) "The way power corrupts is by gradually convincing those who have power that the most important thing is to be effective." (*CET* 213.) For his extended analysis of this theme, see *CET* 199-219.

live",[68] that is, it requires dependency and therefore is not intelligible in a society that makes autonomy primary.[69]

But he stresses also that this patient hope "is not some means to a greater good, but the good itself."[70] It presupposes the recognition that human people are not created violent and that God through Christ has made the non-violent life a possibility. This is the life for which humans are created and redeemed. He has therefore been deeply critical of letting the nuclear threat wholly determine life and theology, a tendency we find in Moltmann's writings. In one of his most eloquent texts with the telling title "Taking Time for Peace: the Ethical Significance of the Trivial"[71] he describes this attitude as totalitarian. It is totalitarian because it lets the bomb, and the struggle to eliminate the threat, determine every aspect of life. Nothing in everyday life can be indifferent to this struggle. Because it lets this threat relativize any other value the risk is also that we will work for a false peace, because any means that might lessen the threat might seem obligatory. But Christians, because of their convictions about God's ultimate rule over the world through Jesus Christ should not accept this attitude. They should not let their lives be determined by this or any other totalitarian claim. Instead they should take the time to go on living, seeing the importance of their daily life. He says

> that there is no more powerful response to totalitarians than to take the time to reclaim life from their power. By refusing to let them claim every aspect of our life as politically significant, we create the space and time that makes politics humane. Therefore, there is nothing more important for us to do in the face of the threat of nuclear war than go on living—that is, to take the time to enjoy a walk with a friend, to read all of Trollope's novels, to maintain universities, to have and care for children, and most importantly, to worship God.[72]

He thus maintains that it is through such a life we can find a worthwhile peace, and also the capacity not to copy the forces, attitudes, and habits that created the

---

[68]*US* 64.

[69]*PK* 113, 144-146, "The Sermon on the Mount", 39f. McClendon's discussion of Bonhoeffer's life in *Systematic Theology: Ethics*, 187-208 is in this context illustrative. He writes for example "that Bonhoeffer's grisly death was . . . an element in the greater tragedy of the Christian community of Germany. Put in briefest terms, it was that they had no effective strand-two moral structure [i. e., roughly 'practical social ethics'] in the church that was adequate to the crucial need of church and German people alike (to say nothing of the need of Jewish people; to say nothing of the world's people). No structures, no practices, no skills of political life existed that were capable of resisting, christianly resisting, the totalitarianism of the times" (p.207). Fowl and Jones have a similar analysis in *Reading in Communion*, 135-164.

[70]*PK* 146.

[71]*CET* 253-266. He takes as an example of this attitude Gordon Kaufman's book *Theology for a Nuclear Age* who like Moltmann stresses the uniqueness of this situation, the exclusive human responsibility, the necessity of radical transformation of society, and the need for theological revisions for making a theology relevant to the situation (although Moltmann would be sceptical towards the way Kaufman does this). See also "The Gospel's Radical Alternative" and *PK* 149-151.

[72]*CET* 256f.

bomb to begin with, and consequently be able to live and work for alternatives. He thinks that peace movements too often only mirror the forces they fight.

d) Pacifism and the Life of Christians in the World

The most common objection against pacifism is that it more or less by definition entails a radical withdrawal from any responsible engagement with society, because state, politics and violence cannot be separated.[73] Hauerwas thinks this is wrong for reasons we have already partly dealt with.

He argues first of all that even, and especially, on this question the most politically significant thing the church can do is to manifest the reality of the kingdom of God and thereby try to free the imaginations of people from the idea of the necessity of war. Instead of just taking a position and theologically legitimate the current conflicting positions, Christians can help open up new perspectives, both through being a visible community that nurtures alternative practices and through the different stories they tell. This can be connected to his theme of taking time for peace. Although the issues concerned are urgent, the church because of its convictions, can take the time for such activities that do not seem to lend themselves to immediate political action. Recognizing this, one prominent non-pacifist theologian, Paul Ramsey, has said that "the charge of 'irresponsibility' or 'ineffectiveness' needs to be withdrawn by those of us in the tradition of Niebuhr and just war."[74]

In addition, Hauerwas strongly argues that pacifism neither excludes co-operation with others, nor, in principle, interaction with the state.

> Christian commitment to non-violence does not require withdrawal from the world and the world's violence. Rather it requires the Christian to be in the world with an enthusiasm that cannot be defeated, for he or she knows that the power of war is not easily broken. Christians, therefore, cannot avoid . . . attempting one step at a time to make the world less war determined. We do that exactly by entering into the complex world of deterrence and disarmament strategy believing that a community nurtured on the habits of peace might be able to see new opportunities not otherwise present. For what creates new opportunities is being a kind of people who have been freed from the assumption that war is our fate.[75]

For Hauerwas the question is not the *if* of co-operation, but the *how*. How can the church, given its locale as living with an alternative history, best contribute to public discussion and co-operation?

We have seen that he does not expect the state to be the church and that he thinks Christians can try to find common language with others. He does not ask the state to become pacifist, but he thinks that it can become less violent and that

---

[73]See e.g. Miscamble, "Sectarian Passivism?". Hauerwas gives a very critical answer in "Will the Real Sectarian Stand Up?", 87-92.
[74]*Speak Up*, 120.
[75]*AN* 198.

Christians might, through their perspective and practices, contribute to this development. He thinks, for example, that just war-language might be helpful both in terms of common language and as a tool for disciplining the power of the state.[76]

The above has moreover given some examples of the sort of contribution Hauerwas himself as theologian has given. Other examples are a discussion of war as moral institution where he tries to understand its hold on our imagination;[77] an elaboration of the sorts of different arguments used in the movement for nuclear disarmament;[78] and a critical discussion of the use of just war-language in the Gulf War (some of which we will meet below).[79] Although he has clear positions, these contributions have not the form of final, well-rounded, position-taking, but are more like interpretative commentaries helping to further conversation and understanding.[80]

But can Christians be active in state activities? Hauerwas does not think this is a question that can be answered abstractly, but only in terms of concrete activities and of specific states. But he does, as we have seen, not accept the view that violence is intrinsic to the nature of the state. That view

> fails to appreciate that the state as a form of community cannot be explained or reduced to a Hobbesian mutual protection society. Violence is necessary not as the essence of community, but when community is no longer sustained by the common will of those that make it up. True authority does not need violence as it is the recognition and obedience given by the citizen to the governors who legitimately lead in accordance with common good of that society.[81]

Furthermore, the fact that he is critical of essentialistic and ahistoric accounts of violence, war and state as well as of non-violence and that he does not defend any strict and clear distinction between what is violence and what is non-violence, gives much space for reflection on how to participate.

Anyhow, most state activities in most states have nothing to do with violence and there is for Hauerwas nothing problematic in Christians participating in such functions, especially as he does not see Christian pacifism as a general theory about state power. Moreover, that Christian citizenship has to be discriminating

---

[76]*DFF* 128.

[77]*AN* 169-208.

[78]*AN* 132-159.

[79]*DFF* 136-152 and "Pacifism, Just War and the Gulf".

[80]*AN* 167. He says that "pacifism is not so much an 'ethic' for judging war as it is the skilled habits of a community that make it possible to give nuanced interpretations to the changing character of war and the state. Such interpretations are the way the church begins to make 'substantive social recommendations,' as they provide the means to free the imagination from the idea that war is a necessity." ("Epilogue", 177.)

[81]*VV* 218. "Rather than disavowing politics, the pacifist must be the most political of animals exactly because politics understood as the process of discovering the goods we have in common is the only alternative to violence. What the pacifist must deny, however, is the common assumption that genuine politics is determined by state coercion." (*AN* 7.) See also *TT* 134, *CC* 62f, and his Review Essay of Ellul, *Violence*, 211-213.

and selective is, he argues, true not only for pacifists but also for advocates of the just war-doctrine, though the area of non-participation likely will be larger for the pacifist.[82] Yet Hauerwas' position would be more concrete if he at some length told and discussed stories of participation and non-participation, as he with such effect has done in other areas, like, for example, in so-called medical ethics.

2. Christian Pacifism and the Just War Tradition

The dominating moral understanding of war in Christianity since the fourth century has been the just war tradition.[83] Although Moltmann seems to defend something like a just revolution, he discards the general just war tradition. He also thinks it is impossible to defend nuclear war and even nuclear armament in terms of just war. Otherwise he has not discussed this tradition of thought much. Hauerwas has however, both in relation to Christian pacifism, its internal coherence, and its use in the Gulf War.

On the first issue he is concerned to show that Christian pacifism should not be understood only as an alternative to just war. The latter pertains to state policy, and presupposes Constantinian assumptions. The former is a description of the church's life and not an abstract position on state policy. It does not assume that the state can live like the church. [84]

If one compares Hauerwas' pacifism and the just war tradition of someone like, for instance, James Turner Johnson, the difference in basic assumptions becomes clear. Johnson assumes the nation-state system and the priority of the community of the nation-state and its values over any other form of community, the church included. The church as church does not play any constitutive role. When he discusses the problem of conscientious objection, the context is only the relation between state and individual.[85] He further sees claims to justice built on religious convictions as illegitimate because they are publicly unverifiable.[86] He consequently also affirms the secularization of the just war tradition, because it has made the tradition which has been thus transformed part of the modern public discourse.[87] The contrast to Hauerwas is obvious point after point.[88]

---

[82]"After all just war theory surely requires its adherents to contemplate the possibility that they will find themselves in deep tension with the war making policies of their governments." (*DFF* 134.) See further *DFF* 132-134 and "Epilogue", 167-181.

[83]See Ramsey, *War and the Christian Conscience,* idem, *The Just War*, Johnson, *Can Modern War Be Just?*, and Walzer, *Just and Unjust Wars*. Hauerwas usually (in the texts mentioned below) discusses Ramsey's account, to which he is most sympathetic. On Johnson, see his review of Johnson, *Can Modern War Be Just?*, and *AN* 135-140, and on Walzer, see "On the Ethics of War and Peace". See also Yoder, *When War is Unjust*.

[84]"Epilogue", 164-166, *DFF* 116-135.

[85]*Can Modern War Be Just?* 153-173.

[86]Ibid., 61.

[87]Ibid., 4-7.

Yet, Hauerwas is generally more supportive of the just war tradition than of so-called "realist" and "survivalist" accounts,[89] because of its Christian roots and because it like pacifism gives the use of violence the burden of proof,[90] and does not make survival primary. There are things worth dying for.[91] For Christian pacifists therefore this might be a way to talk to the state in a language it might accept.[92] He says, however, that the way just war-language was used in connection with the Gulf War made him hesitant.[93] For it is his "contention that the Gulf War was conceived and fought by such political realists who found it useful to justify it on grounds of just war."[94] Hauerwas agrees with the common observation of the importance of crusade language ("freedom and democracy" or "ending all wars") in American warfare—so for example in the World Wars, Vietnam, and the Cold War. When realists used just war language it also easily spilled over into crusade rhetoric (for instance, Saddam Hussein as a new Hitler).

One can also see his criticism of the use of just war language in the Gulf War as an example of his more general criticism of modern moral theory, as the title of his major discussion "Whose Just War? Which Peace?" shows.[95] The just war criteria were used, he contends, as straightforward and self-explanatory and as if the questions who uses it and for what purposes did not make any difference. The analysis could therefore, for instance, be abstracted from the history of "realist" Iraq and Middle East policy of Western nations in general before the invasion of Kuwait and thereby fail to see that many of the important decisions were already made. The theory was instead used as a set of universal and self-evident criteria

---

[88]In his review of Johnson's book, Hauerwas does not deal directly with these sorts of issues, except some comments at the end.

[89]"Realism" here denotes the view that international politics has to be exercised inside the limits a system of sovereign nation-states sets. In such a system war is an inherent instrument of politics that cannot be wished away. The question is how it is used. "Survivalism" stresses the uniqueness of nuclear weapons and consequently the radical discontinuity between conventional and nuclear weapons because of the latter's threat to the survival of humankind. The conclusion often drawn is thus that these weapons have made not only war, but also the nation-state system obsolete. Cf. *AN* 140-153.

[90]"Christians created just war reflection because of their nonviolent convictions; they assumed that those who would use violence bore the burden of proof for doing so." (*DFF* 139f.)

[91]Ramsey's account, which is based on defence of the innocent neighbour and not on self-defence, has as consequence, Hauerwas writes, "that we would rather die as individuals and even as a whole people than directly kill one innocent human being. For Ramsey, that conviction meant that war must be pursued in a manner which may require more people to die in order to avoid directly attacking noncombatants—the innocent neighbors of any war." (*DFF* 142.)

[92]*AN* 135-140, 153-155.

[93]*DFF* 140f.

[94]*DFF* 140. See also *DFF* 148f. For some reflections on the Gulf War by Moltmann, see "Das christlich-jüdische Verhältnis und der zweite Golfkrieg". Concerning the just war-doctrine, he contends that neither Iraq's attack on Kuwait, nor the following attack by the allied forces on Iraq can be justified in terms of the criteria of just war. See ibid., 164. For an overview of the American discussion, see Langan, "The Just-War Theory After the Gulf War".

[95]*DFF* 136-152.This is, of course, an intentional echo of MacIntyre's *Whose Justice? Which Rationality?* See *DFF* 138.

that could be used by anyone without difference. For Hauerwas this is only one instance of an hegemonic power claiming a universal morality that is "meant to create a social and historical amnesia that is intended to make us forget how the dominant achieved power in the first place."[96]

According to Hauerwas, this way of thinking also misses the important historical changes from the use of the tradition in the Middle Ages—on the one side by confessors trying to discipline war participators, and on the other by princes of the Holy Roman Empire—to modern use in nation-states by secular politicians. Or, he asks, what happens when it is not princes, but democracies, that use the theory, when in the latter case secrecy and disinformation are crucial both in relation to the enemy and to the public opinion?[97] To an account like Ramsey's that thinks the theory is coherent because the West is formed by Christian moral assumptions and habits that make it even possible "to consider the possibility of surrender rather than fight a war unjustly" he asks how far that is credible anymore, if it ever was?[98]

This leads up to his perhaps most important point. To make its practice credible the just war tradition, just like pacifism, needs a virtuous people. The question therefore is "how democracies are to develop virtues in their citizens to fight wars with limited purposes, not crusades."[99] Crusade language, however, is most effective in mobilizing the public opinion. In another context, he writes that "[i]t has long been my suspicion that, if we could force just-war thinkers (and churches) to recognize the disciplined kind of communities necessary to sustain the discourse and practices necessary for just war, it would make it increasingly difficult to accuse pacifists of being hopeless 'idealists' and/or 'sectarians.'"[100] From this perspective both the discernment and the practice of just war thus require virtuous people. However, the theory is instead used as an abstract and universal set of principles that ethicists can elucidate, but whose application has to be left to political and military "experts". From Hauerwas' perspective of a virtue ethics it could then be said that "when you first have an ethic that requires further questions about how it is to be applied, then you know you have an ideology."[101]

---

[96]*DFF* 145. The argument of this paragraph goes through the whole chapter.

[97]*DFF* 145-147.

[98]*DFF* 142f. The citation is from p. 143.

[99]*DFF* 147.

[100]"Epilogue", 152.

[101]*DFF* 150. The distinction between "ethics as such" and "applied ethics" has to do with the earlier described modern attempt to develop a rational and neutral ethics for human beings as such abstracted from their histories, communities and views of the good life. To be usable for developing rules for highly institutionalized relationships, like medicine and war, the universal ethical principles have to be applied, through being related to concrete cases and factual findings. But Hauerwas argues that rules cannot be developed separate from applications. For extended criticisms of the idea of applied ethics, see "Casuistry in Context" and MacIntyre, "Does Applied Ethics Rest on a Mistake?".

Finally, Hauerwas thinks that "the saddest aspect of the war for Christians should have been its celebration as a victory" and he deplores the way Christians in America did not resist "the orgy of crusading patriotism that this war unleashed".[102]

3. Critique of Christian Nuclear Pacifism

During the 1980s several churches have written pastoral letters and reports on the issue of nuclear weapons. Hauerwas has, in different contexts, at length discussed three of these: the pastoral letter of the American Roman Catholic bishops *The Challenge of Peace*,[103] his own United Methodist Church's bishop letter *In Defense of Creation*[104] and the British report *The Church and the Bomb* by a working group in the Anglican Church.[105] Although all three are much more positive to pacifism than has been usual, he is nonetheless sharply critical of all three and especially of the latter two. We will here shortly present the main criticisms he directs against his own bishops' declaration, because these are especially telling and because of the clear similarities between this letter and the position of Moltmann, who also has commented positively on this letter.[106]

The decisive criticism concerns the addressee. To whom are the bishops speaking? They claim to speak to the Methodists, but Methodists as American citizens at least as much as Christians, and therefore in practice also to the general public. The stated aim is "to equip the Methodists to engage in a 'political ministry' by exercising political power in the interest of nuclear disarmament."[107] Christians should engage themselves throughout society to make *shalom* into efficient foreign policy. Hauerwas is, of course, critical that they do not clearly differentiate between the church and the American nation. His own conviction is that the bishops first of all should have directed themselves to the Methodist people as a Christian people, helping them see what it might mean to live as Christians in a world of war. But because the bishops do not (in spite of the Methodist stress on sanctification) seem to see much difference, so Hauerwas' argument goes, between being Methodist and being American citizen, they speak to their people primarily as the latter.

This has consequences for how they argue. The question of survival and thereby investigations and predictions about the effects of a nuclear war become

---

[102]Ibid., 104.

[103]*AN* 169-208 (earlier published as the monograph *Should War Be Eliminated?*). Cf. also Yoder's analysis "*The Challenge of Peace*: A Historic Peace Church Perspective".

[104]"A Pacifist Response to 'In Defense of Creation'" and "Epilogue". The latter (which is the longer) is Hauerwas' contribution to his and Paul Ramsey's book on this letter, *Speak Up for Just War or Pacifism*.

[105]"The Need For An Ending"

[106]*CJF* 28f.

[107]"Pacifist Response", 6.

primary. Their argument therefore builds more on people's fear than on Jesus' preaching of the kingdom of God. As a result, Hauerwas continues, the theological discourse is meagre. It consists primarily of making *shalom* into the basic motif. He writes that "what the bishops have done is rhetorically appeal to shalom as a vague and undifferentiated sense of peace such that Jesus is defined by shalom rather than vice versa." Further, "they have used our theological language to underwrite the idealizations and sentimentalities generally accepted by our culture about the importance of peace for our lives without subjecting those idealizations and assumptions to theological examination."[108] Hauerwas maintains that the result is that the peace the bishops talk about is not a peace built on the cross of Christ, but is a peace that first of all seeks for survival. *Shalom* thus works as a Protestant version of a natural law theory that presumes that all yearn for peace. Furthermore, they seem to take for granted that peace can be reached through a transformation of the nation-state system.

> In effect, they want to be Constantinian pacifists fusing church and world so that they can speak to the world without the embarrassment of Christ's cross. Absent the cross, appeals to shalom cannot help but border on mysticism or nature romanticism. God's peace is not the sunny optimism of pastoral scenes but the rough and hard peace that knows truthful witness to the world bent on war may only invite further violence.[109]

The letter's primary problem, from which the others follow, is, according to Hauerwas, that the nation-state and not the Christian church is seen as the primary subject both for the church's reflection and action, and for God's dealing with the world. Hauerwas' claim is that Christians instead should learn to understand what it might mean as followers of the Crucified to be a people of peace, so that the world will have the possibility to imagine new ways of living together. They should show the leaders of the nations that there is a people "who are ready to take the risk necessary for living in a world less determined by spiraling war policy."[110]

So what does Hauerwas then think the bishops should have said? First, he would have wished to see a confession of sin. "I wish they had begun with a confession of sin in which they called on the church to ask God's forgiveness for our failure *as a church* over these many years to discipline ourselves so we might be

---

[108]Ibid., 9f. "Shalom is characterized at such an abstract and ideal level that one never has the sense that it is a way of life that can be lived out in history. We are told that shalom is positive peace, more than the absence of war, denoting harmony, wholeness, health and well-being in all human relations (24); or that in shalom there is no contradiction between justice and peace, peace and security, love and justice (25). It thus appears that what 'pacifism' means throughout Christian history is the Christian's attempt to create a world so just that war is no longer a necessity. But as I have indicated, most Christian pacifism, at least before the Enlightenment, never assumed that the Christian commitment to peace promised a just or war-free world." ("Epilogue", 155. The references inside parentheses are to *The Challenge of Peace*.)

[109]"Pacifist Response", 11.

[110]Ibid., 13.

capable of making a witness for peace."[111] He would then have liked them to discuss the problem of war in general and not nuclear war in isolation and to have
tried to clarify the theological and political issues in terms of just war and Christian pacifism, including discussions about how different policy alternatives look
from these two perspectives. Given the current state of the Methodist church he,
however, does not think it is yet possible for the church to decide for just war or
pacifism. But the bishops should help start the communal process of reflection
about how, as Methodists, to be faithful to that vision of peace Christians already
have in Jesus Christ.[112]

4. Contrasts and Convergences of Two Peace Theologies

With regard to the question of violence, Moltmann's movement in the direction of Radical Reformation theology is unmistakable. While the early Moltmann
could describe the issue of violence and non-violence as illusionary, the later
Moltmann makes non-violence an integral and necessary component of the life of
discipleship. This discipleship ethics is a community ethics, the ethics of the
messianic community that, as a contrast society, lives and proclaims a real alternative to the current world order, made possible by Jesus Christ. In this Moltmann and Hauerwas concur, even if one might ask if Moltmann integrates discipleship and the cross of Jesus the way Hauerwas does, which might have
seemed natural in terms of Moltmann's theological project.

However it is with this, the differences we have repeatedly encountered between Moltmann and Hauerwas, we find here too. The most obvious difference is
Moltmann's hesitancy to follow the logic of his theology into a consistent Christian pacifism. One reason for this is again their different political horizons. For
Hauerwas the primary context is the church as an alternative *polis*. For Moltmann, although his theological argument seems very similar, it is the national and
international struggle for justice and peace, or more specifically the socialist
revolutionary movements and the peace movement, that forms the determining
context. The question he asks is how Christian faith and the church can be relevant and supportive to them. He wants his theology to be partisan theology. Consequently there is little of a critical encounter in the relation between church and
theology on the one side and these movements on the other, which as a result
gives his theological reflections the functional, and therefore sometimes incoherent, character I have noted.

---

[111]"Epilogue", 181.
[112]Ibid., 181f.

a) Christian Theology and "Survivalism"

The preceding description of the contrast between Moltmann's and Hauerwas' positions has several significant consequences that exemplify and illustrate well their divergent ecclesial and theological strategies. One has to do with description and interpretation. Because Moltmann takes the descriptions of the issues provided by the general peace movement for granted, he makes survival into the crucial issue. This was, understandably enough, the starting point and the common denominator for the peace movement of the 1980s.[113] In some of his texts it is this nuclear threat, which he considers to have qualitatively changed the world, that seems to make pacifism realistic, since it is necessary for survival. Hauerwas does not think Christians should describe our situation as first of all a question of survival. He gives several interrelated reasons for this, some of which are clearly pertinent to the case of Moltmann, others maybe less so.[114]

First, he does not think that the nuclear weapons have "posed questions of faith that point beyond just war or pacifism."[115] It is not the nuclear threat that makes the love for one's enemies realistic, but the convictions inherent in Christian faith. Neither does he believe that an imminent nuclear destruction is qualitatively different from a natural cosmic destruction in some billion years.[116]

Second, survival cannot override any other value. We should not seek any peace, but, as Moltmann says, a just peace. The dilemma for Moltmann is that he sees the struggle for justice as the way to peace. If we create a just world, we will also have peace. Every political issue becomes a peace question and therefore the search for peace is reduced to a general utopianism.[117] Moreover, as Moltmann says otherwise (for example when discussing revolutionary violence), the struggle for justice might also endanger the peace. That is, there is a lack of discussion about conflicts between different values. Furthermore, if, as Moltmann says, a just world is necessary for peace and the crisis is urgent, then the situation is rather desperate. Making survival absolutely primary more plausibly seems to make any means, however unjust and oppressive, that lower the specific nuclear threat legitimate.

---

[113]Wasmuth, "Die Entstehung und Entwicklung der Friedensbewegungen der achtziger Jahre", 122f.

[114]For the following, see *AN* 140-146, 160-168 (he here discusses Jonathan Schell's book *The Fate of the Earth*, which was highly influential also in the German peace movement, cf. Wasmuth, "Friedensbewegungen", 123), "Pacifist Response", 7-9, and "Epilogue", 150f.

[115]"Epilogue", 150.

[116]*AN* 145.

[117]Hauerwas writes that the "ideal combination of peace with justice produces a laundry list of social and economic injustice, a list of all the many human needs it would be good to meet if we had unlimited resources. But in the process we are given little sense of how we need to change our lives to do some good when we cannot do everything it would be good to do. Being against nuclear weapons is a far too easy way out to propose to end all the world's injustices." ("Pacifist Response", 9. See also "Epilogue", 157f.)

Third, saying that humanity now has the responsibility for the survival of God's creation implies the sort of Prometheanism that in the first place created the weapons of mass destruction.[118] Moltmann writes that "[i]n the light of a possible nuclear catastrophe, not only do we human beings need God, but God needs us!"[119] God needs us because a nuclear catastrophe would also be a catastrophe for and in God. This sort of language that also absolutizes our survival Hauerwas thinks is behind the will to have nuclear weapons.

> For the peace we desire is the peace of God that comes from the recognition that it is not our task to make history come out right—either through the possession or dispossession of nuclear arms. Rather, we believe that history has already come out right and just because it has we can take the time in a world threatened by its own pretentions of control to seek patiently a truthful peace.[120]

Here we see again the importance Hauerwas gives to the theme of "taking time for peace", i. e., of continuing to live a truthful life, instead of letting the nuclear threat wholly determine one's life.

Fourth, Christians should therefore not appeal to people's fear of death to motivate them to action. The fear Christians should have is for killing others. Instead of witnessing to fear of death, Christians should witness to the good news that the end has already come. He says that the idea that survival overrules everything else is "a strange witness of a people who have been given new life by a God who was willing to die on a cross. If we Christians have a witness to make in the face of nuclear destruction, it is one that will draw on our confidence that we have a destiny given to us by God that cannot be eradicated by our death and even the death of the human species. That is surely a witness that needs making today."[121] Something similar to the conviction that not even the death of the human species could finally destroy the destiny given humankind by God, is also developed by Moltmann. He describes a nuclear annihilation of humankind as "also a catastrophic experience for God himself",[122] but he does not want to follow theologians who see this as also the annihilation of God. As through the Spirit immanent in the world God would suffer a nuclear catastrophe with humanity, and that would mean that "through his own suffering he will bring this annihilated world into the creation of his new world."[123] The murders will not have the final word. This is the basis for the Christian hope. It has, however, not led him, like Hauerwas, to question the central place survival has in the peace movement.

---

[118]Schell exemplifies "a clear case of humanistic eschatology that attempts to secure the eternality of our existence through our ability to control and master our history—exactly the same eschatological presumption that leads to our having nuclear weapons in the first place." (*AN* 161.)

[119]*CJF* 32.

[120]*AN* 166.

[121]"Pacifist Response", 7.

[122]*CJF* 34 (50).

[123]*CJF* 35 (51). See further *CJF* 34-37.

b) The Context of Love for One's Enemies

We have seen that Moltmann does not ask how the love for one's enemies he describes, i.e., the communal discipleship of peace, is to be formed, and that Hauerwas' approach tries to deal with this question. For Moltmann, the result is that there is only a small step from an ecclesial discipleship ethics to an ethics for states and international relations. Hauerwas' problem with this view is that it separates the Christian love for the enemy from the convictions and practices that makes it intelligible and liveable and instead turns it into a generally workable principle for overcoming enmity. What Moltmann seems to do is to argue that the love for the enemy as such overcomes enmity and creates peace. This Hauerwas thinks is naive. "The Sermon does not promise if we just love our enemies they will no longer be our enemy. . . . The Sermon does not promise that if we simply act in accordance with its dictates the world will be free of war."[124] The reason Moltmann hesitates to espouse a consistent pacifism is that he seems to think that, for conflicts on lower levels, loving one's enemy may often not work. In conflicts on the international level it can work since there is no realistic alternative. In this Moltmann is similar to the Methodist bishops' argument in *In Defense of Creation*. Hauerwas thinks that this means that it is not the death and resurrection of Jesus Christ but the common nuclear threat that makes the vision of justice and peace possible and is the ground for their pacifism. He concludes that "they want to be pacifists who continue to rule because now pacifism has become a viable foreign policy due to the threat of nuclear weapons. Yet such a position cannot but be both theologically and politically incoherent."[125] Moreover, for Hauerwas the love for one's enemies and non-violence are embedded in a wider network of practices needed for making such life possible, which makes it impossible for Hauerwas to follow Moltmann when he so easily translates his pacifist ethics into workable policy for international relations. The relation for Hauerwas is much more complex and above all he does not consider Christian pacifism to be a theory about how to create a world without war.

This also makes their relations with various peace movements (or other social and revolutionary movements) different. Because the church for Hauerwas is the source and locus for Christian peace practice, his relation to, say, the peace movement of the 1980s was more critical and discriminating than Moltmann's. In an analysis of the different types of arguments used he concludes that "culturally we lack a coherent morality to sustain the current antinuclear enthusiasm",[126] and that these positions "are based on questionable moral convictions that we would be hesitant to apply in other aspects of our lives."[127]

---

[124]"The Sermon on the Mount", 41.
[125]"Epilogue", 158f.
[126]*AN* 132.
[127]*AN* 153. See further *AN* 132-159.

For Moltmann, in contrast, it is Christian participation in the peace movements that are the locus for his work. The peace movements are the given, his
question is how to mediate Christian faith to them. One effect of this is that political theology so construed will share the dilemmas inherent in a movement like the
peace movement. In a recent study on the European peace movement of the
1980s Thomas Rochon[128] shows the difficulties of sustaining a radical criticism,
when immediate political effect is the aim and the use of media and massmobili-
zation the means. These means are not appropriate to what one wants to attain.
When political theology makes the Christian manifestation of these movements
their base they, Hauerwas would say, fail to see the unique resources the church
represents. The church is not dependent on its immediate effects on the political
system, nor on support from media and temporary trends, but on its own practices
of faith and hope, and has therefore a strength often lacking in the social movements.

c) Eschatology and Power

These reflections again raise the issue of power. We have found that one of
the assumptions behind the rise of political theology was the idea of humanity as
the subject of history and the correlative understanding of politics as the means
for consciously creating a just and peaceful future world. At this point the difference between Radical Reformation theology and political theology is immense.
We have earlier discussed Moltmann's theologically based power critique and its
inherent tensions, and we have seen that Hauerwas can follow Moltmann in his
Christian critique of power, but how Hauerwas instead of talking in *anti*-power
terms, talks in terms of a *different* power. Moreover, unlike Moltmann, he does
not use this critique as an emancipation and celebration of human power. In contrast, Hauerwas extends his power critique to include the assumptions and politics
of modernity that Moltmann celebrates. Hauerwas contends that modernity's assumptions of control are self-deceptive, and as such a cause of violence. To be
able to uphold this illusion of control one is easily tempted to use violence when
other alternatives seem lacking or are less efficient.[129] The church should be free
of this self-deception because it has through Jesus Christ learned to know that
God does not want it to carry out its mission through violence. "For God does not
will that the Kingdom be accomplished through coercion or violence. In the cross,
we see how the Kingdom will come into the world, and we are charged to be
nothing less than a cruciform people."[130] We also saw how he argued that this
hope helps the church to see and risk alternatives.

One factor behind these differences is their different eschatologies. We have
seen how eschatology in the original conception of political theology tended to

---

[128]"The West European Peace Movement and the Theory of New Social Movements".
[129]*PK* 46f.
[130]*CET* 104.

function primarily as, on the one hand, a delegitimation of the present, and, on the other hand, a legitimation of utopian political programs. Its message was that nothing needs to be as it is, and thereby it explicitly underwrote modernity's Promethean assumptions and neglected to critically evaluate the movements promising radical change.

The contrast to Hauerwas' theology, where the eschatology works very differently, is clear. Instead of underwriting the Promethean assumptions that we have to do everything, it, in Hauerwas' interpretation, frees Christians to do one thing, and to do the good thing even if it seems presently ineffective. In an early text Hauerwas criticizes political theology (including a text by Moltmann) for believing that the church or theology has the key to the outcome of history—that is, knowledge about its meaning and direction.[131] Therefore they have the responsibility to be on the right side and to use the means of power available for forming this outcome. Responsibility entails that effective means of power, including violence if necessary, has to be joined to charity.

This was also what we found in our investigation of Moltmann. He joined his eschatology to a semi-Marxist interpretation of history involving the polarization between oppressors and oppressed (which he also identified with the reactionary and progressive forces). Because he knew in which direction history was going, which the progressive forces were, he was confident that it was possible to calculate the costs of the revolutionary violence that would break the reactionary forces, and whose vanishing would open the way for the next step in the history of liberation. Although I am here using the past sense, we found the same type of reasoning even in his latest reflections on revolutionary violence, so I am not sure how much he would like to revise his thinking about this.

In contrast, Hauerwas claims that the church does not have knowledge about how its and the world's actions can bring the world closer to the kingdom of God. Its calling is to witness to the kingdom, not "realize" it. He can therefore not separate means and ends the way Moltmann does, because "the ends are embodied in the means".[132] The church cannot create the just world, but has to in its own life witness to truth, love and justice. The consequence is thus that some means (such as violence) cannot be used by Christians because they are inappropriate for the politics of the kingdom, and would actually destroy it. This is why hope and patience and ability to face tragedy are so important for Christians.[133]

Hauerwas agrees with Moltmann "that the poor have a special place in God's kingdom",[134] but he is critical of collapsing all issues into a conflict between poor and rich, oppressed and oppressors, so that the ethical and political questions are

---

[131]*TT* 132-143. The reference to Moltmann is found at 233 n. 1. Hauerwas refers to "The Cross and Civil Religion" (*PTPE* 34-69).
[132]"What Could It Mean For the Church To Be Christ's Body?", 17.
[133]*TT* 135-143.
[134]*TT* 134.

reduced to the one issue of being on the right side. More important is to ask *how* the church should identify with the poor, *how* it should work for justice.[135]

Also here Moltmann has slowly, but not consistently, moved into Hauerwas' direction. This is most clearly visible in *The Way of Jesus Christ*, where he partly seems to share Hauerwas' eschatological position and he also ends the book with a section on patient hope.[136] In *Creating a Just Future*, a book published the same year (in German 1989), the position is closer to his earlier account. The respective titles, in their English versions,[137] I think, are not without significance for understanding the difference.

To conclude, we thus find the same difference in direction we have seen throughout. Moltmann writes theology for Christian social activists, and therefore discusses political means deemed necessary for creating a peaceful and just world, and formulates a theology that can motivate this struggle for peace and justice. Hauerwas instead discusses how a peaceful community that makes its peace witness credible can be formed and sustained and how this might help the church to show alternatives.

---

[135]"For when the poor become the key to history it is assumed that the aim of the Christian is to identify with those causes that will make the weak the strong." (*TT* 134.) "Moreover, to state the social ethical issue in terms of rich against the poor is to oversimplify, for it makes it appear that the only issue is to be on the side of the poor, but the crucial question is *how* we should identify and work for a more just social system. The *fact* of poverty is certainly the occasion to ask about the justice, but that is just to begin the task." (*TT* 135.) See also *VV* 226f.

[136]*WJC* 338-341 (363-366).

[137]The German title of the latter book is *Gerechtigkeit schafft Zukunft.*

Chapter 14

The Ecclesial Base for a Theological Politics

Political theology emerged in the social and political transformations of the 1960s and especially in relation to the student movements and the New Left. Its primary base has since then been the Christian parts of the so-called new social movements that grew out of the New Left of the 1960s. But we have also seen that it in a wider meaning can be described as one form of a Postmaterialist transformation of Christian theology. We moreover found that this is a source of the severe tensions that characterize the political theology of Moltmann. There is first a contradiction between its professed self-understanding to be a theology grown out of the church's relation with the poor and oppressed and its actual base in one of the so-called progressive elites of modern society. There is a similar tension between its self-description as a theology for the church as contrast society and its actual close alignment with a culturally dominant elite. Substantially this leads to the difficulties Moltmann has in reconciling his ecclesial discipleship account with his attempts to formulate what might be called a Postmaterialist theology.

Moltmann has, especially in *The Way of Jesus Christ*, formulated a very different account of the church. Here the church is depicted as a contrast society and it is as such the social base for a theology of peace and the practice of Christian discipleship. It has been my claim in the previous chapters that Hauerwas more consistently than Moltmann has developed this understanding of church and theology, and that he therefore avoids the specific tensions and contradictions Moltmann's theology is afflicted by. A basic reason for their difference is their divergent understanding of politics. Moltmann's political theology makes the politics of the world primary. The consequence is that the political issues he discusses are already given by the social and political conflicts of the contemporary world. The question becomes on which side the church should be on. In contrast, Hauerwas' theological politics makes the church the primary locus for its politics. As a contrast society the church has its own agenda that challenges the way the world's politics is understood and therefore does not fit current divisions.

In this chapter I will therefore deal with the current prospects in the Western world of the type of church life and theology that Hauerwas represents relative to the prospects of political theology, but before that I will address another issue.

1. Hauerwas and the Agendas of Conservatism and Liberalism

A standard objection from the side of political theology has been that one cannot be neutral. If one does not side with the progressive forces, one will necessarily support the reactionary and conservative forces. A basic reason behind the current sharp polarization between conservative and liberal/progressive forces, a split that for many is much more important than the ones between denominations or even between religions or between religious and secular people, is the extreme expansion of the modern state. It influences, in various ways, most parts of society, including its cultural and moral dimensions. In consequence, the control of the state apparatus is seen as the primary means for forming and changing society. The long-time liberal dominance in the state apparatus has then, as we have seen, led to a conservative reaction when the liberal policy of the state, to a growing extent, has influenced more and more of everyday life. The struggle over the control of the state apparatus has thus become the centre of conflict and this conflict has in its turn increased the polarization. Almost everything can in one way or another be put in terms of this conflict. When the question if you are conservative or liberal is seen as the most important question, it becomes difficult for positions that do not want to be identified with either of them.

Hauerwas does not claim he is neutral, nor that Christian faith is apolitical, only that the church should not let its agenda be defined by the current options of the politics of the world. Yet Hauerwas' strong criticism of liberalism makes many convinced that he is basically on the conservative side in the current cultural wars. I do not know if Moltmann would say so. He has not discussed Hauerwas, but we have seen that he is very positive to Radical Reformation theology in general and to the work of Yoder in particular.[1] For him this theology is basically on the good progressive side. This is furthermore a common judgement among political and liberation theologians.[2] What makes Hauerwas more problematic is that he writes from the inside of so-called mainline Protestantism[3] and that he directs his sharp criticism more clearly against liberal theology and politics than Yoder does, although the differences between them are small. This criticism affects also, as we have seen, Moltmann's Postmaterialist theology and ethics.

a) Hauerwas Described as Conservative

Two examples of this sort of categorization of Hauerwas are provided by Dennis McCann and David Tracy. McCann argues in a response to Hauerwas' critical analysis of contemporary American Catholic theology (including McCann himself) that Hauerwas only sides with the neoconservative strands in Catholic theology against liberal Catholicism.[4] How he reaches this conclusion is not clear to me. It seems to have to do with Hauerwas' criticism of the liberal understanding of freedom, his general "alienation from American cultural values", and his

---

[1]He also wrote the preface to the German translation of Yoder's *The Politics of Jesus.*

[2]See e.g. Duchrow, *Global Economy*, 165-168, and the contributions of Miguez Bonino, Pixley and Shaull to Schipani (ed.), *Freedom and Discipleship.*

[3]"Mainline" is a misnomer of this declining minority of American Christianity. Cf. the criticism of this label by Finke and Stark, *The Churching of America*, 223f.

[4]"Natural Law, Public Theology and the Legacy of John Courtney Murray". The Hauerwas-article he is discussing is "The Importance of Being Catholic".

lack of understanding that the church's "basic cultural strategy at its best has always been open to the world as it is."[5] The odd result of McCann's argument is that Hauerwas is put on the same side as the neoconservative Catholic George Weigel, whom Hauerwas in his analysis includes in his criticism and whose argument, as summarized by McCann, obviously is much closer to McCann's own than to Hauerwas'.

Tracy groups Hauerwas together with Hans Frei, George Lindbeck, Hans Urs von Balthasar, and Joseph Ratzinger and describes them as part of a neoconservative stream of theology. Together with, but also different from, fundamentalism it represents an antimodern option. Tracy expresses much sympathy with this type of theology, but he is critical of its allegedly one-sided criticism of modernity and tendency to idealize the church. He is also afraid that it only in theory, but not in practice, will differ from fundamentalism.[6] He himself defends the progressive theology that continues to align itself with the emancipatory tradition of modernity, although modified by the criticism from neoconservatives and postmoderns.[7]

It is thus Hauerwas' criticism of liberalism and modernity in general that leads to the description of Hauerwas as neoconservative. Behind this terminology is the idea of progress. The progressives stand at the front of a general emancipatory process, the conservatives react and try to restore an older order. Hauerwas, together with many others, questions this way of understanding history and contemporary conflicts. It is furthermore intrinsic to Hauerwas' theology not to make one's position on modernity, capitalism and the state primary. To talk about progress in this way assumes a self-evident direction or moral goal for history. For Hauerwas the church should neither be progressive nor conservative, but different.

Furthermore liberalism, socialism and conservatism as usually understood are all children of modernity. To challenge central aspects of modernity itself, means to go outside the conflicts between these ideologies. From Hauerwas' perspective, conservatives and liberals are thus more similar than dissimilar. Politically they are two versions of a basically liberal polity. Theologically both positions are basically Constantinian.[8] This, of course, does not deny that Radical Reformation

---

[5]"Natural Law", 803.
[6]"On Naming the Present", esp. 75-77, 81f.
[7]Ibid., 80-84.
[8]He (and Willimon) writes: "People often ask us, Is what you are saying liberal or conservative? The question is frankly political. 'Whose side are you on—the progressive, open liberal or the closed reactionary conservative?' We admit that we are quite openly political, but not as that term is usually understood. The conservative-liberal polarity is not much help in diagnosing the situation of the church since, as presently constructed, we can see little difference between the originating positions of liberals or conservatives. Both assume that the main political significance of the church lies in assisting the secular state in its presumption to make a better world for its citizens." (*RA* 156.)

theology will share much with this or that modern perspective. It only denies a systematic correlation.[9]

The confusion of this type of classification is also illustrated by the differences between McCann and Tracy themselves. Both are revisionist liberal Catholics, but while McCann is a strong defender of capitalism and a critic of liberation theology,[10] Tracy defends some semi-socialist perspective and is sympathetic to political and liberation theologies.[11] From the perspective of political theology McCann is thus a conservative.

b) Hauerwas and the Cultural Wars

One way to test Hauerwas' claim not to fit conservatism is to compare him with the agendas of conservatism. What I have said above, however, reveals a problem with this approach of analysing Hauerwas. It is difficult to avoid asking how Hauerwas stands in relation to the "issues" that divide liberalism from conservatism. This assumes that the issues are given, and that the question is on which side you should be. But Hauerwas often questions the very assumptions behind the descriptions of the issues and the understanding of politics that create these issues. Much of his writings consists, as we have seen, of attempts to redescribe such questions and show their relations to specific convictions and practices. In the case of Moltmann, one can make a list of issues, determine on which side he is, and thereby understand him. One cannot do this with Hauerwas, which makes a "list" like the one below misleading. However, it might still have some worth, if for nothing else, it shows that his politics cannot readily be put into one of the current camps.

We earlier met the theme of the cultural wars in the Western world that is especially fierce in America. Discussing Moltmann in these terms we found that he almost wholly subscribes to the views of the elites that constitute the "progressive" Postmaterialist/New Class fraction and culture and which is close to what in America is currently called liberalism.

That Hauerwas is in sharp conflict with the liberal elite outside and inside the churches is, of course, obvious. We see that, for example, in his critique of the idea of the autonomous self as source of moral judgement, in his defence of the importance of the *Christian* tradition and his commitment to the *Christian* community, as well as in his general critique of the modern uses of the languages of freedom, justice and rights. It is such themes which are the basis for McCann's and Tracy's description of Hauerwas as a neoconservative.

---

[9]Michael Northcott, in an article discussing the very different readings of the encyclical *Centesimus Annus* by Ronald Preston (liberal) and Hauerwas (post-liberal), concludes: "Ultimately the philosophical style and mode of thinking which post-liberalism represents is so inimical to the liberal mind that it is difficult for liberalism not to misconstrue its post-liberal antagonist." ("Preston and Hauerwas on *Centesimus Annus*", 31.)

[10]See e.g. Stackhouse and McCann, "A Postcommunist Manifesto".

[11]See e.g. *The Analogical Imagination*, 390-398.

One area where the cultural wars are especially fierce concerns family, sexuality and abortion. Hauerwas has written much in these areas and is again deeply critical of liberal views.[12] For him these issues are not private, but part of the politics of the church. He defends what might be called classical Christian positions. This might seem to put him squarely in the conservative camp. Yet, he is also sharply critical of conservative Christian thinking in these areas. He thinks that what is described as "traditional American values", such as the primacy of individual freedom, the rights language and capitalism, are in conflict with the Christian understanding of family and sex. He also thinks that the family easily becomes a source of idolatry. "Christians believe our first loyalty is to the God who constitutes us first by making us part of the church rather than of the family." He is especially critical of "appeals to 'family values' in the abstract"[13] and says that if fascism comes to America it will appeal to family values.

On abortion he writes that

> I have found it hard to know how to enter the debate about abortion since I do not believe the issue for Christians can be framed in 'pro-life' or 'pro-choice' terms. Such descriptions are attempts to win the political battle on the most minimum set of agreements—that is, that abortion is primarily about the sanctity of life or freedom of women. As a result, abortion is abstracted from those practices through which our lives are ordered that we might as a community be in a position to welcome children.[14]

His writings have therefore concerned itself with redescribing the context for the discussion and the practices that make what he thinks the Christian understanding intelligible.

In some other areas his difference from most conservatism is more obvious. Besides his Christian pacifism, one can mention his critical attitude to the nation-state in general, the American nation and society in particular,[15] to patriotic sentiments,[16] to the American Constitution,[17] and to American foreign policy (for ex-

---

[12]For the family, see e.g. *CC* 155-174, "The Family as a School for Character", and "Marriage and the Family". About sexuality, see *CC* 175-195, *AC* 113-131, *US* 126-133, and "From Conduct to Character". It is worth noting that his longest discussions on these subjects are included in a book on Christian social ethics—i. e., *CC*. On abortion, see *VV* 127-165, *CC* 196-229, and "Abortion, Theologically Understood". To this is related his extensive discussions of so-called medical ethics in general. See *VV* 166-194, *TT* 101-115, 127-131, 147-202, *SP*, and *NS*. These questions are, however, not so easy to put on a conservative-liberal-progressive scale.

[13]Both citations are from *DFF* 158.

[14]*DFF* 11. He started to think about abortion when working with mentally handicapped. His question was which sort of life is required for welcoming mentally handicapped children in our lives and communities. See Stallsworth (ed.), *The Church and Abortion*, 117.

[15]It is not insignificant that Moltmann is much more positive to the American experiment than Hauerwas is. Cf. *OHD* 147-161 (*PTPE* 89-101).

[16]He will not make the Pledge of Allegiance and will not sing *The Star Spangled Banner*. See "Faith in the Republic", 508. Of course, his position is not based on ordinary liberal cosmopolitanism. This text is useful for learning his views on America. One must, however, keep in mind that this is not an article by Hauerwas, but a series of conversations he had with some lawyers and legal experts. Therefore the statements are not very guarded.

ample Vietnam and Iraq). His criticism of the capitalist system and the way the market increasingly dominates all spheres of human life also puts him in conflict with current conservatism. Also suspect from the perspective of much conservative thought is his use of non-foundationalist philosophy (often criticized as "relativism"), radical political theory, feminist thought, and so on.

Finally, he is of course as critical of conservative Christians' endeavours to christianize polity and ethos through the agency of the state, as he is of the liberal endeavour to do the same. For him they are both modern examples of Constantinianism.[18] Hauerwas sees his own work as an attempt to think outside this tradition.

c) Hauerwas and Classical Conservatism

There are many different forms of conservatisms. What is today called conservatism cannot be too closely identified with the classical conservative tradition. One exposition of this more theoretical and sophisticated form of conservatism is Robert Nisbet's book *Conservatism*. Nisbet, for a long time one of the more influential American sociologists and himself a prominent conservative thinker, disassociates sharply the Religious Right and its state interventionist ideas in social life from classical conservatism, shows the multiform and contradictory nature of the coalition behind Ronald Reagan and its only partly classical conservative character, and points to the strong isolationist tendency concerning foreign policy in American conservatism.[19]

Hauerwas has more in common with Nisbet's type of conservatism.[20] Nisbet thinks that the differences between the major modern ideologies can be illuminated by their relation to the individual, the state and the intermediate groups and associations (like church, class, family and guild). While liberalism gives primacy to the individual, and socialism to the state, conservatism defends the right of the intermediate structures against both individualism and statism/nationalism. This has also influenced some forms of early socialism, such as guild socialism, Catholic socialism and, most importantly, anarchism, as well as some forms of

---

[17]"I don't like the Declaration of Independence. I always say that America is the only country that has the disadvantage of being founded on a philosophical mistake, namely the notion of inalienable rights." ("Faith in the Republic", 504f.) So also "Christian Practice and the Practice of Law in a World Without Foundations", 748.

[18]He can thus write "that the reason Falwell is such a challenge to the Christian mainstream in America is not because he is so different from them, but because he has basically accepted their agenda. The Christian right and the Christian left do not disagree about the religious status of the American experiment. They just disagree about what language and/or political theory will allow them to accomplish their common goal of making American democracy as close as possible to a manifestation of God's Kingdom." (*CET* 180.)

[19]*Conservatism*, 102-106.

[20]Nisbet's writings have also been important for Hauerwas. See e.g. his comment in *VV* 253 n. 21. But so have also, from his earliest writings on, socialists and anarchists been, as *VV* 222-260 shows.

pluralist liberalism.[21] As we will see in the next chapter, variations upon this theme have again become common not only in conservative, but also in much post-socialist and communitarian thought. Hauerwas criticizes the predominance of the individual-state polarity in modern society and we will in the next chapter see the fruitfulness of some versions of this perspective for understanding a Radical Reformation perspective.

We have, however, also seen Hauerwas' criticism of the use of these ideas in neoconservative thought. Both empirically and normatively he questions accounts that stress the relative independence of the economic, political and cultural spheres. Even more decisive is the difference concerning the church's role. Nisbet stresses the importance of church and Judaeo-Christian morality for conservatism, but "[i]t is religion as *civil* religion that seems to be the closest to a common essence of conservative belief".[22] Its major functions are to confer "a certain sacredness upon vital functions of government and upon the whole political or social bond" and to "act as a check upon the power of the state".[23] Conservatism is therefore deeply critical of religious claims that go outside its own sphere of competence. Religion "is indeed a good thing provided it is not made the base of the intrusion of personal beliefs into the public body of the nation."[24] Conservatives have therefore always been critical of dissenting forms of Christianity; and Methodism was one of the threats early conservatives reacted against. The radical opposition between this perspective and Hauerwas is obvious.[25]

Another prominent part of the "dogmatics of conservatism" is the emphasis on experience, history and tradition against abstract, rationalist thought and social engineering.[26] This is connected with the centrality given to practical and experiential knowledge learned through history, in contrast to modern political rationalism that stresses knowledge of technique, abstraction and generalization.[27] This also makes the concept of authority crucial for conservatives, but constricted to different autonomous, though ordered, spheres, such as individual, family, church, state and economy. According to conservative theory, it is in such ordered structures that liberty can exist. Division of power and decentralization of administration are thus stressed. Conservatives see also a direct connection between democracy and the growth of government bureaucracy, and between democracy and total warfare.[28]

There are obvious connections to Hauerwas (as well as to much postmodern/postliberal thought in general) in much of this criticism of the Enlightenment

---

[21]*Conservatism*, esp. 21-23, 48-50, 61f, 83f.
[22]Ibid., 73.
[23]Ibid., 70.
[24]Ibid., 74.
[25]Ibid., 15f, 68-74. Cf. Hauerwas' criticism of the similar perspective of a contemporary Conservative like William Bennett, see *AC* 74-88.
[26]*Conservatism*, 23-29.
[27]Ibid., 29-34.
[28]Ibid., 34-46.

tradition. Yet, the crucial questions are again "which tradition?", "which experiences?", "whose authority?", and when such questions are asked, Hauerwas' Radical Reformation theology goes far beyond the compass of classical conservatism.

Conservatives are also deeply critical of liberal views of freedom and of levelling and uniforming equality. In their view "[s]ocial differentiation, hierarchy, and functional rather than mechanical consensus are as vital to freedom as to order."[29] This explains why family property (and especially landed property) is so important for conservatives. They generally also defend the free market and oppose the welfare state. Welfare should be the responsibility of the mediating structures. However, many conservatives have also recognised that capitalism (with its "fluid, mobile, monied property", which creates individualism and egoism),[30] industrialism (with its factory system), and urbanism undermine much of what conservatives value highly.[31]

Hauerwas is likewise critical of liberal views of freedom and equality, but for him freedom is not based and formed on property, but on the new life made possible by Jesus Christ. He has also, as we have seen, pointed out the contradictions between conservatism and capitalism and the severe difficulties this creates for conservative thought. If anything, Hauerwas is closer to the antimodern or postmodern forms of socialism and anarchism mentioned above than to conservatism.[32]

Finally, one might argue that Hauerwas is at least theologically and ecclesially conservative. If this is so, this is also true for Moltmann. Both represent a form of trinitarian orthodoxy and make Christian faithfulness and integrity central. This can be described as a form of conservatism. However, in relation to ecclesial practice and theology of the established Constantinian church neither Hauerwas nor Moltmann can be described as conservative.

The conclusion of this discussion is consequently that it is misleading to describe Hauerwas in terms of a general conservative-liberal dualism. This leads us back to the question of the ecclesial sources of his theology and their current prospects.

---

[29]Ibid., 51. See further ibid., 47-54.
[30]Ibid., 63.
[31]Ibid., 55-68.
[32]So is clearly Milbank. See e.g. *Theology and Social Theory*, 195-203 where he discusses various forms of nineteenth century socialism. He claims that "Marxism stands almost alone in the nineteenth century as a purely 'modernist', Enlightenment variant of socialism" (p. 196) in contrast to most other forms, which "were 'postmodern', in the sense that they had absorbed some measure of a romantic, Counter-Enlightenment critique" (p. 197).

2. The Ecclesial Sources of Radical Reformation Theology

For Hauerwas, theology has its base in the actual historical existence and practices of the Christian church. With this he does not only mean the contemporary church, but the church through the centuries. This makes issues of the integrity and faithfulness of the church to its calling important for theology. For Hauerwas this means, as we have seen, that much of his writings concerns how the church can live faithfully in a liberal society, which in its turn requires an understanding of the liberal society.

Stressing the church's role as the base for theology raises two questions. First, what is the situation and prospect for the sort of *church* life Hauerwas depicts? Second, what are the general prospects for his type of *theology*? In this section, I will describe Hauerwas' own view of the situation for church and theology. Then, in the following section, I will pick up the line from chapter eight and discuss the relative viability of political theology and Radical Reformation theology from a wider sociological perspective. There is a natural connection between these two sections, because Hauerwas is well read in contemporary sociology of religion and often refers to it. This seems to be untrue of Moltmann, who makes few references to sociology of religion. Could this be one reason for the lack of self-understanding he shows?

There is a notable and characteristic difference between how Moltmann and Hauerwas describe and appraise the situation of church, theology and society. Moltmann is more sure of the direction of history, of what should be done, and that political theology and its church affiliates are situated at the front of the progressive development. In his early theology, in addition, he was confident he was on the winning side. This confidence has decreased, but he still knows what must be done, that it can be done, and, if it is not done, that the only alternative is catastrophic for earth, humanity and God.

Although Hauerwas' theology is constructive and though he has strong convictions, he is also more tentative. He offers no general solutions for society or for the church. He often says that he does not know what to do. It is moreover not part of his normal rhetorical strategy to first outline a problem and then come with the solution.[33]

He is also unsure about the future prospects of his own type of theology. He has often commented on his own ambiguous ecclesial situation.[34] As member of the United Methodist Church he is part of the mainline Protestantism that he thinks is dying. Much of his writing is description and analysis of this decline and therefore criticism. Furthermore, as a theologian in a main university he is situ-

---

[33]See e.g. *CET* 247, *AC* 21, and "Faith in the Republic", 472f.
[34]See e.g. *CC* 6, *PK* xiv, *US* 157f n. 10, "The Testament of Friends", 213f, and "The Importance of Being Catholic", 27-29.

ated in an ambiguous situation between the liberal university culture, in itself slowly breaking down, and the church.[35]

But there is also another line of thought. To the criticism that the church described in *Resident Aliens* does not exist and that the book therefore is unrealistic, Hauerwas and Willimon answer: "The whole point of the book is that the church we want *does* exist. . . . that we Christians are sitting on a gold mine called the church, but unfortunately the very categories we have been taught as Western Christians make it difficult for us to notice that it is gold." Therefore this book contains to a large extent reflections on stories of "ordinary saints" in ordinary circumstances. "Through the locating of these heroes, we hope that we have helped situate the church in America. Good communities are known by their saints. By naming these ordinary, but theologically and morally impressive people, we discover resources we did not know we had."[36]

This double attitude to contemporary church life reflects the manifold and diverse character of the modern church and therefore also the complex relation between Radical Reformation theology and the contemporary church. On the one side modernity and liberalism have so transformed the church that Christian practice and tradition, as described by Hauerwas, increasingly become unintelligible. This is especially true of mainline Protestantism, who has made the alliance with the liberal society a main project. On the other hand, he does not describe an ideal future church, which would require heroic efforts to create, but church life and Christian practices that have existed and do exist, but often go unnoticed because of the categories of thought we use.

In a previous chapter we saw how Hauerwas describes the individualization, subjectivization and privatization of Christian faith and practice in liberal society that have made churches into producers of religious market commodities. When the churches lack common language and practices, their inner life becomes instead a mirror of liberal interest politics. Following George Lindbeck, he adds to this picture Western Christianity's "awkwardly intermediate stage"[37] between being culturally established and not yet being wholly disestablished. This makes liberal theological strategies attractive, because there is enough of a Christian heritage left to make translations of Christian faith into modern vocabularies (such as Marxism, existentialism, psychology) seem meaningful. In contrast, it

---

[35]"I teach in a divinity school that is training people for the Methodist ministry, to serve a church that I think basically is dead, or will soon be dead, and probably should be dead." ("Faith in the Republic", 524.) The title of Part I in *DFF* "Positioning: In the Church and University but not of Either" refers to this ambiguous relation to mainline Protestantism and the American university.

[36]Both citations are from "Why *Resident Aliens* Struck a Chord", 424. In *CET* 111-131 he tries to show the empirical realism of his account and the riches in ordinary church life through a theological reflection about an administrative board meeting in the local Methodist congregation of which he was member during his time at Notre Dame. See, furthermore, the section "Politics as Gesture" in chapter 10 above.

[37]*AN* 8, Lindbeck, *The Nature of Doctrine*, 134.

makes a theology of communal discipleship difficult to sustain and make intelligible.[38]

For theology, the fact that the academy is such a strong centre for a Postmaterialist/New Class perspective, with its strong individualism, religious indifference and even anti-Christian attitudes, adds to this difficulty, because the viability of Hauerwas' type of theology is dependent on the participation of theologians in the communal practices of the churches. He quotes Lindbeck, who says:

> Those who share in the intellectual high culture of our day are rarely intensively socialized into coherent religious languages and communal forms of life. This is not necessarily disastrous for the long-range prospects of religion (which is not dependent on elites), but it is for theology as an intellectually and academically creative enterprise capable of making significant contributions to the wider culture and society.[39]

The replacement in many universities and seminaries of theology with religious studies also decreases the institutional space for the type of theology Hauerwas' supports.[40]

Although this situation might support more liberal strategies, he thinks that the weakness of liberal Protestant church life also drains liberal theology. Theology becomes increasingly separate from any base in church practice and becomes private expressions of the thought of individual theologians.[41] He generally thinks that American liberal Protestant theology and ethics have already run out of steam and that the liberal project is now best fulfilled in Catholic theology, that still can build on some theological substance and coherent practices.[42]

But if the negative forces against Radical Reformation theology are strong, Hauerwas also points to forces that might support it. The continuing process of disestablishment of the church could make the long-time prospects for Radical Reformation theology brighter, just as it will make the liberal translation project more and more difficult. This disestablishment means that the church is not expected to supply the ideologies that keep society together and explain why the world is as it is. This can give a space for theology, or so Hauerwas hopes, to develop its own agenda.[43]

On the academic side, the changed philosophical climate, with the collapse of positivism and foundationalism and the re-emergence of substantial moral and political theory have also made Radical Reformation theology intellectually more intelligible.[44]

---

[38]*AN* 8f, *AC* 23.

[39]*The Nature of Doctrine*, 124 and "Christian Ethics in America", 23f.

[40]See also *DFF* 14f.

[41]*DFF* 199 n. 33.

[42]"The Importance of Being Catholic", 29, "Christian Ethics in America", 1.

[43]*DFF* 17, *AN* 40.

[44]In one place he says: "I have been very lucky to live at a time of such rich intellectual developments." ("The Testament of Friends", 215.)

3. Sociological Perspectives on the Relative Social Tenability of Political Theology and Radical Reformation Theology

a) Sociology of Contemporary Church Life

We earlier met Karl Gabriel's claim that the ongoing modernization process only makes one strategy possible as a general project: a pluriform Christianity directed to serve the various religious needs of people. (This is what Hauerwas describes as consumer religion.[45]) If one wants to preserve a general folk religiosity in some relation to the institution of the church, the latter has to accommodate to the various trends of the dominant social groups. Gabriel contends that political theology (and he would say the same about Hauerwas' theological politics) can be one of the products offered as long as it does not make any exclusive claims. As a general strategy for a people's church, it is impossible.

Both for Hauerwas and Moltmann, Gabriel's suggestions are, for both theological and practical reasons, impossible to embrace. They do not espouse a people's church ecclesiology. Moltmann has directly, as we have seen, criticized the sort of double or pluralist strategy Gabriel advocates. However, the difficulty is that Moltmann still wants his committed church to integrate Postmaterialist individualism. This Gabriel thinks is impossible and Hauerwas agrees.

However, the sociological long-time plausibility of the scenario Gabriel provides can also be questioned, and this is relevant also for Moltmann's Postmaterialist theology. Gabriel's intention is to challenge the traditional secularization thesis in which modernity means a disappearance of religion. Gabriel contends that individualization and deinstitutionalization of religion do not mean its disappearance. Instead of deploring these processes the church should positively integrate them in their church practice and theology.

This possibility has been questioned by another German sociologist, Renate Köcher.

> All signs indicate a weakening of religion through the extension of the religious autonomy of the individual, the individualization of religion. This is true also when religion is not defined and measured in terms of the content of the Christian faith, but in more abstract terms . . . Forecasts of a new diffuse religiosity remote from the traditional Christian faith are totally groundless . . . Liberation from the institutionalized and regulated system of faith, in which some people see the future of religion, is ultimately nothing else than the demand to live with a way of thinking that does not mean anything for others and is constantly questioned by others.[46]

The debate exemplified by Gabriel and Köcher reflects the internal struggle inside contemporary Roman Catholicism. In that context, arguments like Köcher's are easily read as supporting the current policies of the Vatican hierarchy, which

---

[45]*AN* 9 and *RA* 142.
[46]Köcher, "Religiös in einer säkularisierten Welt", 184f.

seems enough to make them suspect.[47] If one goes outside this conflict, most American and Swedish studies[48] support Köcher.

American mainline Protestantism does not now perceive issues like church hierarchy, authority and ecclesial moral claims as most urgent, although some conflicts about issues like homosexuality still create debate.[49] Much American sociology of religion, just as much current sociology in general,[50] therefore tends to stress the need to counteract the trends of individualization and deinstitutionalization for both the survival of liberal Protestantism and its possibility for making a public impact.

Wade Clark Roof and William McKinney write "that the enemy of church life in this country is not so much 'secularity' as it is do-it-yourself religiosity.'" This privatized faith "encourages religion à la carte—'picking and choosing' those parts of a religious tradition congenial to the individual."[51] The result is that church life and communal commitment is undercut. This creates a curious contradiction between the strong emphasis on personal autonomy and moral relativism in the personal life, on the one hand, and these churches' "more activist and absolutist" emphasis upon what concerns public affairs, on the other hand. "The result is a disjointed ethic, with the standards applied to social issues differing from the standards applied to private matters. Indeed, the private and public realms for liberal Protestantism have come so uncoupled that the tradition has lost much of its ability to mobilize personal energies on behalf of public causes."[52]

Roof is himself a committed liberal and wants liberal Protestantism to become more consciously liberal. But he also thinks that to be able to uphold a public

---

[47]For a theological critique of Köcher's interpretation, see Fuchs, "Individualization and Institution". The fact that her studies have been used by Roman Catholic authorities seems for him to show their questionable nature. He himself, like Gabriel, wants the church to accept the advancing individualization, but he does not say how he would answer the claims in the quote by Köcher. See also Gabriel's comment in *Christentum zwischen Tradition und Postmoderne*, 183 n. 57. Cf. Metz' claim against views like Gabriel's and Fuchs': "In the long run one can really only be religious by oneself and without 'congregation' in a religious world. The latter is a thing of the past! Therefore, 'congregation' is today more important, more necessary than ever." ("Suchbewegungen nach einem neuen Gemeindebild", 154.)

[48]See e.g. Hamberg, *Studies in the Prevalence of Religious Beliefs and Religious Practice In Contemporary Sweden*.

[49]But cf. the struggles inside the Southern Baptists. See Ammerman, *Baptist Battles*.

[50]Cf. Etzioni who, because of the *current* situation in America, can write the following: "We can act without fear that attempts to shore up our values, responsibilities, institutions, and communities will cause us to charge into a dark tunnel of moralism and authoritarianism that leads to a church-dominated state or a right-wing world." (*The Spirit of Community*, 2.)

[51]*American Mainline Religion*, 56f.

[52]Both citations are from ibid., 227. Wuthnow similarly writes: "Coupled with the hedonistic success ethic, radical freedom of choice further erodes the mobilizing potential of either version of American civil religion by championing privacy in opposition to public involvement. The difficulty with either kind of civil religion is that it demands sacrifices: in the form of public restraints on private morality, or as demands on personal time and resources to become involved in causes of peace and justice. Neither is likely to mobilize a high degree of commitment . . . because the demands of privacy make stronger claims." (*The Restructuring of American Religion*, 282.)

faith, the liberal churches and theology have to go through important changes. He mentions three areas. First, liberals must learn the importance of living with Christian language and stories.[53] Second, they must regain the importance of community against modern privatism and recognize the communal nature of the Christian language. Third, the liberal stress on universality should not blind them to the fact that lives of integrity, passion and conviction are based in particular traditions. "Universality arises out of the particular".[54] This sounds as a liberal version of Hauerwas.[55] For the latter, however, it is not enough to talk about regaining the communal nature of the church. What is important are the *practices* necessary to sustain the life of the church. Individual-community dualism, he thinks, is itself an outgrowth of the liberal practices of modern society.[56]

Interestingly enough, some argue that it is a mistake to identify the decline of mainline Protestantism with a decline of liberal Protestantism. Instead the most vital parts of liberal Protestantism are found among so-called moderate Southern Baptists, Missouri Synod Lutherans and left wing evangelicals.[57] To this could be added progressive Roman Catholics. One could argue that Moltmann has much more in common with the radical wing of evangelicalism that has tried to combine classical Christianity and a Free Church ecclesiology with radical politics than he has with American mainline liberal political theology.[58] This argument is telling, because what it seems to say is that a progressive liberal Protestantism lives upon heritages of communal and committed church life that it itself cannot create, but in fact undermines.

---

[53]"Inevitably the vitality of the Christian church arises out of grass-roots affirmations of faith and commitment, out of the tales and stories told by those sitting in the pews." ("The Church in the Centrifuge", 1013.)

[54]Ibid., 1014.

[55]These themes are also stressed in the various contributions by sociologists, historians and theologians to the book *Liberal Protestantism* (ed. by Michaelsen and Roof) on the crisis and prospects of mainline (or oldline) Protestantism in America. In this book, the most often recurring issue is the necessity of a revitalization of the communal nature of Christian faith and life. See pp. 49, 63f, 123-125,179, 193-197, 215, 237-250.

[56]*US* 149 n. 4.

[57]So Hutchison, "Past Imperfect", 66 and Sweet, "Can a Mainstream Change Its Course?", 235. The latter writes: "Liberal Protestantism is alive and well in left-wing evangelicalism, regardless of its condition in the 'mainline' churches".

[58]Especially interesting may be the once called "Young Evangelicals", whose agenda is close to Moltmann's. Jim Wallis, the editor of the influential journal *Sojourners*, has been one of the more articulate spokesmen for this group. See his books *Agenda for Biblical People* and *The Call to Conversion*. Wallis actually uses Moltmann's writings. Also influential on them—especially in their early days—were the works of Bonhoeffer, Yoder and Ellul. But in practice Wallis and *Sojourners* represent a position which is closer to Moltmann than to Yoder and Ellul, even if they often have been described as neo-Anabaptists. See Quebedeaux, *The Young Evangelicals*, idem, *The Worldly Evangelicals*, 83-172, Bush, "Anabaptism Born Again", Hunter, "The New Class and the Young Evangelicals", and idem, *American Evangelicalism*, 102-119. Cf. also Gish, *The New Left and Christian Radicalism*, which was an (according to Hauerwas unsuccesssful) attempt to relate the New Left and Anabaptism to each other. See *VV* 254.

When Roof and McKinney discuss the future of Protestantism, they thus stress the importance of internal factors. This implies that internal considerations are also important to understand the different developments in various religious communities. Roof and McKinney show that members of more conservative Protestant groups, although many of them have been strongly influenced by modern therapeutic individualism, are more committed to the Christian community and have a stronger sense of responsibility for and accountability to each other. They are more rooted in their religious values and moral principles.[59]

The importance of internal causes has been especially highlighted by three sociologists Benton Johnson, Dean Hoge and Donald Luidens.[60] They have sharply criticized explanations that primarily stress external factors, like the amount of formal education or the value changes of the 1960s, and point to the fact that liberal Protestantism has declined during the whole century (the 1950s was the only exception) and that more conservative Protestantism has grown during the same period.[61] The main reason for the decline is instead the lack of internal conviction and commitment inside these churches. Mainline Protestantism is characterized by a sort of "lay liberalism", a home-made "pick and chose" folk religion, that has had little empowering effect. Christian faith has a low place on the church members' list of priorities. They cannot really answer why Christianity is important or why one should be a Christian. People who leave the churches usually have a background in families where religion has played little role and are from churches that did not expect much commitment. Instead "individual freedom" has been a primary doctrine. Therefore, "the mainline Protestant membership loss is simply the next stage of this process of declining

---

[59]*American Mainline Religion*, 182f. But cf. ibid., 53 and Hunter's books *American Evangelicalism* and *Evangelicalism*. Much Evangelicalism and Baptism share with liberal Protestantism a theological handicap in its encounter with modern liberal individualism in their common basically individualistic view of salvation and a weak ecclesiology.

[60]"Mainline Churches". See also Finke and Stark, *The Churching of America*. Finke and Stark are very critical of much traditional description of the religious developments in America. They do not only argue that internal factors are the most important, but also that factors such as urbanism and pluralism, against what is often said, strengthen religion. In contrast, situations of religious monopoly radically weaken religious participation, which may be an important reason for the European development. See esp. pp. 18-21, 203-207, 250-252. Cf also *PTPE* 19f.

[61]This is extensively argued also by Finke and Stark, *The Churching of America* and Hutchison, "Past Imperfect", 67-74. It is the resurgence in the 1950s which, Hutchison thinks, gives the impression of a break in the 1960s. He does not expect any great resurgence in these denominations. A comparison between Protestantism and Catholicism in Germany is also telling. Protestantism, until very recently in contrast to Catholicism, has long celebrated religious individualism, deemphasized the institutional forms of the church and been closely aligned with the cultural and political centre. The result is that the degree of commitment and practice of Christian faith is much lower than in Catholicism, although the latter community now increasingly follows the Protestant pattern. See the statistics given throughout Gabriel, *Christentum* and Köcher, "Religiös". Köcher writes: "The powerlessness of West German Protestantism, as in other European countries, is not least explained by their characteristic disregard for institutions." (Ibid., 184.)

commitment to the church and to Christian faith and witness."[62] The changes in the 1960s only accelerated this process, but did not create it, as is shown by the fact that more conservative churches went through this period growing.

These three sociologists, furthermore, see little reason to expect any reversal of this process. They also think that the attempt by political theology to reinvigorate liberal Protestantism has failed to get any substantial following among the grass roots, although it did succeed finding support in national assemblies and denominational agencies. The individualistic character of liberal faith and practice, usually strongly supported by political theology itself, has drained the churches of the empowering sources needed for this type of social activism.

In light of this emphasis on the need of theological and ecclesial integrity and commitment, another sociological study is interesting, and relevant for Hauerwas' type of theology. Sociological studies are dependent upon which questions are asked, how they are asked, how the objects of the study are subdivided, and so on. This in its turn is dependent upon the assumptions and theories of the researchers. For example, for a long time, American sociologists concerned with the difference religious beliefs make for political views, only divided religious people into Jews, Protestants and Catholics. The result was that religion did not make much difference. But when one started to subdivide these religious bodies, religion was seen to be a significant influence.

George Gallup and Timothy Jones have in their book *The Saints Among Us* from 1992 tried to see which difference a highly committed Christian faith and practice make.[63] How to define what high commitment is, as the authors recognize, is difficult and differs somewhat between traditions. Their definition includes following: religion as the most important influence in life; the importance of prayer; the striving to put one's belief into practice in the whole of life; trust in God's love; finding comfort and support through one's faith; a high christology and belief in biblical authority; the wish that one's belief were stronger; following what one thinks is the will of God even if it is against one's own desires; practising forgiveness; the practice of evangelism; and a desire to strengthen relationships to other Christians.[64] So defined, they found that the "saints" are more often women than men; more nonwhite (especially black) than white; tend to be older

---

[62]"Mainline Churches", 17. "That problem is the weakening of the spiritual conviction required to generate the enthusiasm and energy needed to sustain a vigorous communal life. Somehow, in the course of the past century, these churches lost the will or the ability to teach the Christian faith and what it requires to a succession of younger cohorts in such a way as to command their allegiance. Admittedly, doing so has become increasingly difficult for churches as close to the very center of American culture and institutional life as the mainline denominations are." ("Mainline Churches", 18.)

[63]They comment that "we have not really known the details about how faith actually makes a difference in the lives of those . . . who seem to take it very seriously. Polling over the years has helped us gauge the breadth, but it has not usually helped us see the depth." (*The Saints Among Us*, 19.) The questionnaire was only one part of the investigation. Other parts where interviews with "saints", and people related to them in various ways.

[64]Ibid., 123 and 11-16.

and having lesser education;[65] more likely to be blue collar than white collar, professional or business; more are found in the South than in other parts of the country;[66] they are more often Protestant than Catholic; and more likely to vote Democratic than Republican.[67] Compared to the "spiritually uncommitted" the committed were much more likely to lack prejudice concerning race; to spend time helping people in various ways; to believe that forgiving is very important; and to follow a strict moral code.[68]

These results do not fit the categories used in other studies we have consulted, neither the liberal-conservative or New Class-Business Class polarities of much American sociology of religion, nor the Postmaterialist-Materialist duality of Inglehart's studies. Although the saints are socially closer to segments that are the primary base for conservatism and Materialist values, they differ from them in questions like race relations and politics. Moreover, the importance of practising forgiveness and reconciliation is not part of the questions most other studies ask. The same is true of the categories they use for identifying the saints. By asking in the way they do and through their analysis of the important role of the saints, they give interesting support to Hauerwas' understanding of the church and the role of the ordinary saints. They thereby also give one indication of where to look for the social base of Radical Reformation theology.

In addition, the authors strongly stress the communal base for the formation and sustenance of the life of these saints. Like Hauerwas, they point to the need for "mentors, guides, and teachers",[69] because "nurturing sainthood requires the corporate resources of the church."[70] They also stress the formative power of Christian language for these people.[71]

b) Prospects

Which conclusions can be drawn from these reflections? How do the prospects for these two types of theology and the church life they presuppose look?[72] Before reflecting upon these questions, a preliminary objection has to be addressed. We have seen that Gabriel argues that there are no alternatives, besides his own pluralistic folk religion. All other strategies will fail. We have in the previous section found reasons to believe that if this is true, there is no future for the

---

[65]Ibid., 33.

[66]Ibid., 20.

[67]Ibid., 23. "They are, in other words, the very ones that society often looks *last* to for help or role models." (Ibid., 15.)

[68]Ibid., 41.

[69]Ibid., 101.

[70]Ibid., 118. See further ibid., 56f, 100f, 109f, and 118f.

[71]Ibid., 64-68. Wuthnow find the same in his study. See *Acts of Compassion*, 50f, and more generally cf. ibid., 121-156.

[72]For writing the following, the work of Lindbeck has been helpful. See esp. *The Nature of Doctrine*, 112-138, "The Sectarian Future of the Church", and "Hans Frei and the Future of Theology in America".

church at all in the long run, because Gabriel's own strategy is implausible. However, there are also other problems with Gabriel's accounts.

Sociological studies like Gabriel's give the impression of a semi-necessary development. The reason is that he uses a modified modernization theory that describes societal evolution in terms of increasing differentiation and rationalization on the structural level, pluralization and reflexivity on the cultural level, and individualization on the level of social relations. The modification in relation to mid-century American modernization theories is that Gabriel does not believe that the American society of the 1960s was the final step in the modernization process. He instead argues that the modernization process can take somewhat different roads, and that different spheres in society can be on different stages in the modernization process. He also, as many do today, questions the idea that modernization means secularization in the sense of disappearance of religion.[73]

Though popular, such evolutionary theories are deeply problematic.[74] First, the very reflexive nature of social life in itself makes social explanation in terms of general causes or laws impossible. Knowledge of history is a means for changing it. Second, "society" or "culture" are not the sort of clear and discrete entities evolutionary theories assume when they talk about the differentiation and rationalization of one society. Third, world history is not one history with the modern West at the front of the development. Fourth, social change is discontinuous and contingent. It cannot be directly derived from social structures abstracted from particular circumstances, crises, events and actors. When this is disregarded, the result is that history does not become much more than illustrations of general theories.

We met a similar criticism of modernization theories in Ron Eyerman's and Andrew Jamison's discussion of the social movements. They see the social movements as forms of cognitive praxis that articulate historical projects which challenge existing politics and offer alternative ways of describing the world and organizing life. The movements' socially embodied cognitive claims are therefore crucial for understanding them. They cannot be understood as just instances of a general theory of modernization.[75]

The significance of such an approach to the study of religion is obvious. Because of Gabriel's use of modernization theory, he does not need to discuss the cognitive claims and distinct practices of churches. The prime actors are instead structures and processes.[76] This makes the evolving and gradual differentiation of society into self-determining subsystems with their own logic, such as the eco-

---

[73]*Christentum*, 13-18.

[74]The following is built on Giddens, *The Constitution of Society*, 236-239 (see further ibid., 227-280) and Nisbet and Perrin, *The Social Bond*, 266-294. See also MacIntyre, *After Virtue*, 76-102.

[75]*Social Movements*, see esp. p. 149.

[76]Wuthnow, although seeing a partial relevance of evolutionary theories, discusses concrete human actors not only as instances of general social processes, but as parts of a struggle for definition and control over the symbolic sphere. This gives his *Restructuring* a different character.

nomy, politics, science, partnership and love, morality and religion, an inevitable development.[77] Religious individualism and privatism are correlates to this process and therefore also inevitable. This is, we have seen, exactly what Hauerwas and Milbank question. They argue that these processes are contingent and not necessary and that sociological accounts of Gabriel's type therefore are legitimations of modern liberal society (and, in Gabriel's case, modern liberal Catholicism) that helps secular society police the church. If this is so, Gabriel's denial of any alternative path is not convincing.[78]

However, even if one can question general evolutionary modernization theories, there is no doubt that they partly are descriptively powerful concerning modern society. Modern society is characterized by strong individualization processes and by the deinstitutionalization and differentiation of religious and moral life. The question is how to meet this situation. Moltmann basically wants church and theology to creatively affirm and integrate the individualizing processes. This is seen most clearly in his reception of a radical therapeutic individualism and in his account of the accepting community. In the short-run this partial accommodation may be an advantage for relating to the Postmaterialist change inside the church. In the long-run it is, we have seen, more likely a counter-productive strategy. It is unlikely that it is a possible strategy for any type of church, but it is especially difficult to combine it with the ecclesial and ethical approach of his type of political theology. He has also questioned the correlate of this process, the privatization of Christian convictions. His early work, in practice although not in word, did integrate also this privatization. We see this, for example, in his acceptance of the autonomy of politics. But in his later theology, he has forcefully (though not wholly consistently) tried to take the path of deprivatization. However, this requires also a rethinking of his radical individualism.

Instead of affirming modern individualism, Hauerwas describes the church as a community of virtue. In the short-run this will be a difficult approach, going against most developments inside the modern Western churches. But in the long-run something like this seems to be the only possibility for a church that claims to be a contrast society. Furthermore, when the consequences of modern liberal individualism are increasingly recognized, counter reactions might be expected both inside and outside the churches. We have seen this recognition already coming in American liberal Protestantism as well as in much current social theory.[79] In this situation a theology of Hauerwas' type can well be seen as providing resources for a more communal approach.

A similar scenario could be depicted concerning the conservative-liberal polarity in current church life. In the short-run this makes it difficult for Radical

---

[77]See Gabriel, *Christentum*, 130-133.
[78]See Milbank, *Theology and Social Theory*, 126-133, as well as above pp. 238-242.
[79]One recognizes that Western society has travelled rather far, when one reads following sentence: "It's hard to believe now, but for a long time the loss of community was considered to be liberating." (Etzioni, *The Spirit of Community*, 116.)

Reformation theology, because it either falls outside the dominant camps as irrelevant or is identified with the conservative side and therefore not understood. Political theology, on the other hand, thrives on this polarity, which it has also helped to create. However, this cultural war can also create counter reactions and/or the social and political situations may change so that the current lines of conflict may seem irrelevant. In such a situation, political theology, which has so closely identified itself with these conflicts, could lose some of its power of attraction. We have already seen one sign of this in the collapse of socialism. Such a development could make Radical Reformation theology more intelligible. In the next chapter, I will argue that this actually is the case in relation to newer developments in sociology and political and moral theory.

These changes are part of the general flux in recent intellectual life, commonly labelled postmodernism. We have seen that political theology is a distinct part of the so-called modern project. It wanted to mediate modernity and Christianity. We have further noted how Moltmann tries to free political theology from this close relation to modernity and how this has created severe tensions inside his theological program. It is difficult to find other North Atlantic political theologians that have done much better. Most of Catholic political theology seems to have identified itself with Habermas' project, which might be the premier defence of the project of modernity. Hauerwas, as has often been noted, can more easily relate to these new intellectual developments. His theology provides resources that might better help church and theology to deal christianly with a postmodern or postliberal culture.

The church lives, as both Hauerwas and Moltmann affirm, in an increasingly post-Constantinian situation. Christianity is no longer an established religion. In many European countries practising Christians constitute a minority. We have seen that Hauerwas thinks the process from establishment to disestablishment creates a difficult situation for his own theology. But when the dechristianization of the general culture advances and church and theology cannot any longer assume a supportive semi-Christian culture, a Radical Reformation approach may have advantages. It does not assume that all people "of good will" already really believe what the church believes, but can take the pluralistic situation seriously. The situation of political theology is again more ambiguous. It claims to be post-Constantinian, but still often identifies itself with what it thinks is the winning forces of history. Despite Moltmann's intentions, his theology risks becoming a new version of Constantinianism, in the sense that he identifies the work of the Spirit of God with special social movements and their hopes for a more just social system. As Yoder writes: "'What God is doing in the world,' or 'hope,' or 'salvation' is spelled out as a better power system yet to come, with which Christians proleptically should identify."[80] And Yoder points out that in this form the church's capacity for criticism is lower than in classical Constantinianism, be-

---

[80]Yoder, *The Priestly Kingdom*, 143.

cause it is not easy to be "concretely critical of a projected future",[81] especially when this is described as a just and peaceful society. Moreover, one can with Paul Ramsey wonder (and this applies to Moltmann) why 'post-Constantinians' can "(1) proclaim with joy the end of that era, yet (2) never hesitate to issue advice to states as if they were Christian kingdoms".[82]

To conclude, the prospects of both these types of theology are unsure. However, in the long run, the prospects for Hauerwas' theological politics may be better. The problems for political theology are reinforced by its internal tensions that partly have their source in an inadequate self-understanding. So one might say that Radical Reformation theology could provide political theology with resources that could help it both to see itself more truthfully and to develop a more consistent and socially more plausible theology. Moltmann's book *The Way of Jesus Christ* could be seen as one important step in this direction.

Even if one should find my argument in this chapter convincing, one worry may yet not be stilled. Moltmann's primary criticism of Radical Reformation theology is that it, because of its strong contrast between church and world, will leave the world to itself. We have seen why Hauerwas thinks this charge is misplaced. And in the next chapter I will argue that, when seen from the perspective of modern social theory, the theological politics of Hauerwas even has certain advantages over political theology in this respect.

---

[81]Ibid., 144. See further ibid., 141-144 and his *The Original Revolution*, 140-153. So also Hauerwas in *DFF* 199 n. 33 and Ellul, *The Subversion of Christianity*, 126f.
[82]*Speak Up for Just War or Pacifism*, 125.

Chapter 15

The Significance of the Politics of the Church
for the Politics of the World

We have seen that the most frequent criticism that Hauerwas faces is that his theology, even if it may be able to make a good case for its biblical and theological faithfulness, leads to withdrawal from responsible political action in the world. To concentrate on the politics of the church is to abandon the responsibility for the politics of the world. We have also seen that Hauerwas does not accept this description. It is for the sake of the world the church is an alternative *polis* offering the world alternatives it otherwise would not have. He thus does not accept the dichotomy faithfulness versus effectiveness. "This church knows that its most credible form of witness (and the most 'effective' thing it can do for the world) is the actual creation of a living, breathing, visible community of faith."[1] The previous chapters have given many examples of how he argues this. We have also seen the failures of political theology in this respect.

In this chapter I will take the argument one step further. Here I will try to show, in terms of Moltmann's own emphasis on the function of church and theology for the world's politics, how Hauerwas' account of the politics of the church can be seen as more relevant and fruitful for the politics of the world than Moltmann's own political theology. In the holistic way of argumentation I use, one can start the argument at different places. In this chapter I will start with the perspective of modern sociology and social theory seen as, so to say, the self-description of the politics of the world, and slowly work my way to a Radical Reformation perspective. In this way I will try to show that even when one starts from such an "outside" perspective, the fruitfulness of Hauerwas' theological politics is clearly seen. If Hauerwas theological convictions are true, that should not be entirely surprising.[2]

1. Political Theology and the Modern Rationalist and Utopian Project

Most modern social thinkers have shared the view that through natural and social science we are able to control our own history. The future is changeable and controllable through human action, and science and technique are seen as central political forces in the modern project. Social change is then a result of intentional and goal-directed choices between different alternatives. In other words,

---

[1]*RA* 47.
[2]Cf. Yoder's highly stimulating similar type of discussions in *The Original Revolution*, 140-176 and in *The Priestly Kingdom*, 80-101, which has inspired parts of the following. My discussion is, however, more sociologically oriented.

first comes the political will, then the process of implementing that will, and finally the desired result. In this view, the important thing, consequently, is how to make the right decisions. The executions of the decisions, however, are seen as relatively unproblematic. The major agent in this process is the state, and consequently the power over the state is important if one wants to control the forces of social change. Most practical political thinking seems to take some variant of this view for granted.

The foregoing has made it clear that this is also basically true for Moltmann. Moreover, the view that society is a human and historical project for realizing the kingdom of freedom and therefore basically formable through planned human action constitutes the basic framework for political theology. This confidence in human power and politics was most pronounced in his early writings, but even if his optimism has abated, the basic view is intact. For him the fundamental problem is antiquated structures and values. Technically, a radical reform of modern society is possible, the problems are wrong values and lack of political will. The basic way to change society is then to get people with the right values and the right political will at the places of decision making or forcing the already powerful to change policy. But he seems to consider the actual implementation of this good political will a rather uncomplicated matter. This is reinforced by the idea that the basic problem is oppression, and if oppression is taken away the realization of freedom is only a technical problem.

Consequently, he regards the struggle for the power over the state as crucial. We have further seen that he tends to take the polarity of state and individual for granted, which means a small place for what we later will call the civil society. The one obvious exception is the role of the social movements in his thinking, but his relation to them is telling. There is often in these movements a tension between building new social forms and a wish to take direct part in the struggle over the political power. In Moltmann's case the second part tends to take the central place.

We have, however, also noted themes in his writings that seem to partly point in another direction. I think of his anti-power theology of the cross, his criticisms of the Enlightenment search for power and concomitant epistemologies, his description of the church as a contrast society, and his newly found (but yet weak) stress on the local communities. However, these ideas do not seem to have as of yet seriously qualified his basic view.

a) The Unpredictable and Undirigable Nature of Social and Political Life

The described rationalist view of politics and social change are one of the most salient parts of the mythology of modern society, but this set of beliefs are also, from the point of view of sociology, political science and philosophy, some of the most discredited.[3] When pressed, few would actually defend them, but they still work as taken for granted, if not explicitly argued, background beliefs, because our political systems as well as our reforming and revolutionary movements assume them. These ideas seem strongest in the type of socialistically inspired radical movements that Moltmann has supported, but they permeate also liberal and conservative thought.

A basic and decisive obstacle for these views is the sheer complexity of society. It is simply impossible to have the sort of overview that is necessary for radical planned changes and the steering of society. It presupposes a knowledge about structures, relations and processes over a long time scale that we just do not have.

Behind the utopian thought of the nineteenth century, that has lived on in somewhat weaker forms in modern ideas of social engineering, was the hope to use the social sciences in the same way that natural sciences have been used. The social sciences should provide political decision-making with a set of law-like generalizations with predictive power. Alasdair MacIntyre, for one, has questioned even the bare possibility of such knowledge and pointed to "four sources of systematic unpredictability in human affairs."[4] The first is that we cannot predict radical conceptual innovations, for doing that would mean inventing the innovation. Consequently we can predict neither the future of science, nor social, moral or religious innovations. Second, because an observer cannot predict his own future action before he has made up his own mind, he cannot predict the impact of his own future action on others, and consequently cannot predict the action of these others. Third, in relation to game-theoretic approaches, he points to "the indefinite reflexivity of game-theoretic situations"[5], the imperfect knowledge that characterizes such situations that derives from the fact that players tend to maximize other players lack of information, the fact that several games are played simultaneously, and that we seldom start with fixed sets of players and definite areas for playing the game. The final source of unpredictability is the contingent nature of human life. If Cleopatra's nose had been shorter, then . . .

MacIntyre finds his view confirmed by the bad record of the predictions by social scientists and economists. If this is right, it has important consequences for

---

[3]On the following, see e.g. Ball, *Modern Politics and Government*, Birnbaum, *La fin du politique,* Brunsson and Olsen (eds.), *Makten att reformera,* Ellul, *L'illusion politique,* Hirdman, *Att lägga livet till rätta,* Nove, *The Economics of Feasible Socialism,* and Wittrock, *Möjligheter och gränser.* I also learned much of this when once engaged in research on Swedish health and care planning. See Rasmusson and Spjuth, *En studie i svensk hälso- och sjukvårdsplanering.*

[4]*After Virtue* 89. See further ibid., 71-102. Cf. also Giddens, *The Consequences of Modernity,* 36-45, 151-158, Ellul, *The Technological Bluff,* 77-99, and Luhmann, *Soziale Systeme,* 635-638. Rosenberg, *Economics* is a sustained argument about why economic theory is not only remarkably unsuccessful in prediction, but also why its predictive power has not increased during the last century and why there is little reason to believe that it will increase. So also McCloskey, *If You're So Smart.*

[5]*After Virtue,* 92.

the idea of social engineering and its basis in the claims of what MacIntyre calls "bureaucratic managerial expertise."[6] His conclusion is that

> [t]he experts' claim to status and reward is fatally undermined when we recognize that he possesses no sound stock of law-like generalisations and when we realise how weak the predictive power available to him is. The concept of managerial effectiveness is after all one more contemporary moral fiction and perhaps the most important of them all. . . . Our social order is in a very literal sense out of our, and indeed anyone's, control. No one is or could be in charge.[7]

Reformers and (post-)revolutionaries need an organization as a necessary instrument. The first requirement is that this organization is largely controllable and predictable, but it must also be efficient and effective. MacIntyre notes that these two characteristics seem to be incompatible.[8] To be effective it has to be very flexible, open for initiatives from below, and having many centres of decision-making, which means that a high level of organizational unpredictability has to be allowed. An organization more strictly controlled from above and therefore more predictable will be more rigid and inefficient.

Innumerable studies of the function of organizations confirm this. One example is the study led and edited by Nils Brunsson and Johan P. Olsen, *Makten att reformera.*[9] They show that modern organizations are continually changing and reformed. Reform is often part of the routine of organizations. But the possibilities to control the content of the reforms are limited. It is not difficult to reform in the direction of the organizational and societal development. Such reforms may be rather extensive, but then the role of reformers tends to be more or less exchangeable agents, rather than as actors that determine the changes in the direction wished by them. An organization, moreover, has a history that forms an organizational culture and identity, which is difficult to break with and which makes large and rapid changes unusual. To be successful, reformers often have to accommodate to the groups and organizations being reformed. The organizations live furthermore in specific societies and are influenced by the general culture and its expectations. Both long term historical and cultural developments and short term trends are important. In modern societies it is, for example, difficult to reform in any other direction than in the direction of more modernization and rationalization.[10] A related problem is that if a reform is wanted and discussed, the

---

[6]Ibid., 101.

[7]Ibid., 101.

[8]Ibid., 100f.

[9]In the following, I have used the more general and summarizing discussions in chapter one and twelve. See also Brunsson, *The Irrational Organization*, idem, *Politik och administration*, and Brunsson and Jönsson, *Beslut och handling*.

[10]One example is the difficulties the European Green parties have had in finding and living with more participatory and radical democratic organizational forms. Even if these forms are more faithful to their ideology, they tend to be less efficient and effective in the political and media struggle. At the time of writing the tendency in several of these parties is to come closer to the organizations of other parties.

opposition against it becomes also mobilized, which may hinder the reform. On the other hand, many of the most important changes occur without being planned or discussed. The authors also show the difference between formal and informal organizational levels, and that reforms are often made at the public formal level, while the more important informal level is left intact. Reforms that stay at the level of ideas and symbols may still have important effects on the public opinion's view of the organization or of the reform mindedness of the politicians behind them. Indeed, the interest of following up the results of reforms seems rather limited. The fact that reforms in themselves may raise hope about future changes and create the impression that changes already are effectuated are often politically more important than the eventual results.

These are some of the problems any reformers face, which make large scale social planning exceedingly difficult. Organizations might be better used if this situation were taken into account. However, the authors think that the rationalist instrumental view is so dominating that all the studies that show this view's lack of reality have little effect. They conclude their book with following words:

> The contents of the reforms are to a large extent determined by culturally determined rules and institutional values, the reformers sit in mental rather than physical prisons. The most important of these rules and values is precisely the idea that organizations should be steerable and reformable. This idea is hard to abandon not only for the reformers but also for others who want to act in the world of formal organizations.[11]

Because politicians are deeply dependent on this "bureaucratic managerial expertise" both when taking their decisions, as it provides the expert knowledge, and in implementing the decisions, which is done through organizations, their ability to intentionally control and determine the development of the society is limited. In addition, there is the problem of the political game itself and the relation to media and public opinion, which also makes a rational and long-term politics difficult.

This criticism of "managerial expertise" involves, as we have seen, a criticism of claims that has often been made by the social and economic sciences. If the criticism is accepted it is better to view these disciplines as parts of social history and practical philosophy. If they do not provide law-like generalizations with predictive power, they still provide historical and practical wisdom. It is in this latter sense I use these disciplines in this book.

b) The Role of Culture

Brunsson's and Olsen's comment that mental prisons often are more important as obstacles to change than the easier seen physical hindrances leads to another argument against the rationalist assumptions: the role of culture. Indeed, as MacIntyre, they see the rationalist perspective on determining organizations and

---

[11]*Makten att reformera*, 267.

societies as one of the most important examples of culturally imprisoned thought. Utopian thinking and social engineering, including the dominant forms of socialism, have usually downplayed cultural and moral factors or seen them as easily mallowable according to rational thought and planning. It is no accident that social engineering and varying emotivist (in Sweden so-called value nihilist) ethical theories have existed closely together.[12] Social change has usually been seen as basically a scientific and technical issue with cultural values and practices as following, or these values and practices in themselves as objects for rationalizing.

Though still dominating, these ideas have become more and more questioned, even in radical and socialist thought. The social movements often see themselves as a form of cultural movement that form alternative values and lifestyles that are better able to form survivable societies. This is also true for Moltmann. He can now discuss the values that "have guided the development of modern civilization" and he writes that

> [t]he political context of science and technology is determined by the sum total of the claims from which the collective behaviour of a society takes its bearings. The sum total of these prevailing wishes, demands and ideas are what we call the accepted values. Through the judgments to which they give rise, these values regulate the way people act, and give practical life its orientation.[13]

He further writes:

> These traditions have emerged from the interplay between the meaning of life as the society sees it, and the social and economic form of that life. Over a long period of history, systems of value and meaning have become very deeply rooted in the human subconscious. Changing them is painful, and usually takes a very long time. Societies which are unable fundamentally to alter their systems of value and meaning, so as to adapt themselves to the new situation, are unable to change as a whole.[14]

Moltmann writes this in relation to the ecological crisis, which has made, he argues, a basic change in the fundamental values of western civilization absolutely necessary. Because the time is short, the change must be rather rapid, which is a problem because of the normal slowness of cultural and moral change. Ronald Inglehart, for example, thinks that people's world-views are formed early. Later radical reconstructions are unusual and presuppose most often traumatic experiences. This means that we live with cultural and moral maps that were formed in relation to the social reality of our youth (and earlier, as we form our world-views from already fabricated concepts), and therefore not adapted to changes in reality. Consequently, radical changes come slowly with new generations.[15] We have also seen that the new social movements may be seen as a cognitive mobilization

---

[12]MacIntyre, *After Virtue*, 22-34, Hirdman, *Att lägga livet till rätta*, Källström, *Den gode nihilisten*.
[13]*GIC* 26 (39f).
[14]*GIC* 24 (38).
[15]*Culture Shift in Advanced Industrial Society*, 422-433.

of newer cultural values and experiences and therefore as shapers of new world-views and political perspectives.

When radical cultural and value shifts are seen, as Moltmann does, to be immediately urgent, the question becomes how to achieve and increase the rapidity of the changes. If, as in this case, part of the hoped for change is to overcome that search for power that characterizes our civilization, one might think that it cannot be done through the ordinary means of power or from above. This is a dilemma that faces the whole alternative movement, and it also shows the difficulty of overcoming rationalist and social engineering assumptions. For example, Karl-Heinz Hillmann, a spokesman for alternative movements, talks in his book *Wertwandel* about the need of a libertarian intentionally-planned value change (!), going from a more or less spontaneous to a rational formation of values. We have seen that Moltmann's thought also has severe difficulties in overcoming these tensions. Views like these tend to (in an unarticulated way) presuppose future harmonious social conditions. Even if pluralism is celebrated, it seems not to be taken very seriously, as it is often argued that the basic political and cultural direction these thinkers hope for is absolutely necessary for survival, and that everyone that gives priority to the universal interest will see reality in the same way. Of course, that is not a very plausible position, but it shows the inherent tensions in much alternative thinking, Moltmann's included.

c) Problems with the Democratic Idea

To the charge that Moltmann's theology, as most political theology, tends to assume some form of rationalist social engineering perspective, one might object by pointing to his strong defence of participatory democracy on all levels of society. But this objection does not hold up, because his view of democracy seems to presuppose the rationalist view that the crucial matter is how and by whom the political decisions are made and that the implementation of these decisions is a rather unproblematic technical matter. It does not by itself lessen the role of the "bureaucratic managerial expertise", because this expertise is needed both for preparing the political decisions and for managing the bureaucracy that shall accomplish them.

We have already seen the problems with this view. But there are further problems with the democratic idea. John Burnheim, in a book that discusses the possibilities of a radical anti-etatistic and minimal bureaucratic socialist democracy, takes up some of the problems.[16] First, how in a world of limits might votes express real preferences? Put differently, if one cannot have everything, one must choose, and the issue then becomes how to relate votes to alternative costs and to willingness to pay the costs? Second, "[i]n practice people do not have

---

[16] *Is Democracy Possible?*, 82-106. He thinks that "the lack of any clear and plausible view of how a democratic socialist society might work is, I believe, the main obstacle to significant radical activity" (p. 13).

definite preferences over the whole range of alternatives that affect them. They have neither the information nor the analytical skill nor the imagination"[17] requi-red by rationalistic models. Third, "there is no procedure, even in principle, by which all sets of expressed preferences can be aggregated into a social decision that guarantees an optimal solution to the task of reconciling them."[18] Fourth, practical social decision-making requires negotiations and the number of parties in a fruitful negotiation process is limited. Consequently, most decisions have to be left to representatives with a large degree of freedom, which makes the role of voting or direct participation small. Fifth, concerning referendums, he thinks that to prevent that "a relatively apathetic majority may block a proposal that is of great advantage to a minority simply out of distaste for change or because it in-volves some relatively trivial adjustment on their part", people ought to "be given votes in proportion to the degree in which they are affected"[19] by the decision. Determining that is of course exceedingly difficult. Moreover, he also thinks that a smaller, informed body often can make better decisions than the general public. Sixth, there are further problems with representative electoral systems. People often vote more on competence and performance than on issues, which is difficult anyhow because of the impossibility of separating different issues from each other, when one has to vote on whole packages. Another problem is that it often pays for parties to mystify issues. The role of media makes this situation even worse. Furthermore, "electoral politics does breed party politics, and party poli-tics breeds mediocrity and corruption."[20] He does not think that decentralization helps, because "decentralized democratic control by electoral processes is likely to produce a static and oppressive local chauvinism of a very conservative kind, the mirror, in fact, of the worst aspects of nationalism."[21]

The consequence of this criticism of the democratic idea need not be that one should give up the western type of democratic systems, as it might well be argued that we do not know any better alternative and because—and that may be the most important reason—it limits the power of the government, makes it replace-able and therefore sensitive to the public.[22]

---

[17]Ibid., 84.

[18]Ibid., 86.

[19]Ibid., 92.

[20]Ibid., 101.

[21]Ibid., 104.

[22]Cf. Yoder, *The Priestly Kingdom*, 151-171. Ian Shapiro writes that "democracy is better thought of as an ethic of opposition than a system of government." (*Political Criticism*, 277.) Burnheim himself, however, prefers a considerably different system, which he calls demarchy, which means "that most of the decisions . . . could be taken by autonomous specialized agencies that are co-ordinated by negotia-tion among themselves or, if that fails, by quasi-judicial arbitration, rather than by direction from a controlling body. Participation in the decision-making process in each body should extend not to 'the people' generally, but to those who are affected by the decision in question to the degree in which they are affected." (*Is Democracy Possible?*, 7f.) In his book he tries to develop what this could mean practically.

To this should be added a theme stressed by Hauerwas that we will return to later in this chapter, namely that democracy is depending on specific virtues and skills, which are not immediately available, but has to be learned. One of the greatest weaknesses of much discourse on participatory democracy is precisely the neglect of this factor, a neglect closely bound up with central commitments of liberal and socialist thought.

One of the frustrating things with Moltmann's writings on this subject is that he gives no clue whatsoever to what he, in terms of concrete institutional and political practice, means by his frequent talk about the necessity of democratic participation on all levels, by his assertion that 'the people' should become subject of its own destiny, or by his claim that the nations must "organize themselves into a collective subject of action".[23] The result is that his view can be used as indiscriminate criticism of every non-ideal state of affairs and as likewise indiscriminate legitimation of any radical demand for more democracy. Alec Nove has said that to say that 'society' should determine and articulate the needs of the society is "literally meaningless . . . It is like saying that 'the people' will decide the timetable of the London-Paris air service or the number of onions to be planted."[24]

This is not to say that state politics is unimportant. Even though it is more a question of administrating society than rationally planning it, it is, of course, an important task. Neither is it unimportant to discuss the direct participation of Christians in this task. However, if we see the limits of politics and planning we may reach a more realistic view of what can be done. Furthermore, it may help us to see the issue of social change from other perspectives that may throw a different light on the church's role. The church may have more important roles than taking part in the political power struggle. To these questions we will now turn.

2. Newer Developments in Social Thought

The above given criticism of the rationalist view of politics and social change ought to be, in its main lines, rather uncontroversial at the level of political science and sociology, even if not at the level of first order political discourse. The following discussion, however, will have a more tentative character. I will point to developments in recent social thought that indicate alternative and arguably more fruitful ways of understanding politics and social change, that make the social and political relevance of the Radical Reformation theology of Hauerwas more plausible than it appears from the rationalist perspective in which Moltmann basically tends to work. I also think that one might cogently maintain that much of Moltmann's theology, especially in his later writings, would make more sense

---

[23]*CJF* 22 (36).
[24]*Feasible Socialism*, 39.

from this perspective, but it would entail radical revisions he may be unwilling to undertake.

Margareta Bertilsson argues in an article on recent tendencies in social thought that modern sociology is a nineteenth century construct formed by the symbiosis between politics and science in the modern project.[25] The fusing of state and society in the welfare state conception[26] has, in addition, tended to degenerate sociology into "social administration" and "social statistics". She thinks, however, that a reformulation process has started in the theoretically informed parts of modern sociology that in a more distinct way separates the social order from the state and from the market. She mentions especially communitarian approaches that "focus on the life-giving, natural and thus more genuine communities (the family, the neighbourhood, the collective) and contrasts these with the artificially created and basically parasitic state community (a community made possible by positive law)."[27] This approach is in the same way and for the same reason critical of the dominating role of the market in modern society.

This type of perspective has become conceptualized in several different ways. One recently revived account of this understanding is the idea of the "civil society". This concept has a complex history and was often used, although in a variety of ways, in the social and political thought of eighteenth and nineteenth century, but then mostly disappeared.[28] It is especially Central and East European intellectuals who are responsible for its recent renaissance, but it has also become used for understanding Western types of societies.[29] As mentioned, it has been used in different ways, but for our general purpose Michael Walzer's definition is enough. "The words 'civil society' name the space of uncoerced human association and also the set of relational networks—formed for the sake of family, faith, interest, and ideology—that fill this space."[30] This idea thus attempts to explicate the fact that social life is much more than market and state and shows this fact's social and political as well as theoretical significance. Other concepts have been used, including "informal" or "voluntary sector", "autonomous sphere" and "mediating institutions". These diverse conceptualizations entail important differences, and an interesting argument concerning their relative adequacy is not in-

---

[25]"Sociologins kärna—i förändring?" On the homology between modern economic and political theory and modern society, and for a Christian deconstruction of these theories, see again Milbank's *Theology and Social Theory*. See also Hauerwas, "In Praise of *Centesimus Annus*", 427.

[26]In modern Swedish language "society" and "public" have become more or less synonymous with state, or more exactly with national, regional and local government.

[27]"Sociologins kärna", 21. She refers to people like Gadamer, MacIntyre, Sandel, Bellah, Bell, and Etzioni.

[28]On its history, see Keane, "Despotism and Democracy". Noteworthy, however, might be Michael Walzer's comment that "[c]ivil society as we know it has its origin in the struggle for religious freedom." ("The Idea of Civil Society", 300.) The Radical Reformation played here, as often noted (e.g. by Moltmann), an important role, even if the different ways the civil society later has become conceptualized not all can be identified with the Radical Reformation theology.

[29]See e.g. Keane (ed.), *Civil Society and the State*.

[30]"Civil Society", 293.

consequential, but still they all point in the same general direction. Theories of civil society, furthermore, often have both a descriptive and normative purport. They first of all help us to understand modern society more adequately. For many of their users, however, they are also important for overcoming the perceived impasses in modern political thought and practice.

First of all, the sheer importance of this sphere for the good life is stressed. Also its role as social space for moral discourse and formation, for the training in democratic skills and habits, and for the practice of and training in communal solidarity is often mentioned. Another common theme is the necessity of a vital civil society both for the proper functioning of the market and of the welfare state. The worry of many is that the bureaucratic welfare state and the institutions of corporate capitalism gradually displace this sphere, with serious results for moral formation, solidarity, the public discourse, as well as for the market and the welfare state themselves.

Alan Wolfe's *Whose Keeper?* is one ambitious (though I think partly flawed) attempt to develop these themes. He does it through an extensive critique of dominating economic, political and social theories and through an analysis of the American market-oriented society and the Scandinavian welfare states. His conclusion is that the civil society in both systems tends to be overtaken by market and state and that the instrumental rationality of the market system as well as that of the welfare bureaucracy erodes and impoverishes the basically non-instrumental moral languages and social practices of the civil society. The rationalist welfare state project was intended partly to defend human life and solidarity from being formed by a purely economic rationality, and partly to rationalize what was conceived as irrational and not systematically planned forms of social life. In the process, however, it contributed to the erosion of the social solidarity grown out of every day life that was the base for the very development of the welfare state. It is so, he contends, because "the welfare state works best when it builds on and strengthens already existing social ties",[31] and does not try to take their place. Significantly, he thinks this weakening of the moral and social ties in the civil society (not least in family life) affects most strongly the weakest members of the society. "Reliance on government instead of the moral ties of civil society to express obligations between people improves the social conditions of most but worsens the lot of those who, already worse off, lack the resources to operate effectively in a system organized around political rules."[32] He does not, however, think that the substitution of a market-oriented system for the welfare state in itself helps, because the market system erodes the civil society as least as much, and again the weakest are most affected.[33] Instead, he recommends the support

---

[31]*Whose Keeper?* 109.

[32]Ibid., 150.

[33]Ibid., 80. Generally, he considers the Scandinavian societies as more successful than the American society.

and the giving of a larger social space for the civil society in relation to the still necessary state and market.

This growing emphasis on the civil society cannot be easily defined in right-left categories, because this polarity is based on the opposition between market and state and on a common devaluation of the civil society.[34] For Wolfe, like for many others on the left, ideas of the civil society seems to have become a way forward for a post-socialist or post-social democratic theory and practice. In France, for example, we find a similar basic questioning of the dominant role of the state and the large economic structures in the writings of such post-socialist thinkers as Cornelius Castoriadis, Jacques Ellul and André Gorz.[35] They all stress the crucial significance of an autonomous sector beside the heteronomous economic and political structures. An important part of their case is their criticism of the dominating role of salaried work in modern life, politics and (not least socialist) ideology, and they emphasize instead the (not non-work!) sectors of life outside formal salaried work.[36]

On the conservative side Peter Berger and Richard Neuhaus have developed somewhat similar ideas.[37] They talk in terms of mediating structures between the individual and the megastructures of the larger society (which include the state and the large economic institutions). Modernity is characterized by a deep dichotomy between private and public life. The importance of these mediating structures is that it is at this level personal meaning and identity is formed, which neither the megastructures nor the isolated individual can realize. They "have a private face, giving private life a measure of stability, and they have a public face, transferring meaning and value to the megastructures." They thereby reduce "both the anomic precariousness of individual existence in isolation from society and the threat of alienation to the public order."[38] Berger and Neuhaus charge most modern political thinking (liberal, conservative and socialist) with being blind to the crucial role of these mediating structures or of seeing them as a cultural lag from a bygone society. The main political debate concerns instead the relative roles of market and government. But both faith in market and faith in government share the abstract, universalist and rationalist thought patterns of the Enlightenment. For Berger and Neuhaus these mediating structures, however, are essential

---

[34]Alberto Melucci thinks that this type of considerations suggests a radical redefinition of politics. He thinks that "the increasing difficulty of maintaining the classic distinction between 'right' and 'left' political traditions" is an indication of this situation. He continues saying that "[t]he analytical vacuity of the term 'left' is now evident. While its sole function is that of empirically defining political agents linked to the Western historical tradition, it no longer reveals anything about either the new conflicts and actors or about the direction of contemporary social and political transformation." ("Social Movements and the Democratization of Everyday Life", 253.) Cf. Wolfe, *Whose Keeper?*, 210.

[35]Castoriadis, *Le Contenu du socialisme*, Ellul, *Changer de révolution*, and Gorz, *Farewell to the Working Class*. See also Rosanvallon, "The Decline of Social Visibility".

[36]Cf. also Christensen, "Lönearbetet som samhällsform och ideologi".

[37]*To Empower People*.

[38]Ibid., 3.

for a democratic society, and they therefore argue that "[p]ublic policy should protect and foster mediating structures, and wherever possible, public policy should utilize mediating structures for the realization of social purposes."[39] It is at this level that people mostly can influence their own lives, from which it follows, that giving a central place to these structures is the best way to empower people, and especially the poor.

A further stream of thought is the one developed in Eastern Europe. Václav Havel's reflections in the text "The Power of the Powerless"[40] are, for my purpose, an especially interesting example. The context of his reflections is the so-called dissident phenomenon in, what he calls, the post-totalitarian societies of Eastern Europe before 1989. Havel here describes an "anti-political politics"[41] that stands in sharp contrast to most ordinary political thinking. Here the struggle for the power over the political system is not in the centre, nor abstract political visions of an alternative system, but the "living in truth" and the many purposeful small steps in everyday life. The context for reflection is not principles but the ordinary practice of everyday life and therefore, he argues, changes on the existential and moral plane have primacy over economic changes. He analyzes how the political system is built on the expectation that people play their expected roles, which makes a consistent "living in truth" dangerous for the system and "the chief breeding ground for independent, alternative political ideas".[42] This individual and communal "living in truth" can, from below and in the pre-political sphere, lead to the development of alternative structures (in, for example, culture, information, education, and even economy), which might develop into a parallel *polis*.[43] This should not be understood as a flight into a ghetto, but as a responsible activity for the world. He therefore discusses how it might lead to changes also in the broader society, at the same time as he criticizes a calculative attitude. This parallel *polis* has its origin not in political calculation, but in the practice of truth in everyday life. He thus stresses the indirect effects in the whole society of changes in moral life and social practice in the civil society, rather than the direct work against the system[44] (even if he reflects on possible political consequences). Dissident movements "understand systemic change as something superficial, something secondary, something that in itself can guarantee nothing"[45] and consequently see violent political revolutions as totally foreign because they are not radical enough.

---

[39]Ibid., 6. Italicized in the original.

[40]*Václav Havel or Living in Truth*, 36-122.

[41]Cf. Havel, "Anti-Political Politics".

[42]*Living in Truth*, 62. The Swedish translation of this text have "politics" instead of "political ideas" (*En dåre i Prag*, 90).

[43]He is here (*Living in Truth*, 100-104) inspired by Václav Benda, "Det alternativa pólis".

[44]"In fact, all eventual changes in the system, changes we may observe here in their rudimentary forms, have come about as it were *de facto*, from 'below', because life compelled them to, not because they came before life, somehow directing it or forcing some change on it." (*Living in Truth*, 102.)

[45]Ibid., 92.

These thinkers obviously do not represent a common position. Their differences and disagreements are often sharp and major. But they all ask radical questions about the rationalistic etatistic project of modernity that for a long time has dominated Western political theory and practice. At the same time, they give what we have called the civil society a more substantial place in the understanding of social existence and politics. A consequence is that the processes of social change are seen from a different angle. The belief in the large-scale rational restructuring of society from above, either through reform or through revolution, is radically revised and complemented or replaced by a stress on the major political importance of the informal spheres of life. Put in more graphic terms, one might speak about "change from below".

Robert Putnam has recently published an important book, *Making Democracy Work*, built on a quarter of a century study of the performance of Italian regional governments. His findings, which he describes as a contribution to an empirical evaluation of the debate between communitarian and liberal political theory,[46] are startling. In 1970 Italy created a new system of regional governments and Putnam and his collaborators have studied the performance of these governments. Not surprisingly, they found great differences between different regions, especially between north and south. However, more interesting is the fact that these differences were much better explained by the degree of civic culture than by any other factor, including economic development, educational level, social stability, and urbanism. With civic culture he means things like social trust, norms of generalized reciprocity, and horizontal networks of civic engagement. It is this sort of social capital that encourage and ease cooperation and make institutions effective and dependable. In a society lacking in civic culture, that is, a society characterized by distrust, shirking, exploitation, and few horizontal networks, cooperation is difficult. For the individual it is rational not to cooperate. In such cultures hierarchical ways of enforcing collective action predominate: coercion, dependence and exploitation. This is both inefficient and expensive. Thus in a society with a strong civic culture both market and government work better and the degree of coerciveness is lower. The more complex a society is the more important is the degree of civic culture. This study does not support the idea that civic culture only can exist in premodern societies. Quite the opposite. It is the modern northern Italy that has the strongest civic culture.[47]

Civic culture is built up slowly. It cannot be engineered. In the case of Italy Putnam has to go back to the twelfth century to find the starting point for the different paths the northern and southern parts of Italy has taken. At this time Sicily was the richest and the most well organized state of Europe, but it was also

---

[46]*Making Democracy Work*, 87.

[47]A recent study, Denvall and Wollinger, *I gemenskapens tjänst?*, of a social project in Arlöv, the town in which I live, shows concretely how the lack of civic culture makes the official ideas of local participation, community and engagement empty. It is also a good illustration of the institutional reality Brunsson and Olsen describe above.

strongly centralized and hierarchical. Southern Italy has since then been characterized by hierarchical relations. In northern Italy arose at the same time city states characterized by a high level of civic engagement and networks that created a very different civic culture.[48]

Putnam believes that this study has much relevance also for understanding the different developments in Eastern Europe after 1989. Many of these countries had weak civic cultures already before they became Communist. The Communist era further weakened the civic traditions there were. He is therefore not too optimistic. Even if institutional reforms help shape civic traditions, the performance of institutions is highly dependent on the civic context. This also explains why some of these countries succeed much better. They can build on a social capital that Communism has not totally destroyed.[49]

In the described views the relative autonomy of the civil society in relation to state and market is defended. Consequently, instead of putting the main stress on more reforms from above or on the necessity of a revolution that totally restructures society, the importance of starting in the civil society when working for social change is stressed. This requires independent social and public spaces where, as Alberto Melucci says, "the signifying practices developed in everyday life can be expressed and heard independently of formal political institutions."[50] Mellucci says this in a discussion of the social movements, whose role is also more understandable in terms of some account of the importance of the civil society.[51] In these perspectives autonomous local experiments and pilot projects become as important for social change as grand government projects and planning.

This is a more modest view than the rationalist utopian vision we have criticized. It takes the limits of the human ability seriously. As Amitai Etzioni says:

> Once one fully recognizes, absorbs, and deeply accepts the limitations of the human ability to know and the pivotal roles of affect and values, one's approach to the world, especially to decision-making, change significantly. Instead of the hyperactive orientation of setting goals, marshalling the 'most efficient' means, and 'implementing'—which assumes that we are God-like creatures and the world (including our fellow human beings) is putty—one

---

[48]Religiosity formed by the Italian Catholic Church does not contribute to these civic attitudes and practices. The modern exception was the Catholic Action, the vigorous federation of lay associations after the World War II. These, however, collapsed in the 1960s. (*Making Democracy Work*, 107-109.) In the middle ages a more congregational form of Catholic Christianity was important for the formation of the civic community in the north. (Ibid., 127.) In the nineteenth century a strongly associational form of Social Catholicism had a similar role. (Ibid., 141.) He also mentions Protestant congregationalism as a historically positive factor outside Italy. (Ibid., 173.)

[49]He also points to the relevance for the Third World. Cf. Hydén, *No Shortcuts to Progress* for strong support.

[50]"Social Movements", 259.

[51]Håkan Thörn and Tomas Eskilsson, two socialists discussing the socialist strategy after 1989, similarly argues that the most important political struggle now takes place at the cultural field outside the formal production sector. This is also, they maintain, the base for the new social movements, who are more concerned with reproduction than production. See "Den gamla vänstern och de nya rörelserna".

grows humble. Most times we lack the knowledge needed for sound decisions. Hence, we must proceed carefully, ready to reverse course, willing to experiment; in short humbly.[52]

3. The Social and Political Fruitfulness of Radical Reformation Theology and Practice

a) Hauerwas' Critique of Rationalist Assumptions

Political theology was explicitly conceived as a Christian response to the rationalist utopian project of modernity. Moltmann's theology of hope was partly a Christian justification of the great optimism of this project in its radical version. As the optimism of the 1960s abated and as new social movements, partly more critical of the modern project, arose, Moltmann has qualified his endorsement, even if he has not withdrawn it. He partakes in the ambiguity often inherent in the social movements he supports toward the modern political project. In contrast, Hauerwas has from the beginning of his writing career been deeply suspicious of the hubris of modern political ideology. We have repeatedly seen that a crucial component of his theology is that the church has to learn to live "out of control". This attitude is based on the belief that God has redeemed the world through the life, death and resurrection of Jesus Christ and that the church is called to live in light of this fact, and that God will use this faithfulness, because it reflects the way God works in the world. Hauerwas does not, as we have seen, believe that these practices stand in opposition to work for a more just and peaceful world. But he questions the illusions of modern Prometheanism.

> To live out of control, however, does not mean that we do not plan and/or seek to find the means to promote justice in the world, but that such planning is not done under the illusion of omnipotence. We can take the risk of planning that does not make effectiveness our primary goal, but faithfulness to God's kingdom. To plan in such a manner involves breaking the self-deception that justice can only be achieved through a power and violence that seeks to assure its efficacy.[53]

My criticisms of the rationalist outlook give this view further support. However, it is important to note that this criticism of political theology is not dependent on a more "pessimistic" anthropology that strongly stresses human sinfulness. For even if humans were angels and totally good, the rationalist project would still fail, because angels still lack omniscience and omnipotence. And as Etzioni says, something like that is in practice presupposed in the rationalist project.[54]

---

[52]*The Moral Dimension*, 244.

[53]*PK* 105.

[54]MacIntyre says the same thing when, discussing the second source of systematic unpredictability mentioned above, he writes: "Another way of putting the same point would be to note that omniscience excludes the making of decisions. If God knows everything that will occur, he confronts no as yet unmade decisions. He has a single will . . . It is precisely insofar as we differ from God that unpredictability invades our life. This way of putting the point has one particular merit: it suggests precisely what project those who seek to eliminate unpredictability from the social world or to deny it may in fact be

One reason for the prominence of consequentialist theories of ethics is the rationalist assumptions of control that dominate modernity.[55] We have seen that at the time when Moltmann in an almost unqualified way subscribed to the ideas of human control of its own history, he justified revolutionary violence in consequentialist terms. However, faced with the overwhelming character of modern means of warfare he has in later writings defended a Kantian approach, which reflects a less optimistic view on the human capability of calculation, but preserves the rationalist idea of seeing the world from a perspective outside history. Hauerwas, in contrast, questions both the assumptions of control that lie behind Moltmann's consequentialist reasonings and the foundationalist assumptions of Kantianism and follows instead the third ethical mode that Moltmann uses, namely that of the ecclesial discipleship.[56]

b) Hauerwas and Accounts of the Civil Society

My suggestion is thus that the critique of the rationalist etatistic project, and the newer developments in social thought that I have outlined, create an intellectual space that makes Hauerwas' theology more intelligible and plausible. The accounts of the civil society should not, however, be understood as providing a systematic context for understanding the place of the church in society. Hauerwas' view of the church makes such an approach impossible. Neither should this understanding be interpreted as a normative defence of the autonomy of the economic and political spheres from a moral and cultural sphere. The recent concern

---

engaging in." (*After Virtue*, 92.) Hauerwas writes: "The view of rationality offered by the standard account is pretentious exactly as it encourages us to try to free ourselves from history. In effect, it offers us the possibility of being like God. Ironically enough, however, this is not the God of the Jews and the Christians since . . . that God does not will himself to be free from history." (*TT* 24.) On consequentialism and Kantianism as moral theories rooted in our "attempt to free ourselves from a finite location within nature and history", see Meilander, *Faith and Faithfulness*, 89-113. The quote is from p. 93. Cf. also Nove, *Feasible Socialism*, 15-20, who makes the point in very concrete terms.

[55] In few countries in the world have these assumptions been such a central part of the official ideology as in Sweden. The dominance for consequentialist theories in Sweden is therefore not surprising. Wolfe thinks that in its politics "[m]arket-oriented societies tend to focus on procedures" while "[w]elfare states, especially those in Scandinavia, tend to be consequentialist". (*Whose Keeper?*, 245). Cf. also Stout, *Ethics after Babel*, 286f.

[56] In addition, two hundred years of violent revolutionary history ought to have given second thoughts. Most violent revolutions have simply failed. The results have instead been more polarization and increased oppression. Most of the violent revolutions that actually have succeeded have furthermore created immensely more oppressive systems than the ones dethroned and the attempts to create radically different and good societies have basically failed. (See e.g. Dunn, *Modern Revolutions*, idem, *The Politics of Socialism*, Eberstadt, *The Poverty of Communism*, Ellul, *The Autopsy of Revolution*, idem, *De la Révolution aux révoltes*, idem, *Changer de révolution*, and Skocpol, *States and Social Revolutions*.) The record of non-violent revolutions as well as of more reformist strategies is clearly better, even if still ambiguous, which Moltmann today seems to recognize, but without always wanting to take the consequences of. (See *CJF* 44f, "Die Christenheit und das Neue Europa", and cf. Hauerwas' comments in *TT* 234 n. 7.)

with the civil society has arisen from the opposite worry, namely that the economic institutions and a bureaucratic welfare state undermine the institutions, practices and solidarity of civil society. In this light my account might be read as an example of "tactic" as described in chapter 10. The usual idea is that without control or decisive influence on the political and economic institutions one is powerless. The accounts of the importance of the civil society and civic culture show that this is not the case. The civil society creates the context for the political and economic life. Putnam's study, for example, gives strong support to Hauerwas' claims for the central political importance of communities that form virtuous people and that a good government, or, say, medical care, is dependent on virtuous communities. And it can have extremely long-time effects, because civic culture is a self-reinforcing resource that creates good circles. The stronger civic culture, the better cooperation works, which in its turn reinforces the virtues of the civic culture and makes defection more difficult.[57]

However, Hauerwas should not be too closely identified with these perspectives. The most important difference is that Hauerwas makes the church and not the national community primary. There will always be an uneasy relationship between a church as Hauerwas understands it and accounts of the civil society that evaluates its effects in terms of how it helps the current nation-state and liberal democracy to function. On the more empirical level he is also more pessimistic than either Berger and Neuhaus or Walzer and Wolfe about the long-term sustainability of these practices and institutions in modern liberal societies. He is consequently more critical of the dominating role of the market, and generally of accepting its autonomy, than is Berger and Neuhaus, more suspicious of the emancipatory ideologies than Wolfe and Gorz, and does not share the establishment perspective (even if oppositional) they all have in common.

In the light of this, it is not surprising that Hauerwas' Radical Reformation theology shows most affinity with the dissident perspective of Havel.[58] In the view of the liberal society this theology is a dissident perspective. There are several obvious similarities that have to do with their common dissident position (when Havel wrote the text we used). The crucial significance of "living in truth" is a theme that goes through most of Hauerwas' writings. Referring to Havel, Hauerwas writes: "Truth and non-violence is the power of the powerless . . . for only through truth can we resist the lies that are the sources of violence."[59] He likewise stresses the political importance of everyday life and concentrates, in Havel's words, more on society than on the power structures as such.[60] Furthermore, his non-control perspective is close to Havel's non-calculative approach. Faithfulness to the truth and not political calculation forms their actions, at the

[57]Putnam, *Making Democracy Work*, 178.
[58]Hauerwas has also, in some of his most recent writings, very positively referred to the text by Havel used above. See *AC* 165 n. 3, *"Centesimus Annus"*, 419f, 423-425, 427f, and "The Splendor of Truth".
[59]*"Centesimus Annus"*, 428.
[60]Havel, *Living in Truth*, 105.

same time as they defend the social and political significance of life in truthfulness. Hope and patience become thus for both central virtues.[61] Connected to this is their scepticism towards general social theories and political utopias. They therefore conceive the church's attitudes respectively the dissident movement's attitudes towards and relations with specific political developments and strategies in ad hoc-terms. That is, they discuss such questions more in terms of concrete situations than in the light of general social theories or abstract utopian ideas. Finally, Hauerwas understands the church as an alternative *polis*, which can develop alternative social practices and institutions.

There are, of course, also differences. The church is something more than a dissident movement in general and has its own specific understanding of reality and concomitant practice and an eschatological hope that goes far beyond Havel's perspective. Another important difference is that Hauerwas has developed his perspective in a liberal society and Havel his in the Communist post-totalitarian world. It might be asked if Havel's perspective has sufficient tools for being sustained in a liberal society.[62] But still, the commonality grounded in their common dissident situation is telling.

c) The Power of the Church as a Contrast Society

Both Moltmann and Hauerwas see the church as the subject of their ethical thinking. Both write ethics for the church, but the way they do it is different. Because Moltmann makes the state or the superstate the primary agent of justice, his ethics is primarily concerned with which side Christians should support and how they should partake in the struggle for control over this agent. In Hauerwas' view, on the other hand, the agency of the state is only one component in the processes of social change. For him, a more important contribution is the church's own life as a social project, which however does not exclude speaking to the government.[63]

In his early theology Moltmann explicitly maintained that a church concentrating on what we have called the civil society would not contribute to change in society, but would only function in compensating ways, and therefore, if anything, more than likely delay change rather than incite it.[64] And his political reflections are still primarily concerned with the state and the market and therefore with direct political activism. But there are exceptions, most clearly seen in an interest-

---

[61]Cf. Havel's more recent text "Godot kommer inte ty han finns ej" on hope and patience.

[62]Havel's hopes, at least when writing this, are clearly post-liberal, or as he says "post-democratic". See *Living in Truth*, 119f. See further ibid., 113-120. There are also consequential philosophical differences between Hauerwas and Havel's phenomenological perspective.

[63]Hauerwas writes that "while I am not opposed to our trying to harness the resources of state power to alleviate the needs of people, I think it is unfortunate when we think only in those terms." ("Will the Real Sectarian Stand Up", 90.)

[64]*TH* 316-321, esp. 320 (292-296, 295).

ing, but little known book titled *Diakonie im Horizont des Reiches Gottes*.[65] It is significant, I think, that in this book it is the care of the handicapped and the retarded that determines his account. A central question in Hauerwas' work has just been which sort of community is needed to be able to welcome handicapped and retarded people.[66] In Moltmann's book we find the central ideas of the modern welfare state: human dignity, rights and the responsibility of the state. But the dominant theme is another, more critical of the welfare state.[67] First, the welfare state is a function of the industrial system and has basically a compensating function. Second, it administrates people's lives and concerns from above, which produces apathy and individualism and therefore a lack of commitment and concern for each others welfare. The state becomes the subject and the people the passive object. His alternative is a society built up from below, which means self-management, base democracy and cooperative enterprises.[68]

The churches are, Moltmann continues, in themselves base communities that can create social forms and practices that provide real alternatives to the welfare state. Crucial here is that the social handicap that follows physical and psychical handicap only can be overcome through community. And the church should be a healing community. The basis is not help, but friendship, common life, and solidarity, where the handicapped and retarded can be integrated in the church's life as community, and where the experiences and life-worlds of these people must become part of the non-handicapped people's world. He thinks that, while the diaconal church cannot make institutions superfluous, many handicapped and retarded people could live outside institutions if the churches functioned as diaconal communities. But such a diaconal church must be a charismatic church, a church where through the gifts of the Spirit all members, and not only professionals, take their responsibilities.

It has been my argument in this book that the wing of the contemporary church Moltmann identifies himself with, and, mirroring this, his own political theology, not only lack the resources needed for the sustenance of this sort of church life and politics, but actually undermine it by their understanding of freedom, community and politics. When life and politics are reduced to questions of oppression and liberation, accounts of the formation of virtuous communities are easily seen as repressive, and politics is reduced to conflicts of interests. The political importance of everyday life is downplayed and political activism is com-

---

[65]A shorter version of *DHRG* 22-41 is found in *HC* 21-36.

[66]For this question, see e.g. *SP* 185. More generally, see *VV* 187-194, *TT* 147-183, *SP* 157-217, and *DFF* 177-186.

[67]The first is primarily found in *DHRG* 42-51 and the second in *DHRG* 18-41 (partly in *HC* 21-36); in other words, they are found in different chapters, and he does not really show how to integrate them. The following is primarily built on the second text.

[68]*DHRG* 18-20, 39f (*HC* 35f). He considers this perspective to be close to the one of subsidiarity in Catholic social thought. In a recent text he likewise says that "[t]he rebuilding of human society will . . . begin with local communities which can be seen and experienced and will restore to the local communities many functions and tasks which have been centralized." (*CJF* 9 [21], cf. 13f [25f].)

mended. The result has been a weakening of the community life and therefore a decline in local impact, which has gone together with a bureaucratization of the social witness and a strong emphasis on the agency of the state.[69]

The emphasis given to political activism and the belief in the power of government policy are, we have seen, typical of the Postmaterialist/New Class fraction, beliefs strengthened by their central location in the power structure of modern societies. Yet most people do not experience themselves as subjects of the history or that they can significantly influence even local or national politics. For them, most Christians included, everyday life is more important. That is a sphere that one can understand and have some control over. Above all, it is there they live most of their life, it is there they find identity and meaning. Family, friendship, neighbourhood, local church life, and work are central. Moltmann's theology, however, has not much to say about everyday life, more than giving the people the impression that they are wrong in being so absorbed in the minor things of everyday life that they do not have time over for the more important political struggles. This might be a significant reason why political theology in the Western world has failed to have a major impact on the local church level in contrast to the level of church agencies and national assemblies.

Hauerwas' different understanding of freedom and politics, and his concrete account of practices and virtues of the communal life, has helped him to begin develop the conceptual resources for understanding the importance of the civil society and therefore also of the everyday life. For him questions of family, marriage, sexuality, child bearing,[70] and work are as much public and political questions as peace and care of the retarded and handicapped are. Everyday life is dependent on the shape of the church, just as the church is dependent on how people live their daily life, because daily life is church life. It is not a sphere that can be separated from the life of the Christian community, for the church is not primarily, in Hauerwas' understanding, a bunch of activities, but a people with a specific identity. He has therefore spent much time theologically analysing these areas of life.[71]

---

[69]Hauerwas comments: "Too often ideals and strategies for 'social justice' are but formulas that attempt to make the poor and oppressed better off without requiring anything of us." (*PK* 105.) About his own Methodist denomination he writes the following: "Indeed I suspect there is almost an inverse ratio between the undisciplined character of the Methodist people and the radical nature of our social statements. We draft radical statements as substitute for being a radical people pledged to witness to the world that God's peace is not just some ideal but a present possibility for us." ("Epilogue", 152f.)

[70]He thus says that "one of the most morally substantive things any of us ever has the opportunity to do is to have children." (*CC* 165.)

[71]Cf. Elshtain's discussion in *Public Man, Private Woman*, 55-99 of the "moral revolution" (p. 56) early Christianity ushered into the world. "Christianity redeemed and sanctified both *each individual life* as well as *everyday life*, especially the lives of society's victims, and granted each a new-found dignity—a *dignitatis*—previously reserved only to the highborn, the rich, or the powerful. At the same time the private sphere, that 'lesser' realm of necessity in Greek thought, was lifted from Greek contempt and elevated to an importance and honor once reserved exclusively for the sphere of 'freedom,'

This concentration on the church's life and on everyday life does not, Hauerwas thinks, prevent the church from speaking to the larger society. Instead it is to make use of the best resources of the church. The church, as a distinct community with its own tradition, can be a carrier of alternative practices and alternative ways of seeing the world. We have noted the difficulty of thinking outside the frame of modernity and liberal and socialist ideologies—even for opponents. The social life and structures tend to work as "grids" that make alternative thinking difficult. We have, for example, mentioned earlier the difficulties of questioning the dominance of the languages of freedom/emancipation and rights, because the concrete structures of social life in a liberal society as well as the internal logic of the basic liberal ideology tend to make them self-evident.

A church with a strong sense of community, living with a tradition and practices that partly stand apart from the dominating stories, traditions and practices of modernity (as a contrast society), might have a larger ability (because of a different "grid") and the social space to see modern society from other perspectives, and to form and sustain new ways of thinking and living. Hauerwas and Yoder are good examples of theological reflection using these resources.

We have seen the importance of forming alternative social practices and institutions outside the government structures. On this Yoder has written:

> The church undertakes pilot programs to meet previously unmet needs or to restore ministries which have collapsed. The church is more able to experiment because not all ministries need to pay off. She can take the risk of losing or failing, more than can those who are in charge of the state. Popular education, institutionalized medicine, and the very concept of dialogical democracy in the Anglo-Saxon world generalize patterns which were first of all experimented with and made sense of in free-church Christianity.[72]

Observe the importance given by Yoder to the freedom for experimentation given by the fact that the church does not assume that it has the control or that its first responsibility is to write ethics or give policy recommendations to the government. It can carry ideas and practices that at the moment seem unrealistic, and therefore are not an option for the power at hand, but that at a later time may become credible. A minority can do this because they do not primarily evaluate their faith and practice according to public opinion or in terms of short-range effectiveness.[73] Yoder also points to the specific strength of a dissident believing community. "The subordinate community with its own internal covenants is able to provide economic and social as well as moral support to individuals standing with it against the stream who could not stand alone."[74] This again points to the impor-

---

that public space within which male citizens debated important things and were heroes together." (Ibid., 58.)

[72] *The Priestly Kingdom*, 92.

[73] Ibid., 96f. Cf. Veldhuis, *Realism versus Utopianism?*, 160.

[74] *The Priestly Kingdom*, 91.

tance of common discipleship and commitment to each other and to the neighbour, where one learns to live a life of service and to put the kingdom of God first. Here the church has resources that both government and market lack.

Moltmann would surely in general agree with much of this, but the primary question his theology has been concerned with has been another: Which sort of church can retain the church involvement of people who are active in the social movements, and which church can mobilize its members to be active in these movements? Therefore the language of dignity, rights and self-realization becomes central for him. This makes the formation of committed communities difficult, and a political discipleship that demands social changes *of the state* easier.

Finally, a common criticism of recent civic republican and communitarian approaches is that they are abstract and implicitly utopian, and that it is better to start with a reconstruction of the sort of moral language most people in modernity live with, i. e., liberalism, than trying to invent or revive languages that are more or less foreign to modern society.[75] However this is answered,[76] the objection is much weakened when directed against Hauerwas, because he starts with an existing and living church and a tradition actually practised. He does not need to invent or reconstruct a public philosophy, but can start with the fact that the Christian tradition is preached every Sunday and that there are actual communities for which the Christian language is a primary language.

To summarize, I have tried to argue that political theology is devised in response to a discredited view of politics and social change, and that much of the criticism of the political irrelevance of Hauerwas' theology assumes this view and becomes groundless without it. Even if Moltmann lately has criticized some of the assumptions of the rationalist view, they are still evident, working as tacit, nonargued background-beliefs in his theology. I have also, more tentatively, tried to show the meaningfulness and fruitfulness of Hauerwas' Radical Reformation theology in the light of recent developments in social thought. Of course, even if my argument is accepted as basically sound, there are no guarantees that churches will have the described effects, but there are good reasons for taking this path instead of the one of political theology. Furthermore, we have also found that there are elements in Moltmann's theology that seem to point in the same direction. These are themes that have become stronger through time, which shows that he slowly moves in this direction.

---

[75]So e.g. Stout, *Ethics after Babel*. Cf. also Shapiro, *Political Criticism*, 121-165.

[76]Stout and Shapiro direct their criticism especially against MacIntyre, who, however, describes his view neither as communitarian nor as civic republican. For MacIntyre's own answer to the charge of utopianism, see *Three Rival Versions of Moral Enquiry*, 234f.

Part Four

Conclusion

Chapter 16

From a Mediating Political Theology
Towards an Ecclesial Theological Politics

1. Radical Reformation Theology Beyond Political Theology

Political theology is a mediating project. It emerged as an attempt to mediate
Christianity and modernity. Central in this mediating project was a positive reception of secularization, which was understood as the liberation of humanity
from nature, fate, tradition and religion into being the free subject of its own history. This interpretation was possible because Moltmann describes the whole
history as a progressive and dialectic history of freedom movements, in which the
church has played a decisive role. The Enlightenment and modernity represent
merely a further stage in this history. In this way he can both give Christian legitimacy to modernity and modern legitimacy to Christianity.

Because humanity is the subject of history and society, politics, understood as
the struggle for control over the processes of social change, becomes the basic
horizon for theology. Everything is embraced by this political horizon. Christian
practice and theology are judged according to their oppressive or emancipatory
functions in this political struggle. In early political theology the autonomy of
politics from theology and ethics is strongly affirmed. The criteria are thus provided by the political struggle. Because of its belief in a progressive metanarrative
of freedom, in which socialism was the latest stage, the direction of history and
the identity of the good side was seldom in doubt. The deprivatization of Christian faith-practice meant thus only that it should be lived out in the political
sphere, but the content of the political practice was given by the movements supported. The modern split between public and private was in addition internalized
into the life of the church. Ethically he usually worked with consequentialist and,
more seldom, natural law perspectives. In practice he thus assumed the modern

idea of religion as a categorial sphere separate from politics and ethics that has gone together with the secularization of knowledge, politics, economy, and so on. This was also part of the apologetic aim of political theology. I have described political theology as a Postmaterialist transformation of Christian theology. Moltmann identifies not only with some of the political aims of specific social movements, but with the whole world-view of the increasingly influential Post-materialist/New Class fraction of the upper middle class.

But there is another prominent line in Moltmann's political theology that has increased in strength with time. Moltmann was formed in the tradition from the Confessing church and the theology of Karl Barth. That he, in addition, is a Re-formed theologian is also important. Parallel to his correlational approach he has stressed the primacy of the Christian narrative. Theology does not start in a general theism or anthropology, but in the particular narratives of Israel and Jesus Christ understood in the context of their universal eschatological claims. Reality should thus be understood in the light of this narrative. This perspective, which has determined Moltmann's theology from the beginning, has lived in an uneasy relationship to his political hermeneutics and correlational approach that make the political horizon interpreted in the light of the modern emancipatory tradition primary. He has not shown how they can be successfully fused.

The publication of *The Crucified God* contained a beginning modification of his political theology. God is no longer only the power of the future, but the "crucified God" who shares the sufferings of people. Moltmann becomes also more concrete in his political stance, but the connection between these political suggestions and his theology is still thin and mainly formal. Yet parallel to this comes also a more critical attitude towards giving the instrumental utilitarian reason of politics such a dominating role and he tries therefore to develop more participatory and doxological concepts of reason and truth. His awakened ecological concern helps him to criticize history as the most comprehensive context and the undifferentiated idea of humanity as subject of history.[1] This exemplifies how the political hermeneutics in part, so to say, undermines itself. Substantial Christian ethical reflection becomes slowly a stronger component in his theology, built into the logic of his theology from the beginning, and developed in trinitarian terms. The climax, until today, comes with the ecclesial ethics of discipleship formulated in *The Way of Jesus Christ*. Here he describes the church as a contrast society whose life of common discipleship witness to an alternative social and political practice. He defends the public nature of Christianity in terms of *solus Christus* in ethics. The church has thereby its own substantial politics. Taking this road,

---

[1]Metz and other Catholic political theologians have not followed Moltmann in this questioning of the primacy of history. John Cobb discusses this difference in *Process Theology as Political Theology*, 111-134. While he praises Moltmann, he criticizes Metz for not wanting to go beyond his Kantian anthropocentrism. He also recognizes that Moltmann's move involves a criticism of fundamental assumptions in political theology and thus means going beyond political theology. Cf. Metz' comment on Moltmann in "Nochmals: Die Marxistische Herausforderung", 418 n. 13.

Moltmann merely follows up not only the logic of his general theological approach, but also his early affirmation of a Radical Reformation ecclesiology.

However, parallel to this development of his theology, the old form of political hermeneutics has continued more or less unchanged. He has not shown which consequences his criticisms of history (and therefore of politics) as most comprehensive context, and of the consequentialist ethics, as well as his development of an ecclesial discipleship ethics have for his political hermeneutics.

We have seen how these two lines in his theology, which have been mixed in various ways, create the sort of tensions that is exemplified in his discussions of violence and human rights as well as of freedom and power. In light of his description of the church as a contrast society and the Christian life as discipleship, the fact that he sees freedom as liberation from restrictions and therefore also tends to describe all forms of power and authority as dominion, is especially bothersome, because it hinders him, I have suggested, from giving plausible and practical content to his accounts of church and discipleship.

It is difficult to avoid the conclusion that the direction this second line has taken in his later theology increasingly undermines the bases of political theology. The strategy in this book has thus been to follow up this line through an exposition and discussion of the theological politics of Hauerwas' Radical Reformation theology. Hauerwas agrees with Moltmann that Christian theology is intrinsically political, but it is the politics of the church and not the politics of the world that forms the primary context. Not an alleged universal history of freedom, that is, some version of the history of the emergence and hoped for fulfilment of modernity, has primacy, but the story of the Bible and its continuation in the church. This leads him to try to redescribe reality from a Christian perspective rather than to redescribe Christianity in the light of current social movements and perspectives. Likewise significant is that Hauerwas comprehends freedom as truthful formation, which means that the goal of politics is the formation of a *different* social reality, not the spontaneous freedom that results from the taking away of all restrictions.

Moreover, Hauerwas attempts to develop an account of the church as a community of virtue formed and sustained by specific practices that help to give concrete content to the description of the church as contrast society. By doing so he shows also the political importance of the practices and small gestures that fill everyday life, in contrast to Moltmann's prevalent account of discipleship as political activism directed towards the struggle for power. Political theology emerged as a Christian reception of the primacy of instrumental reason in modern political theory and it has had great difficulties of showing alternatives to bureaucracy and market for the formation of the communal life. Hauerwas' account of virtue is an attempt to go beyond the polarities of modern political theory and it gives him tools for describing society differently and suggesting other possibilities. This also shows itself in his account of Christian ethics in contrast to the ethical theories of liberalism.

It is the church, as a set of specific discourse-practices, that make theology as social theory possible and therefore also gives theology the perspective from which it can interact with and christianly interpret the societies in which the church exists. While Moltmann constantly wavers between claiming the public nature of the Christian convictions and practices and accepting the primacy of the political reason of modernity (Hauerwas would say the liberal tradition) and the concomitant policing and privatizing of Christian convictions, Hauerwas consistently claims the public nature of Christian practice and theology.

Finally, I have in this book described Hauerwas as a Radical Reformation theologian. I think my investigation has shown that this is essentially an adequate way of reading him. This becomes apparent, for example, in those areas where he tends to be more Catholic than Radical Reformational (such as his theology of sacrament and ministry), because this, as we have seen, creates internal tensions in his theology. Furthermore, when he positively uses Roman Catholic criticism of liberalism, he understands this criticism in the context of his own general non-Constantinian and pacifist Radical Reformation perspective. The same statements understood in a Constantinian context sound very different, which Hauerwas, of course, knows, but too often ignores.[2] This is not to deny what I said in chapter one on the many commonalities between Radical Reformation theology and Roman Catholicism. Furthermore, the more Catholic Christianity becomes deestablished the more Catholic theology will be interpreted in a non-Constantinian way.

2. The Criteria Revisited

Another way of concluding this investigation is to return to the criteria mentioned in the international literature on systematic theology which I outlined in chapter two. I have used these criteria to locate areas for analysis and to assess the strengths and weaknesses of these theological proposals. They have been guidelines in my inquiry, although I have not explicitly discussed them. Now at the end of this investigation, it will be helpful to return to them.

The first type of criterion concerns *consistency* and *coherence*. We have throughout Part Two seen that in this respect there are severe problems in Moltmann's political theology. In contrast, Hauerwas' theological politics is not only inherently more consistent and coherent, it also shows, so I have suggested, how Moltmann's theology might be developed in a more coherent way. Furthermore, the problems in Moltmann's theology are understandable in terms of Hauerwas' theology. For Moltmann to increasingly take up the Radical Reformation tradition is, on the one side, only to follow up the internal "logic" of a central strand of his own theology, but, on the other hand, it also increases the internal tensions of his theology. It comes in conflict with his political hermeneutics and mediating program and, on the substantial level, with his attempt to integrate a Postmaterialist

---

[2]One recent example is the article "The Kingship of Christ".

individualism into his own theology. It thereby helps clarifying the internal tensions his theology has been afflicted with from the beginning.

The second type of criterion concerns *Christian authenticity, aptness* or *faithfulness* and concerns the relation to Scripture and tradition I have not explicitly discussed these issues, because on this level Moltmann and Hauerwas have much in common, and because they are seldom, concerning the issues of this investigation, criticized as being unfaithful to the Bible or the Christian tradition. The criticisms are of another nature. Their positions are said to be unrealistic and sectarian, fail to take modern knowledge and values seriously enough, and so on, even though it is recognized that they can make a good biblical case for them.

I could have discussed areas where they differ, but I have only done this occasionally and then very briefly. One reason is that in the places where they differ Moltmann's theology almost consistently shows an internal incoherence that by itself shows that something is wrong in his account. A second reason is that the basic direction of Hauerwas' theology finds substantial support in Moltmann's reading of the Bible.

I will illustrate this with one example: the understanding of the Christian life. Here Moltmann develops both an ecclesial discipleship ethics that is close to Hauerwas' account and a Postmaterialist expressive individualism that comes in sharp conflict with Hauerwas. We found the latter view both incoherent and implausible in itself, and contradicted by his discipleship ethics. Furthermore, I doubt that anyone would seriously argue that Moltmann's expressivist individualism has much support in the Christian tradition. One has instead to argue that here the tradition needs a radical revision. This Moltmann does concerning the post-biblical tradition, although he can refer to the Lutheran doctrine of justification as the theological basis, but in a way that he otherwise criticizes and that hardly does justice to Luther. However, though he also partly criticizes Paul, he does try to find some support in the biblical tradition. He refers to the importance of the body in the Bible, the unity of the soul and the body, the apocalyptic nature of the statements about the conflict between the flesh and the Spirit, and the bodily nature of salvation, as well as the Spirit-guided nature of the new life. But none of these leads by itself to his expressive individualism. Decisive is instead the modern therapeutic culture. In contrast, his account of an ecclesial discipleship ethics is built on an extensive and careful reading of the biblical texts and exegetical literature. One needs only to compare pages 116-136 (136-157) with 259-267 (282-290) in *The Way of Jesus Christ* to see this contrast in his use of the Bible.

I think that similar arguments could, in varying degrees, be made concerning themes like freedom, power, ethics and ecclesiology. Why this is true is that these incoherences and concomitant tensions with the Bible and the Christian tradition are not random, but systematic. They have to do, as this book has tried to show, with the way Moltmann attempts to mediate modernity (or a version of the worldview of modernity) with Christianity.

Neither the Bible, nor the later Christian tradition is, of course, uniform. Different approaches are possible. There might also be good reasons for more radical revisions and innovations. In relation to the main part of a long Christian tradition, both Hauerwas and Moltmann want, for example, to revise the Constantinian model (they claim, however, support by the New Testament for their revision). But not every innovation or revision is good. The problems with Moltmann's attempts are so consistent and deep, that I think there is enough reason to seriously question their viability. In Hauerwas' case there are many issues that are open for discussion, but we have not found the type of problems that characterizes Moltmann's theology.

The third type of criterion concerns *applicability*. In chapter two I subdivided this type into three aspects: interpretative power, guiding ability, and sustainability. First, how do their theologies perform as interpretative tools in regard to modern society? An initial and maybe surprising finding is that political theology is not too interested in developing this interpretative power, because it takes its interpretations from the social movements it supports. It is therefore short on analysis. Its central task is instead mediating Christian theology to these interpretations. Hauerwas' approach, on the other hand, leads him to spend much of his writing on interpreting society. The fact that Hauerwas is a more interesting social and political interpreter than Moltmann, is thus, at least in part, a consequence of their different theological strategies.

On the substantial level Moltmann's social criticism likewise showed severe weaknesses (in part even on Moltmann's own account). In addition, from the beginning political theology assumed an inadequate rationalist understanding of social change which Moltmann never really has left behind, although important changes have occurred. The unstableness and trendiness of his social criticism further increase one's scepticism. It shows that social trends and movements are more determinative than the inner logic of the theology itself.

However one evaluates it, Hauerwas has developed a more sustained and consistent interpretation of modern liberal society. The primary basis of this interpretation is not current trends, but a theological perspective based on the practices and experiences of the Christian church throughout the centuries. Furthermore, this does not hinder Hauerwas from, more extensively than Moltmann, using and conversing with contemporary social and political theory.

The second question, which concerns how practical and relevant these two theologies are in guiding and assessing Christian social and political practice, is thereby partly already answered. Although many Christians active in or sympathetic to the new social movements or to Postmaterialism in general find political theology highly relevant for their concerns, the mentioned weaknesses of its interpretative power, limit its guiding and assessing capacity. To this one can add the lack of self-understanding Moltmann shows concerning the social base and function of political theology. More important, he has not provided a plausible account of how the church as a contrast society and what he calls a political discipleship can be formed and sustained. His accounts of the personal life and of freedom, power and authority are not only in themselves inadequate, they also, I have argued, undermine the formation of communities of discipleship.

One of the strengths of Hauerwas' theology, on the other hand, is that he has provided an account of the life of the church that not only is coherent with his own theology, but also provides the tools for understanding and analysing the life of the church that Moltmann fails to supply. I have, in addition, suggested that there are some good reasons why Hauerwas' theological politics is politically more fruitful for the world than Moltmann's political theology. There are many gaps in Hauerwas' discussions and his interpretations and suggestions are, of course, open for discussion. He does not want to provide a general theory of society, but he has provided a coherent perspective and a set of interpretative tools that has proven fruitful. One reason for this is that his account of the church as a community of virtue provides tools for analysis of the communal level between the individual and state levels and thereby also enables a redescription of these latter two levels. Moltmann mirrors liberal society's concentration on the individual-state polarity. His lack of adequate account of the communal level leads to an insufficient and inadequate understanding of social change and keeps his ecclesiology on an abstract level.

In answering question one and two, the third question, the long-time sustainability of these two types of theologies and the forms of church life they presuppose, has to a large extent already been answered. Contemporary sociology of religion gives further support to the tentative conclusion that in the long run there is more to be said for Hauerwas' Radical Reformation theology than Moltmann's political theology.

There are no knock down arguments in this type of discussion, but I have at least provided an extended argument that requires a likewise detailed answer from the direction of political theology. My argument is, I think, most persuasive for people that make the theological vision of Moltmann and his emphasis on the identity of the church primary. On the other hand, people who find his theology attractive primarily because of its political hermeneutics, its political views and/or its Postmaterialist apologetics will likely find the argument more difficult to accept. In the introduction to chapter nine I said that another way out of the described impasse would be to take either a constructivist or a radical revisionist road. This may perhaps solve the problem of coherence, though this is an open question, not least because of the internal tensions of modernity. It would, however, increase the problems of Christian authenticity, an area where Moltmann partly is strong. It is his consistent attempt to work creatively inside the biblical and classical Christian tradition that has made his theology so attractive and influential. John Cobb, contrasting Moltmann's work with other political theology, writes: "Moltmann's work stands out partly because of its unequivocally theological cast. . . . the fact that Moltmann has developed his theology simply as theology and has argued his case fully from within the mainstream of the tradition has given it special effectiveness."[3] The risk with constructivist approaches is that it can make Christian theology into a sort of philosophy increasingly abstracted from the practices and experiences of the historical and contemporary church and thereby is in danger of losing its ecclesial base. Two centuries of liberal Protestantism give ample examples of this.

Constructivist or revisionist approaches also face many of the same problems concerning applicability. Most, but not all, political theology show a similar lack of self-understanding. Furthermore, they do not show more interest in substantial Christian social criticism or has not developed a more powerful analysis. Finally, they suffer from the same inadequate understanding of social change. And to the extent Postmaterialist apologetics is in the centre, they will have the same problem of giving a plausible account of community and discipleship. I do not say that this task is impossible, only that I am not aware of any successful formulation. In contrast, I think that Moltmann's theology, with all its problems, has more resources and is more promising than most alternatives.

In this book I have discussed Radical Reformation theology in relation to political theology. There are, of course, other alternatives. Although I have defended Hauerwas against the most common criticisms, I have not systematically related him to other approaches. But my investigation has hopefully shown how such further dialogues might be performed and indicated central areas of investigation that may help further the theological reflection of the Christian church.[4]

---

[3]"Beyond Political Theology", 457.
[4]At Lund University Baldur Sigurdsson, an Icelandic Lutheran, is actually working on a dissertation on the ethics of Hauerwas and Gustaf Wingren.

Bibliography

This bibliography contains only material actually referred to in the book. Thus, it does not contain any full bibliography of the works by and on Moltmann and Hauerwas. A complete bibliography on Moltmann's work up to 1987 is found in *Bibliographie Jürgen Moltmann* (compiled by Dieter Ising with the help of Günter Geisthardt and Adelbert Schloz), München 1987. My practice of giving references to both English and German versions of Moltmann's books and articles creates some difficulties, because Moltmann often publishes the same material in slightly different forms (and sometimes not so slightly) and it is difficult to know whether two texts should be considered as two versions of the same text or as two different ones. Moreover, several of the English translations of Moltmann's books both omit and add material in relation to the German books and sometimes different chapters are published in different books. This is the reason why the German originals of some books are listed both independently and in parenthesis after the English translations.

Jürgen Moltmann

The Church in the Power of the Spirit: A Contribution to Messianic Ecclesiology, London 1977. (*Kirche in der Kraft des Geistes: Ein Beitrag zur messianischen Ekklesiologie*, München 1975.)

Creating a Just Future: The Politics of Peace and the Ethics of Creation in a Threatened World, London 1989. (*Gerechtigkeit schafft Zukunft: Friedenspolitik und Schöpfungsethik in einer bedrohten Welt*, München 1989.)

The Crucified God: The Cross of Christ as the Foundation and Criticism of Christian Theology, London 1974. (*Der gekreuzigte Gott: Das Kreuz Christi als Grund und Kritik christlicher Theologie*, München 1972.)

Diakonie im Horizont des Reiches Gottes: Schritte zum Diakonentum aller Gläubigen. Mit eine Beitrag von Ulrich Bach und einem Vorwort von Theodor Schober, Neukirchen-Vluyn 1984.

Experiences of God, Philadelphia 1980. (*Gotteserfahrungen: Hoffnung – Angst – Mystik*, München 1979.)

The Experiment Hope, Philadelphia 1975. (*Das Experiment Hoffnung: Einführungen*, München 1974.)

The Future of Creation, London 1979. (*Zukunft der Schöpfung: Gesammelte Aufsätze*, München 1977.)

God in Creation: An Ecological Doctrine of Creation, London 1985. (*Gott in der Schöpfung: Ökologische Schöpfungslehre*, München 1985.)

God – His and Hers (with Elisabeth Moltmann-Wendel), London 1991. (*Als Frau und Mann von Gott reden*, München 1991.)

History and the Triune God: Contributions to Trinitarian Theology, London 1991. (*In der Geschichte des dreieinigen Gottes: Beiträge zur trinitarischen Theologie*, München 1991.)

Hope and Planning, London 1971. (*Perspektiven der Theologie: Gesammelte Aufsätze*, München 1968.)

Hope for the Church: Moltmann in Dialogue with Practical Theology (with M. Douglas Meeks, Rodney J. Hunter, James W. Fowler, Noel L. Erskine, ed. by Theodore Runyon), Abingdon 1979.

Humanity in God (with Elisabeth Moltmann-Wendel), London 1984.

Man: Christian Anthropology in the Conflicts of the Present, Philadelphia 1974. (*Mensch: Christliche Anthropologie in den Konflikten der Gegenwart*, Stuttgart 1971.
Menschenwürde, Recht und Freiheit, Stuttgart 1979.
Ohne Macht mächtig: Predigten, München 1981.
On Human Dignity: Political Theology and Ethics, London 1984.
The Open Church: Invitation to a Messianic Lifestyle, London 1978. (*Neuer Lebensstil: Schritte zur Gemeinde*, München 1977.)
Perspektiven der Theologie: Gesammelte Aufsätze, München 1968.
Politische Theologie – Politische Ethik, München 1984.
The Power of the Powerless: The Word of Liberation Today, San Francisco1983. (*Ohne Macht mächtig: Predigten*, München 1981.)
Religion, Revolution, and the Future, New York 1969.
The Spirit of Life: A Universal Affirmation, London 1992. (*Der Geist des Lebens: Eine ganzheitliche Pneumatologie*, München 1991.)
Theology and Joy, London 1973. (*Die ersten Freigelassenen der Schöpfung: Versuche über die Freude an der Freiheit und das Wohlgefallen am Spiel*, München 1971.)
Theology of Hope: On the Ground and the Implications of a Christian Eschatology, London 1967. (*Theologie der Hoffnung: Untersuchungen zur Begründung und zu den Konzequenzen einer christlichen Eschatologie*, München 1964, 1985[12].)
Theology Today: Two Contributions towards Making Theology Present, London 1988. (*Was ist heute Theologie? Zwei Beiträge zu ihrer Vergegenwärtigung*, Freiburg 1988.)
The Trinity and the Kingdom of God: The Doctrine of God, London 1981. (*Trinität und Reich Gottes: Zur Gotteslehre*, München 1980.)
Umkehr zur Zukunft, München 1970.
The Way of Jesus Christ: Christology in Messianic Dimensions, London 1990. (*Der Weg Jesu Christi: Christologie in messianischen Dimensionen*, München 1989.)
Bekennende Kirche wagen: Barmen 1934-1984 (ed. by Jürgen Moltmann), München 1984.

"Abtreibung oder Annahme des Kindes: Thesen zur Diskussion um den § 218" (with Eberhard Jüngel, Ernst Käsemann and Dietrich Rössler), *Evangelische Kommentare* 4, 1971, 452-454.
"Antwort auf die Kritik an 'Der gekruzigte Gott'", *Diskussion über Jürgen Moltmanns Buch "Der gekreuzigte Gott"* (ed. by Michael Welker), München 1979, 165-190.
"Bekennende Kirche werden: Barmen 1934-1984", *Junge Kirche* 45, 1984, 260-263 (with Hans-Joachim Kraus).
"The Challenge of Religion in the '80s", *Theologians in Transitions: The Christian Century "How My Mind Has Changed" Series* (ed. by James M Wall), New York 1981, 107-112.
"Christian Theology and Political Religion", *Civil Religion and Political Theology* (ed. by Leroy S. Rouner), Notre Dame 1986, 41-58.
"Das christlich-jüdische Verhältnis und der zweite Golfkrieg: Eine Stellungnahme von Jürgen Moltmann zu Edna Brockes Beitrag in KuI 1/1991, S. 61ff und der anschließende Briefwechsel zwischen Edna Brocke und Jürgen Moltmann", *Kirche und Israel* 6, 1991, 163-185.
"Christlicher Glaube und Menschenrechte", "*. . . erkämpft das Menschenrecht": Wie christlich sind die Menschenrechte?* (ed by Eckehart Lorenz), Hamburg 1981, 15-35.
"Commentary on 'to Bear Arms'", *Human Rights: A Dialogue Between the First and Third Worlds* (ed. by Robert A. Evans and Alice F. Evans), Maryknoll 1983, 48-52.
"A Conversation with Jürgen Moltmann", Teofilo Cabestrero, *Conversations with Contemporary Theologians*, New York 1980, 121-138.

"Covenant oder Leviathan? Zur Politischen Theologie der Neuzeit", *Zeitschrift für Theologie und Kirche* 90, 1993, 299-317.

"The Cross and Civil Religion", Jürgen Moltmann, Herbert W. Richardson, Johann Baptist Metz, Willi Oelmüller and M. Darrol Bryant, *Religion and Political Society*, New York 1974, 9-47.

"Die Christenheit und das Neue Europa: Die Geschichte der Spaltungen muß überwunden werden", *Lutherische Monatshefte* 30, 1991, 85-88.

"Einführung" to *Annahme und Widerstand* (ed. by Jürgen Moltmann), München 1984, 7-14.

"Einführung" to *Friedenstheologie – Befreiungstheologie: Analysen, Berichte, Meditationen* (ed. by Jürgen Moltmann), München 1988, 7-14.

"Einführung" to *Nachfolge und Bergpredigt* (ed. by Jürgen Moltmann), München 1981, 7-11.

"Einführung" to *Religion der Freiheit: Protestantismus in der Moderne* (ed. by Jürgen Moltmann), München 1990, 7-10.

"Foreword" to A. J. Conyears, *God, Hope and History: Jürgen Moltmann and the Christian Concept of History*, Macon 1988, vii-ix.

"Foreword" to Richard Bauckham, *Moltmann: Messianic Theology in the Making*, Basingstoke 1987, vii-x.

"Foreword" to Robert Thomas Cornelison, *The Christian Realism of Reinhold Niebuhr and the Political Theology of Jürgen Moltmann in Dialogue: The Realism of Hope*, San Francisco 1992, i-v.

"Der Gott, auf den ich hoffe", *Warum ich Christ bin* (ed. by Walter Jens), München 1979, 264-280.

"Has Modern Society any Future?", *Concilium*, no.1, 1990, 54-65. ("Hat die moderne Gesellschaft eine Zukunft?, 26, 1990, 34-41.)

"Human Rights, the Rights of Humanity and the Rights of Nature", *Concilium*, no. 2, 1990, 120-135. ("Menschenrechte, Rechte der Menschheit und Rechte der Natur", 26, 1990, 165-174.)

"Is 'Pluralistic Theology' Useful for the Dialogue of World Religions?", *Christian Uniqueness Reconsidered: The Myth of a Pluralistic Theology of Religions* (ed. by Gavin D'Costa), Maryknoll 1990, 149-156.

"Is Protestantism the 'Religion of Freedom'?", *On Freedom* (ed. by Leroy S. Rouner), Notre Dame 1989, 30-45.

"The Lordship of Christ and Human Society", Jürgen Moltmann and Jürgen Weissbach, *Two Studies in the Theology of Bonhoeffer*, New York 1967, 19-94. (*Herrschaft Christi und Soziale Wirklichkeit nach Dietrich Bonhoeffer*, München 1959).

"Menschenrechte, Rechte der Menschheit und Rechte der Natur" (with Elisabeth Giesser), *Evangelische Theologie* 50, 1990, 437-444.

"On Latin American Liberation Theology: An Open Letter to José Miguez Bonino, *Christianity and Crisis* 36, 1976, 57-63.

"Peace the Fruit of Justice", *Concilium*, no. 1, 1988, 109-120. ("Gerechtigkeit schafft Frieden", 24, 1988, 75-82.)

"Political Theology and Liberation Theology", *Union Seminary Quarterly Review* 45, 1991, 205-217.

"Die Politik der Nachfolge Christi gegen christliche Milleniumspolitk", *Mystik und Politk: Theologie im Ringen um Geschichte und Gesellschaft. Johann Baptist Metz zu Ehren* (ed. by Edward Schillebeeckx), Mainz 1988, 19-31.

"Protestantismus als 'Religion der Freiheit'", *Religion der Freiheit: Protestantismus in der Moderne* (ed. by Jürgen Moltmann), München 1990, 11-28.

"Religion and Politics in Germany and in German-American Relations", *The Federal Republic of Germany and the United States: Changing Political, Social, and Economic Relations* (ed. by James A. Cooney, Gordon A. Craig, Hans Peter Schwatz, and Fritz Stern), Boulder 1984, 98-108.

"Religion and State in Germany: West and East", *Annals of the American Academy of Political and Social Science* no. 483, 1986, 110-117.

"Response to the Opening Presentations", *Hope and the Future of Man* (ed. by Ewert H. Cousin), Philadelphia 1972, 55-59.

"A Response to the Responses", *Dialogue Sequel to Jürgen Moltmann's 'Following Jesus Christ in the World Today'*, Elkhart 1984, 49-62.

"Revolution, Religion and the Future: German Reactions", *Concilium*, no. 1, 1989, 43-50. ("Revolution, Religion und die Zukunft: Deutsche Reaktionen", 25, 1989, 29-33.)

"Der Sinn der Arbeit", *Recht auf Arbeit, Sinn der Arbeit* (ed. by Jürgen Moltmann), München 1979, 59-83.

"Streit um Menschenrechte", *Evangelische Kommentare* 10, 1977, 495-497.

"Theologie im demokratischen Aufbruch Europas", *Christliche Existenz im Demokratischen Aufbruch Europas: Probleme – Chancen – Orientierung* (ed. by Jürgen Moltmann), München 1991, 27-39.

"Thomas Müntzer", *Luther kontrovers* (ed. by H. J. Schultz), Stuttgart 1983, 212-225.

"Versöhnung und Befreiung: der Beitrag der Christenheit zum Frieden", *Begegnung mit Polen: Evangelische Kirchen und die Herausforderung durch Geschichte und Politik* (ed. by Jürgen Moltmann and Martin Stöhr), München 1974, 165-182.

"Vorwort" to Eberhard Arnold, *Salz und Licht: Über die Bergpredigt*, Moers 1982, 7-9.

"Vorwort" to John H. Yoder, *Die Politik Jesu: Der Weg des Kreuzes*, Maxdorf 1981, 5-7.

"Die Zukunft der Aufklärung und des Christentums", *Die Zukunft der Aufklärung* (ed. by Jörn Rüsen, Eberhard Lämmert, and Peter Glotz), Frankfurt a. M. 1988, 73-80.

"Zum Gespräch mit Christian Link", *Evangelische Theologie* 47, 1987, 93-95.

Stanley Hauerwas

After Christendom: How the Church Is to Behave If Freedom, Justice, and a Christian Nation Are Bad Ideas, Nashville 1991.

Against the Nations: War and Survival in a Liberal Society, Minneapolis 1985.

Character and the Christian Life: A Study in Theological Ethics (with a new introduction by the author), San Antonio 1985.

Christian Existence Today: Essays on Church, World, and Living In Between, Durham 1988.

A Community of Character: Toward a Constructive Christian Social Ethic, Notre Dame 1981.

Dispatches from the Front: Theological Engagements with the Secular, Durham 1994.

Naming the Silences: God, Medicine, and the Problem of Suffering, Grand Rapids 1990.

The Peaceable Kingdom: A Primer in Christian Ethics, Notre Dame 1983.

Preaching to Strangers: Evangelism in Today's World (with William H Willimon), Louisville 1992.

Resident Aliens: Life in the Christian Colony (with William H Willimon), Nashville 1989.

Should War Be Eliminated? Philosophical and Theological Investigations, Milwaukee 1984.

Suffering Presence: Theological Reflections on Medicine, the Mentally Handicapped, and the Church, Notre Dame 1986.

Truthfulness and Tragedy: Further Investigations in Christian Ethics, Notre Dame 1977.

Unleashing the Scripture: Freeing the Bible from Captivity to America, Nashville 1993.

Vision and Virtue: Essays in Christian Ethical Reflection, Notre Dame 1974.

Hauerwas, Stanley and L. Gregory Jones (eds.), *Why Narrative? Readings in Narrative Theology*, Grand Rapids 1989.

Hauerwas, Stanley and Alasdair MacIntyre (eds.), *Revisions: Changing Perspectives in Moral Philosophy*, Notre Dame 1983.

"Abortion, Theologically Understood", *The Church and Abortion: In Search of New Ground for Response* (ed. by Paul T Stallsworth), Nashville 1993, 44-66.

"Athens May Be a Long Way From Jerusalem, But Prussia is Even Further", *The Asbury Theological Journal* 45, 1990, 59-63.

"Can Aristotle Be a Liberal? Nussbaum on Luck", *Soundings* 72, 1989, 675-691.

"Casuistry in Context: The Need for Tradition", unpublished.

"Characterizing Perfection: Second Thoughts on Character and Sanctification", *Wesleyan Theology Today: A Bicentennial Theological Consultation* (ed. by Theodore Runyon), Nashville 1985, 251-263.

"The Chief End of All Flesh" (with John Berkman), *Theology Today* 49, 1992, 196-208.

"A Christian Critique of Christian America", *Community in America: The Challenge of* Habits of the Heart (ed. by Charles H. Reynolds and Ralph V. Norman), Berkeley 1988, 250-265.

"Christian Ethics in America: Beginning with an Ending" (manuscript to chapter 1 of *Christian Ethics in America*, forthcoming).

"Christian Practice and the Practice of Law in a World Without Foundations", *Mercer Law Review* 44, 1993, 743-751.

"Christianity and War", *The Charlotte Observer*, February 10, 1991, 1C, 4C.

"The Church and/as God's Non-Violent Imagination" (with Philip D. Kenneson), *Pro Ecclesia* 1, 1992, 76-88.

"The Church's One Foundation Is Jesus Christ Her Lord or In a World Without Foundations: All We Have Is the Church", manuscript, forthcoming in the McClendon Festschrift.

"A Communitarian Lament", *First Things* no. 19, 1992, 45-46.

"Creation, Contingency, and Truthful Non-Violence: A Milbankian Reflection", unpublished.

"Critic's Choices for Christmas: Books I Would Recommend Anyone to Read", *Commonweal* 114, 1987, 708-709.

"The Difference of Virtue and the Difference It Makes: Courage Exemplified", *Modern Theology* 9, 1993, 249-264.

"Embarrassed by God's Presence", *The Christian Century* 102, 1985, 98-100 (with William H. Willimon).

"Epilogue: A Pacifist Response to the Bishops", Paul Ramsey, *Speak Up for Just War or Pacifism: A Critique of the United Methodist Bishops' Pastoral Letter "In Defense of Creation"*, University Park 1988, 149-182.

"The Ethicist as Theologian", *Christian Century* 92, 1975, 408-412.

"Ethics – Christian" (with D. Stephen Long), *New Handbook of Christian Theology* (ed. by Donald Musser and Joseph Price), Nashville 1992, 160-167.

"Faith in the Republic: A Frances Lewis Law Center Conversation" (with Sanford Levinson, Mark V. Tushnet, and Others), *Washington and Lee Law Review* 45, 1988, 467-534.

"The Family as a School for Character", *Religious Education* 80, 1985, 272-286.

"Flight from Foundationalism, or, Things Aren't as Bad as They Seem" (with Philip D. Kenneson), *Soundings* 71, 1988, 675-691.

"Foreword" to Duane K. Friesen, *Christian Peacemaking and International Conflict: A Realist Pacifist Perspective*, Scottdale 1986, 11-12.

"Forgiveness and Political Community", *Worldview* 23, 1980, 15-16.

"From Conduct to Character: A Guide to Sexual Adventure" (with Allen Verhey), *The Reformed Journal* 36:11, 1986, 12-16.

"The Future of Christian Social Ethics", *That They May Live: Theological Reflections on the Quality of Life* (ed. by George Divine), Staten Island, New York 1972, 123-131.

"The Gospel's Radical Alternative: A Peace the World Cannot Give", *The Other Side* 23:6, 1987, 22-27, 45.

"Happiness, the Life of Virtue and Friendship: Theological Reflections on Aristotelian Themes", *The Asbury Theological Journal* 45, 1990, 5-48.

"Honor in the University", *First Things* no. 10, 1991, 26-31.

"The Importance of Being Catholic: Unsolicited Advice From a Protestant Bystander", *Listening* 25, 1990, 27-46.

"In Praise of *Centesimus Annus*", *Theology* 95, 1992, 416-432.

"In Response: Forgiveness and Forgetting", *Sh'ma* 11, 1980, 12, 15-16.

"The Irony of American Christianity. Reinhold Niebuhr on Church and State" (with Mike Broadway), *Insights* 108, 1992, 33-46.

"The Kingship of Christ: Why Freedom of 'Belief' Is Not Enough" (with Michael Baxter), *DePaul Law Review* 42, 1992, 107-127.

"Marriage and the Family: An Open Dialogue Between Stanley Hauerwas and David Bourns", *Quaker Religious Thought* 20:2, 1984, 4-24.

"Medical Care for the Poor: Finite Resources, Infinite Need" (with Larry Churchill and Harmon Smith), *Health Progress* 66:10, 1985, 32-35.

"Messianic Pacifism", *Worldview* 16, 1973, 29-33.

"The Need for an Ending", *The Modern Churchman* 28, 1986, 3-7.

"On Being 'Placed' by John Milbank: A Response", *Christ, Ethics and Tragedy: Essays in Honour of Donald MacKinnon* (ed. by Kenneth Surin), Cambridge 1989, 197-201.

"On Developing Hopeful Virtues", *Christian Scholars Review* 18, 1988, 107-117.

"On God: Ethics and the Power to Act in History", *Essays on Peace Theology and Witness* (ed. by Willard M. Swartley), Elkhart 1988, 204-209.

"On Learning Simplicity in an Ambiguous Age", *Katallagete* 10, 1987, 43-46.

"On the Ethics of War and Peace", *The Review of Politics* 41, 1979, 147-153.

"On the 'Right' to be Tribal", *Christian Scholars Review* 41, 1987, 238-241.

"Pacifism: A Form of Politics", *Peace Betrayed? Essays on Pacifism and Politics* (ed. by Michael Cromartie), Washington 1990, 133-142.

"Pacifism, Just War and the Gulf: An Exchange With Richard John Neuhaus", *First Things* no. 13, 1991, 39-42.

"Pacifism: Some Philosophical Considerations", *Faith and Philosophy* 2, 1985, 99-104.

"A Pacifist Response to *In Defense of Creation*", *The Asbury Theological Journal* 41:2, 1986, 5-14.

"Protestants and the Pope" (with Robert Wilken), *Commonweal* 107, 1980, 80-85.

Review Essay of Jacques Ellul, *Violence: Reflections from a Christian Perspective*, *The American Journal of Jurisprudence* 18, 1973, 206-215.

Review of James Turner Johnson, *Can Modern War Be Just?*, (with L. Gregory Jones), *Theology Today*, 47, 1986, 104-106.

"The Sermon on the Mount, Just War and the Quest for Peace", *Concilium*, no. 1, 1988, 36-43.

"Should Christians Talk So Much About Justice?", *Books and Religion* 14:5-6, 1986, 5, 14-16.

"Some Theological Reflections on Gutierrez's Use of 'Liberation' as a Theological Concept", *Modern Theology* 3, 1986, 67-76.

"The Sources of Charles Taylor" (with David Matzko), *Religious Studies Review* 18, 1992, 286-289.

"The Splendor of Truth" (with David Burrell), *First Things* no. 39, 1994, 21-23.

"The Testament of Friends", *The Christian Century* 107, 1990, 212-216.

"Virtue", *Westminster Dictionary of Christian Ethics* (ed. by James F. Childress and John Macquarrie), Philadelphia 1986, 648-650.

"Virtue Christianly Considered" (with Charles Pinches), manuscript to a chapter in *Virtue Christianly Considered*, Notre Dame (forthcoming).

"What Could It Mean For the Church To Be Christ's Body?", unpublished.

"When the Politics of Jesus Makes a Difference", *The Christian Century* 110, 1993, 982-987.

"Why *Resident Aliens* Struck a Chord" (with William H Willimon), *Missiology* 19, 1991, 419-429.

"Why the Truth Demands Truthfulness: An Imperious Engagement with Hart", *Journal of the American Academy of Religion* 52, 1984, 141-147. (Also in *Why Narrative? Readings in Narrative Theology* (ed. by Stanley Hauerwas and L. Gregory Jones), Grand Rapids 1989, 303-310.)

"Will the Real Sectarian Stand Up", *Theology Today* 44, 1987, 87-94.

"Work as Co-Creation: A Critique of a Remarkably Bad Idea", *Co-Creation and Capitalism: John Paul II's "Laborem Exercens"* (ed. by John W. Houck and Oliver F. Williams), Lanham 1983, 42-58.

Other Works

Alston, William P., *Epistemic Justification: Essays in the Theory of Knowledge*, Ithaca 1989.

Alves, Ruben A., *A Theology of Human Hope*, New York 1969.

Amelung, Eberhard, "Autonomie", *Theologische Realenzyklopädie*, vol. 5 (ed. by Gerhard Krause and Gerhard Müller), Berlin 1980, 4-17.

Ammerman, Nancy Tatom, *Baptist Battles: Social Change and Religious Conflict in the Southern Baptist Convention*, New Brunswick 1990.

Anderson, Benedict, *Imagined Communities: Reflections on the Origin and Spread of Nationalism*, rev. ed., London 1991.

Arens, Edmund, *Christopraxis: Grundzüge theologischer Handlungstheorie*, Freiburg 1992.

Arens, Edmund (ed.), *Habermas und die Theologie*, Düsseldorf 1989.

Arendt, Hannah, *The Human Condition*, Garden City 1959.

Arvidsson, Håkan, "Tystnaden i Sverige och vad den möjligen kan bero på", *Moderna tider* 1:2, 1990, 46-49.

Bainton, Roland, *Christian Attitudes toward War and Peace*, Nashville 1960.

Ball, Alan R., *Modern Politics and Government*, 2nd ed., London 1977.

Barrett, David B, *World Christian Encyclopedia: A Comparative Study of Churches and Religions in the Modern World, AD 1900-2000*, Nairobi 1982.

Battaglia, Anthony, "'Sect' or 'Denomination'?: The Place of Religious Ethics in a Post-Churchly Culture", *Journal of Religious Ethics* 16, 1988, 128-142.

Bauckham, Richard, "Jürgen Moltmann", *The Modern Theologians: An Introduction to Christian Theology in the Twentieth Century* (ed. by David F. Ford), Oxford 1989, vol. 1, 293-310.

————, *Moltmann: Messianic Theology in the Making*, Basingstoke 1987.

————, "Moltmann's Messianic Christology", *Scottish Journal of Theology* 44, 1991, 519-531.

————, "Moltmann's Political Theology", unpublished.

Beiner, Ronald, *What's the Matter with Liberalism?*, Berkeley 1992.

Beker, J. Christiaan, *Paul the Apostle: The Triumph of God in Life and Thought*, Philadelphia 1982.

————, *Paul's Apocalyptic Gospel: The Coming Triumph of God*, Philadelphia 1982.

Bell, Daniel, *The Coming of Post-Industrial Society: A Venture in Social Forecasting*, 2nd ed., New York 1976.

———, *The Cultural Contradictions of Capitalism*, 2nd ed., London 1979.

———, "Kulturkriege: Intellektuelle in Amerika, 1965-1990", *Intellektuellendämmerung? Beiträge zur neuesten Zeit des Geistes* (ed. by Martin Meyer), München 1992, 113-168.

———, "The New Class: A Muddled Concept", *The New Class?* (ed. by B. Bruce-Briggs), New Brunswick 1979, 169-190.

———, *The Winding Passage: Essays and Sociological Journeys 1960-1980*, Cambridge, Mass. 1980.

Bellah, Robert N., Richard Madsen, William M. Sullivan, Ann Swidler, and Steven Tipton, *Habits of the Heart: Individualism and Commitment in American Life*, New York 1986.

Benda, Václav, "Det alternativa pólis", *Frihet och makt: Röster från Charta 77*, Stockholm 1980, 39-47.

Bender, Harold S., "The Anabaptist Vision", *Church History* 13, 1944, 3-24.

Berdesinski, Dieter, *Die Praxis – Kriterium für die Wahrheit des Glaubens? Untersuchungen zu einem Aspekt politischer Theologie*, München 1973.

Berger, Peter, "American Religion: Conservative Upsurge, Liberal Prospects", *Liberal Protestantism: Realities and Possibilities* (ed. by Robert S. Michaelsen and Wade Clark Roof), New York 1986, 19-36.

———, "Capitalism and the Disorders of Modernity", *First Things* no. 9, 1991, 14-19.

———, *The Capitalist Revolution: Fifty Propositions About Prosperity, Equality, and Liberty*, New York 1986.

———, "The Class Struggle in American Religion", *The Christian Century* 98, 1981, 194-199.

———, "Different Gospels: The Social Sources of Apostasy", *Different Gospels: Christian Orthodoxy and Modern Theologies* (ed. by Andrew Walker), London 1988, 225-241.

———, "Ethics and the Present Class Struggle", *Worldview* 21, 1978, 6-11.

———, *Facing Up to Modernity: Excursions in Society, Politics, and Religion*, New York 1977.

———, "On the Obsolence of the Concept of Honor", *Revisions: Changing Perspectives in Moral Philosophy* (ed. by Stanley Hauerwas and Alasdair MacIntyre), Notre Dame 1983, 172-181.

Berger, Peter and Hansfried Kellner, "Life-style Engineering: Some Theoretical Reflections", *Hidden Technocrats: The New Class and New Capitalism* (ed. by Hansfried Kellner and Frank W. Heuberger), New Brunswick 1992, 1-22.

Berger, Peter and Richard John Neuhaus, *To Empower People: The Role of Mediating Structures in Public Policy*, Washington 1977.

Berger, Peter and Thomas Luckmann, *The Social Construction of Reality: A Treatise in the Sociology of Knowledge*, New York 1967.

Berkhof, Hendrikus, *Christian Faith: An Introduction to the Study of Faith*, Grand Rapids 1979.

Bernstein, Richard J., *Beyond Objectivism and Relativism: Science, Hermeneutics, and Praxis*, Oxford 1983.

———, *The New Constellation: The Ethical-Political Horizons of Modernity/Postmodernity*, Cambridge 1991.

———, *Philosophical Profiles: Essays in a Pragmatic Mode*, Cambridge 1986.

———, *Praxis and Action: Contemporary Philosophies of Human Activity*, Philadelphia 1971.

Beronius, Mats, *Genealogi och sociologi: Nietzsche, Foucault och den sociala analysen*, Stockholm 1991.

Bertilsson, Margareta, "Några inledande reflektioner: Moralfilosofi och samhällsvetenskap i ett utvecklingsperspektiv", *Handling, norm och rationalitet: Om förhållandet mellan samhällsvetenskap och praktisk filosofi* (ed. by Margareta Bertilsson and Anders Molander), Bergen 1992, 9-17.

———, *Slaget om det moderna: Sociologiska essäer*, Stockholm 1987.

———, "Sociologins kärna – i förändring?", *Sociologisk forskning* 27:3, 1990, 11-26.

Bexell, Göran, and others, "Ämnespresentation: Etik", *Svensk teologisk kvartalskrift* 69, 1993, 105-143.

Bianco, Lucien, "Croissance démographique et politique antinataliste", *La Chine au XXᵉ siècle. 2: De 1949 à aujourd'hui* (ed. by Marie-Claire Bergère, Lucien Bianco, and Jürgen Domes), Paris 1990, 121-148.

Birnbaum, Pierre, *La fin du politique*, Paris 1979.

Blickle, Peter, *Gemeindereformation: Die Menschen des 16. Jahrhunderts auf dem Weg zum Heil*, München 1987.

Boff, Leonardo, *Church: Charism and Power. Liberation Theology and the Institutional Church*, London 1985.

Bonhoeffer, Dietrich, *The Cost of Discipleship*, New York 1966.

———, *Life Together*, New York 1954.

Boone, Cyril Keith, "The Concept of Political Majesty in the Thought of Reinhold Niebuhr and Jürgen Moltmann. Sociological, Theological and Ethical Appraisals", Diss., Emory University 1978.

Bourdieu, Pierre, *Distinction: A Social Critique of the Judgement of Taste*, London 1984.

Bowles, Samuel and Herbert Gintis, *Democracy and Capitalism: Property, Community, and the Contradictions of Modern Social Thought*, New York 1987.

Brand, Karl-Werner, "Cyclical Aspects of New Social Movements: Waves of Cultural Criticism and Mobilization Cycles of New Middle-Class Radicalism", *Challenging the Political Order: New Social and Political Movements in Western Democracies* (ed. by Russell J. Dalton and Manfred Kuechler), Cambridge 1990, 23-42.

———, *Neue soziale Bewegungen: Entstehung, Funktion und Perspektive neuer Protestpotentiale. Eine Zwischenbilanz*, Opladen 1982.

Brink, Mary Louise, "The Ecclesiological Dimensions of Jurgen Moltmann's Theology: Vision of a Future Church?", Diss., Fordham University 1990.

Brock, Peter, *Pacifism in Europe to 1914*, Princeton 1972.

Brown, Norman O., *Life against Death: The Psychoanalytic Meaning of History*, New York 1959.

———, *Love's Body*, New York 1968.

Browning, Don S., *Religious Thought and the Modern Psychologies*, Philadelphia 1987.

Browning, Don S. and Francis Schüssler Fiorenza (eds.), *Habermas, Modernity and Public Theology*, New York 1992.

Bruce-Briggs, B. (ed.), *The New Class?*, New Brunswick 1979.

Brunsson, Nils, *The Irrational Organization: Irrationality as a Basis for Organizational Action and Change*, Chichester 1985.

———, *Politik och administration: Utveckling och drivkrafter i en politiskt sammansatt organisation*, Stockholm 1981.

Brunsson, Nils and Johan P. Olsen (eds.), *Makten att reformera*, Stockholm 1990.

Brunsson, Nils and Sten Jönsson, *Beslut och handling: Om politikers inflytande på politiken*, Stockholm 1969.

Bubner, Rüdiger, *Modern German Philosophy*, Cambridge 1981.

———, *Theorie und Praxis – eine nachhegelsche Abstraktion*, Frankfurt a. M. 1971.

Buckley, Michael J., *At the Origins of Modern Atheism*, New Haven 1987.

Burnheim, John, *Is Democracy Possible? The Alternative to Electoral Politics*, Berkeley 1985.

Bush, Perry, "Anabaptism Born Again: Mennonites, New Evangelicals, and the Search for a Usable Past, 1950-1980", *Fides et Historia* 25, 1993, 26-47.

Cadoux, C. John, *The Early Christian Attitude to War: A Contribution to the History of Christian Ethics*, New York 1982 (London 1919).

Cartwright, Michael G., "Practices, Politics, and Performance: Toward a Communal Hermeneutic for Christian Ethics", Diss., Duke University 1988.

Castoriadis, Cornelius, *Le Contenu du socialisme*, Paris 1979.

———, *L'institution imaginaire de la société*, Paris 1975.

Cessario, Romanus, *The Moral Virtues and Theological Ethics*, Notre Dame 1991.

The Challenge of Peace: God's Promise and Our Response. A Pastoral Letter on War and Peace. National Conference of Catholic Bishops 1983.

Chapman, Jr., G. Clarke, "Hope and the Ethics of Formation: Moltmann as an Interpreter of Bonhoeffer", *Studies in Religion*, 12, 1983, 449-460.

———, "Jürgen Moltmann and the Christian Dialogue with Marxism", *Journal of Ecumenical Studies* 18, 1981, 435-450.

Chopp, Rebecca S., *The Praxis of Suffering: An Interpretation of Liberation and Political Theologies*, Maryknoll 1986.

Christensen, Anna, "Lönearbetet som samhällsform och ideologi", *Sociala värderingsförändringar*, Stockhom 1983, 1-23.

Christoffersen, Svein Aage, "Etikk for fremtiden?", *Norsk teologisk tidsskrift* 93, 1992, 17-34.

Christsein gestalten: Eine Studie zum Weg der Kirche. Herausgegeben vom Kirchenamt im Auftrag des Rates der Evangelischen Kirche in Deutschland, Gütersloh 1987.

The Church and the Bomb: Nuclear Weapons and Christian Conscience. The report of a working party under the chairmanship of the Bishop of Salisbury. London 1982.

Clark, Kelly James, *Return to Reason: A Critique of Enlightenment Evidentialism and a Defense of Reason and Belief in God*, Grand Rapids 1990.

Clasen, Claus-Peter, *Anabaptism: A Social History, 1525-1618. Switzerland, Austria, Moravia, South and Central Germany*, Ithaca 1972.

Coalter, Milton J., John M. Mulder and Louis B. Weeks (eds.), *The Organizational Revolution: Presbyterians and American Denominationalism*, Louisville 1992.

Cobb, Jr., John B., "Beyond Political Theology", *Gottes Zukunft – Zukunft der Welt. Festschrift für Jürgen Moltmann zum 60. Geburtstag* (ed. by Hermann Deuser, Gerhard Marcel Martin, Konrad Stock und Michael Welker), München 1986, 457-466.

———, *Process Theology as Political Theology*, Manchester 1982.

Cochran, Clarke E., "Authority and Community: The Contributions of Carl Friedrich, Yves R. Simon, and Michael Polanyi", *The American Political Science Review* 71, 1977, 546-558.

———, *Religion in Public and Private Life*, New York 1990.

The Conrad Grebel Review 10:3, 1992.

Conyears, A. J., *God, Hope and History: Jürgen Moltmann and the Christian Concept of History*, Macon 1988.

Cook, Guillermo, "The Evangelical Groundswell in Latin America", *The Christian Century* 107, 1990, 1172-1179.

———, *The Expectation of the Poor: Latin American Basic Ecclesial Communities in Protestant Perspective*, Maryknoll 1985.

Cornelison, Robert Thomas, *The Christian Realism of Reinhold Niebuhr and the Political Theology of Jürgen Moltmann in Dialogue: The Realism of Hope*, San Francisco 1992.

Cox, Harvey, *Feast of Fools*, New York 1969.

Dahlström, Edmund, "Moderniseringens gränser, samhällsvetenskapens självreflexion: Några synpunkter på efterkrigstidens svenska sociologi", *Handling, norm och rationalitet: Om förhållandet mellan samhällsvetenskap och praktisk filosofi* (ed. by Margareta Bertilsson and Anders Molander), Bergen 1992, 53-72.

Dalton, Russell J. and Manfred Kuechler (eds.), *Challenging the Political Order: New Social and Political Movements in Western Democracies*, Cambridge 1990.

Dalton, Russell J., Manfred Kuechler, and Wilhelm Bürklin, "The Challenge of New Movements", *Challenging the Political Order: New Social and Political Movements in Western Democracies* (ed. by Russell J. Dalton and Manfred Kuechler), Cambridge 1990, 3-20.

Dancy, Jonathan, *An Introduction to Contemporary Epistemology*, Oxford 1985.

de Certeau, Michel, *The Practice of Everyday Life*, Berkeley 1984.

de Vylder, Stefan, "Utvecklingsteorier och utvecklingsstrategier igår och idag", *Bistånd i kris: En bok om svensk u-landspolitik* (ed. by Christina Andersson, Lars Heikensten and Stefan de Vylder), Stockholm 1984, 169-186.

Del Colle, Ralph, "God in Creation: A New Theology of Creation and the Spirit of God", *Union Seminary Quarterly Review* 41, 1987, 69-74.

Denvall, Verner and Susanne Wollinger, *I gemenskapens tjänst? Studie av ett boendeprojekt*, Stockholm 1993.

Dialogue Sequel to Jürgen Moltmann's 'Following Jesus Christ in the World Today', Elkhart 1984.

Dorrien, Gary J., *Reconstructing the Common Good: Theology and the Social Order*, Maryknoll 1990.

Duchrow, Ulrich, *Global Economy: A Confessional Issue for the Churches?*, Geneva 1987.

Dunn, James D. G., *Jesus, Paul and the Law: Studies in Mark and Galatians*, London 1990.

———, "The Justice of God: A Renewed Perspective on Justification by Faith", *Journal of Theological Studies* 43, 1992, 1-22.

———, *Romans*, 2 vols., Dallas 1988.

Dunn, John, *Modern Revolutions*, Cambridge 1972.

———, *The Politics of Socialism: An Essay in Political Theory*, Cambridge 1984.

———, *Western Political Theory in the Face of the Future*, Cambridge 1979.

Durnbaugh, Donald F., *The Believers' Church: The History and Character of Radical Protestantism*, Scottdale 1985.

———, "Characteristics of the Radical Reformation in Historical Perspective", *Brethren Life and Thought* 35, 1990, 16-33.

Dworkin, Gerald, *The Theory and Practice of Autonomy*, Cambridge 1988.

Dykstra, Craig, *Vision and Character: A Christian Educator's Alternative to Kohlberg*, New York 1981.

Eberstadt, Nick, *The Poverty of Communism*, New Brunswick 1988.

Eller, Vernard, *Christian Anarchy: Jesus' Primacy Over the Powers*, Grand Rapids 1987.

———, *In Place of Sacraments: A Study of Baptism and the Lord's Supper*, Grand Rapids 1972.

———, *Proclaim Good Tidings: Evangelism for the Faith Community*, Elgin 1987.

———, *The Promise: Ethics in the Kingdom of God*, Garden City 1970.

Elster, Jon, "Is There (or Should There Be) a Right to Work?", *Democracy and the Welfare State* (ed. by Amy Gutmann), Princeton 1988, 53-78.

Elster, Jon and Karl Ove Moene (eds.), *Alternatives to Capitalism*, Cambridge 1989.

Ellul, Jacques, *Anarchy and Christianity*, Grand Rapids 1991.

———, *The Autopsy of Revolution*, New York 1971.

———, *The Betrayal of the West*, New York 1978.

———, *Changer de révolution: L'inéluctable prolétariat*, Paris 1982.

———, *De la Révolution aux révoltes*, Paris 1972.

———, *Ethique de la liberté*, 3 vols., Genève 1973-1984.

————, *L'illusion politique*, 2nd ed., Paris 1977.

————, *The Subversion of Christianity*, Grand Rapids 1986.

————, *The Technological Bluff*, Grand Rapids 1990.

————, *To Will and to Do: An Ethical Research for Christians*, Philadelphia 1969.

————, "Le travail", *Foi et Vie* 79:4, 1980, 1-86. (All author names except "O . . ." are actually pseudonyms for Ellul.)

Elshtain, Jean Bethke, *Meditations on Modern Political Thought: Masculine/Feminine Themes from Luther to Arendt*, New York 1986.

————, *Public Man, Private Woman: Women in Social and Political Thought*, Princeton 1981.

————, *Women and War*, New York 1987.

Engelhardt, Jr., H. Tristram, *Bioethics and Secular Humanism: The Search for a Common Morality*, London 1991.

————, "Bioethics in Pluralist Societies", *Perspectives in Biology and Medicine* 26, 1982, 67-77.

Estep, William R., *The Anabaptist Story*, Grand Rapids 1975.

Etzioni, Amitai, *The Moral Dimension: Towards a New Economics*, New York 1988.

————, *The Spirit of Community: Rights, Responsibilities, and the Communitarian Agenda*, New York 1993.

Eyerman, Ron and Andrew Jamison, *Social Movements: A Cognitive Approach*, Cambridge 1991.

Feyerabend, Paul, *Against Method*, London 1975.

Finger, Thomas N., *Christian Theology: An Eschatological Approach*, 2 vols., Scottdale 1985-1989.

————, "Response to 'Following Christ in an Age of Nuclear War'", *Dialogue Sequel to Jürgen Moltmann's 'Following Jesus Christ in the World Today'*, Elkhart 1984, 45-48.

Finke, Roger and Rodney Stark, *The Churching of America, 1776-1990: Winners and Losers in our Religious Economy*, New Brunswick 1992.

Fiorenza, Francis Schüssler, *Foundational Theology: Jesus and the Church*, New York 1986.

————, "Political Theology and Liberation Theology: An Inquiry Into Their Fundamental Meaning", *Liberation, Revolution, and Freedom* (ed. by Thomas M. McFadden), New York 1975, 3-29.

————, "Political Theology as Foundational Theology", *CTSA Proceedings* 32, 1977, 142-177.

————, "Politische Theologie und liberale Gerechtigkeits-Konzeptionen", *Mystik und Politik: Johann Baptist Metz zu Ehren* (ed. by Edward Schillebeeckx), Mainz 1988, 105-117.

Fish, Stanley, *Doing What Comes Naturally: Change, Rhetoric, and the Practice of Theory in Literary and Legal Studies*, Durham 1989.

————, *Is There a Text in This Class? The Authority of Interpretative Communities*, Cambridge, Mass. 1980.

Forrester, Duncan B., *Theology and Politics*, Oxford 1988.

Fowl, Stephen E., "The Ethics of Interpretation or What's Left Over After the Elimination of Meaning", *The Bible in Three Dimensions: Essays in Celebration of Forty Years of Biblical Studies in the University of Sheffield* (ed. by David J. A. Clines, Stephen E. Fowl, and Stanley E. Porter), Sheffield 1990, 379-398.

Fowl, Stephen E. and L. Gregory Jones, *Reading in Communion: Scripture and Ethics in Christian Life*, Grand Rapids 1991.

Frei, Hans, Review of Jürgen Moltmann, *The Theology of Hope*, *Union Seminary Quarterly Review* 23, 1968, 267-272.

————, *Types of Christian Theology*, New Haven 1992.

French, William C., "Returning to Creation: Moltmann's Eschatology Naturalized", *Journal of Religion* 68, 1988, 78-86.

Friesen, Duane K., "Normative Factors in Troeltsch's Typology of Religious Association", *Journal of Religious Ethics* 3, 1975, 271-283.

Frostin, Per, "Systematisk teologi i ett pluralistiskt samhälle", *Svensk teologisk kvartalskrift* 66, 1990, 154-162.

Fuchs, Ottmar, "Individualization and Institution: Theological Reflection on Some Recent Survey Results in West Germany", *Journal of Empirical Theology* 2, 1989, 69-80.

Gabriel, Karl, *Christentum zwischen Tradition und Postmoderne*, Freiburg 1992.

Gallup, Jr., George H. and Timothy Jones, *The Saints Among Us*, Harrisburg 1992.

Galston, William A., *Liberal Purposes: Goods, Virtues, and Diversity in the Liberal State*, Cambridge 1991.

Gay, Craig M., *With Liberty and Justice for Whom? The Recent Evangelical Debate over Capitalism*, Grand Rapids 1991.

Geertsema, H. G., *Van boven naar voren: Wijsgerige achtergronden en problemen van het theologische denken over geschiedenis bij Jürgen Moltmann*, Kampen 1980.

Gentry, Jerry Lynn, "Narrative Ethics and Economic Justice: Toward an Ethic of Inclusion", Diss., The Southern Baptist Theological Seminary 1989.

Giddens, Anthony, *The Consequences of Modernity*, Cambridge 1990.

————, *The Constitution of Society: Outline of the Theory of Structuration*, Berkeley 1984.

————, *A Contemporary Critique of Historical Materialism*, Berkeley 1981.

————, *The Nation-State and Violence: Volume Two of A Contemporary Critique of Historical Materialism*, Berkeley 1987.

————, *Social Theory and Modern Sociology*, Stanford 1987.

Gilkey, Langdon, *How the Church Can Minister to the World Without Losing Itself*, New York 1964.

————, *Reaping the Whirlwind: A Christian Interpretation of History*, New York 1976.

Gish, Arthur, *The New Left and Christian Radicalism*, Grand Rapids 1970.

Glebe-Møller, Jens, *Den teologiske ellipse*, Odense 1989.

Glendon, Mary Ann, *Rights Talk: The Impoverishment of Political Discourse*, New York 1991.

Godement, François, "La tournamente du vent communiste (1955-1965)", *La Chine au XXe siècle. 2: De 1949 à aujourd'hui* (ed. by Marie-Claire Bergère, Lucien Bianco, and Jürgen Domes), Paris 1990, 35-60.

Goertz, Hans-Jürgen, "The Confessional Heritage in Its New Mold: What is Mennonite Self-Understanding Today?", *Mennonite Identity: Historical and Contemporary Perspectives* (ed. by Calvin Redekop), Lanham 1988, 1-12.

————, *Pfaffenhaß und groß Geschrei: Die reformatorischen Bewegungen in Deutschland 1517-1529*, München 1987.

————, *Die Täufer: Geschichte und Deutung*, 2nd ed., München 1988.

Goldberg, Michael, *Theology and Narrative: A Critical Introduction*, Nashville 1982.

Gorz, André, *Farewell to the Working Class: An Essay on Post-Industrial Socialism*, London 1982.

Gouldner, Alvin, *The Future of the Intellectuals and the Rise of the New Class*, New York 1979.

Gracie, David McInnes, "Translator's Introduction", Adolf Harnack, *Militia Christi: The Christian Religion and the Military in the First Three Centuries*, Philadelphia 1981, 9-22.

Gray, John, *Liberalism*, Minneapolis 1986.

Gregersen, Niels Henrik, "How to Cope with Pluralism in Dogmatics: A Proposal", *Studia Theologica* 44, 1990, 123-136.

————, *Teologi og kultur: Protestantismen mellem isolation og assimilation i det 19. og 20. århundrede*, Århus 1988.

Gunnell, John G., "In Search of the Political Object: Beyond Methodology and Transcendentalism", *What Should Political Theory Be Now?* (ed. by John S Nelson), Albany 1983, 25-52.

Gunnemann, Jon P., "Human Rights and Modernity: The Truth of the Fiction of Individual Rights", *Journal of Religious Ethics* 16, 1988, 160-189.

————, *The Moral Meaning of Revolution*, New Haven 1979.

Gunton, Colin, *The Actuality of Atonement: A Study of Metaphor, Rationality and the Christian Tradition*, Edinburgh 1988.

————, *Enlightenment and Alienation: An Essay towards a Trinitarian Theology*, London 1985.

————, *The Promise of Trinitarian Theology*, Edinburgh 1991.

Guroian, Vigen, *Incarnate Love: Essays in Orthodox Ethics*, Notre Dame 1987.

————, "Tradition and Ethics: Prospects in a Liberal Society", *Modern Theology* 7, 1991, 205-224.

Gustafson, James, *Protestant and Roman Catholic Ethics: Prospects for Rapprochement*, London 1979.

————, "A Response to Critics", *Journal of Religious Ethics* 13, 1985, 185-209.

————, "The Sectarian Temptation: Reflections on Theology, the Church and the University", *Proceedings of the CTS* 40, 1985, 83-94.

————, *Theology and Ethics*, Oxford 1991.

Gustafsson, Ingmar, *Fred och försvar i frikyrkligt perspektiv 1900-1921: Debatten inom Svenska Missionsförbundet*, Uppsala 1987.

Gutierrez, Gustavo, *A Theology of Liberation: History, Politics and Salvation*, rev. ed., London 1988.

Habermas, Jürgen, *Autonomy and Solidarity: Interviews* (edited and introduced by Peter Dews), London 1986.

————, *Kommunikativt handlande: Texter om språk, rationalitet och samhälle*, Göteborg 1988.

————, *Moral Consciousness and Communicative Action*, Cambridge 1990.

————, *The Theory of Communicative Action*, 2 vols., London 1984 and Cambridge 1987.

Hach, Jürgen, *Gesellschaft und Religion in der Bundesrepublik Deutschland: Eine Einführung in die Religionssoziologie*, Heidelberg 1980.

Hamberg, Eva M., *Studies in the Prevalence of Religious Beliefs and Religious Practice In Contemporary Sweden*, Stockholm 1990.

Hampshire, Stuart, "Fallacies in Moral Philosophy", *Revisions: Changing Perspectives in Moral Philosophy* (ed. by Stanley Hauerwas and Alasdair MacIntyre), Notre Dame 1983, 51-67.

Harder, Helmut, "Response to Moltmann's 'Political Theology and Political Hermeneutics'", *Dialogue Sequel to Jürgen Moltmann's 'Following Jesus Christ in the World Today'*, Elkhart 1984, 31-34.

Hargrove, Barbara, *The Emerging New Class: Implications for Church and Society*, New York 1986.

Härle, Wilfried and Eilert Herms, "Deutschsprachige protestantische Dogmatik nach 1945", *Verkündigung und Forschung* 27-28, 1982-83.

Harnack, Adolf, *Militia Christi: The Christian Religion and the Military in the First Three Centuries*, Philadelphia 1981.

Hatch, Natan O. and Mark A. Noll (eds.), *The Bible in America: Essays in Cultural History*, New York 1982.

Havel, Václav, "Anti-Political Politics", *Civil Society and the State: New European Perspectives* (ed. by John Keane), London 1988, 381-398.

――――, *En dåre i Prag: Brev, tal, texter 1975-1990 i urval av Peter Larsson*, Stockholm 1990.

――――, "Godot kommer inte ty han finns ej", *Svenska Dagbladet* December 30, 1992.

――――, *Václav Havel or Living in Truth* (ed. by Jan Vladislav), London 1987.

Hays, Richard B, *Echoes of Scripture in the Letters of Paul*, New Haven 1989.

――――, "Scripture-Shaped Community: The Problem of Method in New Testament Ethics", *Interpretation* 44, 1990, 42-55.

Hedlund, Stefan, *Östeuropas kris: Ekonomi, ekologi och möjliga svenska insatser*, Stockholm 1990.

Heeley, Gerard F., "The Ethical Methodology of Stanley Hauerwas: An Examination of Christian Character Ethics", Diss., Pontificia Studiorum Universitas A S. Thoma AQ. In Urbe 1987.

Helgeland, John, "Christians and the Roman Army A.D. 173-337", *Church History* 43, 1974, 149-163, 200.

Helgeland, John, Robert J. Daly and J. Patout Burns, *Christians and the Military: The Early Experience*, Philadelphia 1985.

Heller, Mikhail and Aleksandr Nekrich, *Utopia in Power: The History of the Soviet Union from 1917 to the Present*, New York 1986.

Herzog, Don, *Without Foundations: Justification in Political Theory*, Ithaca 1985.

Heuberger, Frank W., "The New Class: On the Theory of a No Longer Entirely New Phenomenon", *Hidden Technocrats: The New Class and New Capitalism* (ed. by Hansfried Kellner and Frank W. Heuberger), New Brunswick 1992, 23-47.

Hewitt, W. E., *Base Christian Communities and Social Change in Brazil*, Lincoln 1991.

Hill, Jr., Thomas E., "Autonomy of Moral Agents", *Encyclopedia of Ethics* (ed. by Lawrence C. Becker), vol. 1, New York 1992, 71-75.

Hillmann, Karl-Heinz, *Wertwandel: Zur Frage soziokultureller Voraussetzungen alternativer Lebensformen*, Darmstadt 1989.

Himmelstrand, Ulf, "Den sociologiska analysen av Sverige", *Sverige – vardag och struktur: Sociologer beskriver det svenska samhället* (ed. by Ulf Himmelstrand and Göran Svensson), Södertälje 1988, 13-22.

Hirdman, Yvonne, *Att lägga livet till rätta – studier i svensk folkhemspolitik*, Stockholm 1990.

Holifield, E. Brooks, *A History of Pastoral Care in America: From Salvation to Self-Realization*, Nashville 1983.

Holland, Scott, "The Problems and Prospects of a 'Sectarian Ethic': A Critique of the Hauerwas Reading of the Jesus Story", *Conrad Grebel Review* 10, 1992, 157-168.

Holleman, Warren Lee, *The Human Rights Movement: Western Values and Theological Perspectives*, New York 1987.

Hollenbach, David, *Claims in Conflict: Retrieving and Renewing the Catholic Human Rights Tradition*, New York 1979.

Holmberg, Bengt, "En historisk vändning i forskningen om Jesus", *Svensk teologisk kvartalskrift* 69, 1993, 69-76.

Hornus, Jean-Michel, *It Is Not Lawful For Me To Fight: Early Christian Attitudes Toward War, Violence, and the State*, Scottdale 1980.

Howard, Michael, *War and the Liberal Conscience*, London 1978.

Huber, Wolfgang, *Folgen christlicher Freiheit: Ethik und Theorie der Kirche im Horizont der Barmer Theologischen Erklärung*, Neukirchen-Vluyn 1985.

Huber, Wolfgang and Heinz Eduard Tödt, *Menschenrechte: Perspektiven einer menschlichen Welt*, München 1988.

Hunsinger, George, "The Crucified God and the Political Theology of Violence: A Critical Survey of Jürgen Moltmann's Recent Thought", *Heythrop Journal* 14, 1973, 266-279, 379-395.

———, Review of Jürgen Moltmann, *The Trinity and the Kingdom*, *The Thomist* 47, 1983, 129-139.

Hunter, David G., "A Decade of Research on Early Christians and Military Service", *RSR* 18, 1992, 87-94.

Hunter, James Davison, *American Evangelicalism: Conservative Religion and the Quandary of Modernity*, New Brunswick 1983.

———, *Culture Wars: The Struggle to Define America*, n. p. 1991.

———, *Evangelicalism: The Coming Generation*, Chicago 1987.

———, "The New Class and the Young Evangelicals", *Review of Religious Research* 22, 1980, 155-169.

Hunter, James Davison and James E. Hawdon, "Religious Elites in Advanced Capitalism: The Dialectic of Power and Marginality", *World Order and Religion* (ed. by Wade Clark Roof), Albany 1991, 39-59.

Hunter, James Davison and Tracy Fessenden, "The New Class as Capitalist Class: The Rise of the Moral Entrepreneur in America", *Hidden Technocrats: The New Class and New Capitalism* (ed. by Hansfried Kellner and Frank W. Heuberger), New Brunswick 1992, 157-187.

Hutchison, William R., "Past Imperfect: History and the Prospect of Liberalism", *Liberal Protestantism: Realities and Possibilities* (ed. by Robert S. Michaelsen and Wade Clark Roof), New York 1986, 65-82.

Hütter, Reinhard, "The Church: Midwife of History or Witness of the Eschaton", *Journal of Religious Ethics* 18, 1990, 27-54.

———, "The Church's Peace Beyond the 'Secular': A Postmodern Augustinian's Deconstruction of Secular Modernity and Postmodernity", *Pro Ecclesia* 2, 1993, 106-116.

———, "The Ecclesial Ethics of Stanley Hauerwas", *Dialog* 30, 1991, 231-241.

———, "Ethik in Traditionen: Die Neo-Aristotelische Herausforderung in der philosophischen und theologischen Ethik der USA", *Verkündigung und Forschung* 35, 1990, 61-84.

———, *Evangelische Ethik als kirchliches Zeugnis: Interpretationen zu Schlüsselfragen theologischer Ethik in der Gegenwart*, Neukirchen-Vluyn 1993.

Hydén, Göran, *No Shortcuts to Progress: African Development Management in Perspective*, Berkeley 1983.

In Defense of Creation: the Nuclear Crisis and a Just Peace, Nashville 1986.

Inglehart, Ronald, *Culture Shift in Advanced Industrial Society*, Princeton 1990.

———, *The Silent Revolution: Changing Values and Political Styles Among Western Publics*, Princeton 1977.

Jeffner, Anders, Inge Lønning, and Theodor Jørgensen, "Sakkunnigutlåtande rörande professuren i systematisk teologi vid Lunds universitet", Protokoll för tjänsteförslagsnämnden för teologiska fakulteten i Lund 1989-10-09.

Jenson, Robert, "Hauerwas Examined", *First Things* no. 25, 1992, 49-51.

———, "The Hauerwas Project", *Modern Theology* 8, 1992, 285-295.

Jeschke, Marlin, *Discipling the Brother: Congregational Discipline According to the Gospel*, Scottdale 1972.

Johnson, Benton, Dean R. Hoge and Donald A. Luidens, "Mainline Churches: The Real Reason for Decline", *First Things* no. 31, 1993, 13-18.

Johnson, James Turner, *Can Modern War Be Just?*, New Haven 1984.

———, *The Quest for Peace: Three Moral Traditions in Western Cultural History*, Princeton 1987.

Johnson, Luke Timothy, "The Social Dimension of *Soteria* in Luke-Acts and Paul", *Society of Biblical Literature 1993 Seminar Papers*, 520-536.

Jones, L. Gregory, "Should Christians Affirm Rawl's Justice as Fairness? A Response to Professor Beckley", *Journal of Religious Ethics* 16, 1988, 251-271.

———, *Transformed Judgment: Toward a Trinitarian Account of the Moral Life*, Notre Dame 1990.

Jüngel, Eberhard, *God as the Mystery of the World. On the Foundation of the Theology of the Crucified One in the Dispute between Theism and Atheism*, Grand Rapids 1983.

Källström, Staffan, *Den gode nihilisten: Axel Hägerström och striderna kring uppsalafilosofin*, Kristianstad 1986.

Kammer, Charles L., *Ethics and Liberation: An Introduction*, London 1988.

Kasper, Walter, *The God of Jesus Christ*, London 1984.

———, *Theology and Church*, London 1989.

———, "Die Theologie der Befreiung aus europäischer Perspektive", *Die Theologie der Befreiung: Hoffnung oder Gefahr für die Kirche* (ed. by Johann Baptist Metz), Düsseldorf 1986, 77-98.

Kaufman, Gordon D., *The Theological Imagination: Constructing the Concept of God*, Philadelphia 1981.

———, *Theology for a Nuclear Age*, Manchester 1985.

Kaufmann, Franz-Xaver and Johann Baptist Metz, *Zukunftsfähigkeit: Suchbewegungen im Christentum*, Freiburg 1987.

Kaufmann, Franz-Xaver, Walter Kerber and Paul Zulehner, *Ethos und Religion bei Führungskräften: Eine Studie im Auftrag des Arbeitskreises für Führungskräfte in der Wirtschaft*, München 1986.

Keane, John, "Despotism and Democracy: The Origins and Development of the Distinction between Civil Society and the State 1750-1850", *Civil Society and the State: New European Perspectives* (ed. by John Keane), London 1988, 35-71.

Keane, John (ed.), *Civil Society and the State: New European Perspectives*, London 1988.

Kellner, Hansfried and Frank W. Heuberger, "Modernizing Work: New Frontiers in Business Consulting", *Hidden Technocrats: The New Class and New Capitalism* (ed. by Hansfried Kellner and Frank W. Heuberger), New Brunswick 1992, 49-80.

——— (eds.), *Hidden Technocrats: The New Class and New Capitalism*, New Brunswick 1992.

Kelsey, David, *The Uses of Scripture in Recent Theology*, London 1975.

Kerber, Walter (ed.), *Säkularisierung und Wertewandel: Analysen und Überlegungen zur gesellschaftlichen Situation in Europa*, München 1986.

Klaasen, Walter, *Anabaptism: Neither Catholic nor Protestant*, Waterloo 1973.

Klappert, Bertold, "Christologie in messianischen Dimensionen", *Evangelische Theologie* 50, 1990, 574-586.

Köcher, Renate, "Religiös in einer säkularisierten Welt", Elisabeth Noelle-Neumann and Renate Köcher, *Die verletzte Nation: Über den Versuch der Deutschen, ihren Charakter zu ändern*, Stuttgart 1987, 164-281.

Kolakowski, Leszek, *Main Current of Marxism: Its Origins, Growth and Dissolution*, 3 vols., Oxford 1978.

Koontz, Ted, "Mennonites and the State: Preliminary Reflections", *Essays on Peace Theology and Witness* (ed. by Willard M. Swartley), Elkhart 1988, 35-60.

Kovesi, Julius, *Moral Notions*, London 1967.

Krogh, Thomas, "Frontlinjer i moderne moralfilosofisk debatt", *Handling, norm och rationalitet: Om förhållandet mellan samhällsvetenskap och praktisk filosofi* (ed. by Margareta Bertilsson and Anders Molander), Bergen 1992, 175-193.

Kuhn, Thomas S., *The Structure of Scientific Revolutions*, 2nd ed., Chicago 1970.

Kukathas, Chandran and Philip Pettit, *John Rawls: En introduktion*, Göteborg 1992.

Lakatos, Imre, *The Methodology of Scientific Research Programmes* (*Philosophical Papers*, vol. 1), Cambridge 1978.

Lane, D. A., *Foundations for a Social Theology: Praxis, Process and Salvation*, Ramsey 1984.

Langan, John, "The Just-War Theory After the Gulf War", *Theological Studies* 53, 1992, 95-112.

Lasch, Christopher, *The Culture of Narcissism: American Life in an Age of Diminishing Expectations*, London 1980.

Lash, Nicholas, *Theology on the Way to Emmaus*, London 1986.

Lauritzen, Paul, "Emotion and Religious Ethics", *Journal of Religious Ethics* 16, 1988, 307-324.

Levenson, Jon D., *The Hebrew Bible, the Old Testament and Historical Criticism: Jews and Christians in Biblical Studies*, Louisville 1993.

Lindbeck, George A., "The Church's Mission to a Postmodern Culture", *Postmodern Theology: Christian Faith in a Pluralistic World* (ed. by Frederic B. Burnham), New York 1989, 37-55.

————, "Confession and Community: An Israel-like View of the Church", *The Christian Century* 107, 1990, 492-496.

————, "Hans Frei and the Future of Theology in America", unpublished.

————, "Modernity and Luther's Understanding of the Freedom of the Christian", *Martin Luther and the Modern Mind: Freedom, Conscience, Toleration, Rights* (ed. by Manfred Hoffmann), New York 1985, 1-22.

————, *The Nature of Doctrine: Religion and Theology in a Postliberal Age*, London 1984.

————, "The Sectarian Future of the Church", *The God Experience: Essays in Hope* (ed. by Joseph P. Whelan), New York 1971, 226-243.

Lindquist, Curtis George, "The Church as a Christian Community of Hope: A Comparative Study of Moltmann and Hauerwas Using a Cultural-Linguistic Style of Thinking", Diss., Emory University 1990.

Link, Christian, *Schöpfung. 1. Schöpfungstheologie in reformatorischer Tradition. 2. Schöpfungstheologie angesichts der Herausforderungen des 20. Jahrhunderts* (Handbuch Systematischer Theologie Band 7/1-2), Gütersloh 1991.

————, "Schöpfung im messianischen Licht", *Evangelische Theologie* 47, 1987, 83-92.

Littell, Franklin H., *The Anabaptist View of the Church: A Study in the Origins of Sectarian Protestantism*, 2nd ed., Boston 1958.

————, *The Free Church*, Boston 1957.

Lobkowicz, Nicholas, "On the History of Theory and Praxis", *Political Theory and Praxis: New Perspectives* (ed. by Terence Ball), Minneapolis 1977, 13-27.

————, *Theory and Practice: History of a Concept from Aristotle to Marx*, Notre Dame 1967.

Lohfink, Gerhard, *Jesus and Community. The Social Dimension of Christian Faith*, Philadelphia 1984.

————, "Jesus und die Kirche", *Theologische Jahrbuch* 1990, 64-106.

————, "Die Not der Exegese mit der Reich-Gottes-Verkündigung Jesu", *Theologische Quartalschrift*, 168, 1988, 1-15.

————, *Wem gilt die Bergpredigt? Beiträge zu einer christlichen Ethik*, Freiburg 1988.

Lønning, Per, "Die Schöpfungstheologie Jürgen Moltmanns – eine nordische Perspektive", *Kerygma und Dogma* 33, 1987, 207-223.

Luhmann, Niklas, *Soziale Systeme: Grundriß einer allgemeinen Theorie*, Frankfurt a. M. 1987.

Lundkvist, Sven, *Folkrörelserna i det svenska samhället 1850-1920*, Stockholm 1977.

Lyttkens, Lorentz, *Den disciplinerade människan: Om social kontroll och långsiktiga värderingsförändringar*, Stockholm 1985.

————, *Politikens klichéer och människans ansikte*, Stockholm 1988.

MacIntyre, Alasdair, *After Virtue: A Study in Moral Theory*, London 1981.

————, "Does Applied Ethics Rest on a Mistake?", *The Monist* 67, 1984, 498-513.

————, "Epistemological Crises, Dramatic Narrative and the Philosophy of Science", *The Monist* 60, 1977, 453-472.09.06

————, "Nietzsche or Aristotle? Alasdair MacIntyre", Giovanna Borradori, *The American Philosopher: Conversations with Quine, Davidson, Putnam, Nozick, Danto, Rorty, Cavell, MacIntyre, and Kuhn*, Chicago 1994, 137-152.

————, "Objectivity in Morality and Objectivity in Science", *Morals, Science and Sociality* (ed. by H. Tristram Engelhardt, Jr. and Daniel Callahan), Hastings-on-Hudson 1978, 21-39.

————, *Three Rival Versions of Moral Enquiry: Encyclopaedia, Genealogy, and Tradition*, Notre Dame 1990.

————, *Whose Justice? Which Rationality?*, Notre Dame 1988.

Macken, John, *The Autonomy Theme in the* Church Dogmatics*: Karl Barth and His Critics*, Cambridge 1990.

Macquarrie, John, *In Search of Deity: An Essay in Dialectical Theism*, London 1984.

Mansbridge, Jane J., "The Rise and Fall of Self-Interest in the Explanation of Political Life", *Beyond Self-Interest* (ed. by Jane J. Mansbridge), Chicago 1990, 3-22.

———— (ed.), *Beyond Self-Interest*, Chicago 1990.

Marshall, Bruce D., "Absorbing the World: Christianity and the Universe of Truths", *Theology and Dialogue: Essays in Conversation with George Lindbeck* (ed. by Bruce D. Marshall), Notre Dame 1990, 69-102.

Martin, David, *Tongues of Fire: The Explosion of Protestantism in Latin America*, Oxford 1990.

Matic, Marko, *Jürgen Moltmanns Theologie in Auseinandersetzung mit Ernst Bloch*, Frankfurt a. M. 1983.

Matzko, David, "Postmodernism, Saints and Scoundrels", *Modern Theology* 9, 1993, 19-36.

McCann, Dennis P., "Natural Law, Public Theology and the Legacy of John Courtney Murray", *The Christian Century* 107, 1990, 801-803.

McCarthy, Thomas A., "Philosophical Foundations of Political Theology: Kant, Peukert, and the Frankfurt School", *Civil Religion and Political Theology* (ed. by Leroy S. Rouner), Notre Dame 1986, 23-40.

McClendon, Jr., James Wm., "Balthasar Hubmaier, Catholic Anabaptist", *Mennonite Quarterly Review* 65, 1991, 20-33.

————, "In the Light of Last Things: A Theology for the Believer's Church", *Perspectives in Religious Studies*, 18, 1991, 71-78.

————, *Systematic Theology: Ethics*, Nashville 1986.

McClendon, Jr., James Wm. and James M. Smith, *Understanding Religious Convictions*, Notre Dame 1975.

McCloskey, Donald, *If You're So Smart: The Narrative of Economic Expertise*, Chicago 1990.

————, *The Rhetoric of Economics*, Brighton 1986.

McFague, Sallie, *Models of God: Theology for an Ecological, Nuclear Age*, Philadelphia 1987.

McGovern, Arthur F., *Liberation Theology and Its Critics: Toward an Assessment*, Maryknoll 1989.

Meeks, M. Douglas, *God the Economist: The Doctrine of God and Political Economy*, Minneapolis 1989.

——, *Origins of the Theology of Hope*, Philadelphia 1974.

——, "Political Theology and Political Economy", *Gottes Zukunft – Zukunft der Welt. Festschrift für Jürgen Moltmann zum 60. Geburtstag* (ed. by Hermann Deuser, Gerhard Marcel Martin, Konrad Stock and Michael Welker), München 1986, 446-456.

Meeks, Wayne A., "A Hermeneutics of Social Embodiment", *Harvard Theological Review* 79, 1986, 176-186.

——, *The Moral World of the First Christians*, London 1987.

——, "Understanding Early Christian Ethics", *Journal of Biblical Literature* 105, 1986, 3-11.

Meilander, Gilbert C., *Faith and Faithfulness: Basic Themes in Christian Ethics*, Notre Dame 1991.

——, *The Theory and Practice of Virtue*, Notre Dame 1984.

Melucci, Alberto, *Nomader i nuet: Sociala rörelser och individuella behov i dagens samhälle*, Göteborg 1991.

——, "Social Movements and the Democratization of Everyday Life", *Civil Society and the State. New European Perspectives* (ed. by John Keane), London 1988, 245-260.

Metz, Johann Baptist, *The Emergent Church: The Future of Christianity in a Postbourgeois World*, New York 1981.

——, *Faith in History and Society: Toward a Practical Fundamental Theology*, London 1980.

——, *Followers of Christ: The Religious Life and the Church*, London 1978.

——, "Nochmals: Die Marxistische Herausforderung: Zu einem Problemansatz politischer Theologie", *Gottes Zukunft – Zukunft der Welt. Festschrift für Jürgen Moltmann zum 60. Geburtstag* (ed. by Hermann Deuser, Gerhard Marcel Martin, Konrad Stock and Michael Welker), München 1986, 414-422.

——, "Political Theology: A New Paradigm of Theology?", *Civil Religion and Political Theology* (ed. by Leroy S. Rouner), Notre Dame 1986, 141-153.

——, "Suchbewegungen nach einem neuen Gemeindebild", Franz-Xaver Kaufmann and Johann Baptist Metz, *Zukunftsfähigkeit: Suchbewegungen im Christentum*, Freiburg 1987, 148-165.

——, *Theology of the World*, London 1969.

Meyer, Ben F., *The Aims of Jesus*, London 1979.

Michaelsen, Robert S. and Wade Clark Roof (eds.), *Liberal Protestantism: Realities and Possibilities*, New York 1986.

Midgley, Mary, "Strange Contest: Science Versus Religion", *The Gospel and Contemporary Culture* (ed. by Hugh Montefiore), London 1992, 40-57.

Miguez Bonino, José, *Doing Theology in a Revolutionary Situation*, Philadelphia 1975.

——, *Towards a Christian Political Ethics*, London 1983.

Milbank, John, "'Between Purgation and Illumination': A Critique of the Theology of Right", *Christ, Ethics and Tragedy: Essays in Honour of Donald MacKinnon* (ed. by Kenneth Surin), Cambridge 1989, 161-196.

——, "Critical Study: Stanley Hauerwas, *Character and the Christian Life* and *Against the Nations*", *Modern Theology* 4, 1988, 211-216.

——, "The End of Dialogue", *Christian Uniqueness Reconsidered: The Myth of a Pluralistic Theology of Religions* (ed. by Gavin D'Costa), Maryknoll 1990, 174-191.

————, "On Baseless Suspicion: Christianity and the Crisis of Socialism", *New Blackfriars* 69, 1988, 4-19.

————, Review of Paul Nelson, *Narrative and Morality: A Theological Inquiry*, *Religious Studies* 25, 1989, 393-396.

————, "'Postmodern Critical Augustinianism': A Short *Summa* in Forty Two Responses to Unasked Questions", *Modern Theology* 7, 1991, 225-237.

————, "Problematizing the Secular: The Post-Postmodern Agenda", *Shadow of Spirit: Postmodernism and Religion* (ed. by Philippa Berry and Andrew Wernick), London 1992, 30-44.

————, *Theology and Social Theory: Beyond Secular Reason*, Oxford 1990.

Mirowski, Philip, *Against Mechanism: Protecting Economics from Science*, Totowa 1988.

Miscamble, Wilson D., "Sectarian Passivism?", *Theology Today* 44, 1987, 69-77.

Mitchell, Basil, *The Justification of Religious Belief*, London 1973.

————, *Morality: Religious and Secular. The Dilemma of the Traditional Conscience*, Oxford 1980.

Moll, Peter G., "Liberating Liberation Theology: Towards Independence from Dependency Theory", *Journal for Theology of South Africa* no. 78, 1992, 25-40.

Moore, Stephen D., *Literary Criticism and the Gospel: The Theoretical Challenge*, New Haven 1989.

Morse, Christopher, *The Logic of Promise in Moltmann's Theology*, Philadelphia 1979.

Mouw, Richard, "Abandoning the Typology: A Reformed Assist", *TSF Bulletin* 8:5, 1985, 7-10.

————, "Creational Politics: Some Calvinist Amendments", *Christian Scholars Review* 23, 1993, 181-193.

————, *The God Who Commands: A Study in Divine Command Ethics*, Notre Dame 1990.

Mouw, Richard and John H. Yoder, "Evangelical Ethics and the Anabaptist-Reformed Dialogue", *Journal of Religious Ethics* 17, 1989, 121-137.

Mulkay, Michael, *Sociology of Science: A Sociological Pilgrimage*, Bloomington 1991.

Murphy, Nancey, *Theology in the Age of Scientific Reasoning*, Ithaca 1990.

Nelson, John S. (ed.), *What Should Political Theory Be Now?*, Albany 1983.

Nelson, Paul, *Narrative and Morality: A Theological Inquiry*, University Park 1987.

Nelson, Robert H., *Reaching for Heaven on Earth: The Theological Meaning of Economics*, Lanham 1991.

Neuhaus, Richard J., *The Catholic Moment: The Paradox of the Church in the Postmodern World*, San Francisco 1987.

————, "Challenging the Culture: The Hauerwas Enterprise", *Commonweal* 109, 1982, 269-272.

Newbigin, Lesslie, *Foolishness to the Greeks: The Gospel and Western Culture*, London 1986.

————, *The Gospel in a Pluralist Society*, London 1989.

Niebuhr, H. Richard, *Christ and Culture*, New York 1975.

Niebuhr, Reinhold, *An Interpretation of Christian Ethics*, New York 1979.

————, *Moral Man and Immoral Society: A Study in Ethics and Politics*, New York 1960.

Niewiadomski, Jósef, *Die Zweideutigkeit von Gott und Welt in J. Moltmanns Theologien*, Innsbruck 1982.

Nisbet, Robert, *Conservatism: Dream and Reality*, Minneapolis 1986.

Nisbet, Robert and Robert G. Perrin, *The Social Bond*, 2nd ed., New York 1977.

Nordin, Svante, *Från Hägerström till Hedenius: Den moderna svenska filosofin*, Lund 1984.

Nortcott, Michael S., "Preston and Hauerwas on *Centesimus Annus*: Reflections on the Incommensurability of the Liberal and Post-Liberal Mind", *Theology* 96, 1993, 27-35.

Nove, Alec, *The Economics of Feasible Socialism*, London 1983.

Nozick, Robert, *Anarchy, State, and Utopia*, Oxford 1980.

Nussbaum, Martha, "Narrative Emotions: Beckett's Genealogy of Love", *Why Narrative? Readings in Narrative Theology* (ed. by Stanley Hauerwas and L. Gregory Jones), Grand Rapids 1989, 216-248.

O'Collins, G., "The Principle and Theology of Hope", *Scottish Journal of Theology* 21, 1968, 129-144.

Ohne Rüstung leben ed. by "Ohne Rüstung Leben", Arbeitskreis von Pro Ökumene, Gütersloh 1981.

Österberg, Dag, *Metasociology: An Inquiry into the Origins and Validity of Social Thought*, Oslo 1988.

Packull, Werner O., "Between Paradigms: Anabaptist Studies at the Crossroads", *Conrad Grebel Review* 8, 1990, 1-22.

Pannenberg, Wolfhart, *Ethics*, Philadelphia 1981.

———, *Systematic Theology*, vol. 1, Edinburgh 1991.

Peaslee, Amos J. and Dorothy Peaslee Xydis, *Constitutions of Nations*, 4 vols., The Hague 1970.

Petrén, Erik, *Kyrka och makt: Bilder ur svensk kyrkohistoria*, Lund 1990.

Pettersson, Thorleif, *Bakom dubbla lås: En studie av små och långsamma värderingsförändringar*, Stockholm 1988.

———, "Välfärd, värderingsförändringar och folkrörelseengagemang", *Mot denna framtid: Folkrörelser och folk om framtiden* (ed. by Sigbert Axelsson and Thorleif Pettersson), Stockholm 1992, 33-99.

Peukert, Helmut, *Wissenschaftstheorie – Handlungstheorie – Fundamentale Theologie: Analysen zu Ansatz und Status theologischer Theoriebildung*, Düsseldorf 1976.

Phillips, Steven, "The Use of Scripture in Liberation Theologies: An Examination of Juan Luis Segundo, James H. Cone, and Jürgen Moltmann", Diss., The Southern Baptist Theological Seminary, 1978.

Piepkorn, Arthur Carl, *Protestant Denominations (Profiles in Belief: The Religious Bodies of the United States and Canada*, vol. 2), San Francisco 1978.

Placher, William, "Postliberal Theology", *The Modern Theologians: An Introduction to Christian Theology in the Twentieth Century* (ed. by David F. Ford), Oxford 1989, vol. 2, 115-128.

———, *Unapologetic Theology: A Christian Voice in a Pluralistic Conversation*, Louisville 1989.

Plantinga, Alvin, "Coherentism and the Evidentialist Objection to Belief in God", *Rationality, Religious Belief, and Moral Commitment: New Essays in the Philosophy of Religion* (ed. by Robert Audi and William J. Wainright), Ithaca 1986, 109-138.

Plantinga, Alvin and Nicholas Wolterstorff (eds.), *Faith and Rationality: Reason and Belief in God*, Notre Dame 1983.

Pocock, J. G. A., "Political Ideas as Historical Events: Political Philosophers as Historical Actors", *Political Theory and Political Education* (ed. by Melvin Richter), Princeton 1980, 139-158.

Polanyi, Michael, *Personal Knowledge: Towards a Post-Critical Philosophy*, London 1962.

Powell, H. Jefferson, *The Moral Tradition of American Constitutionalism: A Theological Interpretation*, Durham 1993.

Poole, Ross, *Morality and Modernity*, London 1991.

Putnam, Hilary, *Realism and Reason (Philosophical Papers*, vol. 3), Cambridge 1983.

———, *Realism with a Human Face* (ed. by James Conant), Cambridge, Mass. 1990.

———, *Reason, Truth and History*, Cambridge 1981.

Putnam, Robert D., *Making Democracy Work: Civic Traditions in Modern Italy*, Princeton 1993.

Quebedeaux, Richard, *The Worldly Evangelicals*, New York 1978.

———, *The Young Evangelicals: Revolution in Orthodoxy*, New York 1974.

Quine, Willard Van Orman, *From a Logical Point of View*, 2nd rev. ed., Cambridge, Mass. 1961.

Quinn, Philip L., "Is Athens Revived Jerusalem Denied?", *The Asbury Theological Journal* 45, 1990, 49-57.

Quirk, Michael, "Beyond Sectarianism?", *Theology Today* 44, 1987, 78-86.

Rajchman, John and Cornel West (eds.), *Post-Analytic Philosophy*, New York 1985.

Ramsey, Paul, *The Just War: Force and Political Responsibility*, New York 1968.

———, "A Question (Or Two) For Stanley Hauerwas", unpublished.

———, *Speak Up for Just War or Pacifism: A Critique of the United Methodist Bishops' Pastoral Letter "In Defense of Creation"* (with an Epilogue by Stanley Hauerwas), University Park 1988.

———, *War and the Christian Conscience: How Shall Modern War be Conducted Justly?*, Durham 1961.

Rasmusson, Arne and Roland Spjuth, *Kristologiska perspektiv: Om möjligheter och återvändsgränder i modern teologi med speciell referens till Edward Schillebeeckx, Wolfhart Pannenberg och Walter Kasper*, Örebro 1986.

———, *En studie i svensk hälso- och sjukvårdsplanering*, Örebro 1980.

Rawls, John, *Political Liberalism*, New York 1993.

———, *A Theory of Justice*, Cambridge, Mass. 1971.

Redekop, Calvin, *Mennonite Society*, Baltimore 1989.

Rendtorff, Trutz, *Theologie in der Moderne: Über Religion im Prozeß der Aufklärung*, Gütersloh 1991.

Richardson, Robert N., "Christian Community and Ethics: Critical Reflections on the Nature and Function of the Church in the Ethics of Stanley Hauerwas", Diss., University of Natal 1986.

Rieff, Philip, *The Triumph of the Therapeutic: Uses of Faith After Freud*, Chicago 1987.

Ritschl, Dietrich, "Die vier Reiche der 'drei göttlichen Subjekte': Bemerkungen zu Jürgen Moltmanns Trinitätslehre", *Evangelische Theologie* 41, 1981, 463-471.

Ritter, Joachim, *Metaphysik und Politik: Studien zu Aristoteles und Hegel*, Frankfurt a. M. 1977.

Roberts, Robert C., "What an Emotion Is: A Sketch", *The Philosophical Review* 97, 1988, 183-209.

Robertson, Roland, *The Sociological Interpretation of Religion*, Oxford 1980.

Rochon, Thomas R., "The West European Peace Movement and the Theory of New Social Movements", *Challenging the Political Order: New Social and Political Movements in Western Democracies* (ed. by Russell J. Dalton and Manfred Kuechler), Cambridge 1990, 105-121.

Roloff, Jürgen, *Die Kirche im Neuen Testament*, Göttingen 1993.

Roof, Wade Clark, "The Church in the Centrifuge", *The Christian Century* 106, 1989, 1012-1014.

Roof, Wade Clark and William McKinney, *American Mainline Religion: Its Changing Shape and Future*, New Brunswick 1987.

Rorty, Richard, *Contingency, Irony, and Solidarity*, Cambridge 1989.

———, *Objectivity, Relativism, and Truth* (*Philosophical Papers*, vol. 1), Cambridge 1991.

———, *Philosophy and the Mirror of Nature*, Oxford 1980.

Rosanvallon, Pierre, "The Decline of Social Visibility", *Civil Society and the State: New European Perspectives* (ed. by John Keane), London 1988, 199-220.

Rosenberg, Alexander, *Economics: Mathematical Politics or Science of Diminishing Returns?*, Chicago 1992.

Rosenblum, Nancy (ed.), *Liberalism and the Moral Life*, Cambridge, Mass. 1989.

Roth, Roland and Dieter Rucht (eds.), *Neue soziale Bewegungen in der Bundesrepublik Deutschland*, Frankfurt a. M. 1987.

Ruhbach, Gerhard (ed.), *Die Kirche angesichts der konstantinischen Wende*, Darmstadt 1976.

Salisbury, Harrison E., *The New Emperors: China in the Era of Mao and Deng*, Boston 1992.

Sandel, Michael J., *Liberalism and the Limits of Justice*, Cambridge 1982.

Sanders, E. P., *Paul and Palestinian Judaism: A Comparison of Patterns of Religion*, London 1977.

Schell, Jonathan, *The Fate of the Earth*, New York 1982.

Schillebeeckx, Edward, *Christ: The Experience of Jesus as Lord*, New York 1981.

Schipani, Daniel S. (ed.), *Freedom and Discipleship: Liberation Theology in an Anabaptist Perspective*, Maryknoll 1989.

Schmidt, David P., "Theological Ethics and Public Policy: An Analysis of Argument in Public Policy. Testimonies by Paul Ramsey and Stanley Hauerwas", Diss., The University of Chicago 1987.

Schmitt, Carl, *Politische Theologie: Vier Kapitel zur Lehre von der Souveränität*, München 1922.

Schnädelbach, Herbert, *Philosophie in Deutschland 1831-1933*, Frankfurt a. M. 1983.

Schrage, Wolfgang, *Ethik des Neuen Testaments*, Göttingen 1982.

Schuurman, Douglas J., *Creation, Eschaton, and Ethics: The Ethical Significance of the Creation-Eschaton Relation in the Thought of Emil Brunner and Jürgen Moltmann*, New York 1991.

Schweitzer, Don, "The Consistency of Jürgen Moltmann's Theology", *Studies in Religion* 22, 1993, 197-208.

Scott, Gregory Mahlon, "A Comparison of the Political Thought of Jacques Ellul and Jurgen Moltmann", Diss., University of Virginia 1989.

Scriven, Charles, *The Transformation of Culture: Christian Social Ethics After H. Richard Niebuhr*, Scottdale 1988.

Segundo, Juan Luis, "Capitalism Versus Socialism: Crux Theologica", *Frontiers of Theology in Latin America* (ed. by Rosino Gibellini), London 1980, 240-259.

Selznick, Philip, *The Moral Commonwealth: Social Theory and the Promise of Community*, Berkeley 1992.

Sennett, Richard, *The Fall of Public Man*, Cambridge 1977.

Shaffer, Thomas, *American Lawyers and their Communities. Ethics in the Legal Profession* (with Mary M. Shaffer), Notre Dame 1991.

Shapiro, Ian, *The Evolution of Rights in Liberal Theory*, Cambridge 1986.

⸺, *Political Criticism*, Berkeley 1990.

Shaw, Earl, "Beyond Political Theology", *Communities of Faith and Radical Discipleship* (ed. by G. McLeod Bryan), Macon 1986, 33-67.

Sigismund, Paul, *Liberation Theology at the Crossroads: Democracy or Revolution?*, New York 1990.

Skocpol, Theda, *States and Social Revolutions: A Comparative Analysis of France, Russia, and China*, Cambridge 1979.

Smith, Gudmund and Nils-Erik Sahlin, "Forskaren och vetenskapsidealen", *Tvärsnitt* no. 1, 1992, 56-61.

Snyder, Howard A., *The Radical Wesley and Patterns for Church Renewal*, Downers Grove 1980.

Sobrino, Jon, *Christology at the Crossroads: A Latin American Approach*, London 1978.

Soskice, Janet Martin, *Metaphor and Religious Language*, Oxford 1985.

Spencer, Richard Leroy, "Marx, Bloch and Moltmann: Dialectical Models of History and the Question of Ends and Means", Diss., Princeton Theological Seminary 1973.

Spjuth, Roland, *Creation, Contingency and Divine Presence in the Theologies of Thomas F. Torrance and Eberhard Jüngel*, Lund (forthcoming).

Spohn, William C., "The Return of Virtue Ethics", *Theological Studies* 53, 1992, 60-75.

Spotts, Frederic, *The Churches and Politics in Germany*, Middletown 1973.

Stackhouse, Max, *Creeds, Society, and Human Rights: A Study in Three Cultures*, Grand Rapids 1984.

Stackhouse, Max and Dennis P. McCann, "A Postcommunist Manifesto: Public Theology After the Collapse of Socialism", *The Christian Century* 108, 1991, 44-47.

Stallsworth, Paul T. (ed.), *The Church and Abortion: In Search of New Ground for Response*, Nashville 1993.

Stayer, James M., *Anabaptists and the Sword*, 2nd ed., Lawrence 1976.

———, "The Early Demise of a Normative Vision of Anabaptism", *Mennonite Identity: Historical and Contemporary Perspectives* (ed. by Calvin Redekop), Lanham 1988, 109-116.

Stayer, James M., Werner O. Packull, and Klaus Deppermann, "From Monogenesis to Polygenesis: The Historical Discussion of Anabaptist Origins", *Mennonite Quarterly Review* 49, 1975, 83-121.

Stendahl, Krister, *Paulus bland judar och hedningar*, Stockholm 1977.

Stoll, David, *Is Latin America Turning Protestant? The Politics of Evangelical Growth*, Berkeley 1990.

Stout, Jeffrey, *Ethics after Babel: The Languages of Morals and Their Discontents*, Boston 1988.

———, Review of Stanley Hauerwas, *Suffering Presence: Theological Reflections on Medicine, the Mentally Handicapped, and the Church*, *Theology Today* 44, 1987, 124-126.

Stroup, George W., *The Promise of Narrative Theology*, London 1984.

Sullivan, William M., *Reconstructing Public Philosophy*, Berkeley 1986.

Surin, Kenneth, "A 'Politics of Speech': Religious Pluralism in the Age of the McDonald's Hamburger", *Christian Uniqueness Reconsidered: The Myth of a Pluralistic Theology of Religions* (ed. by Gavin D'Costa), Maryknoll 1990, 192-212.

Swartley, Willard M. (ed.), *Essays on Peace Theology and Witness*, Elkhart 1988.

Sweet, Leonard, "Can a Mainstream Change Its Course?", *Liberal Protestantism: Realities and Possibilities* (ed. by Robert S. Michaelsen and Wade Clark Roof), New York 1986, 235-262.

Swift, Louis J., *The Early Fathers on War and Military Service*, Wilmington 1983.

Sykes, Stephen W., "The Dialectic of Community and Structure", *Love: The Foundation of Hope. The Theology of Jürgen Moltmann and Elisabeth Moltmann-Wendel* (ed. by Frederic B. Burnham, Charles S. McCoy and M. Douglas Meeks), San Francisco 1988, 113-128.

———, *The Identity of Christianity: Theologians and the Essence of Christianity from Schleiermacher to Barth*, Philadelphia 1984.

Taylor, Charles, "Cross-Purposes: The Liberal-Communitarian Debate", *Liberalism and the Moral Life* (ed. by Nancy L. Rosenblum), Cambridge, Mass. 1989, 159-182.

———, *Explanation and Practical Reason*, Helsinki 1989.

———, *Multiculturalism and "The Politics of Recognition"* (with commentary by Amy Gutmann [ed.], Steven C. Rockefeller, Michael Walzer and Susan Wolf), Princeton 1992.

————, "Overcoming Epistemology", *After Philosophy: End or Transformation?* (ed. by Kenneth Baynes, James Bohman, and Thomas McCarthy), Cambridge, Mass. 1987, 464-488.

————, *Philosophy and the Human Sciences (Philosophical Papers*, vol. 2), Cambridge 1985.

————, *The Sources of the Self: The Making of the Modern Identity*, Cambridge 1989.

Thiemann, Ronald F., "Gotthold Ephraim Lessing: An Enlightened View of Judaism", *Journal of Ecumenical Studies* 18, 1981, 401-422.

————, *Revelation and Theology: The Gospel as Narrated Promise*, Notre Dame 1985.

Thörn, Håkan and Eskilsson, Tomas, "Den gamla vänstern och de nya rörelserna – Från arbetets etik till skapandets logik", *Socialism utan ansikte* (ed. by David Karlsson and Per Månsson), Uddevalla 1991, 125-141.

Tillich, Paul, *Perspectives on 19th and 20th Century Protestant Theology*, London 1967.

Torstendahl, Rolf and Thorsten Nybom, *Historievetenskap som teori, praktik, ideologi*, Södertälje 1988.

Touraine; Alain, *La Société post-industrielle*, Paris 1969.

————, *The Voice and the Eye: An Analysis of Social Movements*, Cambridge 1981.

Tracy, David, *The Analogical Imagination: Christian Theology and the Culture of Pluralism*, London 1981.

————, *The Blessed Rage of Order: The New Pluralism in Theology*, New York 1978.

————, "On Naming the Present", *Concilium*, no. 1, 1990, 66-85.

Tripole, Martin R., "A Church for the Poor and the World: At Issue with Moltmann's Ecclesiology", *Theological Studies* 42, 1981, 645-659.

Troeltsch, Ernst, *Protestantism and Progress: The Significance of Protestantism for the Rise of the Modern World*, Philadelphia 1986.

————, *The Social Teaching of the Christian Churches*, 2 vols., London 1931.

Ulrich, Hans, "Theologische Ethik im englischsprachigen Kontext: Zur neueren Diskussion in Nordamerika", *Verkündigung und Forschung* 38, 1993, 61-84.

———— (ed.), *Evangelische Ethik: Texte zu ihrer Grundlegung und Durchführung*, München 1990.

Van Gerwen, Josef, "The Church in the Theological Ethics of Stanley Hauerwas", Diss., Graduate Theological Union 1984.

Veldhuis, Ruurd, *Realism versus Utopianism? Reinhold Niebuhr's Christian Realism and the Relevance of Utopian Thought for Social Ethics*, Assen 1975.

Verhey, Allen, *The Great Reversal: Ethics and the New Testament*, Grand Rapids 1984.

Vidich, Arthur J. and Stanford M. Lyman, *American Sociology: Worldly Rejections of Religion and Their Directions*, New Haven 1985.

Vroom, H. M., *De Schrift alleen? Een vergelijkend onderzoek naar de toetsing van theologische uitspraken volgens de openbaringstheologische visie van Torrance en de hermeneutisch-theologische opvattingen van Van Buren, Ebeling, Moltmann en Pannenberg*, Kampen 1978.

Wacker, Bernd, "Politische Theologie", *Neues Handbuch theologischer Grundbegriffe* (ed. by Peter Eicher), vol. 3 , München 1985, 379-391.

Wadell, Paul J., *The Primacy of Love: An Introduction to the Ethics of Thomas Aquinas*, New York 1992.

Wallach, Michael A. and Lise Wallach, *Psychology's Sanction for Selfishness: The Error of Egoism in Theory and Therapy*, San Francisco 1983.

Wallis, Jim, *Agenda for Biblical People*, New York 1976.

————, *The Call to Conversion*, Tring 1981.

Walzer, Michael, "The Communitarian Critique of Liberalism", *Political Theory* 18, 1990, 6-23.

———, "A Critique of Philosophical Conversation", *Hermeneutics and Critical Theory in Ethics and Politics* (ed. by Michael Kelly), Cambridge, Mass. 1990, 182-196.

———, "The Idea of Civil Society: A Path to Social Reconstruction", *Dissent* 1991, 293-304.

———, *Just and Unjust Wars: A Moral Argument with Historical Illustrations*, New York 1977.

———, "Retrospective", *Religious Studies Review* 16, 1990, 193-197.

———, *The Spheres of Justice: A Defense of Pluralism and Equality*, New York 1983.

Wasmuth, Ulrike C., "Die Entstehung und Entwicklung der Friedensbewegungen der achtziger Jahre: Ihre geistigen Strömungen und ihre Beziehung zu den Ergebnissen der Friedensforschung", *Neue soziale Bewegungen in der Bundesrepublik Deutschland* (ed. by Roland Roth and Dieter Rucht), Frankfurt a. M. 1987, 109-133.

——— (ed.), *Alternativen zur Alten Politik: Neue soziale Bewegungen in der Diskussion*, Darmstadt 1989.

Weaver, J. Denny, "Atonement for the NonConstantinian Church", *Modern Theology* 6, 1990, 307-323.

———, *Becoming Anabaptist: The Origin and Significance of Sixteenth-Century Anabaptism*, Scottdale 1987.

Webber, Robert and Rodney Clapp, *People of the Truth: The Power of the Worshipping Community in the Modern World*, San Francisco 1988.

Weber, Max, *Economy and Society. An Outline of Interpretative Sociology*, 3 vols., New York 1968.

———, *The Protestant Ethic and the Spirit of Capitalism*, London 1930.

———, "The Protestant Sects and the Spirit of Capitalism", *From Max Weber: Essays in Sociology* (ed. by H. H. Gerth and C. Wright Mills), London 1970, 302-322.

Weber, Otto, *Foundations of Dogmatics*, 2 vols., Grand Rapids 1981-1983.

———, *Versammelte Gemeinde: Beiträge zum Gespräch über Kirche und Gottesdienst*, Neukirchen 1975.

Weintraub, E. Roy, *Stabilizing Dynamics: Constructing Economic Knowledge*, Cambridge 1991.

Werpehowski, William, "Political Liberalism and Christian Ethics: A Review Discussion", *The Thomist* 48, 1984, 81-115.

Westerståhl, Jörgen and Folke Johansson, *Bilden av Sverige: Studier av nyheter and nyhetsideologier i TV, radio och dagspress*, Stockholm 1985.

Westin, Gunnar, *Den kristna friförsamlingen genom tiderna: Martyrer och frihetskämpar*, Stockholm 1957.

Weston, William J., "The Invisible Church: The Missing Element in Hauerwas' *A Community of Character*", *Journal of Religious Studies* 13, 1987, 95-105.

Weth, Rudolf, *"Barmen" als Herausforderung der Kirche: Beiträge zum Kirchenverständnis im Licht der Barmer Theologischen Erklärung*, München 1984.

Whitmore, Todd, "Beyond Liberalism and Communitarianism in Christian Ethics: A Critique of Stanley Hauerwas", *The Annual of the Society of Christian Ethics*, Knoxville 1989, 207-225.

Wiebe, Ben, *Messianic Ethics: Jesus' Proclamation of the Kingdom of God and the Church in Response*, Waterloo 1992.

———, "Revolution as an Issue in Theology: Jürgen Moltmann", *Restoration Quarterly* 26, 1983, 105-120.

Wiedenhofer, Siegfried, *Politische Theologie*, Stuttgart 1976.

———, "Politische Theologie", *Denken und Glauben*, no. 19, 1985, 7-11.

Williams, Bernard, *Ethics and the Limits of Philosophy*, Cambridge, Mass. 1985.

Williams, George H., *The Radical Reformation*, Philadelphia 1962.

————, "The Radical Reformation Revisited", *Union Seminary Quarterly Review* 39, 1984, 1-24.

Wilson, Bryan, *Religious Sects: A Sociological Study*, London 1970.

Wingren, Gustaf, "Reformationens och lutherdomens ethos", *Etik och kristen tro* (ed. by Gustaf Wingren), Lund 1971, 112-147.

Wittrock, Björn, *Möjligheter och gränser: Framtidsstudier i politik och planering*, Stockholm 1980.

Wogaman, J. Philip, *Christian Perspectives on Politics*, London 1988.

Wolfe, Alan, *Whose Keeper? Social Science and Moral Obligation*, Berkeley 1989.

Wolterstorff, Nicholas, *Reason within the Bounds of Religion*, 2nd ed., Grand Rapids 1984.

Wright, N. T., *The New Testament and the People of God* (*Christian Origins and the Question of God*, vol. 1), London 1992.

Wright, Nigel, *Makt och lärjungaskap: En frikyrklig teologi om förhållandet församling – samhälle*, Örebro 1993.

Wuthnow, Robert, *Acts of Compassion: Caring for Others and Helping Ourselves*, Princeton 1991.

————, *The Restructuring of American Religion: Society and State Since World War II*, Princeton 1988.

————, *The Struggle for America's Soul: Evangelicals, Liberals, and Secularism*, Grand Rapids 1989.

Yearley, Lee H., "Recent Work on Virtue", *Religious Studies Review* 16, 1990, 1-9.

Yoder, John H., "The Believers' Church Conferences in Historical Perspective", *Mennonite Quarterly Review* 65, 1991, 5-19.

————, "The Believers' Church: Global Perspectives", *The Believers' Church in Canada* (ed. by J. Zeman and W. Klaasen), Winnipeg 1979, 3-15.

————, "Binding and Loosing", Appendix to *Healing the Wounded: The Costly Love of Church Discipline* by John White and Ken Blue, Downers Grove 1985, 211-234.

————, "*The Challenge of Peace*: A Historic Peace Church Perspective", *Peace in a Nuclear Age: The Bishops' Pastoral Letter in Perspective* (ed. by Charles J. Reid, Jr.), Washington, DC 1986, 273-290.

————, *Christian Attitudes to War, Peace, and Revolution: A Companion to Bainton*, Elkhart 1983.

————, *The Christian Witness to the State*, Newton 1964.

————, *The Fullness of Christ: Paul's Revolutionary Vision of Universal Ministry*, Elgin 1987.

————, "How Richard Niebuhr Reasons: A Critique of *Christ and Culture*", unpublished.

————, "The Lord's Supper in Historical Perspective", unpublished.

————, *Nevertheless: The Varieties and Shortcomings of Religious Pacifism* (Revised and Expanded Edition), Scottdale 1992.

————, "A Non-Baptist View of Southern Baptists", *Review and Expositor* 67, 1970, 219-228.

————, *The Original Revolution: Essays on Christian Pacifism*, Scottdale 1977.

————, *The Politics of Jesus: Vicit Agnus Noster*, Grand Rapids 1972.

————, *The Priestly Kingdom: Social Ethics as Gospel*, Notre Dame 1984.

————, "Reformed Versus Anabaptist Social Strategies: An Inadequate Typology", *TSF Bulletin* 8:5, 1985, 2-7.

————, "Sacrament as Social Process: Christ the Transformer of Culture", *Theology Today* 48, 1991, 33-44.

————, *When War is Unjust: Being Honest in Just-War Thinking*, Minneapolis 1984.

Young, Norman, *Creator, Creation and Faith*, Philadelphia 1976.

Zinger, Don H., "Are Grace and Virtue Compatible?" Lutheran Forum 23:1, 1989, 12–13.

Abbreviations

AC	Hauerwas, *After Christendom*
AN	Hauerwas, *Against the Nations*
CC	Hauerwas, *A Community of Character*
CCL	Hauerwas, *Character and the Christian Life*
CET	Hauerwas, *Christian Existence Today*
CG	Moltmann, *The Crucified God*
CJF	Moltmann, *Creating a Just Future*
CPS	Moltmann, *The Church in the Power of the Spirit*
DFF	Hauerwas, *Dispatches from the Front*
DHRG	Moltmann, *Diakonie im Horizont des Reiches Gottes*
EG	Moltmann, *Experiences of God*
EH	Moltmann, *The Experiment Hope*
FC	Moltmann, *The Future of Creation*
GHH	Moltmann-Wendel and Moltmann, *God – His and Hers*
GIC	Moltmann, *God In Creation*
HC	Moltmann et al, *Hope for the Church*
HIG	Moltmann-Wendel and Moltmann, *Humanity in God*
HP	Moltmann, *Hope and Planning*
HTG	Moltmann, *History and the Triune God*
IGMEB	Moltmann, *Im Gespräch mit Ernst Bloch*
MRF	Moltmann, *Menschenwürde, Recht und Freiheit*
NS	Hauerwas, *Naming the Silences*
OC	Moltmann, *The Open Church*
OHD	Moltmann, *On Human Dignity*
OMM	Moltmann, *Ohne Macht mächtig*
PdT	Moltmann, *Perspektiven der Theologie*
PK	Hauerwas, *The Peaceable Kingdom*
PPL	Moltmann, *The Power of the Powerless*
PTPE	Moltmann, *Politische Theologie – Politische Ethik*
PtS	Hauerwas and Willimon, *Preaching to Strangers*
RA	Hauerwas and Willimon, *Resident Aliens*
RRF	Moltmann, *Religion, Revolution, and the Future*
SL	Moltmann, *The Spirit of Life*
SP	Hauerwas, *Suffering Presence*
TH	Moltmann, *Theology of Hope*
ThT	Moltmann, *Theology Today*
TJ	Moltmann, *Theology and Joy*
TKG	Moltmann, *The Trinity and the Kingdom of God*
TT	Hauerwas, *Truthfulness and Tragedy*
US	Hauerwas, *Unleashing the Scripture*
UZ	Moltmann, *Umkehr zur Zukunft*
VV	Hauerwas, *Vision and Virtue*
WJC	Moltmann, *The Way of Jesus Christ*

Index